The First Ladies

Fact Book

The First Ladies

Fact Book

The Stories of the Women of the White House from Martha Washington to Laura Bush

Bill Harris

BLACK DOG
& LEVENTHAL
PUBLISHERS
NEW YORK

Copyright © 2005 by Black Dog & Leventhal Publishers, Inc.

Published by:
Black Dog & Leventhal Publishers, Inc.
151 West 19th Street
New York, NY 10011

Distributed by:
Workman Publishing Company
708 Broadway
New York, NY 10003

Manufactured in the United States of America

Jacket and book design by Scot Covey

Contributing Writers:
Jim Callan
Michael Lewis
Stephen Spignesi
Richard Steins

Photo Research:
Sarah Parvis

ISBN: 1-57912-468-2

g f e d c b

Library of Congress Cataloging-in-Publication Data

Harris, Bill, 1933-
    The first ladies fact book : the stories of the women of the White House, from Martha Washington to Laura Bush / Bill Harris.
        p. cm.
    ISBN 1-57912-468-2
        1. Presidents' spouses--United States--Biography. 2. President's spouses--United States--History. 3. President's spouses--United States--Social life and customs. I. Title.

E176.2.H368 2005
973'.09'9--dc22   2005048235

Contents

Martha Washington

Lady Washington

When sixty-year-old Martha Washington arrived in New York in the spring of 1789 to join her husband, the newly inaugurated president of the United States, she had no notion of what to expect, nor of what was expected of her as the First Lady of the United States.

George Washington himself was facing a similar challenge. The Constitution outlined most of his state duties, but it was quite silent on the ceremonial roles he would have to play. He had recently given eight years of his life to freeing the American people from a monarchy, and they regarded him as one of their own; but, in fact, President Washington was a wealthy Southern planter and by nature a patrician in a society that had, in theory, done away with such social distinctions. With no role model before him, George had to figure out what it meant to be "presidential," and how to conduct himself as the leader of this fledgling nation of free people. The new office itself was different from any other the world had ever seen. The American president is the head of state with all of the ceremonial obligations that go with it, and he is also the head of the government, directly responsible to the needs of the people he serves. George was also very sensitive to the fact that the ways he handled the office would establish a precedent for all of the American presidents who would follow him.

The members of his official family had debated for weeks over how the citizenry should address him and, by custom, his successors. Vice President John Adams was firmly on the side of the Senate, which had voted that the proper way ought to be "His Highness, the President of the United States and Protector of Liberties." The House of Representatives, however, in a less formal and more democratic frame of mind, insisted that it should simply be "Mr. President." Although Mr. Adams said the latter fell on his ear as "the officer of some local insignificant organization," the egalitarian "Mr. President" won out in the end.

The debate extended to how the First Lady should be addressed as well, and although it, too, came down to a simple "Mrs.," Martha had come to New York enthusiastically hailed as "Lady Washington," an honorific given to her by the soldiers under her husband's command—for it was plain for anyone to see that Martha was every inch a lady. One of the French officers who served in the Revolution once said that she reminded him of a Roman matron, and nothing suited her bearing more aptly.

Martha Dandridge Custis Washington

Born
June 2, 1731,
Chestnut Grove, New
Kent County, Virginia

Parents
John Dandridge and
Frances Jones Dandridge

Marriage
1750 to Daniel Parke
Custis

Children
Daniel Custis (1751-56);
Frances Custis (1753-57);
John (Jacky) Custis
(1755-81); Martha (Patsy)
Custis (1757-73)

Widowed
1757

Remarried
1759 to Colonel George
Washington (1732-99)

Died
May 22, 1802, Mount
Vernon, Virginia

Above: Painter Gilbert Stuart created many images of George Washington. This one appears on the dollar bill in a reversed engraving.

It was what was expected of the daughter of one of the first families of Virginia. Born Martha Dandridge, the daughter of a wealthy tobacco planter, John, she grew up in a world of private tutors, attentive servants, and spirited horses. And after she was introduced into society at age fifteen, her life was filled with a constant round of balls, parties, and formal dinners. When Martha was seventeen, she married Daniel Parke Custis, a man even wealthier than her father, and she became the mistress of the Custis plantation, called the White House, not far north of the Virginia capital at Williamsburg, which was the epicenter of the colony's social life.

Martha's status grew, especially among eligible bachelors, when Daniel died eight years later, leaving an estate that made her the wealthiest widow in Virginia, not to mention the most attractive, at the age of twenty-five.

She chose to shun their advances, concentrating instead on running the Custis plantation and raising the surviving two of her four children: four-year-old John, who was called Jacky; and a girl of two named for her mother but, like her, affectionately known as Patsy. But then a new man caught her eye. His name was George Washington.

Colonel Washington had made a name for himself as a hero of the frontier war against the French and Indians, and Martha had met him several times when he appeared at Williamsburg for consultations with the governor. She had been impressed by his appearance, tall and lithe with cool blue eyes, and she was quite taken by his quiet dignity, formality, remoteness, and even his

Martha Washington married her first husband, Daniel Parke Custis, in 1750 and moved into his mansion, which he called the White House!

Below: Martha Dandridge Custis as she looked at about the time she married Colonel George Washington at the age of twenty-eight.

shyness around women, all qualities that were glaringly in short supply among the swains who were pursuing her. But it was all just a passing fancy—she was certain of that.

Martha met him again at a dinner party in the early spring of 1758, and they lingered in the parlor together after the other guests had left. It was an evening of polite conversation between two plantation owners, and only George had any inkling that it was anything more than that. His intentions finally dawned on Martha when her children were brought in to say goodnight and the soldier enchanted them as well.

Martha and George met again soon afterward when he invited himself to her home on his way back from another trip to Williamsburg. She had talked herself out of any idea of romance by then, but he brought it back to the top of her mind by the way he treated her servants and, more important, in the easy bond he established with her children. There would be two more visits before he asked Martha to marry him, and by then she was joyfully ready to accept his proposal. But first, he went off to take care of some urgent unfinished business with the French, which he promised her would be his last military campaign.

He didn't come back again until six months later, just in time for Christmas. He had been elected to the Virginia House of Burgesses in the meantime, and he had resigned his military commission. (This was a relief to Martha, who was interested in a stable home and family life for herself and her children.) All that remained for George to complete his own new role in life was to take a wife, and he and Martha were married at her plantation house in January 1759. While his own estate, Mount Vernon, was being readied for its new mistress, the newlyweds went to live for the rest of the winter at the Custis townhouse in Williamsburg.

The couple moved into Mount Vernon in April, and they went right to work on the routine running of the plantation and improving it as a home. They had plenty of people to help them. With Martha's servants joining the new household, there were fourteen people on the house staff and seven more working its grounds, while more than forty ran the adjoining farms that were part of the estate. In addition to supervising the servants, George and Martha were responsible for feeding and clothing all of them, as well as looking after their health.

George's daily routine invariably started with a twenty-mile horseback tour of his holdings, and Martha began her days with an hour of complete solitude for herself. No one knew how she spent those hours locked away from all, including her children. She may have read from her Bible, written letters to old friends, worked on her needlework, or just meditated. Everyone was well aware that it was strictly forbidden to intrude on her alone time.

Dinner was at three each day, and there were usually guests to share it. George always rode home to change into more formal clothes in time to welcome the old friends and family members, many of whom just showed up without an invitation, and all of whom were assured a warm welcome. It wasn't uncommon for some of the less affluent among them to ask their host for cash loans, and he rarely disappointed them.

The round of nonstop entertaining came to an abrupt halt the following January when Martha came down with a case of measles. Her recovery was slow, but complete by spring, and nothing more was said of it. But it seems likely that the disease left her unable to have any more children, and George Washington would never have a direct heir.

But he had two stepchildren in Jacky and Patsy, and he doted on them every bit as much as if they were his own. It was obvious that he loved them as much as he loved their mother. They may not have been so easy to love, because Martha seemed to go out of her

Above: George's first meeting with Martha was strictly formal, following the demands of custom in Virginia in the 1750s.

Below: The Washington-Custis wedding took place at her plantation, "The White House," with Martha's two young children, Jacky and Patsy Custis, among the honored guests.

Family Gathering

At Mount Vernon, George and Martha Washington were surrounded not only by friendly neighbors but by their own families, as well. George had two half brothers, three brothers, and a sister. One of the half brothers, Augustine, married Anne Aylette, and had several daughters and a son, William Augustine. George's sister, Betty, married Fielding Lewis, and together they had five sons and a daughter. His brother Samuel was married five times, and had three sons and a daughter. Another brother, John Augustine, married Hannah Bushrod, and had two sons and two daughters. His brother Charles married Mildred Thornton, and among their several children, George's nephew George Augustine served as his aide during the Revolutionary War and as steward at Mount Vernon during his presidency. Another nephew, John Augustine's son Bushrod, was ultimately named as George Washington's heir, after Martha, in his will.

Martha Dandridge was one of eight children, and she remained close to all of them after she married George. She was especially close to her brother Bartholomew, whose son Bartholomew II was her husband's personal secretary during his presidency. She was also close to her sister Anne, known as Nancy, whose children by Burwell Bassett included Fanny Bassett, who married George's nephew George Augustine. After he died, she married Tobias Lear, the president's personal secretary.

Martha's son John (Jacky) Parke Custis had four children by his wife, Eleanor Calvert: Eliza Parke Custis, who married Thomas Law; Martha (Patty) Parke Custis, who married Thomas Peter; Eleanor (Nelly) Parke Custis, who married George's nephew Lawrence Lewis, and George (Little Wash) Washington Parke Custis, who married Mary Lee Fitzhugh.

Above: Later in their lives, George and Martha's family grew to include several of their grandchildren, along with nieces and nephews, whom they helped raise.

way to spoil them. They could do nothing wrong as far as she was concerned, and no indulgence was ever out of the question. Her husband was notoriously easygoing and tried not to interfere (possibly because his own mother had been a domineering woman, and during his youth, he never seemed able to find a way to get her approval). But he believed that children were tough little creatures who needed to experience some hard knocks so that they could deal with the problems they would surely face as adults, and he didn't mind saying so. But Martha would have none of it. These were her children, she informed him, and George had no experience in such matters anyway. He backed down and never mentioned the problem again.

Life at Mount Vernon was close to idyllic. The estate was constantly being improved, and George had switched to growing wheat instead of tobacco because there was a good market for it locally and he was leery of depending

Above: Martha Parke Custis, known as "Patsy," died when she was just a teen.

on the London market. Transatlantic arguments over prices were only part of it. As a member of the House of Burgesses, he was involved in discussions about an onerous new tax from the Mother Country that required a stamp to be pasted on legal documents and newspapers. Patrick Henry had been accused of treason for his fiery opposition to it at Williamsburg, and there were rumors that passions were running far higher up in Massachusetts.

The situation festered when new import taxes were imposed, and Virginians as well as people in the other colonies responded by boycotting British imports. There was a quiet understanding among them that if Great Britain sent more troops to North America, as had happened at Boston, they would fight back. But many people, including Martha, couldn't help wondering, with what army?

By their tenth wedding anniversary, the Washingtons were beginning to enjoy a new prosperity. After a great deal of agonizing soul-searching, Martha agreed to allow young Jacky to leave home for life at a boarding school in far-off Fredericksburg, Virginia, and they indulged themselves by ordering a gilded four-horse coach with the Washington coat of arms painted on its doors and engraved on the harness. About the only thing that troubled them was young Patsy's poor health. She had been prone to seizures all her life, but now that she was becoming a teenager, they were coming more frequently and more violently. Beyond endless consultations with doctors, who didn't seem to have any idea what to do, there was nothing Martha could do but shower her daughter with love and rain gifts on her. Patsy died of her ailment in the late spring of 1773, and the following winter, her eighteen-year-old brother, Jacky, by then a student at Kings College in New York, married fifteen-year-old Nelly Calvert, the daughter of another of the first families of Virginia. Martha and George had only each other now, but their lives would change again, and soon.

Below: Although he retired from the military when he married Martha, George rode his daily plantation tours in full uniform. Their household slaves dressed in the formal scarlet and white livery of the family.

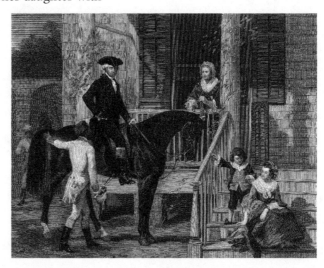

The Fight for Independence

The anticipated troubles with the Mother Country had still not materialized, even after British soldiers fired into a crowd on Boston Common, killing three Colonists. But things began to come to a head in the fall, when George went to Philadelphia as a delegate to

Above: George Washington spent his life expanding and improving his plantation and its manor house. It is his most impressive monument.

Below: Martha had help running her kitchen at Mount Vernon, but she was an accomplished cook and she spent much of her time there.

the Continental Congress to help decide how the Colonies could accomplish a clean break with Great Britain. He had already told the Virginia assembly that he would "raise one thousand men, subsist them at my own expense, and march myself at their head for the relief of Boston," and he had ordered a new uniform—blue with buff facings, the colors of the Fairfax County militia.

He spent more and more of his time drilling that militia, and when the call came for him to join the Second Continental Congress, he arrived at Philadelphia in full uniform with a sword on his side. It might have been a subconscious advertisement for his military resume, but if it was, he needn't have bothered. When Congress authorized the raising of ten companies of riflemen to march on Boston, everyone at the Philadelphia statehouse knew that there was only one man among them with the experience that it would take to lead them.

In a letter he wrote to Martha the day after his appointment, George said that he was leaving immediately to take command of the new Continental Army in far-off Massachusetts. That meant only one thing to Martha. They would be separated from each other over a greater distance than they had ever known, and neither of them had any idea for how long. She supported her husband wholeheartedly, but Martha knew very well that she wasn't going to be seeing her husband again anytime soon.

Before he left Philadelphia, George had asked Jacky and his wife, Nelly, to move to Mount Vernon to keep Martha company. He also sold a piece of land to pay off their debts, and he passed along the duties of overseer to his cousin Lund, who had been his right-hand man for some time, even though Martha herself had years of experience in the day-to-day running of a plantation. Finally, in one last gesture before leaving for Boston, he ordered two suits of "the prettiest muslin" for his wife. "I wish it may please you," he wrote.

George and Martha had been separated before, but he had never been so far from her as when he established his headquarters at Cambridge overlooking Boston. Apparently the British didn't know that George's army had just about run out of ammunition, because they had not attacked yet, even after their reinforcements had arrived.

Then as summer turned to autumn, a letter from George arrived at Mount Vernon asking Martha to join him, and suggesting that if she left right away, she could be in Cambridge in time for Christmas. Martha had never been any farther north than Alexandria, Virginia, and at best, the trip would take three weeks, even for an experienced traveler, not counting breakdowns and the problems that come with traveling in the winter. It was already the middle of November. There was no time to waste.

Martha and her family arrived in Cambridge a few days before Christmas, always an important holiday in the lives of the Washingtons, and Martha took up residence in the general's headquarters, a cheerful yellow mansion that had been the home of a Loyalist who abandoned it in the wake of the advancing Minutemen. George and Martha hadn't seen each other in seven months, but his duties as commander in chief left them little of the quiet time that had been so precious to them back home. She was given a parlor across the entry hall from his office and was largely left to fend for herself among strangers with odd accents. But as she had learned on her journey north, her husband was the most widely respected man in all the Colonies, and that affection had rubbed off on her. She knew that she was among friends, and she made the most of it with all the graciousness she could muster.

She made some confidantes among the officers' wives, many of whom became her friends for life. Among them was Kitty Greene, the wife of General Nathanael Greene, who showed up for her first visit with her new son, named George Washington Greene. Martha always had a soft spot for babies, but this was the first one she'd met outside their own family who had been named for her husband, and that made him all the more precious. Before the war was over, she would dandle dozens more babies named George Washington on her knee.

After celebrating Christmas, then New Year's, and then their seventeenth wedding anniversary, George began to realize that all work and no play wasn't good either for him or for his homesick soldiers, and Martha's stay made him understand that morale was as important to them as the ability to fire a musket.

But Martha did more than pour glasses of wine, serve cake, and make engaging conversation. Her husband hired her as an assistant to his private secretary, and she spent long hours copying official letters. He left it up to her to negotiate a salary with the Congress, warning that they hadn't been very forthcoming with his requests for money to buy powder and shot. She must have smiled at that because he himself had agreed to serve without any pay except for his expenses, and Congress hadn't been forthcoming about that, either. As it turned out, the job was priceless to Martha. Transcribing her husband's letters gave her a deep insight into his job as a military leader, and it opened the door to conversations with his generals and aides that otherwise might have been vapid and forgettable. Martha also learned the value of military secrets and how to guard them, an insight that she used very well in the political wars that would follow years later.

Martha was in Philadelphia when Thomas Jefferson's Declaration of Independence was first read on July fourth, and she knew it meant that the United Colonies were now the United States of America. She also knew that as the wife of the man who was leading troops against the Mother Country, her neck was more firmly in the noose of treason than it had been before. But the British had to catch her first, and she had no intention of allowing that to happen.

Meanwhile, George's neck was being measured for that same noose, and he was on the run after a serious defeat in Brooklyn with British-led Hessian mercenaries hard on his heels, occupying Manhattan Island along the way. There was no possibility of Martha's joining him again, and Congress arranged an escort for her as far as Baltimore,

Above: Martha's granddaughter Nelly went along with her parents to live at Mount Vernon when George went off to war.

Below: Martha and the children were always on hand to welcome George and his guests back from a hunt.

Above: George and Martha were as close to their grandchildren as they had been to her son and daughter when they were young.

Below: It was a cold day when Martha arrived at the army's winter quarters in Morristown, New Jersey, but her welcome, as always, was a warm one.

where she was met by Jacky and Nelly, along with a new addition to the family, a baby girl named Eliza Parke Custis, Martha's first grandchild. There would be three more grandchildren later on: two girls, and a boy who would be named George Washington Parke Custis and would be known as "Little Washington" for most of his life.

Once she was back at Mount Vernon, there was nothing for Martha to do but wait, worry, and pray. The war was not going at all well for her husband. But then at the end of December, George wrote to her with details about how he crossed the Delaware River on Christmas Day, surprising the Hessians who were camped at Trenton, New Jersey. It brightened an otherwise bleak holiday for her, and then another letter told her that his army had scored a major victory at Princeton. The situation had turned around in the twinkling of an eye, and he suggested that it would be safe for her to make the trip to his new winter headquarters at Morristown. Worries of an attack on Philadelphia postponed an actual summons, but by early March, Martha was on her way again. This time their absence from one another had lasted ten months.

The staff she had known at Cambridge was changed. Some had been killed, some had been promoted, and new men were assigned to replace them. Among the newcomers was young Alexander Hamilton, a colonel of artillery who was valuable on the general's secretarial staff, especially because he was fluent in French, a skill that was essential now that Europeans were making their mark in the Continental Army. Martha was no longer needed as an assistant secretary, so her stay at Morristown was devoted to socializing, visiting the wounded, and, as always, knitting. When George's sock drawer was filled, she turned to making stockings for his men, not to mention mending their shirts and making blankets, which were in short supply.

When the war heated up again in the spring, Martha went home to Mount Vernon again. During that summer of 1777, the British attacked and occupied Philadelphia, and from her vantage point, it looked as though the tide had turned again. Her husband had lost New York to the enemy the previous year, and now he hadn't been able to save Philadelphia, either. There were calls for him to be replaced, but not everyone took them seriously, least of all Martha, although she may have secretly wished that he would be relieved of his command.

Her worst fears were realized when, as he prepared to make his winter camp at Valley Forge, the expected summons for her to join him there didn't arrive. The invitation finally came, though, and Martha arrived at Valley Forge in time for her husband's birthday in February, the coldest month of an unusually cold winter. Martha had plenty of experience with military camps by then; the sound of cannons and mortars didn't startle her, and she had grown accustomed to the sounds of drumrolls from dawn to sunset. But this camp was primitive compared to the others she had seen, and she must have been longing for the comforts of Mount Vernon. Valley Forge was no place for the fainthearted.

There was no local population for Martha to charm, but there were several other officers' wives who had become close friends. Most of the officers were maintaining bachelor quarters, though, and she realized that their accommodations were not at all like her own, Spartan as they were. She reached out to them, listening to their letters from home, memorizing their children's names, and getting out her sewing basket to mend their threadbare uniforms.

Above: Whenever Martha visited her husband in the field, she always took her knitting needles along with her, and she encouraged other officers' wives to follow her example.

Always a horse lover, Martha was heartbroken at the sight of starving horses for whom there was simply no food to be had. She was moved to tears by the soldiers who were starving, too, and who sat around smoky fires all night to keep from freezing to death. Many had no shoes and wrapped their feet in moth-eaten blankets or tied their hats around them, leaving bloody tracks in the snow. And as for the field hospitals, she was forbidden to go near them. Lack of provisions and lack of space made entertaining out of the question, but Martha presided over evening gatherings where the guests themselves provided the entertainment by singing songs, telling stories, and sharing memories of home.

In the spring, the men who had survived spruced themselves up, and because they had lived through such a hellish winter, they had a new kind of pride. Martha was proud of them, too, and when she left for home, she had hope that the war would be over before another winter set in.

Below: The winter encampment at Valley Forge is remembered as one of the most terrible experiences in the history of the United States army. Martha was there to share it.

> *"The general's headquarters have been made more tolerable by the addition of a log cabin to the house, built to dine in. The apartment for business is only about sixteen feet square, and has a large fireplace. The house is built of stone. The walls are very thick, and below a deep east window, out of which the general can look upon the encampment, he had a box made, which appears to be part of the casement, with a blind trap door at top, in which he keeps his valuable papers."*
>
> —*Martha Washington on life at Valley Forge*

WASHINGTON AT THE DEATH BED OF YOUNG CUSTIS.

Above: Martha's son, John Parke Custis, died soon after the decisive victory at Yorktown that led to the end of the war. His passing was a tragic postscript for George and Martha.

But when the snow came down again, her husband was encamped north of New York, where the enemy was still entrenched. He had been ordered to Philadelphia, which the British had abandoned by then, to meet with Congress, and Martha met him there. The opportunities for socializing were more abundant than they had known since the war began, and George and Martha made the most of it. It was the first time that they had enough leisure time for quiet conversation, too. That winter was much milder than the previous one had been, and when they moved into the new headquarters at Middlebrook, New Jersey, early in February, Martha welcomed the change. So did her husband. She hadn't seen him so relaxed and happy in years.

When the army marched north, Martha headed south again. It was a quiet summer both on the Hudson highlands, where George was keeping an eye on the enemy, and at Mount Vernon, where his long absence had cast a pall over his family and friends.

The good news during the summer of 1779 was that the British seemed to have lost interest in fighting. The bad news came in early winter after their halfhearted attack on Savannah had failed, and George couldn't spare more than a token force to take the battle to the South. Martha set out to join him at headquarters, which had been established at Morristown again, yet she was snowbound in Philadelphia, and didn't arrive there until January.

Martha's next winter sojourn was spent at a small stone house overlooking the Hudson above New York City. The war, at least in this part of the country, had settled into a dull routine, but she had no sooner gone back home than the British general Lord Cornwallis took Williamsburg. He didn't head for Mount Vernon after his triumph, but rather marched in the opposite direction toward Yorktown. He had backed himself into a trap, but the main force of George's army was hundreds of miles away getting ready to fight for New York.

George made a quick decision to head south to spring the trap, and his path would take him home for a few days. She didn't have much advance notice, but Martha organized a welcome for him and his guests that was fit for a king. Among the local guests were Jacky and Nelly, and before he left, his stepson talked George into taking him along so that he could watch the battle. He became sick with a fever on the way, but he saw his stepfather's greatest victory from a carriage parked at the side of the road, and he saw Lord Cornwallis surrender his sword. But a few days afterward, Jacky was dead.

The joy of her husband's victory was tempered by her profound grief, but Martha knew that the war still wasn't over, and she stoically packed her trunks for yet another winter away from home. This year it would be spent at Newburgh, New York. The war had come down to breaking the British occupation of New York City, and waiting for news from Paris, where a peace treaty was being forged. It was all an anticlimax, and the men began to drift away in the direction of home again. It wasn't very long before the Washingtons themselves joined them. George lingered awhile waiting for the enemy troops to evacuate the city, and then he marched in to formally reclaim it. Martha, meanwhile, had gone on ahead to get their house ready for his final homecoming. He left New York on November 25, and after resigning his commission at Annapolis, he rode up the drive to Mount Vernon a month later, just in time for their first Christmas at home in eight years.

A Classic Roman Matron

The retired General Washington and Martha were older now, and pleased that the pace of their lives had slowed down. He needed spectacles to respond to hundreds of letters from well-wishers and to study his accounts, and Martha needed a pair of them, too, to keep up with her incessant needlework.

There were children at Mount Vernon again, which made Martha blessedly content. Daughter-in-law Nelly had married again, but two of her children, Nelly, five, and George, two, stayed with their grandmother at Mount Vernon while their two older sisters lived nearby at the estate Jacky had built outside Alexandria. The path between the two mansions was well worn, and all four children were frequently together with George and Martha, who delighted in them no end. It was as though the clock had been turned back to the first days of their marriage.

But the outside world was threatening them again. The new nation that George had helped build was having growing pains. An armed rebellion in western Massachusetts had all the earmarks of a civil war in the making, and troubles in other states hinted at a nasty general trend toward anarchy. A new congress was being formed with the purpose of drafting a constitution, and naturally George was urged to head the Virginia delegation again. But he was dogged in his refusal. He knew that oratory would be key to the deliberations, and it was well known that he was a poor public speaker. He made it clear that he was retired and that he had no intention of leaving home ever again, noting that the new generation was more capable than he was of uniting the states.

George might have realized that fate was working against his dream of living out his days as the squire of Mount Vernon when the Constitutional Convention made him its president. The document they drafted was signed in September and he went home again, but Martha could tell from his mood that this wasn't going to be the end of his public service.

Her fears were realized as the individual state legislatures debated ratification of the Constitution and the one thing that they all seemed to agree on right from the start was that George Washington should be the country's first president. When he protested, he was assured that it would only be for a little while until the new system could take root, although the Constitution clearly stated that he would have to serve for at least four years.

When the votes were counted, every last one of them was for the only candidate, George Washington, and he left home to serve his country once again, this time in New York City, where the new government had been established.

Below: With the end of a long and frustrating war, George eagerly looked forward to going home to his former life as a country squire among his friends, neighbors, and family.

Martha joined him there after his inauguration along with her grandchildren, Nelly, who was ten years old, and George, known as "Wash," a rambunctious lad of eight. They also had a retinue of servants, including Martha's two personal maids, who had been at her side during all of her travels. They were settled in a three-story mansion on Cherry Street, where fourteen white servants augmented the seven slaves who had been brought up from Virginia, all of them dressed in the scarlet-and-white Washington livery. It was obviously very different from Martha's other homes-away-from-home during the war years.

The household staff also included Samuel Fraunces, who had given up his famous local tavern to work wonders in the Washington kitchen. And a valet brought over from France set and powdered Martha's hair every morning while she sipped coffee that she insisted on making for herself.

Martha's grandson George Washington Parke Custis (right), built the Virginia mansion he called Arlington House (below) overlooking the new capital city as a memorial to the first president. The building, known today as the Custis-Lee Mansion, has become the focal point of the Arlington National Cemetery.

The Custis-Lee Mansion

In 1802, the year Martha Washington died, her grandson George Washington Parke Custis finished building the first section of a mansion on a Virginia hillside overlooking the District of Columbia across the Potomac. It was the centerpiece of an 11,000-acre estate he eventually inherited from his grandmother, and it became his family home when he married Mary Lee Fitzhugh two years later. But the place he called Arlington House was much more than that. It was a memorial to his grandmother's husband, and he filled it with the president's personal papers, portraits, clothing, and other memorabilia that he had been collecting all his life.

In 1831, his only child, Mary Anna, married Robert E. Lee, and she inherited the estate when Custis died twenty-six years later. She was given control of the property until her death, at which time the title was to pass to her eldest son, George Washington Custis Lee.

Fate stepped in when the Civil War broke out and Robert E. Lee left home to take command of Virginia's military forces. He had no sooner left than federal troops commandeered the Arlington estate and turned it into a military installation.

Within a few years, the estate was appropriated as a military cemetery and efforts were undertaken to make the mansion itself uninhabitable if the Lees should ever attempt to reclaim it. After General Lee died, his grandson G. W. Custis Lee sued the government for unlawful seizure, and the property was returned to him after the U.S. Supreme Court ruled in his favor. The government responded by buying it from him for $150,000. Today, the shell of the house is the heart of Arlington National Cemetery.

In spite of that French touch, Martha never attempted to follow foreign fashions, even though European styles were all the rage among well-dressed women at the time. She wasn't interested in making a fashion statement, preferring the understated elegance of muslin gowns and homespun dresses that had a made-in-America look. The style had served her well most of her life, and she didn't see any reason to change.

When Martha's dresses began to show signs of wear, she had them unraveled, the fabric recycled, and the threads rewound on spools.

Abigail Adams, the vice president's wife, hadn't met Martha before they both went to New York City, but her first impression was one of instant admiration. A letter to her sister in Massachusetts began by saying, "She [Martha] is plain in her dress, but that plainness is the best of every art." Abigail went on to report, "Her hair is white, her teeth are beautiful, her person is rather short." After adding that Martha had a fine figure, she went on to say, "Her manners are modest and unassuming, dignified and feminine."

The house on Cherry Street was a crowded and busy place, and there was a severe problem with crowds of visitors, some of whom were war veterans dropping by to pay their respects to the old general, and some who were looking for a path to the government payroll. George wasn't inclined to turn anyone away, but he realized that he needed time to get his work done; he settled the problem by ordering a weekly levee, or reception, every Tuesday afternoon, a formal dinner on Thursdays, and a formal reception, which Martha would preside over, on Friday evenings. He set aside bits of time for close friends, but he made it clear that no one at all would be welcome on Sundays. It wasn't nearly as intense a social schedule as they had followed back home, but he was running a country now, not a plantation.

Even before Martha arrived in New York, Congress established some strict ground rules for her behavior. She and her husband were forbidden to accept dinner invitations from private citizens, and the rules put tight limits on visits she could make among her new neighbors, word of which meant that she didn't get many invitations. After a lifetime of socializing, it made her feel isolated: She wrote to a friend, "I am more like a state prisoner than anything else." But Martha being Martha, she said in another letter, "I am determined to be cheerful and to be happy, in whatever situation I may be; for I have also learned from experience that the greater part of our happiness or misery depends upon our dispositions, and not upon our circumstances."

In spite of Martha's characterization of a life under house arrest, the presence of her grandchildren made the house a home. The youngsters, who had never lived in a city, were

Below: Martha preferred to sit on the sidelines at the round of balls that she and her husband hosted, but George loved to dance. It was one of the few things he enjoyed about his official life in New York and Philadelphia.

enchanted by pantomimes and puppet shows, and fascinated by museums and waxworks. Martha and George also took advantage of the city's cultural life; he was especially fond of the theater, and they went to plays as often as they could.

In addition to her personal servants, Martha had an unofficial social secretary in the person of Polly Lear, the wife of Tobias Lear, who had served as George's secretary and a tutor for the Custis children back home and was now the president's chief aide. She also relied on Robert Lewis, one of George's many nephews, who assumed the role of her escort and a companion for the children.

Although the Washingtons were generally careful not to behave like royalty, Martha made an exception with her Friday receptions, which she unapologetically modeled on the customs of the courts of England and France. She was eager to establish respect for the office of the president, and she believed that the respect should extend to the Europeans, who she hoped would interpret her imitation as a form of flattery.

Guests were formally announced when they entered and were escorted into Martha's presence, where their curtsies were acknowledged with a slight, almost imperceptible, nod. Then they were led to chairs arranged in a semicircle around their hostess, where they were told not to engage in any conversation. The president strolled around the edge of the gathering, stopping for a few words at each chair before moving on to the side of the room, and then the guests were led into another room, where buffet tables were set with the equivalent of an English high tea, and the president and his wife joined them for coffee. Martha retired promptly at nine and the party was over. Men were welcome at these affairs, but they were forbidden to engage in ribald storytelling or playing cards or, worse, in flirting with any of the ladies, with the result that men usually tried to find more pressing business on Friday evenings.

These formal gatherings were invitation-only affairs, but following the established New York custom of New Year's Day open houses, Martha also threw open her doors to anyone who cared to come calling on the first day of the year. Naturally, the open houses, which were held throughout the Washington presidency, were well attended. They were the only time that Lady Washington had an opportunity to see how the other half lived, and they earned her a reputation as a solid supporter of the new democracy—even if it only happened once a year.

Near the end of their first year in New York, the French minister went home to Paris and his mansion on Broadway next to Trinity Church was leased for the Washingtons. It was much larger and more elegant, not to mention closer to the center of government, than the Cherry Street house was, and they moved in on the president's fifty-eighth birthday before the renovations were finished. The building was eventually demolished, as was the one on Cherry Street, which along with most of the street itself, disappeared to make way for the Brooklyn Bridge. Another historic landmark, Federal Hall, where George took his first oath of office, was also torn down.

The president and his wife were no sooner settled in their new home than Congress voted to move the government to a new federal city near their family homestead, and to relocate to Philadelphia while it was being built. They lived in the mansion on Broadway for less than a year, but Martha had grown fond of the place even though her husband had gone through another life-threatening experience there as a victim of an influenza epidemic. Still, she looked forward to the change. She knew Philadelphia well, and many of her old friends from the war years were settled there. The Washingtons had lived in New York for seventeen months, but Martha never established any ties there, and she never looked back.

Their new home on Philadelphia's Market Street was rented from Robert Morris, an old family friend who had served on George's wartime staff. His wife, Marcia, and Martha were close friends, too, and it pleased Martha that they would be living next door in a mansion that shared a garden with hers.

As the end of her husband's first term approached, Martha's hope that there wouldn't be a second began to vanish. Political parties were beginning to rear their ugly heads, and the war of words between the states rights–oriented Thomas Jefferson and James Madison and the Federalists represented by George Washington and John Adams sometimes became direct attacks on the president and his wife. But because George was a godlike figure in the minds of most Americans, attacking him wasn't a good idea for his political opponents, and so Martha became their lightning rod instead. It was all very subtle, to be sure; she, too, had an adoring constituency.

Above: Martha Washington never lived in the White House, but this portrait of her hangs there.

The position of the men who were calling themselves Democratic-Republicans was that the United States had an obligation to set an example of democracy at work to the rest of the world, and here the wife of its chief executive was behaving like royalty with her exclusive levees and receptions. Why, she had even organized lavish balls to celebrate the president's birthday, an honor previously reserved only for the crowned heads of Europe! Not only that, but the Old World versions paled in comparison to Martha's birthday balls, at least that was the opinion of one French nobleman who had seen his share of them.

Newspaper publishers with Anti-Federalist leanings jumped into the controversy, attacking Martha for "frivolities, fripperies and needless expense," and suggesting that she was single-handedly destroying America's republican principles with her "queenly" ways. One suggested that she had inherited her European attitudes from her English-born father, but that charge didn't get very far with his readers, some of whom had themselves been born in England or who, like Martha, had relatives there. Another published an engraving of Martha dressed in her usual modest muslin, but trimmed with ermine and silk ruffles.

But Martha herself was unruffled. Although she slightly, even imperceptibly, reined in some of her courtly ways, she knew that approval abroad was vital to the country's place in the world, and she was passionate about projecting an image of dignity. She didn't feel any obligation to explain her motives, and she effectively silenced her critics without saying a word.

Still, Martha had had enough of being the wife of a president, and when her husband's first term began to wind down she was one of the few Americans who wished that he wouldn't run for a second. In the end, she knew that the will of the people was stronger than her own and she agreed that he should accept a second term "[a]ccording to his ideas of duty." Once again, George ran unopposed for the presidency in 1792.

The world was beginning to turn ugly before the election was held. A republic had been declared in France as an outgrowth of its own revolution, and King Louis XVI and Queen Marie Antoinette had been arrested and were doomed to be beheaded. It gave new strength to radical Democratic-Republicans like Thomas Jefferson, who were rabidly against monarchies and squarely in favor of anything French, including a Reign of Terror that was looming just over the horizon. On the other side of the gulf were the Federalists, led by John Adams and Alexander Hamilton. Once again George Washington was a man in the middle, but, of course, that was the point. He had been perceived as the only one who could settle the Hamilton-Jefferson feud, but he couldn't do it without the people behind him, and when he looked around after taking the oath of office for the second time, they were divided along party lines. Those who were backing Jefferson were pushing for American involvement on France's side in the inevitable European war, while the Federalists were insisting that America should stay neutral.

In the midst of the battle, both Jefferson and Hamilton began talking of retiring to private life, but the president, who had been coerced into a second term as the only man who could reconcile their differences, had no such option. It was Martha who persuaded him to let Jefferson go home if he wanted to. She was determined to avoid a war, and she perceived that there would be one if Jefferson had his way. Their fellow Virginian "had never tasted gunpowder," she told her husband, but Hamilton had. Although Martha was quite fond of Hamilton's wife, the former Betsy Schuyler, she didn't seem to think much of the man himself, but she convinced George that he was the lesser of the two evils and that the time had come for him to take sides.

George's decision opened the floodgates of criticism, and he was accused of deserting an old ally in the French by some, and of abandoning the principles of the Revolution by others. But, as Martha had done before him, the president quietly ignored his critics and went about the business of government with all the dignity he could muster. Only Martha knew that he had been hurt deeply.

Long before his last days in the presidency, George wrote to a friend, "Unless someone pops in unexpectedly, Mrs. Washington and myself will do what has not been done within the last twenty years by us—that is to set down to dinner by ourselves."

> *"The General and I feel like children just released from school or from a hard taskmaster, and we believe that nothing can tempt us to leave our sacred roof-tree again … the twilight is gathering around our lives. I am again fairly settled down to the pleasant duties of an old-fashioned Virginia house-keeper, steady as a clock, busy as a bee, and as cheerful as a cricket."*
>
> —*Martha Washington on life postpresidency*

The political vitriol cooled somewhat during the summer of 1793, when a yellow fever epidemic struck Philadelphia. One of its first victims was Polly Lear, who died at the age of twenty-three. She had been Martha's closest companion.

Life came to a standstill in the wake of increasing sudden death, but although Martha was worried about her grandchildren, she refused to go home to Mount Vernon without her husband, who faced the epidemic with his usual calm. When they finally did go home in the fall, they found their plantation in a state of virtual ruin from mismanagement in their absence. Neither George nor Martha had wanted a second term as the head of the government, and this was the icing on the cake of what may have been the worst year of their lives.

They managed to bring back order to their plantation, but the mess in Philadelphia seemed to be getting worse. A British blockade of French West Indian ports was putting American sailors at risk of capture in spite of their country's neutrality, and George sent John Jay to London to negotiate a treaty. At the same time, trouble was brewing in western Pennsylvania over a whiskey tax, and the president put on his uniform once again to supervise the mobilization of the militia. But even that reminder of his previous service to his country didn't stop a new round of nastiness by the press over what they characterized as John Jay's sellout in his treaty with Great Britain. This time, the attacks reached all the way back to 1776 with questions on his war record.

Then the public apparently had had enough, and they turned out in enthusiastic droves to celebrate the president's sixty-fourth birthday, in 1796. As far as Martha was concerned, it marked the beginning of their final year in office, and she was counting the days.

The red-letter day finally came on March 4, 1797, when George went to Congress Hall dressed in black velvet with a powdered wig and a military headpiece to witness the presidential inauguration of his successor, John Adams. Five days later he was on his way home again—he hoped for the last time.

Below: A letter in Martha's own hand to her friend Henrietta Liston. It was written at Mount Vernon a year after she returned from Philadelphia.

Home Again

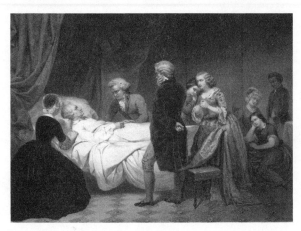

John and Abigail Adams had decided not to buy the furnishings in the Philadelphia presidential mansion, and George left his aides Tobias Lear and Martha's nephew Bart Dandridge behind to dispose of them and organize the move to Mount Vernon. As for himself, George was pleased that his wife had stopped referring to him as "the president," in favor of "the general."

George and Martha had been away from Mount Vernon for the better part of the previous twenty years, but after a few short weeks, they slipped back into the old routine as if nothing had happened in the meantime, Their family was gathered around them again and as granddaughter Nelly Custis wrote to a friend, "I never have a dull or lonesome hour, never find a day too long." George never strayed far from his vine and fig tree, but he did make frequent trips upriver to watch the building of the new federal city that would one day be named for him. "A century hence," he wrote to an old friend, "if this country keeps united … will produce a city, though not as large as London, yet of a magnitude inferior to few others in Europe, on the banks of the Potomac… where elegant buildings are erecting and in forwardness, for the reception of Congress in 1800."

In the meantime, though, in Philadelphia there was talk of war with France, and the secretary of war made the trip to Mount Vernon to present George with a new commission as commander in chief. Martha, needless to say, was appalled. But he accepted the honor stoically. Both were fairly certain that push wouldn't come to shove, and that there would be no war. Still, it was a threat more real to the Washingtons' happiness than to the country's security.

It became a moot point by the end of the year, when the general rode through a snowstorm and contracted a sore throat that wouldn't go away. His doctor, James Craik, was called, and he in turn called in two consultants, but none of their tried-and-true home remedies worked and their patient's condition grew worse. Bleeding him, they concluded, was their only hope, but the bloodletting, which was done over Martha's objections, only weakened him, and he died of a cold, with Martha at his side, at around sunset on December 14, 1799.

Although their home was filled with well-wishers, Martha was lonely in the big house. She closed the bedroom they had shared, and moved into an attic room above it, which had no heat but did have a view of her husband's burial

Above: George Washington's death, probably from a common cold, could easily have been prevented today, but in 1799, "cures" such as bloodletting often proved to be deadly.

The first American currency bearing the portrait of a woman was a $1.00 silver certificate honoring Martha Washington, issued in 1886.

vault. As she had done in an earlier time, she locked herself in the room for an hour each morning with strict orders that she was not to be disturbed.

At other times, she was the perfect hostess she always had been, but gradually she began spending more and more time alone in that upstairs room. Then, two years after her husband's death, Martha knew that the prediction she made at his deathbed—"I shall soon follow him"—was about to come true. She had but one more thing to do. She had saved all of George's letters to her, and she intended to burn them to protect their private memories from prying eyes. She managed to destroy all but two of his letters, which she put into a writing desk drawer when her chore was interrupted.

She was never able to retrieve them. The next morning, May 22, 1802, Martha Washington died of what was diagnosed as a fever. She was seventy years old. An obituary that appeared in the Alexandria *Advertiser and Commercial Appeal* said, "She was the worthy partner of the worthiest of men."

Visiting Mount Vernon

The home George and Martha Washington loved is sixteen miles south of Washington, D.C., on the George Washington Parkway. It is open every day of the year, including all holidays. The site includes the twenty-one-room mansion house and several outbuildings, including the kitchen, stables, greenhouse, and slave quarters, as well as a sixteen-acre working farm. The extensive gardens, which George Washington designed, are open for strolling and contemplation. The home is open from 9:00 A.M. to 5:00 P.M. most times of the year, and an admission fee is charged.

Boat tours are available spring through fall both from Washington, D.C., and Alexandria, Virginia, and organized bus tours are operated from Washington, D.C.'s Union Station year-round. The address is 3200 George Washington Memorial Parkway, Mount Vernon, Virginia 22121. The mailing address is P.O. Box 110, Mount Vernon, Virginia 22121. You can find information on the Web at www.mountvernon.org.

Above: The tomb George Washington designed for himself near the Mount Vernon manor house also became Martha's last resting place.

Abigail Adams

Family Tradition

Abigail Smith Adams grew up in the village of Weymouth, one of the first settlements of the Massachusetts Bay Colony. Her mother, Elizabeth Quincy, had been from a family that was among the first to arrive at next-door Braintree in 1637 when Edmund Quincy established a seaside estate there that he called Mount Wollaston.

On her father's side, Abigail traced her family back to Thomas Smith, a butcher who settled in Charlestown, across the river from Boston, in the early 1660s. He married Sarah Boylston, a member of one of the Bay Colony's most prominent families. Their grandson, William Smith, a Congregationalist minister who graduated from Harvard College in 1725, married Elizabeth Quincy, uniting the two locally important families.

As the highly regarded parson of Weymouth's Puritan congregation, Reverend Smith was near the top of the pecking order among the town's elite, and his son and three daughters grew up sharing his status.

Reverend Smith became pastor of Weymouth's North Parish almost as soon as he graduated from Harvard, and he kept the job for more than forty-five years—highly unusual among New England divines, who served at the pleasure of congregations that were often easily displeased. Chief among his talents was his ability to base his sermons on biblical texts that related directly to local events in the here and now, but he also seemed always to be able to find the right solutions to family problems within his flock without offending anyone, and they loved him for it. It didn't hurt his status a bit when he married Elizabeth Quincy, whose father was the area's leading citizen, a perennial moderator of the town meeting and the local justice of the peace.

The Smith parsonage was the center of Weymouth's intellectual life, and the parson's enviable personal library was a local treasure. He was generous about sharing it, and he welcomed anyone who was interested to gather around his fire for discussions of what they were reading. Plenty of local men were, indeed, interested, and the Smith household had all the earmarks of a literary salon.

But it was also his family's home, and it began to grow when their first child, Mary, was born at the end of 1741. Abigail, their second daughter, was born three years later, followed in another two years by a son, William, and their third daughter, Elizabeth, who arrived in 1750.

Abigail Quincy Smith Adams

Born
November 11, 1744, Weymouth, Massachusetts

Parents
Reverend William Smith and Elizabeth Quincy Smith

Marriage
1764 to John Adams (1735-1826)

Children
Abigail (Nabby) Amelia (1765-1813); John Quincy (1767-1848); Susanna (1768-70); Charles (1770-1800); Thomas Boylston (1772-1832)

Died
October 28, 1818, Quincy, Massachusetts

Above: The house in Weymouth, Massachusetts, where Abigail Smith grew up is a "saltbox" style house; the style has grown popular over the years.

The four Smith children were raised in a home where education ranked just a hair below godliness, but having three daughters made it a difficult goal, especially considering that, as their father noted, each of them had "an uncommon force of intellect." In those days, although schools had been established for boys, girls weren't expected to learn much more than how to read and write and do simple sums. Their mothers could teach them that—along with the more essential skills of cooking, weaving and sewing, and running a household—and few mothers were better teachers than Elizabeth Quincy Smith.

Except one: In Abigail's case, it was her mother's mother, grandmother Elizabeth Quincy. Abigail remembered her as "an oracle of wisdom" who had "a happy method of mixing instruction and amusement." Nabby, as Abigail was called, spent a great deal of time with her grandparents, frequently staying at Mount Wollaston for weeks at a time. It was a common practice among New England families who believed that the change of scenery had a broadening effect on a youngster, not to mention that it gave their mothers a bit of a rest. In Abigail's case, she recalled that as a young girl, she had a "volatile disposition," which others described as "headstrong," and the family apparently concluded that some extra time at her grandmother's patient knee would help calm her down.

But the Smith children spent more time at home than farmed out with relatives, and their father encouraged them to read anything in his library that struck their fancy. As far as Abigail was concerned, everything did, and she read through translations of the ancient classics, from Homer to Cicero, and dipped into contemporary works on politics and theology. By the time she was a young woman, she was as well-read as any college-trained man, and more so than any woman she knew, including her sisters, who were as enthusiastic about reading as she was.

The Smith children also had the advantage of being able to eavesdrop on the discussions in the family parlor, and as they got older they were encouraged to join them. The people who came every evening for these enlightening conversations were more often than not their own relatives, but there were some notable exceptions. Among them was Richard Cranch, a bookish, self-taught young man whose belief that women ought to be well read bordered on obsession. He was pleased to have found such eager students as the Smith girls, and he enthusiastically introduced them to great literary works. Abigail was especially smitten with Brother Cranch, although he ended up marrying her sister Mary, and she always gave him credit for making her a "lover of literature." But admiration and love are two different things, and if Abigail ever had any romantic notions about Cranch, she kept them to herself.

As a teenager, Abigail spent a lot of time visiting her aunt and uncle, Isaac and Elizabeth Smith, in Boston. But Weymouth was her home, and there was another young man there, a struggling young lawyer named John Adams who had a practice in Braintree, Massachusetts. They had met many times, but John wasn't very impressed with Abigail or her sisters, and while she was silent about her own feelings, she also generally made it a point to ignore him. But John Adams was hard to avoid. His closest friend, Richard Cranch, encouraged the young lawyer to join him on his visits to the parsonage, and when Cranch started to court Mary Smith, the visits became more frequent. It could hardly be called an instant attraction, but John couldn't help being impressed with Abigail's intellect, and before long he was showing up with books that he knew she'd find interesting. It wasn't much longer before they began to realize that they were as much alike as two people could possibly be, and not much longer after that, they realized that they were in love with each other. She said that their two hearts were "cast in the same mold," and she never changed her opinion up until the day she died.

After a long courtship, Abigail's father married John and his second daughter in October 1764. The bridegroom was twenty-eight, and she was nineteen. Nabby's mother tried to stop the wedding because she considered John's ancestry beneath her, and besides, he was a lawyer, and that didn't speak well for his future. But he had just inherited a house and a ten-acre farm, and his law practice was thriving; anyway, there was no stopping the stubborn Abigail, who was clearly very much in love with this man.

Above: Abigail's daughter, Abigail Adams Smith.

Abigail and John

The newlyweds moved into a small saltbox house next door to a similar one where John had grown up and was still the home of Abigail's mother-in-law, whom she loved and admired, fortunately. Her own parents were less than five miles away, and her sister, Mary Cranch, lived even closer, and they all visited one another often. The couple shared the work of running their farm, which supplied most of their needs, and John eagerly anticipated a long life as a country squire. Indeed their lives changed very little until late in the following summer, when their first child was born. They named her Abigail, but called her Nabby, and her presence brought them even closer. John's law office was in their house, and they were never far apart, except when he was riding circuit to courts from Plymouth to Maine. But not long after baby Nabby arrived, the outside world was beginning to change, and their lives would soon change along with it.

Bostonians had long been annoyed by the way the British treated them, but injury was added to insult when London decreed that legal documents

Below: Abigail's husband, John Adams.

Abigail and John were married for fifty-four years, longer than any other First Couple thus far.

---

and other printed material, including playing cards, should be taxed through the purchase of a special stamp. It was a relatively minor thing, but it was the straw that broke the camel's back, and it led to rioting in the streets of Boston so violent that the stamp administrator quit his job and left town. But no replacement came forward, and without one there was no way for anyone to buy the stamps. Court business came to a standstill, and that meant lawyers like John Adams were virtually out of business.

It was only a matter of time before the Stamp Act was repealed, thanks in large part to a petition John wrote and circulated, but in the meantime, he took advantage of the lull to become politically active. He was a founding member of the revolutionary Sons of Liberty, and he joined with his second cousin Samuel Adams in forming the Committees of Correspondence, which encouraged united action among the Colonies. John also wrote newspaper articles favoring the budding revolution, and he spoke eloquently about it at town meetings, which built his reputation as a local firebrand. After the courts reopened, his law practice burgeoned, too, and his time away from home could often be counted in weeks rather than days.

John and Abigail's second child, John Quincy, was born in 1767, making it impossible for Abigail to join her husband on even brief trips to the far-flung courts. They solved the problem, at least partly, by renting a house in Boston where they could be together more often. It also gave John more time to get involved in political discussions at local coffeehouses, and to contemplate his future. He was torn between supporting his family through his law practice and serving his country, which had become a passion to him. At first, he compromised by taking on high-profile politically significant cases, the first of which was a defense of John Hancock, a local businessman, against smuggling charges, followed within weeks by securing the acquittal of four sailors who stood accused of killing an officer who attempted to shanghai them into the British navy.

Below: Five generations of Adams babies slept in this cradle, including two American presidents, John and John Quincy Adams.

Meanwhile, Abigail's own interest in politics was strengthened through deep discussions with men like Sam Adams and John Hancock. Like most women of her time, she had always regarded politics as the business of men, but little by little she made it her business, too, and few men in town had more highly developed political opinions, nor more eagerness to share them, than she did.

During this time, Abigail gave birth to another daughter, whom she named Susanna after John's mother. The child died, as many did in those years, shortly after her first birthday. It was not long afterward that British soldiers fired on a crowd in the Common, killing three in an incident that became known as the Boston Massacre. John took on the unpopular job of defending the soldiers, even though he knew that his reputation for patriotism would be compromised. But he strongly believed that every man was entitled to his day in court, and that the trial would send a message to London that the rule of law was still important in Boston.

He proved his point with acquittals, and his neighbors showed him that his reputation was as solid as ever when the town meeting elected him their representative in the legislature. It meant time away from his law practice that would cut into his income at the very moment his family was growing again. A third child, Charles, had just been born.

With three babies to care for, Abigail wasn't able to go to meetings of the legislature, but she received detailed reports on the sessions, as well as what was going on behind the scenes, from her husband. The anti-British sentiments they both shared intensified, and Abigail broke with the tradition that women should stay out of politics by becoming as outspoken as any of the Boston radicals.

> *"I long to hear that you have declared an independency and by the way in the new Code of Laws which I suppose it will be necessary for you to make I desire you would remember the Ladies, and be more favourable and generous to them than your ancestors. Do not put unlimited power into the hands of their Husbands. Remember all Men would be tyrants if they could. If particular care and attention is not paid to the Ladies we are determined to foment a Rebellion, and will not hold ourselves bound by any Laws in which we have no voice, or Representation."*
>
> —Abigail to John Adams, March 31, 1776

Then she took on a cause of her own. Breaking with Great Britain was important, to be sure, but just as important to Abigail was the role women should play in the new order of things. She sought out like-minded women and began long correspondences with them that continued for years. But her established responsibilities as a wife and mother grew when she gave birth to her fourth child, Thomas Boylston, in 1772. Her eldest, Nabby, was only seven years old.

Two years later, the English Parliament levied a tax on tea, and gave the British East India Company a monopoly on it. It infuriated the Boston radicals, and a group of them quietly dumped the company's first shipment into the harbor in what they called the Boston Tea Party.

The royal chess game continued with another round of laws. One required the Colonists to quarter British troops, another made it easier to prosecute radicals for inciting riots, and in the case of Massachusetts, the royal governor was given dictatorial powers. It meant that John Adams would be devoting more time to politics and less to his law practice. He moved Abigail and the children back to Braintree, where he felt they'd be safer, and closer to their extended family, and then he left for Philadelphia as a Massachusetts delegate to the Continental Congress.

John and Abigail exchanged letters almost every day when he was away making the rounds of the courts, but they were predominantly love letters and exchanges of family news. Now that he was in Philadelphia, she demanded more insight from him into the day-to-day deliberations of the Congress. John tried to satisfy her, but in an early letter, he warned her that the historic proceedings might be a bit dull, even for her.

By the time John was elected to the Second Continental Congress, Abigail wrote that she had become firmly convinced that the only option for lovers of liberty was "to die [the] last of British freemen than to live the first of British Slaves."

Below: One of Abigail's most treasured possessions, this locket was a gift from her husband, John. She wore it through her married life.

Not long before the Congress convened, George Gates, the royal governor of Massachusetts, ordered troops to Lexington to confiscate rebel guns and ammunition, but the patriots were ready for them, thanks to signals relayed by Paul Revere and William Dawes, and the first shots of the Revolution were fired there on April 18, 1775. The redcoats moved on to nearby Concord, where they took the arsenal without a fight, but when they reached a bridge outside of town on their way back to Boston, more than three hundred Minutemen blocked their way.

Abigail melted down her pewter spoons to make bullets for her brother-in-law Elihu, a Minuteman.

Braintree was about the same distance south of Boston as Concord Bridge was west of it, but Abigail, who would be left alone there when John went off in a few days to serve in Congress, refused to panic. There was a real threat that the British, cut off from the west, would attack coastal towns like Braintree and Weymouth, and a few of her neighbors were already making evacuation plans. Recognizing Abigail's stubbornness, John agreed with her decision to stay where she was, but he made her promise that she would "fly to the woods with our children" at the first sign of trouble.

Less than a month later, Abigail's life was intruded upon again, this time by cannon fire. Taking her boys with her, she climbed to the top of a hill where they'd have a clear view of Boston and the serious battle that was taking place there. Because of the distance, they had no idea what was happening, but it was obviously a major encounter. Several days passed before she found out that she had been watching the defense of Breed's and Bunker Hill in Charlestown, which the Minutemen ultimately lost, but at great cost of life to the enemy. It was the first major conflict of what was now a full-scale war, and Abigail and her children were at the center of the war of nerves that came with it. Refugees from Boston poured down the road, and Abigail opened her house to them. She lived in a world of wild rumors and far-off cannon fire that no one could explain; she endured shortages of basic necessities, and she was forced to spend more of her time tending their farm as hired help went off to enlist in the Continental Army.

Then, late in the summer, things went from bad to worse. A dysentery pandemic swept though the area, wiping out entire families, and Abigail was one of the first to be infected. She recovered quickly, but it left her weakened, and she had to gather up her strength to nurse her son Tommy and care for two of her servants who were also bedridden. Then her mother was stricken, and Abigail shuttled between her house and the parsonage to take care of her before she died of the disease after a few weeks.

Her mother's death devastated Abigail. "I have been like a nun in a cloister," she wrote, and she stopped her rounds of visits to friends and family, except her father and her sisters, and lost herself in running the farm and caring for her children, spending long evenings staring into the fire and wondering what the future held. She was pregnant again, for the sixth time, and she faced the prospect of bearing a child without her mother or her husband at her side. The baby girl died during birth the following summer.

In the midst of it all, John and Sam Adams requested a leave of absence from Congress, and John arrived home in Braintree in November. John and Abigail had recently marked their thirteenth wedding anniversary, and she noted ruefully, "Three years of that time we have been cruelly separated." But now she and her husband were together again, although within two weeks he went off to try an important legal case in Portsmouth, New Hampshire. But Abigail didn't mind that he was back in harness. The family needed the money almost desperately, and she knew that he'd come back to her before too long.

Above: The kitchen was the most important room in John and Abigail's first home at what was then called Braintree. In cold winters the fire was as welcome as the meals cooked over it.

But while he was gone, a letter arrived informing him that he had been elected commissioner to the court of France. He didn't have to accept, the letter said, but it urged him to consider it his patriotic duty. In conclusion, his fellow congressman James Lovell wrote, "Your dear amiable partner may be tempted to condemn my persuasions of you to distance yourself from her farther than York Town." Tempted she was, but never in their married life had Abigail ever attempted to stand in John's way, and she wouldn't this time.

At first they decided that Abigail and the children would go with him to Paris, but they simply couldn't afford it and in the end John agreed to take only ten-year-old John Quincy along. He was at an age when most boys entered into apprenticeships, and this was an opportunity for him to learn what his father regarded as the greatest trade of all: public service.

Five months after John and John Quincy arrived in Paris, Benjamin Franklin was elected minister to France, and with the dissolution of the mission, John was effectively out of a job. There were rumors that he'd be sent to Vienna, but without letters from either her husband or son, Abigail turned to friends in Congress to find out what was going on. All she got was a runaround, and finally she wrote to Sam Adams to help her get to the bottom of it. He responded that John was, indeed, on his way home. What he didn't say was that their boat had already dropped anchor and that John and John Quincy were being rowed up to the Braintree beach. They had been away from home for a year and a half.

John and Abigail were together again, but four months later another letter arrived from Congress, informing him that he had been elected minister to negotiate peace with King George III. Peace was still a long way off, but he sailed back to France as soon as he could, this time taking along their nine-year-old son Charles as well as young Johnny, who was an experienced transoceanic traveler by then. Abigail was left at home with Nabby and Tommy, facing another aching loneliness that had no end as far as she could see.

With two of her children abroad and Nabby at school in Boston, Abigail found herself with time on her hands, and she used it to manage the family's financial affairs, investing in real estate, currency exchange, and safe securities.

Above: John Singleton Copley's portrait of fourteen-year-old John Quincy Adams at the start of his diplomatic career in the Russian court.

She was a hardheaded businesswoman, but she relied on trusted friends to help her avoid "persons who would take advantage of me"—as if anyone could. When John finally got settled in Europe, he began sending her shipments of things that were cheap overseas but expensive in New England. She sold them for cash, and soon began requesting gifts that could bring higher prices. Eventually she started ordering directly from merchants in places like Holland and Spain, and commissioned women in her wide network of friends to help her sell the goods that arrived. Abigail had developed into a merchant princess.

In spite of John's involvement in her cottage industry, letters from him were as rare as they had been on his previous mission. Ten months went by before she heard from him. He was having a discouraging time dealing with the Byzantine politics of the French court, and he wasn't getting much cooperation from Benjamin Franklin, either. He responded by packing his bags and taking his sons to Holland, where he hoped to persuade the Dutch to support the American Revolution. He enrolled his sons in the University of Leyden, which pleased Abigail no end, but the boys were as poor at writing of their experiences as their father had become.

Back in Philadelphia, Congress appointed Benjamin Franklin, John Jay, and Thomas Jefferson to join John in the peace negotiations. Abigail learned of it from newspaper accounts, and she smelled a rat. She pressed John for details, and he responded by sending a coded message to Sam Adams. Although John was often subject to paranoia, it was clear that Franklin and the others were smearing his name, and that sent Abigail off on a crusade to set things right, writing to everyone she knew defending her husband because, "when he is wounded I bleed."

In the midst of the storm, their son John Quincy went off to Russia with the new minister to the court of Catherine the Great, Francis Dana, a family friend and an associate of his father's. The Adamses' son, Charles, was homesick for his mother, and his father put him aboard a ship headed for America. The normal five- or six-week voyage took more than five months, which also explained why mail service from abroad was so erratic. Charles's arrival was supposed to be a surprise for Abigail, but she heard that he was on his way about a month after he left, and his late arrival gave her one more thing to worry about. She was pleased that John Quincy had gone to Saint Petersburg, even though she realized it was hopeless to expect that mail to and from the frozen north would get through. As it was, she'd only had one or two letters from John in an entire year, and he was in Amsterdam, one of the world's busiest port cities.

After the British surrender at Yorktown, John went back to Paris to rejoin the peace negotiations, but not until after he had negotiated a series of loans from the Dutch that kept the American confederation afloat. As soon as an armistice was declared early in 1783, the commissioners went to work on what was called the Peace of Paris, formally ending the American Revolution. It was accomplished, John reported, "with as little ceremony, and in as short a time as a Marriage Settlement."

Sojourns

John and Abigail's marriage had suffered during his long absence, but if their love was wounded, it was still impressively strong. Each of them had been making plans to get back together. Abigail had packed her trunks several times to go to Europe; at the same time, John was forever promising to resign and go home. But their plans were always checkmated. The game seemed to have come to an end after the peace treaty was signed and his work was finished, but even as he contemplated giving up public service altogether, he was appointed to a committee charged with forging an important commercial treaty with Britain. That meant that he had to cancel his plans to sail home, but this time he had a better idea. He sent a letter to Abigail asking her to "come to me this fall and go home with me this spring." He also asked that she take sixteen-year-old Nabby along with her. They left early in the spring.

John was in Holland when Abigail arrived in London, but he sent John Quincy, who had just come back from Russia, to meet her and tour London with her. She hadn't been prepared to like London after the recent unpleasantness with the English, but she was captivated by the city in spite of herself, and she was happier than she had been for as long as she could remember to be reunited with her son, whom she hadn't seen in more than six years. Then in another week, John himself appeared at her door, and the unhappiness of the recent past was forgotten in an instant.

Within a month, they were settled in an elegant house in Auteuil, a Paris suburb that was unlike anything Abigail had ever seen or even imagined back home. She was overwhelmed by the number of servants she needed to hire, and she wasn't too pleased by their strict division of labor, which made them more of a burden than a help. She concluded that they were a "pack of lazy wretches." They also had to furnish the place, which was expensive, and John's salary had been cut.

Still, Abigail was happy that they were living out of the city, which didn't impress her at all. She found Paris dreary and dirty, although she enjoyed its theater, music, and the endless round of public entertainments, not to mention the fashions, which fascinated her. She was shocked by the lack of morals among the Parisians, compared to the New England Puritans she had been raised among, but over time, thanks to such women as the Marquise de Lafayette, she came to admire French manners and style, although she still strongly believed that American ways were the right ways.

After nine months in Paris, John was appointed minister to the Court of St. James, and as they were planning their move to London, John decided that young Johnny should go back to America, where he and Abigail agreed he would get a better education. It was arranged that he would enroll in Harvard College, where their son Charles had also been accepted.

Below: Abigail at the age of thirty-seven, just before she left for her first trip to Europe.

Abigail was apprehensive about John's going to England as the first representative of the breakaway United States, but when John presented himself to the old villain, George III, the audience went well, with the king telling him, "I cannot but say I am gratified that you are the man chosen to be the Minister." But John and his wife had been among those who had talked the rebellion against the king into existence, and as expected, the press received him with less courtesy.

Abigail and Nabby did their country proud when they were formally presented, along with John, at court a few weeks after their arrival. Abigail instructed the dressmaker that she wanted to be as plain as possible, but her white silk and crepe dress with a huge hoopskirt and a train three yards long may not have seemed so plain back in Boston. Abigail wrote to her sister that she thought both she and Nabby looked "very tasty," but she also admitted that she felt ridiculous.

Abigail took on the job of house hunting and settled on a townhouse in Grosvenor Square, a new and fashionable neighborhood favored by diplomats and government officials. It was smaller than their house in France had been, but with the higher cost of living in London it was a good deal more expensive. It required a large staff of servants, who turned out to be as difficult and as mysterious about what they would and wouldn't do as the ones in France had been.

Like other ambassadors, John was expected to entertain lavishly and often, but unlike the others, he had to do it on his salary, with the result was that the diplomatic community didn't gather very often on the northeast corner of Grosvenor Square. The Adamses were frequently invited to other diplomatic receptions, but Abigail found all of them a waste of time. She did, however, cultivate close friendships, as she always did wherever she was, so they weren't completely isolated socially.

But they were never regarded as a part of London society, and that made young Nabby a kind of wallflower. Before she left home she had become engaged to Royall Tyler, a young Boston lawyer, but her absence from him hardly made her heart grow fonder. She was thinking about breaking the engagement when Colonel William Smith, the secretary to the legation, began calling at the Adams house with more and more regularity. He was obviously entranced by the Adams daughter, but Abigail waved him off by telling him that Nabby was already spoken for. It wouldn't be proper for the girl to jilt her fiancé just because somebody better had come along, especially because Abigail herself had engineered the engagement in the first place. On the other hand, she very much approved of Smith and contrived with John to send him off to Prussia to observe military operations there for a couple of weeks so he would be out of the way while Nabby freed herself from Tyler, who hadn't written to her in months.

Nabby didn't waste a day firing off a letter to Tyler, breaking off their engagement and returning all of the letters he had sent her along with the portrait of himself that he had given her. But then Smith's absence grew. What was supposed to be couple of weeks extended to three months of anxiety for the Adams family. When he finally did come back, the very first thing he did was to ask for Abigail's permission to marry her daughter. Though it was customary to ask the woman's father, Colonel Smith knew very well how the Adams household was run. The wedding date was set for June, four months after the engagement became official.

Nabby and William settled in a house near her parents and they joined them for dinner every day, but Abigail felt a deep sense of loss; her boys were back in America, and her daughter was beginning a new family. Nabby gave birth to a son, named William for his father, the following spring. After her husband took a diplomatic post in Portugal, she and the baby went to live with Abigail, who reveled in her new title, "Grandmama." The household grew again when Thomas Jefferson's eight-year-old daughter, Maria, and her maid, a slave named Sally Hemmings, moved in for an extended time of rest on the long journey to join her father in Paris.

Later that same year, John asked Congress not to renew his commission and he began talking of going home again. In the meantime, Abigail's financial advisor, Cotton Tufts, had told them of a large house in Braintree that was for sale, and they authorized him to buy it for them. Abigail had been in the house many times, and she began right away sending instructions for redecorating it, including a future plan to add a room big enough for John's massive library, which never would have fit in their old house. Before they left England, Abigail wrote to Thomas Jefferson, "'Tis Domestick happiness and Rural felicity in the bosom of my Native land, that has charms for me. Yet I do not regret that I made this excursion since it has only more attached me to America."

Home Again

Their new house was far from ready when they arrived, and Abigail was annoyed to have to dodge painters, carpenters, and stonemasons while she arranged her furniture, which hadn't weathered the transatlantic voyage very well. But beyond that, she was displeased with the size of the house. With seven rooms, it was much bigger than their saltbox cottage, but she had remembered something grander than the reality of this place she described as a "wren's house." She wrote to Nabby that she was eager to welcome

Below: The Adamses's oldest child, Abigail, known in the family as Nabby, delivered the first Adams grandchild, William Smith. The boy was named for his father.

her there, but warned her not to wear high heels or feathers in her hat or she would have to hunch her shoulders to get through the front door. Her memory had played tricks on her, of course, but after her houses in France and England, it was comparatively tiny, although much bigger and more elegant than the rural felicity that she said she longed for. Over the next few years, she doubled the size of the house and imported fine furniture to turn it into a showplace, which the couple named Peacefield.

In the meantime, it was home, and Abigail was grateful to be reunited with her sons. Both Charles and Thomas were nearby at Harvard, and John Quincy had graduated and was clerking for a prominent lawyer in Newburyport. Nabby was in America, too, living in New York, in Jamaica, Long Island, which she described as a "land of strangers." Her husband was undecided about his future, and John advised that he should avoid public service in favor of becoming a lawyer, a suggestion that Nabby rejected, sensing that her father was ruminating on his own future.

As was typical of him, John was aloof to the rumors that he was slated for high office. Although he wouldn't admit it, when the electors cast their votes the following March, three months after the official election day, he was pleased to hear that he had been chosen to serve as George Washington's vice president. Abigail was also pleased, of course, but she wasn't too happy with the idea that she was going to have to move again.

Below: The first addition to the Adams house was a wing containing the kitchen. The appliances that are there today are more representative of the nineteenth than eighteenth century, because the family lived there until 1927.

A Wren's Nest

John and Abigail's new house had a paneled living room, an entry hall, and a dining room. The previously detached kitchen had been joined to the house, but that was small pleasure for Abigail, who found all of the rooms too small and the ceilings too low. There were two bedrooms upstairs, but they were tiny, too. Her daughter was married by then, but Abigail still had three sons at home, and the place was as crowded as a rabbit warren, although she characterized it as a "wren's house." John called it "the old house" from the time they moved in, although it was only five years older than he was. It took Abigail a dozen years to turn the house into the home that she thought she was getting in the first place.

She didn't go with him when John went to New York to help set the new government in motion. But he urgently requested her presence a couple of days later, when he found out that Congress hadn't designated residences for the president and vice president and, worse, that they had decided they'd have to pay for it out of their own salaries, which had yet to be set.

It was her son-in-law, William Smith, who found a house for her. It was the same house, part of an estate called Richmond Hill in what is now New York City's Greenwich Village, that had been rented for Martha Washington during her brief stay in New York during the war. It was perched on a hillside with a striking view of the city about a mile away, and its extensive garden stretched down to the edge of the Hudson River.

Abigail loved the Richmond Hill house, and she despaired that it might actually be making her too happy, considering that it was a temporary home at best. Just how temporary it was came front and center to her when Congress decided to move the capital to Philadelphia and she was forced to make moving plans yet again. By the time the move took place, she had worried herself into a weakening illness that was so real she couldn't travel, and it took her five days to make the journey from New York to Philadelphia, a little more than a hundred miles away.

Above: When John became vice president, he and Abigail moved into a suburban estate called Richmond Hill, at the northwest corner of what is now Greenwich Village in Manhattan.

Abigail's day-to-day routine didn't change much in her new surroundings, but Philadelphians were more sociable than New Yorkers, and she and John were invited to more balls and parties. There were so many distractions that in their second year there, they gave up their suburban existence for a house in town. It was smaller, though, and that meant Abigail had to entertain more often to accommodate the same number of guests she felt required her attention. But if their lives were frantic, John and Abigail were comfortable there. Abigail was enchanted by the people of Philadelphia, and the feeling was mutual, although over time she became wearied by the social whirl.

As his term wound down, President Washington was coerced into running for a second one, which he said he certainly didn't want, and John was duty-bound to run for the vice presidency again, although, like the president, he was eager to retire to a farmer's life. But while preparations were being made for the election, he went back to his hometown, which had recently been renamed Quincy for Abigail's grandfather, leaving his sons Thomas and Charles to keep their ear to the ground for political developments. It was contrary to John's nature to campaign for his job, and he didn't want it anyway. But it would have been devastating to lose it in the face of Washington's unanimous vote, which was a foregone conclusion, and he needed to keep well informed, if not involved.

Above: Abigail Adams had a fetish about refusing to follow current fashions, but she made an exception with her hair, which she kept stylish and fresh with a curling iron that she heated in her bedroom fireplace.

Abigail didn't go back to Philadelphia for John's second term. She'd had enough of playing the part of the vice president's lady, and she resented the expense of maintaining two households—the previous four years had left them $2,000 in debt, well over $38,000 in today's dollars. Her poor health allowed her to gracefully slip out of the bondage, and in those days when precedents were being set, she freed all future vice presidents' wives of social obligations that were already becoming as proscribed as the First Lady's.

Abigail's time alone in Quincy brought back unpleasant memories of their separations when John was serving in Congress and when he went abroad, but this time she was lonelier than she had been before. In was even harder for John, who continually pleaded with her to join him, but Abigail stuck to her guns, pleading her own poor health and the unhealthy Philadelphia climate.

All she missed was the opportunity to listen in on congressional debates, but John kept her up to the minute on them through his letters. Those debates had become more interesting as the French Revolution changed the European political landscape, and the question of jumping into the war between Great Britain and France was dividing Americans as nothing ever had before.

For all her talk of equality a few years earlier, Abigail's views had become stridently conservative. She didn't think that ordinary people had the interest or the capacity to deal with the subtleties of politics, and that they might easily be led astray by some silver-tongued orator one day. She believed in a society with distinct social divisions, knowing that the educated class would, and should, produce the country's future leaders, although she still drew the line at a hereditary ruling class.

But she had other things on her mind. She was completely in charge of running two farms, the one where she lived now and the one that had been their first home, and she bought a third and converted it into a dairy. They also owned a house in Boston, but John Quincy, who had his law office there, cared for it and collected the rents from tenants who shared the space with him. But then he was appointed minister to Holland, and when he left, he took his brother Thomas along with him as his secretary. Nabby and the Adams grandchildren were in New York, and Charles was practicing law there. With her children scattered, Abigail was lonelier than ever, but she was much too busy to let it get her down.

At the beginning of 1795, Nabby gave birth to a daughter, and Abigail went to New York for an extended visit. While she was there, Charles introduced her to Sally Smith, Nabby's sister-in-law, whom he said he intended to marry. Both John and Abigail considered him too young to take such a step—he was twenty-five—but he was prospering and they couldn't think of any reason to object.

The following year, President Washington told John that he was planning to retire at the end of his second term. John was his logical successor, but both he and Abigail had mixed emotions about it.

John felt that he really didn't have any choice, and when the president formally announced his intention to retire in the fall of 1796, the Federalists nominated the vice president as their candidate to replace him, and the Democratic-Republicans named Thomas Jefferson to oppose Adams. Neither of them was expected to campaign for the job, but the party faithful and their allies in the press had no such restrictions.

By the end of the year, enough electors had been canvased to make it fairly certain that John Adams would be the next president, but who would get the second spot was very much in doubt for several more weeks. When the votes were finally tallied, Thomas Jefferson, the candidate of the opposition party, won the vice presidency by three votes.

Abigail's old friendship with Jefferson had cooled, but she was nevertheless pleased by the prospect of a bipartisan executive branch, which she felt would help lessen the differences between the Federalists and the Democratic-Republicans. But politics was the least of her concerns at the moment; she was about to have a new role thrust on her.

The President's Wife

The only role model Abigail had when John was elected president was Martha Washington, who had been as well loved by the people as her husband was. Abigail had come to know Martha quite well, and her admiration bordered on hero worship. She despaired that she didn't have the "patience, prudence, discretion to fill a station so exceptionally." And she worried that, "I have been so used to freedom of sentiment that I know not how to place so many guards about me, as will be indispensable, to look at every word before I utter it, and to impose a silence upon my self, when I long to talk."

In the months leading up to the March 4 inauguration, Abigail was kept busy getting their Massachusetts farms in order, and nursing John's sick mother, who eventually died a month after her son became president, and she didn't arrive in Philadelphia until nearly the middle of May, long after John had assumed his new office, and she her role as First Lady.

Fortunately, by the time Abigail reached Philadelphia, summer was approaching, and she wasn't expected to begin the round of receptions and state dinners for a couple of months. Still, she wasn't without obligations to receive and entertain members of Congress and the cabinet, as well as others considered important to their new existence. She also had her hands full organizing the former president's house, which had become their home, and needed to be furnished. She rankled at the expense, which had to be covered out of John's $25,000-a-year salary.

Abigail had originally liked almost everything about Philadelphia except the climate, but now after her long absence, she thought it had been transformed into a "depraved" place, as "vile and debauched as the city of London." She might have meant Paris, which, at the time she lived near it, she regarded as just a cut above a cesspool. But Abigail was undoubtedly being politically correct. The problem of dealing with France that had made President Washington's life miserable during his second term had not only not gone away, but seemed to be getting worse. John's opposition, including his vice-president Thomas Jefferson who was strongly in favor of France, disagreed when he proposed a diplomatic commission to negotiate with Paris rather than risking a war. The pro-French press came down hard on John, and Abigail read every word of their "impudent abuse," and every word made her angrier than the last.

The war on her husband became more personal when John transferred his son John Quincy from Lisbon to become minister to Berlin. What cut her to the quick were the venomous attacks in the *Boston Independence Chronicle*, her hometown paper, suggesting that John Quincy's $10,000-a-year salary was nothing less than a gift from his father, and a raid on the U.S. Treasury.

Abigail sent letters by the dozen to the friendly newspaper editors supporting John and his policies, always with instructions on how to edit them so that her own identity would be hidden, and her views almost always made it into print. Her influence over the president was no secret, either, and many on both sides thought he couldn't make an important decision without Abigail's whispering in his ear; many sarcastically called her "Mrs. President."

In the meantime, they were facing family problems. Nabby's husband, William, was in deep financial trouble, and Charles had become an alcoholic, neglecting both his business and his family. John Quincy had left Charles to manage his own financial affairs, and he had managed to make nearly all of his money disappear.

John blamed himself, telling Abigail that if he had kept up his law practice and not distanced himself from his children by going into public service, things might have turned out differently. At the very least, he said, he would have the resources to bail them out now that they were in trouble. Of course, Abigail didn't agree. "You have the satisfaction of knowing that you have faithfully served your generation," she wrote. "You do not know whether you would have been a happier man in private, than you have been in publick life."

Abigail was well enough to go back to Philadelphia the following winter. It was the city's final season as the capital, and that was a reason for the local society to stage more parties, balls, and receptions, with the president's wife as the biggest party giver of them all. Fortunately, her health was better than it had been in years, and she was able to give two receptions a week and sit through

Below: Abigail missed John's inauguration, but she sent him this letter containing a prayer: "And now O Lord my God thou hast made thy servant Ruler over the people, give unto him an understanding Heart, that he may know how to go out and come in before this great people."

"My thoughts and my meditations are with you, though personally absent; and my petitions to Heaven are that, 'the things which made for peace should not be hidden from your eyes.' My feelings are not those of pride or ostentation upon the occasion. They are solemnized by a sense of the obligations, the important trusts, and numerous duties connected with it. That you may be enabled to discharge them with honour to yourself, with justice and impartiality to your country, and with satisfaction to this great people, shall be the daily prayer of your A. A."

—*Abigail to John Adams, February 8, 1797*

a seemingly endless round of visits from well-wishers, sometimes reaching as many as fifty or sixty a day. She had become the center of attention, and she was thoroughly enjoying it.

Martha Washington had made it a point not to set any style trends during her years as first lady, but Abigail said, "At my age, I think I am privileged to set a fashion." She thought that current trends were silly, especially that women were wearing flimsy muslin dresses in the wintertime, which she didn't think kept them warm enough. Silk was her idea of proper winter attire. She was also scandalized by the popular new "empire" style, which stressed high waistlines and low necklines, as well as flowing skirts, that was the fashion equivalent of the classical art and architecture that had caught the public's fancy. She wrote, "Not content with the show that nature bestows, [women] borrow from art, and literally look like Nursing Mothers."

The new president was elected after a campaign that saw the Federalists more seriously divided than ever, with Alexander Hamilton once more working against his party's candidate, and the Democratic-Republicans were even more united than before. Abigail was disgusted. She didn't believe in elections anyway; she thought a president ought to be able to serve until he reached retirement age or abused the public trust. As she put it, "No engine can be more fatally employed than frequent popular Elections to corrupt and destroy the morals of the people." Besides, she had come to love her own job, and she was distraught to think that she might lose it. Yet, lose it she did, and even though she still had a respectful fondness for Thomas Jefferson, she believed with all her heart that John's loss was a far greater loss to the country—a disaster, in fact.

Even though defeated at the polls, John was still president, and he would serve out the last months of his term in the new federal city that was already being called Washington. After a debate that was typical of them, Abigail agreed to go with him when he moved into the new presidential home, even if it might be for only a short stay.

When she arrived several days behind him, she was appalled by the unfinished state of the city, but even more by the "castle of a house" that she was expected to call home. Of course, she had coped with unfinished houses before, but this one was much larger—too large, in fact—and the huge public rooms hadn't yet been plastered and painted. Work hadn't even been started on the central section, and the grounds, like the roads leading up to the mansion, were a muddy mess. In spite of it all, Abigail was expected to preside over receptions and parties there, and she made the best of a bad thing.

They weren't sure of John's defeat until after they had been in the new capital for about a month, and they were surprised that Jefferson had won by only eight electoral votes, although John himself served with a majority of only three. Abigail smiled through it all, writing, "At my age and with my bodily infirmities, I shall be happier at

Below: Abigail was an old-fashioned woman who preferred the "full dress of bombazine" of the 1740s to the new century's "undress of bum-be-seen" shown in this British cartoon.

When Abigail arrived in the new capital, her carriage driver became lost in the woods and they had to ask for directions to the presidential mansion.

Quincy." Abigail was already packing her bags to go home, and after a weather delay, she was on her way by mid-February. John left town on inauguration day long before the ceremonies began, without bothering to say good-bye to anyone, least of all Mr. Jefferson.

A New Life

John was bitter about his defeat, and long months passed before he seemed to become resigned to it, but Abigail had no such problem. They were together again, and there would be no more painful discussions of separations. It was all she ever really wanted. Her children were grown, but her grandchildren made up for the loss. Charles's recently orphaned daughter, Susan, came to live at Peacefield, and Nabby's sons, William and John, spent their school holidays there. Others came and stayed for long visits, and over time, there would be still more grandchildren to keep Abigail feeling young. There were ten of them in all, five of whom would eventually live under her roof.

John Quincy, meanwhile, was on his way home from Berlin, with his new son, George Washington Adams, and his English-born wife, Louisa. John and Abigail's other son, Thomas, was still in Philadelphia struggling with his law practice, and his parents set up a barrage of letters begging him to come home to Quincy. Thomas eventually did go back to Quincy. Not only that, but he married Nancy Harrod, a childhood friend, and together they moved into Peacefield. Abigail couldn't have been more pleased, not only to have her son living with her, but to have a fellow New Englander for a daughter-in-law.

Abigail was also happy to have come back to the familiar life of tending her garden, running her farms, and smothering her family with maternal love. She also went back to her old habits of observing the political scene—John Quincy had become a United States senator, and he helped keep her well informed on what was happening in Washington—and to share her strong opinions in letters to her wide circle of friends. She read several newspapers every day.

Below: The federal city was still largely untamed wilderness when Abigail went there as First Lady. She was not impressed, but as always, she managed to adapt to living in the woods.

Abigail was sixty-five years old by then, and her health was deteriorating. But she was more cheerful than she had ever been, less strident in her politics and more willing to let her children and grandchildren live their own lives and make their own mistakes. Her "ancient friends" were dying with great regularity, and she accepted the deaths stoically. Except, that is, the death of her sister Mary in 1811, followed within days by the death of Mary's husband, Richard Cranch—a double funeral Abigail had hoped she'd never have to see. The presence of death made old friends all the more precious, and Abigail went to work patching up old feuds. John followed her example by reinstating his old friendship with Thomas Jefferson, beginning a new correspondence that lasted the rest of their lives.

Abigail's greatest regret was that she didn't think she'd ever see John Quincy again, but another new president, James Monroe, named him secretary of state, and she calculated the number of days it would take him to get back to Quincy. He and his family were with her for a long vacation before he went back to Washington, and then they came back for another long visit during the summer. A few days after they left, Abigail contracted yellow fever, and she died two weeks before her seventy-fifth birthday.

John was nine years older than Abigail, and he lived another eight years after her death. For the last two of those years, he had the satisfaction of seeing his son John Quincy become president of the United States, as he had been. John died as quietly and peacefully as Abigail had, at the age of eighty-one, on July 4, 1826, the fiftieth anniversary of the signing of the Declaration of Independence. It was the same day that death came to Thomas Jefferson, the only other survivor among the country's founding fathers.

As for Abigail, she would have been amazed to know of her own legacy as one of America's founding mothers; more important, she'd have been pleased that future governments finally took her advice to "Remember the Ladies."

Tragedy

After John and Abigail retired to Peacefield, their daughter, Nabby, was diagnosed with breast cancer. She had no choice but to undergo a mastectomy, which was performed without anesthesia in the family home. Her suffering was almost unspeakable, but she went into remission and the cancer didn't come back for two more years. Her husband, William, was a bit of a wanderer, and she was left on her own; when her condition worsened, she moved back to Peacefield, where she could die surrounded by her loving family.

Visiting Peacefield

The Adams National Historic Site, administered by the National Park Service, is at 135 Adams Street in Quincy, Massachusetts, about ten miles south of Boston at the Furnace Brook Parkway, exit 8 on Route 93. The site includes eleven historic structures, including Peacefield, the "old house," surrounded by fourteen landscaped acres. It is open daily, and an admission fee is charged for adults; children under sixteen are admitted free of charge.

The Stone Library contains more than 14,000 historic volumes, including John Quincy Adams's personal library. The John and John Quincy Adams birthplaces at 133 and 141 Franklin Street are open, with guided tours, between mid-April and mid-October. There is no admission charge. In the same area, Mount Wollaston, the Quincy homestead at Hancock Street and Quincy Road, features period furnishings gathered by four generations of the family. It is open daily, except Mondays, April through October. Abigail and her husband, as well as John Quincy Adams and his wife, are interred in the family crypt at the United First Parish Church on Hancock Street. Unlike other presidential homes, Peacefield was continuously occupied by the Adams family, and none of the original furnishings has had to be replaced. It represents a span of history from 1788 to 1927 with its parts intact.

Below: Looking back, Abigail wrote: "I shall have reason to say that my Lot hath fallen to me in a pleasant place and verily I have a goodly Heritage." (Portrait by Gilbert Stuart.)

Martha Jefferson

An Interrupted Career

Thomas Jefferson had been a widower for twenty years when he became president, and many historians have speculated that had his wife, Martha, lived, it is likely that he never would have moved into the White House.

There were plenty of signs during his early political career that Thomas's love for his wife more than trumped any feelings he had for public service. When he went to Philadelphia to serve in the Second Continental Congress, she adamantly refused to join him there, and less than two months after he wrote the Declaration of Independence, he dismayed his colleagues by resigning from Congress so that he could go home to her. Four years later, he turned down an offer to join Benjamin Franklin as commissioner to Paris, saying that he didn't want to expose Martha to the dangers of a long sea voyage and he couldn't bear to leave her behind. Later, he also resigned as governor of Virginia and promised his wife he would never leave her again to accept any other public office, nor would he ever involve himself in politics.

In nearly every case, he cited Martha's poor health as the reason for "the state of perpetual solicitude to which I am unfortunately reduced," as he described his self-enforced retirement in a letter to George Washington. It is true that she had given birth to six children during their ten-year marriage, not to mention one with her previous husband, and she had lost all but three of them. It is also true that she was bedridden for four months after giving birth for the last time, with her husband at her side during virtually every minute of the delivery. But although her last delivery was difficult—the baby girl was said to have weighed sixteen pounds—the cause of Martha's death in 1782 isn't known. Neither are many details of the nearly thirty-four years of her life. When she died, her husband destroyed all of her letters, and he never again mentioned her name in any of his voluminous writings over the rest of his life. His final tribute to her was the epitaph he had placed on her tomb, a quotation from Homer's *Iliad*:

> *If in the melancholy shades below.*
> *The shades of friends and lovers cease to glow,*
> *Yet mine shall sacred last; mine undecayed*
> *Burn on through death and animate my shade.*

Martha Wayles Skelton Jefferson

Born
October 19, 1748,
Charles City County,
Virginia

Parents
John Wayles and Martha
Eppes Wayles

Marriage
1766 to Bathurst Skelton

Children
John Skelton (1767-71)

Widowed
1768

Remarried
1772 to Thomas Jefferson
(1743-1826)

Children
Martha (Patsy)
(1772-1836); Jane
Randolph (1774-75);
unnamed son (1777);
Maria (Polly)
(1778-1804); Lucy
Elizabeth (1780-81); Lucy
Elizabeth (1782-85)

Died
September 6, 1782,
Monticello, Virginia

Left: Martha Jefferson Randolph, Thomas and Martha's daughter. There are no known portraits of Martha Jefferson.

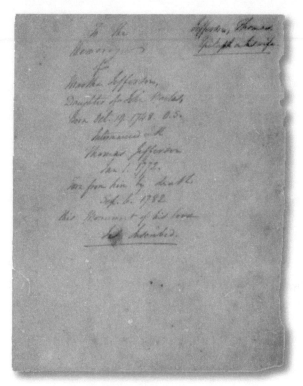

Above: The epitaph that Thomas wrote upon Martha's death is the only record of her in any of his writings, including his biography.

He ordered it carved in stone in the original Greek, as he had often done in letters whose details he preferred to keep private.

None of this is any indication that Thomas Jefferson wanted to deny that his wife had ever existed. Like many public figures of his time, he was determined to keep his private affairs within the family.

After Martha died, his grief kept him confined behind his library door for three straight weeks, and when he was finally coaxed out, all he could do for several more weeks was ride silently with his ten-year-old daughter, Patsy, through mile after mile of deserted forests.

Uncharacteristic of him, several more weeks passed before he wrote any letters, and the first of them was to Martha's sister Elizabeth, to whom he confided: "This miserable kind of existence is really too burdensome to be borne. ...Were it not for the infidelity of deserting the charge left me, I could not wish its continuance a moment. For what could it be wished?"

Not long afterward, he confided to a friend: "Before that event, my scheme of life had been determined. I had folded myself in the arms of retirement, and rested all prospect of future happiness on domestic and literary objects....A single event wiped away all my plans and left me a blank which I had not in my spirits to fill up."

Remarriage was not an option. As she lay dying, Martha had made him promise that he would never marry again, because she didn't want her daughters

> "The violence of his emotion to this day I dare not describe to myself."
>
> —Patsy Jefferson on her father after the death of Martha

Below: Gilbert Stuart's portrait of Thomas Jefferson.

to be raised by a stepmother as she herself had been. It is also quite likely that he never could have found a love that would ever measure up to the feelings he'd had for Martha.

His old friend James Madison, at the time a delegate to Congress, brought him out of his malaise by arranging to have Thomas appointed minister plenipotentiary to negotiate peace with Great Britain. It meant that he would have to go to Paris, a journey he had rejected not so long before, but he welcomed the prospect this time with enthusiasm.

"I will comply in the arduous charge, with diligence and integrity, the best of my poor talents, which I am conscious are far short of what it requires," his acceptance letter said.

His attempt to cross the Atlantic with his daughter Patsy at his side was aborted because the ship was locked in winter ice, and when it was eventually freed, a fleet of British warships blocked its passage.

The mission was delayed a second time while Congress rewrote Thomas's instructions, and he used the time to update himself on America's preparedness for peace. He didn't like what he found. It became apparent to him that his country was doomed to remain a loose connection of individual states that would turn against one another before long. "I know no danger so dreadful and so probable as that of internal contests," he wrote in an unsolicited report to Congress. "And I know no remedy so likely to prevent it as strengthening the band which connects us." With that, Thomas Jefferson came out of a retirement that had kept him sidelined during most of the Revolutionary War, and he was more than ready to take on the challenge of serving his country again.

But in the meantime, the peace treaty had been signed in Paris, and Thomas was no longer needed there. Instead of taking her to Europe, he escorted Patsy back to their home at Monticello, and his new lease on public life seemed to have expired.

He considered himself retired from the Virginia Assembly, and felt that his colleagues there had forgotten him. But during a stopover at Richmond he discovered that his alma mater, the College of William and Mary, had given him an honorary degree of doctor of civil law. The citation was written in glowing terms that helped him realize that his reputation was still intact, even though he had been virtually out of sight for the larger part of a decade. He knew that his political comeback was waiting for him right there in Virginia, where his career had begun.

Connections

In the small world of colonial Virginia, it seemed unlikely to people who kept track of such things that young Thomas would ever marry into a family as highly regarded as the Wayleses. The Jeffersons were from the still partly wild western edge of the colony, far removed from the tidewater where people who mattered lived, and they were poor compared to many of them. On the other hand, Martha's father, John Wayles, had become quite wealthy, even by Virginia standards, as a lawyer, a land speculator, and a slave trader, and his estate near Williamsburg, called The Forest, was among the biggest and most productive in all of Virginia. When his father-in-law died, Thomas and the husbands of the other two Wayles daughters offered 5,400 of their inherited acres for sale, after each of them reserved large choice parcels for themselves.

About all the Jefferson and the Wayles families had in common was their Welsh background; John Wayles himself had emigrated from Wales and, many years earlier, so had Thomas Jefferson I. The future president's great-grandfather, a farmer, had married well, and he was able to buy a 167-acre farm in Henrico County, becoming moderately wealthy, buying several slaves and producing almost two tons of tobacco a year. His son Thomas II acquired the status of "gentleman," which had eluded his father, becoming a court justice and interacting with the best of Virginia society. He enhanced his status by marrying Mary Field, a close relative of the Randolphs, who owned more land than any

Above: Jefferson's daughter Martha, whom he called "Patsy," became his "constant companion" at the age of ten when her mother died. She served as his hostess when he became president and at Monticello after he retired.

Martha's first husband, Bathurst Skelton,
died when she was twenty years old.

other family in the colony, and he added to her estate by buying hundreds of acres on his own.

His son Peter Jefferson eventually inherited his father's extensive landholdings after his older brother died, but by then the estate had become so encumbered with debt that he couldn't even stay on his own small farm. He moved farther west where he cleared land and worked as a surveyor, mapping territory that was familiar only to the local Indian tribes. Large and powerful, Peter Jefferson was what would be called a man's man today, but he also dazzled the ladies with his rugged good looks and his charming ways. Among the smitten was Jane Randolph, who looked past a long line of suitors to become his wife. She gave him a social connection, not just to her own illustrious family but also to all of the first families of Virginia, including the Byrds, the Dandridges, and the Washingtons. Yet when their son Thomas began to court Martha Wayles, her father dismissed him as an "upstart."

But Thomas Jefferson was hardly that. His father died when he was fourteen, leaving him more than 3,700 acres of land, with an equal amount to come to him when he turned twenty-one. At that time, he would also inherit twenty-five slaves and large numbers of livestock, including some of the best horses in Virginia. More important to Thomas than any of that, though, was that his father also left him his library of forty books and a fervent wish that he would continue his classical education.

At seventeen, Thomas followed his father's wishes and went off to Williamsburg to study at the College of William and Mary, as well as to experience the life of a gentleman away from the rough frontier. He took advantage of the opportunity to cultivate important friendships. It came easily to him, and his family connections with the Randolphs gave him entree into the local society. His closest friend there was John Page, a fellow student who confessed, "I was too sociable and fond of the conversation of my friends to study as Mr. Jefferson did." Although he insisted that his friends should study along with him, Thomas shared their enthusiasm for having a good time, even though he was torn with guilt over it. He spent long evenings at Williamsburg's Raleigh Tavern, and he was often a guest at private homes, flirting with the girls and gossiping among his friends, even though he considered all of it a waste of his valuable time. But he also found time to become part of the royal governor's social circle: He was regularly invited to play the violin for the guests' dancing pleasure, and he took part in intellectual discussions with them, too.

It was all a heady experience for a young man like Thomas, but he knew he couldn't be a student forever, and he eventually went home to Shadwell, the family estate, to take responsibility for running it and to settle down as a country lawyer. Settling down would also mean getting married, if for no better reason than to produce an heir. Yet he was busy improving his mind, and he had his hands full already with a burgeoning law practice. Additionally, he was coping with his mother, his sisters, and his brother, whose needs were forcing him to dip heavily into his own inheritance, which he endured although he resented it.

After his father died, Thomas had drifted further away from his mother and his much younger siblings, and during his stays at Shadwell, he largely kept himself out of sight in his own room. The house was destroyed by fire in the winter of 1770, and he lost all of his books and records (fortunately, his precious violin, reputed to be a Stradivarius, was saved by a quick-thinking slave), but at least he had a place to live. He had begun construction of a mansion of his own on a nearby mountaintop that he called Monticello, and a one-room stone cottage on the site gave him a place where he could begin to reconstruct his life. His mother and her other children weren't so lucky; they were forced to crowd together in a small farmhouse on the property, and he chose to leave them to their own devices. Over time after that, Thomas ignored his mother nearly altogether, and his siblings as well, except for his older sister, Martha. He was twenty-seven years old and finally free, he felt, for the first time to live his own life among his books.

Love Walks In

While Thomas was getting his life in order, he started making regular visits to Williamsburg, but by this time he had become something of a dandy, sporting powdered hair, silver shoe buckles, and embroidered jackets, affectations that he had mocked during his student days. He seems to have overcome his shyness with women, too, and he avidly, even aggressively, began to court a pretty young widow named Martha Wayles Skelton.

The twenty-two-year-old Martha was by all accounts strikingly beautiful, with large hazel eyes and auburn hair. It was also said that she was "exquisitely formed." She had been widowed when her husband Bathurst Skelton, a young attorney, died when she was just twenty. When Thomas met Martha, he realized they had a great deal in common, including a love of reading, spirited riding, and taking long walks. The icing on the cake, though, was Martha's love of music; she was the best harpsichordist he had ever heard, and her sweet singing voice left him stunned. He had not heard such singing since his beloved older sister Jane had died a few years earlier.

Above: Their shared love of music was what drew Thomas Jefferson to Martha Wayles, and he bought this handcrafted mahogany fortepiano for her. "Do not neglect your music," he wrote to her. "It will be a companion that will sweeten many hours of life to you."

Performance of a Lifetime

One day while Thomas was visiting the Wayles plantation, a couple of local boys rode up hoping for a chance to visit Martha. They made it as far as the veranda, where they were stopped dead in their tracks by the sweet sounds coming from inside the house. Young Thomas was playing the violin and Martha was accompanying him on the harpsichord. They knew right away they had been upstaged, and they left behind any thoughts of courting the mistress of the house.

Martha's father was uncommonly wealthy, and all of the bachelors in Williamsburg, eager to have her take notice of them, literally formed long lines around her father's house at about teatime every day. But the formerly shy Thomas Jefferson had a bold plan to outshine them all.

Work on Monticello had progressed by then to a point where he could do a bit of entertaining there. He had been advising his friend Robert Skipwith on building his personal library at the same time that he was rapidly rebuilding his own, and he invited Skipwith and his wife, Tibby, for a visit so they could have a look at the new house and its new collection of books. He also casually suggested they might bring Martha Skelton, Tibby's sister, along with them, reminding his friend that as a book lover, she'd undoubtedly be interested in browsing through the library, too.

Above: Thomas Jefferson sold his library, which had grown to 6,000 volumes, to the government to rebuild the Library of Congress after it was destroyed during the War of 1812. The collection has been duplicated and replaced in the Book Room at the restored Monticello.

Thomas's original library had been destroyed, but by the time Martha visited Monticello, his new one contained 1,256 books.

It all seemed perfectly innocent, but of course, it wasn't. It was a carefully planned scheme to get Martha out of her father's house and away from all those other young men. Obviously, he never could have invited her to his house without a chaperone, but her sister's presence covered him there. His new library, already quite impressive, would also help prevent any attacks of his old shyness, because their common interest in books would make conversation easy. The plan worked beautifully.

But the visit only gave him a foot in the door. Thomas impressed Martha, but it would all be meaningless if he didn't also impress her father, and that was much harder to do. Whenever he was in Williamsburg after that, Thomas rode out to the Wayles plantation, always with his violin and several gifts of books in his saddlebags. Music and books drew Martha closer to him, but John Wayles still wasn't impressed. Thomas was a country boy as far as he was concerned; his house was still far from finished, and his estate comparatively puny. Thomas's worst fear was "the unfeeling temper of a parent who delays, perhaps refuses to approve his daughter's choice."

But he didn't give up. Over frequent visits, his love for Martha deepened through her "spriteliness and sensibility," and he couldn't believe his good fortune at finding someone who shared all of his tastes and his interests. He'd always had a habit of singing out loud when he rode on horseback, but now instead of snatches of Italian opera and chamber music, he switched to love songs and other romantic pieces that he and Martha sang together whenever they weren't deep in discussions of poetry and the current crop of fiction, another interest he had acquired in his father's drawing room.

No matter how hard Thomas tried, Martha's father still didn't seem inclined to give the union his blessing, even though both men had come to admire each other. But Thomas threw caution to the wind and ordered an expensive custom-built pianoforte from a London company as a wedding present for his intended but still unapproved bride. Nearly ten more months passed before he finally wore her father down, and Martha, age twenty-three, and Thomas, age twenty-eight, were married at the Wayles plantation house on New Year's Day in 1772. The celebration of the event went on for two and a half weeks before they set out for the hundred-mile journey to Monticello, which Thomas had been preparing feverishly for months to get into proper shape to receive his new bride.

On the Jeffersons' application for a marriage license, Martha was identified as a "spinster," but the word was crossed out and "widow" substituted.

Snow began falling as they hurried west, and eventually chest-high drifts stopped their horses in their tracks. They managed to reach a plantation seven or eight miles from Monticello, and abandoned their carriage there, setting out overland on horseback as the blizzard raged around them. It was well after midnight before they finally made their way home, and by then the servants had all gone to their own houses and the fires had burned themselves out. But if it was cold, dark, and dreary at Monticello, Thomas and Martha didn't seem to notice. He got fires going right away, and then he found a bottle of wine on a shelf. Family tradition has it that they passed the night "with song and merry laughter." It didn't seem to matter that they were snowbound, and they would be for well over two weeks.

Thomas Jefferson was a supremely happy young man. He had a beautiful, accomplished wife, whom he deeply loved, and his personal fortunes were better than ever. In his first year of married life, he earned $3,000 with his law practice and another $2,000 from his farms—a total of well over $106,000 in today's money. Life was sweet for the Jeffersons. They spent lavishly on

Below: There was never a time in Jefferson's adult life when he wasn't either changing Monticello or planning to. It had eight rooms when Martha died, but it had grown to twenty-one by the time he died.

Builder's Assistant

When Thomas Jefferson began planning Monticello, he hadn't been thinking of getting married, and when he took his bride there, his house plans began to change, and Martha's hand can be seen in it. She wanted more space for dining and bedrooms, and two semi-octagonal additions were made to each wing. He also altered his scheme for the dependencies to make the house more functional for domestic purposes, and although Martha didn't live to see them built, she had the satisfaction of seeing, through his constantly changing drawings, that their house would have all the earmarks of a home and not a bachelor's retreat. He added several very large storerooms, too, reflecting a housewife's need for more closet space.

Home Brew

Martha was well trained in domestic arts by the time of her second marriage. She personally made all of the candles she and her husband needed, and she turned out soap two hundred pounds at a time. But her greatest skill seems to have been in brewing beer. The first thing she did when she arrived at Monticello was to brew fifteen gallons of what was called small beer, brewed from wheat and bottled and drunk as soon as it had fermented, about a week later. In her first year as mistress of Monticello, Martha brewed one twenty-gallon and ten fifteen-gallon casks of regular beer, adding up to about 1,700 twelve-ounce servings. Considering that her husband's preference was cider or wine, it is an amazing statistic. In his final design for the house, Thomas placed a beer distillery under the south pavilion.

Above: The tools of Martha's spirituous trade.

furnishing and improving Monticello and its grounds, and they devoted two hours of every afternoon to full-gallop horseback riding. Both Thomas and Martha loved horses, and he insisted on owning only the best of the old Virginia stock. He was also meticulous about his gardens, and they worked together developing what became the finest landscape in all of Virginia, where such things were taken as a sign of status, although to the Jeffersons it was much more than that: It was a symbol of their happiness together.

Their first child, Martha, whom they called Patsy, was born in September. A small, sickly baby, she was nursed by a slave, and by the time she was a year old, she had become a healthy, cheerful little girl. Her mother, on the other hand, had been left frail and weakened by her pregnancy, and the job of nursing her back to health fell on Thomas's shoulders. He missed the term of the general court, as well as the 1772 session of the House of Burgesses, where he was a delegate, and he bowed out of several law cases. What time he had left for himself, after tending to Martha's needs, he spent studying and supervising work on the still unfinished Monticello, distancing himself from the fast-changing political scene that was never far from his mind.

By the following spring, Martha's condition had improved, and Thomas went to Williamsburg for the next session of the House of Burgesses. The spark of revolution was in the air, and he was prominent among the radicals who favored it. Among the issues under discussion was Great Britain's taxation policies and the colony's boycott of imports, and for Thomas, it was a personal matter. The pianoforte he had ordered for Martha had still not arrived because of the restrictions, and he worked hard to have them lifted, even though he himself had been one of the prime movers of the boycott in the first place.

Of course, quickening delivery of his wedding present wasn't the only thing on his mind, and before the session ended Thomas had drafted a series of resolutions that, among other things, would "maintain a correspondence and communication with our sister colonies." They were passed unanimously, and Virginia's fate was tied to the rest of British America for the first time, with Thomas Jefferson leading the way.

As he became more and more involved as a spokesman in the growing fight against Great Britain, Thomas made a decision to give up the law practice that had consumed thirteen years of his life. While he had many clients, not many of them paid his fees, and he was weary of being a part-time bill collector chasing down "the unworthy part" of his clientele. Besides, the death of his father-in-law in 1773 had left him a comparatively wealthy man. He treasured the long days at Monticello, where he and Martha had the time to read to each other and dote on their little daughter, Patsy, and where he could work on his garden; and he eagerly looked forward to having more time for such pleasures.

Thomas was an ardent abolitionist all his life, but much of Martha's father's wealth had come from the slave trade, and when he died, the couple inherited 169 slaves, including a large number who had only recently arrived from Africa. At the time, Thomas himself owned thirty-four adult slaves, including the ones he had inherited from his own father, and those whom Martha had brought with her when they were married. He only bought slaves once in his life, a family of four, which he had accepted as payment of a debt that was owed to Martha.

Thomas and Martha accepted the responsibility of their human legacy, and Thomas remained a slave owner until the day he died, intending, as George Washington also did, to grant them all their freedom in his will. It was the only legal way a slave could be freed in Virginia, and he was reluctant to sell them because he knew their slavery would only continue if he did.

When Thomas was called to serve in the Second Continental Congress in 1775, Martha was again in poor health and he was reluctant to leave her for his first mission outside Virginia. But there may have been more than his wife's frailty involved. He didn't seem too eager to get there, and it took him more than two weeks to make the four-hundred-mile trip from Monticello to Philadelphia, much longer than it should have, especially considering his phenomenal skill with horses, and he had four of them pulling his coach.

Congress had already been in session for more than six weeks by the time he arrived, and the delegates were all putting in long hours. But Thomas spent a great deal of his time browsing through the stores buying trifles for Martha and

Above: It isn't known whether Martha played the guitar, although it is likely. Thomas bought this one in Paris for $14 for his daughter Maria.

Sally Hemmings

In an ironic twist, Sally Hemmings, one of the slaves Martha Jefferson inherited from her father, was also her half sister. Sally's mother, Elizabeth Hemmings, had been born on John Wayles's plantation, and she became his mistress after his wife died. They had six children together. She gave birth to Sally the same year Wayles died, and together with her mother and her siblings, the baby went to live with the Jeffersons at Monticello. When Martha died in 1782, Sally was nine years old, and employed as a house servant whose responsibilities were mostly playing with the Jeffersons' two daughters.

Five years later, when Thomas was in Paris, he sent for his younger daughter, Maria, to join him there, and Sally, who was fourteen by then, went along as her companion. Under French law, she was no longer considered a slave there, but she and her older brother James, who had gone to Paris with Thomas to study culinary arts, went home to Monticello with the family two years later. It was said that Sally was visibly pregnant when she arrived.

Some years afterward, Sally's sixth child, Madison Hemmings, wrote in an Ohio newspaper that during her time in Paris, "My mother became Mr. Jefferson's concubine and when he was called back home, she was pregnant by him." The account also stated that Sally hadn't wanted to go home, where she would become a slave again, and that Thomas "promised her extraordinary privileges and made a solemn pledge that her children should be freed at the age of twenty-one years." Sally gave birth to seven children at Monticello before she died in 1835.

During the second year of the Jefferson presidency, the Richmond Recorder *titillated its readers with a lurid account of his purported relationship with his mulatto slave, and broadly hinted that the president was the father of all seven of her children. But there was no way for anyone to prove it, and Thomas himself kept his silence.*

Historians have been divided over the truth of the story ever since, but in 1998, DNA tests of known descendants of the Jefferson and Hemmings families proved a genetic link between them. But the link didn't lead directly to Thomas Jefferson himself—his brother Randolph and his two sons, the president's nephews, also lived at Monticello a good deal of the time. And so the guessing game continues until genetic testing is refined enough to be able to prove conclusively that Thomas Jefferson was, indeed, the father of Sally Hemmings's children.

books and musical scores for himself. On Thomas's second day in Philadelphia, a messenger arrived from Boston with a report of a pitched battle between British regulars and a ragtag army of colonials who called themselves Minutemen in a small Massachusetts town named Lexington.

Martha had taken Patsy and her one-year-old baby, Jane, for an extended visit to her sister Elizabeth and her husband, Francis Eppes, and Thomas wrote of the news from Boston to her brother-in-law, cautioning him to keep it from Martha until more details were known. It was clear to him, he said, that the Colonies were at war and the time for negotiation had passed, and he was concerned about worrying Martha too much over the prospect.

The job of throwing the fat into the fire fell on his shoulders when he was chosen to draft "a manifesto on arming," the Declaration of Independence.

Thomas left Philadelphia before the congressional session ended so he could hurry home to Martha, and he arrived just in time for the funeral of their second daughter, seventeen-month-old Jane. Although he kept detailed records of his daily activities, he didn't mention it in his writings.

After burying her child, Martha went back for another extended stay with her sister and brother-in-law at The Forest, her own former home, but when the threat of a British attack by sea emerged, Thomas took her and little Patsy back to the relative safety of Monticello. He spent the next several months there living the life of a country squire, setting an elegant table and enjoying the contents of his admirable wine cellar, as the war raged on far away.

Not long afterward, Thomas went to Williamsburg for the House of Delegates session, and he took Martha and Patsy with him, along with an entourage of servants. They were able to move into George Wythe's house while his old mentor was in Philadelphia as a member of Congress, and they settled in for a season of lavish entertaining. They had no sooner arrived when a letter from Congress informed Thomas that he had been appointed to join Benjamin Franklin's mission to France. It wasn't really a surprise—he had conspired with Franklin to make the recommendation in the first place—but Thomas agonized over the decision for three days before rejecting the offer. The appointment had specifically included a promise to pay for the voyage to France, not only for Thomas but for his wife and daughter as well, but Martha would have none of it, and he couldn't stomach the idea of a separation from her that would last months if not years. During the time he had been away at Philadelphia, his wife had gone into a deep depression and didn't answer any of his letters to her. In an anxious letter to her brother-in-law, Thomas had written, "I have never received a scrip of a pen from any mortal in Virginia since I left it, nor been able to make any inquiries I could make to hear of my family.... The suspense under which I am is too terrible to be endured." It was an experience he didn't want to repeat.

> *"When the question of Independence was before Congress, it had its meetings near a livery stable. The members wore short breeches and silk stockings, and, with handkerchiefs in hand, they were diligently employed in lashing flies from their legs. So very vexatious was this annoyance, and to so great an impatience did it arouse in the sufferers, that it hastened, if it did not aid, in inducing them to promptly affix their signatures to the great document that gave birth to an empire republic.... This anecdote I had from Mr. Jefferson at Monticello, who seemed to enjoy it very much, as well as to give great credit to the influence of flies. He told it with much glee, and seemed to retain a vivid recollection of an attack, from which the only relief was signing the paper and flying from the scene."*
>
> —*Henry S. Randall in* Life of Jefferson

Below: Jefferson brought back elegant table settings from Europe, including this crystal condiment server. He served traditional Virginian fare, but also impressed his guests with such things as macaroni and ice cream.

During their stay in Williamsburg, the Jeffersons entertained old friends and enjoyed the good life. It isn't known whether Martha was celebrating her little victory, or even if her husband had any regrets.

Except for occasional short trips to Williamsburg, Thomas stayed with his family at Monticello during most of 1777, using his own library as a reference point for his writing, which would revolutionize the laws of Virginia. The war was being fought far to the north, and occasionally to the south of them, but it was peaceful in the Jeffersons' corner of Virginia. Martha was pregnant again, and when he left her for the legislature's spring session, he took a leave of absence after two weeks to hurry home to her. Their only son was born soon afterward, but he died, unnamed, after only three weeks. It would be another year before their third child was born. It was another daughter, named Mary, but she was more often called Maria and sometimes Polly. At the same time, the facade of Monticello was finally finished, and it was everything Thomas had hoped it would be.

Two years later, the war had finally begun to turn in America's favor, but Thomas, who hated war, had stayed aloof of it, spending all of his time with what he considered the more important work of changing the laws of Virginia. That work done, he made a decision to take Martha's advice and give up politics. His announced retirement was scorned, though, and then the war came to Monticello.

Some five thousand British troops who had surrendered after their defeat in the Battle of Saratoga were force-marched almost seven hundred miles south to Albemarle County, and they became Thomas's responsibility as colonel of the local militia, a title he had considered nothing more than honorary until then.

He was honor-bound to build barracks and other facilities for them, but Governor Patrick Henry wasn't very forthcoming with supplies to get the job done. "Is an enemy so execrable that, though in captivity, his wishes and comfort are to be disregarded and even crossed? I think not," Thomas wrote in exasperation.

In spite of the governor's foot-dragging, Thomas arranged to rent a nearby plantation house, which was vacant at the moment, for the Hessian general in charge of the British troops and his family, and Thomas and Martha accepted an invitation to join them for dinner as soon as they were settled. They took Patsy along, and she acquired new playmates in the general's daughters. Thomas was also pleased to find accomplished musicians among the officer corps, and as long as they were there, he and Martha had other people to share their music. One of them later wrote, "As all Virginians are fond of music, he is particularly so. You will find in his house an elegant harpsichord, pianoforte [it had finally been delivered], and some violins. The latter he performs well upon himself, the former his lady touches very skillfully, and who is in all respects a very agreeable, sensible, and accomplished lady."

In the spring, Thomas reluctantly accepted the legislature's decision that he should run for governor of Virginia against two

Below: Jefferson loved chess as much as he enjoyed music and reading. This fanciful ivory chess set, made in France, was one of his favorites.

other men, including his oldest and best friend, John Page, who had been his advisor on affairs of the heart. It was a close victory, and Thomas wasn't at all pleased by it; he had said all along that he was irresistibly drawn to "private retirement," and he regretted running against his old friend. He wrote to Page that he was in "much pain that the zeal of our respected friends should ever have placed you and me in the situation of competitors."

Martha, Patsy, and baby Maria went with Thomas when he moved into the governor's palace, but life in Williamsburg wasn't as gay as it had been in their younger days. Virginia's economy, once the strongest of all the Colonies, was in shambles, and a British fleet was lurking in nearby Chesapeake Bay. It was not only blockading Virginia's ports, but staging raids on the coastal towns. Life was so bleak for Martha and the girls that Thomas packed them off to The Forest for another long visit with his sister-in-law, and he settled down to long days of dealing with the problems at hand.

Among those problems was Virginia's westward expansion, which had been accelerated by the war, and with so much of the population hundreds of miles away from a capital threatened by war, he arranged to have it moved farther inland to Richmond. It was a sleepy country town at the time—Thomas himself had declared it "disagreeable"—but the architect of Monticello accepted it as a challenge, envisioning a city of broad squares and handsome public buildings that he would design himself. But when he moved his wife and family there, there wasn't anything good that could be said of it. They made the best of it, living in a rented hilltop mansion that they furnished with pieces from Monticello.

About a year after they arrived in Richmond, Martha gave birth to a girl they named Lucy Elizabeth. It had been a difficult delivery, and Martha was bedridden for most of the winter. Because of the state of her health, Thomas made up his mind to resign the governorship, but the war put his plan on hold. Some British ships, including a troop transport, were heading up the James River, and it became apparent that Richmond was their ultimate destination. When an army of some 1,500 loyalists, led by the traitor Benedict Arnold, was already within twenty-five miles of the new capital, Thomas mobilized his own militia and hustled Martha and their children off to the safety of his father's old farm at Fine Creek. Then he rode twenty miles back in the direction of Richmond, rousing the thin lines of would-be defenders along the way. It was such a wild ride that his horse fell from under him, and he had to commandeer another. When Arnold took Richmond, with little or no resistance, Thomas Jefferson, his intended target, had disappeared. The troops had no problem finding the governor's mansion, though, and they ransacked the place, destroying nearly all of Thomas's books and papers, drinking freely from his wine cellar and smashing the rest. They also kidnapped all of the servants, intending to sell them as the spoils of war.

Thomas gave a good account of himself during the days leading up to and following the raid, but he was roundly criticized for what

Below: One of the very few of Martha Wayles Jefferson's possessions that survived her is this pincushion that she made for herself.

many characterized as cowardice. He still hoped to be able to give up the job of governor, which he hadn't wanted in the first place, and now the job was even more frustrating. Although he had called the legislature into session several times, the required majority never showed up. After their third child died in the spring at the age of five months, he couldn't bear to leave Martha, and instead sent a note saying, "The [cold and rainy] day is so bad that I hardly expect a council, and there being nothing there I know of that is pressing, and Mrs. Jefferson in a situation in which I would not wish to leave her, I shall not attend today." Days later, he announced that he wasn't going to run for another term as governor. "I think public service and private misery inseparably linked together," he confided in a letter to his longtime associate, James Madison. During the time left of his term, he moved the government to Monticello, and he never went back to Richmond.

Martha narrowly escaped the British attack on her Richmond home, and she rode out of town with her new baby, Lucy, in her arms.

Apparently few of the members of the legislature realized that Thomas considered abandoning his job, and neither had the British general Lord Cornwallis. Because Thomas was the author of the Declaration of Independence, the British had put a price on his head, and capturing the legislature of the biggest colony would have been a prize in itself. It seemed worthwhile to him to attack Richmond again—although, for the second time, his real targets were nowhere to be found.

It was the last straw. Thomas submitted his resignation with a strong recommendation that General Thomas Nelson, the head of the militia, should take over. He pointed out in his letter that "the union of civil and military power in the same hands at this time would greatly facilitate military measures." In truth, the governor had little real power—Thomas himself had written the laws that gave it directly to the people through their elected legislators—and his attempts to call out the militia had generally fallen on deaf ears.

Below: Martha kept meticulous household accounts in books that rarely left her side. They chronicled every detail of plantation life. Notice her bird doodles on the right page.

But Cornwallis didn't give up. He knew where Thomas was, and he sent out his best legion of cavalry to mount an attack on Monticello. The plan might have worked, but Captain Jack Jouette, a militia officer, saw the soldiers riding out and he knew where they were going. He also knew a shortcut to Charlottesville, seventy miles away, and he reached Monticello at dawn, a short time ahead of the enemy. Thomas took the news calmly, but he didn't waste any time packing Martha and his daughters into his fastest carriage for their third dash for safety in as many months. He himself rode into the woods to have a look around, and while he was training his telescope on the streets of

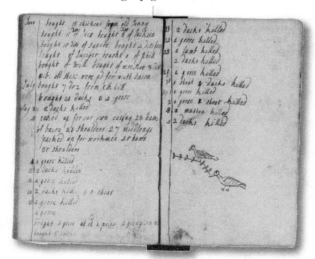

Charlottesville, the vanguard of the British force reached Monticello itself, only to find it empty.

Thomas caught up with his family later in the morning, and he and Martha and the girls set out for a ninety-mile southwesterly flight to a house Martha had inherited from her father. They would stay there, out of sight, for the next six weeks.

With Cornwallis's surrender at Yorktown in October, the war was effectively over, and Virginia was safe again. Thomas and his family had settled down at Monticello again, and he was reelected to another term in the House of Delegates, but he refused to serve, even in the face of possible arrest. Martha was pregnant again, for the sixth time, and her husband was beside himself with anxiety about her weakened condition. Each of her pregnancies had been difficult, but this time it seemed worse. She had gained a frightening amount of weight, and she couldn't endure sitting through the ordeal of entertaining visitors. She turned her household responsibilities over to the servants and stayed aloof of a continual round of visiting friends and neighbors. Yet one of them wrote that he had found her "mild and amiable," and that she didn't seem fazed by a houseful of children, including two of her own and six of her widowed sister-in-law. She gave birth to a girl, whom they named Lucy Elizabeth, honoring their previous child who had died the year before, in May of 1782, and Mrs. Jefferson was bedridden for the rest of the spring and summer. She eventually sank into a coma, and at the moment she did, her husband passed out, as well. He was unconscious for more than an hour, alarming the other women of the house, who thought that he must be dying, too. Martha, whom Thomas had affectionately called Patty, died on September 6, 1782. It was the end of everything Thomas loved, but it was also the rebirth of his career in public service.

Above: Patsy's son, Thomas Jefferson Randolph, known as Jefferson, lived near Monticello and helped in the settling of his grandfather's devastating burden of debt.

President Jefferson

Martha Jefferson's background was remarkably similar to Martha Washington's, and it is easy to speculate what sort of First Lady she might have been. They had both been raised on plantations in tidewater Virginia, where courtly manners and lavish entertainments were a way of life. The two Marthas' personalities may have been different, but their basic instincts about relating to guests in their home were nearly identical.

But of course, Martha Jefferson had been dead for nearly twenty years by the time her husband became president, and we'll never know. We'll also never know what her husband would have expected of her. Like George Washington, Thomas Jefferson had lived his early years among the Virginia elite, and he had believed that social graces were the key to a successful life. But during those years of bachelorhood, Thomas had seen much more of the world, and he developed a distaste for showy public display. The inaugurations of both of his predecessors had been marked with elaborate parades, and both of them had

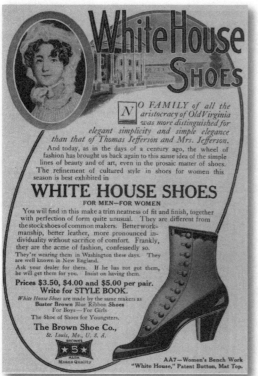
been driven to the scene of their oath-taking in the most splendid carriages available. But on March 4, 1801, the day of Thomas's inauguration, he chose to walk from the boardinghouse where he had been living through the muddy streets of Washington to the unfinished Capitol. A local newspaper reported that "his dress was, as usual, that of a plain citizen without any distinctive badge of office." No powdered wig, no ceremonial sword, no formal jacket would mark him as any different from anyone in the crowd that gathered to watch him pass.

Thomas Jefferson's common-man image nearly created an international incident when he shocked and dismayed the new British ambassador by welcoming him to the White House dressed in a soiled dressing gown and heel-less house slippers. Later, when the ambassador and his wife showed up for a formal dinner in his honor, the president allowed his guests to find their own places at a very egalitarian oval table with no head or foot. And when he followed them into the room, rather than taking the arm of the ambassador's wife, as protocol required, he accompanied Dolley Madison, the wife of his secretary of state, instead.

Thomas realized that he needed a feminine hand to help with the social side of his presidency, and he picked Dolley Madison, the wife of his old friend James Madison, to be his official hostess. Dolley was a natural. She was pretty, she was witty, and she was an enthusiastic entertainer. No woman in Washington loved a party more than she did, and that was all the new president had in mind for her.

During his travels in Europe, Thomas had soured on the openly political scheming of the women he met there. He wrote: "Our good ladies, I trust, have been too wise to wrinkle their foreheads with politics. They are contented to soothe and calm the minds of their husbands returned ruffled from political debate. They have the good sense to value domestic happiness above all other … there is no part of the earth where so much of this is enjoyed as in America." He also wrote, "The tender breasts of ladies were not formed for political convulsions."

What he hadn't noticed was that Dolley Madison loved politics almost as much as she loved having a good time. She became a fixture in the congressional visitors gallery, where she hung on every word of every debate; when her husband became secretary of state, she pressed him for every detail on international affairs, and she wasn't shy about pressing her own opinions on him. She also sometimes forced her opinions on White House guests, much to the chagrin of the president, who would have much preferred that she just kept smiling and pouring wine, as he believed a good hostess ought to do.

Both of Thomas's daughters were married to congressmen and were living in Washington, and he frequently called on them to help with his official entertaining. But Dolley was in charge nearly all of the time, not knowing, as Patsy and Maria did, of Thomas's aversion to political women. He never let her know. He admired Dolley Madison in spite of her political opinions, which, after all, mirrored his own.

She became a problem to him near the end of his second term. It had been a foregone conclusion for him that his friend Madison would succeed him, but when James Monroe announced he would oppose Madison, the press took sides. The same Richmond newspaper that had revealed the Sally Hemmings

Thomas's daughter Patsy, who became Mrs. Thomas Randolph, gave birth to the first child born in the White House.

affair burst forth with reports that Dolley was Thomas's mistress. Not only that, the papers said, but Dolley was a sex fiend who routinely offered her body to congressmen and diplomats to assure their support for the president's domestic and foreign policies.

Above: Meriwether Lewis Randolph, Patsy's son, was named for the president's old friend and confidential secretary, Meriwether Lewis, who led the Lewis and Clark Expedition to the Pacific and opened the West for settlement.

Thomas himself chose to consider the source and ignored the charges, except to write that he believed "[m]y age and ordinary demeanor would have prevented any suggestions in that form." But Dolley was deeply hurt, and when the allegations began appearing in speeches on the floor of Congress, she promised her husband that she would never allow a gentleman into her room "unless entitled by age and long acquaintance."

The scandal blew over long before the election. Monroe removed himself from the ballot, saving the battle for a better day, and Madison won the election. When Thomas Jefferson became a private citizen again, Dolley Madison became First Lady in her own right.

Visiting Monticello

The house that Thomas Jefferson designed, built, and loved, and where his wife, Martha, died, is on Route 53, about two miles southeast of Charlottesville, Virginia. It is open every day of the year, except Christmas Day. The admission fee includes access to the grounds, a tour of the house, and other seasonal tours. The Charlottesville Visitors Center is a clearinghouse of local information, from restaurants to hotels to other sites to visit in the area, including the campus of the University of Virginia, which was designed and founded by Thomas Jefferson. Very near to Monticello is Ash Lawn, a working plantation that was once the home of President James Monroe. Jefferson, Monroe, and James Madison often met at the nearby Michie Tavern, now a museum and still operating as a restaurant in a two-hundred-year-old log building. Not far from Charlottesville, more than a half dozen caverns and several Civil War historic sites are in the gorgeous Shenandoah Valley, less that a day's drive away. Charlottesville is about 125 miles from Washington, D.C., 100 miles from Williamsburg, and 70 miles from Richmond.

Above: Among Jefferson's innovations at Monticello are the double doors he installed between the dining room and tea room to conserve heat.

Dolley Madison

A Foe to Dullness

When Dolley Madison died in 1849 at the grand old age of eighty-two, the Washington newspaper *The National Intelligencer* reflected the deeply felt opinion of its readers: "Beloved by all who personally knew her, and universally respected, this venerable Lady closed her long and well-spent life with the calm resignation which goodness of heart combined with piety can only impart."

Her funeral was attended by her friend President Zachary Taylor and all of his cabinet, most of the members of the House and Senate, the diplomatic corps, and justices of the Supreme Court, as well as representatives of the army and the navy and every department of the federal government, along with tens of thousands of ordinary citizens. It marked a day of national mourning usually associated with the death of a president.

But Dolley Madison didn't have any official status at the time she died. She hadn't been America's First Lady for thirty-two years, and her husband, former president James Madison, had been dead for thirteen of them. Other presidents had come and gone over that time; other First Ladies, too, but Dolley was the queen of them all. And today, more than 150 years later, she still is.

Margaret Bayard Smith, a chronicler of Washington society for decades, wrote, "Mrs. Madison was a foe of dullness in every form, even when invested with the dignity which high ceremonial could bestow." But if Mrs. Smith had known Dolley as a girl, she might have thought twice about singling her out as a foe of dullness. Dolley was brought up as a Quaker, a religion that celebrates dullness, at least in appearance, and she lived under the strict teachings of its Book of Discipline until she was twenty-six years old.

Her mother, Mary Payne, was the granddaughter of one of the earliest Quaker immigrants from Great Britain, but her father, John, had been raised outside the faith. He accepted the Quaker Truth eagerly when he married Mary, and like most converts, he quickly became a zealous pillar of the church, eventually becoming, along with his wife, a clerk of the Cedar Creek Meeting in rural Virginia. They were responsible for all of the meeting's records, and they saw to it that the members of the flock toed the straight and narrow path of the Society of Friends. John was also named public friend, similar to a minister in other religions, and he was allowed to preach whenever the spirit moved him.

Mary Payne had a total of eleven children, three of whom died in infancy. The Paynes' first daughter and third child was born in 1768 during a brief

---

Dolley Payne Todd Madison

Born
May 20, 1768,
New Garden Quaker
Settlement, North
Carolina

Parents
John Payne and
Mary Coles Payne

Marriage
1790 to John Todd, Jr.

Children
John Payne Todd
(1792-1852); William
Temple Todd (1793-93)

Widowed
1793

Remarried
1794 to James Madison
(1751-1836)

Died
July 12, 1849,
Washington, D.C.

In the eulogy he gave at Dolley Madison's funeral,
President Zachary Taylor was the first to refer to her, or anyone else,
as "First Lady." "She will never be forgotten because she was
our First Lady for half a century," he said.

period when they were living on the North Carolina frontier. They named her Dolly, but the clerk of the local Quaker meeting wrote it as "Dolley" on her birth certificate, and although she herself sometimes dropped the extra letter during her lifetime, as far as the official records were concerned, she was spelling her name wrong when she did.

The family moved back to Virginia when Dolley was less than a year old, and she was brought up under strict Quaker rules. As more brothers and sisters came along, Dolley, as the eldest daughter, took on the new duties of helping to look after them, added to an already long list of chores that were considered vital lessons in moral responsibility.

She was fifteen years old when her father moved the family to Philadelphia in 1783. The Revolution was finally over, and the city, no longer a colony, was the largest in the just-born United States. It was also the worldliest, and although Dolley was far from the only girl in town dressed in the plain gray of the Quakers, she found herself surrounded by women and men wearing delicious bright colors, and she couldn't help being impressed. Neither could she resist sidelong glances into store windows that were filled with fashions and fabrics she had never known even existed. But she resisted dreaming any new dreams. Hadn't William Penn himself told the first Philadelphians, "Let thy garments be plain and simple"? It was good enough for Dolley Payne. For the time being, anyway.

The Payne family—John and Mary and their children, William Temple, Isaac, Dolley, Lucy, Anna, Mary, and John—was accepted into the Quaker

Below: At a time when Paris ruled the fashion world, its designers produced quality dresses and bonnets in the plain style of the Quakers, many of whom were wealthy customers.

Worldly Influence

As a child, Dolley often visited her grandmother Coles, who was not a Quaker, and she discovered colorful clothes there. Although Dolley wasn't allowed to wear the clothes home, her grandmother gave her a gold brooch, a family heirloom, which Dolley began to wear as a necklace concealed under her drab Quaker dress. Her grandmother also taught her how to dance when Dolley's distant cousin the statesman Patrick Henry came to call and needed a partner. It was another of her closely kept girlhood secrets.

Northern District Monthly Meeting within days of their arrival, and John and Mary were received as elders. The Northern District was the most prestigious Quaker meeting in Philadelphia, bringing together the city's oldest and wealthiest families. Considering that John Payne was a fairly recent convert and a relatively poor man, the family's acceptance into the district says a great deal about his reputation. He became an even bigger fish in the smaller pond of the Pine Street Meeting, where he transferred three years later, resuming his activities as public friend.

THE DIGNITY OF POWER.

Chorus: "Who is she, anyhow?"
Tilly MacAllister: "She comes from Philadelphia, an' her father's a butcher. She wants to get into our set, but we ain't got no use for butchers' daughters nor Quakers."

Above: In places like New York, Quaker children such as Dolley were ostracized just for being "different."

It was traditional for Philadelphia Quakers to run small manufacturing or retail businesses, and John followed their lead by buying a small starch-making business. But he had been a farmer all his life, and he knew almost nothing about making and selling starch. His problems were compounded by the fact that he had lived off the land all his life and now he had to buy everything his family needed, from milk to firewood, and in postwar Philadelphia that was an expensive proposition. John Payne may have been good at being a Quaker, but he was very bad at being a city slicker, and his business crashed around him.

There are plenty of things the Quakers consider sinful, but high on the list is not paying one's debts, and because John couldn't pay his creditors, the Pine Street Meeting publicly disowned him. He retired in disgrace behind the closed doors of his home, and he stayed there until he died three years later.

By then Dolley had already married John Todd, Jr., a successful Quaker lawyer, and before her father died, she had given birth to a son whom she named John Payne Todd to honor him.

By most accounts, Dolley hadn't been too interested in getting married, but she apparently did it to please her father, whom Todd had helped get through his business failure, saving the family from poverty. She was a devout Quaker, to be sure, but not so eager to be married to one.

Living in the city had broadened Dolley's outlook. She loved everyone she met, and everyone she met loved her—especially the boys. She was emerging as one of the great beauties of hers or any other age; reflecting her father's Irish background, Dolley's hair was raven black, her eyes bright blue and lively, and her complexion was what was described as "peaches and cream." When Dolley was a little girl on the Virginia plantation, her mother had devised a muslin cover, like a ski mask, to keep the sun from drying her daughter's beautiful skin.

As a teenager, Dolley wasn't enrolled in a "worldly" school, although many of the schools were accepting young ladies by then; but she did learn to read and write along with the moral lessons taught to young people at the Pine Street Meeting. Ironically, those worldly schools kept boys and girls segregated, but the Quakers believed they should mix freely. Although dancing and public entertainments were forbidden, the adolescents were encouraged to socialize within the brotherhood, and chaperones were never anywhere to be seen.

Pretty and flirtatious, Dolley became the centerpiece of most of the young people's gatherings, and it was through them that she acquired an ease in mixed company. It was a talent that would serve her very well later in her life, but one that most young women of her generation had to wait until after they were married to learn for themselves.

The house where John and Dolley Todd lived at Fourth and Walnut Streets in Philadelphia is now a restored historic landmark. Before its restoration, it was an ice cream parlor— serving Dolly Madison ice cream, of course.

In spite of her earlier misgivings about marriage, Dolley Todd was a perfect Quaker wife. There was no question that she had come to love her husband, and as far as he was concerned, there had never been any doubt about how she felt. Five years older than Dolley, John had been pursuing her since the day he first saw her, when he was a young law student and her family joined the Pine Street Meeting. His own family had been Philadelphians for three generations and was highly regarded in Quaker society. And in spite of her father's recent embarrassment, Dolley was accepted warmly by the most august members of the society.

Dolley's mother, meanwhile, had been reduced to a life of relative poverty, with children to feed and a husband to care for. There weren't many ways for a woman to earn her way in those days, but Philadelphia offered an unusual opportunity in the form of congressmen and other government officials, as well as visiting businessmen, who needed a temporary place to live. Many women accommodated them by turning their homes into boardinghouses, and Mary Payne ran one of the best of them. One of her earliest boarders was Aaron Burr, the senator from New York, who stayed with Mrs. Payne long enough

Just Friends

Aaron Burr and Dolley Payne became good friends while he was her mother's boarder, but there wasn't much opportunity for them to become romantically involved under mother Mary Payne's watchful eye. Besides, there were other more compliant young women in Philadelphia who were attracted to the rising young senator from New York. Later he became a willing go-between when James Madison asked Burr to introduce him to Miss Payne. After her marriage, Dolley, probably leery of gossip, kept Burr at arm's length. But when he was tried for treason during the Jefferson administration, Dolley interceded on his behalf; and after his exile to France, it was she who pushed for the issuing of a passport so he could come home. Dolley also kept in close touch with Burr's daughter Theodosia and helped her rise in Washington society in spite of her father's tarnished name.

Right: Aaron Burr, the young senator from New York, was a boarder at Dolley's mother's house.

to become a close family friend. In fact, rumors persist to this day that he was romantically involved with her daughter Dolley. Burr wasn't a Quaker as she would have preferred, but he was a charmer, and he brought an unaccustomed breath of the outside world into her household.

That may or may not have influenced her daughter Lucy, who at the age of fifteen announced that she was getting married. The seventeen-year-old prospective bridegroom wasn't a Quaker, and Mary did all she could to stand in Lucy's way, but her efforts were too little and too late. The smitten Lucy eloped to Virginia against her mother's wishes and married George Steptoe Washington. He may have been what the Quakers called a libertine, but he was a well-connected one. He was the president's ward, his namesake, and his favorite nephew.

Lucy managed to make her getaway while her mother was busy tending to Dolley, who had just given birth to another son, named William Temple after her brother. The Pine Street Meeting had other things to deal with at the moment, too. Cases of yellow fever were being reported, and a plague soon developed that affected nearly every family in the city.

Those who could left town, and John Todd moved Dolley and his sons to a former resort—already filled with refugees—on higher ground across the Schuylkill River. But he didn't stay there himself. As a Quaker, he believed he had a duty to the less fortunate, and that his place was among them. His father and mother had also stayed behind to do what they could, and they quickly became yellow fever victims themselves. Both of them died, as more than four thousand did that summer. John worked among the sick for more than two months before he himself contracted the disease. He knew he was dying, but he managed to make it to Dolley's side before he did. Dolley herself became desperately ill a few days later, and so did her baby, Temple. She eventually recovered, but he didn't.

When Dolley and her mother finally went back home in the fall after the danger had subsided, both were widows with cloudy prospects for the future. Mary's boardinghouse was closed, and Congress wasn't eager to go back to Philadelphia, leaving her with little hope that she'd be able to reopen it again anytime soon.

Lucy and her new husband, still teenagers, took Mary into their home, a Virginia plantation called Harewood, and Lucy and Dolley shared the responsibility of caring for their two younger sisters, Mary and Anna. Dolley's inheritance from her late husband allowed her to live comfortably, and his surviving family took her and her son under its wing. She seems to have loved her comfortable independence, and the responsibility of raising her son and caring for her sister, gave her a new lease on life.

Above: The Schuylkill River as it appeared during the time Dolley lived in Philadelphia. Its opposite bank was her haven during the yellow fever epidemic that took both her husband and her newborn child from her.

Below: Dolley Payne and James Madison were married at Harewood, the Virginia plantation of Dolley's sister Lucy and her husband, George Steptoe Washington.

Dolley called her husband "The Great Little Madison." There was no question of his greatness, but he was also little. He was five feet, four inches tall and weighed a hundred pounds.

Not one to give in to the self-pity of mourning, Dolley emerged smiling, and by all accounts more beautiful and more desirable than ever before. She literally turned heads on the streets of Philadelphia; a friend noted in her diary that "gentlemen would station themselves where they could see her pass." It was a good bet that the widow Todd wouldn't be a widow for long if she didn't want to be.

Then in the spring of 1794, Dolley had a note from Aaron Burr that shook her quiet world. She dashed off a note to her friend Elizabeth Collins: "Thou must come to me—Aaron Burr says that the great little Madison has asked to be brought to see me this evening."

Virginia congressman James Madison was, as the father of the Constitution, one of the most important men in Philadelphia at the time, and Dolley's nervousness about entertaining him probably had more to do with his status than any idea that he might have romantic intentions. He was seventeen years older than she was, for one thing, and it was well known that he was oblivious to the fact that there were women in the world, and that there might be something interesting about them.

But perhaps that was all just a rumor, because James Madison was very interested in Dolley Todd. And as was typical of him, he had done his homework before arranging the visit. He knew that her Virginia family background was very much like his own. One of her mother's cousins, Patrick Henry, had served with him in Williamsburg, and he admired her father, who had sold his plantation rather than continue as a slave owner. It didn't take James long to come to the point, but although the local gossips had Dolley and James engaged, they themselves kept silent about it. The truth was that Dolley still wasn't sure.

Dolley still couldn't make up her mind, and she decided to take a little trip back to Virginia with her son and her sixteen-year-old sister, Anna. They stayed there all summer, and she used the time to weigh the pros and cons of marrying a forty-three-year-old man at the age of twenty-six, a time when she was thoroughly enjoying life. She was well aware that James would probably always be a public servant, and she never had even the slightest interest in politics. That was against Quaker principles. So, for that matter, was marrying an outsider.

Yet as she made her way back home, she sent a letter on ahead of her addressed to James Madison accepting his proposal. They were married on September 15, 1794, just a few days after her return, at her sister's Virginia plantation. Although it was noted and recorded how elegantly the groom was dressed, not a word was written about the bride. But the ceremony was conducted by an Episcopalian clergyman hundreds of miles from the Quaker meetings in Philadelphia, and it is reasonable to assume that Dolley appeared for the first time in her life not wearing the chaste gray dress and bonnet of the Quaker girl she had been up until that day. It is also highly likely that she wore flowers in her hair.

Below: James Madison was seventeen years older than his bride when he and Dolley were married, and their backgrounds and personalities were light years apart.

A Public Life

Dolley was expelled from the Pine Street Meeting less than three months after the wedding. As far as the members of the meeting were concerned, she was no longer a Quaker. But she still considered herself one, and she was determined to go right on living by the Quakers' strict codes of conduct. But now she was free to dress as she pleased, and to buy the clothes that had always tantalized her from behind shop windows.

Her husband, meanwhile, was making serious plans to retire from public life and to move back to his beloved plantation, Montpelier, in the Virginia Piedmont. His friend, neighbor, and mentor Thomas Jefferson was dead set against it, and compared it to an impending shipwreck, noting in a letter, "This must not be, except to a more splendid and officious post." But even dangling the presidency under his nose didn't change James's mind, and Jefferson changed his pitch with an appeal to "present me respectfully to Mrs. Madison and pray her to keep you where you are for her own satisfaction and the public good."

He may have been right that Dolley was a city girl at heart and that she would have been happy to stay in Philadelphia, but she would have been completely happy anywhere with her husband. Respect had turned to love almost overnight—just as it had in the case of John Todd—and she was pleased with the way James had become a doting father to her three-year-old son, Payne, and her teenage sister Anna.

Dolley and James learned from each other. She taught him her own brand of Quaker domesticity, and he initiated her into the strange world of politics. Both learned quickly, but both held onto their original strengths, he with his powerful intellect, she with her wide-open heart. It was an unlikely combination, but it worked wonderfully, and people were attracted to them as a couple. The Madisons entertained often, and each dinner party added to their blossoming reputation.

Dolley was still going through her political tutorials, but although she was in lockstep with her husband's philosophies, she never let them influence her guest lists, which crossed party lines and was like mixing roosters and foxes in the combative political climate of the day. Just as others found the contrasts between her and her husband fascinating, she was fascinated by the way philosophical differences could stimulate conversations. Most of the time, however, her own outlook on life was all the stimulation that was needed. She was deeply interested in anything anyone had to say about everything under the sun, and all of her guests went away believing that Dolley had never met anyone quite as interesting as they.

Above: Dolley sat for this Gilbert Stuart portrait in a dress that would have scandalized her Quaker parents. But this was the new Dolley.

"She welcomed all classes of people, greasy boots and silk stockings."

—Senator Elijah Mills on Dolley Madison

After a lifetime as an outsider in the world of fashion, Dolley suddenly became its queen. French Empire style was all the rage in Philadelphia in those days, and she would easily have been a standout at Versailles. The fashion, high-waisted and flowing, called for deep décolletage, and Dolley had both the body and the complexion to enhance it. The plunging necklines also provided a stage for displays of elegant necklaces, and she acquired boxes full of them; richly jeweled necklaces were her husband's most frequent gift.

In the meantime, she made up for her own lost time by launching her sister Anna into Philadelphia society, and she watched the younger set adoringly from the sidelines. It was all still a learning process for Dolley, and she learned her lessons well.

Dolley left the gaiety behind when she and James moved home to Montpelier after President Washington retired to his own plantation and John Adams replaced him in Philadelphia. James had kept his vow to retire from politics, and he expected to live out his days as a country squire. He made that apparent with a single-minded effort to expand his mansion and to add to his landholdings. Dolley had spent her childhood on a smaller plantation not very far away; she developed a close and loving relationship with the elder Madisons, whose home she shared, and she was more than happy with the prospect of raising a family of her own in such an idyllic setting. Both she and James hoped to have many children, a dream that was never fulfilled.

Soon James got back into public life as a member of the Virginia Assembly, which many saw as the great hope of Republicans in other parts of the Union. As one legislator put it to him, "If you will not save yourself and your friends, yet save your country."

James knew he couldn't refuse, but he had Dolley to consider. His only dream was to see her and young Payne, as her son was known, settled comfortably in his country seat, but Dolley wouldn't ever stand in his way, and once he had her approval, he announced his candidacy.

The 1800 presidential election took center stage near the end of his second year of service in Richmond. The Federalists had nominated John Adams to succeed himself for another term, and the Democratic-Republicans fielded Jefferson as their candidate, with Aaron Burr as his running mate. After one of the nastiest campaigns in history, Burr and Jefferson each wound up with the same number of electoral votes. Under the rules at the time, the man with the highest number of votes would be president, and the second highest, vice president. The tie meant that the House of Representatives would have to decide, but it took them nearly thirty ballots to give the highest office to Thomas Jefferson.

The new president had long since extracted a promise from James that he would serve as his secretary of state, and now the promise had to be kept. After four years out of national politics, he and Dolley packed up to move to the new capital city that many were already calling Washington.

They arrived there without a place to live, and the family—James, Dolley, Payne, and Anna—moved into the president's mansion. The widower Jefferson

was living there all alone except for his servants, and there was plenty of room for the Madisons. He'd have been pleased if they stayed there indefinitely, except for the Federalist humorists' jokes about the propriety of a president taking in boarders. The laughing came to a stop when Dolley found a small house after three weeks of hunting. It was too small for them, and too far from the center of Washington life, but in another three months they moved back to Montpelier for the summer; by the time they returned to the capital city, Dr. William Thornton had found them a fine house next door to his own, conveniently located between the president's mansion and the Capitol. Thornton, a Philadelphia architect, and one of James's closest friends, had been appointed planning commissioner for the new capital city. His wife, Anna Maria, already a shining light in the newly emerging Washington society, became Dolley's close friend, too. There would be many, many more.

Dolley would entertain often and elegantly in her new house, but she was soon given a grander stage. President Jefferson didn't have a wife to preside with him over official social functions, and neither did Vice President Burr. But propriety demanded a woman's presence whenever the president entertained female guests, and the job naturally fell to the wife of the secretary of state, who was third in line for the presidency at that time. Even without theis connection, if Jefferson had been given his choice of any woman in the city, it surely would have been Dolley Madison.

A new style of entertaining was being established, and that was exactly what President Jefferson wanted to happen. He regarded himself as a man of the people, and after his sojourns in Europe, he had developed a strong aversion to pomp and glitter. He wanted his own entertainments to be as low-key as the situation allowed, and he wanted to set an example that

Among her many talents, Dolley never forgot a face, or the name that went with it.

Queen of Ice Cream

It is often said that Dolley was the first to serve ice cream to presidential visitors, but actually, Martha Washington beat her to it. Her husband liked the frozen dessert so much that he bought an ice cream machine for their home at Mount Vernon. Thomas Jefferson was introduced to ice cream in Paris, and he encouraged Dolley to make it the crowning touch at the dinners she served for his guests. An early visitor recalled,: "Last night I was bid by our President to the executive palace, and it was a most unusual affair. Mrs. Madison always entertains with grace and charm, but last night there was a twinkle in her eyes that set astir an air of expectancy among her guests. When finally the brilliant assemblage, America's best, entered the dining room, they beheld a table set with French china and English silver laden with good things to eat, and in the center, high on a silver platter, a large shining dome of pink ice cream." Dolley might not have been the first, but as in most things, she was the best at creating a new sensation. The president's cook, Augustus Jackson, went on to start the first ice cream store in America.

other men and their wives could comfortably follow. There was no question that he had found the perfect woman to accomplish it for him. If for some reason Dolley wasn't available when he needed her, he almost never called on the wives of his other cabinet ministers, but on her sister Anna, who, although less beautiful than Dolley, was very nearly every bit as charming.

Dolley also helped the president as a kind of personal shopper, trusted to select exactly the right gifts for Jefferson's daughters, and other men in the government relied on her services to shop for their absent wives and daughters as well; but most of all, she loved to shop for herself, ordering the latest fashions from Paris by way of Philadelphia, and haunting the local stores whose owners bent over backward to please her as their most valued customer. It was a girlhood dream come true. Dolley Madison adored shopping.

She also loved a good party, and when she wasn't charming guests at the president's mansion, the lights were burning brightly at her own house. Some went so far as to say that Dolley's own parties were bigger and even more enjoyable.

There were no fashion magazines at the beginning of the nineteenth century, and newspapers, edited mostly for male readers, rarely concerned themselves with such things as women's clothes. But discussions over Washington breakfast tables invariably came around to "What did Dolley wear last night?" and the message to the women was "go thou and do likewise." Many of them went straight to Dolley herself for advice, and she was pleased to give it. What she wore last night wasn't nearly as important to her as what she would be wearing tonight.

Though she preferred getting attention by dressing in the latest, most colorful fashions—yellow was her favorite, and she only wore white for the most formal of receptions—Dolley also resorted to a bit of trickery to attract people to her side. She wasn't much of a reader, but she sometimes carried a book that served as a conversation starter. Of course, she wasn't always prepared to discuss what the book was about, but she was very good at changing the subject, usually to her guest's own interests. All she needed was a foot in the conversational door.

Dolley was also very good at steering conversations away from political discussions even in gatherings of men who had strong political differences. It was quite a feat in a city whose lifeblood was politics, but she was determined that the subject should be left at the door. "I confess," she said, "I do not admire contention in any form, either political or civil. I would rather fight with my hands than with my tongue." She had no problem getting her guests to talk about other things, and she seemed able to talk, at least a little bit, on just about any subject, as long as it didn't involve fighting words. "She talks a great deal, and in such quick, beautiful tones," gushed one admirer.

Above: Dolley's parties were legendary right from the start. A poem that was published with this drawing said, in part: "Less heed was paid to rank and station, In Madison's administration. They say that Dolley Madison Was wont on country legislators To lavish smiles, and plain homespun Was not tabooed by style's dictators, That brains instead of clothes were prized."

When all else failed, Dolley's snuff box would come to the rescue. She nearly always carried one. Dolley used snuff herself, which was quite acceptable among women back then, and she freely shared it with her guests. After all, her husband owned a thriving tobacco plantation and she had a practically unlimited supply.

Political figures, their wives, and hostesses in general have, from time immemorial, invariably arrived late for their own parties, but that was never true of Dolley Madison. She always made her entrance on the dot of the hour—four in the afternoon for dinner parties—that was noted on her invitations. Even though she was a perfectionist about her dress (and the styles were elaborate enough that things could easily go wrong as she was getting it all together), she always managed get it done on time. It was likely she considered it rude to keep her guests waiting, but it is just as likely that she wanted to squeeze every last minute out of the enjoyment of the evening.

When Jefferson first arrived in the capital, he expected to keep the doors of the president's mansion open all the time, encouraging guests to drop in whenever they felt like it, but he quickly realized that if he intended to ever get any work done, he'd have to limit his socializing to formal calls in the morning. But twice a year, on New Year's Day and Independence Day, his home became the people's house that he had envisioned, and the whole city was invited to drop in. He was the official host, of course, but Dolley was always on hand as well. She had a reputation for being able to handle large crowds and for seeing to it that even the most reluctant to leave would move on, unoffended, to make room for people who were waiting at the door, and she honed the art at these affairs. It was for these occasions that she also started wearing the turbans that became her trademark and her most lasting contribution to American fashion. A couple of generations later, the Broadway impresario Florenz Ziegfeld adopted Dolley's headgear style for his stage versions of the ideal American beauty. More than an affectation, her headdresses, usually adorned with feathers or flowers, made it easy to spot her in a crowded room.

Above: Dolley's turbans became her trademark and established an entirely new fashion. But that impish smile of hers couldn't be imitated.

The city's social life was enhanced by two popular annual events: One was the dancing assembly, which was intended to show that the new capital was as culturally aware as the old one at Philadelphia had been; the other was the Washington horse races, which, although instituted by the former Philadelphian Dr. Thornton, reflected the city's Southern roots. Nearly everyone who could walk turned out for the races, and the ladies watched from their finest carriages, strung out along the road outside the track. Naturally, Dolley presided over the festivities, her turban towering over the richest and most well-connected women out for a day in the country. Her husband, who was sometimes sidelined as Dolley went about her social duties—probably because he wanted to be—was an especially prominent participant at the races. Before his elevation to the president's cabinet he had been a well-regarded breeder of racehorses, and he was one of America's leading connoisseurs of horseflesh.

Dolley's presence was more notable at the dancing assembly, a more feminine affair, where she learned a great deal about organizing and staging formal balls. But although she presided over them, she never stepped out onto the dance floor herself. She had never learned to dance as a child, and her still-strong Quaker leanings made learning as an adult out of the question. Over her long career as the undisputed leader of Washington society, Dolley Madison never danced a step.

Jefferson's first term eventually merged into his second in 1805. His new vice president, George Clinton, like Aaron Burr who had preceded him, had no wife, and so Dolley continued on as the president's official hostess. It was obvious to everyone that Jefferson didn't regard the aged Clinton as his successor and that he intended to have James follow him. If that were to happen, it meant that Dolley would be donning her turbans and her ball gowns for at least eight more years, possibly even twelve. But if it bothered her, she didn't show any sign of it—at least outwardly.

Within several days of the inauguration, she took to her bed with a leg problem that went undescribed in the circumspect society of the day. She wrote to her sister Anna, who had married Richard Cutts and moved off to his estate in Maine, about it: "My dear husband insists on taking me to Philadelphia to be under Dr. Physick's care, but he cannot stay with me, and I dread the separation."

Dolley was in Philadelphia for four months before her leg finally healed, and she used the time to reflect on her past life in the place where it had begun, as well as her future, which to many women might have been terrifying. She had already gotten more than she bargained for, and although she thoroughly enjoyed it, there was much more to come. She had decided to welcome the future with open arms long before she was able to walk again, and as

Dolley loved to bet on horse races, and she was lucky at it. She was luckier still at poker, and she played for high stakes whenever she could.

soon as she could, she celebrated the decision by going shopping. She bought presents for everybody, including new outfits for the president's daughter Martha Randolph, who had taken over some of her entertaining duties, and a pair of fine carriage horses for her husband. In her triumphal return, she was accompanied by her sister Anna, and her husband, Richard Cutts, who were moving back to Washington.

She returned home in time for Jefferson's retirement. As Jefferson had wished, James Madison had quietly become his successor, and he was inaugurated in the brand-new House of Representatives chamber on March 4, 1809.

First Lady

It was predictable that Dolley would be the star of the inaugural show, but no one was prepared for the way she was dressed for the ceremony. James wore a brown suit made by American tailors of American-grown wool, and Dolley picked up the theme, intended to recall the great American Revolution.

Margaret Bayard Smith reported in her newspaper column: "She looked extremely beautiful, was dressed in a plain cambric dress with a very long train, plain round the neck without any handkerchief, and a beautiful bonnet of purple velvet and white satin, with white plumes. She was all grace, dignity and affability."

The reception that followed wasn't at the president's mansion, but rather at "Dolley's," their house on F Street that was open to as many well-wishers as could be shoehorned inside. The main event was scheduled for that evening at the Inaugural Ball, held at Long's Hotel. It had been Dolley's idea—neither previous First Lady had attempted such a gala—and it was advertised in the local papers as "A Dancing Assembly." Readers were directed to the hotel's manager to get their tickets, which cost $4 each. The room, which boasted one of the city's biggest dance floors, was filled to suffocating capacity. The new First Lady arrived—on time, naturally—dressed as elegantly, possibly even more so, as anyone had seen her before.

Dolley was seated at the center of a long dining table with the British ambassador on one side of her, and the representative of France on the other. All their old animosities were forgotten, at least for the evening. Mrs. Madison had, even if temporarily, brought them to conciliation. It was her night and she made the most of it. She was the real First Lady now.

The Madisons didn't move into the president's mansion until a week later, allowing Mr. Jefferson time to pack leisurely for his trip back to Monticello. After the couple began entertaining there, even the Federalists, who weren't inclined to give President Madison much credit for anything, had to admit that he was the perfect host. It went without saying that his wife was beyond perfect as a hostess. As she had in Jefferson's White House, Dolley followed the president's lead in entertaining with a minimum of ceremony.

Below: This miniature of Dolley by James Peale was mass-produced and became a best-selling item among her admirers around the country.

Above: The shell of the president's house after it was burned in 1814. Rebuilt, it was painted white, and in a city of red brick residences it was commonly called "The White House," although the designation didn't become official until Theodore Roosevelt's day.

Building on Success

The day after the Madison inauguration, Dolley went to Congress with a request for funds to redecorate the executive mansion. The former president had preferred homey furnishings and low-key entertaining, but now that it was her home, Dolley wanted to entertain more lavishly in more elegant surroundings. After she charmed the money from the legislators, Dolley went right to work transforming the house into a showplace, and then she hired a French chef and expanded her old guest lists. She had entertained only people important to the government during the Jefferson years, but now she invited writers and artists and other guests that intrigued her.

She reinstituted Martha Washington's weekly levees, but in Dolley's hands these Wednesday-evening receptions were remarkably different. She managed to meet every guest personally, and made it a point to engage each one of them in conversation, even if a brief one. One dazzled guest wrote: "It became evident in the course of the evening that the gladness which played in the countenances of those whom she approached was inspired by something more than respect. We have not forgotten how admirably the air of authority was softened by the smile of gayety; and it is pleasing to recall a certain expression that must have been created by the happiest of all dispositions—a wish to please, and a willingness to be pleased."

The president, though genial, was an intellectual with little taste for small talk, quite unlike his wife; but he gamely appeared at all the White House dinner parties that were held almost every week during the months when Congress was in session. But it was Dolley, and not James, who sat at the head of the table. He sat at her side, avoiding the duties of serving his guests and, more to the point, of engaging them in conversations that he often considered too trivial to be worth the bother. No one seemed to notice, or even care. These were her husband's public gatherings, but it was Dolley everyone came to see and talk with. He shone in after-dinner conversations with his old friends, where he made his mark as a gifted storyteller.

During Jefferson's years there, the president's mansion was a rather drab place, brightened only by his own and Dolley's presence. Now that the Madison family was in residence, the time had come to spruce it up and furnish it. Congress grudgingly appropriated $6,000 to do the job, and it appointed Benjamin Latrobe, the designer of the Capitol and chief planner of the city, to oversee the work. Of course, he deferred to Dolley's taste, agreeing that a woman's touch was necessary and recognizing the importance of the opinions of the woman who would have to live there. They got along beautifully, and by all accounts the result of their collaboration was beautiful, too. The drawing room was especially striking, with draperies and upholstery in Dolley's favorite color, yellow; and all of the public rooms were made to look bigger and more elegant with huge mirrors in gilt frames that endlessly reflected the dancing light of candles and oil lamps. Dolley also bought a pianoforte and a guitar to add musical accompaniment to the gay laughter of her parties. She selected richly carved mantelpieces, and she ordered new china, table linens, and silverware. It was all accomplished within the budget and far ahead of schedule. There was little left to be finished by the time the family left for their summer break at Montpelier.

The Madisons' own furniture rounded out the transformation, and Dolley personally saw to it that it was kept shipshape. She appeared every morning wearing a Quaker frock and white apron, supervising the servants and lending a hand herself at the daily round of dusting, scrubbing, and straightening up.

During the first three years of his administration, James, like Jefferson before him, had little on his mind other than avoiding a war that seemed to be inevitable. The British had been playing a cat-and-mouse game, making repeated peace overtures and then withdrawing them. Both the Royal Navy and Napoleon's fleets were seizing American ships, stealing their cargoes, and kidnapping their crews. By 1812, as James was getting ready to run for a second term, the country was divided between the Federalist North calling for appeasement and the Republican South that was all for a declaration of war. Six months before the election, with unwelcome prodding from Congress, James was forced to declare war on Great Britain. That he even managed to be nominated for a second term after that was a mystery to most observers, and when he was, the smart money was on his opponent, DeWitt Clinton. But even smarter bettors knew that Dolley's popularity would carry the day. Also in James's favor, the voters were relieved that the war that had been threatening for so many years had finally come to a head, and for better or for worse, sufficient numbers of them still trusted James enough to give him a second term.

The New Year's reception went on as usual in spite of the war, and James's second inauguration was almost as elegantly celebrated as his first. His political

Above: Table settings are as often a part of a First Lady's legacy as her ball gowns. Dolley's dishes were her own special pride and joy.

Below: Dolley's imported mirror in the White House's Blue Room raised eyebrows, but not because of its appropriateness for the room.

When Dolley spent $40 for a mirror for the White House, the Senate, furious that it had been imported from France, called for an investigation. The probe cost the government $2,000. The mirror stayed where it was.

"The President's house is a perfect palace. You enter the front door, and are at once in a large hall, which is an entry, etc. Pillars of immense size are dispersed thro' this, and it is handsomely furnished, etc., and has large lamps for the whole length. On the side opposite to the entrance are doors opening to four rooms. The corner is the dining room and is very spacious, and twice the height of modern parlours, and three times as large. This is furnished in the most elegant manner, and the furniture is so large that Mrs. Cutts says the sideboard would cover the whole side of a large parlour. At the head of the room, George Washington is represented as large as life. This room opens by a single door into Mrs. Madison's sitting room, which is half as large. This is furnished equally as well, and has more elegant and delicate furniture."

—Elbridge Gerry, Jr., Diary, 1813

enemies denounced such showiness in wartime, but Dolley soldiered on and the people loved her for it.

As was customary, the entertaining stopped in the summer when the president and First Lady went back to Virginia for their annual vacation. They had planned to skip it that year, even though Mr. Madison's War was now being called the phony war, and no one felt in any particular danger. But in June, James was attacked by a nearly fatal case of malaria and as soon as he was able to travel, they were off to Montpelier for his recuperation. It gave Dolley a chance to catch her second wind as well.

During the weeks she had been nursing her husband in Washington, she'd had a nagging dread that the British might take it into their heads to attack the capital. The British admiral George Cockburn, whose fleet was in the Chesapeake Bay, had bragged that he would soon "make his bow in Mrs. Madison's drawing-room," and she wrote to a friend, "All the city have expected a visit from the enemy, and were not lacking in their expressions of terror and reproach. … I therefore keep the old Tunisian sabre within reach."

In spite of Dolley's fears, the fleet stayed where it was for almost a year. The British army had recently defeated Napoleon, and the navy waited until the battle-hardened troops arrived to take part in this new war. After they did, about five thousand soldiers went ashore in late August 1814 and began marching on Washington itself. The defending militia, never very notable, had been lulled into a sense of complacency, and the path to the Capitol was wide-open, with only token resistance. As one soldier put it, "The militia ran like sheep chased by dogs."

Below: The British attack on Washington on October 24, 1814, left most of the city in ashes, including the presidential mansion, and it came close to costing the First Lady her life.

When they stormed into the city, the British troops headed straight for the Capitol and set fire to it, completely destroying the House chamber and ruining the Senate almost beyond repair. Their next stop was the president's mansion, and they torched private houses and public buildings as they marched down Pennsylvania Avenue. Before setting fire to the executive mansion, Admiral Cockburn kept his promise to visit Mrs. Madison's drawing room, picking up a couple of souvenirs—the president's hat and a cushion from the First Lady's chair—but ordering everything of value to be stacked in the center of the rooms to feed the fire his men were about to set.

Dolley and James had fled the mansion by then, but they could easily see what was happening. The entire city appeared to be burning, and the light from the fires could be seen as far as forty miles away.

James and Dolley were not together, and neither of them had any way of knowing whether the other was safe. The commander in chief had gone off to see if his presence might have a positive effect on the troops, and he had been cut off on his way back and forced to move in the opposite direction. He had promised Dolley that he'd be home by dinnertime, and that he would bring his cabinet, who had accompanied him, back for dinner.

Dolley knew she might have to flee the capital city, so she had spent most of the day packing for an evacuation. She wasn't able to cram more into her coach than a few boxes of state papers, some clothes, and the velvet draperies from her sitting room. Other valuables were also packed in hopes that a wagon could be found to haul them out of harm's way, but that seemed like a hopeless gesture. As a messenger was riding up to the door to warn her to leave right away, Dolley was struggling with the irreplaceable Gilbert Stuart portrait of George Washington. It was screwed to the wall, and she finally opted to cut it from its frame. At the last possible moment, she rolled it up and entrusted it to two men who had come to help, with orders to take it, along with whatever other presidential papers they were able to carry, to the nearby farm of a friend. Dolley, meanwhile, made her escape in her own carriage and headed across the river into Virginia.

Dolley made her escape well before Admiral Cockburn arrived, but she apparently just missed James, who arrived home within an hour of her flight. Assuring himself that she wasn't there, he moved on rather quickly himself because the enemy was already within the city. The president spent the night in a house near the river, and just before sunrise, he and his party crossed over to the safety of the Virginia forest. By afternoon, they had reached the farm where it had been prearranged he would find his wife, and he was relieved to find her already there, and none the worse for her terrifying experience.

The next morning, Dolley and James went their separate ways in the interest of safety. Dolley disguised herself as an ordinary farmer's wife, traveling alone without her ever-present

Above: Dolley Madison became a national hero when she saved her husband's papers and a rare portrait of George Washington as British troops came in sight, bent on destroying the house and everything in it.

"Anyone would have done what I did."

—*Dolley Madison on her daring flight from Washington*

The Gilbert Stuart portrait of George Washington, which is in the East Room of the White House today, was originally bought by Congress for $800.

Above: Dolley's firsthand account of the British attack and her narrow escape is detailed in this letter to her sister.

"My husband left me yesterday morning to join General Winder. He inquired anxiously whether I had the courage, or firmness, to remain in the President's House until his return, on the morrow, or the succeeding day; and on my assurance that I had no fear but for him and the success of our army, he left me, beseeching me to take care of myself, and of the Cabinet Papers, public and private. I have since received two dispatches from him, written with a pencil; the last is alarming, because he desires I should be ready at a moment's warning to enter my carriage and leave the city; that the enemy seemed stronger than had been reported and that it might happen that they would reach the city with the intention to destroy it.

"At this late hour a wagon has been procured; I have it filled with the [silver] plate and most valuable portable articles belonging to the house; whether it will reach its destination, the Bank of Maryland, or fall into the hands of the British soldiery, events must determine. Our kind friend, Mr. Carroll, has come to hasten my departure, and is in a very bad humor with me because I insist on waiting until the large picture of General Washington is secured and it requires unscrewing from the wall. This process was found too tedious for these perilous moments; I have ordered the frame to be broken, and the canvas taken out; it is done—and the precious portrait placed in the hands of two gentlemen from New York for safekeeping."

—Dolley Madison to Lucy Washington Todd, August 23, 1814

maid and the elegant presidential carriage filled with the historic papers she had saved. Both were carefully concealed, and Dolley rode off in a rough wagon with two armed men who were also disguised as farmers. Their whereabouts were unknown for the next two days.

Dolley finally turned up at the Potomac ferry and made her way to her old house on F Street, which was still standing and had become the home of her sister Anna Cutts. She never said where she had been during her flight, and even later when her husband asked her about it, she brushed him off as though it wasn't of any importance. As far as Dolley was concerned, it wasn't; she never liked to talk about unpleasant things. She had seen the ruined shell of her official home, though, and she wrote a letter to Benjamin Latrobe's wife about it. It was as close as she ever came to revealing her feelings about what had happened: "Two hours before the enemy entered the city, I left the house where Mr. Latrobe's elegant taste had been justly admired, and where you and I had so often wandered together. ... It would fatigue you to read the list of my losses, or an account of the general dismay or particular distress of your acquaintances."

Indeed, there was destruction everywhere. The only public building left undamaged was the patent office; most of the others, including the president's mansion, were beyond repair. The common wisdom was that the capital city should probably be abandoned, and other cities, especially Philadelphia, quickly put out the welcome mat for the federal government.

But the president would have none of it. Within days of his return, he and his secretary of state, James Monroe, who was also serving as the secretary of war at the time, were hard at work reorganizing the government and requisitioning private homes for its various departments. The president also ordered that rebuilding should start immediately, if not sooner. The patent office was converted into a temporary Capitol, and James and Dolley moved into a mansion called the Octagon House, which had been saved from the fire. Next to the president's house itself, it was the most impressive residence in the city; graced with Dolley's presence, it became a kind of symbol of hope that all was right with the world in spite of the war.

Above: With the President's House destroyed, the West Room at the Octagon House became the scene of Dolley's entertaining for a year.

All through the war, Dolley had made it a point to dress even more gaily than she had before. She was aided by her friend Mrs. Joel Barlow, who had gone to Paris with her husband on an abortive peace mission and was commissioned by Dolley to shop for her. The result was a representation of the latest from the Paris shops—the duty alone came to more than $2,000—which Dolley pronounced "enchanting."

Much of the finery was destroyed in the fire, but Dolley had been able to rescue some of it, and she didn't lose any time augmenting her wardrobe. She was back in stride by midwinter. A guest at an early-December ball noted that she was dressed in "sky-blue striped velvet—a frock—fine. Elegant lace around the neck and lace handkerchief inside and a large ruff, white lace turban starred in gold, and white feathers. She had neat little ornaments, emeralds set in gold."

Less than a month later, a guest at her New Year's Day reception reported that Dolley wore "yellow satin embroidered all over with sprigs of butterflies, not two alike in her dress; a narrow border in all colors, made high in the neck; a little cape, long sleeves, and a white bonnet with feathers."

By February 1815, the War of 1812 was over at last. The great general Andrew Jackson had whipped the British in the Battle of New Orleans, and while the victory was being celebrated at one of Dolley's receptions, a peace treaty, negotiated weeks earlier, arrived by ship from Europe. The president signed the agreement on Valentine's Day, and that night the Octagon House was the scene of the most exuberant party Dolley Madison ever staged.

The Madisons moved from the Octagon House a few months later into a smaller house at the corner of Pennsylvania Avenue and Nineteenth Street. It was a townhouse built flush to the sidewalk, and passersby could look into the windows. Dolley had retrieved her pet parrot by then, and she charmed children

Above: Dolley's husband, James, didn't share her enthusiasm for entertaining, but he never stood in her way, and toward the end of his presidency he actually seemed to enjoy it.

who gathered on the sidewalk to watch her feed it every morning, encouraging the bird to say a few words for them.

Although the house was comparatively small, Dolley didn't cut her guest lists, and her entertainments became known as "squeezes." The grandest of them was her reception for Andrew Jackson, the hero of the Battle of New Orleans. On that occasion, she stationed servants with torches at the ground floor windows. It not only brightened up the room, which wasn't normally very well lighted, but it also delighted the crowds gathered outside on the sidewalk and made them feel like they were a part of the celebration.

When the army was disbanded, each company in the parade down Pennsylvania Avenue stopped in front of the house and gave three cheers for the First Lady, which she graciously acknowledged from her window. Rather than allowing the small house to cramp her style, she had turned it into an advantage by making ordinary citizens feel a part of her circle of admirers.

Dolley's years at the head of Washington society came to an end with the inauguration of James Monroe on March 4, 1817. She and her husband were on hand for the Inaugural Ball, but this was Elizabeth Monroe's party, and Dolley was careful not to upstage her. The Madisons quietly left town before the ball was over.

On that same day, Elizabeth Lee, one of Dolley's oldest friends, summed up what everyone felt:

"How much greater cause have I to congratulate you at this period, for having so filled it as to render yourself more enviable this day than your successor, as it is more difficult to deserve gratitude and thanks of the community than their congratulations. …You will retire from the tumult and fatigue of public life to your favorite retreat in Orange County and will carry with you principles and manners not to be put off with the robe of state. … Talents such as yours were never meant to remain inactive; on retiring from public life, you will form a more fortunate arrangement of your time, be able to display them in the more noble and interesting walks of life."

The First Lady was retiring. But Washington hadn't seen the last of Dolley Madison.

After Dolley retired as First Lady, the House of Representatives voted to reserve a chair for her in its chambers for "whenever it shall be her pleasure to use it."

Retired, but Not Retiring

The Virginia plantation that became the Madisons' permanent home had been established by James's father in 1756. Like all of the Virginia plantations, Montpelier was the scene of endless rounds of parties and the destination of hordes of guests, both invited and casual drop-ins, especially during the summer months, and with Dolley as its mistress, it was much more active than most of them. The house was furnished with pieces sent from France, first by James's neighbor Thomas Jefferson, and then by James Monroe, who was in Paris after the French Revolution and whom James commissioned to pick up bargains among the detritus of the deposed royalty. Dolley added her own touches to the decor, and the result was described as "modern." In many ways, it was more elegant than the president's mansion back in Washington had been, and by all accounts it was the most charming house in all Virginia. The charm, of course, wasn't the house; it was Dolley Madison's presence there.

Above: A great deal of the furniture James and Dolley collected during their marriage is displayed at Montpelier today. Included is a mahogany side chair thought to have come from Dolley's first house in Philadelphia.

They settled in quickly, with James managing his farms, and Dolley tending the gardens. After they had been settled there for ten years, Margaret Bayard Smith visited her old friend and wrote of Dolley, "She certainly has always been, and still is, one of the happiest of human beings. … She seems to have no place about her which could afford a lodgement for care or trouble. Time seems to favor her as much as fortune. She looks young and she says she feels so. I can believe her, nor do I think she will *ever* look or feel like an old woman."

The legendary entertaining at Montpelier continued for twenty years, longer than Dolley's reign in Washington, but age seemed to have caught up with James when his friend Thomas Jefferson died in 1826. That his friend had been reduced to poverty weighed heavily on James. Bad crop years had cut into James's own prosperity, and at seventy-five he knew that his own death wasn't far off (he would live another ten years). What worried him most was that he wouldn't have enough time to organize the papers he had assembled as a participant in the birth of the nation. They were the most detailed of any of the founding fathers, and he knew that future historians would be in the dark without them. By mutual agreement, such eyewitness accounts were to remain private for fifty years, but now the time had nearly passed, and he was already at work organizing them for publication. But now it became an obsession. It was then that Dolley became his helpmate in every sense of the word. He had no secretary, and she filled in, even transcribing the notes when his eyesight began to fail and his rheumatic hands couldn't hold a pen. These were the same documents that she herself had saved from the burning of Washington; in addition to their being her husband's legacy to the American people, Dolley had

Above: Dolley's base of operations during her last twelve years in Washington was the former Richard Cutts House on H Street. It had been built by her brother-in-law, but acquired by her husband, and she invested in making it a showplace as glittering as any in the capital.

a personal stake because he planned to leave all the publishing rights to her in his will.

While she was serving as her husband's scribe, Dolley was also his nurse. James suffered from a variety of ailments, but he bore them all stoically. Yet in the last months of his life he was confined to his bed. A visitor during that time wrote, "She looks just as she did twenty years ago, and dresses in the same manner with her turban and cravat; rises early and is very active, but seldom leaves the house, as her devotion to Mr. Madison is incessant, and he needs all of her constant attention."

After her husband died, Dolley stayed at Montpelier for another year. The historic papers were ready for publication, but she had made the mistake of allowing her son John Payne Todd to negotiate their sale.

James had always regarded Payne as his own son, and he had hoped that the boy would be educated at Princeton as he had been. But Dolley's son seemed more interested in living the life of a crown prince, much to the delight of the young ladies in Washington. He was an unusually handsome young man, and he had inherited his mother's charm. He was also popular among the young men who became his drinking buddies, and the gamblers who loved to take his money.

When the family went back to Montpelier, Dolley was happy that her son would be removed from the temptations of the capital city, and that he would finally be able to get his act together, which to her meant finding a wife. She was wrong on both counts.

After her husband died, Dolley, ever optimistic about Payne's abilities, turned the running of Montpelier over to him. He had been teetering on the brink of alcoholism, and the comparatively dull life of a country squire pushed him over the edge. He also fell victim to a variety of illnesses, both real and imagined, and all the while the plantation's income plummeted.

Dolley had gone back to Washington in the meantime, but she intended to use Montpelier as a summer retreat. One of her visits extended to two years when she put her own hands to work to slow the obvious decline of the place in her son's hands. With her usual positive outlook, she wrote to a friend that she wanted to try her hand at being a "farmeress." Although she had never learned much about agriculture, she was able to bring her brand of cheerfulness back to the plantation. Payne, meanwhile, had bought some nearby land and was at work building a place of his own—he said he was going to make a fortune here raising silkworms. Although he had already shown he had no talent for business, he did have unlimited funds thanks to his mother. Dolley's main interest in holding on to Montpelier had been to leave it to Payne, but now that he would have a place of his own, she decided to sell it.

She had already removed herself to Washington again; it had become urgent that she sell her husband's papers and she needed the help of her friends there. An opportunity of a different sort was knocking when she arrived. President William Henry Harrison had recently died after only a month in office, and the wife of the new president, John Tyler, was an invalid. His son's wife, Mrs. Robert Tyler, assumed the role of First Lady, but she was uncomfortable with it, and Dolley had a new assignment as her advisor. She organized the White House wedding of the president's daughter, and it was such a huge success that Dolley had a seat reserved for her in the presidential carriage for every state occasion during the rest of the Tyler administration.

Dolley also did a great deal of entertaining on her own, and she couldn't recall a happier social season in all her years as a Washington hostess. But there was still that problem of selling the Madison manuscript. She had empowered her son to act as her agent, but after several unproductive trips to New York, he still hadn't produced a publisher. Using that as an excuse, Dolley went up to New York herself, but her diaries don't indicate that she saw any editors while she was there. She did, on the other hand, visit with all the people who mattered among the New York Knickerbockers, including her friend John Jacob Astor, with whom she negotiated a mortgage on her Washington house. Dolley was rather desperate for money, and she had already sold some of the land from her husband's estate, even before she decided to sell the entire plantation.

She had been able to sell the Madison papers to the government, but the price, $30,000, was far below what she had expected—her late husband had predicted that she would get at least $100,000. As part of the deal, Congress had agreed to let her retain the reproduction rights, which she offered to Harper Brothers for commercial publication. Her friend George Tucker had taken the material to the New York publishing house, but he reported back to Dolley, "I accidentally met with Mr. Todd on the street [and] he informed me that he had come on for that purpose and I thought any further efforts on my part were unnecessary." Payne apparently made no further efforts, either, even though his mother was covering his expenses. Two years passed without a sale, and Dolley decided to offer Congress the second volume of her husband's papers. She knew that the price would be low, but by that point was more important to her seeing her husband's work published for future generations than her own financial security.

The Senate approved the sale almost as soon as the offer was received, but the House dragged its feet, and the matter wasn't settled for another four long years. The war with Mexico gave Congress other priorities, but in the end it was revealed that Payne Todd's self-important meddling had muddied the waters. Mr. Todd had a reputation in Washington that was the direct opposite of his mother's.

Another new president, James Knox Polk, had moved into the White House by then. He and his wife, Sarah, had known and loved Dolley since he was a congressman and she the First Lady. The Polks kept their entertaining to a minimum, but no matter how small the guest list, Dolley was always on it. Sarah Polk kept her parties as low-key as they were rare, but the glitter-starved could always find satisfaction across Lafayette Square at Dolley's house. Sarah didn't

Below: Secretary of State Daniel Webster's political views didn't square with Dolley's, but she never let a thing like that get in the way of a friendship. He came up with a scheme to help her when her finances hit rock bottom.

mind, as long as they weren't drinking in *her* presence.

At the end of his presidency, Polk decided to go out with a bang by organizing a grand party at the White House. As a climax, the president strolled through all the crowded rooms, chatting amiably with his guests. It was reminiscent of Dolley's style as presidential hostess, even down to the detail that the woman on the president's arm was Dolley herself. Sarah didn't mind playing second fiddle at all. In fact, none of the first ladies Mrs. Madison befriended ever showed the slightest sign of jealousy or resentment at being upstaged by her.

Dolley's own entertaining put a strain on her already reduced financial resources, and Daniel Webster, who was famous for his own parties as secretary of state, decided to help. Friends and admirers were forever giving him money, and he proposed sharing some of it with Dolley in the form of a perpetual annuity. But the scheme fell apart when the actuaries asked for her birth date. Dolley had lied about her age so often that there was no reliable source save Dolley herself. She refused Webster's offer, not to avoid revealing her true age, but because it didn't seem to her to be ethical for the widow of James Madison to take political funds that had been donated to a Whig. The new party had replaced the Federalists as a thorn in the side of the Democratic-Republicans, and many Whigs resented Dolley's presence in Washington, in fact. But even the pettiest among them had to admit that she brightened the place up.

When Congress finally agreed to buy the remaining Madison papers, the price was set at $25,000, to be paid through the same kind of annuity Daniel Webster had proposed in order to give Dolley a secure income for the rest of her life. The deal also included a $5,000 advance to clear up her outstanding debts, including the mortgage on her house.

Payne turned up again more than a year later and coerced Dolley into signing a will he had written that made him the beneficiary of her remaining trust fund. She was too weary to protest, and all that remained was to produce witnesses to her signature on the document he had brought with him. Dolley had close friends literally everywhere, but Payne chose to go out and collar the first three men he found on the street, who wouldn't have any reason to question what his mother was doing.

In the cold light of dawn, Dolley regretted what she had done and she fell into a deep depression. When she recovered, she contacted her nephew Madison Cutts, who had served her as a financial advisor, and explained what had happened to her. He went to work to correct the situation—the document she signed hadn't yet been legally registered—and by the time he came back, Dolley was suffering from what would

Below: Dolley was the first president's wife to sit for a photograph. The resulting daguerreotype is a true image of her.

prove to be her final illness. The new will Cutts had drawn up divided the remainder of her trust fund equally between Payne Todd and Dolley's niece Anna Payne, who had been her constant companion for many years. It left everything else—her house, her furniture, and her art collection—to her son. She died a few days later, confident she had done the right thing.

Of course, her son didn't think so, and he went to court to break his mother's second will. The final decision upheld the second version, which, in fact, had actually expanded and not reduced Payne's inheritance, considering the value of the property involved. He himself died less than two years later, broke again, and his funeral party consisted of a single mourner and two slaves whom he had set free on his death. It was probably the only decent thing John Payne Todd had done in decades.

It was a striking contrast to his mother. Dolley Madison established precedents for every First Lady who has followed in her footsteps. Fortunately, when she died they didn't break the mold.

Visiting Montpelier

James Madison's plantation, Montpelier, is one of the properties owned by the National Trust for Historic Preservation, which acquired it in 1983. After Dolley Madison sold Montpelier, the estate had six different owners over the next half-century, and each of them altered it to their own tastes. The most extensive changes came after William DuPont, Sr., bought it in 1901. He added second floors to each of the wings, and covered the original brick with beige stucco. His daughter, who lived there for many years, added a very modern exercise room in the basement for her husband, Randolph Scott, the movie star. In 2003, the Montpelier Foundation, an arm of the National Trust, began a massive restoration project that is expected to take several more years. When the work is completed, the house will be returned to its appearance at the time of James Madison's death. Most of it remains open while the restoration is in progress. The house is open from 9:30 A.M. until 5:30 P.M. for most of the year, and an admission fee is charged for adults and children older than six.

Montpelier is located at 11407 Constitution Highway, Montpelier Station, Virginia 22957. To get there from Washington, D.C., take Route 66 West, to Route 29 South to Culpepper, exit at Route 15 South toward Orange onto Route 20 South. Montpelier is about four miles past the town. To get there from Richmond, Virginia, take I-64 West to Zion's Corner, exit to Route 15 North to Orange. Continue about four miles past the town. Please note that there is a town called Montpelier on Route 33 near Richmond. This is not where you'll find the Montpelier plantation.

Below: Montpelier as it appeared in the Madison era. The plantation changed hands six times after Dolley Madison sold it in 1844.

Elizabeth Monroe

Queen Elizabeth

Dolley Madison had often been called "the Presidentess," but although Elizabeth Monroe took on a far more active, if behind-the-scenes, political role during her husband's presidency, it was evident from the first day that she would never be called anything but Mrs. Monroe. The only exception was among catty women who were put off by her regal attitude and referred to her as "Queen Elizabeth" behind her back.

The reconstruction of the White House wouldn't be finished until nearly a year after James Monroe's inauguration in 1817, and in the meantime, formal presidential functions were held in the First Family's own house on F Street. Lack of space was usually cited as justification for their infrequency and their subdued atmosphere, but more often the excuse was Elizabeth's fragile health.

In the first half of the nineteenth century, it was considered gauche to discuss a woman's health, and details of what might have ailed Elizabeth Monroe were never revealed; however, in her rare public appearances, guests were frequently surprised at how youthful and radiant Elizabeth looked.

Medical experts have since concluded that Elizabeth suffered from epilepsy, a condition that was little understood in her time, and was usually called "the falling sickness" because those stricken were prone to unpredictable convulsions and fainting spells. At one point during Elizabeth's years in the White House, she blacked out and fell into a fireplace and was left with severe burns. There is some evidence that former president James Madison had also been an epileptic during his early years, and it was epilepsy that shortened the life of Martha Washington's daughter Patsy. Both of them had found some relief in the waters at White Sulfur and Warm Springs in Virginia, and Elizabeth's husband had tried the same remedy for her.

Throughout their life together, James Monroe devoted a great deal of attention to his wife's health, which he said was "impaired by many causes," but he never discussed any of those causes except among her doctors, and in Washington, where rumors and gossip are a way of life, it was whispered that Elizabeth suffered from only one thing: snobbishness.

It seemed to be an inescapable conclusion. When she left her husband's first Inaugural Ball "before supper was served," the opinion among the guests who stayed for the whole celebration was that as a native New Yorker, it was probably likely that Elizabeth found the event a bit too provincial for her tastes.

Elizabeth Kortright Monroe

Born
June 30, 1768,
New York, New York

Parents
Captain Lawrence Kortright and Hannah Aspenwall Kortright

Marriage
February 16, 1786,
to James Monroe
(1758-1831)

Children
Eliza (1786-1840); James Spence (1799-1801); Maria Hester (1803-50)

Died
September 23, 1830,
Loudon County, Virginia

When she didn't take part in official entertainments in her own home, they said it was because she found her guests boring. As if to prove them right, sometimes when she did appear, Elizabeth didn't have much of anything to say to anyone, and she seemed incapable of even the shadow of a smile. On the other hand, on many occasions, possibly proving that she was indeed in poor health in spite of what the cynics may have believed, she was capable of brilliant conversation, and although she didn't have a bubbly personality, she could be a warm and charming hostess.

The fact that Elizabeth's frequent absences were never explained only added to the criticism that was leveled at her, and there were times when she herself added fuel to the fire. When the sponsors of a charity ball approached her for support, she agreed to put in an appearance, but only on the condition that they were forbidden to use her name in their fund-raising and would forbid the press to report her presence at the ball itself. When her daughter Maria was married at the White House to Samuel Gouvernour, the president's secretary and Elizabeth's cousin, she kept the wedding a closed family affair and adamantly refused to invite any diplomats or government leaders; and if any of them chose to send a wedding gift, she ordered that no thank-you notes should be written.

During her later years as First Lady, Dolley Madison had organized and actively supported a group of women to upgrade and support the local orphan's asylum, and the work was expected to continue after her retirement. It seemed to be a foregone conclusion that Elizabeth would take on the cause as her own, and the organization's leaders invited themselves to her home to talk it over. Although she was cordial to them, Mrs. Monroe never invited them back and she quietly withdrew her active support.

Louisa Adams, the wife of Secretary of State John Quincy Adams, and Elizabeth's close friend, diplomatically told the First Lady's critics that their expectations were probably unfair. "Tastes differ and dear Dolley was much more popular," she pointed out. She also wrote that Elizabeth was, in her own way, every bit as stylish as Mrs. Madison. "She dresses in the highest style of

Below: Maria Hester Monroe, Elizabeth's youngest daughter, was the first presidential daughter to be married in a White House ceremony.

Family Connections

Elizabeth's family, the Kortrights, were among the first settlers in New York after it was established as a Dutch colony and settled by Walloons, who were brought over as indentured servants from present-day Belgium. The Walloons became wealthy merchants over time, and their children intermarried into other successful Walloon families, forming the colony's first upper class. Among those families were the Gouverneurs, and Elizabeth's sister Hester followed the tradition by marrying into the Gouverneur family. Hester's son Samuel married his cousin Maria Monroe at the White House.

fashion, and moves not like a queen—for that is an unpardonable word in this country—but like a goddess." Dolley, being Dolley, had nothing to say about how the new First Lady seemed to be completely changing all of the social rules that she had established over her sixteen years as their number-one arbiter.

Among the first traditions Elizabeth did away with was the custom of paying the first call on newly arrived foreign dignitaries and the wives of newly elected congressmen. In fact, she let it be known that she didn't plan to make social calls on anyone at all, and anybody who wished to call on her would be allowed to appear at the White House only on Tuesday mornings at ten. At that time, she said, they would need to first meet with her daughter Eliza Hay, who would determine whether they would be admitted into the First Lady's drawing room. Elizabeth made it clear that, her health permitting, she was quite happy to meet and greet anyone who arrived at her door at the appointed hour; but she wouldn't, under any circumstances, return the visit. Instead, Mrs. Hay would return calls for her.

But there was a problem. In many cases, Elizabeth's daughter felt that some of those calls amounted to casting pearls before swine. Right or wrong, it was her own opinion, and she had probably come by it naturally.

According to protocol, the wives of invited White House guests couldn't accompany their husbands unless there was a woman there to receive them, and Elizabeth Monroe was away quite often.

Eliza was eight years old when her father was named minister to France, and during the years that they were in Paris her parents enrolled her in the exclusive Madam Campan's seminary in Saint-Germain, where she studied among young duchesses and future queens. Among her classmates was Caroline Bonaparte, Napoleon's youngest sister, and her best friend there was Hortense Beauharnais, the daughter of Josephine Bonaparte and Napoleon's stepdaughter, who would become queen of Holland. The friendship lasted over the years, and the queen was the godmother of Eliza's daughter Hortensia. Although she had been lifted from the heady atmosphere of the seminary at age eleven, Eliza acquired a feeling there that she had been born to royalty herself, and when her father became president, the feeling was enhanced. Call it snobbishness. Everybody else did.

Foreign ministers expected the president's wife to make the first call on them as a welcoming gesture, and when Elizabeth didn't appear at their embassies, they refused to visit the White House until she did. A compromise might have been reached had Eliza Hay agreed to make those first ceremonial calls as her mother's representative, but she refused to do it. Not only that, but she convinced her father that he himself ought to distance himself from the diplomats, especially the ones that she had decided were beneath her. Fortunately, Secretary of State John Quincy Adams and his wife, Louisa, smoothed their ruffled feathers as much as possible.

Below: Elizabeth's oldest daughter, Eliza, took charge of most of the White House entertaining, often with disastrous results.

Above: The Monroes lived in this house on "Eye" Street in Washington when he was secretary of state and secretary of war during the Madison administration. They stayed after he became president, and it became the temporary executive mansion from March through September in 1817.

Below: It isn't surprising that Elizabeth was often called "Queen Elizabeth." She looked the part.

Elizabeth had lived in Europe for several years, and she and her husband frequently conversed with one another in French, considered to be the language of diplomacy, but she had no words for the Washington diplomatic corps, and the perceived slight wasn't taken lightly. The bad feelings became especially strong when the president refused to accept an invitation to the French embassy. He had been invited to celebrate the Congress of Vienna, which had brought peace to Europe after years of warfare. He refused the invite because he said there was no precedent for it, and he didn't believe he ought to set one. Elizabeth also refused to attend, because she thought it would be unseemly for her to go anywhere that her husband would not.

It was one of many perceived slights, and the president ignored them at first, but as plans were being made for the New Year's celebration that would be his first social function in the newly restored White House, he worried about protocols that might cause international tensions if they weren't followed properly. He was relieved to learn that, unlike the customs that prevailed in the courts of Europe, there had never been an established pecking order at such functions in Washington; but in view of the social undercurrents, he agreed to receive foreign ministers on a first-come-first-recognized basis during the half hour before the doors were opened to the general public. No one was offended, and the reception was an unqualified success on every level.

No one could upstage the First Lady who, as expected, was the star of the show. Others who were there had nothing but good things to say about her. It was generally agreed that she rose to the occasion with dignity and grace, and that she was easily the most stately and regal-looking woman ever to preside over the annual event. "Stately and regal-looking" were the adjectives most often used to describe Elizabeth during her eight years as First Lady.

Rumor had it that Elizabeth ordered her dresses directly from Paris and that the one she wore that day had cost $1,500, an extravagance that translates to well over $21,500 in today's dollars. It was of white-figured silk trimmed with white point lace, and her hat—a turban, following the Dolley Madison tradition—was trimmed with rare white feathers.

Elizabeth reinstated the custom of biweekly drawing rooms, putting to rest the old-fashioned designation of "levees," although she wasn't always able to attend them herself. First Lady watchers worked the grapevine to determine when she would be most likely to put in an appearance, and when she did, the rooms were as full as they ever had been in the past. Eliza, who had moved from her own home into the White House, attended all of them, either by herself or at her mother's side, and her guests were always impressed by her appearance. The president, of course, stuck to tradition by putting in an appearance at all of the drawing rooms, receiving his guests with a level of charm that was more comparable to that of Dolley Madison than to other presidents who had accepted the duty in the past. Elizabeth also sat at her husband's side for most of their small dinner parties, and she always captivated the guests with her own natural conversational skills.

The population of the capital city had grown dramatically by the time the Monroes moved into the White House, and the country itself was growing, too—four new states were added to the Union during the Monroe administration—and that created an influx of new members of Congress. In slower times, greeting these newcomers and other VIPs might have been taken in stride, but considering Elizabeth's poor health, and her daughter Eliza's attitude, it would have been foolish to even think of sipping tea with all the people who considered it their right.

No one was pleased with Elizabeth's "no first calls" policy and she seems to have felt the sting. She scheduled a meeting with Louisa Adams, and between them they decided that Elizabeth was doing the right thing, but that the public perception of it was wrong. Louisa's advice was to emphasize her frail health and spin the criticism away from any suggestion of rudeness. The strategy worked rather well, replacing anger with sympathy, but many in official Washington, especially senators' wives, still had their noses out of joint.

They might have been able to understand why the president's wife didn't call on them, but when Mrs. Hay, her daughter and designated surrogate, avoided them, too, they found it unforgivable, and they did what any self-respecting, self-important woman would do: They boycotted the White House, and Mrs. Monroe's drawing rooms became a "beggarly row of empty chairs." One of them, it was said, was attended by only five women, "three of whom were foreigners." Many senators decided that because the vice president didn't have a wife to send into the breech, Louisa Adams, as the wife of the secretary of state, ought to be taking up the slack, and when she didn't, the Adamses became pariahs as well.

Finally, the president had enough and, as if they didn't have any more important things to do, he called a meeting of his cabinet to discuss the "uneasiness, heart-burnings, and severe criticisms" that he felt were beginning to gnaw at the dignity of the presidency itself. Vice President Daniel Tompkins led the debate, telling his colleagues that members of the Senate "[are] peculiarly tenacious of their claim to a first visit, and the principle on which they rest their claim is that the Senate being, by their concurrence to appointments, a component part of the Supreme Executive, and therefore the Senators ought to be first visited by heads of Departments." Not all of the cabinet members agreed with him, and the diplomatic James Monroe suggested that he himself was "inclined to think it would be well for the heads of departments to indulge the humor of the Senators, and then, to avoid an invidious discrimination between the two Houses to do the same thing by the members of the House, and at the commencement of every session of Congress." In other words, he didn't think the vice president's idea was a very good one. He called on John Quincy Adams to come up with a better plan.

Above: The turban that Dolley Madison popularized became the style known as "Costume Parisian" and it was all the rage in Washington well into the Monroe presidency.

Below: The Capitol building hadn't been completely rebuilt when James and Elizabeth went there for his inauguration on March 4, 1817.

Below: Elizabeth bought furniture for the White House designed by the French cabinetmaker Pierre-Antoine Bellange, in spite of a mandate to "buy American." This armchair upholstered in blue and gold satin with woven eagles is still in the White House.

Adams took it personally. It was his opinion that the whole controversy was based more on social climbing by a few parvenus rather than a desire to reinstate an established tradition. He concluded his report by saying, "Those Senators who have set up the pretension are ashamed of avowing it, and yet are too proud to renounce it."

In the end, it was made official that neither the president nor the First Lady was under any obligation to make or return any visits. That had been the informal policy of all of the previous presidents, but now it was backed up by a specific presidential order, and what had been called a "senseless war" within Washington society came to a merciful end. But Elizabeth Monroe's reputation as an antisocial woman went right on keeping tongues wagging.

The president's woes over protocol didn't end there, either. It had become customary to invite the secretary of state to White House dinners that were attended by members of the diplomatic corps. James's other cabinet appointees resented that they weren't included on those guest lists, and they took advantage of the firestorm over protocol to put pressure on him to make a change in the custom to include the other secretaries and their wives as well. But the foreign ministers completely rejected the idea. Except for ambassadors, and there were relatively few of those, ordinary ministers were outranked by the secretary of state, and that was understood. But they resented the idea of having to play second fiddle to their inferiors among the other cabinet secretaries, and they threatened to start ignoring White House invitations. President Madison solved that problem with a masterstroke of diplomatic compromise by simply rotating cabinet members one at a time from one dinner party to another.

Of course, although she was always invited, the First Lady rarely put in an appearance at these affairs, and that meant invitations didn't always extend to the wives of the president's guests, which resulted in some pretty dull parties. Because political discussions were off-limits, the men who gathered in the Oval Room more often than not seemed to be at a loss for conversation; most of them didn't have much else on their minds.

The president was very proud of his own new home, which was now informally being called the White House because the charred stones that remained after the fire had been painted white, making it stand out in a city of red-brick mansions. During the time they lived in Europe, Elizabeth and James had bought a large number of outstanding pieces of French furniture. And when they moved into the White House, they augmented their collection with more items they ordered from Paris. Those purchases were made at government expense largely because the new president, who despised debt, already owed creditors more than $35,000 and, in spite of the pressures of inflation, his salary was still the same $25,000 that his predecessors had struggled with. He justified every purchase in a special report to Congress, pointing out that he and Elizabeth had carefully selected each piece of furniture with an eye to its appropriateness as an adornment for the home of presidents yet to come, and in fact, many of the things they bought are still in the house. The inventory included Empire gilt chairs upholstered in crimson satin and Americanized with carved eagles, ornate mantelpieces in the French style but reworked with American iconography, and ormolu clocks that, in the interest of American sensibilities, had been stripped of their traditional nude figures. James also requested the creation of an office of superintendent of buildings, which

Eagles, a symbol of the French Empire, were out of fashion in post-Napoleonic France, so Elizabeth had them especially carved for the presidential furnishings that she imported from there.

would keep the house in repair and keep track of the furnishings that would be handed down from president to president. Congress grudgingly paid the bills, but the lawmakers wouldn't buy into creating a new bureaucracy to keep track of what they were paying for, and the selection reflected the taste of the First Lady alone. The furnishings she chose were a testament to her cultured sensibilities, but at the same time, their bow to American expectations didn't go unnoticed.

Still, the overall effect was worthy of a French château, and the accent of White House entertainments was decidedly French as well. Servants were carefully instructed on how to attend guests in the highly formal manner of the old French aristocracy, which the Monroes had observed firsthand and admired. During their years in Washington, the Monroes brought back a kind of European formality that was reminiscent, at least to those old enough to remember, of George Washington's presidency.

La Belle Americaine

George Washington was still three years away from taking his first oath of office as president when James Monroe and Elizabeth Kortright were married in New York. They had been together for thirty-one years by the time he took his own oath of office.

Elizabeth's mother, the former Hannah Aspenwall, died when the girl was nine years old, and she was raised by her grandmother Hester Kortright, an accomplished woman who ran a successful business of her own in New York. Her son, Elizabeth's father, Lawrence, had been a wealthy merchant in the West Indian trade before his business collapsed during the British occupation of the city during the Revolutionary War. Earlier, in the French and Indian War, he was a privateer in the service of the British government, and he held the rank of captain in the British army right through

Above: Among the objects that Elizabeth imported from France for the White House is this bronze "Hannibal" clock. It still keeps perfect time after all these years.

When First Lady Jacqueline Kennedy restored the White House, she said that the furnishings Elizabeth Monroe had selected were the best pieces she had available to her.

Below: Elizabeth Kortright and James Monroe were married at Trinity Church in Manhattan on February 16, 1786. The building, the second one built on the site at Broadway and Wall Street, was still under construction at the time. It was replaced by this present church in 1839.

the occupation. He was still a highly regarded member of New York society after the war was over, though, and his daughter was its most accomplished debutante.

Elizabeth was seventeen years old when she married the twenty-eight-year-old James at Manhattan's Trinity Church. A strikingly beautiful young woman, she had raven-black hair and violet eyes, and although she was only five feet tall and slender, she was said to have had a "fine figure."

James, the heir to one of one of the lesser plantations in the Virginia tidewater, had joined the militia at age eighteen. As a lieutenant in the Third Virginia Infantry, he fought in the Battle of Harlem Heights, a small victory for the Continentals, but their first of the war. When General Washington crossed the Delaware River for his surprise attack on Trenton on Christmas night in '76, James was among the small party of officers and men who crossed the river a few hours ahead of him. He was promoted to captain for his gallantry in the battle that followed, but he was severely wounded, and his fighting days seemed to be over. After a long recovery, he became an aide-de-camp, with the rank of major, to Lord Stirling, one of General Washington's most important brigade commanders. It was an opportunity for James to learn military tactics, but also to turn his life in a new direction. Among his new associates were Aaron Burr and Alexander Hamilton, as well as the Marquis de Lafayette, all of whom became his lifelong friends. But perhaps most important among his new acquaintances was another young French officer, Pierre Du Ponceau, who introduced James to the philosophies of the Enlightenment, which they discussed endlessly during the long winter encampment at Valley Forge.

It was this philosophical epiphany that brought James and Thomas Jefferson together as like-minded close friends. James had no idea what to do with himself when his wartime service had come to an end, and Jefferson, who was governor of Virginia at the time, encouraged him to reenter the College of William and Mary to study law, and he gave his new protégé access to his own library. When the state government was moved from Williamsburg to Richmond, James went along to be close to the governor, who had become a father figure to him.

Jefferson's influence could lead to only one conclusion: James Monroe decided to become involved in politics. He was elected to the Virginia House of Delegates in 1782, and the following year, the legislature tapped him to represent the state in Congress. Four years after that, Congress was meeting in New York and the former soldier's life came full circle. Young James Monroe had a date with destiny in New York. Her name was Elizabeth Kortright.

The teenage Elizabeth was regarded as not only the most beautiful but also one of the most accomplished belles of New York society. But she was more than just another pretty face. James's uncle, Judge Joseph Jones, who had taken his father's place when James inherited the family estate at the age of sixteen, advised him to look for a wife with "sensibility and kindness of heart—good nature without levity—a modest share of good sense with some portion of domestic experience and economy [which] will generally if united in the female character produce that happiness and benefit which results from the married state." Elizabeth filled the bill absolutely perfectly.

Her friends weren't so sure that this paragon wasn't too good for the "not particularly attractive Virginia congressman," and it was said that some of her closest friends "twitted her with the amiable reflection that she could have done better." As their life together turned out, it's hard to imagine how she possibly could have. James and Elizabeth were very happily married for forty-four years, and they were rarely separated from each other for more than a few days during all that time.

As newlyweds they lived with Elizabeth's father in New York until the congressional session ended, but James had no intention of either becoming a New Yorker or remaining a congressman, and he arranged to rent a simple house for them in Fredericksburg, Virginia. He had decided to establish a law practice there, not only because it was where his uncle, Judge Jones, lived, but also because the competition for new clients was less a problem there than it would have been in Williamsburg or Richmond. Although neither of those cities, nor certainly Fredericksburg, would seem cosmopolitan enough to satisfy a woman like Elizabeth, who had been recently plucked from the top tier of New York society, she adapted quite quickly.

Above: James established his first law office in this building in Fredericksburg, Virginia.

"Domestic cares" came into her life when the couple's first child, Eliza, was born near the end of their first year of married life. James wrote that "Mrs. Monroe hath added a daughter to our society, who tho' noisy, contributes greatly to its amusement."

It was James, and not Elizabeth, who grew tired of Fredericksburg, and in 1788, not long after their second wedding anniversary, he traded a piece of land he owned in Kentucky for eight hundred acres and a house in Charlottesville, which years later would be part of the campus of the University of Virginia. He had been dreaming for years about settling in Albemarle County, not only because he loved the countryside, but because it would put him within hailing distance of Jefferson's Monticello. He and Elizabeth and the baby moved there a few months after buying the property. James also had dreams of becoming a gentleman farmer, but the land he had acquired was disappointingly barren, and he redoubled his efforts to build up his law practice. At the same time, at Jefferson's urging, he jumped back into the world of politics, and when he went to Philadelphia as a senator in 1790, it gave Elizabeth her first chance to visit her family and friends in New York since her wedding four years earlier.

When they went home to Virginia after his second term, Elizabeth told her husband that nothing could have made her happier, for she had become tired of city life. The truth was that he was weary of it, too, but he had become as enamored with politics as she had with her quiet life as a plantation mistress, and they both knew that they'd be traveling again before long.

Neither James nor Elizabeth ever seemed to be interested in moving to New York, but their Virginia neighbors, his legal clients, and his political colleagues all accepted it as an article of faith that it would be only a matter of time before they left. The speculation became intense when James, who had become a leader of the Democratic-Republican wing in the Senate, refused to accept any committee assignments so that he could be free to go to New York with Elizabeth, whose visits were becoming more frequent. The rumors came to an end when her father died, and after several weeks of sorting out his depleted estate, the Monroes left New York and they didn't look back.

Their next destination, as it happened, was Paris. James wasn't his first choice, but President Washington appointed him minister to France in spite of his earlier misgivings about their widening political differences. James himself wasn't so sure it was a good career move for him, but he recognized the mission's importance, and he and Elizabeth, with young Eliza in tow, were on their way less than a week after he got his orders. He didn't even take the time to go home to organize his affairs, relying on his friends James Madison and Thomas Jefferson to keep an eye on things while the Monroes were gone.

Below: Gilbert Stuart had established a kind of tradition of painting presidential portraits by the time he made this one of James Monroe.

Despite their warm reception, the Monroes found Paris a cold place, both figuratively and literally. The scars of the revolution were everywhere, the streets were a filthy mess, and most of the shops were shuttered; and although the Reign of Terror had ended, most Parisians were still living in a state of anxiety, suspicion, and fear. The winter of 1795 was the coldest in anyone's memory, and firewood was both hard to find and unconscionably overpriced. Food was in short supply, too, and rationing put tight limits on the Monroe household, which included the family, James's staff, and the inevitable servants, all of whom had to be fed.

The Monroes' social life was almost nonexistent, at least at first, because the French government had put a stop to all diplomatic entertaining. The situation improved eventually, and before long, Elizabeth was entertaining not only influential French officials but also many Americans who had gone to Paris to show their support for the revolution. Among these was Thomas Paine, the pamphleteer whose fiery writing had encouraged his fellow Americans to stage their own revolution. When he first arrived in France, he was made an honorary French citizen, but he had been imprisoned there for more than nine months by the time the Monroes arrived. James secured his release, but as an example of the theory that no good deed goes unpunished, he was obliged to make Paine a guest in his house. The author of *Common Sense* stayed there for a year and a half, all the while issuing insensitive polemics against the United States in general and President Washington in particular for not getting him out of prison sooner. Although James curbed his venom, his guest's attacks had a negative effect on James's reputation among the Federalists back home. As far as President Washington was concerned, a recall of James was all but inevitable.

James not only managed to save Paine from the French prison system, but he was also soon able to force the release of all the other Americans who had been jailed. Yet he couldn't do anything to end the suffering of the hundreds of imprisoned French citizens, and there was one in particular whom he desperately wanted to help. Madame Adrienne de Lafayette, the wife of James's close friend the Marquis, was a prisoner in the Bastille and she had been sentenced to be guillotined as her grandmother, her mother, and her sister had been. James used his influence to delay her execution, but there was no way he could arrange her freedom. That, he hoped, might be accomplished with a visit from Elizabeth. When word spread through Paris that the wife of the American minister had called on Madame de Lafayette, public sympathies shifted. James was able to convince the authorities to let her free.

Madame de Lafayette left Paris right away to voluntarily join her husband in an Austrian prison until they were both exiled a short time later. Elizabeth, in the meantime, had become the toast of Paris, where she became affectionately known as *la belle americaine*.

Whenever she appeared at the theater, which was frequently, the audience rose to its feet while the band offered a sprightly rendition of "Yankee Doodle." She was also routinely cheered whenever she appeared on the streets in her carriage.

The honeymoon came to an end not long afterward, when the French Directory reconsidered its love for the Americans, principally because of John Jay's treaty with Great Britain, which its members regarded as an affront to France. Back in Philadelphia, where the treaty wasn't universally hailed, a new Federalist secretary of state questioned the usefulness of a member of the opposition party as his man in Paris, and he began leaking papers that put James's tenure in a bad light. The Monroes left France under a cloud at the end of 1797. James was disappointed at the way he had been treated, but even more dismayed to be leaving. Both he and Elizabeth had become confirmed Francophiles.

Their spirits brightened when they went home to Virginia's Albemarle County to the estate James had begun calling "Highland," and which would later be known as Ash Lawn, where he could expand the house and try to coax a profitable crop from its fields. He also worked to clear his reputation, which had become stained by Federalist calumny over his tenure in France, and he worked with his neighbors Thomas Jefferson and James Madison to refine the

Above: Thomas Paine became famous as a pamphleteer with his Common Sense, *which called for a break with England in 1776.*

Above: During the time she was in Paris, Elizabeth was instrumental in saving Madame de Lafayette from execution and reunited her with her stepdaughters and husband, the Marquis de Lafayette, a hero of the American war.

The Lafayettes

Of all the receptions Elizabeth Monroe staged, the most memorable was when the Marquis de Lafayette came to America at the president's invitation. The French general had been one of James's close friends during the Revolutionary War, and Elizabeth was credited with saving his wife from the guillotine, so the event was a highly personal one for both hosts and guest.

The hero, whose full name was Marie-Joseph-Paul-Yves-Roche-Gilbert du Motier de Lafayette, had joined the French army by the time he married Adrienne de Noailles, the daughter of the Duc d'Ayen, in 1773. He left her behind four years later to go to America to help in the fight against Great Britain, France's traditional enemy. The American Congress immediately gave him the honorary commission of major general, and assigned him as an aide to General Washington. He was eventually given command of a division of American troops, but was soon sent back to France to gain more support there for the American cause. He returned in 1781 with a French force that was pivotal in the battle at Yorktown, Virginia, that effectively ended the war. He received a hero's welcome in Paris when he went home again, and he was made a brigadier general in the French army. Lafayette was influential during the first months of the French Revolution as commander of the Parisian National Guard, organized to protect the new government. He fell out of favor with that regime, however, and he was forced to resign. He reemerged when war broke out between France and Austria and Prussia, but he became a prisoner of war. He was released through the influence of the victorious Napoleon and allowed to retire quietly. President Monroe invited Lafayette to visit America in 1824, and he was hailed as a great hero everywhere he went during his fifteen-month tour of the country. He was presented with a gift of $200,000 and an estate in northern Florida.

principles of the Democratic-Republican party. Both missions accomplished, the legislature elected James governor of Virginia. The office carried little power, but plenty of prestige, and James made the most of it, finally removing any lingering doubts about his ability and his patriotism. Elizabeth captivated her new neighbors by bringing new life into the drab governor's house, ironically called "the palace." It was in such a state of disrepair that she refused to move into it until she had a chance to spruce it up. But by the time she was finished, it was indeed a palace, and she became the most popular hostess in Richmond.

Thomas Jefferson's election to the presidency opened the door for his fellow Democratic-Republican and protégé, James Monroe, to get involved on the national scene again. But when his third term as governor ended, James decided to stay in Richmond to practice law. He needed the money more than he needed a political career. But before he could settle down, a note from the president informed him that he had been tapped to become special envoy to France, where he would work with the American minister, Robert Livingston, to negotiate the use of the port of New Orleans at the mouth of the Mississippi River, which the Spanish had recently ceded to the French. Even before James received the news that he was being considered for it, the Senate had already confirmed his appointment.

James, Elizabeth, Eliza, and the newest member of the family, a new baby named Maria, arrived back in Paris in the springtime of 1803, and his mission was accomplished by the end of April. Napoleon offered the Americans all of Louisiana rather than just the port city, and Livingston and James, acting without consulting either the secretary of state or the president, agreed to his price of $11,250,000, plus another $3,750,000 to cover existing claims against the French government. Naturally, the news was received enthusiastically back home, although no one, least of all James and Livingston, had any clue just how big this territory was. That would sink in later, but for now, it was enough that they had secured Mississippi River access for Americans settled on the frontier.

Above: During his White House years, James added more rooms to his country house, anticipating the comforts of retirement.

The Monroes stayed in Paris for four months while details of the purchase were being worked out, and they took advantage of the opportunity to renew old friendships there, especially with the Lafayettes, who had finally been allowed to come out of exile. At the end of their sojourn, James and his wife, *la belle americaine*, were honored guests at the ceremony that made Napoleon an emperor.

James had also been ordered to go to London and to Spain with the status of minister to negotiate international backing for the Americanization of the Mississippi. He chose to go to England first.

Leaving Eliza behind in France—where she was back under the wing of Mme. Campan for a kind of booster shot for her already regal attitude—James, Elizabeth, and the baby Maria crossed the English Channel with no idea of how they were going to be received in London. The Monroes' love for the French was no secret, and James carried the extra burden of his heroism during the American Revolution against King George III, who was still on the throne; but his presentation to the king muted that liability right away. It wasn't exactly a love fest, but the regent's attitude toward America had softened a great deal over the twenty years since the war ended, and he seemed pleased to pledge his friendliness to the former colonies. War hero or not, the friendliness extended to James personally, although it probably didn't hurt at all that he had the lovely Elizabeth on his arm.

Below: Before their presidential years, Elizabeth and James went to Paris where he was empowered to buy the port of New Orleans. The emperor, Napoleon I, surprised everyone, by offering to include the whole Louisiana Territory in what became the biggest real estate deal in history.

In spite of their warm welcome at court, James and Elizabeth found a chill in the July air in the form of a general distrust of anything that smacked of Americanism. Elizabeth followed the protocol of calling on the ladies of the court, but none of her visits were ever returned. By the end of the winter, the snubbing, along with the nasty English weather, had them both longing for home. Elizabeth had been suffering from painful bouts of rheumatism, the baby was sick, and the Monroes were generally miserable.

When James left London for his mission to Madrid, he took Elizabeth and the baby with him as far as Saint-Germaine in France, where Eliza had remained as a student. He picked them up again on his way back to London, and they spent several weeks in Paris before finishing the trip. Another year would pass before they were able to go home again, and by the time they did, they were more than pleased to put Europe and its convoluted politics behind them after four years.

They found American politics almost as Byzantine. There was some enthusiasm for James to run for the presidency to succeed Jefferson, and his name was actually placed on the ballot against James Madison, his good friend and Jefferson's own choice. In the end, James Monroe withdrew, and he considered it the end of his political career. Before backing out, James suggested that Jefferson might save face by sending him back to England, even saying that he would leave his family behind which, considering his well-known love for Elizabeth, was a strong statement of his loyalty to the party, as well as to Jefferson. The appointment never came, and after another brief tenure as Virginia's governor, President Madison appointed him secretary of state.

James and Elizabeth moved to Washington, which was still a sleepy country town but had developed a lively social scene, thanks largely to Dolley Madison. Elizabeth was a welcome addition to the mix, although she arrived with the chilly reserve that would work against her later. Still deep in debt after his European experience, the new secretary of state didn't stage as many of the parties as may have been expected of him, and that surprised the British ambassador, who wrote that the Monroes lived a rather Spartan life and, "entertained very sparingly, which does not fail to be commented upon in a place where good dinners produce as much effect as in any part of the world." Butu, with the possible exception of George III, not many British officials ever had a good word for James Monroe.

From the other side came the gushing report of a Madison dinner party from the wife of the secretary of the navy, who wrote, "It was the most stylish dinner I have been at." She went on to report, "Mrs. Monroe is a very elegant woman. She was dressed in a very fine muslin worked in front and lined with pink, and a black velvet turban close and spangled. Her daughter, Mrs. Hay, a red silk sprigged in colors, white lace sleeves and a dozen strings of coral round her neck."

It was Elizabeth's introduction to the ladies who mattered in the capital city. She made it a point to put in an appearance at nearly every official function at the presidential mansion and at every public celebration in the city, at a time when James and Dolley Madison were hosting a breathless round of them. Little did anyone know that it would all cool down when Elizabeth Monroe became First Lady herself.

Below: Elizabeth was as lovely at the end of her eight years as First Lady as she had been at the start, but her failing health took its toll.

> "Mrs. Monroe paints very much, and has besides an appearance of youth which would induce a stranger to suppose her age to be thirty [she was forty-five]: in lieu of which she introduces them to her daughter, Mrs. Hay of Richmond."
>
> —A guest at the Monroe mansion on Elizabeth

The End of an Era

When James Monroe retired from the presidency, he was the last of what are regarded as the nation's founding fathers, even though he was only eighteen years old when the Declaration of Independence was written. He was to be succeeded by John Quincy Adams, the son of one of those men, who wrote, "Thus strengthening and consolidating the federative edifice of his country's Union, till he was entitled to say, like Augustus Caesar, that he had found her built of brick and left her constructed of marble."

A lot had changed during James's eight years in the White House, but the most striking transition was a social one. Elizabeth Monroe had found the structure covered with veneer, and she left it with a fine natural dignity that hasn't worn off right through the present day. Well before her husband's second term began, she had already overcome her earlier unpopularity, and replaced it with genuine admiration. She had captivated everyone at her husband's second Inaugural Ball, which became the turning point for her acceptance among the local elite. It was also observed that she was more than her husband's official hostess, but his sounding board and advisor as well. John Quincy Adams called her the president's "partner," and James himself agreed. She was "the partner of all the toils and cares," he wrote, "exposed in public trusts abroad and at home … devoted to the honor and interests of the country … her burdens and cares must have been great." He went on to say, "It was improbable for any female to have fulfilled all the duties … with more attention."

It was well known that Elizabeth's life experience served her husband well as he was grappling with the creation of the Monroe Doctrine, which ordered the Europeans to stop colonizing the Americas, a daring and difficult process. She also knew from her experience as a diplomat's wife when and how to advise the former diplomat himself of the pitfalls of his dealings with other countries, and her advice seems to have been given freely and frequently.

Elizabeth was much more forthcoming as a hostess during the second four years of her husband's presidency, but it was always on her own terms. The last important affair at the Monroe White House was the 1825 New Year's reception, although it would be more than three months before they would take their leave. One of the guests wrote: "We passed on and were presented to Mrs. Monroe and her two daughters, Mrs. Judge Hay and Mrs. Gouverneur, who stood by their mother and assisted her in receiving. Mrs. Monroe's manner is very gracious, and she is a regal-looking lady. Her dress was superb, black velvet; neck and arms bare and beautifully formed; her hair in puffs and dressed high on the head and ornamented with white ostrich plumes; around her neck an elegant pearl necklace. Though no longer young, she is still a very handsome woman. … Mrs. Judge Hay's dress was crimson velvet, gold cord and tassel round the waist, white plumes in the hair, handsome jewelry, bare neck and arms. The other daughter, Mrs. Gouverneur, is also very handsome—dress, rich white satin, trimmed with a great deal of blonde lace, embroidered with silver thread, bare neck and arms, pearl jewelry and white plumes in the hair."

It was Elizabeth's last act as a Washington hostess, but the biggest reception of the year that preceded it had taken place a few weeks earlier, when the Marquis de Lafayette was a guest at the White House. He had come back to America at the invitation of Congress, which presented him with $200,000 and an estate in the recently acquired territory of Florida. Of course, the president enthusiastically approved the gifts, despite the fact that former president Thomas Jefferson was bankrupt and that he himself was facing a retirement in poverty—even though Congress had been dragging its feet on a bill to repay him $30,000 that was still owed to him, after all these years, for his European service. But he begrudged Lafayette nothing, and emotionally served as the host at a reception honoring the other hero of the revolution, which was also, as far as the two hundred guests were concerned, a tribute to his own his recent service as president.

As the Monroes were about to leave the White House, Elizabeth became too ill to travel, and their tenure at the mansion was extended. When they arrived at Oak Hill, the house he had built for his retirement in Loudon County, Virginia, James and Elizabeth settled down to enjoy a quiet life surrounded by family and friends. James had always been against the idea of granting political jobs to relatives, but he made an exception in the case of his sons-in-law. George Hay, who was a brilliant lawyer and a Virginia judge, was given a more prestigious federal judgeship, mostly because of his qualifications, but also out of respect for James. His other son-in-law, Samuel Gouverneur, had fallen on hard times, but he got a new lease on life when he was appointed postmaster of New York, a high-paying job that came directly through his father-in-law's intervention. Other than that, James generally avoided politics and the law and concentrated on his real first love, running a farm, raising sheep, and enjoying life with his beloved Elizabeth. He also put a great deal of time and effort into seeing the University of Virginia through its growing pains.

The Monroes' domestic bliss was marred by Elizabeth's declining health, but the Hays family moved in with them, and Eliza took charge of the running of the household. Her father said that she "walked, and worked, and bustled off

Below: George Hay, Eliza's husband, was a highly successful attorney and he became a valued advisor in the Monroe White House.

The Monroe Daughters

When Eliza Monroe's husband, George Hay, was made a federal judge, it only heightened the already high opinion of herself that had rubbed many White House guests the wrong way when she filled in for her mother as hostess. After the deaths of her husband and her mother and father, Eliza moved to Paris, converted to Catholicism, and disappeared behind the walls of a convent. Her sister, Maria, was only fourteen when their father became president, and she finished her education in Philadelphia before joining the family at the White House, where her marriage to Samuel Gouverneur took place. Like many others, Samuel couldn't get along with his sister-in-law, Eliza, and the couple quickly moved to New York. After his wife, Elizabeth, died, the former president moved to New York to live with the Gouverneurs, and was part of their household when he himself died.

some thirty or forty pounds of flesh." Eliza's daughter, Hortensia, lived there, too, until she was married four years later. Elizabeth doted on her grandchildren, but Maria's three children were too young to come visit her, so she did the next best thing and went off to visit them herself. She and her husband made a similar extended visit together three years later.

When Elizabeth died in 1830, the former president was so grief-stricken that he couldn't bring himself to make funeral arrangements for several days. After Elizabeth died, life became a burden for James. He wrote to a friend who had also recently lost his wife: "We have both suffered the most afflicting calamity that can befall us in this life, and which, if time may alleviate it, it cannot efface. After you have lived with your partner in so many vicissitudes of life, so long together, and afforded to each other comforts which no other person on earth could do, as both of us have done, to have her snatched from us, is an affliction which none but those who feel it, can justly estimate."

> "I shall never forget the touching grief manifested by the old man on the morning after Mrs. Monroe's death, when he sent for me to go to his room and with trembling frame and streaming eyes spoke of the long years they had spent happily together."
>
> —A close friend on James Monroe after Elizabeth's death

Although they had lived at Oak Hill for only five years, James couldn't deal with the memories there, and he moved to New York to live with Maria and her husband. He died there on July 4, 1831.

Visiting Ash Lawn

Ash Lawn, which James Monroe called his "cabin castle," and is still known by its former name, Highland, is the only one of several properties he owned in Virginia that is open to the public today. It is owned by his alma mater, the College of William and Mary. James and Elizabeth lived there between 1793 and 1826, and it was their official residence after 1799. Although James sold some of its acreage to pay debts during his lifetime, Ash Lawn is still a 535-acre working farm and performing arts center. It has been faithfully restored to its original early-nineteenth-century glory, and the house contains much of the original Monroe furniture.

Ash Lawn is open daily, and an admission fee is charged to adults and children ages six and up. To get to Ash Lawn, take Route I-64, exit 121 from the east or 121A from the west, to Route 20 South. Turn left onto Route 53, then right on Route 795. Roadside signs will direct you to the site, which is at 1000 James Monroe Parkway, Charlottesville, Virginia 22902. The telephone number is 434-293-8000.

Above: Attilio Piccirilli, the sculptor of the James Monroe statue at Ash Lawn, specialized in translating sculptors' clay models into stone.

Louisa Adams

A Different World

The Constitution is quite clear that no person "except a natural born citizen" is eligible to be president of the United States, but there is no such restriction placed on a president's wife. Louisa Adams is the only one of a long line of First Ladies who were born abroad, and although her father was an American and citizenship her birthright, it became an issue that was used against her husband, John Quincy Adams, when he ran for the presidency. It was a whispering campaign, to be sure, because most people knew very well that Louisa was as much a citizen as they were. A large number of people didn't understand that children born to Americans abroad inherited their parents' rights, and in Louisa's case, even some of those who did know this weren't so sure that the rule applied to her because her mother was a British subject.

Louisa's father, Joshua Johnson, had been born into an aristocratic Maryland family and as a young man was sent by his partners in an Annapolis trading firm to London to manage their interests there. He managed very well. A charming man, he was able to defuse the hostility of his British competitors and, more important, to stay above the battle as the Colonies and the Mother Country drifted toward war. He also charmed sixteen-year-old Catherine Nuth, and they were married not long after he arrived in London. Their first daughter, Nancy, was born soon afterward, followed in 1775 by Louisa Catherine. The third of their seven daughters was given the cumbersome name of Carolina Virginia Marylanda to honor the votes of those states for independence.

In spite of the gesture, the Johnsons still felt welcome in the enemy camp after the vote for independence led to war, but by 1778, when Louisa was three, Joshua began to feel the heat and decided that the time had come to get out of town. He had planned to go home to Maryland, but rather than face the dangers of a sea voyage in wartime, he decided to go in the opposite direction and settled in the French port city of Nantes. It was a good business move; he was given lucrative trading commissions both by the American Congress and the Maryland legislature, and he mastered the intrigues and scheming of his more experienced rivals well enough to be able to beat them at their own game.

As far as Louisa and her sisters were concerned, she wrote later that, "we were to all intents and purposes, in manners, language, and dress French children." By the time they went back to England after their father was

---

Louisa Catherine Johnson Adams

Born
February 12, 1775,
London, England

Parents
Joshua Johnson and
Catherine Nuth Johnson

Marriage
July 26, 1797, to
John Quincy Adams
(1769-1848)

Children
George Washington
(1801-29); John II
(1803-34); Charles
Francis (1807-86); Louisa
Catherine (1811-12)

Died
May 15, 1852,
Washington, D.C.

Above: Louisa spent her early girlhood in the French city of Nantes, near the mouth of the Loire River in Brittany. As the country's oldest seaport, it was ideal for her father's shipping business during the Revolutionary War.

Below: This miniature of Louisa Catherine Johnson was painted near the time of her marriage to John Quincy Adams; she was twenty-one years old.

appointed U.S. consul, the girls had to learn English all over again after twelve years of living in France.

At fourteen, Louisa was painfully shy, overshadowed by her older sister, Nancy, who everyone agreed was turning into a great beauty and developing enviable social skills. But Louisa and her younger sister Carolina, both pretty teenagers themselves, were anything but wallflowers. Their mother, Catherine, wouldn't have stood for it.

Catherine Johnson was one of London's great beauties, and Louisa remembered her as "lively … her understanding highly cultivated, and her wit brilliant." She entertained lavishly and often as a way of helping her husband in his business, but by the time the family arrived back in London, she had three daughters approaching marriageable age—another reason for her to dazzle her guests, not to mention to lure younger men into her drawing room.

Because her goal was to showcase her eldest daughters, each of them was required to contribute to the evening's entertainment. Louisa's talent was for music, and she was called upon to sing a song or two whenever there were guests in the house. Her voice was so pleasing that her father frequently requested songs from her even when there was no one but the family on hand to listen.

Louisa and Nancy were both introduced into London society at the same time, and both were welcomed as among the best educated, most highly desirable young women of the season. Their home on Great Tower Hill had striking views of the Tower of London and the Thames River, but young men came to their door with an entirely different view in mind—that of the Johnson sisters. Louisa was five feet tall, with a fair complexion, hazel eyes with green flecks, and curly auburn hair. She had a slender figure, sloping shoulders and expressive hands. Nancy looked a great deal like her younger sister, except that she had a dimpled mouth and beautiful teeth, both of which Louisa envied. Louisa herself, a lifelong chocoholic, had to have several of her teeth pulled at an early age, and although they had been replaced with artificial dentures, it made her feel obliged to keep her lips pressed together, an affectation that gave her a kind of Mona Lisa smile that was generally regarded as mysterious and seductive.

Carolina had also turned sixteen by this time, and she was no less attractive than her older sisters. Yet their father began to discourage young gentleman callers on the advice of his brother back in Maryland, who recommended that he should have his daughters "form connections with none but men of note and distinction from [their] own country." Naturally, the girls thought that the advice was "silly," but their father's word was law, and Louisa said that, "although we lived in the midst of the city of London we were kept almost entirely out of English society and visited only one family on the street where we lived."

As the American consul, Joshua Johnson's home would have been a natural destination for visiting Americans even if he didn't have three lovely daughters, and the girls weren't starved for suitors. Nancy eventually married her cousin Walter Hellen, but Louisa played the field, although it proved to be a narrow one—not because of the number of possibilities, but because her father exercised the right of refusal over any young man who seemed to be thinking of marriage, and his standards were tough.

Louisa's hopes of avoiding spinsterhood took a small step upward in the winter of 1795 when young John Quincy Adams came to call. He easily filled the bill as a "man of note." He was serving as minister resident to the Netherlands, and he was the son of the vice president of the United States. But although Joshua Johnson dismissed him as a New England Yankee, a race of men he believed made poor husbands, the rest of the family worried that they had made a bad impression on him.

> "I am the daughter of an American Republican merchant."
>
> —Louisa Adams

After dinner, Nancy and Louisa gathered around the piano for a marathon of singing, but although John Quincy liked music, he wasn't too fond of female vocalizing. He put up with it for as long as he could, finally grabbing his coat and hat and leaving when the Johnson sisters started to sing a song he didn't like.

But the Johnsons hadn't seen the last of John Quincy Adams. He was back again the next night and almost every other night during his brief sojourn in London. He had never shown much interest in women up until then, and his parents had discouraged any liaisons that might get in the way of the career in public service that they had planned for him. But John and Abigail Adams were thousands of miles away, and John Quincy was nearly twenty-nine years old and on his own. It was time, he thought, to find a wife and produce an heir. Young Louisa Johnson seemed to be the perfect candidate. She was only eight years younger than he, and she was quite beautiful, intelligent, and socially well accomplished, not to mention apparently rich. But most important of all, as far as he was concerned, was that she was shorter than he was. He didn't want a wife whose height would make her look superior to him.

Below: John Quincy Adams later in his life.

There was room for improvement, of course, and young John Quincy made no bones about things he expected to have her change before they marched down the aisle. For her part, Louisa wasn't so sure that he was Mr. Right, either. She wasn't impressed by his status as an American minister, which she thought was a "very small personage," and she found his personality too frosty, forcing her to be "coaxed into an affection" on her own.

It was a gloomy courtship, with quiet walks in the park and carriage rides, and lots of little spats. Neither John Quincy nor Louisa had any experience with the opposite sex, and their conversations were strained, even though they were both well educated and well-read. John Quincy seemed to have two left feet on the dance floor, where Louisa was the picture of gracefulness; she was always elegantly dressed, but he had a fashion sense that was more appropriate for a field hand than a foreign minister. On that score, Louisa felt entitled to ask him to buy himself a stylish suit for a fancy party they had been invited to. He complied, but when she complimented him on how nice he looked, she said that "he immediately took fire" and coldly informed her that as his wife she must never interfere with his dress.

John Quincy kept his mother, Abigail, in the dark about his courting of Louisa. He knew that she would force an arranged American marriage if she could.

His tone was "high and lofty," she said, and she responded by breaking off their engagement and leaving his side for the rest of the evening. They patched things up the following day, but they both had a preview of what their life together was going to be like. He made a mental note that his intended had a "strong fixedness of opinion," and Louisa realized that he had a stinging temper. The incident may have seemed trivial, but for Louisa, it left her with a "secret and unknown dread of something hidden beneath the rosy wreath of love."

She probably should have quit while she was ahead, but Louisa went right on making wedding plans. Her fiancé, on the other hand, decided that he had wasted enough time in London, and he left again for The Hague, where his public duty awaited him. Leaving Louisa with a reading list that he hoped would improve her mind, he told her he'd come back when he could, but he didn't offer any clues about when that might be.

Back in Massachusetts, his mother, Abigail, was pleased that he had gone back to his duties and hadn't taken the drastic step of getting married. She didn't know much about Louisa Johnson, but she wasn't so sure that she approved of her son's choice.

Their personalities were completely different from each other, but John Quincy and Louisa found common ground in their love for reading.

"I would hope for the love I bear my country that the Siren is at least half-blooded," she wrote. Her husband, John, added a postscript noting, "You are now of an age to judge for yourself," but he couldn't help adding that "I wished in my heart that it might have been in America."

As any parent ought to know, such warnings only serve to strengthen young resolve, and John Quincy let them know by return mail that his mind was already made up. But Abigail still wasn't satisfied. She switched her tack to wondering whether the girl, raised in an English household, even an upper-class one, would turn out to be a proper companion for him in formal European courts. John Quincy didn't buy that as a problem, either, and he closed the debate by writing to his mother: "If upon the whole I have done wrong, I shall be the principal sufferer. ... Prudence is a sorry matchmaker."

John Quincy and Louisa were married on the same day his father was inaugurated as president.

In the meantime, Louisa's father rented a small house for her so she could study without distraction, to reduce, as she put it, "the immense distance which existed in point of mind and talents between myself and my future husband." It was an ordeal that she said made her "miserably dull, stupid and cross," but her diary is silent on her reaction when John Quincy demanded a written report on what she was accomplishing. Their courtship was entirely by mail, with long delays between each letter from Holland, and Louisa made up her mind that she wouldn't write to him except in response to his own letters. The prospective bridegroom didn't get back to London for fourteen months, and then he suddenly announced that he and Louisa would be married in two weeks' time because he had been appointed minister plenipotentiary to the court of Portugal and he needed to be on his way. While Louisa and her mother rushed to put the wedding together, John Quincy got a letter from his father, now the president, directing him to Berlin rather than to Lisbon. He considered rejecting the order, but duty was duty, and after an angry exchange of letters with his parents, young John Quincy agreed to go. But first, he had a wedding to attend.

John Quincy Adams and Louisa Catherine Johnson were married at All Hallows Barking on London's Tower Hill on July 26, 1797. His parents learned of the event by reading about it in the newspapers. Her parents waited until after the wedding to reveal that Joshua had been forced into bankruptcy after one of his partners embezzled the company's funds. Not only had John Quincy lost the handsome dowry he had been anticipating, but his father-in-law's creditors came to him for satisfaction after the Johnson family disappeared to America. Louisa was shamed; John Quincy was disgraced. She quickly realized that she had hopelessly lost "all of my husband's esteem."

Above: The time Louisa spent as a foreign minister's wife in Berlin was a stressful period in her life.

The newlyweds sailed for Berlin four months after the wedding, a trip she described as "dreadful." She suffered a painful miscarriage soon afterward—there would be six more in her married life—and she took to her room and stayed there for three months alone and homesick. Her husband ignored her, preferring to tend to his state duties, and rumors spread through the Prussian court that she was either deformed or embarrassingly ugly, or perhaps she didn't exist at all. As far as John Quincy was concerned, she didn't seem to.

Fortunately, she was befriended by Pauline Neale, a countess and a member of the royal court, who saw to it that Louisa appeared at concerts and the theater, where she could put a lie to the rumors about her, and then she arranged for the wife of the American minister to be presented to the king and queen. It was the start of a four-year tour on what Louisa described as "the giddy round of fashionable life." But "giddy" is a word that wasn't in John Quincy Adams's vocabulary, and her escort to balls, dinners, and parties wasn't her husband, but the legation secretary, his brother Thomas.

By the time Thomas went home after their first year in Berlin, Louisa said, "I became a Belle." With her friend Countess Neale to open doors for her, she didn't need to depend on her husband to be part of the glittering scene that was the Prussian court. For his part, John Quincy found it dissolute, indolent, and depraved, and he avoided socializing whenever he could. He also found life in Berlin boring, with no opportunities for a man like him with political ambitions. He used the time to negotiate a new treaty that helped his father maintain American neutrality, and he also kept the president informed on events elsewhere in Europe. In his spare time, he mastered the German language, but he relied on books and poetry to work his way through it. Louisa, on the other hand, learned it as it was spoken. She had a good ear and a great talent for languages.

When John Quincy and Louisa arrived at the gates of Berlin, a guard turned them away because he had never heard of the United States.

These first years of the Adams marriage were stressful to the extreme. Louisa, not unlike Abigail Adams at her age, was a determined champion of the rights of women, but her husband held the view that wives should be kept on a tight leash, and dominating this particular wife was almost too much for him to handle. They quarreled often about money. He blamed her for her father's financial difficulties and the loss of his anticipated dowry. He demanded frugality, and Louisa, stung by her sense of shame, willingly sewed all of her own ball dresses. They made do with a minimum of servants, entertained little, and furnished their apartments with secondhand furniture.

After Louisa's fourth miscarriage, they took a long vacation at a mineral spa, and after a few weeks of bathing and hiking and relaxing, both John and Louisa had a new lease on life. Best of all for a man who had married to produce an heir, Louisa gave birth to their first child the following year. It was a son, whom they named George Washington Adams, much to Abigail's distress. She had expected the baby's namesake to be the second president, not the first.

The English Bride

The baby was less than two months old, and Louisa still bedridden after a difficult delivery, when John Quincy was recalled from his Berlin post and they packed their bags to sail home. But the United States had never been Louisa's home, and she boarded the ship with mixed emotions. She was already well aware that she was facing mother-in-law problems, and she knew very well that the family referred to her as "the English bride," and expected that she'd be a fish out of water in American society. On the plus side, her own family was living in Washington, and she was eager to see them again after a four-year separation.

John Quincy had been away from his own family even longer, and after their ship landed, they each went their separate ways, he to Massachusetts and she and the baby to Washington. They were apart for two months. John Quincy produced excuse after excuse for not making the six-hundred-mile trip to escort Louisa and George to the Adams home, but he eventually ran out of reasons why he couldn't. He finally arrived in Washington near the end of October, at the beginning of the worst possible time for stagecoach travel. The trip, predictably, was disastrous.

But their welcome in Quincy was a warm one, with hordes of Adamses arriving to meet the English bride and the new grandson. Louisa found herself a stranger in a strange land, listening to the odd accents of the New Englanders and adapting herself to what passed for food among them. They couldn't do much about their speech or their peculiar way of dressing, but they did prepare special dishes for her, a gesture of kindness that had the effect of making her feel like the outsider that she obviously was. "Though I felt grateful," she wrote, "it appeared so strongly to stamp me with unfitness that I often would not eat my delicacy and thus gave offence."

Her mother-in-law, Abigail, was no help. Though cordial, she didn't make much effort to hide the fact that she thought her son had made a poor choice. "She has added a weight of years to his brow," she confided to a friend. The former president, though, had his own opinion. "The old gentleman took a fancy to me," Louisa said, adding, "he was the only one."

After a brief time in Boston, John Quincy had established a law practice, and the Federalists appointed him to fill a vacant seat in the United States Senate. In the meantime, Louisa was pregnant again, and gave birth—on the Fourth of July—to John Adams II. The choice of name pleased Abigail no end, but she still wasn't so sure that she was pleased with her daughter-in-law.

But the woman had produced two male heirs, and now John Quincy could get on with the business of politics, with time out for raising his sons as he thought the Adams heirs out to be brought up; he had little time left over to devote much attention to Louisa. He would serve in the Senate for six years, and Louisa would accompany him to the presidential mansion in response to frequent dinner invitations. She would also enjoy the hospitality of Dolley Madison, who entertained often as President Jefferson's official hostess.

The Washington climate left Louisa ill much of the time, and the city's frontier atmosphere bored her. When Congress adjourned for the summer, John Quincy went home to Massachusetts alone, leaving Louisa and the boys with her sister Nancy Hellens and her now widowed mother. Louisa didn't like

Above: Louisa dressed in the style of the London fashion scene, and when she arrived in America, it marked her as the foreigner the Adams family was expecting.

it, but she didn't have any other choice. Her husband made all the decisions, and that was that. He allowed her to go along with him when he went home the following summer, but when it ended, he decreed that the boys should stay behind and that they should go back to Washington without them. Louisa knew that it was futile for her to object, but she tried anyway. In a letter to her mother-in-law, she complained that she had been "compelled" to separate herself from her children, and had been treated as though her opinion didn't matter at all. Abigail had an opinion of her own. In a cold tone, she suggested that Louisa had better get with the program. The children were where they ought to be, she said, and not "at any boardinghouse in Washington."

The following spring, John Quincy went home alone again. Louisa was pregnant and in no condition to travel, but he didn't let a thing like that stand in his way. When the child was stillborn, John Quincy was hundreds of miles away.

By 1804, political differences made it apparent to him that his days as a senator were numbered, and John Quincy accepted a part-time professorship at Harvard and bought a house in Boston in anticipation of an early retirement. When he went back to Washington for yet another Senate term, Louisa, pregnant again, was left behind with her boys in the house that she found "gloomy beyond description."

John Quincy was back in Boston by the time the baby was born, and it seemed that this one, too, had been born dead. But Louisa thought otherwise. Resorting to a primitive version of mouth-to-mouth resuscitation, she got the baby breathing on his own, and then watched his every move for three days until he began nursing and showed signs that he was going to live after all. "He is born to be lucky," she wrote. The Adams family named the child Charles Francis, without bothering to ask Louisa if she had any suggestions.

When the time came for them to go back to Washington again, the family decided that George and John should stay behind again, but Louisa put her foot down and refused to surrender baby Charles to them. The scenario was repeated again the following year, but their stay in Washington was brief this time. The Federalists abruptly tossed John Quincy out of his Senate chair, and they went back to Massachusetts. Louisa was outspoken about the political turn of events that she found appalling, but she was just as happy that "we were a family again."

They had no sooner unpacked their bags when word came from President Madison that he wanted to make John Quincy minister plenipotentiary to Russia, and the former senator accepted without thinking of asking Louisa what she thought of the idea. She didn't like it. Moving abroad again was "a thing perfectly abhorrent to me and I hoped was done with forever." Her husband said that her objection was just an "affectation," and that there was to be no further discussion. He left it to his brother Thomas to tell her that her two older sons would be left behind. Only Louisa's sister Catherine and little Charles Francis would go along to Saint Petersburg.

"In this agony of agonies, can ambition repay such sacrifices? Never!!!"

—*Louisa Adams on moving to Saint Petersburg*

Land of Darkness

Of all the courts of Europe, only Napoleon's Paris was more splendid than Czar Alexander I's Saint Petersburg in 1809. Yet when the Adamses arrived there, Louisa was completely oblivious to the glitter. Another pregnancy had ended in a miscarriage; she desperately missed her two older sons; and her only companion, apart from her son Charles, was her sister Catherine. John Quincy, on the other hand, was at the pinnacle of his political career and he intended to make the most of it. Louisa was almost constantly ill, but he dismissed it as hypochondria and insisted that she be on his arm at every social event—in dresses that she made for herself.

The position he held turned out to be more important than he had anticipated. Russia had become one of America's most important trading partners, and the two countries needed each other in a world that Napoleon seemed determined to make completely his. The changing fortunes of the countries of Europe put the diplomatic corps in a constant state of flux, and the Adamses acquired the furniture of some of the departing ministers and the former home of one of them, although during their time in Saint Petersburg, rising rents kept them on the move themselves. They hadn't been there more than a few months when Louisa found herself the only wife of a foreign diplomat left in the city.

Protocol was absolutely essential in the court of the czar, and although John Quincy found the formalities "trifling and insignificant," he swallowed his pride and learned the required rituals. It all began when he was formally received by the czar, and he was surprised at how informal the meeting turned out to be. They met alone in the Russian ruler's private chamber and engaged in friendly conversation as though they were old friends meeting in a gentleman's club.

In this way, John Quincy and Louisa became accepted into the strange and confusing maze of Saint Petersburg society. In a place where the czar knew everything and worked at making sure that no one else knew anything, it was incumbent on them to attend every ball, every dinner party, and every reception where gossip would fill the gap between what they could glean from censored newspapers and what they could see with their own eyes. In this, Louisa became her husband's eyes and ears as well as his right hand. It was an exhausting experience. In a place where winter darkness made clocks redundant and turned familiar routines upside down, a typical day found them getting out of bed at 11:00 in the morning, dining at 5:00, stopping for tea at 10:00, and then partying until 4:00 the following morning. There were nearly always two or three parties to attend each night.

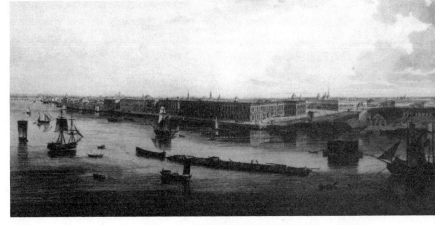

Above: The city of Saint Petersburg was the showplace of Europe when Louisa and John Quincy became part of the royal court in 1809.

Friend in High Places

Both John Quincy and Louisa were favorites of Czar Alexander I when they were in Saint Petersburg. Alexander's father, Paul, was the son of Catherine the Great, who took Alexander from his father to raise him herself as the heir to her throne. When she died in 1896, her own son became czar, but his reign lasted only five years, ending with his murder by disgruntled aristocrats. Alexander was crowned immediately, and he instituted a policy of reform in the direction of freedom for his subjects. But he slowly became an autocrat, finding it the easiest way to impose his will. He trusted no one, and no one was sure where he stood at any given moment. His greatest challenge came with the Napoleonic War, which was destroying the great cities of Europe, and was threatening Saint Petersburg itself at the time the Adamses were there. When the Allies were victorious, Alexander personally rode at the head of the triumphal procession into Paris, but his mind became troubled and he started neglecting his subjects because of an all-consuming personal obsession with the Orthodox Church. In 1825, he disappeared into the Siberian forest, and there were rumors that he had committed suicide. Others said that he had changed his name and become a monk.

Alexandre 1er
Empereur de toutes les Russies

Above: Czar Alexander I wasn't easy to get along with, but he liked Louisa and John Quincy, and they were given special access to his palace.

Below: What passed for entertainment among the people of Saint Petersburg was sliding down ice hills without sleds or skis. The city was a kind of theme park, and the theme was ice.

As always, the family was plagued with money problems, and Louisa and John Quincy argued endlessly about it. Back home, when Abigail found out about their situation, she contacted her friend President Madison and asked to have her son recalled. The president responded by offering John Quincy a seat on the Supreme Court, an honor he refused out of hand. Money aside, he was proud of the job he was doing, and besides, Louisa was pregnant again and she couldn't leave even if she wanted to.

Their relative poverty in the midst of showy opulence didn't seem to raise any eyebrows among John Quincy's fellow diplomats, and the czar himself seemed to understand. The two men frequently met during their morning walks, and on one of those occasions, Alexander told him how important he thought it was for one to balance one's "income and outgo"—a maxim that he himself never seemed to follow.

Louisa and Catherine also often met the czar when their paths crossed during daily walks. Alexander sometimes seemed to go out of his way to cross their path. He seemed especially entranced by Catherine, and on one occasion he delayed a state dinner for half an hour so he could go on dancing with her. It produced "a buzz of astonishment," Louisa noted, but that was only the beginning. Catherine had never been formally presented at court, but Alexander issued an order that she must be invited to every royal function. To avoid a scandal, which seemed inevitable, Louisa and Catherine stopped taking their daily walks. They discovered through the gossip mill that Alexander was offended, and fearful that they may have put John Quincy in hot water, they picked up the routine again, this time planning their route so a chance meeting with Alexander would be likely. When he did catch up with them, he lectured them on the health benefits of brisk walks and requested that they meet him every day. It was a simple request, but Louisa characterized it as "a real Imperial command." Sometimes they took little Charles along with them, which charmed the czar even more. Of all the members of the diplomatic corps, John Quincy Adams seemed to have become the ruler's favorite. He and his family were given special privileges that weren't extended to the others, such as access to a private entrance at the Hermitage. He owed it all to his wife—or more likely to his wife's sister.

During the summer of 1811, Louisa gave birth to a girl, whom they named Louisa Catherine. Both parents were delirious with joy, and closer to one another than they had ever been in the fourteen years since they were married. After ticking off their considerable differences, John Quincy wrote that Louisa was "a faithful and affectionate

When Louisa's only daughter was born, the czar banned traffic near their house so the baby could rest.

wife, and a careful, tender, indulgent, and watchful mother to our children." Louisa had never been happier at any time in her life. The ice had finally broken.

In 1812, when the winter ice had shut down Saint Petersburg until spring, Napoleon's armies were marching northward. By Easter week, hundreds of thousands of Russian troops had marched out to meet him, and the French ambassador urged the Adamses to leave the capital while there was still time. But Louisa couldn't; her baby was desperately ill. She and Catherine nursed her through the summer until the day Louisa sadly told her diary, "My child gone to Heaven." Louisa went into a deep mourning that lasted for well over a year.

Life went on in the court of the czar in spite of the war, and the Adamses were on hand for the round of balls and parties in spite of their personal loss. But the end was clearly coming. Napoleon's army had entered Moscow and burned it to the ground, and it seemed inevitable that Saint Petersburg would also be snuffed out.

At the same time that Russia was at war with France, the United States had declared war on Great Britain, and Alexander offered to help negotiate an end to it. It was finally agreed to hold peace talks under his auspices

"My heart is almost broken and my temper which was never good suffers in proportion to my grief. … My heart is buried in my Louisa's grave and my greatest longing is to be laid beside her."

—Louisa Adams on the death of her daughter

in the neutral city of Ghent in present-day Belgium. While preparations were being made, the czar's own army had dramatically turned Napoleon back.

Louisa and John Quincy were on hand for the great celebrations that followed, but then he left for the long journey to Ghent to help bring the other war to an end. Louisa was left behind to wind up their affairs, and to keep her husband's name and his country's interests at the forefront of the diplomatic community by attending social functions as though he were at her side. She had expected him to return to Russia after the peace treaty was signed, but instead he sent her a letter with instructions to meet him in Paris.

It goes without saying that she was shocked at the news. Women of her time never traveled alone, yet Louisa was being asked to pack herself and her eight-year-old son into a carriage and travel 1,800 miles over the frozen Russian steppe right behind the defeated French army. She feared the worst, and her worst fears were almost realized.

She sold all the family's furniture and obtained a document that served as a letter of introduction, a letter of credit, and a passport. She bought a carriage and outfitted it with a bed for her son, and provisions including chocolate, which she couldn't live without, and on February 12, 1815, her fortieth birthday, Louisa and Charles and a French maid were on their way, followed close behind by a smaller vehicle with two well-armed menservants on board.

For the first leg of their journey, they attached runners to the carriage, converting it into a sleigh. But by the time they reached Riga, the snowdrifts were so deep that the runners became useless and they frequently had to hire local people to dig them out. In the meantime, their provisions were frozen solid, and they themselves, with only fur blankets to protect them, were in real danger of freezing to death.

By the time they reached Poland, they were able to shed the sled runners and use the carriage wheels. The road ahead was passable, though sandy, which slowed their pace, and they began encountering more and more small bands of French soldiers making their way home in defeat. Sensing danger, Louisa hung Charles's toy sword in the carriage window, and her armed guards made it a point to keep their pistols drawn and in plain sight. Eventually a rumor flew up and down the road that she was Napoleon's sister hurrying to Paris, and she did all she could to look the part. They arrived safely in Paris on March 23, after six weeks on the road.

A few months later, the Adams family was on the road again. John Quincy had been named minister plenipotentiary to Great Britain, a post his father had held many years before, and they were off to London. Louisa rented a country house at Ealing, just outside the city, and they settled down for two of the most enjoyable years either of them had ever known.

There wasn't much for John Quincy to do but bask in the bosom of his family. He and Louisa played music together, took long walks through the English countryside, and enjoyed the London social life on their own terms. It gave Louisa a chance to indulge her passion for fishing, a pastime that had been impossible most of their time in the frozen north.

Above: When Louisa made her dash across Europe, she relied on her passport to prove her identity. But in many cases, local officials couldn't read it, and soldiers and innkeepers had never heard of the United States of America.

Below: Her husband wasn't fond of singing, but Louisa was quite good at it, often accompanying herself on the harp.

Though he was forty-nine years old, overweight, and fighting a battle with thinning hair, Louisa thought that her husband "never looked so well or so handsome as he does now." He had also become, in his way, a devoted husband. Their two older sons, George and John, had gone to England to join them, and along with young Charles, they were enrolled in a prestigious boys school close to their new home. They were a family again, and they savored every waking minute of it.

Their idyll came to an end when President Monroe made John Quincy his secretary of state. It meant taking a cut in pay, a painful thing for the Adamses, but the post had become a traditional stepping-stone to the presidency. It was an offer John Quincy Adams couldn't refuse.

A New Life

After several weeks visiting the family in Quincy, during which time Abigail buried the hatchet and ended her subtle feud with her daughter-in-law, John Quincy and Louisa left their sons behind to get on with their schooling and set out for Washington. The new secretary found the State Department almost hopelessly disorganized, and he worked nearly around the clock to restore order. Before long, he was reading every letter and scrutinizing every report, and he demanded that responses be sent immediately, and usually drafted them himself.

In this new age of political parties, men were beginning to line up to become James Monroe's successor only weeks after he took his first oath of office. Few of them, though, lusted after the job quite as much as John Quincy Adams did. Like his father before him, he loved politics but hated political campaigning, and Louisa realized that if his dream were ever to come true, it couldn't be done without her.

She had never liked the social obligations of the political world, and after all those years as a diplomat's wife, Louisa was hoping to be able to fade into the woodwork at this stage of her life. But while her obligations abroad had been in the interest of her country, here in Washington her efforts would be completely personal, making sure her husband's star was raised high enough that people who mattered couldn't help but notice.

It was a foregone conclusion that Monroe would be elected to a second term in 1820, but John Quincy and others had their eyes fixed on the 1824 election, and the jockeying for position went on in earnest for six years. No one was more active during that time than Louisa Adams.

It was a rare day that didn't find her out making calls on congressional wives or receiving them in her own home. Illness didn't stop her, bad weather never got in the way of her schedule, and distance and muddy roads were no obstacle. She and her husband never turned down an invitation to a dinner, a reception, or a ball, and although John Quincy found socializing difficult, Louisa saw to it that he was always smiling, and she made sure that he left his sarcastic tongue at home.

All of the contenders staged their own entertainments, but Louisa's drawing rooms, held once a week, were the brightest, recalling the days of Dolley Madison. During the months that Congress was in session, as many as one hundred well-dressed guests crowded into her home every Tuesday evening. Schooled in European hospitality, Louisa entertained them with her singing, accompanying herself on the harp or pianoforte, and she read poetry, often written by her husband. All the rival hostesses worked to snare visiting celebrities, but Louisa seemed to have a knack for finding famous authors and actors before anyone else knew they were in town, and announcing their presence at an Adams affair.

Louisa carefully planned every detail of every gathering, from selecting the musicians to creating the menu and hiring and dressing the servants. Her charm, her wit, and her beauty took care of the rest. It was quite an expensive proposition, but although John Quincy Adams was famous for his frugality, he didn't object. He knew very well that without the investment and his wife's talents he would never make it to the White House.

One of Abigail Adams's early objections to her son's marriage had been that the European-raised Louisa would never fit into the still rough-around-the-edges American culture. But it was her European manners and Old World sensibilities that made her such a hit among culture-starved Washingtonians, and few of her guests realized that she hadn't even seen America until she was twenty-six years old. One of them gushed that she was "the most accomplished American I have seen," and it was a natural reaction. Louisa had an unusual talent for languages, and its corollary was a gift for mimicry. By the time she began her election campaign, she had developed a very charming American Southern accent.

Below: Louisa's most successful ball was the one she held in honor of General Andrew Jackson, John Quincy's toughest political opponent.

Louisa's campaigning intensified during the 1823 season as the election grew closer, and at the beginning of the fateful year of 1824, she pulled out all the stops by organizing a ball for General Andrew Jackson, now a senator and John Quincy's chief rival for the presidential nomination. The occasion was the tenth anniversary of the Battle of New Orleans, which had turned Jackson into a national hero; but it was also an opportunity for the Adamses to show off their new house, whose ballroom, combined with the adjacent drawing room, was the largest of any private home in the capital. Louisa was proud of the fact that six sets of couples could dance cotillions at the same time "with ease."

It had been her intention to open four rooms for the event, but as more guests seemed imminent, Louisa decided to expand it to eight. Doors were removed to combine them. The four lower rooms served as a ballroom for dancing, and food and punch were served on the upper floor, although guests would be required to eat standing up because of the crush of people.

The house was filled to capacity and beyond when Louisa met the general at the door. She led him through the rooms introducing him to her guests, making certain that she was as much the center of attention as he was, and when dinner was announced, she led him upstairs where tables were set, as *Harper's* reported, "with natural and candied fruits, pies, sweetmeats, tongues, games, etc. … prepared in French style, and arranged with the most exquisite taste." Jackson and Louisa were nearly trampled in the rush for the food, but he managed to shout a toast to his hostess above the din and then he made a retreat. There were other celebrations planned in his honor that evening, and he was expected elsewhere. But nobody seemed to care much. The Adams house was the place to be. It was the most lavish party that had been seen in Washington since Dolley Madison left town, and it was easily the most successful.

The Goal

Under the prevailing system in 1824, voters in the individual states selected presidential electors, and when the counting was done, Andrew Jackson had won ninety-nine electoral votes to John Quincy Adams's eighty-four, and Treasury Secretary William H. Crawford had gathered forty-one. The required majority was 131, and so it was up to the House of Representatives to choose the president from among these top three candidates.

When the vote was finally taken early in February, after some adroit arm-twisting, John Quincy Adams became president of the United States, with the backing of thirteen states to Jackson's seven. His administration was uninspired. He made the mistake of leaving the Monroe cabinet in place in spite of their self-serving squabbling, and he was forced to deal with a hostile Congress that opposed him repeatedly.

Louisa had predicted that the White House would become her prison, and it turned out to be a self-fulfilling prophecy. She followed Elizabeth Monroe's precedent of not accepting invitations to outside events, and she limited her entertaining to one dinner party a week, a drawing room every two weeks, and the traditional New Year's Day open house. For the most part, they spent lonely evenings at home, with the president usually reading until he fell asleep with the book in his hands. They didn't turn uninvited guests away, but more often than not their visitors were turned off by the chilly White House atmosphere. One of John Quincy's guests wrote, "He himself is very dull and his neighbors at table when he gives formal dinners have a very hard time of it."

Her husband had no time for Louisa at all, and she felt that her role was only as an ornament and that she was obliged to stay out of sight in her "prison" until she was needed. But except for her obligatory appearance as a hostess for scheduled functions, that was almost never. She hated everything about the White House itself, regarding it as an impersonal barn of a place without even the comforts of "any private mechanic's family."

Like other women in similar circumstances, Louisa was plagued

> *"There is something in this great unsocial house which depresses my spirits beyond expression and makes it impossible for me to feel at home or to fancy that I have a home anywhere."*
>
> —Louisa Adams on living in the White House

by frequent illnesses during her four years as First Lady. She suffered from chest pains, nagging coughs, and other ailments that were diagnosed as "nerves," and she spent nearly all of her time confined to her room wallowing in self-pity. She wrote plays and poetry to pass the time, and she worked on an autobiography, all the while gorging herself on chocolate, as she had been doing since her girlhood, although by now it had become an addiction. Fortunately, the sweets never added a pound to her still slender figure, although she had none of her own teeth left.

> *"Do for once gratify me [and campaign for the presidency]—If harm comes of it, I will promise never to advise you again."*
>
> —*Louisa to John Quincy Adams*

John Quincy fell into bouts of depression as well. He was discouraged by the political infighting he had to deal with, and months before his term ended he wrote that "my career is closed." If that were so, he would be, like his father, a one-term president. Much as she dreaded four more years as First Lady, Louisa took it on herself to campaign for him again.

By the time the presidential campaign began in earnest, Andrew Jackson was John Quincy's opponent once again. It was quite probably the nastiest election campaign in American history, starting with a ruckus over a billiard table that the president had installed in the White House. His son John, in his capacity as the president's secretary, had put together a list of White House furnishings acquired through a congressional appropriation, and he mistakenly included the billiard table on it. When the opposition press got wind of it, they suggested that this was but one example of the president's playing fast and loose with public funds, and although John Quincy was able to prove that he had paid for the thing out of his own pocket, it didn't really matter. "Billiards," to most Americans, was just a polite name for pool, and images of the White House as a den of iniquity offended them. A friendly newspaper tried to pour oil on the troubled waters by pointing out that billiard tables were "a common appendage in the houses of the rich and great in Europe," but that only raised a new issue. The president was not only a spendthrift but also a closet aristocrat. And, furthermore, his wife was a foreigner—and the mudslinging went on and on.

The pro-Adams press latched onto the issue of Andrew Jackson's marriage, which they painted as adulterous. And besides, they said, the backwoods Tennessean not only played pool, but he played it for money. Worse, he gambled at the racetrack, at cockfights, and in poker games at low saloons. And for extra emphasis, the critics revealed that his wife was a pipe smoker.

John Quincy's political career seemed to come to an end in the fall, when only the New England states, New Jersey, Delaware, and Maryland (thanks, in part, to Louisa's efforts there) gave their votes to him. All the others were overwhelming in their support for Andrew Jackson. All that Louisa had to say was that "we are all in good spirits." She had been sprung from the birdcage that had held her fast for four years, and it is highly likely that "good spirits" was an understatement. As if to show that there were no hard feelings, Louisa's last

Below: Louisa's oldest son, George Washington Adams, died before he reached thirty; it was an apparent suicide, ending a disappointing life.

drawing room was attended by more people than had shown up for her Jackson ball. She was radiant and joyful that evening, and when the party ended at two in the morning, long after John Quincy's bedtime, she told a friend, "I can positively assure you that there was no wailing or gnashing of teeth."

The next great event in Washington was President Jackson's inauguration on March 4, 1829. The Adamses had moved out of the White House the day before into a rented farmhouse less than two miles away because Louisa refused to face another New England winter, even though spring was just around the corner.

Into the Breech Once More

John Quincy went home to Massachusetts for the summer, but Louisa stayed behind in Washington, mourning for her son George, who had just died, most likely a suicide, and wondering about what the future held. She attempted the trip north but turned around at New York, where bad memories came rushing back to haunt her.

Her son John had been married while they were still in the White House and presented them with their first grandchild, Mary Louisa Adams; her other son, Charles, was planning to get married in the fall.

Louisa arrived in Quincy shortly after the wedding took place, and once again, the Adamses were together as one big happy family. Then, in September 1830, eighteen months after John Quincy had signed off on his political ambitions, the local newspaper suggested that he should represent the district in the House of Representatives. The former president didn't say what he thought of the idea because he still believed it was improper for a man to seek any office until after the voters had weighed in.

What he did was allow his name to be placed before the voters, and they responded by electing him by a margin of almost five to one. He wrote in his diary, "I am a member-elect of the Twenty-second Congress. My election as president of the United States was not half so gratifying to my inmost soul. No election or appointment conferred upon me ever gave me so much pleasure." He was sixty-two years old, but he would win seven more elections, and would serve as a congressman a few days short of seventeen years.

Louisa realized how important this election was to him, and she knew that his salary would help them avoid the poverty that had ruined the retirement years of other former presidents. Besides, the climate was better in Washington than in Quincy. She arrived there less than a month after her husband's election.

John Quincy had arrived ahead of her, and when he took his seat in the House his intentions were a blank slate. Before very long, though, he was swept up in "the Slave and Abolition Whirligig." Southern slaveholders dominated Congress at the time, and John Quincy, though no abolitionist, believed that the issue of slavery was going to pull the Union apart one day, and

Above: Louisa's son John Adams II gave up on politics at the end of his father's presidency and managed a flour mill in his last years.

Below: Mary Louisa "Looly" Adams, Louisa's first grandchild, was baptized at the White House. The baby's father, John Adams II, was married to his cousin, and Looly, too, eventually married one of her cousins.

Bad Seed/Good Seed

Louisa had high hopes that her son John II would follow the family tradition in public service, but the political enemies he made as his father's secretary put up a roadblock he couldn't surmount. He went home to Quincy to manage the family's finances, but he wasn't up to the job, and he began drinking heavily, which led to an early death. His brother George was also a problem drinker and a poor money manager. He vanished from a steamboat on Long Island Sound on April 30, 1829, and his body, an apparent suicide, washed up on shore two weeks later. Louisa's third son, Charles Francis, on the other hand, became a member of the Massachusetts House of Representatives and later a state senator. He formed the Boston Whig party, but he ran, and lost, as Martin Van Buren's vice-presidential candidate on the Free Soil ticket in 1848. He was twice elected to the U.S. Congress, but resigned to become President Lincoln's minister to England, as both his father and grandfather had been. He served in London as a watchdog to curb British support for the Confederate cause. One of his sons, Charles Francis Adams II, saw service in the Civil War and was promoted to brigadier general for his heroism at the Battle of Antietam. He went on to become chairman of the Massachusetts Board of Railroad Commissioners, and wrote a book exposing the financial skullduggery of the Erie Railroad. He also served for twenty-four years on Harvard's Board of Overseers, and he went on to become chairman of the Board of the Union Pacific Railroad.

Above: Charles Francis Adams was twice elected to the U.S. Congress.

he felt driven to prevent it. Louisa was opposed to slavery, too, but in her case it was based on the idea that no human being should ever have to live under the yoke of a master. As far as she was concerned, that included women as well.

During her years as First Lady, Louisa hadn't put forward any special cause, but now she had one that she could get passionate about. Women's organizations began funneling their petitions through the Adams household, and Louisa was impressed that so many of them were calling for freedom not for slaves, but for themselves, an issue that went straight to her heart. She went to work sorting through them, cataloging and organizing them so that John Quincy could more easily frame his own arguments, when he was able to slip them past his noisy colleagues.

Louisa also became deeply religious, and her Bible reading strengthened her passion for the rights of women. Her religious awakening led her to a close involvement with Angelina and Sarah Grimké, the first female abolitionists, and Angelina's husband, Theodore Weld, would work closely with John Quincy. The sisters' books, pamphlets, and accounts of their speaking tours inspired Louisa, and their correspondence with her turned her into an activist. At Louisa's urging, John Quincy addressed meetings and rallies they staged, and he became not only a spokesman for the abolition-

After Louisa died, both houses of Congress took the unprecedented step of suspending all business on the day of her funeral.

ists but, uncharacteristically, a voice for the rights of women, a concept that had been completely alien to him before.

Without the help of the people Louisa had brought into his life, Congressman Adams might have been censured and expelled from his post, but when hearings were staged to make that happen, John Quincy held off his enemies for six solid days, reeling off facts fed to him by his new colleague Theodore Weld. In the end, John Quincy knew that without his wife's help, he never could have accomplished it. But of course, he didn't stop there. The problem of slavery hadn't gone away, and he kept right on battling in spite of Louisa's concern for the state of his health.

To many, John Quincy's greatest achievement had been the defense of Blacks who had revolted on the high seas aboard the ship *Amistad*. At the age of seventy-four, he argued their case for two days before the Supreme Court, which declared them innocent and, more important, free.

John Quincy's career came to an end on February 21, 1848, when he collapsed at his desk in the House chamber and then died two days later. Louisa suffered a stroke that April, and thereafter she lived in "quiet and contented infirmity," although she kept abreast of politics and received guests, including President Zachary Taylor and Vice President Millard Fillmore, who discussed slavery with her. She died in Washington on May 25, 1852.

Above: Angelina Grimké (left) and her sister, Sarah Grimké (right), were America's first antislavery activists. They had a powerful influence on Louisa and John Quincy, who enthusiastically took up the abolitionist cause late in life.

Visiting Peacefield

Louisa and John Quincy Adams had many homes during their life together. Their house at 1333-5 F Street in Washington, D.C., the same one that James and Dolley Madison occupied when he was secretary of state, remained in the Adams family until 1884. Their memory is kept alive at the Adams National Historic Site, administered by the National Park Service, at 135 Adams Street in Quincy, Massachusetts. It is located about ten miles south of Boston at the Furnace Brook Parkway exit (8) on Route 93. The site includes eleven historic structures around Peacefield, "the old house," and fourteen landscaped acres. It is open daily and the admission fee is $3.00.

Below: The Stone Library at Peacefield.

The Stone Library contains more that 14,000 historic volumes, including John Quincy Adams's personal library. The John and John Quincy Adams birthplaces at 133 and 141 Franklin Street are open, with guided tours, between mid-April and mid-October. There is no admission charge. In the same area, Mount Wollaston, the Quincy homestead at Hancock Street and Quincy Road, features period furnishings gathered by four generations of the family. It is open daily except Monday, April through October. Louisa and her husband, as well as John and Abigail Adams, are interred in the family crypt at the United First Parish Church on Hancock Street. Unlike other presidential homes, Peacefield was continuously occupied by the Adams family, and none of the original furnishings has had to be replaced. It represents a span of history from 1788 to 1927 with its parts intact.

Rachel Jackson

Backwoods Romance

After Andrew Jackson was elected to the presidency, his wife, Rachel, bluntly told him that he would be going to the White House alone. Paraphrasing the Bible, she said, "I had rather be a door-keeper in the house of God than live in that palace in Washington. ... For Mr. Jackson's sake, I'm glad; for my own part I never wished it." She changed her mind, however, after being convinced that dropping out of her husband's life at that point would only give credence to the vitriolic press attacks on her during the recent election campaign; and she bought a white dress to wear to his Inaugural Ball. But more than three months before her husband took his oath of office, Rachel died of an apparent heart attack. She was buried in her new dress on Christmas Eve, 1828, at their estate, the Hermitage, in Nashville. Her husband never recovered from his grief, and he blamed her death on the way the press had dragged his wife's name through the mud during the campaign. He called it part of a conspiracy against him. Although she never lived in the White House, Rachel Jackson's memory haunted the place for the next eight years.

Thanks to the innuendo of the hostile press coverage during the campaign, many people—even today—believe that Rachel Jackson had been a bigamist and an adulterer. But there are no official records that can back up such a conclusion or even prove it was a case of slander; and whether it was all just a misunderstanding or a tale of willful flouting of the marriage laws depends on which contemporary accounts one chooses to read.

The simple facts are that the young lawyer Andrew Jackson boarded in the home of the recently widowed Rachel Donelson when he first went to Nashville, and that he was attracted to her daughter, also named Rachel, a beautiful dark-eyed young woman his own age. Young Rachel had been married while she was still a teenager to Lewis Robards, who turned out to be tyrannical and jealous, and she had since moved out of his home in Kentucky and gone back to Nashville to live with her mother. By the time Andrew appeared on the scene, Lewis Robards had moved in, too, in an apparent attempt to save his marriage, and before long he accused Andrew of improper

---

Rachel Donelson Robards Jackson

Born
June 15, 1767,
Halifax County, Virginia

Parents
Colonel John Donelson
and Rachel Stockley
Donelson

Marriage
c.1785 to Lewis Robards;
1791 to Andrew Jackson
(1767–1845)

Children
None. Andrew Jackson
Donelson, the son of her
younger brother, adopted
1809; Lyncoya, a Creek
Indian boy, adopted
1813. She also raised
several other nieces
and nephews.

Died
December 22, 1828,
Nashville, Tennessee

"May God almighty forgive her murderers as I know she forgave them. I never can."
—*Andrew Jackson on his wife's early death*

As a young woman, Rachel Donelson was well known as the best dancer and the best horsewoman in the county.

behavior toward his estranged wife. Andrew denied it to the point of calling for "gentlemanly satisfaction," a duel, but he quickly moved out of Mrs. Donelson's boardinghouse instead as a more civilized way of defending the young woman's virtue. Rachel moved out, too, and she went to live with her sister Jane, who was married to the respectable Revolutionary War hero Robert Hays. For his part, Robards went home to Kentucky.

Before Robards left Nashville, he threatened Rachel that he would come back to haunt her and make her life miserable. She didn't intend to be there when he did, and left for an extended visit with her sister in Natchez, a Spanish colony at the time. She traveled with a migrating family, but because there were hostile Indians along the way, the party also included armed guards, one of whom was Andy Jackson. He said later that he fell in love with Rachel during that three-hundred-mile journey; yet, be that as it may, he turned right around and went back to Nashville so he could get on with his law practice. That was his version of the story, and if it is to be believed, it had been a completely innocent chivalrous excursion. But he made several more trips to Natchez alone over the next few months, and before long, after he was told that Robards had been granted a divorce, he hurried back there again, married Rachel, and took her home to Nashville.

They lived as man and wife in Nashville for two years before they found out that her former husband had only *filed* for divorce, on grounds of desertion, but that the Virginia legislature, which had jurisdiction in the case, had not yet acted on it. Technically, Rachel was married to two different men, and because of it, Robards changed his plea to add bigamy to the charges against Rachel, and he refiled his divorce petition. After the divorce became legal, Andy and Rachel were married a second time, by the bride's brother-in-law Robert Hays, who was a justice of the peace.

It all seemed to be perfectly aboveboard, and although their relationship became an issue in many of Andrew's quarrels over the years, little was said about it until the presidential election campaign of 1828. It was at that time that a Cincinnati newspaper began publishing its own versions of candidate Jackson's past and other opposition papers turned it into a steady drumbeat. Nothing could be proven beyond any doubt by either side, and there were plenty of gray areas to pick at. But whether Andrew and Rachel Jackson had been guilty of "gratifying their own appetites" outside the law, or if it was true that they had

Below: Major General Andrew Jackson, hero of the Battle of New Orleans in the War of 1812.

Rachel's mother was a well-off widow, but she took boarders into her home to protect her from marauding Indians.

Extended Family

Rachel and Andy had no children of their own, but they adopted two sons—a Native American boy whom Andrew had rescued during a skirmish, and Andrew Jackson Donelson, the son of Rachel's younger brother, who became known as Andrew Jackson, Jr. The Jacksons also raised, but didn't formally adopt, several more of Rachel's nephews and nieces, thirteen in all. One of them, Jack Hays, her sister's boy, went on to become one of the first and best-known Texas Rangers.

Above: Rachel and Andy adopted one of the twin sons of her brother Severn Donelson and renamed him Andrew Jackson, Jr. When Jackson became president, Andy Jr. took over the management of his Nashville estate.

behaved out of total innocence, was all in the eye of the beholder, but it is likely that where there was smoke, there was fire.

Andrew Jackson's fellow Tennesseans were generally satisfied that the only sparks involved were those of true love, but not everyone forgot the couple's alleged indiscretions. The issue came up again a few years after their marriage when Andrew's political rival, Territorial Governor John Sevier, told him in front of a large crowd that "I know of no great service you have ever rendered your country except taking a trip to Natchez with another man's wife." Andrew shouted back, "Great God! Do you mention her sacred name?" and wrestled him to the ground. When others separated them, the offended Andrew challenged Sevier to a duel. What happened next was worthy of a comic opera.

Dueling was illegal in the Tennessee Territory, and the governor suggested the affair would be better settled elsewhere, which Andrew brushed off as "a subterfuge." He published an ad in the local paper calling Sevier a "base coward and poltroon." As if to prove otherwise, the governor responded by naming a dueling ground in nearby Virginia, but he called for a delay, citing "pressing business."

Below: Andy's bizarre duel with Governor John Sevier didn't give either man any satisfaction, but it added to Jackson's reputation as a defender of womanhood.

Andrew met Sevier on the road a few days later, by chance, and jumping down from his horse, he pulled out his pistol and approached his enemy waving it and shouting obscenities. In the commotion, the governor's horse bolted, dumping him on the ground, and galloped off with Sevier's own guns flapping in their holsters still attached to the saddle. Sevier took cover behind a tree and plaintively called out to Andrew, asking if even a man such as he would have the gall to fire on "a naked man." Meanwhile, Sevier's son, who was with him, drew his own pistol and aimed it at his father's raving attacker, but Thomas Vandyke, who had been riding with Andrew, retaliated by drawing his gun and threatening to kill him if he made another move. The standoff was ended after a heated shouting match, and all the guns were holstered again, but Andrew was left without getting his satisfaction. The discussions over the site

of a proper dueling ground went on for weeks after that, and the war of words got even more heated. The governor called Andrew "one of the most abandoned rascals in principle my eyes ever beheld," and he publicly accused Vandyke of an attempted assassination. Andrew responded by writing an angry letter of protest to President Thomas Jefferson, hoping to head off charges against his friend, and adding a few charges of his own against the governor, who was the president's appointee. The whole affair finally died of its own overblown weight, and no blood was shed, but Andrew Jackson never, ever forgave the offense to Rachel's honor.

The issue came up again in 1806, three years later, when Andrew and one Charles Dickinson got into a fight about the outcome of a horserace. In the midst of it, Dickinson changed the subject of the argument and began attacking Rachel's virtue. Though Dickinson apologized when he quickly realized he was heading toward dangerous ground, Andrew simmered over the blurted insult for days before he asked for satisfaction on the dueling field.

Dickinson, who was well-known as the best pistol shot in the area, fired first, and Andrew clutched his chest, although he didn't show any sign of pain. He aimed his own pistol but it misfired, and a quick second shot sent a bullet into his opponent's stomach. Leaving Dickinson on the ground bleeding to death, Andrew strode off, himself bleeding profusely from a chest wound. But he still wouldn't acknowledge that he was in any pain. He carried the bullet, which had lodged near his heart, for the rest of his life, a constant, sometimes painful, reminder of his love for his wife.

Below: Rachel had been an attractive young woman, but after she turned matronly, Andy's political opponents attacked what they called her backwoods ugliness, even if she still retained much of her earlier loveliness.

The list of charges that followed him throughout his political career had included adultery and bigamy, but it was expanded to include murder that day. Andrew Jackson was satisfied with the self-righteous belief that he was nothing more or less than a devoted husband, ready at any time to defend his wife's honor no matter what it might take.

Many of the political attacks that were leveled against Rachel Jackson in the 1820s involved her appearance. She was still an attractive woman, but she had put on weight in her fifties. And even though such a thing was far from uncommon, she was often described in the press as a dumpy matron. Her complexion was dark, but the ideal woman of the day was blonde and fair-skinned, and that worked against her, too. As the wife of Nashville's leading citizen, she was well dressed by Tennessee standards, but not quite up to the Paris-inspired style sense that was preferred by Washington socialites, and that became a strike against her as well. Rachel often enjoyed puffing on a pipe after dinner, even smoking an occasional cigar—a fairly common thing among countrywomen, but a sign among city folk that she was an ill-bred product of the backwoods, certainly not worthy to represent a great cosmopolitan nation. Finally, it was frequently reported that she was illiterate, but like many things that were written about Rachel Jackson, it wasn't true at all. It *was* true that she hadn't had any formal schooling—few girls of her generation did—but she did learn to read and write, and in fact, she developed an early lifelong interest in reading, especially about politics. During the years of her marriage, she kept herself informed of every development that might affect her husband's public career, and in turn, she kept him informed, too.

Rachel's father, John Donelson, was a well-regarded Virginia gentleman, a surveyor and land speculator, and a member of the House of Burgesses. As a young girl, she frequently traveled with him, and she had often visited the homes of both George Washington and Thomas Jefferson. John Donelson was also an adventurer, and he was one of the first to lead settlers to the wilderness settlement at Boonesboro, Kentucky. When Rachel was thirteen, he guided a flatboat flotilla carrying fifty families, including his own, with their livestock and everything else they owned, to a place along the Cumberland River known as French Lick, which would one day become Nashville.

Rachel had a busy life of her own, but new settlers to Tennessee were usually directed to her for help. She not only loaned them tools but also worked side by side with them clearing their fields.

John Donelson was dead by the time Andrew Jackson appeared there, but he would have admired the young man's talent for acquiring land, which had been one of his own great passions. Over time, Andrew acquired thousands of acres of farmland in and around Nashville, and although he collected heavy rents on it, he was always ready to sell his land at almost unconscionable profits, and he often did. But there was one piece of land that he would never part with—a 425-acre plot that would become the estate he called the Hermitage.

Rachel had picked the site for them, and she insisted that Andrew take her there to live. They had made their home for several years at a small plantation called Hunters Hill, which had, ironically, originally belonged to Lewis Robards, her former husband. Andrew sold the place, paid off his debts with the proceeds, and built a square two-story cabin on the new site two miles away. The house was rebuilt, expanded, and improved many times after that, always at Rachel's insistence, but from 1804 on it was her only home, and one that she never had had any desire to leave, even for the White House. Andrew wasn't interested in farming, and he was away frequently, either as a soldier or a circuit-riding lawyer, so Rachel took over the job of running the Hermitage as a working plantation. The Jacksons also followed the Virginia tradition of almost continuous entertaining, and Rachel became a legendary hostess. She was proud of her home and proud of her husband, and everyone who visited the Hermitage couldn't help noticing.

The only time Rachel moved away from her Nashville home was when her husband was made territorial governor of Florida, a post he held for only

Below: The Jacksons' tomb is to the right of the Hermitage manor house in this 1856 view.

Above: Among the memories of Rachel at the Hermitage is her day cap, pieces of jewelry, and a book of poems. Rachel enjoyed reading, and was especially fond of poetry.

Below: Andy built the Hermitage Church on their plantation as a gift to Rachel. She spent peaceful hours there when he was away, but she was happier when he was at her side.

a few months before resigning because "Mrs. Jackson is anxious to return home." During that brief time, though, her devotion to fundamentalist Christian principles gave Florida its first law banning the sale of spirituous liquors on Sunday. Andrew wasn't especially religious, but he generally did whatever Rachel asked of him, including a rule against traveling on Sundays. She also greatly impressed her husband's colleagues with an uncommon ability to remember the name and the title of everyone she met, always addressing them correctly when they met again.

During his military campaigns, which propelled him to fame and led to a bright political future, Andrew's most treasured goal in life was "that moment when I could retire from the bustle of public life to private ease and domestic happiness" at Rachel's side. His life would take a much different turn, and he never realized that dream.

Andrew Jackson's victory at the Battle of New Orleans, the final engagement of the War of 1812, made him a national hero. Other military adventures strengthened his popularity, and the Tennessee legislature appointed him to the United States Senate in 1823, with nothing more or less in mind than putting him forward for the presidential nomination the following year. He managed to beat three other candidates in 1824, but no one had a majority of electoral votes, and the House of Representatives chose John Quincy Adams. Without skipping a beat, Andrew started working for the 1828 election, which he would win impressively.

Rachel didn't approve of Andy's political aspirations, and she never did anything to advance any of his candidacies. But she did visit Washington during both of his presidential campaigns, although she was like a fish out of water there. Her impression of the capital city was so negative that she made up her mind that if her Andy became president, she'd stay in Nashville. She eventually changed her mind, but while she was getting ready to go to Washington after the election, she suffered an apparent heart attack and died. Her husband was convinced that the attack had been brought on by her almost cruel treatment by the press during the campaign; but Rachel Jackson was a daughter of the frontier with strong religious faith, and she was better able to deal with such issues than most women.

White House Women

When Andrew Jackson moved into the White House, he took along Andrew Jackson Donelson, the son of Rachel's brother, whom he had raised. The young man was Andrew's favorite among a number of Rachel's nieces and nephews whom they had taken into their home, and he was known as Andrew Jackson, Jr. His guardian had arranged for him to study at West Point and made him his aide-de-camp during the war in Florida. He was a twenty-nine-year-old lawyer when he went to Washington as the president's secretary. He had married his cousin Emily Donelson, who went along to assume the duties of White House hostess. Twenty-one years old, Emily was a graduate of the Nashville Female Academy, where she had learned the required social graces, and she had acquired a striking sense of fashion. Washington society welcomed her with unabashed enthusiasm, and she established herself as its leader almost overnight. But there was a serpent in the garden. Her name was Margaret Eaton.

Andrew Jackson had first met Margaret (often called Peggy) in 1823, when he went to Washington as a senator and lived in a boardinghouse that was run by her parents, William and Rhoda O'Neale. He bonded with the entire family, but he was especially impressed by their daughter Peggy.

Later, when Rachel Jackson was in Washington during the congressional debate over the inconclusive 1824 election, she and Peggy became fast friends,

Above: Among the children the Jacksons raised, Andrew Jackson, Jr., the son of Rachel's brother Samuel was Andy's favorite. Andy later served as President Jackson's secretary.

and that tied the young woman even closer to Andrew. But an even tighter bond developed between Peggy and John Henry Eaton, Andrew's closest friend and his fellow senator from Tennessee. In fact, many Washington gossips said that Peggy and Eaton's friendship was something much more than platonic, and when Peggy's sailor husband died at sea, the rumor was that he had committed suicide over his wife's brazen affair with the man from Tennessee.

Even if she were a saint, which she probably wasn't, Peggy was a barmaid in her father's tavern, and even though she was serving senators and other high-ranking government officials, she was shunned by women who thought they mattered in Washington society. She scandalized all of them when she made a decision to marry John Henry Eaton just a few months after she learned of her husband's death.

Eaton had considered the ramifications of such a marriage long before he proposed to Peggy. He was especially concerned about Andrew's opinion, considering the attacks that had been made on his wife, Rachel, and they had long discussions about it. Andrew was quite fond of Peggy, and her abuse in the local gossip mill seemed to parallel Rachel's own experience. Always ready to defend the virtue of a maligned woman, he gave his unqualified approval, even though his political advisors cautioned him that the wedding would turn out to be a disastrous mistake. Andrew took a little time to think it over, but he came

Below: Among the greatest pleasures in the White House came from the antics of little Rachel Jackson, who became the Jacksons adopted granddaughter.

to the conclusion that not only should Eaton and Peggy marry each other, but they should do it "forthwith." Andy Jackson was a strong believer in marriage.

As everyone but Andrew and Eaton might have predicted, the union started a firestorm. One newspaper reported, "J. H. Eaton has made an honest woman of his mistress." Another chimed in that he had "just married his mistress and the mistress of eleven dozen others." Margaret Bayard Smith, whose newspaper column represented the thinking at the highest levels of society, had for some reason not heard of the death of Rachel Jackson and wrote, "The General's personal and political friends are very much disturbed about it; his enemies laugh and divert themselves with the idea of what a suitable lady in waiting Mrs. Eaton will make to Mrs. Jackson and repeat the old adage, 'birds of a feather will flock together.' "

Andrew was in deep mourning for Rachel throughout his presidency. He wore a cameo with her image around his neck, and he placed it at his bedside so it would be the first thing he saw when he woke up in the morning.

The new president linked the two women as well, and as he had done in the case of his wife, he was determined to protect Peggy Eaton from any slander that might come her way.

They knew that there was trouble ahead when the Eatons paid their first courtesy call on Vice President John C. Calhoun, who had served in the same capacity during the previous administration. The vice president himself wasn't there, but his wife, Floride, received the Eatons cordially. By the time her husband came home, though, she was beginning to wonder if that had been a good idea. On the vice president's advice, she decided to snub the Eatons and she didn't return the visit, as protocol required. Other snubs followed quickly, quite likely on the advice of Floride Calhoun—a conclusion President Jackson eventually reached.

A lot of the husbands of those women were afraid that the rough-and-ready Andrew Jackson was going to lead the country down the path of immorality, too. All that could save him from himself, they were saying, was to appoint able and experienced statesmen to his cabinet. Margaret Bayard Smith wasn't so sure that would happen. Having finally found out that Rachel was dead, she wrote that it would surely be a bad thing that "this restraining and benign influence [has been] withdrawn.... A wife could control the violence of his temper, soothe the exacerbation of feelings always keenly sensitive and excessively irritable."

But Andrew didn't read Ms. Smith's column, and he was deaf to the other pundits, too. He made his own decisions, and as he announced his choice of cabinet ministers one by one, that became more and more apparent. When the list dwindled down to secretary of war, the president confided to a friend that he needed "a personal and confidential friend to whom [I] could unbosom [myself] on all

Below: Peggy Eaton brought both joy and grief into Andy's life. He was as quick to defend her honor as he had Rachel's, and it gave him a serious problem during his presidency.

subjects." There were several possibilities, but only one possible conclusion: John Henry Eaton.

Before the appointment was announced, the wife of a British diplomat, one of the few women who would still speak to Peggy Eaton, told her it was rumored that John would be named ambassador to France to cover up the fact that she was prematurely pregnant. Peggy angrily confronted the president with the news and told him that she had no intention of leaving the country for at least ten months. Andrew wasn't pleased with the rumor, either, and he reassured her that the story wasn't true. "I had rather have live vermin on my back," he told her, "than the tongue of one of these Washington women on my reputation."

The first salvos in the war against Peggy Eaton exploded during the Inaugural Ball, when every female guest, led by Floride Calhoun, made it a point to pretend that Peggy Eaton wasn't even there. Even Emily Donelson, the official White House hostess, snubbed her.

At first, Emily seemed to respect the president's feelings on the subject, and she and her husband called on the Eatons frequently. But as she also visited with other Washington women, the calls dwindled and her friendly attitude began to chill. Emily had been told that Rachel Jackson herself had been cautioned to "avoid a certain woman [who was] not a proper character for her to associate with." But what she hadn't been told was Rachel's response: "I did not come here to listen to little slanders and to decide upon people's characters." After Peggy told Emily the rest of the story about her aunt's attitude, she only pulled further away. She apparently didn't know whom to believe, but she made a decision to join, or perhaps even lead, the Peggy Eaton boycott.

John Eaton made an attempt to change Emily's attitude, suggesting to her that she was quite young and unfamiliar with the "malice and insincerity of the world," and that she should consider the source of the slanders against his wife, which he suggested was standard practice in Washington society. It only served to strengthen Emily's resolve, however, and she responded that as the anointed White House hostess, her own reputation was secure from calumny and she would continue to run the social side of the Jackson administration as she saw fit. What she didn't seem to see was the president's own opinion of Peggy Eaton.

The whole business put a damper on the work of the Jackson administration, so the president called a meeting of a few key cabinet members, whom he told that the Eaton affair was doing great harm to the government, and that he wanted them to know he was prepared to fire them in the interest of harmony. Of course, they denied that they themselves were party to any conspiracy, but pointed out that they didn't have much control over their

Above: Emily Donelson, the wife of Andrew Jackson, Jr., served as the official hostess in the early years of the Jackson White House.

The Rats leaving a Falling House

Above: Political cartoonists had a field day when Jackson's cabinet resigned en-masse over the Peggy Eaton affair. Thousands of reprinted copies of this one were sold.

families. Still, they promised to do what they could, and over the next several months, a truce seemed to have settled over Washington. Mrs. Eaton was treated with polite, though restrained, civility at dinners and receptions, and members of the diplomatic corps, who seemed to feel sorry for her, went out of their way to treat Peggy with kindness. But still waters run deep, and the little war went on.

By the time the president went home to Tennessee that summer, the tension between Emily Donelson and Peggy Eaton had reemerged. Both families went along with Andrew to Nashville, but when many of his old friends snubbed the Eatons in the same way Washington society had done, Andrew became more convinced than ever that it was all the result of a carefully orchestrated conspiracy aimed at him. And now, he decided, his secretary, whom he was proud to call Andrew Jackson, Jr., and his wife, Emily, had not only joined the conspiracy but were actually encouraging it.

By the time fall arrived, Andrew had decided that the best way to defuse the Eaton problem was to have Peggy stay in Nashville until the end of the Washington social season. It may have worked—at least John Eaton thought so—but Peggy wouldn't allow him to go back into the lion's den without her. Andrew also made a similar suggestion to John and Emily Donelson, and they agreed, even if it meant leaving the White House without an official hostess. The president's niece Sarah Jackson accepted the assignment, although there wasn't much need for a hostess in a White House that women were avoiding. Emily never went back.

In the meantime, the cabinet ministers had resumed their old ways, and although the president repeatedly threatened to fire them all, he never seemed to really mean it. The ice was broken when Martin Van Buren, Andrew's secretary of state, offered to resign as a way of forcing the others to follow suit. Andrew rejected the idea

Right: The Federal Theatre Project, part of President Franklin Roosevelt's New Deal, produced a successful play based on Jackson's life that was called Rachel's Man.

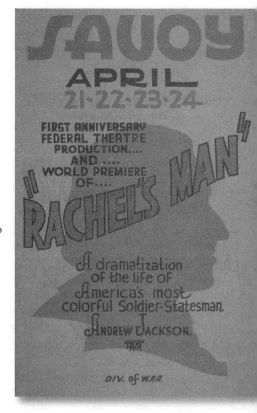

SAVOY
APRIL
21·22·23·24

FIRST ANNIVERSARY
FEDERAL THEATRE
PRODUCTION....
AND....
WORLD PREMIERE
OF....

"RACHEL'S MAN"

A dramatization
of the life of
America's most
colorful Soldier-Statesman
ANDREW JACKSON.

DIV. of W.P.A.

at first, thinking it would be a victory for the faction that he was convinced was conspiring against him. But he finally accepted it, and even before Van Buren made his resignation official, John Henry Eaton quit his post, over Peggy's tearful objection that it would hand a victory to the women who had been hounding her. But she had been overruled.

Over the next several days, each of the other members of the Jackson cabinet handed in his resignation, and when it was all over, only Postmaster General William Barry was still a member of the president's official family. Andrew pointed out that Barry wasn't officially a member of the cabinet anyway, but it was well known that he and his wife were the only ones who had been cordial to Peggy Eaton. They lived in the Eaton home, in fact.

All the resignations were made public at the same time, and press and public weren't sure what to make of it. *The Washington National Journal* gave them something to think about by pointing out that the crisis had a precedent in "the reign of Louis XV when Ministers were appointed and dismissed at a woman's nod, and the interests of the nation were tied to her apron string." As far as Andrew Jackson was concerned, it was a fitting defense of womanhood, easily his overriding passion. In his mind, Peggy Eaton and his wife, Rachel, were interchangeable in their need for his chivalrous protection. He was a president without a First Lady, and as far as he was concerned, Mrs. Eaton deserved the same respect that would be due to his wife.

Above: Both Rachel and Andy were laid to rest in this tomb at their Nashville plantation, the Hermitage, where they had spent so many happy days together.

Visiting the Hermitage

Operated by the Ladies' Hermitage Society, an organization similar to the one that welcomes visitors to George Washington's Mount Vernon, the home of Andrew and Rachel Jackson contains original furniture and mementos of the family. The president left the furnishing up to Rachel and other family members, but he had one firm rule: "Keep the bedposts plain or you will not be able to keep them clean." The house is surrounded by virgin forest, and its grounds include a formal garden, which Rachel designed and planted. Also on the property is Tulip Grove, an 1836 Greek Revival mansion built for Rachel's nephew and adopted son, Andrew Jackson Donelson, who was known as Andrew Jackson, Jr., and his wife, Emily, who served as White House hostess during the early part of the Jackson presidency. The Hermitage Church, built in 1823, is also part of the estate.

The Hermitage is located twelve miles east of downtown Nashville, at exit 221A off Interstate 40, and exit 92 off I-65 North. It is open daily from 9:00 A.M. to 5:00 P.M., except on Thanksgiving, Christmas, and during the third week in January.

Above: The grand double parlor at the Hermitage.

Hannah Van Buren

Childhood Sweetheart

In the early nineteenth century, gentlemen—especially gentlemen with political careers—worked very hard to keep their private lives to themselves. They rarely spoke of their wives in public, and if the woman closest to them died, they destroyed all references to her and carried her memory only in their hearts. Thomas Jefferson had been careful to wipe the record clean after his wife, Martha, died, and the final act of Martha Washington's life was to burn the personal letters that her late husband had sent to her.

Some people were more efficient at wiping out public memories of their spouses, and the methodical Martin Van Buren was among them. After his wife, Hannah, died in 1819, ending their twelve-year marriage, he never spoke of her again outside his own family. He had a twenty-foot granite obelisk erected over her grave, engraved with her name and the dates of her birth and death, and he withdrew in deep grief for a week. But then he got on with his life, which by then was an unusually busy one. He was serving in the New York State senate, and he was knee-deep in political infighting.

Both Martin Van Buren and Hannah Hoes had been raised in the village of Kinderhook, New York, about a hundred miles north of New York City on the Hudson River. Hannah was a distant cousin of Martin's mother, and they had known each other since they were babies. Everyone in town knew they would eventually marry each other, but young Martin waited until he was twenty-five years old before he took the step. Hannah was a year younger, which by the customs of that time and place had put her on the doorstep of spinsterhood. He had been waiting to marry until his law practice was well enough established to be able to support a family.

It was customary at the time for bridegrooms to entertain the entire village at their weddings, and the frugal Martin decided not to get married in Kinderhook, but in the town of Catskill, about a dozen miles away. Only their immediate families were invited, but still there were several dozen guests there—both Martin and Hannah seem to have come from large families.

Martin Van Buren never mentioned Hannah in his autobiography.

Hannah Hoes Van Buren

Born
March 8, 1783,
Kinderhook, New York

Parents
John Dirchsen Hoes and
Maria Quachenboss Hoes

Marriage
February 21, 1807, to
Martin Van Buren
(1782-1862)

Children
Abraham (1807-73);
John (1810-66); Martin
(1812-55); Winfield Scott
(1814); Smith Thompson
(1817-76)

Died
February 5, 1819,
Albany, New York

Above: Hannah spent all of her short life in a setting very much like this peaceful representation of the Catskill Mountains of New York State.

Below: This miniature, painted four years before Hannah died at age thirty-six, is one of the few images that were made of her.

Although the groom had three sisters and two brothers, as well as three half siblings from his mother's previous marriage, almost nothing is known of Hannah's family. In those days, people recorded vital statistics in their family Bibles, and kept the records to themselves. But it is reasonable to assume that Hannah Hoes had several brothers and sisters, as all of her friends did.

Hannah was, by some accounts, small and slim, and her Dutch heritage was reflected in her fair complexion and blonde hair. She had been brought up in the strict traditions of the Dutch Reform Church, and she was both devoutly religious and very proper. One of the rare descriptions of her notes that she was "a woman of sweet nature but few intellectual gifts." Another said that she "had no love of show [and] no ambitious desires, no pride of ostentation."

Before their marriage, Martin had long since made up his mind that he wasn't going to stay in Kinderhook. He thought remaining there would stifle his ambitions, which were lofty. He had considered relocating to New York City, but he didn't feel qualified to practice law there, and the transition from small village to big city, frankly, frightened him. He rejected the state capital at Albany for the same reasons, but he found a berth that was just right in the growing town of Hudson, about thirty miles south of there.

Unlike the other river-valley towns that he might have considered, Hudson had been settled not by the Dutch, but by Quakers from New England. Their qualities of thrift and industriousness were familiar to Martin, but their town itself wasn't. Its streets were lined with saltbox houses—some of them brought down from New England and reconstructed there—rather than the steeply gabled structures with high stoops that were common everywhere else along the Hudson River. The people were different, too. Even the dour Quakers were more worldly than the Dutch. Kinderhook had provided the inspiration for many of Washington Irving's Hudson Valley characters and it was said that Sleepy Hollow's Ichabod Crane himself might have taught in the one-room school there where young Martin Van Buren had learned to read and write.

>
>
> *Martin's parents served as godparents at Hannah's baptism.*

Hannah and her new husband, Martin, moved to Hudson in 1808, almost a year after they were married. Their first son, Abraham, had been born by then, and the family grew in stages, with three more sons who would live to adulthood. Martin's law practice grew at an even faster rate. Hudson was the seat of Columbia County, which eventually became his power base, but he would be away from home a lot of the time. He went north to Albany for Supreme Court sessions during the winter, and south

Family Ties

Both Hannah and Martin grew up speaking Dutch as their first language, even though each of them represented the fifth generation of descendants of immigrants from the Netherlands who had originally settled New York's Hudson River Valley in the early seventeenth century. She was called "Jannetje," by everyone who knew her, including her husband. Martin's mother was Maria Hoes, and after she died, he was pleased that his stepmother was a member of the Van Alen family, whose Dutch roots went back as far as his mother's did. Martin was the first American president who wasn't born a British subject, and the first with no English ancestry.

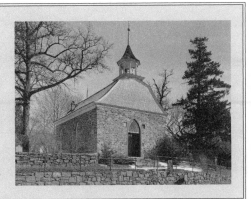

to New York in the spring to attend the important courts that were quaintly named "courts for the correction of errors." At other times during the year, he ranged all over New York State taking cases to various local courts. Hannah, the dutiful wife that she had been brought up to be, made sure that the home he returned to was peaceful, quiet, and in sharp contrast to the boardinghouses and taverns he stayed in while he was on the road, or the tavern he had been raised in, for that matter.

Above: The Dutch influence is found on both sides of the Hudson River. When Washington Irving wrote his tales of Sleepy Hollow, set around the Dutch Reformed Church in Tarrytown, he found his characters among people like the Van Burens.

Martin used the time he was away from home to build a political career. He had a natural talent for it. His schooling in the law was relatively meager, but he had a natural talent for that, too. There wasn't a lawyer in the county, or in Albany, either, who could get the better of him in a courtroom. He had also become a staunch Democratic-Republican in those early years of his career, but that was about all anybody knew for sure about him.

Martin and Hannah Van Buren spoke Dutch at home, which was the language most commonly spoken in the Dutch-settled town of Kinderhook, New York.

Whenever the conversation turned to politics, as it often did among traveling lawyers like himself, he mostly listened and absorbed their ideas without making any specific comments except for the tried-and-true party line. It helped him avoid falling into opposition traps that were concealed everywhere in upstate New York, a Federalist stronghold in those days.

Martin never took politics home with him. Hannah wasn't interested anyway, but he enjoyed the peace and quiet she had brought into his life, and he was content to leave his political ambitions at the front door. The Van Burens' fifth son was born in 1814, and only lived for a few weeks. Hannah named him after General Winfield Scott, a recent war hero, whom her husband admired and was hoping to propel into state politics. It may have been the only political gesture Hannah Van Buren ever made, although she repeated it by naming her next son Smith Thompson for her husband's patron, a future justice of the U.S. Supreme Court.

Below: Sunday mornings in Kinderhook never varied; every man, woman, and child headed for the Dutch Reformed Church wearing their Sunday best.

THE TRAP SPRUNG! THE KINDERHOOK FOX CAUGHT!
SOLD BY MURPHY & Co. 104 NASSAU-ST. N. Y.

The Red Fox

Martin Van Buren had a way of making anyone who listened to what he had to say think that he agreed completely with the listener's own point of view. In his autobiography, he tells the story of a congressman who tried to get him to take a stand. "It has been rumored that the sun rises in the East," he said, "do you think that it is true?" "Well," said Martin, "I heard that too, but I never get up until after dawn, so I really can't say." It was not for nothing that they called Martin Van Buren "The Red Fox of Kinderhook."

Left: A cartoon published during Van Buren's campaign for a second presidential term.

In January 1815, Martin Van Buren's political orchestrations came to a temporary halt when Hannah became seriously ill. She had been bedridden for most of the previous year, and had been ailing since the birth of her son Smith. Her doctor diagnosed her condition as tuberculosis. Martin stayed at her side for days, but he left to take part in the final days of the state legislature's session; he wasn't with her when she died on February 5, which was, ironically, the session's closing day. He left with her body for the funeral in Kinderhook the following day, and then took her to Hudson for burial.

Martin was left with four sons to raise on his own: Abraham, a quiet ten-year-old who, it was said, had his mother's meek disposition; seven-year-old John, a rambunctious little boy; Martin, Jr., two years younger, who was prone to childhood illnesses and seemed frail; and the baby, Smith, who had so far been raised by a nurse during the almost two years of his life. Another man in

Above: Hannah's second son, John, had an unremarkable political career, although he showed great promise as a younger man.

The Van Buren Boys

Hannah didn't live to see her sons grow up. But she would have been proud of Abraham, who graduated from the Military Academy at West Point and saw service as an officer on the frontier before he resigned his commission to become his father's secretary at the White House. He rejoined the army later and saw service in the Mexican War. His brother John graduated with honors from Yale University while he was still a teenager, but his life seemed to go downhill from there. He went to England with his father, and developed a taste for drinking, gambling, and womanizing, which earned him the nickname "Prince John." He served in Congress, but his bad habits made it a short and unremarkable career. Martin, Jr., who was known as "Mat," never married, and he devoted his life to editing his father's papers. When he developed tuberculosis, his father sent him to Paris to recover, but he didn't survive the voyage. Hannah's youngest son, Smith Thompson Van Buren, was married twice and fathered seven children. He, too, devoted his life to building his father's reputation. While their father was president, all four of them were popular in Washington society, which called them "The Van Buren Boys."

*Two years before Hannah Van Buren died, at the age of thirty-five,
Martin Van Buren buried his father, Abraham, who had lived to eighty-
one. Martin's mother, Maria, died the following year.*

his position might have tried to find a second wife, but Martin Van Buren was
inexorably married to politics, and he was convinced that no other woman
could ever measure up to his beloved Hannah. He arranged for relatives and
servants to run his household and raise his children. It was a poor substitute for
his own presence as the head of the family. He knew that and he agonized over
it. But he couldn't resist the thrill of debate, and the power he had built in the
world of politics. He was very good at it, and he couldn't give it up.

John and Smith Van Buren both inherited their father's political talents.
John went abroad with his father during Martin's brief tenure as minister to
Great Britain, and stayed on there when the mission ended. Smith, who had an
uncanny physical resemblance to his father, was a student at the time, but he
spent his vacations in Washington. He was living in New York with Alexander
Hamilton's family when the elder Van Buren was elected to the presidency, and
he went with his older brother Abraham to be part of his inauguration. Smith
didn't like Washington, and he went home to become a power in New York
State politics and, from a distance, a thorn in the side of future president, James
K. Polk. Martin, Jr., lived with his father during his term as secretary of state,
and when they moved into the White House, he served as a copyist, rendering
private and official correspondence into a readable form. His penmanship was
nearly perfect, a trait that had been handed down from his mother.

Substitute First Lady

Martin Van Buren became president and moved into the White House
in 1837, after eighteen years as a bachelor, six years longer than he had been
married to Hannah, in fact. Except for their home in the Hudson Valley, he had
spent his entire adult life in boardinghouses, taverns, hotels, and other temporary
rented homes. He knew that the White House was a temporary home, too,
but it was the biggest, grandest place he had ever lived in. He was a man with
a legendary wit, and a finely developed knack for charming visitors, but he
couldn't get his arms around the problem of White House entertaining without

*Above: Martin Van Buren during the
single term he served as President of
the United States.*

*Before she died, Hannah made her husband promise not to spend much
on her funeral and to give the money he saved to the needy.*

a woman at his side. He realized right away that he needed a housekeeper to supervise the servants—there were more than twenty of them—to plan menus, and to organize the round of receptions and parties that were expected of a president. He hired a professional who had been highly recommended by friends, and she was very good at what she did. But in the end, she was just another servant. Martin himself was a charming host, but there was something missing, and no matter how hard he tried, the White House was still a cold and lonely place. Most of his guests didn't notice, but one woman who knew him fairly well was disturbed that his old ebullience seemed to have disappeared and that he was depressed. "He goes out little," she said, "and then seems to take little pleasure in society." It wasn't the old Martin Van Buren she knew. He had always been the life of every party, and he took a great deal of pleasure in the petty gossip that was always whirling around Washington.

The problem, of course, was that he was living in an all-male household, isolated from the city's social scene. His son John was still in England, and Smith was away at school; only Abraham and Martin, Jr., were living with him. The rest of the household consisted only of Benjamin Butler: Butler was Martin's former law clerk as well as his biographer, and also attorney general in the second half of the Jackson administration, a post he still held temporarily in Martin's. The

Below: Benjamin F. Butler was attorney general during the first year of the Van Buren presidency. A former law partner of Van Buren's, he served in Andrew Jackson's cabinet, but resigned from Van Buren's.

four men routinely gathered over evening glasses of sherry in the White House residence quarters, and they shared the behind-the-scenes news of the city outside. But it wasn't a very satisfying experience for any of them, least of all the president. Then, like a breath of fresh air, Dolley Madison burst on the scene again.

The widow Madison had come to Washington to lobby Congress to buy her husband's memoirs, and she took up residence in their former home on Lafayette Square, across from the White House. As far as she was concerned, lobbying meant partying, and her house quickly became the focus of the Washington social scene as though she had never been away. She was welcomed with wide-open arms because, as one of her old friends told her, "Ah! Madam, your successors have been sickly, tame, spiritless, and indifferent." Fashion had long since passed Dolley by, but she insisted on appearing in her old outdated Empire gowns and yesterday's turbans. Nobody minded a bit. It was a welcome reminder of better times. Even Washingtonians too young to remember her days there were fascinated by the tales she had to tell of men like Washington and Jefferson; and Dolley was possibly a more popular hostess than she had ever been.

She crossed over to the White House often, and nobody was more pleased than Martin Van Buren. He knew Dolley well, and had often escorted her to parties. Now, history seemed to be repeating itself. Dolley stepped in as the White House hostess, but no party she staged there was as important to her instinct for matchmaking as the private White House dinner party she organized during the 1837 season.

Her two young cousins, Marion and Angelica Singleton, had traveled from South Carolina for a visit, and she saw a golden opportunity waiting for them in the still-single Van Buren sons. Marion found both Abraham and young Martin "pleasant, unpretentious, unpretending, civil amiable young men," but no bells began ringing her head. Her younger sister, Angelica, on the other hand, was quite impressed by the older son, Abraham, and before the after-dinner wine was poured, she had decided to set her cap for him. If Abraham was as instantly smitten, he kept it to himself, but Angelica was hard to resist. She had the finely carved features of a Roman goddess and expressive dark eyes; her face was framed by the corkscrew curls that were fashionable among young Southern ladies of the time, and she had a long and lovely neck. At twenty-one, she was a student at one of the most highly regarded finishing schools in Philadelphia, and her manners were impeccable. What was there not to like? Abraham certainly couldn't think of anything, and after a few weeks during which she subtly courted him, he asked Angelica to marry him. The wedding took place at her father's plantation eight months after they met. The president wasn't able to get away for the ceremony, but he was a completely happy man—the White House had an official hostess at last, nineteen months into his administration.

Above: Martin and Hannah's son Abraham brought Angelica Singleton into the Van Buren family by marrying her; she served as the White House's charming new hostess.

Angelica made her debut as surrogate First Lady at the annual New Year's Day reception in 1839, after several weeks of rehearsal that began with an anxious note to her cousin Dolley that said, "I am very anxious to consult with you for a few minutes on a very important matter." The former First Lady gave her much more than a few minutes of her time, and after her first official appearance, a newspaper reported that Angelica Van Buren was "a lady of rare accomplishments, free and vivacious in her conversation."

Abraham and Angelica waited until the social season wound down, and then they left for their honeymoon, a grand tour of Europe. Although both of the Adams First Ladies had traveled abroad, Angelica was the first to make an overseas voyage as part of a president's family, and she was received like royalty wherever she went, especially in England. The American ambassador there was a relative of hers, and he arranged to have his country's royal couple formally presented to Queen Victoria. The queen was noticeably pleased. Abraham's younger brother John was still in London when they arrived, and he accompanied them to Paris, where they had a similar audience with the French king Louis Philippe. The result was an education in courtly etiquette for Angelica, and it served her quite well in her new position.

Angelica perfumed her duties as White House hostess, in a style that reminded everyone of her cousin Dolley Madison's best years, for the next two seasons, until her father-in-law was replaced by a new president, William Henry Harrison.

Five wives of future presidents died without becoming First Lady. In addition to Hannah Van Buren, they were Martha Jefferson, Rachel Jackson, Ellen Arthur, and Alice Roosevelt.

It was a foregone conclusion that Martin would go home to New York after that, and he had already prepared for his retirement by buying a mansion in Kinderhook, the village that he couldn't wait to leave as a young man. He had paid $14,000 for the estate, which was established on land that had originally belonged to his grandfather, the second generation of the Van Burens in America. By the time Martin bought it, it was a slightly rundown, square Georgian-style building whose main feature was a large ballroom. He had ambitious plans for changing it, and the work was well under way by the time Abraham and Angelica arrived, an event that had been delayed by her first pregnancy, which she spent back on the plantation with her mother, looking "prosperous and ponderous," her husband said. As soon as the baby was born, a boy they named Singleton, they traveled to the house the former president called Lindenwald, but they only stayed until the snow began to fly, and then they went back to the more pleasant climate of South Carolina.

Southern Charm

Angelica Singleton had spent her childhood on a South Carolina plantation called Home Place that was owned by her father, Colonel Richard Singleton. It was an impressive place with a huge house built for frequent lavish entertaining, surrounded by formal gardens and lush greenswards. Its stables housed the finest horses, and they proved their mettle on a private racetrack on the grounds; and there were miles of roads through the forest where Angelica and her sister Marion developed their uncommon skills on horseback. The Singleton family was linked by marriage to nearly all the important families of the southeast, including James Madison and his wife, Dolley, the matchmaker who brought the Van Burens into their circle.

Even though he was theoretically out of politics by then, politics wasn't out of Martin Van Buren's blood, and he invited Democratic congressional candidates from around the state to make Lindenwald a campaign stop. On the appointed day, he made a speech that the *Albany Argus* said was Martin Van Buren at his very best. "[It was] one of the most beautiful and effective addresses I have ever heard," wrote the reporter. "All hearts were melted and he himself was almost overcome."

It wasn't a political speech, as it turned out, but rather a valedictory tribute to the scenes of his youth that were no more, and to people they all remembered but were now gone. Then he gazed across the square to the spot where his parents were buried and where he had reinterred his beloved Hannah. Their spirits, he said, were still very much alive in the depths of his heart. It was the first time Martin Van Buren had uttered his wife's name in public since the day she died.

Above: Lindenwald, Van Buren's retirement home at Kinderhook, was built by Judge Peter Van Ness, one of his former law associates. The judge's son was Aaron Burr's second in his duel with Alexander Hamilton, and fled to the house for safety in its aftermath.

Visiting Lindenwald

Hannah Van Buren never lived at Lindenwald, but she is buried beside her husband in the nearby village of Kinderhook, New York, where they both grew up. The former president's retirement home is administered by the National Park Service as the Martin Van Buren National Historic Site. It is open every day from the end of May through October 31. There is normally a small admission fee, which includes a guided tour, but while extensive renovations, begun in 2004, are under way, the admission fee has been suspended.

Lindenwald is southeast of the village of Kinderhook on New York Route 9H, the Old Post Road. From Albany and points north, use Interstate 90 to exit 12 (from Boston, the exit is B1), U.S. Route 9 at Hudson. Follow Route 9 South to New York Route 9H (about 4.5 miles), turn right onto Route 9H for another 4.5 miles. Note that Lindenwald is not on U.S. Route 9, the Boston Post Road, but New York Route 9H. From New York and points south (including the Franklin D. Roosevelt home at Hyde Park), follow U.S. Route 9 North to Kinderhook, turn right onto Hudson Street, and then make the first left, following signs to New York Route 9H. Lindenwald is about 1.5 miles south of the village.

Above: Hannah's gravesite at Kinderhook Cemetery is close to where she and her husband grew up.

Anna Harrison

Absentee First Lady

The day had dawned brisk and cold, but the sun was shining when William Henry Harrison took the oath of office as the ninth president of the United States on March 4, 1841. It hadn't been mentioned often during the recent election campaign, but he was starting this new job at an age when most men had long since retired. William needed to show the American people that he was still fit as a fiddle, so the sixty-eight-year-old former general opted to ride up Pennsylvania Avenue to the Capitol on his favorite horse, Old Whitey, even though a handsome coach had been provided for him. The ceremonies began inside the Senate chamber with the installation of his vice president, John Tyler, and then the crowd of VIPs moved outdoors to a platform where other dignitaries, including members of the new cabinet, the diplomatic corps, and Supreme Court justices, were all waiting. Also among them were William's daughter-in-law Jane Findlay Harrison, and his youngest daughter, Anna Tuthill Harrison. His wife, who was also named Anna, was not there that day. Although her husband had served in both houses of Congress, and he was in familiar territory, Anna had never been to Washington, D.C. On this occasion, she was too ill to make the journey from her home in Ohio, and she had asked her daughter and daughter-in-law to represent her. She would wait to go to the White House herself, she said, until she felt better and travel conditions improved after the spring thaw.

Patience was among Anna's admirable qualities, but she might not have been able to summon up enough of it to smile through her husband's inaugural address. Standing hatless and coatless in the blustery March wind, he looked out at more than 50,000 well-wishers, and began a speech that lasted an hour and forty minutes. Those who actually listened to every word were pleased with what he had to say, and it was agreed that President Harrison was a man of great integrity and sincerity and that he had an "undoubted sense of patriotism." After

Anna Tuthilll Symmes Harrison
Born
July 25, 1775, Flatbrook, New Jersey
Parents
Judge John Cleves Symmes and Anna Tuthill Symmes
Marriage
November 25, 1795, to William Henry Harrison (1773-1841)
Children
Elizabeth Bassett (1796-1846); John Cleves Symmes (1798-1830); Lucy Singleton (1800-26); William Henry II (1802-38); John Scott (1804-78); Benjamin (1806-40); Mary Symmes (1809-42); Carter Bassett (1811-39); Anna Tuthill (1813-45); James Findlay (1814-17)
Died
February 25, 1864, North Bend, Ohio

Anna Harrison was sixty-five when she became First Lady, making her the oldest of them all. Barbara Bush is a close second; she became First Lady at sixty-four.

Above: Anna did not make it to her husband's inauguration, but if she had, the pageantry would have impressed her.

the oath of his office was administered by Chief Justice Roger B. Taney, the new president finally put on his hat and coat, waved to the cheering crowd, and then rode back down the avenue to take possession of the White House.

The president-elect had arrived in Washington about three weeks before Inauguration Day, and after a long journey interrupted by rounds of banquets and receptions, his right hand had become swollen and he couldn't shake anyone's hand for more than a month afterward. But he patiently received many a glad-hander lining up for the government jobs that he would soon have the power to dispense.

He also used the time to put his cabinet together, and in the midst of all the activity, he was able to pay a visit to the outgoing president, Martin Van Buren, at the White House. It was a notable break with tradition, and Van Buren responded by breaking another, when he assembled his entire cabinet for a return visit to William. Although he had been disappointed by his loss in the presidential election, Van Buren didn't seem to harbor any animosity and he wrote that his successor "is the most extraordinary man I ever saw. He does not seem to realize the vast importance of his elevation. He talks and thinks with much ease and vivacity. He is as tickled with the presidency as is a young woman with a new bonnet."

All in all, it seemed reasonable to predict that the Harrison administration was going to be a memorable one. Although the Whigs had nominated him because they thought his personal popularity would carry them into the White House, they expected that the old man would lie down after that and let them run things. The new president didn't show many signs that they had guessed right, though, and he was unusually attentive to his job. William was busy getting himself ready for a special session of Congress that would set the pattern for his presidency, and he worked long hours lining up support for his ideas. That left little time for his daughter-in-law Jane to demonstrate an aptitude for her job as White House hostess in the absence of her mother-in-law, Anna. Jane welcomed the members of the diplomatic corps, who arrived in a body one afternoon to meet the new president and his cabinet, a formality that had been stretched out over many individual receptions in previous administrations. Jane also planned a dinner party for William's old friend, General Solomon Van Rensselaer, who had gone to Washington hoping to be made secretary of war but wound up with his old job as postmaster of Albany, New York, and needed a bit of ego massaging before he left. Except for that, there were no receptions, no drawing rooms, and no other dinner parties. The president was simply too busy. Perhaps the White House would brighten when Anna arrived in the spring, he hoped.

Above: President William Henry Harrison.

After a couple of weeks of this intense activity, the president was caught in a rainstorm during one of his morning walks and he came down with a cold. It hadn't helped that he gone coatless and hatless on that frigid day of his inauguration, and his condition steadily worsened until he was finally forced to call a doctor. His symptoms of pneumonia and intestinal irritation were diagnosed as "bilious pleurisy" and bed rest was recommended. But the cure didn't seem to have much effect, and a couple of days later, he told a servant, "I am ill, very ill, much more so than they think me." Specialists were called in from Baltimore and Philadelphia, but before they arrived, the president had sunk into delirium, and he died not long after midnight on April 4, exactly one month after his inauguration day.

Within hours, all of Washington's major thoroughfares were draped in black bunting, and many private homeowners hung crepes on their doors, as they would have done if they had lost a member of the family. The president's body was laid in the White House East Room, and on the day of the funeral, a capacity crowd gathered there. Along with the new president, John Tyler, the ranks of mourners included cabinet members, a delegation of congressmen led by former president John Quincy Adams, and what was described as "the faithful women," his daughter and daughter-in-law. His widow, Anna, was not there. She stopped packing her trunks for the trip to join her husband in Washington as soon as news of his death reached her, and she stayed at home in North Bend, Ohio, where she waited for his body to rejoin her for his second funeral and burial there.

Although Washingtonians had hardly gotten to know William Henry Harrison, thousands of them gathered outside the White House the day he died, while thousands more lined Pennsylvania Avenue for the procession to the Capitol building where he would lie in state. The procession included fourteen military companies, with William's horse, Old Whitey, leading the way, riderless with the stirrups on his empty saddle facing backward. William was the first president to die in office, and new rituals had to be devised.

Anna Harrison's own health was relatively robust by that time, and she probably could have gone to Washington for her late husband's state funeral. But

Below: When death came to William, he was in the company of some of his cabinet ministers and his niece, the daughter of Jane Irwin Findlay, who had come to Washington to help with White House entertaining.

she refused. It would be enough to oversee her own family's tribute right there in Ohio, she decided. Anna was much more interested in politics than most women of her time, but she was very much opposed to the turn her husband's political career had taken, and her refusal to go to Washington was quite possibly a subtle political statement. When he was nominated to run for the presidency, she was completely opposed to the very idea. "I wish that my husband's friends had left him where he is, happy and contented in retirement," she said. At other times during their life together, he had almost always bowed to her wishes, even when he didn't agree with her. As one of their friends put it, "She rules the General." But on this occasion, General Harrison had decided to run for president without his wife's support.

Life on the Frontier

William made a name for himself as an army lieutenant under General Mad Anthony Wayne fighting Indians on the frontier of the Northwest Territory, which would one day become Ohio, Indiana, and Illinois. A truce had been forged in 1795, and when William went to Lexington, Kentucky, to pick up the official printed copies of Wayne's peace proclamation, he met and fell instantly in love with Anna Tuthill Symmes, whom he described in a letter as "a remarkably beautiful girl."

The twenty-year-old, dark-eyed, and cultured Anna had been born in New Jersey, but by that time her father, Colonel John Cleves Symmes, was among the most important men in the territory, and he was well-known, at least by reputation, to the young lieutenant. Anna's mother died not long after Anna was born, and when New Jersey became a Revolutionary War battleground, her father put on a British uniform and rode with the baby tied to his saddle to the home of her grandparents Henry and Phebe Tuthill, on eastern Long Island. Then he rode home, changed his uniform, and fought the British on his home ground. After the war ended, he served in the Continental Congress, where he made a connection that allowed him to buy a million acres of land in present-day Ohio and to obtain a judgeship there.

Below: Anna is remembered as a First Lady who never visited Washington, D.C.

One for the Books

Apart from her one month as First Lady, a record, Anna Harrison is also the only First Lady who never visited Washington, D.C., and except for Martha Washington, the only one who never lived in the White House. She is also the only First Lady who was both the wife and the grandmother of a president; her grandson Benjamin Harrison was elected in 1889. Her son John Scott Harrison, the father of the future president, was the fifth of her ten children, the largest number of children surviving to adulthood who were born to any of America's First Ladies. Anna outlived all but one of them. She was also the first First Lady to be given a widow's pension, a lump sum of $25,000.

In the meantime, his second wife died and his older daughter, Maria, had married and moved to Lexington, Kentucky. A lonely man, he went to New York, where he courted and married Susanna Livingston, the sister of a local judge, and a member of one of the city's oldest families. During this time, Anna, who had already graduated from a Long Island academy, was enrolled in a private school in New York, but she cut her education short to go with her father and her stepmother to their new home in North Bend, Ohio, a short distance from Cincinnati. While their house was being built, the two women went to live with Anna's older sister in Kentucky, and it was there that William Henry Harrison came into her life.

William wanted to stay and get to know Anna better, but duty called in the form of a grand council of Indian chiefs. The long negotiations ended with a treaty that divided the territory between the White men and Native Americans, and William was given the new job of patrolling the area to keep an eye

out for infractions on either side. But before he took on his new assignment, the lieutenant borrowed money to organize a pack train to carry supplies to North Bend. Anna had apparently not been far from his mind, and he knew that the Symmes house in North Bend had been finished and that's where he would find her. She had been thinking about him, too, and she was obviously more than just glad to see him. But her father, the judge, didn't share her enthusiasm. When William asked for permission to marry his daughter, he adamantly refused. There had been some gossip making the rounds about this young man who had previously courted another girl whose money seemed to interest him more than her charms, and more important, his financial future didn't look too bright. He was living on his army pay, and he had no family money to speak of, even though he had been raised on a thriving Virginia plantation that had been given to his family by Great Britain's King James. His father had been a signer of the Declaration of Independence, but the judge wasn't interested in that. It was William's future that he worried about.

The judge was so firm in his denial that he ordered William from his house and told him never to darken his door again. As evidence that William was truly in love, he arranged to meet Anna away from her father's house as often as possible. Among the people they visited was General Wayne, who gave his own blessing to their marriage plans. Then, when her father left town on business for a few days, the happy couple called on Dr. Stephen Wood, an official in the territorial government who was a justice of the peace. After he married them, they moved themselves to the safety of the nearest army fort.

Not too many weeks passed before Symmes and his new son-in-law met again. "How do you expect to support my daughter?" the judge asked, and William responded, "My sword is my means

Below: General "Mad Anthony" Wayne, a hero of the American Revolution, earned his nickname for his quick temper. During the later Indian Wars, his battlefield victories opened the Northwest Territory to American settlement.

of support, sir." It must have been the right answer, because the man's attitude softened. He didn't completely accept William into his family, though, until three years later when the couple named their first son after him. John Cleves Symmes Harrison was the second of the Harrisons' ten children.

Shortly before their first child, Betsey Bassett Harrison, was born, William resigned his position on General Wayne's staff and devoted much of his time to running a whiskey distillery, although he was still in the army at the time. He had been promoted to captain, in fact. He quit the army and made a move to politics when the territorial secretary left to become governor of the Mississippi Territory and he applied for the job. President John Adams gave it to him, with obvious pleasure, almost as soon as his petition reached Philadelphia. It was one of those political jobs with not much else to do but endorse the paychecks, and William spent most of the next year running his farm and his distillery. But he also used some of his time to get involved in local politics, which was a messy business at that time. The governor was an ardent Federalist, but William, his assistant, was an enthusiastic follower of Thomas Jefferson's Republican principles. Their differences came to a head when the territory's population grew to the point that it merited a representative in Congress. William agreed to run as a Democratic-Republican against a Federalist candidate, who happened to be the governor's son. He won by a vote in the legislature of eleven votes to ten.

His tenure was highly successful. Among other things, he redrew the lines of the Northwest Territory to allow for the creation of new states, and he was appointed governor of the Indiana portion. When his congressional term ended, he got ready to move to Vincennes on the Wabash River, and Anna, who hadn't gone to Philadelphia with him, joined him there in the spring. She had three babies to care for by then. Their third child, Lucy Singleton Harrison, had been born the previous September.

Their fourth child, William Henry Harrison II, was born at Vincennes, prompting his father to start building a bigger and more elegant house, the first brick building in town. It was William Henry Harrison II's wife, Jane, who would be Anna's substitute as First Lady.

Work on the new house, which William named Grouseland, was just about finished when John Scott Harrison, their fifth child, was born. His son, Benjamin Harrison, would one day become the twenty-third president of the United States.

During the years the Harrisons lived there, the town of Vincennes grew from a tiny little frontier trading post to home for nearly a thousand people, mostly emigrants from the big eastern cities. Governor Harrison enriched their lives by establishing a circulating library and encouraging the establishment of several churches, including one of the Presbyterian denomination, where Anna and the children could be found every Sunday and often on weekdays as well. He also laid the foundations for the establishment of a university there. And following the wishes of President Jefferson, he had acquired nearly all of present-day Illinois and most of southern Indiana as public land.

Above: Jane Irwin Findlay Harrison, the widow of Anna's son William Henry, Jr., accepted the job of substituting for her ailing mother-in-law as the official White House hostess.

Thanks largely to William, there was general peace among the Native Americans there. But as they saw their ancestral lands shrinking, two Shawnee leaders, Tecumseh and his brother, who was known as "the Prophet," began to conspire among the other local tribes to stop the sale of their land. Tecumseh rallied the other chiefs, threatening violence, to stop selling their lands, and his brother used his self-styled kinship with the Great Spirit to goad their braves into calling for open war.

In the meantime, President Jefferson extended Governor Harrison's tenure at about the same time his sixth child, Benjamin Harrison, was born. In his letter thanking the president, the by-then experienced father said, "The emoluments of my office afford me a decent support and will, I hope, enable me to lay up a small fund for the education of my children. I have hitherto found, however, that my nursery grows faster than my strongbox."

The doctor who was on hand for all of Anna's pregnancies had traveled all the way from Lexington, Kentucky, to Ohio to be with Anna when her fifth child was born. As an honor, the Harrisons named their new son John Scott after him. The doctor's own wife had a baby boy at about the same time, and they named him William Henry Harrison Scott.

A few years later, William invested in land in southern Indiana and built a sawmill, which kept the contents of his strongbox growing and provided a more comfortable life for Anna and the children. She took on the job of running the business for him, and keeping track of its accounts, as she had done with his distillery and their farm. She confessed that she didn't have much of a head for business, and she blamed herself that the family's income from these ventures wasn't as high as it might have been.

It wasn't as though Anna didn't have other things to do. Her large family was a distraction, to be sure, but she also served as hostess for the official meetings that were commonly held at Grouseland. What taxed her energies and her state of mind most was a steady round of councils with the local Native Americans that were held in her home, and frequently at Indian encampments that were set up on their front lawn. They were usually peaceful encounters, but Anna, like most of her Vincennes neighbors, was fearful of the Indians, who had the little town virtually surrounded.

Most of the local tribes were friendly, and Governor Harrison valued their friendship, but Tecumseh's Shawnees were another matter. Anna's pastor, Reverend Samuel Scott, circulated a petition to be sent to the president demanding "the exertion of some vigor" against the chief and his brother, the Prophet, whom everyone feared most. Both Anna and her husband signed it. While Congress debated its demands, William mobilized the local militia and it was already on the march, with the governor in the lead, when the federal government sent in troops to help. By the time they reached the Prophet's village, known throughout the territory as Prophetstown, the force numbered nearly a thousand men.

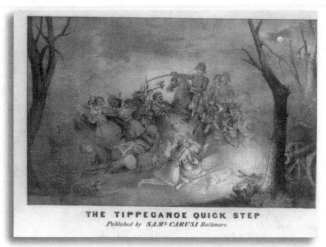

THE TIPPECANOE QUICK STEP
Published by SAM. CARUSI Baltimore.

Above: William's fame as the hero of the Battle of Tippecanoe led to many tributes, including music for a dance, "The Tippecanoe Quick Step," that was illustrated with a painting of his battlefield exploit.

Below: William went on to greater glory with his defeat of the Shawnee chief, Tecumseh, at the War of 1812 Battle of the Thames.

The battle that followed on the banks of the Tippecanoe River, the site of present-day Lafayette, Indiana, was an easy victory for William's men, especially compared to other encounters he would lead. But the Battle of Tippecanoe gave William the status of national hero, and he was known forever afterward as "Old Tippecanoe."

After defusing the threat from Prophetstown in the Battle of Tippecanoe, William resigned as governor and rejoined the army with the rank of general. The United States had declared war on Great Britain by then, and both Tecumseh and the Prophet had gone north to fight alongside the British forces. William's mission was to follow them and remove the threat. His forces met the enemy along the Thames River north of Detroit and killed nearly all of the British troops, as well as most of their Indian allies, including Tecumseh and his brother. It was the first important victory of the War of 1812, to be sure, but Tippecanoe was the victory that Americans preferred to remember.

William served with distinction in many frontier battles during the War of 1812. When it was over, Anna gave birth to her tenth child, James Findlay Harrison, and all ten children were living with their mother at Grouseland. It had been built for a family of five, and as if it weren't already bursting at the seams, Anna also took in the daughter of a soldier killed at Tippecanoe, and the family was putting the orphaned son of another of William's comrades-in-arms through West Point. A great many men who fought the war of the frontier had retired rich, but General Harrison wasn't one of them. He and his family were living on his army pay, the very thing Anna's father had predicted would happen. Judge Symmes had died recently, and Anna inherited his extensive lands at North Bend, Ohio. They couldn't afford to build a house there, but they could, and did, expand a log cabin William had bought from his father-in-law, and which had served as the couple's first home. Their children were growing and leaving for college but, of course, Anna still had younger ones to look after. But, when her husband was sent to Congress, she found their expanded cabin much roomier than she had expected. The Harrisons had dabbled in a few other small businesses to help make ends meet, but they failed one by one, and when his congressional career ended, he was deep in debt. Anna had taken on the task of keeping the business ventures afloat, and whenever her husband traveled on his continuing political business, she stayed home to save money. William's next trip east was as a United States senator. Anna kept up with him by devouring the contents of several different newspapers that found their way to North Bend.

Anna stayed behind when William was made minister to the new Latin American nation of Colombia, and no one was more pleased than she when it turned out to be a short-lived appointment. Anna was resigned to being a homebody, and she preferred her husband to be closer to home than that.

When he came home, briefly, after more than a year away, a family problem was waiting for him. His son, William, had all but given up his law practice, and his problem with alcohol had worsened. Trying to get his life back together, he moved to North Bend, where Anna was caring for him. The others were in a better state. John Symmes lived nearby and had become reasonably successful as a local magistrate. John Scott had taken over running the family farm in his father's absence, and was living with his wife in Vincennes, where after an unsuccessful tenure at the local land office, which left him several thousand dollars in debt, he had become one of its leading citizens. He was serving not only as chairman of the town's board of trustees but also as supervisor of the local library, which had been moved into Grouseland, the Harrisons' former home.

The other children were doing reasonably well, too. Benjamin had earned a medical degree; Carter had enrolled at Miami University to study law; and Betsey and her husband, John Cleves, were running a successful farm. The Harrisons' daughter Lucy had died, as had James, their youngest son; Mary was married to Dr. John H. Thornton, who had a successful medical practice in a nearby town; and the baby of the family, Anna, lived with her mother. All things considered, Anna Harrison had a lot to be proud of with the children she had raised.

Above: Grouseland, the Harrison home in Vincennes, Indiana, was filled to the rafters with Anna's ten children and a war orphan she took in to raise as her own.

Presidential Hopeful

Although he kept his hand in and his contacts active, William Henry Harrison declined offers to run for Congress again, and he looked for better ways to earn money for his family than public service had to offer. Then things began to change in 1836 when the Whigs dusted off his military record and nominated him to run for the presidency against Martin Van Buren. Anna would have preferred it if he had turned the honor down, but at least she knew that he'd stay close to home while the campaign was going on. And if she didn't wish it out loud, there was always the chance that he might lose. Campaign swings were unheard of in those days, and William generally stayed at his wife's side in North Bend and Cincinnati up until Election Day. He knew very well that his military record had been the reason for his nomination, but he hoped that the voters would take his other qualifications into consideration as well. The fact was that he had a lot of good ones.

As Election Day grew nearer, the Whigs began to worry that that they might lose, and they talked William into traveling a bit to show the flag. He rejected most of their invitations, but he and Anna went to Virginia for the wedding of their daughter Anna to Colonel William Henry Harrison Taylor in

Above: William was not born in a log cabin, but his political managers thought it would help his image as a son of the great West, and so they invented one for campaign posters.

the midst of the run-up to the election. The bridegroom was a grandson of Lucy Singleton, the candidate's sister, and so the setting was appropriate. When William did leave home, local reporters almost always zeroed in on his frailty and apparent poor health. As a way of putting those rumors to rest, he finally agreed on a junket that would take him to New York, Van Buren's home turf. Anna went along this time, too, not to support her husband, but to visit her son Carter, who was establishing a law practice there.

In the end, William made a good showing in the West, but he lost the election, and Anna could look forward to four more years with her husband to herself. But she had to share him with a steady stream of politicians who had become convinced that if he ran again, he could win, and slowly William started to believe them himself. He cordially received any delegation that cared to make the trip to North Bend, and in four years, he turned only one away. They had arrived on a Sunday, and he said, "I have too much respect for the religion of my wife to encourage a violation of the Sabbath." He didn't seem to have much respect for her opinion that he shouldn't run, though. She did, however, make every visitor welcome in her home, and her homespun charm went a long way toward convincing them that William Henry Harrison was a man of the people who deserved to be president.

Right after he was nominated, Anna became seriously ill and he was forced to stay at her side for more than a month. A local newspaper made visitors to North Bend aware that their presence "interrupts the quiet of the family and retards recovery of the invalid," and they stopped going there. But the strange campaign went on elsewhere, and on Election Day, "Tippecanoe and Tyler too" were on their way to Washington.

The deluge of visitors to North Bend escalated again, but this time the well-wishers weren't trying to get a job for the presidential candidate but rather to get government jobs for themselves from the president-elect. He and Anna avoided them by going off to Kentucky to tend to what he characterized as "family business," and in a way it was. They were trying to save their family from all these so-called friends. Then they went home to wind up their affairs, and it was then that Anna was afflicted with the illness, real or imagined, that would make moving on to Washington impossible, at least until spring.

Opposed to slavery, Anna encouraged her sons to join the Union army during the Civil War.

Life Postpresidency

When William left for Washington and Anna remained behind, it was the last time they would see each other. President Harrison died on April 4, 1841, and Anna waited for his body to return to Ohio to be buried on their family land. While never having set foot in Washington, D.C., after the president's death, Anna began to flex her own political muscles and started a largely successful campaign to secure federal jobs for members of her family. She also routinely made her positions on issues known to members of the new administration and of Congress. Other First Ladies, before and after her, rarely did such things, but she had power and she knew how to use it. It is a fascinating clue to how she might have conducted herself if her husband had lived and she had become First Lady in more than just name.

Anna continued to live in her home on the Harrison family land in North Bend until a fire destroyed it in 1858. She then went to live with her son John Scott Harrison at his farm nearby. It was there that she died in 1864 at the age of eighty-eight.

Anna was the first First Lady to be given a franking privilege— she had authorization to send mail without paying postage!

Visiting Grouseland

Grouseland, the house Governor Harrison built at Vincennes, Indiana, and where Anna lived for many years, is now a national shrine run by the Grouseland Foundation. It is open every day in January and February from 9:00 A.M. to 5:00 P.M.; and from March through December, it is open Monday through Saturday, 9:00 A.M. to 5:00 P.M., and Sundays 11:00 A.M. to 5:00 P.M. It is closed Thanksgiving, Christmas, and New Year's Day. An admission fee is charged for adults and children over age six. The house is located at 3 West Scott Street, Vincennes, Indiana 47591. Telephone: 812-882-2096.

Below: Grouseland was more than just a home. Its main parlor was used as a council chamber.

The tomb where Anna and her husband are interred is surrounded by a golf course today. It is all that remains of North Bend, Ohio, the town that Anna's father founded.

Letitia & Julia Tyler

Hidden Away

John Tyler didn't move into the White House until a couple of weeks after William Henry Harrison died. At first, there was some question whether he was president at all. The Constitution wasn't clear about it, and many constitutional authorities believed that the vice president inherited powers of the presidency, but not the rights to the office itself. As for John Tyler, he thought otherwise, and while the debate was going on, he rose above it and conducted himself in a presidential manner. Still, he couldn't ride roughshod over them by moving into the White House with his wife, Letitia, as soon as they arrived in town, even though he had taken the oath of office as president of the United States before he left his Virginia plantation near Williamsburg.

While the men debated the issue, John temporarily left Washington, D.C., making a trip home to Virginia to gather up his family and transport them back to the capital city. The little caravan included five of his seven children, his servants, and Letitia, who had suffered a stroke two years earlier and was partially paralyzed. It had been John's intention to fulfill most of his vice presidential obligations from home so that he could be at Letitia's side and spare her the painful trip north.

By the time the family arrived in Washington, Congress had decided that even if the Tylers did have the temerity to move into the White House, John wasn't entitled to collect a president's salary. He was forced to dig into his own pockets to pay for upkeep of the mansion, and for all the entertainment he was still expected to provide—even if many of his guests were those same penny-pinching congressmen. He made it a point to include his political enemies as well as his friends on all of his guest lists. And, as if to rub their noses in the expensive problem they had saddled him with, he entertained often. He had,

John Tyler replaced the oldest president and, at fifty-one, he was the youngest man ever to take over the office—a distinction he would lose in 1901 when another vice president, Theodore Roosevelt, moved into the White House at the age of forty-one. John F. Kennedy, the youngest president to be elected, was forty-four when he was inaugurated sixty years later.

Letitia Christian Tyler

Born
November 12, 1790,
Cedar Grove Plantation,
near Richmond, Virginia

Parents
Robert Christian and
Mary Browne Christian

Marriage
March 29, 1813, to
John Tyler (1790-1862)

Children
Mary (1815-48); Robert (1816-77); John, Jr. (1819-96); Letitia (1821-1907); Elizabeth (1823-50); Anne Contesse (1825); Alice (1827-54); Tazewell (1830-74)

Died
September 10, 1842,
Washington, D.C.

Above: John Tyler discovered that he had become president when a messenger arrived at his door with the news that Harrison had died.

after all, grown up in the Virginia tidewater, where entertaining was a way of life.

His wife, Letitia, was the daughter of a Virginia planter, and she, too, had been raised in the tidewater tradition, but because of her physical incapacity, she wasn't able to put her experience in entertaining to use. She spent her life at the White House generally hidden away upstairs on the second floor, and some of his guests weren't aware that John Tyler even had a wife.

The job of planning and running the endless round of dinners, balls, and receptions fell to Letitia's daughter-in-law Priscilla Cooper Tyler, the wife of her son Robert. The young woman had the abundant advice of the experienced Dolley Madison, a close friend of John's, who knew the ropes better than just about anyone. But Priscilla's parties weren't a reflection of Mrs. Madison's glory days. Just about everyone who remembered those days couldn't help saying that Priscilla's celebrations were, if anything, much more enjoyable.

During her first eight months as White House hostess, Priscilla planned and presided over a reception every night of the week during the social season, eventually scaling back to twice a week in the interest of economy. (Congress still hadn't untied the purse strings.) There were also two formal dinners every

> "[The president's] natural courtesy, simple dignity, and the manner in which he puts his guests at ease made a favorable impression on all present."
>
> —The New York Herald

week, a public drawing room once a month, and, of course, the annual New Year's Day open house. If all that wasn't enough, the Tylers brought back the Fourth of July reception, opening the White House doors to anyone who cared to come; and Priscilla organized weekly concerts by the marine band on the White House lawn during the summer months.

Priscilla hadn't come to the job without experience. Her father, Thomas Cooper, had been the most famous Shakespearean actor of his day, and she was a former actor herself. Her husband, Robert, had first been attracted to her when she was playing Desdemona to her father's Othello in a Richmond theater.

> "The party at the President's house last evening consisted of about a hundred persons invited by Mrs. Robert Tyler. There was dancing in the now gorgeously furnished East Room, and an elegant supper. The courtesies of the President and Mrs. Robert Tyler to their guests were all that the most accomplished European court could have displayed."
>
> —John Quincy Adams on entertaining by the Tylers

Their marriage put an end to her acting career, but it led to her greatest role when she became White House hostess. At twenty-four, Priscilla was as beautiful as she was charming, and she clearly enjoyed the role every bit as much as her guests enjoyed her attentions.

Letitia Tyler was more than pleased with Priscilla's entertaining, and she encouraged it. "Because I am ill is no reason why the young people should not enjoy themselves," she said. Even though she was partially paralyzed, she took part in White House life as much as she could. For the first few months after her stroke, she had lost her ability to speak, but by the time John became president she could talk again, even if haltingly. She frequently received visitors informally and discussed politics with them—and she did so "intelligently," it was reported. It was apparent to anyone who conversed

Above: Priscilla Cooper Tyler, Letitia's daughter-in-law, filled in for her as White House hostess. A former actor, Priscilla reveled in the new role.

"Mother attends to and regulates all so quietly that you can't tell she does it."
—Priscilla Tyler on Letitia

with Letitia that she was an avid newspaper reader, as she had been in her younger days, in spite of the rumors that she spent all her time reading the Episcopalian Book of Common Prayer.

In earlier years, Letitia had served as her husband's closest advisor. One of her children remembered: "I have frequently heard our father say that he rarely failed to consult her judgment in the midst of difficulties and trouble, and that she invariably led him to the best conclusion." But by and large, her main role throughout their life together was managing their plantation. Her skills made it a profitable venture, and even allowed them to buy more land to expand their holdings on at least two occasions and eventually to buy an even larger plantation. She also provided her husband with the financial acumen that made his political career possible. Like most upper-class young women who were raised in Virginia, including Martha Washington, Letitia learned business management at her father's knee, and like Martha, she became better at it than many men who called themselves planters.

Letitia Christian and John Tyler met when they were both eighteen years old. He was a recent graduate of the College of William and Mary, and at the time he was studying law under his father, who had become governor of Virginia. There was no question that they were attracted to one another, but there were no visible sparks apart from John's subsequent proposal of marriage. Her father wasn't forthcoming with his approval; it wasn't enough, apparently, that John's family background was above reproach or even that his father was governor of the state. The fact was that the Tyler family, like many in the tidewater, was rich in land, but poor as far as income was concerned, and that may have been one of Robert Christian's objections, although he didn't say so. But young John regarded his family's financial embarrassment as proof

Below: John Tyler was the first vice president to become president. It wasn't an easy transition for a maverick like him.

Above: Lizzie Tyler,
White House bride.

that Letitia's love was true, and that she wasn't interested in marrying him merely for his money. (And there didn't seem to be speculation that it might have been the other way around, either.)

Mr. Christian gave the couple his approval, but not his blessing. That would come, he told them, if they were still interested in getting married after five years had passed. John and Letitia agreed that they would wait, and they embarked on a quiet, chaste five-year engagement. There were never any public displays of affection between them during all that time, and none that any close family members were aware of, either. It was said that the young man wouldn't even kiss his fiancée's hand until three weeks before they were married on John's twenty-third birthday.

John Tyler was already a member of the Virginia legislature by that time, and four years later he went to Washington as a member of the House of Representatives. But his bride stayed behind to tend to the plantation, which she had inherited when both of her parents died not long after her wedding. When John became Virginia's governor in 1825, their home was close enough to the capital that people who mattered came to visit her and she still almost never left home. After John was elected to the United States Senate, Letitia went up to Washington only for one season during his nine years there. She had seven children by then, and her eighth was born in the middle of his Senate tenure. She also had a plantation to run, and Letitia was clearly much too busy to play the role of a Senate wife.

"Lizzie looked surpassingly lovely [but] our dear mother was far more attractive to me."

—Priscilla Tyler on Letitia

Her role as a president's wife was limited by her paralysis, but she did manage to make one public appearance during her time in the White House: when her daughter, Elizabeth, was married to William N. Waller, another prominent Virginian, in January of 1842. Letitia had been upstairs in the White House, largely out of sight, for ten months by then.

The oppressive heat of the Washington summer, along with Letitia's constant worries about the family's finances, led to her second stroke, and Letitia died in September 1842, eight months after her daughter's wedding. The White House was once again draped in black, as it had been when President Harrison died, and crowds gathered outside "sobbing and wringing their hands." Letitia was the first wife of a president to die while her husband was in office, and although very few in Washington had ever actually seen her, the mourners wailed that they had lost a good friend.

> "Nothing can exceed the loneliness of this large and gloomy mansion, hung with black, its walls echoing with sighs."
>
> —Priscilla Tyler on the death of her mother-in-law

Two of Letitia's nine children were dead by then: One, who was unnamed, died at birth, and a daughter they named Anne had lived for only a few months. Five of the remaining seven children were married. Fifteen-year-old Alice and her twelve-year-old brother, Tazewell, lived at the White House, and so did Robert and his wife, Priscilla, along with John, Jr., his father's secretary. Robert and Priscilla moved out two years later, and another Tyler daughter, Letitia Semple, moved in to assume the duties of White House hostess with Dolley Madison at her side. A few months later, both women would be upstaged by John Tyler's second wife, the former Julia Gardiner, who had already taken Washington by storm.

Below: Robert Tyler, Priscilla's husband, was the oldest of Letitia's three sons. She also had five daughters by the time she became First Lady.

The Rose

At the moment Letitia Tyler died, she was clutching a rose in her hand, which was mentioned in nearly every obituary and every tribute that was written about her. Some years later, people who like to believe such things said that it had been a deathbed prediction that she would be replaced by a woman named Rose, and as proof they pointed out that John Tyler's second wife was well known as "The Rose of Long Island."

Julia Gardiner had shocked New York society, which regarded her as one of its up-and-coming stars, and her parents as well, when she agreed to endorse a local dry goods store and the title was engraved under her portrait in its advertising. Refined young women simply didn't do such things in the nineteenth century, but Julia always made her own rules.

> "I'll purchase at Bogert and McCamby's. Their goods are Beautiful and Astonishingly Cheap."
>
> —*Julia Gardiner in a newspaper advertisement*

The family connection with Long Island went back seven generations to Lion Gardiner, who bought a three-thousand-acre island off its north shore from the Montauk Indians, and turned it into a private estate. Julia and her younger sister, Margaret, lived there as young girls, and later generations of the family still do.

Julia and her sister were raised in an atmosphere of bottomless wealth and privilege. Not only was their father's family at the very top of New York's upper crust, but their mother was heir to an unusually large fortune as well.

Both girls were educated at the highly fashionable Madame N. D. Chagary's Institute for Young Ladies in New York, where they studied French, arithmetic, literature, history, and composition, and minored in partying. But as glittering as the New York social scene was at that time, Julia didn't find it stimulating enough, and by the time she was fifteen she had begun thumbing through the pages of the social register of the era searching for a young man who might be wealthy enough to change her life.

After she scandalized the family by posing for that newspaper ad, she and Margaret were hustled off to Europe. Margaret was considered prettier than her sister, but at nineteen, Julia was quite a head-turner herself. And she had a flirtatious streak that kept heads turned in her direction. She dazzled counts and barons, and even King Louis Phillippe of France couldn't take his eyes off her. For her part, Julia couldn't turn her eyes away from the queen's diamond-studded headdress. It was at that moment she was infected with what was known as "queen fever." An invitation to call on Queen Victoria took away any hope that she would ever recover from it.

Left: Julia Gardiner Tyler

Julia Gardiner Tyler

Born
May 4, 1820, Gardiner's Island, New York

Parents
David Gardiner and Juliana McLachlan Gardiner

Marriage
June 26, 1844, to John Tyler (1790-1882)

Children
David Gardiner (1846-1927); John Alexander (1848-83); Julia (1849-71); Lachlan (1851-1902); Lyon Gardiner (1853-1935); Robert Fitzwalter (1856-1927); Pearl (1860-1947)

Died
July 10, 1889, Richmond, Virginia

Below: Julia Gardiner, John Tyler's second wife, scandalized local society with this newspaper ad that called her "The Rose of Long Island."

Buried Treasure

Captain William Kidd was regarded as a successful businessman by his neighbors in New York, but he was also a privateer, which his English victims called a pirate. On his last voyage before being taken to London to be hanged, he approached New York by way of Long Island Sound to avoid British warships, and he stopped for a spell to visit with his friend John Gardiner of Gardiner's Island. It is said that he buried his pirate treasure on the island before he moved on, and to this day rumors persist that it is still there. But if it truly had been buried, the Gardiners themselves would probably have found it by now. On the other hand, they didn't need it. The family became uncommonly rich following in Lion Gardiner's footsteps and dabbling in New York real estate.

Right: The windmill on Gardiner's Island.

When they came home from their grand tour of Europe, the Gardiner girls found New York more boring than ever—it was too *American*, they said—and their father, who was ready for a change himself, took them down to Washington for some husband hunting during the social season. He rented a whole floor in one of the better rooming houses to give the girls enough elbow room to spread their nets for eligible bachelors, and Julia proved to be better at it than her sister. They stayed for three seasons, and during that time she had considered proposals of marriage from two congressmen, one of whom was future president James Buchanan, as well as Supreme Court Justice John McLean. She kept all three on the string and dozens more still hopeful, and she went right on looking around. One place she looked was on the floor of the House of Representatives, and she was in the visitors gallery just about every day, to "educate herself," she said. But she was also up there to flirt, and as if she needed it, she always wore a large hat to call attention to herself.

David Gardiner, Julia's father, was a businessman, not a politician. But he had served for a time in the New York State senate, and when he took his daughters to Washington, he insisted on being called "Senator," as if Washington didn't already have enough of them.

Julia and her sister were invited to every important party in town, and they made a splash at every one of them. Naturally, that included White House parties, and their presence didn't go unnoticed by the recently widowed president. It was said that after one reception, John was seen running down the stairs in pursuit of Julia, and that during another he invited her to the White House for a quiet evening of cards. At one point, he kissed both sisters on the cheek, but Margaret complained that she got only two while her sister was favored with three.

Finally, the president cornered Julia at a party and told her that he wanted to marry her. "No, no, no," she remembered saying, "and shook my head with each word which flung the tassel of my Greek cap into his face with every move." But that still wasn't the last word. Although she was only twenty-four years old and he was fifty-four, and her mother, who was nine years younger than her daughter's suitor, didn't think that the president was nearly rich enough to be able to support her, John wasn't ready to give up. There is no fool like an old fool, after all. At least that was what the Washington gossips were saying.

When John wasn't making a fool of himself chasing young Julia between the tables at White House parties, President Tyler kept his nose to the grindstone, and he was too busy to get out of the executive mansion for vacations and public ceremonies. He was especially attentive to military affairs, with the growing navy his special pride. When it built the most up-to-date warship, the USS *Princeton,* and sailed her up the Potomac for a round of demonstrations, a presidential reception for the crew was held in the East Room. But although he had been among the dignitaries invited to an excursion aboard the ship the following day, John wasn't planning to accept.

Among his own guests that evening, though, was the old matchmaker, Dolley Madison, and she had a special reason to make him change his mind. David Gardiner and his two daughters were going to be there. What could possibly encourage romance more than an afternoon cruising on the river? President Tyler had a special affection for this great iron ship, and it didn't tax Dolley's powers of persuasion to talk him into going on the excursion as her escort.

The *Princeton,* with two giant swivel-mounted cannons, was the last word in fighting ships. The cannon at the bow, called the "peacemaker," was, at fifteen feet, the largest naval gun ever made up until that time; and another, smaller but equally impressive, called the "Oregon," was mounted at the stern. Peacemaker was fired twice as the ship shoved off from the navy yard before the guests, their ears still ringing, went below to enjoy the lavish banquet that had been set for them.

As they approached Mount Vernon, it was announced that the gun would be fired again as a salute to the first president, and many of the partiers went up on deck to add their cheers to the cannon's roar. But they got more than they expected. The great gun exploded. Chunks of shrapnel rained on the crowd; the ship was shrouded in black smoke, and a twenty-foot slice of the *Princeton's* hull was sheared off into the river. Eight people were killed, including the secretary of the navy, the secretary of state, and the ship's commander, as well as David Gardiner, Julia's father.

The president was below at the time, and so was Julia, who fainted when she heard what had happened—right into John Tyler's arms. When she came to, he was carrying her down the gangway to a rescue ship.

Four months later, the president who never went anywhere mysteriously disappeared from the White House. Even his family had no idea where he had gone. But the Washington gossips thought that they knew. The Gardiner sisters were in New York. Where *else* would he have gone?

Above: Julia was thirty years younger than her presidential husband.

Below: Julia's father and two cabinet ministers were killed when a gun exploded aboard the USS Princeton. *The blast also propelled Julia into President Tyler's arms, and the die was cast.*

They were right, of course, but when John Tyler checked into a New York hotel, the staff was sworn to secrecy, and he didn't show his face until Wednesday morning, June 26, 1844, when he appeared at the Church of the Ascension on lower Fifth Avenue, where Julia was waiting for him. She was dressed in a simple white dress with a gauze veil trailing from a headpiece adorned with white flowers. Her mother was there, and so were Margaret and their two brothers. There was no one from the Tyler family on hand, except for the bridegroom, and more significantly, there were no reporters on hand, either. By the time the New York press corps found out that there had been a presidential wedding in their city, the bride and groom were well on their way to a Virginia honeymoon.

The Tyler sons approved of their new stepmother, but their sisters Letitia, who was a year older than Julia, and Alice, who was only seven years younger, refused to speak to her. Both eventually came around when they could see how deeply their father loved his new wife. It may also have been the result of the breath of fresh air that Julia brought into the White House.

Their wedding was formally announced at a White House reception in the Blue Room two days after the president and his new wife arrived back in Washington. Tongues were still wagging around the capital over their May-December relationship, but Julia charmed "the gossips" into forgetting what she considered their narrow-mindedness. "She was a born ballroom lobbyist," one historian said.

Her trip abroad had been unsuccessful in her search for a husband, but it gave Julia a taste of Old World courtliness, and she reigned over the White House with a style that any queen would recognize. But she also discovered that the Europeans had some better ways of having fun than were common in either New York or in Washington. Chief among them was the waltz, a style of dancing that was considered scandalous on the western side of the Atlantic because it involved couples touching one another. It didn't take Julia very long to show her guests that this was a pleasure that they had gone without far too long. She also introduced them to the polka, which in those days was considered about as decadent as disco dancing was to the older generation in the 1970s.

Father of His Country

Letitia Tyler had eight children, and Julia Tyler seven. The total of fifteen is by far the largest number of children fathered by any American president. The last of John Tyler's children was born when he was seventy years old. John seems to have enjoyed being a father. In his retirement he wrote to a friend, "I have a houseful of goodly babies budding around me."

Above: The Tylers' son Lyon was named for Julia's ancestor, the founder of her family fortune.

Below: Julia's influence on fashion was evident in this page from an 1845 issue of The Columbian *magazine.*

She caught her guests by surprise at one of her receptions when she dashed out onto the floor and grabbed every convenient male arm, guiding the men though the moves that they had been brought up to believe were the first steps on the road to perdition. Both dance styles quickly spread from Washington to other parts of the country, and although preachers railed against them, young people took to them like surfers to a perfect wave, and they were indebted to Julia Tyler for the pleasure.

Pleasure was the key word at the White House during the eight months of Julia's reign. The mansion itself was rather dowdy when she took over, and her public relations man, F. W. Thomas, who had been recruited from the newsroom of *The New York Herald* to work with Margaret, her social secretary, wrote that it was "a disgrace to the nation. Many of the chairs in the East Room would be kicked out of a brothel." Congress had consistently refused funds to even keep the place clean, but as what seemed to be a kind of wedding present, it came forward with a $20,000 appropriation to buy new furnishings. It turned out to be an empty gesture, however, and the bill became bogged down in committee; some congressmen still weren't convinced that the man who lived in the house ought to be called president. Julia took the bull by the horns and prevailed on her mother to come up with the money to make her new stage set more presentable.

The president, meanwhile, concentrated on Julia's own appearance. He bought her an impressive Italian greyhound to add a touch of elegance when she went out for strolls, and he ordered a fancy coach pulled by six white Arabian horses to call attention to her when she rode about town.

It was fairly obvious that John wasn't going to win a second term, although Julia worked hard to change his destiny. After

"Almost everything in the polka depends upon the fascinating expression of countenance."

—Julia Tyler on her love of dance

Julia Tyler was the first president's wife to hire a press agent. Her husband, who considered it unseemly and unnecessary, never had one.

Letitia died, he had sold their old plantation and bought a bigger and better one, a 1,600-acre estate eighteen miles from Williamsburg that he called Sherwood Forest because he considered himself a political outlaw. He and Julia used it for quick getaways, and when retirement was forced on him, they moved there permanently.

In the meantime, Julia made the most of her life in Washington. She had developed a strong attraction for the rituals of the European courts she had visited, and she copied every elegant detail that appealed to her. A newspaper reported that she "is attended on reception days by twelve maids of honor, six on either side, dressed all alike.... Her serene loveliness received upon a raised platform wearing a headdress formed of bugles and resembling a crown." The First Lady, still in mourning for her father, was limited to wearing white, black, or purple, but it didn't dull her appearance a bit. Her headpieces always included a string of jet-black beads that featured a black stone at the center of her forehead. When the mourning period ended, she replaced the black beads with diamonds.

Julia broke with tradition by frequently accepting invitations to other

Some of the land that became John Tyler's Sherwood Forest plantation had once belonged to former president William Henry Harrison.

Washington parties, and she always took the twelve maids, who had become known as the "vestal virgins," along with her. Needless to say, they always arrived late to be sure that they would be noticed, although that was just a kind of insurance. Julia Tyler never had a problem making herself noticed.

In spite of the cynics who believed that it wasn't possible for a twenty-four-year-old woman to love a fifty-four-year-old man who wasn't her father, no one who saw them together had any doubts that it was entirely possible. Julia's mother was scandalized, in fact. "You spend so much time in kissing," she sniffed, "things of more importance are left undone." Julia ignored her mother's advice, and she and John went right on behaving like a couple of teenagers.

But it was quite true that Julia was an incurable and highly accomplished flirt, and she used the talent to help her husband with some of those things of more importance. Congressmen, cabinet members, and foreign dignitaries were all putty in her hands.

Julia Tyler loved attention, but she also loved her husband. She ordered the band to play "Hail to the Chief" whenever he arrived for a reception so that attention would be focused on him.

One of her critics said that she conducted her endless lobbying "partly in the bedrooms of men other than her husband," but Julia didn't have to. Her charms were open and completely public, and a bat of her eyelashes could accomplish every bit as much as lifting her skirts. Besides, her husband's bedroom was where the real power lay—hers, not his. Julia had more influence over John Tyler than any other person on earth.

She was especially interested, possibly for her own personal reasons, in securing a second term for the president, and she started off her marriage conspiring with her brother Alexander to build a power base for John in New York, a must-win state. She scrutinized every name on patronage lists, and she made recommendations on them to her husband, sometimes bypassing him to whisper her opinions in the ears of the appropriate cabinet members.

Julia also worked hard for causes that the president embraced, especially the question of the annexation of Texas. "At least fifty members of Congress paid their respects to me," she wrote, and each of them got the message that the president needed their support. When the issue came up for a vote in the House, she reappeared in the visitors gallery to remind the members of her desire. Then she invited herself to dinner with her old flame Supreme Court Justice John McLean, and wheedled him into issuing a public statement supporting the issue. One of her toughest challenges was with Secretary of State John Calhoun, who at the time hoped to delay the issue so that the next administration could take the credit, and had said of the First Lady's lobbying effort that "there is no honor in politics." During a White House dinner, she slipped him a note suggesting that he should offer a toast to "Texas and John Tyler." It must have pained him, but he nodded and said, "for your sake," before he raised his glass and did as he was told.

When all was said and done, the public was convinced that the Texas annexation wouldn't ever have been accomplished without Julia, and the president seemed to agree. After he signed the proclamation, he handed the gold pen to his wife, and she wore it on her necklace. There was no question that she had earned it. As for himself, John Tyler considered it the greatest accomplishment of his presidency.

His future had already been settled by then. James K. Polk had been elected to replace him, and their lease on the White House was about to expire. Less than two weeks before it did, the Tylers held a farewell ball that turned out to be the most memorable party that Julia, or any other First Lady for that matter, had ever staged. Two thousand invitations were sent out, and more than three thousand people showed up. In the jargon of the day, the crowd was "squeezy," even in the ample space of the White House. Eight cases of Champagne were consumed, the punch bowls refilled scores of times, and the flames of more than six hundred candles flickered merrily. Julia and her attendants waved seductively

Above: Julia introduced bright colors into women's wardrobes while she was First Lady. It brought her attention, and she enjoyed that.

to the crowd before she came down from her perch to lead the dancing in spite of the cramped space.

Julia was never lovelier. She was dressed in a silver-embroidered white dress under a white cape that was looped with white rosebuds. Her white satin headdress was also embroidered with silver, and it was topped by two ostrich feathers and festooned with diamonds. Her press agent gushed that she "looked like Juno ... which no Court of Europe could equal."

When the Tylers left the White House, Julia was only twenty-five years old. The first of her seven children was born the following year, and she settled down at Sherwood Forest in her new role as a typical Southern wife. But, of course, the word "typical" could never describe her—her own personal motto was, "The full extent or nothing." The president had remodeled the manor house and doubled its original size, but Julia went to work making it bigger and better, including adding a sixty-eight-foot ballroom, big enough to dance the Virginia reel, which they both adored as much as the waltz and the polka. Of course, she arranged big parties at the drop of a hat. It was a local tradition, and it was in Julia's blood. All of this was very expensive, far beyond John Tyler's means, but Julia had an inheritance to dip into, and her wealthy mother was always available whenever the need for more cash came up. The former president wasn't interested in the political jobs that were offered to him, although toward the end of his life he agreed to serve in the Confederate House of

Above: The facade of Sherwood Forest, the Tyler plantation near Charles City, Virginia.

Representatives when Virginia seceded from the Union the year before he died. He refused to run for the Senate because he believed that he wouldn't live long enough to finish the six-year term. He did his duty for Virginia, but not until after he had made an attempt to head off secession. He had served as chairman of a special peace conference, and pleaded with President Buchanan to hold the Union together.

Even though she was a New Yorker, Julia stood with her adopted South on the question of slavery. When British women published a plea for the women of the American South to help end slavery, Julia wrote an indignant letter to the magazine defending slavery as "a civilizing influence," and informed the British ladies that "our slaves live better than the poor of London." When war finally came, she encouraged her older sons to join the Confederate army.

Julia was forty-one when John died, and she stayed at Sherwood Forest until it was eventually commandeered by the Union army. She fled to New York, but her views made her a pariah there and she went back to try to sell the plantation, which of course wasn't possible. She was back in New York when her mother died in 1864, and she was left comfortable enough to send her children to school in Europe.

Julia went back to Washington many times, and on one occasion she co-hosted a White House reception alongside First Lady Lucy Hayes. Financially pinched after the Panic of 1873, she went back to lobbying Congress again, this time on her own behalf, and eventually she was granted a widow's pension of $1,200 a year, which was later increased to $5,000. First Lady Anna Harrison had been given a one-time payment in lieu of a permanent pension, but in Julia's case, and in the case of future First Ladies, it would be a recurring payment over the rest of her life. In her case, that would be eight more years. Julia died on July 10, 1889, at the age of sixty-nine.

Above: John's simple gravesite in Richmond, Virginia.

Julia Tyler died in the same Richmond hotel room where her husband had died twenty-seven years earlier.

Visiting Sherwood Forest

The James River plantation where John and Julia Tyler lived is still owned by members of the Tyler family, who live there, and it is still a working farm. The manor house, at over three hundred feet, is the longest frame house in America. It is furnished as it was when Julia decorated it. It was originally built in 1720, but the former president and his wife expanded and updated it to its present state. The house and grounds are open every day except Thanksgiving and Christmas Day from 9:00 A.M. to 5:00 P.M. The admission fee is $5.00.

The plantation is eighteen miles west of Williamsburg, Virginia, and thirty-five miles east of Richmond. From Richmond, follow Virginia Route 5, the John Tyler Memorial Highway. From Washington, D.C., use I-95 South to I-295 South, exit 22A, Route 5, Charles City. On I-64 East from Virginia Beach, use exit 242A (Jamestown) to Route 5 West.

Above: Southern comfort is the guiding principle in the rooms at the Tylers' Sherwood Forest.

Sarah Polk

Accomplished Politician

Sarah Polk, the incoming First Lady, turned down her invitation to Julia Tyler's blowout farewell party, claiming an "indisposition." But everybody in Washington was well aware that Sarah just wasn't disposed to dancing and drinking, and no one was fooled. Julia took it in stride without comment; she wasn't so sure that she even liked the new president and his wife, anyway. But the outgoing president couldn't help remarking to his wife, "Imagine the idea of her being able to follow you."

Mrs. Polk was quite able, thank you. But there was no question that there were going to be some changes made. The first clue came at President Polk's Inaugural Ball when the orchestra members started packing up their instruments as soon as Sarah arrived. She was a devout Presbyterian, and she didn't approve of dancing, especially at the White House, where she felt it was disrespectful to the dignity of the presidential mansion. She also shunned cardplaying, attending the theater, being seen at the horse races, or doing anything at all on Sundays except going to church. She also decreed that there would be no drinking—with the exception of wine served at dinners—allowed in *her* White House.

A very large number of Americans believed that Sarah was on the right track. Religious revivalism was sweeping the country at the time, and people were being "saved" by the score every night of the week by traveling preachers who had ridden into their towns to wrestle with the devil for their souls. Even James Polk, who had walked away from religion early in his life, was moved by one of them to take up the cross, although he managed to resist the impulse after a few days. It was Sarah who eventually made a churchgoer out of him.

When they first went to Washington after James became a congressman, she accepted every party invitation that came their way—yes, Sarah loved a good party—and James, who wasn't the sociable type at all, asked her to stop wasting so much of their time. She agreed to cut back, but only on the condition that he would go to church with her every Sunday. From then on, he was seen at the Presbyterian church more often than many of the regular parishioners, and he was often

---

Sarah Childress Polk

Born
September 4, 1803,
Murfreesboro, Tennessee

Parents
Joel Childress and
Elizabeth Whitsett
Childress

Marriage
January 1, 1824, to James
K. Polk (1795-1849)

Children
None

Died
August 4, 1891,
Nashville, Tennessee

Below: Outdoor revival meetings introduced thousands to Christian fundamentalism in Sarah's day.

seen a two or three different churches on the same Sabbath day, although he refused to become a member of any of them.

If worldly pleasures were off-limits to Sarah Polk, the world of fashion fascinated her, and from the time she and her sister Susan were little girls back in Tennessee, they always wore satins, silks, and velvets stitched together by the finest dressmakers in the region. "We never knew," she said, "what it was to be simply clothed."

*Like Julia Tyler, Sarah Polk went to the White House
with a substantial family fortune to support her.*

Her sense of style had become honed to an art form by the time she reached Washington, and long before she became First Lady fourteen years later, she was highly regarded as one of the most elegantly dressed women in town.

To say that Sarah's girlhood was a privileged one would probably be an understatement. Her father, Joel Childress, moved to the Tennessee wilderness from Virginia in his early twenties, and before he was thirty he had become a wealthy planter and owned more land than any other landowner in the region. He also established a tavern and a general store in the center of Murfreesboro, and he was a confidant of every important person in the territory. Sarah was their third child; her mother, Elizabeth, had already given birth to a son they named Anderson and a daughter named Susan. Another son, John, was born a short time afterward.

*Below: Sarah was about twenty-five
years old when this portrait was made,
not long after she was married to the
young lawyer James K. Polk.*

Joel Childress wanted nothing but the very best for his four children, and he could afford to give it to them. There was no question that his sons would be well educated, but their father took the radical view that his daughters ought to be as well. When they finished their education at the town's public school, he prevailed on the headmaster of the private local boys academy to give the girls special classes after the regular school day ended. After they graduated from the academy, they were sent to Nashville to board with family friends and attend Mr. Abercrombie's School for Young Ladies. Sarah was fourteen by the time she had learned all the social skills Mr. Abercrombie could teach her, and she and Susan went on to Salem, North Carolina, to continue their studies at the Moravian Female Academy, which was considered the very best girls school in the South. Their father died in 1819, a year afterward, and the sisters were called home to Murfreesboro, which they both believed was far beneath their educational achievements.

But the town had changed a great deal while they were gone. It was a contender to become the capital of Tennessee, and the legislature was already meeting there in its courthouse. James Polk, a young lawyer and a friend of

Sarah was usually called Sally by her family and close friends.

Sarah's brother, was serving as chief clerk of the state senate, and it didn't take long for him and Sarah to become interested in each other when their paths crossed at parties and receptions. But James had strong political ambitions, and he didn't have much time for Sarah; and he had no plans to get married, either. That changed the day he asked his mentor, Andrew Jackson, for advice on how to climb the political ladder. "Stop dilly-dallying," General Jackson recommended, "and get married." When James suggested that he might want to marry Sarah Childress, Jackson grabbed him by the shoulders and pointed him in her direction. He knew the Childress family well, he said, and he couldn't imagine a better choice.

Above: President James Knox Polk.

Sarah wasn't so sure, when it came right down to it, that she herself might not have some better choices. The town was full of eligible young men. James's father was a planter like her own father had been, but he wasn't nearly as prosperous, and James almost never went to church, a black mark against him if ever there was one. Still, in spite of those things, Sarah loved James. They had so much in common: an almost unnatural belief in themselves, along with dogged determination and uncommon intelligence. So her answer in response to his marriage proposal added up to a "yes," but Sarah made it a conditional one. His salary on the senate staff was only $6 a day, and although he was qualified to hang his shingle as a lawyer, it was obvious he was dreaming of a career in politics and didn't have time for that. Sarah accepted his proposal, but she told him that she wouldn't set a wedding date until he proved that he could support her.

He had no choice but to announce his candidacy for the state House of Representatives. The campaign lasted all summer, and nobody was taking any bets that he'd win—except Sarah and her mother, who spent the time planning her wedding. It was a close election, but James won, and Sarah named the date. The wedding was set for New Year's Day, 1824, three months after the bridegroom took his seat in the legislature. Among the wedding guests were several of his new colleagues, including Colonel David Crockett.

> "That girl is wealthy, pretty, ambitious, and intelligent."
> —Andrew Jackson on Sarah Polk

The wedding itself took place at the Childress plantation after a memorable seven-course dinner, and the round of parties lasted for five days before the bride and groom finally went off to his hometown, Columbia, Tennessee, to meet the Polk family. According to custom, the Polks had not gone to the wedding, but waited patiently for the newlyweds to come to them. It was the first time Sarah met any of her in-laws, but she won them over almost instantly. She brightened any social situation like a shooting star, and the Polk family was completely captivated by her almost as soon as she walked through their door.

Their next stop was the two-room cottage James had rented near the new Capitol in Nashville. It was a far cry from the huge plantation house he had taken her away from, but Sarah was delighted with it. She had a great many

Above: James was at home in the halls of the state legislature, but like most Tennesseans he was also in his element on long hunting trips.

talents, but an aptitude for housework wasn't one of them, and freed from the routines of dusting and scrubbing, she would have the time to watch legislative sessions over at the capitol every day. Sarah loved political debates, and she also loved Representative Polk, who was developing into one of the best debaters in the state of Tennessee.

James and Sarah quickly became the toast of Nashville. She was bright and beautiful at the age of twenty, and he, at twenty-eight, was highly regarded as a rising star. His friendship with Andrew Jackson didn't hurt at all, and when the general ran for president in 1824, James Polk was on the Democratic ticket as a candidate for Congress. Both of them lost that year, but James tried again in the next election and he won a seat in Congress by a narrow margin.

Sarah had an opinion about everything, but when she shared them, she always began by saying, "Mr. Polk believes... "

No one was happier, or more proud, than his wife, Sarah. And it was obvious to her that Jackson was going to be president one day, and soon, and that James would likely be in Washington to share in his reflected glory. Where that might lead, she couldn't say, but she surely could dream.

His election to Congress meant that they would be parted frequently, but Sarah had the Polk family for company, and there were dozens of them eager to provide it. Each of James's nine brothers and sisters had a large number of children, and although Sarah hadn't provided them with any cousins, all of them thought of her as their second mother. Sarah became especially close to her mother-in-law, Jane Polk, largely because of the religious fervor they shared, and they visited one another almost every week. And she visited her own mother as often as she could, even though her Murfreesboro plantation was sixty miles away over dusty dirt roads.

Washington was even farther away, and the roads no better, and James decided to make his first trip there without Sarah at his side. While he was gone, she wrote to him every day. Her letters were always long ones, filled with the tiniest details of what was going on in his congressional district, and what his constituents were concerned about. She enjoyed the partnership, but she longed to experience the excitement of Washington for herself, and when her husband went back the following year, he bought a stagecoach so that she could go along. Most congressmen made the trip on horseback, and another member

"Mrs. Polk early learned to be silent where anything was at stake."

—*James K. Polk on Sarah*

> "The Speaker, if the proper person, and with the correct idea of his position, has even more influence over legislation and in directing the policy of Parties, than the President or any other public officer."
>
> —Sarah Polk on politics

of the Tennessee congressional delegation, Sam Houston, was pleased to accept their offer to share the coach with them.

Like most other married members of Congress, the Polks moved into a boardinghouse that catered to couples, and once again Sarah escaped the drudgery of housework. That made it possible for her to spend her days watching congressional debates, which were much more stimulating than the ones back in Nashville. Her release from domestic chores also gave her plenty of time to live the life of a congressman's wife to the fullest. She never turned down an invitation to a ball, a dinner, or a reception, and her charming personality propelled her to the top of everyone's A-list.

Because of her frequent visits to the House visitors gallery, Sarah was unusually well versed on both sides of every issue, and the men she met at social affairs were overwhelmed by her knowledge, even if the other women weren't. More often than not, when a reception reached the point where the women retired to gossip and the men stayed behind to talk politics, Sarah stayed with the men, even if the cigar smoke offended her, and occasionally she dominated the discussions.

During those years, she took on the job of James's private secretary, and she was as busy as he was. When putting out political fires or campaigning took him away from Washington, she stayed behind to keep an eye on his interests. She devoured every newspaper and mailed news items and editorials to him, along with letters explaining why she thought they were important to him. Much more than his private secretary, Sarah was her husband's political advisor, and he always completely trusted what she had to say.

Many Washington wives criticized Sarah for her strong political opinions, which women weren't supposed to have, and that separated her from many of them. But James encouraged her interest, and whenever it was possible, he invited her to attend meetings with him, even if she would be the only woman there. "He always wished me to go," she wrote, "and he would say, 'Why should you stay at home? To take care of the house? Why, if the house burns down we can live without it!' "

James and Sarah spent fourteen years in Washington, and during that time, under the patronage of President Jackson, he became Speaker of the House. It put the Polks near the top of Washington society, and although James wasn't impressed, Sarah was completely in her element.

Below: First Couple James and Sarah were among the first to sit for a photograph.

> "[Conduct yourself] with a fair and just interpretation [of the Bible].... Greater worth and wisdom will be expected...you will have to be more than human, the presidency is no idle thing...commence it now in the multitude of counsel."
>
> —A fellow Christian's advice to James Polk

Then he decided not to run for Congress again, opting instead to run for governor of Tennessee. For Sarah, it meant leaving behind a circle of close friends that included the best-educated, most interesting women in Washington. For James, it meant his best shot at going back to Washington was as president some day.

Washington was sorry to see Sarah go. A Supreme Court justice who said that he would miss this "gentle graceful" woman, wrote a poem in tribute to her "playful mind." Other similar tributes were read at the round of parties that were held in Sarah's honor.

Nashville would pale by comparison, but Sarah made the best of it, especially as the hostess of rallies, picnics, and parties during the summer-long election campaign. James won the governorship in 1839, but he served only a single term. He ran again in both 1841 and 1843, but a backlash against Andrew Jackson and the Democrats gave both elections to Whig candidates, not only in Tennessee but around the country as well.

The Polks had been married for seventeen years by then, and for the first time they were out of politics. He established a law practice in Columbia, and he managed his family's plantation, which had expanded and become much more profitable. For her part, Sarah trawled the newspapers and kept her ears open at public gatherings, listening for a change in the political climate.

Change came in 1844 when the dying Whig party refused to renominate John Tyler to succeed himself as president. Instead, they trotted out their old warhorse, Henry Clay, to lead them. The Democrats saw it as an opportunity, but they couldn't agree on the right man to pull it off. Their nominating convention became almost hopelessly deadlocked, and it wasn't until after ten ballots had been taken that James Polk emerged as America's first "dark horse" candidate. But he hadn't come out of nowhere— James had worked long and hard for the honor, and Sarah had, too.

Still, no one was more surprised than the candidate and his wife that they might be on their way to the White House. The Whig campaign centered on the slogan "Who is James Polk?" but it wasn't a hard question to answer. If memories were short, every newspaper in the country had thick files on him, and most had more than routine campaign biographies on Sarah. Her name came up often as a reason to vote for Clay, and the negative comments usually concentrated on two issues that might

Below: James was welcomed back from obscurity when the Democrats chose him to run against Henry Clay for the presidency in 1844. Street rallies sometimes brought supporters of both men to the same corner.

turn women against her: that she had no children, and that she was a less than careful housekeeper. It didn't seem to matter that women couldn't vote anyway. One of the most often repeated statements was that Mrs. Clay's house was immaculate and that she churned her own butter, to which Sarah sniffed, "If I get to the White House, I expect to live on $25,000 a year and I will neither keep house nor make butter."

Above: The new president gave his wife this fan with the images of the first eleven chief executives.

Partners in the Presidency

The folks back home in Tennessee were not only delighted at James's victory, even if it had been close, but pleased that one of their own would be First Lady. Needless to say, none of them was as pleased as Sarah. She rode to the inauguration carrying a fan decorated with portraits of all the previous presidents, a gift from her husband that she treasured for the rest of her life.

James wasn't the most popular of presidents, and his doggedness about handling tough issues like continental expansion kept him engrossed in his work and generally out of sight. When he did appear in public, he appeared to be a humorless man, and Sarah worked hard to brush up his image with her own personal charm. She insisted, no matter how busy he might be, that he should put in an appearance at all of her White House receptions. And although she had banned music at her parties, she made an exception by bringing in the marine band to play "Hail to the Chief" whenever he walked into the room. Otherwise, she thought, nobody would notice him. She may have been right.

Most people who arrived for White House receptions brushed past the president after a quick handshake to get on to what they considered the main event, a nod from the First Lady. James didn't mind at all. It was where he wanted to be, too.

Sarah greeted her guests dressed in the fashion of the day, full floor-length skirts supported by hoops that made them billow. Her dresses were trimmed with fancy ruffles with puckered shirring on the sleeves and bodices—think Scarlett O'Hara. Bright colors, even plaids and checks, were all the rage in the 1840s, but Sarah preferred dark blue or purple velvet, although she often wore red or maroon to complement her coloring.

Sarah was an attractive women, but she wasn't usually described as beautiful, although "handsome" was a frequently used description of her.

Below: The official portrait of Sarah Polk, the eleventh First Lady of the United States.

Sarah changed the character of White House receptions by opening them to ordinary people so that she and her husband could keep in touch with public opinion.

Above: The Polk's White House dinner service was made in Paris by Edouard Honore. The president's insignia is on the green border.

She was relatively tall, with black hair parted in the middle and cascading in ringlets along the sides of her oval face. She had prominent teeth, which she disguised by tightening her lips, and that made her appear disapproving, but she also had a dazzling smile that would light up the room whenever anyone asked for her opinion on a political issue. Her complexion was described as "sallow," which led many to call her "Sahara Sarah," but others referred to her as the "Spanish Madonna."

Even as First Lady, Sarah continued in her role of private secretary to her husband, which gave her uncommon insight on the issues he was facing. To give those issues an airing, she invited policymakers to the White House for a casual dinner every week, and while policy and politics had previously been forbidden topics for presidential dinner guests, Sarah insisted on bringing them out into the open in the relaxed setting. Her White House entertainment was never planned just for the fun of it, but always to advance the president's goals. She took her job seriously, but she handled it in a gracious way that hid her real intentions. One surprised admirer said that she "had a great deal of spice."

Because of Sarah's religious scruples, almost no one would have described her parties as "spicy." But those same scruples gave her an image of integrity and honesty, and after the unbridled gaiety of the previous First Lady, Washington society was ready for a rest. Indeed, Sarah was more popular with the public than Julia Tyler had been.

One thing that added to Sarah's popularity was her frugality. Few remembered that the Tylers had run the White House with their own money, but they were impressed at Sarah's efforts to save the public's money. When Congress finally appropriated funds to refurbish the White House, she carefully saved half of it, although she spent the other half admirably well. Among her improvements was the installation of gaslights throughout the mansion, but acting on a romantic impulse, she left the East Room to be lit with old-fashioned candles. She and her guests were glad she did when the gas failed after

While Sarah served as the president's personal secretary, one of his relatives, Mrs. Knox Walker, served as her social secretary.

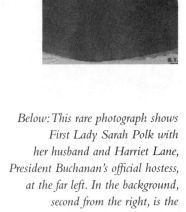

it was turned on during her first reception, which was staged to show off the modern lighting.

Some people thought that it was unseemly for a First Lady to be so deeply involved in the inner workings of the presidency, but Sarah said that she did it because she had to keep an eagle eye on her husband's schedule out of her concern for his health. James had never been robust, but from the earliest days of their marriage, Sarah harbored a constant fear that his obsession with hard work was going to kill him. His years in the White House may well have. He was completely exhausted, and Sarah breathed a sign of relief when he announced that he wouldn't run for a second term.

In anticipation of their retirement, the Polks bought a house in Nashville that they called Polk Place. Sarah took on the job of furnishing it, even taking a trip to New York, one of her rare absences from Washington, to buy the things she needed to turn it into a showplace. She had been ecstatically happy in her role as First Lady, but she was eager to finally have some peace and quiet and the role of retired First Lady.

As for James, he was even more eager. "I am heartily rejoiced that my term is so near to a close," he wrote. "I will soon cease to be a servant and will become a sovereign. As a private citizen, I will have no one but myself to serve.... I am sure I will be happier in this condition than in the exalted one I now hold." He would only have three months to enjoy it.

Below: This rare photograph shows First Lady Sarah Polk with her husband and Harriet Lane, President Buchanan's official hostess, at the far left. In the background, second from the right, is the ubiquitous Dolley Madison.

Above: Sarah bought this chandelier, one of a pair, for Polk Place from A. T. Stewart's New York department store for $54.

When he and Sarah left the White House, their journey back to Nashville was planned as a grand farewell to the people. There were celebrations in every city they passed through, and by the time the weakened former president arrived in New Orleans, he collapsed with a fever and never recovered from it. He died at Polk Place on June 15, 1849. The new president, Zachary Taylor, had been in office for only a few months.

Widowhood

Sarah lived on at Polk Place for forty-two years after her husband died. She went into deep mourning during the first few years, wearing nothing but black and never leaving the house except to go to church on Sundays. She received occasional visitors, mostly family members, and always met with them in James's study, which she had carefully not changed. His papers were where he left them, and his personal effects were where he had decided they should be.

Sarah tried to recover her former sociable disposition, but her grief always got in the way, and most of her friends reached the conclusion that she would be in mourning for the rest of her life.

> *"None but Sarah knew so intimately my private affairs.... She was politician, counselor, nurse, and emotional resource."*
>
> —James K. Polk on Sarah

But that wouldn't be Sarah. Little by little, she invited friends and family to visit her, and Polk Place began to brighten up. When her grandniece Sarah Polk Jetton was orphaned, Sarah invited the girl to come live with her as the daughter she never had, and when young Sarah grew up and was married, her husband was invited into the widow's household as well. Before much longer the house was filled with children, and Sarah Polk was happy again.

People who had known her in Washington began calling on her in Nashville, and many of her fellow Tennesseeans did, too. It gave her a chance to do what she enjoyed most—entertaining—and everybody who came to visit was given a warm welcome. The entire Tennessee legislature came calling on New Year's Days, and as had been customary back at the White House, the doors of Polk Place were opened wide to anyone else who cared to pay their respects. Hundreds did. Whenever a parade was planned in Nashville, the route was always arranged so that it would pass Sarah's house, and every marching unit paused there so that she could wave to them from her window.

When the Civil War came to Nashville, families were divided in their loyalties, but both the Polks and the Childresses were strong supporters of the Confederacy. The former president had been a slave owner, but he had also been strongly opposed to the idea of secession, and that left Sarah divided within herself. She announced that she regarded Polk Place as neutral territory, and to everyone's surprise, including Sarah's, the generals on both sides agreed that it should be. Sarah welcomed troops from both sides into her home, and she even sipped tea with the despised Union general William Tecumseh Sherman when he passed through town.

Like many women of the South, Sarah was left destitute by the war. Her family's plantation had been overrun, and she had no other source of income until Congress awarded a widow's pension to her and to other former First Ladies almost twenty years after the war ended. She died ten years after that, on August 14, 1891, a few weeks before her eightieth birthday.

Visiting the Polk Home

Nashville's Polk Place, where Sarah spent the last four decades of her life, was torn down in 1901. The only remaining home of her husband, except for the White House, is the one built by his father, Samuel Polk, in Columbia, Tennessee, in 1816. The future president lived there from the time he graduated from the University of North Carolina until he married Sarah Childress. The Federal-style house contains furniture, paintings, china, and other objects that Sarah collected for their other homes. It is open Monday through Saturday from April through October, from 9:00 A.M. to 5:00 P.M.; and from November through March until 4:00 P.M. It is open every Sunday from 1:00 P.M. to 5:00 P.M. A small admission fee is charged for both children and adults. The house is in downtown Columbia, off U.S. Route 31, a few miles south of Nashville.

Below: Polk Place was intended to be the president's retirement home, but he died before he could enjoy it. It became Sarah's last home.

Margaret Taylor

Woman of Mystery

Like the presidents themselves, America's First Ladies don't often appear to have a lot in common with one another except that as long they are in Washington, they are topic one of conversations among their temporary neighbors. The buzz about presidential wives frequently runs to gossip, and though it is usually confined to capital insiders, every now and then, wild tales about a First Lady become a national obsession.

This happened when Zachary Taylor became president and his wife, Margaret (Peggy), vanished into the upper reaches of the White House—some said into the attic. She had her reasons, her defenders claimed, but they couldn't agree on what those reasons might be.

The president was a popular hero of the recent Mexican War, and he had put his life on the line time after time serving his country. His wife, who was never far behind the front lines herself during his military career, became worried that he was going to stop an enemy bullet, and, as the story goes, she made a promise to God that if he survived, she would completely remove herself from any kind of social activity and give her husband the quiet retirement that he had earned.

She kept that promise when Zachary retired to a seven-room cottage they owned at Baton Rouge, Louisiana, on the site of the present-day state capitol. It was very much off the beaten path in those days, and that was the point. The general was as interested in avoiding the obligations of society as his wife, Peggy, was, even if it wasn't the result of his own sacred promise. If the Taylors were out of sight, though, they weren't out of the minds of political movers and shakers who believed that the man everybody called "Old Rough and Ready" was surefire presidential timber. He repeatedly said that he thought political parties were an abomination, but he kept the door open to run as the "people's candidate." For her part, Peggy slammed the door shut as forcefully as she could. She said that the whole idea of making him president was a conspiracy to cut his life short and deprive her of her husband. It was at that point, the gossips claimed, that she put her foot down and decided that if her family should suffer the misfortune of occupying the White House, she would have no part of it herself.

With two perfectly clear and plausible reasons why the First Lady was almost never seen—nor had she fulfilled what her Washington neighbors

---

Margaret Mackall Smith Taylor

Born
September 21, 1788, Calvert County, Maryland

Parents
Walter Smith and Ann Mackall Smith

Marriage
June 21, 1810, to Zachary Taylor (1784-1850)

Children
Ann Margaret Mackall (1811-75); Sarah Knox (1814- 35); Octavia Pannel (1816-20); Margaret Smith (1819-20); Mary Elizabeth (Betty) (1824-1909); Richard (1826-79)

Died
August 14, 1852, East Pascagoula, Mississippi

Above: General Zachary Taylor became a hero of the Mexican War at the Battle of Buena Vista.

Below: Peggy enjoyed smoking a pipe. In the 1840s, many ladies did the same thing.

The only special preparation Peggy made for their move to the White House was ordering her husband to buy a new suit. He did as he was told, but he bought one a size too large— for comfort, and possibly to show her who was boss.

considered her duties—the wagging tongues came up with a couple of others. As they had done with Rachel Jackson, the rumormongers painted Peggy Taylor as a boorish backwoods type of woman who was an embarrassment to her family. She was addicted to the undignified habit of pipe smoking, they said; she was illiterate, unable to put her thoughts into anything resembling a cultured conversation; and she was a slightly mad recluse. Not a bit of this was true, but the stories were repeated over and over again anyway.

The fact was that Margaret Taylor was as cultured as most Washington women of the time, and more so than many of them. It was true that she had spent most of her adult life on army posts spread across the frontier, but as the wife of an officer, she lived a relatively comfortable life everywhere he was assigned, and she made sure that her children were well educated. She herself had been educated on her father's Maryland plantation just as other upper-class daughters of the South were. Her father was a wealthy planter and a Revolutionary War veteran, and her mother a prominent heiress. Young Peggy not only learned how to read and write, but she was exposed to classical literature and she learned the basics of business management. She was also well drilled in the social skills that had become the basic requirement of a First Lady. The decision not to use these skills was her own choice and not something that was forced on her out of fear that she wasn't up to the job. The few who actually met Mrs. Taylor remembered her as a genteel woman with a kindly manner.

When she was twenty-one, Peggy Smith went to Louisville, Kentucky, for an extended visit with her older sister, and it was there that she met Zachary Taylor, the son of her sister's neighbor. He had joined the army in 1807, anticipating a war with Great Britain, and thanks to his family connections, he had joined up as a first lieutenant. It was the only time in his career that merit had little to do with his rank. He had just come back from a nearly year-long assignment in New Orleans, where disease and fatigue had killed 686 of the two-thousand-man garrison, but Peggy didn't let that stand in the way of her

Peggy Taylor was probably the only First Lady who was a crack pistol shot. She honed the skill on the frontier, and if she hadn't, she might not have lived to become First Lady.

Zachary's trip to Washington to accept the presidency
was a kind of triumphal tour. His wife took
a different route to avoid the celebrations.

Above: Peggy's calling
card was as elegant as many
people wrongly thought she was not.

decision to accept his proposal when he asked her to marry him the following year.

Zachary and Peggy were married at her sister's home on June 10, 1810, and began their life together on a nearby farm that her father-in-law gave to them as a wedding present. They wouldn't stay there long. Zachary had been promoted to captain by then, and there was a war to be fought. He left his wife behind when he went to bring order to the troops at Fort Knox, Kentucky, but a year later when he was put in command of Fort Harrison in Indiana, she was at his side, and nearly everywhere he went after that, Peggy went, too. Their lives were in constant danger at Fort Harrison, not only from hostile Indians, but from a fever that weakened all of them. Captain Taylor saved the fort and the troops, as well as the women and the children inside—including his own first daughter, Ann—from an Indian raid, and he was promoted to major on the spot. The exploit also gave him widespread publicity, and Zachary Taylor became one of the most celebrated heroes of the War of 1812.

In spite of the promotion, he was angry that others had risen through the ranks faster. As the army was drawn down at the end of the war, Zachary was reduced to captain again, and he answered the insult with his resignation. He took Peggy and the baby back to the farm, where their second daughter, Sarah Knox, was born (she would always be known to the family as "Knox"), but he wasn't happy commanding slaves in his tobacco fields rather than soldiers, and when he was offered a restoration of his major's rank, the family was off again. They moved from one frontier post to another, building roads and fortifications. By 1819, after their family had grown with the births of two more daughters, Octavia and Margaret, Zachary was given the

Below: Fort Harrison in Indiana was
the first home the Taylors knew. They
lived in such military outposts during
most of their married life.

There are no pictures of Margaret Taylor known to exist, but there are
several artists' renderings of what she might have looked like, based on
pictures of her daughters who it were said to resemble her.

rank of lieutenant colonel, an especially significant honor at a time when many other officers were being either demoted or discharged.

Both Octavia and Margaret died the following year from a fever that swept through the post, and Peggy came close to death herself. For a few years afterward, the family moved to the healthier surroundings of a plantation Zachary bought a few miles north of Baton Rouge, Louisiana, but eventually they traveled north again when he assumed command of various forts in the upper Mississippi region. He became a hero in the Black Hawk Indian War, but he was appalled at the way White settlers rushed in to appropriate Indian lands. With Peggy's help, he built and ran a school for Winnebago Indian children, and constantly railed against the government's policies toward the Native Americans. The gesture made him popular among the Indians, if not with officials back in Washington, but he was also highly regarded among the ordinary soldiers whom the Indians regarded as their enemy. Zachary was a relaxed commander with little patience for protocol, and what little he might have lacked in personal charm, his wife and his daughters more than made up for. It became a Zachary Taylor trademark that his men would follow him anywhere, and they always stood their ground in battles no matter what the odds against them might have been.

Above: These children on the Winnebago Reservation might well have attended the school Peggy ran there.

A Twist of Fate

Twenty-seven years after Sarah Knox Taylor married Jefferson Davis, he became president of the Confederate States of America. Had she lived, Sarah would have been the First Lady of the Confederacy. That honor went to President Davis's second wife, the former Varina Howell, a Mississippi plantation owner whom he married in 1845. At the time he wedded Sarah, Davis had retired from the army, which pleased his new father-in-law. He reenlisted during the Mexican War and served under General Taylor with a distinction that pleased the old man even more.

Left: Confederate President Jefferson Davis was once married to Peggy's daughter Sarah; she died before his political career began.

His own experience as a military man turned him completely against any idea that one of his daughters might marry a soldier. But they lived their lives on military posts, and it was inevitable that one would. Zachary flew into a rage when his eighteen-year-old daughter, Knox, announced that she intended to marry Lieutenant Jefferson Davis, a dashing young Mississippian. The lieutenant was a West Point graduate, and on a track to become a career soldier, and so Zachary decided it would be best to get him out of the way and ordered his transfer to a post a few hundred miles away.

Of course, the axiom "out of sight, out of mind" is often trumped by the one that says "absence makes the heart grow fonder," and after a two-year separation, love won out and Knox's father finally gave his consent, although a grudging one, for her to marry the officer. But he let his daughter know in no uncertain terms that he didn't approve. He had never liked Jefferson Davis the man, and he hated the idea that she would have to endure the hardships that came with being a soldier's wife.

His own wife knew from hard experience what that life was going to be like, but she was very much in favor of the match. She worked hard putting a trousseau together, and twisting her husband's arm to come up with a "liberal supply of money." Then mother and daughter left for Kentucky, where the wedding was held in the same house where the Taylors themselves had been married. Tragedy struck when, within a few weeks of their wedding, Knox contracted malaria at her new husband's Mississippi plantation and she died.

The Taylors were transferred to Florida next, where Zachary was promoted to brigadier general and took command of the war against the Seminoles. Peggy went along, of course, and she built an enviable reputation among the other military wives for her work in field hospitals and for her ability to improve the morale of the troops. It was during this time that the Taylors bought what they called their "Spanish cottage" in Louisiana. It was the first real home Peggy had in her thirty years of married life, and she lavished all of her time on decorating it. It was also where she would stay when her husband went off to Texas to fight in the Mexican War, and where they enjoyed his all too brief retirement.

In his extended leave after he came home from the Seminole War, Zachary took the family on a tour that ranged as far north as Niagara Falls and east to Boston, where he left his thirteen-year-old son, Richard, in the care of a tutor who would prepare him to enter Harvard. The preparation took the boy to Europe, where he spent three years studying the classics at Edinburgh and another year of study in Paris. When he came home, he enrolled at Yale rather than Harvard, and he was accepted there as a junior.

General Taylor had put a strong emphasis on his only son's education because the last thing in the world he wanted to see was Richard in a uniform. He didn't get his wish. Richard managed his father's plantations after he graduated from Yale, and in the 1850s he served in the Louisiana state senate, eventually becoming a colonel in the Ninth Louisiana Volunteers at the outbreak of the Civil War, arriving just in time to serve in the First Battle of Manassas.

Richard fought with distinction in dozens of battles, often at the side of General "Stonewall" Jackson, and by time the war came to an end, he had been promoted to lieutenant general and commanded the Departments of Louisiana, Mississippi, and Alabama. When the war ended, he went back to Europe, where he stayed for nearly twenty years.

All the Taylor children received a first-rate education; the girls matriculated at convent schools. Elizabeth (Betty) was sent to Philadelphia for her schooling, and it was there that she acquired the social skills that made her a perfect choice to substitute for her mother to fulfill the duties of First Lady. Like her sister, she had gone against her father's wishes at the age of nineteen by marrying William W. W. Bliss, her father's military aide for many years, who eventually became

Above: (Top, bottom): The Taylors' son, Richard Taylor; son-in-law William Bliss (with the President).

Above: Betty Bliss, the Taylor White House hostess.

the president's private secretary. Although he was still dead-set against military matchups, Zachary pronounced their marriage "perfect bliss."

The Taylors' oldest daughter, Ann, married a civilian, a doctor named Robert C. Wood. They had four children, who frequently visited the White House from their home in nearby Baltimore, much to the delight of their grandparents. There were many other family members living close to Washington, and following the long-standing Southern tradition, they visited the First Family often and frequently stayed for long periods. Even though Peggy had turned the official role of hostess over to her daughter, Betty Bliss, she was unquestionably the head of the private household, and she graciously received family and personal friends upstairs. She had redecorated her sitting room to resemble her beloved Spanish cottage, and she had brought fifteen slaves from one of the family plantations to serve as her personal servants, completely separate from the ones who served in the public rooms of the White House.

Quite likely, the president was happiest of all. After having spent so much of his life far away from those friends and family members, thanks to his wife Zachary now had a real home, even if it did happen to be the White House. Peggy did appear at his side once in a while when protocol demanded it, and she went out every Sunday to worship at St. John's Episcopal Church, as have a host of other First Ladies. But she was a phantom presence in the official Taylor White House, and it was her choice that it remained that way.

Other First Ladies who shunned the limelight usually had poor health as an excuse. But while Peggy Taylor had her ups and downs, she was generally in very good health, probably the result of the rigors her body had become accustomed to while living in remote military outposts. In this First Family's case, it was the president whose health failed. During the hot summer of 1850, Zachary Taylor became overheated during an outdoor Fourth of July celebration and cooled down too fast by overeating. He was dead five days later.

Peggy was beside herself with grief, and had to be dragged away from his body. She felt for a pulse and leaned close to look for signs of breathing. It was inconceivable to her that her husband was dead. He wouldn't leave without speaking to her, she said. During the funeral ceremony, she trembled violently, still not able to accept what had happened to her family. During her moments of grief, the gossip mills cranked up again and a rumor was started that she had poisoned him. She left the White House under that cloud, and the gossip persisted until nearly a century and a half later when his body was exhumed and an autopsy confirmed that he had died a natural death from a form of cholera.

> *"[Mrs. Bliss] blends the artlessness of a rustic belle and the grace of a duchess."*
>
> —*A White House guest on Betty Bliss's style of entertaining*

Peggy Taylor didn't go back to her Spanish cottage in Louisiana as she had hoped, but rather went to live at Betty Bliss's plantation in East Pascagoula, Mississippi. She died there a few weeks short of her sixty-fourth birthday, on August 14, 1852. She died of unknown causes, but it was very likely a broken heart. Her husband had died two years before her, and never once during that time did she even mention the White House again except to relive the events of his death, which she was still convinced was the result of a conspiracy.

The Footsteps of Zachary and Margaret Taylor

The Taylors had many, many addresses besides the White House during their life together, but none of them has been turned into a shrine to them. The house where they were married and lived for a time, at 5608 Apache Road in Louisville, Kentucky, had been sold even before their White House years, and it has changed owners dozens of times since. One of those owners began to restore it to its original appearance in the 1970s, but a tornado set the work back and it wasn't restarted for several more years, when the current owners began accumulating some of the original furnishings. The house is not open to the public, although the current owners sometimes open their doors for special events and special tours.

Right: The Taylor house in Kentucky.

Abigail Fillmore

Career Woman

When Abigail Fillmore arrived at the White House after her husband, Millard, became president, she discovered to her complete amazement that there were no books there—not even a Bible. She was even more surprised when Congress turned down her request to establish a library in the mansion because of a fear that it might be a threat to congressional power. They didn't want the executive branch to compete with their own Library of Congress.

The nub of the problem was that President Fillmore was a Whig faced with the daunting job of dealing with a Democratic Congress. The Whig party was badly split internally, leaving the president all but toothless, and the Democrats were in a rush to deal with new territory that had been added to the country since the Mexican War. The issue of slavery was very much on everybody's mind, too, and although Millard signed the Fugitive Slave Law, it was obvious that it was all he was going to do to satisfy the Southern bloc. He was a Northerner after all, and he had been put on the ticket in the 1848 election as a counterbalance to the slave-owning Zachary Taylor. The sword cut both ways, and Millard Fillmore wasn't likely to get any favors from a Congress dominated by Southerners.

The issue of a White House library had nothing to do with any of that. It wasn't even the president's idea; it was his wife who was pushing for it. She prevailed on George Stempleman of the Library of Congress to advise her, and he responded with an offer of congressional documents that he thought he might be able to transfer over to what he believed should be called the "Library of the President of the United States." He followed it up with an opinion that, "as there may be some other books that the President may select, it may be well to say that $2,500 will get a very useful reference library for the President's House."

Within days, John Houston, a Whig congressman, offered a resolution to form a committee that would decide whether it might be a good idea to furnish the White House with a complete set of documents from both houses of Congress. His action also suggested that the committee ought to be formed to explore the very idea of establishing a White House library in the first place.

The issue quickly became a political football. A few Democratic congressmen objected strenuously, and Houston's resolution was rejected out of hand. But he didn't give up. On the theory that the suggested price tag was too steep, he resubmitted his proposal with an amendment that called

Abigail Powers Fillmore

Born
March 13, 1798, Saratoga County, New York

Parents
Reverend Lemuel Powers and Abigail Newland Powers

Marriage
February 5, 1826, to Millard Fillmore (1800-74)

Children
Millard Powers (1828-89); Mary Abigail (1832-54)

Died
March 30, 1853, Washington, D.C.

for a $500 appropriation to make it possible. He told his colleagues that until Abigail Fillmore had brought it to his attention, he had always assumed that the president was furnished with congressional documents just as the cabinet departments were. He said in his speech that whenever the president needed to refer to any of these books, "he is compelled...to send to some one of these departments." He concluded by saying that passing his bill would allow the president to "hereafter have the means of reference at hand."

It made sense to him, but none whatsoever on the other side of the aisle. As one Democratic opponent pointed out, they were being asked to come up with $500 to establish an executive library, but he predicted that next year it would be $1,000, and $2,000 the year after. It was a Trojan horse as far as he was concerned, and there would be no end to it. The House voted on it and the measure failed, but just by a single vote.

Above: James Alfred Pearce, the Maryland Senator, was Abigail's first target in her campaign to get authorization for a White House library.

Abigail responded by organizing a dinner party. Her guest of honor was Senator James A. Pearce, chairman of the Joint Committee on the Library, which was charged with overseeing the Library of Congress as well as other government libraries. She also invited all the other members of the committee, which included the famous educator Congressman Horace Mann. It was only natural that the conversation would turn to books, a subject that Abigail Fillmore was passionate about, and in the midst of it, she casually lamented the fact, as though she were the only one who realized it, that there were none at all in this, the people's house.

By the end of the evening, she had won the entire group over to her idea of a White House library, and they promised the president that they would stand behind him if he would send a bill to Congress. He did, and they kept their promise. Senator Pearce led the way with a proposal from his subcommittee to appropriate $2,000 to buy books for the White House and to allow other government libraries, including the Library of Congress, to supply any duplicates of public documents that they might have to the president's collection. The amendment sailed through both houses of Congress, and Abigail Fillmore had scored one of the greatest political victories of any First Lady up until her time.

Like Abigail Adams, Abigail Fillmore loved books from the time she was a little girl growing up in Saratoga County, New York. Her father, Lemuel Powers, was a respected Baptist minister, and she was given free access to the library he had accumulated. She was two years old when he died, but her widowed

After the library bill passed, Abigail was also successful in lobbying Congress to install indoor plumbing in the White House. She complained that she had found the White House without a Bible or a bathtub.

mother packed up his books, her only legacy, and took her children to Cayuga County, in the center of New York State, where the cost of living would be lower. She educated Abigail at home, and by the time the girl was sixteen, Abigail became a teacher herself at the local one-room school, and in her spare time, she established and ran the first lending library in the county.

One of the patrons of the library was Millard Fillmore, who, with the aid of a pocket dictionary, taught himself to read in the library in what spare time he had while he was working in a textile mill. It cost $2.00 a year for the privilege to use the library, which he could barely afford, but he got his money's worth by visiting the library often. But he didn't meet Abigail until he was seventeen, and she nineteen, when he enrolled for classes at the New Hope Academy, where she was his teacher. It was a case of love at first sight, but any thoughts of marriage were out of the question. Millard could barely afford the tuition.

Yet Abigail encouraged him to make something of himself, and when an opportunity came along for him to work and study in a lawyer's office in another town halfway across the state, she came up with a plan that would make it possible. Law

> *"I then, for the first time in my life, heard a sentence parsed, and had an opportunity to study geography with a map. I pursued much of my study with and was stimulated by the companionship of a young lady whom I afterward married."*
>
> —*Millard Fillmore on his education courtesy of Abigail*

clerks didn't make much money, and he needed to get together enough of it to buy out his apprenticeship at the mill; Abigail suggested he should open a school and make teaching a part-time job. It could bring him as much as $10 a month and it would give him free room and board in the bargain. It didn't matter that he wasn't very well educated himself; neither was she. But she knew that he had enough native intelligence and determination to make it work. The fact that he would be miles away from her—for three years as it turned out—was a sacrifice they were both willing to make.

They were engaged to one another for seven years before Millard got his law practice established and could begin to think about supporting a family. All the while, Abigail continued her teaching job. She kept right on teaching for another two years after their marriage in 1826, until her first child, Millard Powers Fillmore, was born. He was called "Powers" all of his life.

The Fillmores started their married life in East Aurora, New York, about twenty miles south of Buffalo, where Millard built their first home with his own hands. It was across the street from his law office, which had already made him one of the most important people in town.

He had started his law career in Buffalo, a city with a bright future in anticipation of the opening of the Erie Canal, and he worked in the most prestigious law firm there. But in spite of the advantage it gave him, the city was swarming with young lawyers and he felt intimidated by them. It led to a decision to go down to East Aurora, where his family lived, and become a big fish in a small pond. Four years later, after he had proven it was the right decision, he was ready to marry Abigail.

Abigail Fillmore was the first First Lady who had been raised in poverty, and she was the first to have worked for a living in her life before the White House.

Above: President Millard Fillmore.

Below: The Fillmore's' daughter, Abby, was a teenager when her father became president.

In less than three more years, he was admitted as a counselor to the New York State Supreme Court, and he took his family back to Buffalo. They swapped their country cottage for the grandest house in what had by then become a boomtown. Years later, when Millard's father visited him at the White House, he looked around and said, "Nice place you have here, but not as nice as your house in Buffalo."

As mistress of the Fillmore mansion, Abigail entertained the great and the near great of the Niagara frontier with an almost endless circuit of balls, receptions, and dinner parties, all calculated to make her husband the natural leader of the Whigs in western New York.

The combination of Abigail's charm and Millard's reputation as a fair-minded lawyer propelled him to the state legislature in the 1828 election, which was otherwise swept by the Jacksonian Democrats. Four years later he went to Washington as a congressman, and the same year, Abigail gave birth to their daughter, Mary Abigail. While Millard was in Congress, he was empowered to practice before the United States Supreme Court. Eventually the family went back to the New York State capital at Albany after he was elected state comptroller by a historic margin.

With Abigail at his side, Millard Fillmore didn't seem to have an enemy in the world, but they were both surprised when the Whigs nominated him to run for vice president. When he went back to Washington to join the new Taylor administration in 1849, Abigail stayed behind in Buffalo with her children—her daughter, known as Abby, was seventeen by then, and Powers had just turned twenty-one, and both were students there. It wasn't as though Abigail lacked for anything to do; the Fillmores' personal library had grown to four thousand volumes by then. And she worked at maintaining her husband's reputation back home while he was in Washington. Considering the general climate of Buffalo, it might have seemed odd that the reason she gave for staying behind was that she found the Washington weather disagreeable and unhealthy. Abigail had lived there for six years when her husband was serving in Congress, leaving the youngsters behind with relatives in New York City, and although her life there had been a happy one, she wasn't eager to go back.

During the time Abigail was a Washingtonian, she was a regular at the congressional visitors galleries, and she developed a fascination for listening to debates, an addiction that many other First Ladies acquired. The Fillmores were also popular guests at Washington social affairs. When President Zachary Taylor died suddenly in July 1850, Millard Fillmore assumed the presidency and Abigail never hesitated. She arrived with her children at the White House a few days after he took the oath of office—only to discover that there was nothing there for her to read.

Once Congress authorized funds to create a presidential library, Abigail called on Charles Lanman, the War Department librarian, to help her decide how best to spend the money. He was "extensively acquainted with the booksellers of the North," he had told her, implying that he could save money. He also said that he had connections in the scientific community who would be invaluable in selecting books in their fields.

With the president's blessing, Lanman went up to New York and Boston, and came back with an eclectic book list that ranged from *Arabian Nights* to Adam Smith's *Wealth of Nations.* He also donated about 2,500 volumes of government documents from his own War Department library; they were duplicates, of course.

MRS. FILLMORE'S CARRIAGE.

Above: Abigail's friends in Albany presented her with this coach, which is said to have been the most elegant in the country at the time.

While Lanman's contribution was significant, it leaned heavily on politics and law, and Abigail took on the job of rounding it out. She was especially interested in contemporary authors, and among other selections, she ordered the complete works of Dickens and Thackeray as well as Washington Irving and Nathaniel Hawthorne.

As the shipments started arriving, Abigail had enough reading material to last several lifetimes. But she didn't have a place to put all those books. She picked a room on the second floor that had always been used as a reception area but that Sarah Polk had turned into a private dining room filled with enough small tables to discourage guests wandering up from downstairs from stepping any farther into the First Family's living quarters. Abigail didn't feel the need for such a barrier, and the room, now called the Yellow Oval Room, was completely transformed.

> "Her [Abigail's] face lighted up when she was engaged in conversation, and her manner was winning, though marked by a retiring modesty, bordering on reserve."
>
> —Elizabeth Ellet, historian of American women

Below: Abigail was a resourceful woman with many talents, but she was like a fish out of water in a house that didn't have books.

There was some precedent for her decision. By the middle of the nineteenth century it had become fashionable for grand homes to include a library, and they were invariably placed on the second floor in the interest of peace, quiet, and privacy. Abigail was generally praised for her choice of the space directly above the well-known Blue Room as a sign that she was conversant with the fine points of house decoration, but the reality was that it was the only space available that was big enough. She kept the impression alive by not changing any other rooms.

She began the transformation by hiring a cabinetmaker to build two mahogany bookcases that were curved to suit the oval walls, and a matching unit for the center of the room. The following year, as the collection grew, he built two more long bookcases for her.

A library is more than just books, though, and Abigail was up to the challenge of furnishing hers. "It was a nondescript room," she wrote, "with a tobacco-stained matting on the floor." Obviously, the matting had to go, and when it was taken up she was pleased to discover "a Brussels carpet of wonderful design" underneath. All it needed was a thorough cleaning. Next she made the rounds of local stores, buying inexpensive yet attractive upholstered

Above: Powers Fillmore, Abigail and Millard's son, worked for his father in the White House. The president constantly nagged him about his appearance.

Below: Daughter Mary Abigail Fillmore often doubled as the White House hostess, which became a full-time job during the last year of Millard's presidency.

chairs and picking up screens for parts of the room that she considered unattractive but couldn't afford to furnish.

She had her piano and a harp sent down from Buffalo, and when they were hauled up to the second floor, the new library was ready to serve double duty as a music room. Both Abigail and her daughter were accomplished pianists, and young Abby was also proficient on the harp as well as the guitar. A friend later reported, "Here Mrs. Fillmore surrounded herself with her own little home comforts… [and] received the informal visits of the friends she loved, and for her, the real pleasures and enjoyments of the White House were in this room."

Not all of the First Lady's receptions in the room were the informal visits of close friends. Abigail had spent a lifetime promoting her husband's career and she wasn't going to stop now. The library/music room became a kind of salon. Political bigwigs found their way there, and many of them called it the most comfortable room in the whole city, but she also invited writers and musicians and other artists to add an unprecedented air of culture to the presidential mansion. Sometimes the First Family itself provided the entertainment, with

Abigail could play the piano like a graduate of a musical conservatory. She was self-taught, picking up the ability around the same time she taught herself French … when she was in her forties!

Abby and her mother singing duets, Powers offering "old-time melodies," and the president himself frequently demonstrating his talents as a singer. Some of the songs they all sang weren't old-timers. Millard's favorite was Stephen Foster's "Old Folks at Home," and he sang it for the composer himself, when he was a guest at the White House.

One of the Fillmores' most celebrated guests was Jenny Lind, the wildly popular "Swedish nightingale," who arrived on the arm of her American producer, P. T. Barnum. The author Washington Irving, a longtime friend of the Fillmore family, showed up frequently, and two guests who especially pleased the First Lady were Charles Dickens and William Makepeace Thackeray, her favorite authors. Abigail may have been frail of health, but she still loved to entertain. She was known for her elegant, formal dresses and witty conversation.

Allowing for Tradition

Abigail's cozy music room relieved her of the necessity of entertaining downstairs in the White House. When protocol demanded more formal dinners and receptions, she designated her daughter, Abby, as the official White House hostess. Abby was an educated girl, and formal entertaining was a pleasure for her. For Abigail, like many of her predecessors, her frail health made entertaining a chore. Because of an old injury to her ankle, she couldn't stand at her husband's side to receive guests for more than very short periods.

The End of the Fillmore Term

This early version of what would be called "Camelot" in later presidential years ended too soon. President Fillmore didn't run for a presidential term of his own, and the Fillmore White House tenancy lasted just two years and eight months. The Fillmore library was a legacy that kept growing after they left, especially during the Lincoln presidency, when First Lady Mary Todd Lincoln bought more books for the collection. The library had become a sitting room by then, and it was where the president went to relax and read his Bible. In other administrations it became the Oval Office for some presidents and an office for the wives of some of the others.

Abigail Fillmore didn't live to see what her library would mean to future presidents. She insisted on attending the inauguration of Franklin Pierce, her husband's successor, in the absence of his own wife, who was grieving over the recent loss of her son. Abigail had never come to grips with the Washington climate and the day, as often happens in Washington during the month of March, was cold, damp, and miserable. It made her lingering cold worse, and after a few days that the Fillmores spent at the Willard Hotel, where her husband had lived as vice president, it developed into pneumonia, and she didn't live to make the trip back to Buffalo. Her life as a former First Lady lasted less than four weeks. Her daughter, Abby, died at the age of twenty-two, just sixteen months later.

Above: Singer Jenny Lind, a guest at the Fillmore White House, was an international sensation on a level that was unheard of before the 1850s.

> *"[Abigail was] a lady of great strength of mind, dignified manners, genteel deportment, and of much energy of character."*
>
> —The New York Times

Visiting the Fillmore House

The house Millard Fillmore built for his wife is located in East Aurora, New York, twenty miles south of Buffalo. It is operated by the Aurora Historical Society, which acquired it in 1974. The society restored the property to its original appearance and has furnished it with many pieces that Abigail Fillmore herself selected. It is open Wednesdays, Saturdays, and Sundays between June 1 and October 15 from 2:00 P.M. to 4:00 P.M., when costumed guides conduct tours and demonstrate such things as open-hearth cooking.

In the village nearby, the Aurora Historical Museum contains artifacts from the town's earliest days, and includes one of the largest collections of Indian arrowheads in the state. The Elbert Hubbard Library and Museum contains examples of items produced in the famous Roycroft Shops, which reflect Hubbard's philosophy of "the beautiful and the good, the plain and the simple." Both museums are open on the same schedule as the Fillmore House.

For travel directions and other information, write to: Millard Fillmore House, 24 Shearer Avenue, East Aurora, New York 14052; or call 716-652-8875.

Below: The Fillmore House in Buffalo, New York.

Jane Pierce

Puritan Heritage

A great many nineteenth-century American women lived tragic lives, but Jane Pierce's life was poignant enough to have been the subject of a Victorian novel. She had three children and lost all of them, including a son, Bennie, who suffered a violent death before her eyes at the age of twelve. She was ill during most of her adult life, and she never weighed more than a hundred pounds. Seeing her husband, Franklin, become president of the United States weighed on her like a millstone around her neck. Even her deep religious faith failed her. Jane believed in a vengeful God who visited these things on her as punishment for sins that she wasn't even aware of committing. Other women with similar faith regarded such setbacks as a way of building the inner strength of their soul, but Jane Pierce had very little inner strength to build on.

Her father, the Reverend Dr. Jesse Appleton, was a Congregationalist minister and highly regarded as one of the great theologians of his day. But while the church had outgrown most of the sternness of its Puritan roots, he seemed to be stuck in the past. Even some members of his flock thought he was a little strange. He never allowed himself more than three or four hours of sleep each night, and he ate just enough to keep him alive. He believed that it was God's will that he should deny himself even the simplest pleasures of eating and sleeping. It didn't surprise anyone that he went to an early grave—Jane was thirteen years old when he died.

When Reverend Appleton became president of Bowdoin College, he moved his wife and six children to the campus, at Brunswick, Maine, and proceeded to adopt an even more ascetic life as a way of setting an example for the young men who were his students. One of the professors serving under him said that he had a "morbid sense of responsibility." Naturally, Jane and her brothers and sisters were expected to follow his example.

After he died, his widow, Elizabeth, moved the family to Amherst, Massachusetts, where they could live a comparatively normal life among her relatives. Jane had become a striking young beauty by then, and that wasn't lost on the local boys, but she was almost painfully shy and introverted, and none of them stood a chance.

That changed when she was twenty and she met Franklin Pierce. He had moved to nearby Northampton, and as a recent Bowdoin graduate, he decided to call on the Appletons to pay his respects to the family of his alma mater's

---

Jane Means Appleton Pierce

Born
March 12, 1806, Hampton, New Hampshire

Parents
Reverend Jesse Appleton and Elizabeth Means Appleton

Marriage
November 19, 1834, to Franklin Pierce (1804-69)

Children
Franklin, Jr. (1836); Frank Robert (1839-43); Benjamin (1841-53)

Died
December 2, 1863, Andover, Massachusetts

Above: In addition to Franklin Pierce, Bowdoin College alumnae also include writer Nathaniel Hawthorne and poet Henry Wadsworth Longfellow.

Below: A cartoon published during the 1852 presidential campaign shows Franklin leaning against a tree offering a drink to a Quaker man. "I'll stand as long as this tree will stand by me," he says. Maine at the time had just enacted the country's first prohibition law.

Jane showed great promise as a pianist at an early age, but gave up playing as an adult.

legendary president. He was obviously more interested in Jane than he was in the rest of the family, and he kept going back to see more of her.

Her mother and her relatives weren't too pleased, even if the attention was bringing Jane out of her shell. They took note of the fact that Franklin wasn't much of a churchgoer and that as a young man with a passion for politics, he was spending far too much time in taverns discussing political issues. And there were also those rumors that his mother drank herself to death. All of the family members, except Jane of course, breathed a collective sigh of relief when he decided to open a law practice up in Concord, New Hampshire. It was eighty miles away, and they didn't think they'd ever see him again.

Bad roads notwithstanding, eighty miles isn't really all that far when love is involved, and the only thing that kept Franklin from making the trip more often than he did were the demands of his law office. The young couple also wrote long letters to each other, and his were filled with news of his new involvement with New Hampshire politics. Jane despised politics and politicians to the very core of her being. She especially hated Democrats, whose ideas went against the principles of the Federalists she had grown up among; and Franklin Pierce was a Democrat. In spite of it, she thought that she might be able to reform him. She had already made him more regular in his attendance at church, and if she could sour him on politics she'd be killing two birds with one stone, because it would leave him without a reason to spend so much of his time in taverns.

When he was elected to the New Hampshire legislature, she began to realize that changing him was going to be more difficult than she anticipated, and then he won a seat in the United States Congress. But love overcame her objections. Her family's attitude had softened, too, and Jane and Franklin were married by her brother-in-law in 1834, eight years after they first met.

They began their married life in Hillsborough, New Hampshire, where Franklin's family lived, but Jane's shyness worked against her, and after two years there, she made friends with almost no one. Sensing her unhappiness, Franklin suggested that they move to Concord, where he had been practicing law, and she was happier there. But she suffered through bouts of depression when her husband went to Washington for congressional sessions.

She accompanied him enough times to know that she didn't like the place. She was too withdrawn to enjoy the constant barrage of parties and balls, and she was irritated that politics, that hated evil, was the only topic of conversation wherever they went. Most of the time, Franklin went to the capital alone, and Jane stayed home. It was a fact of nineteenth-century life that a woman should be subservient to her husband, but it was also considered a wife's duty to guide him to a proper life, and Jane was determined to do her duty and lead him away from a life in politics. It was an uphill battle, but one she never stopped fighting through all of their married life.

Their first child, Franklin Pierce, Jr., died when he was three days old, and when Franklin, Sr., was elected to the Senate a few months afterward, he decided that the change of scene might soften his wife's grief, and she went to Washington with him. But it was the wrong scene for her, and she was back in New Hampshire by the time her second son, Frank Robert, was born. He died at the age of four, but in the meantime, a third boy, Benjamin, had come into their lives. Jane smothered him with all the hope and affection she'd developed for her other two children. The grief she had been enduring was transformed to an unnatural worry over the health of the little boy she called Bennie.

Above: Franklin's birthplace at Hillsborough, New Hampshire, was where he and Jane began their married life. She wasn't happy there, and they moved away after two years.

Her concern rubbed off onto her husband, and he resigned from the Senate in the middle of his term to go home to her and their son. Jane had finally found a way to wean him away from a life in politics. It appeared that he had made a clean break, and he was willing to settle down to the life of a small-town lawyer. If Jane needed proof, it came when President Polk offered him the post of attorney general in his cabinet. He brushed the honor aside, writing to the president: "You know that Mrs. Pierce's health while at Washington was very delicate. It is, I fear, even more so now, and the responsibilities which the proposed change would necessarily impose on her ought probably in themselves to constitute an insurmountable objection to leaving our quiet home for a public station in Washington." Two years after that,

Rather than leave Jane alone at home when he went to Washington, Franklin Pierce hired a local couple to live with her while he was away.

he refused an appointment to go back to the Senate, and he turned away a movement to make him governor of New Hampshire.

It seemed that Jane had won her battle, but she had no control over a war that broke out with Mexico. Franklin considered it his patriotic duty to enlist in the army, and he left Jane and five-year-old Bennie behind so he could take command of a regiment in far-off Mexico. He was quickly promoted to brigadier general and he gave a good account of himself as a military leader. Except for a leg injury that he sustained when he was thrown from his horse, he went home unscathed, and his anxious wife was grateful to have him back.

But his battlefield exploits had put him back in the public eye, and as the Democrats began searching for a candidate to run for president in 1852, Franklin's name came up much too often as far as Jane was concerned. She was appalled by the idea that his love of politics might not have died after all, and she extracted a promise from him not to encourage the party leaders to work for his nomination. But he wouldn't promise to turn down the nomination if they came to the conclusion on their own and his presence on the ticket was needed.

When the Democrats met for their nominating convention, it seemed that few of them thought that they needed Franklin Pierce. But the country was widely split between North and South by that time, and so was the

Above: Franklin's career as a general in the Mexican War helped relaunch his political career, which he had promised to give it up.

Below: Son Bennie was Jane's only interest in life after the deaths of her two older sons. He, too, would die a tragic death.

> *"I hope he [his father, Franklin] won't be elected, for I should not like to live in Washington and I know you would not either."*
>
> —*Bennie Pierce in a letter to his mother*

party. After forty-eight ballots, the delegates began looking around for a compromise candidate, and to Jane's horror, it turned out to be former senator Franklin Pierce. She fainted when she heard the news. But there was nothing she could do except make the best of a bad thing. "If what seems so probable is to come," she wrote, "I pray that Grace be given where it is and will be so much needed." She braced herself against the prospect of four miserable years in the White House, but she justified it in her mind as a rare and wonderful experience for her son, Bennie. By the time Franklin won the election in a landslide, Jane actually seemed to be looking forward to going back to Washington.

A few days before they were scheduled to leave, one of Jane's relatives died and the family went to Andover for the funeral. A new railroad had just been built, and they decided that it would be a treat for Bennie if they went by train; they had no way of knowing that the return trip would be the boy's last adventure on earth.

A few miles outside of Concord, the car they were riding in jumped the tracks, separated from the others, and cartwheeled down an embankment, coming to rest at the bottom in a mass of twisted metal and broken glass.

Neither Franklin nor Jane was hurt, but Bennie, who had been sitting next to his mother, was struck on the head by an iron bar and died instantly.

After she was pulled from the wreckage, Jane was inconsolable, and when she searched her mind for a reason why this terrible tragedy had come to her, she came to the conclusion that it was her husband who was to blame. A few days earlier, she had been told that Franklin had broken his promise to her and had, in fact, brokered his own nomination to run for the presidency. While that wasn't quite true, he had in fact been keeping up his contacts in the Democratic party behind her back, and it was difficult for him to deny it. As far as she was concerned, he had betrayed her, and God had punished him for it by taking away their son. It was a strange conclusion, considering that she, the betrayed one, was more affected by the punishment. She must have thought so herself, because as she thought more about God's mysterious ways, she eventually came to the conclusion that He had taken Bennie home to free the new president from any distractions as he guided the country through perilous times. And that, she decided, was all the more reason why she should stay at home when he went down to Washington, since she would only be a distraction, too.

Above: Jane had a dress made for her husband's inaugural ball, but she never got to wear it.

The Shadow of the White House

Jane was determined to sit out her husband's presidency back home in New Hampshire, but her perceived duty to the man with whom she shared her life overcame her resolve. When he boarded the train that would take him to Washington, Jane, dressed in the prescribed black of mourning, was on his arm. But during a stopover in Baltimore, she refused to go any farther. Her husband was forced to go on without her, and he was inaugurated without his wife at his side. The Inaugural Ball was called off, and he moved into the White House alone.

Jane arrived a few days later, accompanied by her uncle's widow, Abigail Kent Means, whom she had asked to assume the duties of White House hostess. There wasn't much for her to do. The president was in mourning, too, and social events were scaled down to a bare minimum. At Jane's insistence, the public rooms were all draped in black, taking all hints of gaiety away from any receptions or dinner parties. She made a couple of attempts to appear at formal dinners, but her deep depression and her obvious discomfort made them as unpleasant for her guests as for herself, and she soon stopped appearing in public at all.

Jane took to her room and she rarely came out for two years, spending most of her time in near darkness writing long sad letters

When Franklin Pierce arrived at the White House, First Lady Abigail Fillmore hadn't bothered to prepare the way for him, and he and his secretary had to spend their first night sleeping in chairs.

to her son Bennie. She never received visitors there, except for a pair of famous mediums who claimed to be able to communicate with her dead son, but all they produced was a mysterious rapping on the table. Of course, they claimed that it was Bennie who was doing the knocking, and Jane believed them with all her heart.

Although Jane was almost never seen, the black bunting draped all over the White House served as a constant reminder of her presence, and she became known around Washington as the "Shadow of the White House."

Then one day, halfway through her husband's presidency, Jane suddenly emerged from her exile. She put in an appearance at a few receptions and dinner parties, and she even organized a few. Not only that, but it seemed to have become less painful for her to smile. Franklin's close friend Nathaniel Hawthorne escorted her around town, and they discussed books, especially his own, although she had to admit that she hadn't read much more than the Bible since Bennie died. Jane's own friend Varina Davis, the wife of Secretary of State Jefferson Davis, and the future First Lady of the Confederacy, took her on shopping trips and excursions outside the city.

Jane also started going out on her own, and her usual destination was the Capitol building, where she gave rapt attention to congressional debates. This woman who always abhorred politics seemed to have gone through a complete transformation, but nobody could figure out why. She even started offering political advice to her husband, and he couldn't figure it out, either.

What he, if nobody else, finally realized was that Jane had become an abolitionist. While the president was struggling to avoid a civil war, she had made up her mind that freeing slaves would make such a war worthwhile. There are still no clues what brought on this sudden epiphany, but it is likely, considering her New England upbringing, that she hadn't changed her opinion but simply made up her mind to bring it out into the open.

The president was strongly in favor of the Kansas-Nebraska Act, which would allow people in the new territories to determine whether they would allow slavery there, but Jane believed that it would only encourage the spread of slavery. For what may have been the first time in her life, she had become passionate about an issue, and she lost her shyness in making sure that everyone she met knew how she felt. Most of all, she let the president know, but he signed the bill in spite of her. In the end, she might have said "I told

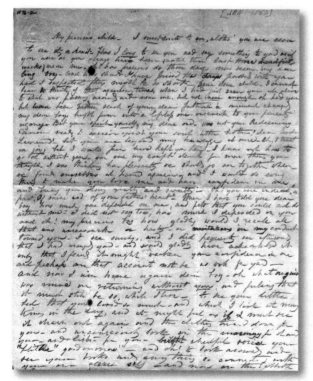

Below: One of many letters Jane wrote to her dead son Bennie from the White House.

The Spiritualists

The two women who visited Jane Pierce in her darkened room were Kate and Margaret Fox, who are generally credited as the founders of the spiritualism craze that swept the country in the 1850s. They claimed to have discovered an ability to communicate with the dead in 1848, when they said that a murdered man led them to his hidden grave through a series of mysterious rappings. They moved on to conducting séances in private homes and demonstrating their talents on the vaudeville circuit. Former First Lady Julia Tyler hired them to amuse her guests at a party, and later Mary Todd Lincoln called on them to help her get in touch with her assassinated husband. Much later, Maggie publicly confessed that she and Kate were a couple of frauds, but they had started a large industry in communications with the dead, and their followers dismissed their confession as their greatest fraud.

Right: Spiritualists Kate and Margaret Fox (and sometimes their sister, Leah) visited Jane to communicate with her dead son.

you so," because signing the bill put an end to President Pierce's hopes of running for a second term.

Still wearing nothing but the black of mourning, Jane took on the duties of White House hostess during the last two years she lived there. But she wasn't a cheerful hostess; her heart was broken beyond repair, and her health was deteriorating. Her guests understood. Jane Pierce was regarded as an invalid, and there were rumors that when she left the White House for the last time, she had to be carried out. It wasn't true, but there was no mistaking that she was not at all well.

As much as Jane hated Washington, she and her husband stayed there for two months as private citizens after his single term ended, and as spring began breaking out in New England, they made their way back north. Doctors had determined that she was in the advanced stages of tuberculosis, the disease they called "consumption" in those days, but they couldn't agree on what to do for her. Some said that she needed to relax in fresh mountain air, but there was plenty of that in New England and it didn't seem to be helping. Others said that she'd

Above: White House parties were depressing affairs while the Pierces were living there.

Jane was especially fond of Varina Davis's son, Samuel, who helped fill the huge gap in her life. The boy died at the age of two, plunging Jane into even deeper depression.

find relief breathing salt air, and as the rivers began to freeze, Franklin and Jane set out for the Madeira Islands off the coast of North Africa. Even that didn't seem to help, and in the spring they moved on to Spain and then to France and Italy, visiting the vaunted European spas along the way. But what pure air hadn't been able to accomplish, the healing waters were no more effective at doing, and they sailed off to the Bahamas for another season in the sun. But Jane continued to waste away, and she realized that she probably didn't have much longer to live. She had carried Bennie's Bible, as well as locks of hair from all three of her children, her "precious dead," she called them, everywhere they went during their two years of searching for a cure, and now she said that she needed to be closer to their graves.

Going home seemed to check Jane's decline, and she was soon well enough to entertain nearby friends and to restart correspondences with old ones. She began going to church again, too, and she insisted that Franklin should join her. And just to make sure that he had been paying attention, she quizzed him on the sermon after they went home.

Southern states began seceding from the Union at around the same time the Pierces went back to Concord, and when war broke out between the states, the war between Jane and Franklin broke out again as well. Neither of them was able to change the other's mind. Franklin still insisted that the war was "cruel, heartless, aimless, unnecessary," and Jane stuck to her resolve that ending slavery was worth whatever it might cost.

Eleven months after President Lincoln issued the Emancipation Proclamation, which must have been a happy day for Jane, she died at her sister's home in Andover on December 2, 1863. Her final words were, "Other refuge I have none." She was buried in Concord, next to her beloved son Bennie.

Above: Jane aged prematurely during her years as First Lady. She considered her service an almost unbearable ordeal.

After Franklin's presidential term ended, the Pierces went back to New England, but he went to New Hampshire and she stayed with her sister in Massachusetts.

Left: During their post-presidential years, Jane and Franklin often returned to New England to visit with her sister Mary Aiken (left), and nephew Charles Packard (right).

Visiting the Pierce Manse

The house where Franklin and Jane Pierce lived in Concord, New Hampshire, from the time he resigned from the Senate until he went to serve in the Mexican War, has been completely restored by the Pierce Brigade and is furnished with family heirlooms, including some of the furniture the Pierces bought during their time at the White House. It is open Monday through Friday, except holidays, between mid-June and Labor Day, from 11:00 A.M. to 3:00 P.M. Adults are charged $3.00; children and students, $1.00.

The house is located at 14 Penacook Street in the heart of the Concord Historic District near exit 15 on I-93.

Jane and her sons Bennie and Frank Robert, as well as her husband, are buried nearby at Concord's Old North Cemetery. Their first son, Franklin, Jr., is buried at Hillsborough, New Hampshire, not far from the Pierce Homestead, where the future president was born. The house, three miles west of Hillsborough at the junction of Routes 9 and 31, has also been restored and furnished as it was in 1804. It is open to the public on weekends between Memorial Day and Labor Day.

Right: The Pierces' Concord, New Hampshire, home.

Harriet Lane

Lady in Waiting

While John Quincy Adams was the only president who was brought up to assume the office, Harriet Lane was the only First Lady to have been trained in advance for the job. But according to the modern definition, Miss Lane wasn't really a First Lady at all, since she wasn't married to a president. But the fact is that she was the first woman to be given the title of "First Lady."

Americans didn't know what to call the president's wife for the first sixty-five years of the republic. Some of the titles included Lady Washington, Mrs. President Adams, and even Presidentess Dolley Madison. In Harriet's case, she was known as the "Democratic Queen" during the first years of her service in the White House.

The term "First Lady" was used frequently over the years, to be sure, but it never appeared in print until *Frank Leslie's Illustrated Newspaper* ran a full-page engraving of Harriet Lane in its issue of March 31, 1860. The caption read: "The subject of our illustration, from the semi-official position which she has long sustained with so much honor to herself and her country, may justly be termed the first lady of the land." A short time later, *Leslie's* magazine referred to her as the president's "amiable niece, the lady of the White House, and by courtesy the first lady of the land." With that, it became a part of the national vocabulary. America had a First Lady and her name was Harriet Lane.

Julia Tyler was the youngest First Lady; she was twenty-four years old when she moved into the White House and took charge of its social side. Harriet, at age twenty-seven, was just three years older when she arrived there. Official Washington was generally pleased to welcome her after four years of the dour Jane Pierce, but many people in the establishment believed that she was too young to take on the responsibilities of the role. Mrs. Tyler had married into the job, and there wasn't much anybody could do about that, but Miss Lane was merely the president's niece, and the gossip held that he should have picked someone a little bit older.

The reason President James Buchanan had the option of choosing a First Lady was because he didn't have a wife, and he didn't have any plans to look for one. He had no intentions to search for anyone else to represent him in Washington society, either. He had carefully trained Harriet in all the social skills that she would need for the job, and he couldn't possibly have found anyone who was better qualified.

Harriet Rebecca Lane Johnston

Born
May 18, 1830,
Mercersburg,
Pennsylvania

Parents
Elliot Tole Lane and
Jane Buchanan Lane

Marriage
January 11, 1866,
to Henry Elliot Johnston
(? -1884)

Children
James Buchanan Johnston
(1868-81); Henry Elliot
Johnston (1869-82)

Died
July 3, 1903,
Narragansett,
Rhode Island

A SERVICEABLE GARMENT—
OR REVERIE OF A BACHELOR.

Above: During James's presidential campaign, a cartoonist drew him as a needy bachelor, although he was quite a wealthy man. All he needed was a higher office.

Except for Grover Cleveland, James Buchanan was the only bachelor who was ever elected president of the United States. In James's day, bachelorhood was considered un-American in most circles. Among the principles codified by the founding fathers, one that was left unspoken, but very well understood, was that it was the civic duty of every American citizen to get married and have children. It has perhaps been the most important rule in the creation of every nation in history that the only way to secure a country is to populate it. Indeed, during James's lifetime, only three out of every one hundred American men were single by choice.

James Buchanan understood the rule as well as anyone did, and he started out with the best of intentions. While other young men his age were getting married, he was busy getting rich as a lawyer in Lancaster, Pennsylvania. His social life was limited to joining organizations that would help him meet well-heeled clients, and working to curry favor among the local Federalists, which earned him a seat in the state legislature.

Once his career was established to his liking, he decided that it was time to find a wife. He had a lot to offer. At twenty-five, James was six feet tall with blond hair and a smooth face that never showed a sign of a whisker; he was charming and he was always elegantly dressed in the height of fashion—and he was earning $8,000 a year, more than $150,000 in today's dollars, and the sky seemed to be the limit. It was no wonder that dozens of young local ladies had their eyes on him. He encouraged all of them—James was an unabashed flirt all of his life—but he only had eyes for Ann Coleman. She was practically the girl next door, and her father, who owned an iron mine and was reputed to be the richest man in Pennsylvania, had emigrated from the same county in Ireland as James's own father. It seemed to be a perfect match.

James and Ann were seen everywhere together during the summer of 1819, and they considered themselves engaged to be married. But then the local gossips started spreading the rumor that in spite of Ann's dark-haired beauty all that really interested James was her father's money. The rumor reached the Coleman household, and both father and daughter believed it. To add insult to the injury, Ann was weary of playing second fiddle to James's law practice, and when she heard that he was seeing another girl on the sly, she broke off the engagement and her mother hustled her off to Philadelphia to get over the emotional strain. Soon afterward, the healthy twenty-three-year-old girl suddenly died of what a doctor diagnosed as "hysterical convulsions."

Her father refused to allow James to attend Ann's funeral, and in the midst of rumors that she had committed suicide, and that she had probably been pregnant, the would-be bridegroom swore off the idea of ever marrying anyone because of his loss of "the only earthly object of my affection." He wrote to one of his neighbors, "The time will come when you will discover that she, as well as I, have been much abused. I may sustain the shock of her death, but I feel that happiness has fled me forever." Soon afterward, he found happiness as a congressman, and he went off to Washington, where he spent the next ten years without a woman at his side.

When his father died, James became the head of his family, with several orphaned nieces and nephews to care for. The number grew twenty years later when the six children, four boys and two girls, of his late sister Jane Buchanan Lane, came into his life as his wards. Of all of them, he became especially attached to eleven-year-old Harriet, whom everyone called Hal. She was a gawky, gangly kid, a tomboy who liked reading well enough, but only if she could climb a tree to do it.

Like the mythic Pygmalion who turned his stone creation, Galatea, into an ideal woman, James set out to transform Harriet into a "proper lady." Her late father, Elliot Tole Lane, had been a successful businessman, and he and his wife made sure that their children got the best education available to them in southeastern Pennsylvania. Harriet had already learned the basics of writing and arithmetic and she had been exposed to classical literature. She also had basic training in the social graces, even if her uncle only saw the rough edges. He wasn't happy with the local school, and he sent her off to what he considered a better one in western Virginia.

"Your day will come," he told her, "after your education shall have been completed and your conduct approved by me." He promised her that when the time came, he would introduce her into his world "in the proper manner." When Harriet became a teenager, she began complaining that she didn't like the school he had chosen for her, and he responded by enrolling her in what was highly regarded as the very best girls school in the country, the Visitation Convent School in Georgetown. It had the added advantage of being near to the Capitol, where he could keep an eye on her progress. James had no religion himself at that stage in his life, and this would be Harriet's first real brush with it, although she was nominally an Episcopalian. But he assured himself, and Harriet as well, that "your religious principles are doubtless so well settled that you will not become a nun." Religion had nothing to do with it. Harriet was the least likely candidate for taking holy vows among all of her classmates. She loved nothing more than having a good time, and it seems likely that her exuberance must have gotten in the way of her studies often, to the consternation of the nuns who watched over her.

Above: By the time he ran for president, James had already had a quite distinguished career.

Below: Harriet began training for her career as her uncle's hostess at the Visitation Convent School in Washington, D.C.'s Georgetown section.

James Buchanan hated to part with money, but when Harriet came into his home, he spent $17.50 to buy a piano so that she could add music to her cultural accomplishments.

James hated nicknames, and the only one that he ever allowed in his presence was Harriet's affectionate, but slightly flippant "Nunc," which he accepted as a loving father might. He also played a role in her life that went beyond the usual father-daughter relationship. When he became minister to Russia and couldn't have a face-to-face influence over her, he wrote to Harriet several times a week from Moscow to pass along life lessons that he felt were important for her to learn. In one of his letters, he suggested that she should be wary of men who tend to be "shortsighted and know not the consequence of their own actions." Fearing that she might be giving too much attention to the opposite sex, he cautioned her, "The most brilliant prospects are often overcast, and those who commence life under favorable auspices are often unfortunate." He was right that Harriet was boy-crazy, but he needn't have worried. She usually found the young men who pursued her to be "pleasant, but dreadfully troublesome." Still, she couldn't resist leading them on. According to one story that made the rounds, when an admirer tried a line on her—"Your hands are fitted to play the harp"—she couldn't resist a quick comeback, "or awake to ecstasies the living lyre."

Her uncle realized, of course, that times had changed and that young ladies of Harriet's generation were prone to make up their own minds in matters of the heart, and in spite of his own lack of experience along those lines, he switched to giving her more specific advice on the proper way to select a partner for life. Be wary of flattery, he told her, and don't rush into anything that you might regret later. He strongly urged that she should look for good moral habits in a prospective husband and by all means to make sure that he had plenty of money. As a fail-safe position, he commanded her to "never engage yourself to any person without my previous advice." It was no wonder that poor Harriet didn't get married until she was thirty-six years old. Her final choice was Henry Elliot Johnston, one of the most successful bank executives in Baltimore. And, yes, dear old Nunc had advised her to take the step, although he insisted on a much longer than normal engagement.

When her formal education was finished, nineteen-year-old Harriet went back to Pennsylvania to take charge of the estate in Lancaster that her uncle called Wheatland. It was already a massive house, but he added a library and several other rooms to it, and he gave Harriet the responsibility of furnishing them, as well as the other rooms that the previous owner had decorated in the French style. Left to her own devices, she selected heavy walnut furniture that gave the place a solid all-American look, which was exactly what her uncle had in mind. Harriet's main responsibility at Wheatland was keeping all of her family members entertained, but she also took on the role of her uncle's hostess. Because Lancaster was on the main route to Washington from the north, her ambitious uncle insisted that his home ought to serve as a way station for congressmen and cabinet members who were passing through. It was a kind of

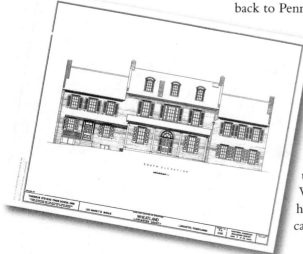

Below: Wheatland, James's estate in Lancaster, Pennsylvania, was already beautiful when he bought it, but he set out to make it better.

test for her abilities, and Harriet passed it as though it were second nature to her. It was a test for Nunc's presidential ambitions, too. He called his home the "grand theater of President making," and he relied on Harriet to match his own impressive personal charm and win Democrat movers and shakers over to his point of view.

Along with Harriet and six other orphaned relatives whom James adopted, the Buchanan household included twenty-two nieces and nephews and thirteen grandnieces and grandnephews, all of whom depended on him for their support.

She had already established herself as an able politician during the 1852 presidential election when her uncle sent her out to campaign for candidate Franklin Pierce in western Pennsylvania. No woman, not even a candidate's wife, had ever done such a thing before. The head of the party was impressed, and happy to report that she had proven herself as a "figure in the political world." When James eventually ran for the presidency himself, Harriet hosted banquets and rallies and other events to push his candidacy forward, setting the stage for future candidates' wives, many of whom were happy to be able to rise above the old rule that political wives should be seen but not heard.

James himself claimed that he had retired from public life at that point, living the life of a family man among his nieces and nephews and enjoying his status as "the Sage of Wheatland." But nobody was fooled. He had become a leading Democrat and he was angling to become president of the United States, a quest that had failed him several times in the past. When he lost the nomination to Franklin Pierce for the 1852 election, he turned down an offer to place him on the ticket as the vice presidential candidate, saying, "After a long and stormy public life, I will go into retirement without regret and, with perfect consciousness that I have done my duty faithfully to my country in all public circumstances which I have been placed.... I only mean that I shall never hold another public office."

"Never" in this case turned out to be six months. President Pierce asked James to become minister to Great Britain, and he turned down the honor twice before he finally accepted it. He had already held the higher rank of secretary of state, and he cited concerns about the division of responsibilities between himself as minister and William Marcy, the current secretary. In the end, he accepted the post, and he sailed for England in the summer of 1853 with Harriet Lane as his traveling companion.

As it had always been, the post of minister to Great Britain was an important one, but although there were significant issues for James to deal with, Great Britain was distracted by its war with

The Entertainer

Minister Buchanan wasn't always welcome at parties and dinners during his time in London. Staged by members of the Court of St. James, these parties required that he dress the part of a courtier. When he refused, he was refused entrance. But he himself staged some of the most brilliant parties in London at his own residence. It was one more stage of Harriet's training as a hostess, and as usual, she upstaged her uncle at every one of them, and he loved her for it.

Above: Britain's Queen Victoria was always surrounded by a group of admirers, but it was she who greatly admired Harriet.

the Russians in the Crimea, and fast-moving changes at home made Americans uninterested in foreign affairs. But James was able to attract attention to himself anyway.

It was official policy that American diplomats should wear simple American clothes, and although James had always been something of a dandy, he complied with the order. Yet the English insisted on "court dress" as the only acceptable attire for state functions and dinner parties among the gentry, and James thumbed his nose at the tradition by not showing up for the opening of Parliament.

Dinner with Queen Victoria was another matter. James refused to put on the required ruffles and lace and gold braid for the occasion, and instead he wore a sword at his side, which was the emblem of a gentleman in both countries. It was a bit of a gamble. He had been mistaken for a servant at other functions, but the sword was good enough for the queen, even though one London newspaper denounced him as "the gentleman in the black coat from Yankee land." Back home, though, the press painted him as a supporter of American principles in dress as well as in attitude, and his political career took a huge leap forward among potential voters.

For her part, Harriet had no such problem. She loved the fashions of the English court, and she wasn't restrained by any official order. The British adored everything about her, and the queen was no exception. She ordered that "dear Miss Lane" should be given all the privileges of an ambassador's wife rather than the lesser acceptance that was ordinarily due his relatives, and Harriet was invited to balls and parties, each one of which took her reputation to new heights. She even danced with Prince Albert himself on one occasion, an honor that was denied to many English women and to nearly all foreigners. Queen Victoria had become so fond of Harriet, in fact, that she attempted to arrange a marriage between her and an English peer so that she would stay on in England. The man was much more than twice her age, and Harriet respectfully declined, even before her uncle could register his own objection. During their nearly three years there, James was given an honorary degree by Oxford University in the same ceremony that honored Alfred Lord Tennyson, but Harriet upstaged both of them with her entrance: The students welcomed her with a deafening round of cheers.

Harriet had the status of an ambassador's wife in Great Britain, but her uncle held the title of "minister." Up until that time, the Americans refused to call their foreign diplomats anything else because the title "ambassador" seemed to be too close to a royal rank.

America's Sweetheart

If there had been such a thing in 1857, Harriet Lane might have been the prototype of a Barbie doll. She was tall with long blonde, almost golden, hair and blue eyes that leaned toward violet. She had a full figure, perfect posture, and a regal bearing, and she had impeccable taste in clothes. It was no wonder that people called her a queen, even if they felt obliged to modify it to "Our Democratic Queen."

After having conquered British society, Harriet burst on the American scene like a dazzling comet when her uncle was inaugurated as president. The ball that followed was the biggest yet staged for any president. A special building was constructed to accommodate the more than six thousand guests who danced to the music of a forty-piece orchestra in a massive room that was painted red, white, and blue, and whose twenty-foot ceiling was decorated with gold stars. They drank the finest wines and rye whiskey by the barrel, and the tables groaned with food that ranged from oysters to ice cream, with plenty of mutton, venison, chicken, ham, and other delicacies in between. But the main attraction was Miss Harriet Lane. No one could take their eyes away from her, dressed as she was in a low-cut white gown trimmed with roses and pearls, showing off her fine figure to perfection. Those who were lucky enough to get to talk to this vision of loveliness were completely entranced by her gaiety, her smile, and her captivating manner. Even Julia Tyler paled by comparison.

They hadn't seen anything yet. The level of presidential entertaining was stepped up to a pace that hadn't been seen since Dolley Madison's time, possibly even greater than the days of George and Martha Washington. James Buchanan was, at sixty-five, the oldest president the country had yet seen, and Washington society wasn't expecting much in the way of entertainment from such an old-timer. But James Buchanan had always loved a good party and he was not going to stop now. He was also a very wealthy man, and although he usually squeezed every dollar, he didn't mind dipping deep into his own purse to entertain lavishly. Washingtonians were ready for some fun, too, after the less-than-glittering social seasons during the terms of the three previous presidents. They also welcomed the distraction from the problems that were being faced by a country that seemed to be falling apart around them.

Harriet and the president held a large dinner party every week, usually averaging forty guests. Because the country was on the brink of a civil war, it took a great deal of effort to keep the Northerners and Southerners separate from one another and at the same time to be able to make them all feel comfortable and welcome. Harriet's sensitivity equaled her ebullience, and whatever their other differences, every political figure in Washington agreed that she was not only a delightful hostess but also a cherished friend. She held receptions even more often than state dinners, and almost no one ever turned down an invitation

Above: Twenty-seven year old Harriet provided a queenly presence to the White House, and she was loved for it.

Below: Harriet was introduced to all of American society on the night she appeared on her uncle's arm during his inaugural ball.

> *"Uncle places so much confidence in me that he gives himself no uneasiness."*
>
> —*Harriet Lane on James Buchanan*

to one of them. About the only negative note was that some of James's closest supporters were opposed to dancing, and although he rather enjoyed spinning around the dance floor himself, he took their advice and banned it at the White House. Harriet loved to dance, too, and she was very good at it, but she accepted the ban gracefully. She was very much in demand at parties outside the executive mansion, so she was able to find plenty of opportunity to lead quadrilles and to waltz and polka to her heart's content.

> *"[She was] silent whenever it was possible to be silent, watchful and careful, she made no enemies, was betrayed in no entangling alliances, and was involved in no contretemps of any kind."*
>
> —*A frequent White House guest on Harriet Lane*

Harriet's most memorable conquest was no less a person than the Prince of Wales. Edward Albert, Queen Victoria's oldest son, and the future King Edward VII, visited Washington during an 1860 North American tour, and Harriet was designated to be his escort. There were two elaborate state dinners, which she planned and presided over, and she was at his side during the obligatory tour of public buildings that included a stopover at Mrs. Smith's Young Ladies Institute. The nineteen-year-old prince seemed especially fascinated by the gymnasium, which had a bowling alley (they called it ninepins back then)—something he had never seen before. Harriet challenged him to a game and then, quite undiplomatically, beat him in what may have been the only time in his life that the prince was ever allowed to lose at any game.

Below: When the Prince of Wales came to Washington, Harriet introduced him to bowling, but she made the mistake of beating him.

Apart from a fireworks display, which, as usual, was billed as the greatest ever seen, and was watched by Harriet's friends from upstairs windows at the White House, the main event of the prince's visit was a boat trip down the Potomac to Mount Vernon. The excursion was aboard the SS *Harriet Lane*, a cutter that had recently been built for the Coast Guard and was, as the first government sidewheel steamship, the pride of the American fleet. Edward Albert was dutifully interested in the former president's estate and all the artifacts that it contained, but *The New York Times* reported that he "seemed more interested in the fascinations of Miss Lane than in the reminiscences." By the time the prince left on the next leg of his tour, Washington gossips had become convinced that a royal romance was smoldering, and there was wide speculation that Harriet had an inside track to becoming the consort of the next king of England. Naturally the English have rules about such things, but that didn't discourage the gossips who were quite sure that Queen Victoria would bend the rules because of her fondness for Harriet.

Be that as it may, they didn't give any consideration to her uncle, who demanded the last word on the subject of Harriet's choice of a husband. And they both had their eye on Baltimore banker Henry Elliot Johnston, whom they had met during a presidential vacation trip to Bedford Springs in Pennsylvania. Harriet loved him from the start, and her uncle loved his financial outlook, but they all agreed to keep the romance a secret until their White House days were behind them.

Congress had appropriated funds to spruce up the White House, and Harriet took charge of spending the money. She managed to keep within the budget, but only barely, and she transformed the mansion into a showplace. Most notable was her choice of fresh flowers that filled every room. She herself attached roses to her gowns, and she usually carried a bouquet, as a bride would, as she received guests at her uncle's side.

Above: SS Harriet Lane *was a 750-ton sidewheel gunboat. She took part in the attempt to relieve Fort Sumter and fired the first U.S. navy shot in the Civil War. The ship was eventually boarded and captured by the Confederate Army off Galveston, Texas.*

After the SS Harriet Lane *was launched, Harriet sent out invitations to several dozen of her closest friends to a party on board. She had to withdraw them when it was pointed out that the vessel was the government's property and not hers.*

Harriet became the darling of Washington society, but thanks to press coverage of her accomplishments, she caught the imagination of people all over the country as well. Women named their baby girls after her, and she established a national fashion by often wearing a lace bertha, a kind of scarf placed over the shoulders above a low-necked dress. Every well-dressed woman was soon wearing them, but few of them did as much justice to them as Harriet herself. One newspaper account said that her name "was bestowed upon flowers, perfumes, garments, poems, songs, pet animals, horses, neckties, ships, clubs, and societies." One of the most memorable of those tributes was the popular song "Listen to the Mockingbird," whose verse begins, "I'm dreaming now of sweet Halley" (by then, everyone knew about Harriet's childhood nickname). The sheet music sales reached into the millions, and the tune still ranks high among the standards in the American songbook.

During the last months of the Buchanan administration, Abraham Lincoln was elected to follow him and South Carolina seceded from the Union. Worse, as far as his administration was concerned, both James's secretary of state and his secretary of war resigned to throw in their lot with the emerging Confederacy. When treasury secretary Howell Cobb turned in his resignation, James sent Harriet to his home to try to get him to change his mind and keep "the family" from breaking up. But, for what may have been the first time, Harriet's charms failed her, and Cobb's wife, Mary Ann, told her that "I feel as light and happy as a bird. I am out. Yes, and out of the Union, too."

Below: Even when James's popularity began to fade with the approach of the Civil War, Harriet's star never dimmed at all.

Above: The bertha, a lace scarf that Harriet popularized, often trailed down the back.

Below: Harriet received many gifts from her admiring public, including this large cache brought over by a delegation from Japan.

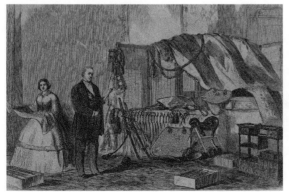

Harriet had always been a close advisor to her uncle, and now he relied on her more than ever. "[She is] a fit adviser in difficulty, a sympathetic companion in sorrow," he wrote, "and the comfort at last of [my] lonely hearth." But Harriet's star had begun to fade, too. The press branded her as a Southern sympathizer, and one paper reported that she had prevailed on her old friend Queen Victoria to keep Great Britain neutral in the war that was just around the corner. Another "exposed" her for systematically stealing paintings and state gifts from the White House. Harriet's only comment was that it all made her feel "very sad."

The truth was that Harriet hadn't removed anything from the White House that wasn't her own personal property. During her time in Great Britain, she had begun collecting art, and in her White House years, she invited prominent artists to her receptions to boost her own dream of establishing a national art gallery as had been done in London. She bought paintings of every kind that appealed to her, but her special interest was Native American art, at a time when the arts of Asia and Africa were beginning to attract the attention of the Western world.

That led to an interest in minorities in general, and American Indians in particular. As First Lady, she welcomed the ideas of reformers and presented them to lawmakers in hopes of bringing attention to the medical and educational needs of the Native Americans, with a strong emphasis on pushing for legislation to ban the sale of liquor on the reservations. Her efforts, even when they weren't as successful as she hoped, didn't go unnoticed, and the Chippewa nation made her one of their own blood brothers with the designation of "Great Mother."

Harriet was married on January 11, 1866, five years after she and her uncle had retired to Wheatland, and she moved with her husband to Baltimore. Their first son, James Buchanan Johnston, was born in November that same year, and their second son, Henry Elliot Johnston II, was born four years later. Young James died of rheumatic fever at the age of fourteen, and the family took a trip to France where they hoped that the weather would help their ailing son, Henry. The cure didn't work out, and the boy died at the age of twelve, a year after his older brother had passed away.

On their way back from France, Harriet and her husband decided that a proper memorial to their sons would be a special hospital for children. There was no such institution in America at the time, and the medical establishment was doing very little to find cures for childhood diseases, which were all too common and devastating to parents like them. They called their new hospital the Harriet Lane Home for Invalid Children, and it has since become the nucleus of the children's wing of the Johns Hopkins Medical Center in Baltimore, regarded today as the most important pediatric research institution in the world.

The hospital had barely opened when Harriet's husband, Henry Elliot Johnston, died of pneumonia, and she was at another crossroads in her life. Her uncle had died years earlier and left her Wheatland, but she chose to spend only her summers there. She moved to Washington to lobby for the creation of a national art gallery, and at one point she joined with Julia Tyler as a co-hostess at Chester A. Arthur's White House. Later she worked closely with First Lady Caroline Harrison in a project to rebuild the White House. During her years there, she was fascinated by the long construction of the Washington National Cathedral, and she provided the funds to establish St. Albans, its world-famous school for choristers.

Although he obviously had other things to do, James had an annoying habit of opening Harriet's mail, which she resented. He wrote on one envelope, "I know not whether it contains aught or love or treason."

After Harriet died of cancer at the age of seventy-six, her huge art collection was acquired by the Smithsonian Institution and became the seed of the present-day National Gallery of Art. It had been her dream for half a century.

For all her impressive accomplishments, Harriet Lane is sometimes forgotten in the roster of America's First Ladies, even though she was the first woman to officially carry the title. It has something to do with the fact that she wasn't married to a president, of course, but it is also a sign of the times that she lived in. It was during her uncle's administration that the country started to become formally divided, North and South, and everything else about his administration, good and bad, has faded into the background of the public's consciousness. But Harriet Lane was one of the best loved of all of our First Ladies, and she deserved every bit of the love that was lavished on her in her own time.

Below: The Harriet Lane Home for Invalid Children, which she endowed at Johns Hopkins Hospital in Baltimore, was the first such facility associated with a teaching hospital, and it is still known as the country's best.

Visiting Wheatland

Harriet Lane's taste is reflected in the furnishings and nineteenth-century decor at Wheatland in Lancaster, Pennsylvania, the heart of Pennsylvania Dutch country. It is run by the James Buchanan Foundation for the Preservation of Wheatland. The Romanic Victorian parlor is unchanged from the day Harriet was married there. Guided tours of the house and its four-acre grounds are available every day from 10:00 A.M. to 4:00 P.M., April through October, and on weekends in November and December. A small admission fee is charged.

Wheatland is about a mile west of central Lancaster at 1120 Marietta Avenue. From points west, take Route 30 to the Millersville/Roherstown exit to Route 741 East. From Philadelphia and the Pennsylvania Turnpike, leave the turnpike at exit 286, Lancaster/Reading, and follow Route 222 South to Route 30 West, exit at 741 East. From points north, use Route 283 East from I-83, exiting at Millersville/Roherstown to Route 741 East.

Mary Todd Lincoln

A Girl With a Future

While she was growing up in Lexington, Kentucky, Mary Todd's two greatest heroes were her father, Robert Smith Todd, the president of the local bank, and their neighbor Henry Clay, a man who wanted to be president of the United States. She once told her father that she wished he would run for president so she could go to Washington and live in the White House, but as she explained to Mr. Clay, "He only laughed and said he would rather see you there than be president himself." In that case, she added, "If you were not already married, I would wait for you." Clay responded with an invitation to visit him when he got to the White House, and although at the age of twenty-two Mary was active in his campaign for the presidential nomination in 1840, even her enthusiastic charm wasn't enough to make Clay's dream come true.

She would have to take her own dream elsewhere, and eventually she was courted by two presidential hopefuls, Stephen A. Douglas and Abraham Lincoln. When she made her choice, love had more to do with it than ambition, but it was a curious romance that fired it.

Mary was the daughter of Eliza Parker and Robert Smith Todd, who settled in Kentucky. Mary's mother died when she was young, and at thirteen and finished with her basic schooling, Mary was enrolled at Mentelle's Academy, a local finishing school for young ladies. There she learned to appreciate English and French literature and to speak French with a perfect Parisian accent. She also became an accomplished dancer, and the steps of the polka, the schottische, the waltz, and all the other popular dances of the day became as natural to her as walking. The rules of etiquette were at the center of the curriculum and Mary learned them well, but if she learned to control her sharp tongue, she frequently forgot to put that lesson into practice. Mary Todd was smarter than most of her classmates, and she didn't suffer fools gladly.

At a time when young women weren't expected to have opinions of their own, Mary had a lot of them and she wasn't the least bit shy about expressing them. She grew up in a household where local political leaders gathered, and she had always been encouraged to sit in on their discussions and to participate in them after she was old enough. She read more than most girls her age and she had a fascination with human nature, and the result was that she had something to add to just about any conversation. The problem was that she also

---

**Mary Ann
Todd Lincoln**

Born
December 13, 1818,
Lexington, Kentucky

Parents
Robert Smith Todd and
Eliza Ann Parker Todd
(Eliza died when Mary
was seven; her father
remarried Elizabeth
Humphrey)

Marriage
November 4, 1842, to
Abraham Lincoln (1809-65)

Children
Robert Todd (1843-1926);
Edward Baker (1846-50);
William Wallace (1850-62);
Thomas (Tad) (1853-71)

Died
July 16, 1882,
Springfield, Illinois

had a biting wit and a flair for mimicry that usually left others either at a loss for words or ready to box her ears.

But for all that, Mary Todd was usually sought after as the life of any party. She knew quite well how to win people over and she was generally considered a delightful young woman. She was also an attractive one; although not a raving beauty, Mary was, in the expression of the day, "becoming." She had an

> "She now and then indulged in sarcastic, witty remarks that cut. But there was no malice in it. She was impulsive and made no attempt to conceal her feelings. Indeed, it would have been an impossibility had she desired to do so, for her face was an index to every passing emotion."
>
> —Lizzie Norris, Mary Todd's school roommate, on Mary

upturned nose and bright blue eyes below a wide forehead that was crowned by soft brown hair. Her hands and arms were animated and expressive, her complexion was rosy, and her buxom figure was ideal for the fashions of the time. She not only had good taste in clothes but an obsession with them.

All these qualities served but toward one goal for a young woman in the 1830s, because the only career path that was open to her was the march down the aisle. By the time Mary graduated from school when she was seventeen, her older sister Frances was already on an extended visit to Springfield, Illinois, where their married sister, Elizabeth (or Betsey) Edwards, had recently found a prospective husband—a doctor, no less—for Frances. Mary was next in line.

Above: This series of images was captured when Mary sat for her official photograph as First Lady.

Mary's cousin John Todd Stuart was a prominent lawyer in Springfield, and his firm included a junior partner named Abraham Lincoln, who was also serving in the legislature. He had a good reputation around town as a lawyer and a storyteller, but he was too recently out of the backwoods and still very much a diamond in the rough, which made him unwelcome at Betsey's salon; so Mary didn't get to meet him.

She didn't meet anyone else who struck her fancy, either, and she went back to Lexington for two years of more intense education, which most people considered a waste of time for a woman. Eventually she gravitated back to Springfield, which had become the state capital in the meantime and was filled with all sorts of eligible bachelors, including lawyers and businessmen, and Betsey Edwards knew all the ones who mattered.

She had formed a circle known as "the coterie" that met regularly in her parlor for serious discussions and a bit of matchmaking. There were as many attractive girls in the group as there were men with obvious bright futures, but Mary quickly became the star, mostly because she could do more than bat her eyelashes and flutter a fan. She was well read and she had grown up in the midst of political discussions and gossip. She always had something to say, and when she spoke people usually listened. Her brother-in-law Ninian Edwards said she "could make a bishop forget his prayers."

"She is the very creature of excitement, you know, and never enjoys herself more than when in society and surrounded by a company of merry friends."

—James C. Conkling, of "the coterie," on Mary Todd

Young Abe Lincoln had kicked enough of the mud from his boots to be allowed into the group by then, and he was accepted in the rest of the community as well for his accomplishments, his native intelligence, and most of all his knack for telling a good story. But he still wasn't quite like any of the other men who gathered at the Edwards house, from his background to his appearance and his manners, and that may be why Mary Todd couldn't resist him.

Abraham Lincoln didn't have a very high opinion of himself, and although he was attracted to Mary, he didn't think he could support a wife, and more to the point, he was overwhelmed by her abundant charm, which only served to force him to retreat into his shell. In spite of his discomfort, he became a regular fixture in the Edwards parlor, where he could bask in the glow of the girl he called Molly.

Whether it's true or not, a Todd family tradition has it that Mary and Abe met for the first time at a ball. He was six feet, four inches tall, and she was five feet, two inches. He overcame his shyness and said to her, "Miss Todd, I want to dance with you in the worst way."

Mary had made the gangly lawyer a special romantic target, but she wasn't so sure she wanted to marry him or anyone else, and she left town again, this time to visit her uncle Judge David Todd and her cousin Ann in Columbia, Missouri. She stayed there for several months, but while she found plenty of suitors there, none of them compared to the man she had left behind in Springfield.

While she was away, Abraham had become the law partner of her cousin Judge Steven T. Logan; he was dressing better, he was more comfortable among people who considered themselves his betters, and after four terms in the legislature, he was ready to spread his wings in a wider world of politics.

But as Abe and Mary began seeing more of each other and discovering the depth of interests they had in common, her sister Betsey started to panic. There was no way she would approve a marriage between her sister and this country bumpkin who was ten years older than she was. With sister Frances as an ally, she started whispering to Mary that the Lincoln family was beneath them,

Above: One of Mary's early suitors was Stephen A. Douglas, who became Abe's opponent in the presidential election.

that his education was inferior to her own, and that he had no social graces whatsoever, not to mention that he was as homely as a mud fence.

In one of her rebuttals to their arguments, Mary told them that she had a premonition that Mr. Lincoln would be president one day. After calling her insane and seriously suggesting that she needed to see a doctor, they countered with a prediction of their own that another member of the coterie, Stephen A. Douglas, had a better chance, and not only was he more eligible as far as they were concerned, but he and Mary had already been romantically involved and it wouldn't take much to rekindle the fire. As it turned out, Douglas ran against Abraham in the 1860 presidential election, so their argument probably made some sense, except that they were backing the wrong horse.

But Mary's mind was already made up. She and Abe considered themselves engaged to each other, or as they characterized it, they had "reached an understanding." But then almost without warning, Abe appeared to have a change of heart. He told her that he thought he couldn't support her in the style she deserved, and he went on to say that it was probably impossible for him to make any woman happy. Then he broke off their engagement. After he left town, Mary bided her time. He'd be back after he came to his senses, she was certain of it. It took a year and a half.

In the meantime, Abe wrote, "I am now the most miserable man in the world. If what I feel were equally distributed to the whole human family, there would not be one cheerful face on the earth."

Eventually, a local woman who admired Abraham and approved of the match brought them into her home for a series of encounters out of sight of Mary's sisters so the couple could "be friends again." They were already much more than friends, and they decided to get married immediately, if not sooner.

But Mary's home was in the house of her sister and brother-in-law, and they initially refused to allow the ceremony to take place in their parlor. It took some doing, but they finally agreed, still against their better judgment, that the wedding should be a family affair. It delayed their plans, but Abe and Mary were married "at home" on November 4, 1842. She was just shy of twenty-four years old; he was thirty-three.

A New Life

Abraham was impoverished at the time they were married; he had debts to pay and he was helping to support his relatives. But Mary was determined to live within his income, and that meant living in a room above a local tavern, where the rent was $4 a week. She was part of a wealthy family that ranked high

Mary did not have a wedding dress made, but was married wearing a white muslin dress that she washed and ironed for the occasion.

in local society, but because of the way her sisters had treated her over her choice of a husband, she pointedly avoided going to the Edwards house, where she had spent so many happy hours socializing with the elite of Springfield. Even later in her life, when it appeared that she had made the right decision and her sisters and their circle tried to lure her back, Mary never softened toward them again. Both she and her husband regarded them as incurable snobs, and they probably were.

Above: The Lincolns spent their early married life in rooms above a tavern. It was a comedown for Mary, who was used to more genteel homes, but she never complained about it.

She could have used the company, because Abe's legal business took him away from home for long periods. He was on the road for three months each in the spring and the fall. But she used the lonely time to read more books and to search for ways that she could help advance her husband's career. When he was at home, they had plenty of time for conversation; their discussions of the books they were both reading, and

> *"Nothing new here, except my marrying, which to me is a matter of profound wonder."*
>
> —*Abraham Lincoln in a letter to a friend*

the ones that she read to him, added a great deal to his own limited formal education.

The routine, which was far removed from the life she had been leading but seemed to appeal to her, was broken when their first son, Robert Todd Lincoln, was born. Mary discovered that she had a talent for motherhood as well. Her father, pleased that his grandson had been named for him, arranged to have $120 a year deposited into their bank account—nearly $3,000 in today's dollars.

It was enough to move them out from above the tavern, where patrons were grumbling about the crying baby upstairs. They moved into a three-room house, where Mary got her first taste of housekeeping, and the following spring they moved into a larger house in Springfield that is now known as the Lincoln House. At about the same time, her father gave them eighty acres of land outside of town.

About the only domestic skill Mary had learned as a girl was sewing, and her new neighbors criticized her as a poor housekeeper, which was about as

Mary never called her husband Abe or even Abraham; it was always "Mr. Lincoln," although she called him "Father" after their children were born.

Above: Mary had never learned to cook before she was married, but she did the best she could, and by the time they moved into their new house, she knew her way around the kitchen.

Below: Abe and his son Tad were shot through the lens of Matthew Brady's camera in 1864.

low-down as a woman could be in their eyes. And although Abe never seemed to complain about it, she wasn't much of a cook, either.

Eventually, Mary had three other sons to care for: Edward Baker Lincoln was born in 1846, and William Wallace Lincoln, whom they called Willie, arrived four years later, followed in 1853 by a son they named Thomas. He was a spindly-legged baby with a large head, like a tadpole, which prompted his father to call him Tad. All the births were difficult ones for Mary, and she suffered from the complications of Tad's birth for a dozen years.

Although the Lincolns were happy together in their way, nobody would have called them a "fun couple." He was frequently moody and given to unexpected outbursts, and he was also a restless sleeper who had frightening dreams that often drove him to wake up screaming. He was given to roughhousing with his sons, which must have grated against Mary's genteel instincts; and his earthy language, even around the children, must have annoyed her, too. He was much too casual about his appearance for Mary's tastes, and she found it disgraceful. And then, of course, there was Mary's lifelong history of migraine headaches, temper tantrums, and sudden crying spells that Abe had to deal with. But he treated Mary like a fragile porcelain doll—he called her "my child-wife"—and she treated him with loving respect in spite of the annoyances each visited on the other. His sharp wit also helped bring lots of laughter into their home, and Mary herself had no problem seeing humor behind every dark cloud.

Her strong will allowed Mary to become a model housekeeper and a tolerable cook. Even her neighbors said so. She made all her own clothes using pictures in magazines as her inspiration, and she made her husband's clothes as well, although that was a challenge considering his frame, which was all right angles. But Abe Lincoln could never be called a slave to fashion.

Over time, their prosperity increased as his law practice flourished, but his political career didn't take hold until he was elected to Congress in 1847. They had two sons at that point, and the whole family packed up to go to Washington with him. They spent some time on the way in Louisville with her family, whom she hadn't visited in seven years, and Mary had the opportunity to introduce her husband to her other idol, Henry Clay, who had just been defeated in his third run for the presidency, and whom, like Mary, Abe had admired all of his life. The meeting was a kind of passing of the torch from one presidential hopeful to another. At least that was how Mary saw it.

The Lincolns moved into a boardinghouse near Capitol Hill, and Mary began exploring her new neighborhood. Washington at the time was a Southern town without any of the charms; the streets were mostly unpaved and there were fewer stores than in Springfield. What it had that Springfield didn't was a slave market, and the sight of people in chains on their way to lives of hard labor offended Mary as much as it had while she was growing up Louisville.

After a lifetime dreaming of going to Washington, Mary was disappointed in the place. There wasn't much social life for the wife of a freshman congressman, and her rambunctious sons were a problem while their father was too busy to keep them amused, as he had always done back home. After a few months she decided to go back to Louisville to spend the rest of her husband's term getting reacquainted with her family and showing off her youngsters.

After she left, he wrote to her, "I thought you had hindered me some in attending to business but now, having nothing but business—no variety—it has grown exceedingly tasteless to me. I hate to stay in this old room by myself."

It had been their plan to reunite in Lexington at the end of the session, but Abe was tapped to go to New England to make speeches for Whig presidential candidate Zachary Taylor, who was in trouble up there. Mary and the boys joined him in Buffalo, New York, where they boarded a steamer to take them to Chicago. She had followed press reports of his campaign swing, and she was more proud of her Abe than ever. Her pride swelled even more when she listened to a two-hour speech he made, which the Chicago *Daily Journal* called "one of the very best we have heard or read since the opening of the campaign."

The Lincolns returned to Springfield, but their house had been rented; so they went to live at the Globe Tavern, where their married life had begun. When Abe went back to Washington for the rest of his term, Mary stayed behind at the tavern, an arrangement that relieved her of household chores (although she had mastered them, she still found them unpleasant). The arrangement also reassured her husband that she wouldn't be alone at night, a thing both of them dreaded.

Tragedy came into her life in 1849 when Mary's father died, followed soon afterward by her grandmother, who had been a strong influence on her while she was growing up. When word of the second death reached her, Mary was fearful that a third was about to follow. Her youngest son, Eddie, was suffering from what seemed to be diphtheria. Mary stayed at his bedside day and night for nearly two months, and when he died, she collapsed, deep in grief. She refused to take any food until her husband coaxed her to "eat, for we must live." She realized, though, that he needed her, for he was deep in depression, too, and their son, Robert, needed both of them. Writing provided some relief, however. One of her poems ended with the lines, "Angel boy—fare thee well, farewell/ Sweet Eddie, we bid you adieu." Mary was pregnant again soon after her son's funeral, and their third son, Willie, was born on December 17, 1850, ten months after they buried their sweet Eddie.

Both Mary and Abe loved children, and they seemed to understand them better than most parents did. They indulged their

Mary's grandmother operated a way station on the Underground Railroad to speed slaves to the safety of the North, and young Mary helped her.

Faith of Our Fathers

Abraham Lincoln's strong faith in God is one of his most enduring legacies. Few American presidents have had such sincere beliefs. But he grew up in a world of revivalists and fearsome preachers for whom emotionalism was more important than faith and understanding; and Abe didn't care for that kind of religion. Mary had been raised as a Presbyterian, but she went to the Episcopal church with her sister after she arrived in Springfield, and she and Abe were married in an Episcopalian ceremony. When their son Eddie was buried, a Presbyterian minister, Dr. James Smith, conducted the service. Not only did his words comfort them, but Smith impressed Abe with his philosophy. Abraham didn't formally join the First Presbyterian Church as Mary did, but he was there at her side most Sundays and he cheerfully paid rent for their family pew. He was a regular churchgoer for the rest of his life, which greatly pleased Mary, who always had been.

Right: Mary and Abe with sons Robert Todd and Thomas, whom they called Tad.

boys beyond what would be called permissiveness today. Their father always let them have the run of his office, usually with the result of hopelessly scattered papers and rearranged furniture. Mary was no less indulgent. She proudly brought the boys out for visitors to fawn over, she arranged elaborate parties for them even if there was no special occasion to celebrate, and she put her ingrained dignity aside to join them in their games.

The Lincolns became well established in their Springfield neighborhood, and they became frequent hosts of dinner parties and socials. The old coteries had nearly disappeared, and the "in crowd" had become young married couples with children, and the Lincolns were at the head of it. On one occasion, Mary wrote of a party for three hundred guests at their home that was "a very handsome and agreeable entertainment, at least our friends flatter us by saying so." A guest at a dinner party wrote in his diary, "It was the genial manner and ever kind welcome of the hostess, and the wit and humor, anecdotes and unrivaled conversation of the host which formed the chief attraction and made dinner at the Lincolns an event to be remembered."

The intellectual scene had shifted, too. Springfield had a theater by then, and Mary and Abe, both of whom got special pleasure out of plays, especially those of Shakespeare, almost never missed a traveling production when it passed through town.

Abe stayed interested in the political scene, but he concentrated on his law practice for several years after his term in Congress ended, and Mary began to worry that her dream of living in the White House might never come true. The situation changed in 1855 when the legislature got ready to appoint a new United States senator and he started lobbying for the job. Abraham lost his bid and it was painful to him, but bigger changes were in the air. Both he and Mary had been lifelong supporters of the Whig party, but a new party that called itself Republican was being formed.

Below: Road company productions of Shakespeare, including Thomas Keene's Macbeth, *frequently played Springfield.*

Although Abe wasn't happy to "de-Whig" himself and leave behind old friends and associates, he became one of its earliest members. The issue that drew him was Republican opposition to the extension of slavery into new territories. He had often said that seeing slaves was a "continual torment" that made him "miserable," and there was never any question that Mary completely agreed with him, even though she had been raised among slaveholders. Neither of them cared to be called abolitionists, which was too strong a position for them, but they were solidly behind the idea that slavery shouldn't be allowed to spread.

A chance to become a U.S. senator came up again three years later when their old friend Stephen A. Douglas ran for reelection as a Democrat and Abraham was nominated to oppose him. The historic debates of the campaign turned him into a national figure, and Mary was bright-eyed with pride. Stephen Douglas, the so-called Little Giant and the man her sisters thought she ought to marry, was, she said, "a very little, little giant by the side of my tall Kentuckian, and intellectually my husband towers above Douglas just as he does physically."

Still, although Abraham forced Douglas into a corner time after time during their debates, he lost the Senate seat again. It didn't matter, though; he was on his way to bigger things, just as Mary had been predicting almost since the first day she met him. She often went on the road with him during the next eighteen months as he traveled the country making speeches that would turn his defeat into the ultimate victory they both wanted. Mary Todd Lincoln had never been happier. Her joy increased when the Republicans nominated her husband to run for the presidency, and she threw her heart and soul into campaigning with him. Part of the irony was that her old beau Stephen Douglas was one of the men running against him.

Mary stayed home, worrying, watching, and waiting on Election Day, and her husband, the candidate, spent the evening at the telegraph office waiting for returns. When it appeared that he had won, more than ten thousand people had gathered outside and they sent up a loud call for a speech. But all they got from the president-elect was a smile and a wave. "I need to go down and tell Mary about it," he said.

National Figure

Americans were holding their breath, waiting to find out what they could expect of this hick from the West whom they had just made their president. They were even more apprehensive about his wife. What could she possibly know about dressing for the part? Or even about presiding over Washington society?

They needn't have worried about Mary Lincoln. After spending a postelection Christmas with her family and friends, she set out for New York on a shopping spree. She found gowns and dresses and jewelry, hats and furs and fancy shoes that not even the magazines had prepared her for. More important, she quickly discovered that she didn't need the money she had taken along with her. The big-city merchants, who knew a good thing when they saw it, gave unlimited credit to the First Lady-elect.

Her new status gave her instant entrée to important people there, and reporters followed her around town like homeless puppies. She was invited to glittering parties where her opinions were eagerly solicited on everything from fashion to politics, and especially about other prominent personalities. Of course, Mary had never been a shrinking violet, but she had never occupied such a prominent stage. From the days she sat in on her father's political gatherings, she always had an opinion to put forward, and she never did learn that silence is sometimes golden. She didn't hold back then, and she wasn't holding back now. It wasn't enough that she was expounding to complete strangers and often dealing in rumors, but there were usually reporters in the room taking down every word.

Her tongue had created enemies for Mary nearly all her life, but they had been social in nature, and although she understood politics better than most women, she didn't seem to realize that her husband might have some political enemies. After her New York trip, so did she.

Abe had always confided his personal opinions to Mary; he shared his political ideas, too, and he often asked for her advice, which more often than not he didn't take. But now that Mary had become a national figure in her own right, she became a convenient target for the political opposition, which was frustrated by Abraham's own subtlety and his ability to keep his own counsel. An early charge leveled against Mary was that she was behind some of his choices for cabinet appointments, even to the point of accepting bribes to finance her love for shopping. There is some evidence that the former was true—that she at least tried, but not that she ever succeeded—but it was totally out of character for her to accept money from anyone except her husband.

Their trip east was like a triumphal tour, with celebrations at every city along the way, but by the time they reached Pennsylvania, Abraham had a visit from the detective Allan Pinkerton, who had news of a plot to derail the train and kidnap him as the train passed through Baltimore. The facts of the plot were thoroughly documented, and Abe agreed to be separated from his family and continue on alone in an unmarked, unscheduled train. Naturally, Mary was distraught, but she agreed to the arrangement in spite of the panic she was feeling. The rest of the trip was a nightmare for her, and she acquired an overwhelming dread that never left her mind for very long throughout the entire Lincoln presidency.

The city of Washington, where the family was reunited after arriving like thieves in the night, was completely divided. Even a woman with a more stable personality than Mary Lincoln might have been driven over the edge by what she found there. The Confederacy was being formed in response to Abraham's election, and Washington was becoming an island in the middle of a hostile country.

From the time the city was established as the capital, the Washington gentry had been dominated by Southern planters and their wives, and although many of them had gone home, there were enough of them still around to give the place an atmosphere of hostility. They hated Yankees, they couldn't

Above: Abe started the 1860 presidential campaign without his familiar beard, which he grew near the end of it. It was not Mary's idea, but came from an eleven year-old girl who wrote to him suggesting it. He didn't top off his beard with a mustache, which. It was the emblem of a soldier back in those days.

stand Republicans, and they despised the Lincolns even more because they were Westerners. Mary got a double dose of their contempt. Union supporters, even some who were also supporters of the new administration, spread rumors that Mary was loyal to her Kentucky roots and was almost certainly a secessionist.

She had her first inkling that the road ahead was going to be a rough one when the city's socialites refused to call on Mary at Willard's Hotel, where the Lincolns were living before the inauguration. She was being dismissed for the first time in her life, and it affected her until the day she died. To make matters worse, she began to get hate mail, and the press never missed an opportunity to put her down, from negative comments on her appearance, to hints that she was a woman of the frontier with no social graces, to references to her ties with the despised South. It was even rumored that Mary was a Confederate spy, a charge that prompted a Senate committee to hold hearings to find out if the rumors were true.

Abraham's inauguration was a somber affair. Other presidents had been escorted to the Capitol by military units in their smartest uniforms, but in this case, the troops were not an honor guard, but a protective one. The crowds along Pennsylvania Avenue were either apprehensive or downright hostile, and Mary was quite aware of the sharpshooters stationed on rooftops along the way. The only bright note for her that day was her husband's inaugural speech, which, like all of his speeches, she believed was the greatest oratory since the days of the noble Romans.

Above: Mary's first home in Washington before the inauguration was at Willard's Hotel, but few ladies came to call on her there.

The following evening, Mary appeared at the Inaugural Ball wearing a stunning blue gown with gold and pearl jewelry and a blue feather in her hair. She entered the room not on the arm of her husband, but accompanied by their old friend Stephen A. Douglas. At least one old wound had been bound up, but there were new ones to deal with. Although five thousand people came to the party, the old guard of local society boycotted it and so did the Southerners who were still in town. There was no question that Mary noticed the snub, but she refused to let it drag her spirits down. This was her moment and she made the most of it.

Mary had come to Washington with an entourage of her own: seventeen relatives, every one of them well accomplished socially. Her sister Betsey Edwards was among them, ready to eat a little crow after her opposition to her sister's marriage. She brought along her two grown daughters, Elizabeth and Julia, and their cousin Elizabeth Todd Grimsley, who wrote later that "there were a hundred Todds on deck, all of them seeking appointments."

"Thousands of soldiers are guarding us, and if there is safety in numbers we have every reason to feel secure."

—Mary Lincoln

The Eldest Lincoln Son

Robert Todd Lincoln was eighteen years old when the family went to Washington, and he was generally considered the life of the party. He was old enough to join the men in the smoking room at the hotel that was their temporary quarters, but even he felt the sting of his mother's enemies when he was away from her side. On one occasion when he showed up at the male inner sanctum, the piano player struck up a rendition of "Dixie," the marching song of the rebels. As his father most likely would have done, Robert casually lit a cigar and pretended not to notice, but he requested that the next tune should be "Hail Columbia."

Left: Robert Todd Lincoln, Mary and Abe's first son.

Mary found the White House in an abysmal state, especially the family quarters. Paint was peeling from the walls of the public rooms, the carpets were frayed and stained with tobacco juice, wallpaper was peeling off, and chandeliers were dusty and corroded. Fortunately, Congress agreed and provided the funds to make the mansion more presentable. It was an opportunity for Mary to show the local establishment that in spite of what they might be thinking, she was a woman of refined taste. It took her some time because troops were billeted in many of the rooms, but by the time Mary finished the work, the White House was more tastefully decorated than it had been by any other First Lady. But not many of them had such expensive tastes as Mary Lincoln had.

When the work was finished, Mary held a reception to show it off, and her guests were delighted by what she had accomplished. Older furniture had been revarnished and chairs and settees reupholstered in crimson satin, folded and tufted in the very latest fashion. The wallpaper in the East Room had been replaced with maroon, crimson, and gold velvet paper with a French pattern; the carpeting, of the newly fashionable wall-to-wall variety, had a custom design of wreaths and flowers. The windows were covered with lace curtains and framed by crimson, gold-fringed drapes. Both the Green Room and the Red Room had been completely refurnished and redecorated. The only reminder of the past was the Washington portrait that Dolley Madison had rescued from the White House fire, which was hung in the Red Room. The State Bedroom had been redone in royal purple, and the huge canopied bed was draped with purple satin and gold lace. The private section of the residence was redone, too, with modern furniture and fresh wallpaper.

Mary had gone way over her budget, but the president wasn't aware of it until the bills started coming in. He wasn't happy about it, but he said he'd pay them out of his own pocket. Mary went in tears to Major B. B. French, the commissioner of public buildings, who agreed with her view that it was "common to over-run appropriations," and he agreed to do something about it. But he needed the president's approval to ask for more money, and Abraham

Below: This is a sampling of the ladies who showed up for President Lincoln's inaugural ball, which was notable for the ones who refused the invitation.

put his foot down. "It would stink in the nostrils of the American people to have it said that the president of the United States had approved a bill over-running an appropriation of $20,000 for flub dubs for this damned old house, when the soldiers cannot have blankets," he thundered. Major French was able to have the obviously padded bills reduced, and it all ended well enough, but he had to admit that Mary Lincoln was indeed a "curiosity."

As a further attempt to prove she wasn't a vulgar frontier woman, Mary set out to dress better than any of her critics. As she explained to her dressmaker, Elizabeth Keckley, "I must dress in costly materials. The people scrutinize every article that I wear with critical curiosity. The very fact of having grown up in the West subjects me to more searching observation." This was after a discussion of the dressmaker's salary in which Lizzie was told, "I cannot afford to be extravagant…we are poor." Mrs. Keckley, a former slave who had been in the service of Varina Davis, the First Lady of the Confederacy, became Mary's close friend and confidante as well as her dressmaker. She may have been the only person in Washington, if not the country, who could deal with Mary's unpredictable temper and her sometimes unreasonable demands about how she should be turned out and how she expected to live her life.

Above: The Capitol building still wasn't completely rebuilt when Abraham Lincoln was inaugurated there, even though forty-seven years had passed since it was destroyed.

Below: Tad hardly ever had a dull moment during the time he lived in the White House.

Children's Hour

"Let the Children have a good time," was the watchword in the Lincoln White House. Their two boys and their friends, sometimes street urchins they befriended, had the run of the place. The president could often be found wrestling with them on the floor of his office, and he sometimes invited his sons to sit at the foot of the table during state dinners. Willie and Tad loved playing pranks, which was understandable considering that both their parents did, as well, and there was no telling where they'd turn up. They were especially intrigued by the bell system that was used to summon servants, and no one knew when the bell rang whether it was the real thing or not. Once Tad set up a tollbooth at the foot of the stairs frequented by office seekers and charged each of them a nickel to pass. The boys' favorite playground was up on the White House roof, which sometimes doubled as a fort where they played war games, and sometimes it was a setting for circuses with the family pets doubling as the menagerie. The house was full of animals, especially dogs. There were a couple of ponies, too, and also goats, all of whom could wander, or be led, anywhere they wanted to go. One of the goats wanted most of all to lie on Tad's bed. The president had a dog of his own that he called Jip. Abraham allowed it to sit on his lap while he ate lunch, which the animal shared as he was gently stroked by his master.

The Other First Lady

When Varina Howell Davis's (1826-1905) husband, Jefferson Davis, resigned from the United States Senate on his way to becoming president of the Confederate States of America, Varina Davis told friends it would be just a matter of time before she'd be back and living in the White House. Like Mary Lincoln, she had been expecting that would happen for nearly all of her life.

The lives of the two First Ladies were remarkably similar in other ways as well. Varina was born and raised in Natchez, Mississippi, in a family very much like the Todds of Kentucky, and their early educations were alike. Varina was fascinated by politics as a young woman, and she was a strong advocate of the Whig party, which represented the Southern aristocracy. Both she and Mary switched their allegiance later in their lives; Varina became a Democrat, and Mary a Republican.

Both women were highly regarded as lively conversationalists and accomplished hostesses. But as First Ladies, both were unfairly scorned as crude women with sharp tongues. Varina was an outcast in many circles because of her family's ties to the North, as Mary was for her Southern roots. Both had been congressional wives: Davis entered the Senate in 1847, the same year Abraham became a congressman, and although Varina had already been a congressional wife for two years before Mary arrived, each of them shared the frustrating experience of getting accepted into Washington's closed society.

When Varina Howell married Jefferson Davis in 1845, her family opposed the match, another parallel with the Lincolns. He was eighteen years older than she was, but they couldn't find much else to complain about—except that they just didn't like him. Davis was a successful plantation owner with a brilliant military career behind him and a promising political career ahead of him. He had just been elected to Congress.

Varina adapted well to life in Washington. Both she and her husband were obsessively ambitious, and her talents as a hostess pushed him along faster than he probably could have on his own. He was extremely sensitive to criticism, but she was outstanding in her efforts at keeping him from making enemies he didn't need, as well as encouraging him to hide his hurt feelings. They were in Washington for sixteen years, some of them when he was secretary of war in the Franklin Pierce administration, but their life there came to an end in 1861, two months before President Lincoln arrived.

After her husband was made president of the Confederacy, Varina became his brilliant First Lady. The parties at the executive mansion in Richmond were always stunning affairs, even by Southern standards. But by the Davis's second year there, Richmond had become a beleaguered city and people who were suffering began attacking Mrs. Davis as insensitive to what was becoming of them. On the other hand, some of them complained she wasn't giving enough parties, which they saw as a way of boosting overall morale. Varina was criticized for having too much influence over her husband, too. Whether or not that was the case, anyone who dared to challenge his abilities as a politician got a withering taste of her biting sarcasm.

Varina and Jefferson had six children, only one of whom survived her. One was born at the Richmond White House, and another died there.

After the war ended, the former president was arrested and jailed. The Davis children were sent to Canada to the safety of her mother's home, but Varina herself was forbidden to leave Georgia where her husband was serving his sentence. She spent nearly all of her time working to get a parole for him, and it took her more than two years to succeed.

The Davises lived in virtual poverty for the next few years until a friend made it possible for them to buy a Mississippi plantation called Beauvoir, which became their retirement home. Varina stayed on there writing her memoirs after her husband died in 1889, and eventually she turned the plantation over to the state to become a home for Confederate veterans. She moved to New York after that, and she supported herself writing magazine articles until she died in 1905.

It was much easier to attack the First Lady than the president, and Mary had more than her share of outright lies to deal with. To her credit, she almost never had temper tantrums in public, but White House servants, whom she fired with uncommon regularity, delighted in informing the public that they were frequent, real, and sudden, and no fun to witness. The scorned hired help also spread tales about Mary's vanity and her obsession with clothes. On that score, she had hoped to use her style sense to prove she was no farm wife, but her critics charged that she was overdoing it, especially considering that the nation was at war.

Mary was also scorned by the New England elite, who regarded her as a parvenu. John Quincy Adams, still a keen observer, wrote in his diary, "If the President caught it at dinner, his wife caught it at the reception. All manner of stories about her were flying around; she wanted to do the right thing but, not knowing how, was too weak and proud to ask." The elder statesman didn't bother to figure out why those stories were flying around, but after a lifetime in politics and diplomacy, he should have known that he ought to take them with a grain of salt. But then, no one did.

Newspaper columnists, a new breed at the time, competed with each other to heap dirt on Mary Lincoln. She was good copy, but not all of what appeared in the papers was good news for the First Lady, nor was all of it true.

At times, it seemed as though Mary's only real supporter was her husband. He understood her moods, and he had long since learned how to deal with them. He was entranced by her face, the way she dressed, and her conversational skills. "My wife is as handsome as when she was a girl," he said, "and I, a poor nobody then, fell in love with her, and what is more I have never fallen out." As far as he was concerned, they were still a young couple in love.

Above: The Lincolns' last reception at the White House was attended by victorious Union generals and members of his Cabinet.

The Smell of Success

One of Mary's earliest successes as a hostess was a dinner party for the diplomatic corps, which the Washington Star reported was "the most brilliant affair of the sort that has ever taken place in the Executive Mansion." Its story continued, "Through the good taste of Mrs. Lincoln, the stiff artificial flowers heretofore ornamenting the presidential tables were wholly discarded and their places delightfully supplied by fragrant, natural flowers. The Blue Room was decorated with cut flowers; and the chandeliers gracefully festooned with wreaths and flowers, indeed the senses of sight and smell were delighted at every turn by beautiful and fragrant pyramids and wreaths from the floral riches of the White House conservatories and grounds. The dinner was served in a style to indicate that Mrs. Lincoln's good taste and good judgment had exercised supervision in this department also."

A Family Tragedy

Above: Mary in her finest ball gown.

Not long after the traditional White House New Year's reception in 1862, Mary began planning her own drawing room receptions. Then, in the midst of her preparations, she had an idea. It was customary for the president to host a series of state dinners during the congressional season, but in the interest of economy and in deference to the war, Mary suggested that the dinners should be canceled in favor of three large receptions.

Abraham wasn't so sure it was a good idea. He considered the dinner parties a good venue for candid conversations with his generals, and more important, he knew it would give the public, which hated change even in wartime, another excuse to criticize him. Still, Mary was a persuasive woman, especially as far as her husband was concerned, and he agreed to give the idea a try.

There was criticism, lots of it, when Mary sent out invitations to her first reception of the year. Some of it came from hard-nosed abolitionists who thought partying at a time like this was unseemly. "Don't Mr. and Mrs. Lincoln know there is a civil war?" huffed one of them as he tore up his invitation. Most of the hostility came from people who didn't get an invitation at all, but Mary defused them by sending out more of them, even though it meant she would be entertaining her husband's political enemies and members of a hostile press corps.

The reception was a magnificent success in spite of everything. Mary appeared wearing a stunning white satin dress trimmed with black lace, symbolically mourning Prince Albert, Queen Victoria's consort who had recently died. The gesture might also have been in memory of the thousands of Union troops who had been slaughtered in the war, but no one bothered to make that connection.

The East Room was filled with the cut flowers that had become Mary's trademark, and the decor spilled over into the Blue Room, where she and her husband received their guests. A great many of those guests were European military experts brought over to train the Union army officers, and they arrived in full uniform with acres of medals on their chests and miles of gold braid on their arms and shoulders, adding unprecedented glitter to the occasion.

The dinner was catered by a chef from New York, and his presentation was more than dramatic. It included a replica of a warship made of spun sugar, and a fountain with water nymphs fashioned out of nougat candy.

But for all the opulence of her party, Mary wasn't smiling as usual, and she disappeared from the receiving line several times. Her son Willie needed her. What had started as a cold had developed into a fever, and it was only after their doctor reassured her that he wasn't in any danger that she decided not to cancel the reception. But at some point during the evening, the doctor changed his mind. Willie had developed a type of malaria, and his life was indeed in danger. The twelve-year-old boy was dead the following afternoon.

Both Mary and the president were beside themselves with grief. She was led to her bed, where she stayed behind drawn curtains sobbing uncontrollably. She was still there on the day of her son's funeral, which she couldn't gather the strength to witness. The rooms downstairs that had been so gaily decked out the night before were draped in black bunting, and she refused to allow it to be taken down for several weeks. Mary was always subject to sudden crying spells, but they came more frequently and she couldn't function at all for most of the next three months. As had been the case when she lost her little Eddie, she finally snapped out of it because of her feelings of duty to her husband. "If I had not felt the spur of necessity urging me to cheer Mr. Lincoln, whose grief was as great as my own," she wrote, "I would never have smiled again."

Mary never completely recovered from her grief. Deep religious faith sustained both her and her husband, but she believed that Willie was always near to her, even in death, and she consulted several mediums and spiritualists who said they could help her talk with him. None of their séances worked, but Mary claimed that her dead son appeared at the foot of her bed every night, sometimes in the company of his brother Eddie. As her friend Lizzie Keckley said, Mary was "a peculiarly constituted woman."

Mary eventually forced a change of scene on herself with a trip to New York and Boston to assemble a new wardrobe of mourning clothes, and she went again a few months later, seeming to be her old self again. Among the changes that had taken place was a stronger interest in the abolition of slavery. Her traveling companion, Mrs. Keckley, had started raising funds for relief of newly freed slaves, and Mary not only gave money to the cause and encouraged her husband to do the same, but she gave Lizzie introductions to wealthy New Yorkers who were more than happy to help.

Mental Problems

It had been rumored for years that Mary Lincoln was mentally unstable, but such things were a gray area of medical practice in her day, and there was no way to confirm or deny what was being whispered about her. It is true as well that she was a target of malicious gossip by people who were prone to make outlandish charges. But it seems apparent that after her son Willie died, she went through what would be diagnosed as a nervous breakdown today.

Her husband was a hands-on war president and much too distracted to give Mary all the attention she needed. Her sister Betsey moved into the White House for a time to take care of her, but it was her husband who put her on the road to recovery. He led her to a window that had a view of a mental institution and gently said, "Mother, do you see that large white building on the hill yonder? Try and control your grief or it will drive you mad, and we may have to send you there."

Right: Willie, the third son of Mary and Abe, died in the White House at age twelve.

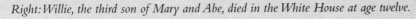

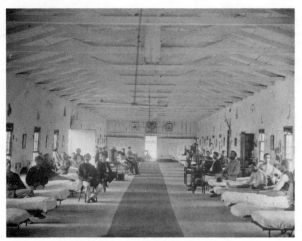

Above: The military hospital on Washington's Armory Square was one of several that Mary visited frequently with flowers in hand.

Below: Robert Todd Lincoln, in his uniform as a captain in the Union army, left college to enlist, against Mary's wishes.

After a year with no receptions, dinners, or band concerts at the White House, Mary was ready to entertain again for the New Year's Day reception in 1863—the same day her husband's Emancipation Proclamation went into effect. Although the party was an unqualified success, and in spite of the special reason for a celebration, Mary's heart wasn't in it, and she left soon after it began.

In the meantime, she was seen frequently, usually alone and unannounced, at military hospitals, where she indulged her strong maternal instincts by ministering to the wounded. She never appeared without bouquets of flowers from the White House conservatory and samples of food from its kitchens, as well as gifts that she herself had received from well-wishers. Of course, her visits weren't made with newspaper reporters in tow, and so they went unnoticed. Even her donation of $1,000 to one of the hospitals wasn't made public until after Mary died.

Death came into Mary's life again when two of her half brothers, Sam and Alexander Todd, were killed fighting for the Confederacy, but she had to keep her grief to herself this time, real though it was. In another time, she wouldn't have been so sensitive to public opinion, but times had changed and so had Mary.

Her biggest concern was the fast-approaching presidential election. It was vital to Mary that her husband be reelected, and she was relieved when he was, by more than 400,000 votes. But she had mixed emotions. She said, "Now that we have won the position, I almost wish it were otherwise. Poor Mr. Lincoln is looking so broken-hearted, so completely worn out, I fear he will not get through the next four years." The chief reason for her happiness was that his dedication to his job would delay his discovery of her mountain of debts or of her backstage dabbling in politics. He may already have known, because he had been taking her into his confidence less and less in recent months.

A happier day than Election Day for all of the Lincoln family came when General Robert E. Lee surrendered to General Ulysses S. Grant five months later and the war was over at last. But for Mary the worst was yet ahead.

"I Didn't Raise My Boy to Be a Soldier"

Robert Lincoln, Mary's oldest son, was safely at Harvard Law School, but she had an overwhelming dread that army service was inevitable for him. She had already lost two sons and she wasn't ready to part with a third, but the boy had pleaded with his parents to allow him to join up, and the president was worried that his son might be painted as a shirker if he didn't. Over his wife's tearful objections, he had Robert assigned to General Grant's staff, offering to pay his salary and upkeep out of his own pocket. Robert was commissioned as a captain and placed far behind the front lines, but Mary was never convinced that he was out of harm's way.

On April 14, 1865, the First Lady and the president spent the day touring Washington and sharing dreams of the future. "We must be cheerful," he told her, "between the war and the loss of our darling Willie, we have both been very miserable." They planned long trips together, to California, to Europe, and to Jerusalem, which he said he had always dreamed of seeing.

They were the first presidential couple since George Washington to attend the theater regularly, and after months of denying themselves the pleasure, they were planning to go to Ford's Theater to see Laura Keane's production of an English play called *Our American Cousin*. It wasn't Shakespeare, as they would have preferred, but it starred John Wilkes Booth, one of the great Shakespearean actors of the day. It would turn out to be one of the most dramatic evenings in American history.

The Lincolns and their guests were seated in the presidential box, he in an upholstered rocker and she in a chair pulled close to it. As they always did, they joined hands for the rest of the evening.

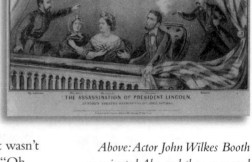

Well into the third act, there was a sudden sharp sound and a frantic flurry in the presidential box. John Wilkes Booth had shot the president and stabbed one of the other guests. Mary knew before anyone else that her husband had been shot, and it was her terrified screams that alerted everyone else to what had just happened. She followed, completely dazed, when the wounded president was carried to a house across the street, and she fell to her knees beside his bed, sobbing uncontrollably and begging him to try to speak. She asked that her sons be brought to their father's side, and Robert appeared soon afterward. Tad, his father's favorite, couldn't be found.

Mary sat at her husband's side through the night, until he died at 7:22 in the morning. Robert took her home to the White House, and it wasn't until then that the reality of an unthinkable evening came home to her. "Oh, my God," she screamed, "and have I given my husband to die?" Deep worry that something like this would happen to her husband had never been far from Mary's mind since they left Springfield a lifetime ago, but she'd finally had reason to believe that he was safe at last now that the war was over.

She was in her room when the president's body was brought back to the White House, but she didn't come out, not that day or any other, for days on end. Elizabeth Keckley wrote that the sounds from the room were "the wails of a broken heart, the wild unearthly shrieks, the wild tempestuous outbursts of grief from the soul."

Above: Actor John Wilkes Booth assassinated Abe and then managed to escape in spite of having shattered his leg in a leap to the stage of the crowded theater, and despite the fact that his face was as familiar to most people as Abe's was.

Mary took it upon herself to have a local policeman assigned to watch over the presidential box at Ford's Theater, but he was on the wrong side of the door when John Wilkes Booth entered the box, fired the fatal shot, and then leapt to the stage to his escape.

The theater had always been one of Mary Lincoln's greatest pleasures, but she never set foot in one again after the night her husband was assassinated.

Thousands passed through the East Room, where Abraham's funeral was held, but Mary was not among them. Thousands more went to the Capitol to pay their respects when his body lay in state there, but again, Mary wasn't one of them. When the fallen president was placed on a special train for the slow journey back to Springfield, Robert was with him, but Mary was left behind in her room, tormented by the phantoms of her memory.

Over the next month, Mary alternated between hysterical grieving and the sad task of winding up her husband's personal affairs. She packed their possessions into boxes to be shipped to Chicago, where she chose to live because it was near enough to Springfield that she could visit her husband's grave but far enough away that she could be spared the memories that the city held for her.

As Mary left Washington, her old enemies couldn't resist taking one final shot at her. They accused her of absconding with the people's property from the White House. Other former residents of the mansion, before and since, have been accused of the same thing, but unlike nearly all of them, Mary Lincoln had a problem defending herself. While she was still there, looters had invaded the place and made off with "souvenirs" that were never recovered.

The Widow Lincoln

A crowd estimated at more than ten thousand people filled the train depot in Washington when the president's funeral train left for Springfield, but a month later when his widow boarded a train there, no one was on hand to say good-bye. Along with two members of the White House guard, she was accompanied by her two sons and her friends Elizabeth Keckley and Dr. Anson Henry, who had been her late husband's physician.

The Lincoln family took up residence in a new hotel at Hyde Park, a Chicago suburb. It was comfortable but quite a step down from the White House, although that didn't matter to Mary, at least at first. She never left her room, sitting in a chair dressed in her black widow's weeds, overcome with grief. She had many friends nearby, but none was invited to call on her and she didn't call on them. Not even her sisters came to console her. Mary Lincoln was completely alone except for her sons. She wrote hundreds of letters to old friends back east, and all of them were filled with anguish over what had become of her. The fact that she was alone, nearly penniless, and completely miserable was repeated over and over again. Her only reason for living, she said, was to preserve her husband's memory.

What galled Mary most was the ingratitude of the nation that

The night before his assassination, Abraham said he dreamed that he saw mourners filing into the East Room.

her husband had given his life to saving. Civil War generals, Grant in particular, whom she had never liked, were being given grand homes and handsome annuities, while she was reduced to living in a boardinghouse, as she insisted on calling the hotel. She didn't know whom she despised more, the new president, the Congress, the Republican party, or the American people themselves. She believed that all of them had abandoned her and, by inference, the memory of her late husband.

Although Abraham left an estate of some $160,000 in cash, bonds, and real estate, he didn't leave a will, and the amount was divided between Mary and her sons. Tad's portion was placed in trust for nine years until he turned twenty-one, and Mary's share yielded an income of about $1,800 a year. She sniffed that it was a "clerk's salary," and complained that because she couldn't touch the principal, she wouldn't be able to afford even a small house. And then there was the matter of her debts.

Even Mary herself had no idea how much she owed from her profligate years, but it seems to have been in the neighborhood of $20,000—more than $225,000 in today's dollars. Not even her son Robert was aware of the debt, but her creditors were threatening to have their outstanding accounts "published," and then the fat would be in the fire. She sincerely planned to pay everyone, if for no better reason than to protect her husband's memory, but she needed time to do some scheming.

Among her hopes was that Congress would grant her a widow's pension. There was some precedent for it, but it wasn't automatic; she was given a one-time grant of $25,000, as others before her had received, and she netted $22,000 after the inevitable deductions. With this money, plus some funds that had been raised by public subscription, Mary was able to buy a small row house in Chicago, but there wasn't enough money left over for her to maintain it.

Mary rented out her house after less than a year and put her furniture up for auction, resigned to the fact that she would have to move into a rooming house with her son Tad, whom she enrolled in a private school, even though she didn't think she could afford it. She had even spent a few months in New York trying to sell her wardrobe, but no one was interested except rag pickers, and she lost money in the bargain. Even her trusted friend Mrs. Keckley betrayed her by writing a book about her experiences at the White House. While she was kind to the former First Lady, she was also very candid, and it started tongues wagging all over again.

Above: The president's body was taken by train from Washington to Springfield, Illinois, and thousands of people turned out along the way as the coffin was removed from the train for special memorial ceremonies.

Below: Mary stayed behind at the White House while the country was paying its final tribute to her husband on the route to Springfield.

After Abraham's death, Mary unsuccessfully petitioned Congress for $100,000, the amount her husband would have earned as salary during the rest of his unexpired term.

Things began to change for the better late in 1867 when Abraham's estate was settled and Mary and her sons received relatively large cash legacies. In the meantime, Robert had been working to clear his mother of some of her debt, but it had been difficult for him and it drove a wedge between them. With the new infusion of cash, Mary decided to take Tad to Europe, where she thought the stricter schooling would be good for him. Besides, she thought the change would also be good for her health, which had been failing her. And it would be nice to live in a place where she might find some respect for a change. Robert, who had plans to get married, didn't go along with them.

Above: William Henry Herndon wasn't fond of Mary, and the feeling was mutual.

Adding Insult to Injury

Mary Lincoln quite possibly had more enemies than any other woman in United States history. One of the nastiest of them was William H. Herndon, who had been a partner in Abraham's law practice back in the early Springfield days. He felt that Mary had dismissed him much too often back then, and he never forgave her for it. And he never missed an opportunity to slip a knife into her back in the form of "revelations." He wrote a Lincoln biography after the president's assassination that was filled with enough calumny and character assassination to warrant a libel suit, and because there was no such suit, much of what he wrote is accepted as fact today.

Not content with smearing Mary's name, Herndon apparently decided to also hurt her memory of her dead husband's love for her. In a lecture in 1866, he revealed that it was not Mary whom Abe was in love with, but a young girl named Ann Rutledge, whom he loved "with all his soul, mind and strength." When she died of malaria, he said, the despondent Abraham, whose love for Ann never cooled, drifted into a loveless marriage with Mary Ann Todd.

It was true that Abraham knew a girl named Ann Rutledge in New Salem, Illinois, but she was engaged to another man, and there is no evidence that it was anything more than a casual friendship. As for his signs of grief, the girl's death occurred during the period after young Abraham had broken his engagement to Mary, and his spirits couldn't have been lower.

Mary was carefully reading all of the newspapers she could get her hands on at the time Herndon delivered his revealing lecture, but for some reason word of it escaped her eye. She wasn't made aware of it for more than four months, but when she was, she was furious. The man was trying to take away the only thing she had left, the assurance that Abe Lincoln had never loved anyone but her.

For once in her life, Mary decided to consider the source, and she had no comment except to call him a "dirty dog." Neither she nor Herndon could prove whether or not Abraham had been romantically involved with Ann Rutledge anyway. But it became an American love story that took on a life of its own, even if it might not have been true.

They settled in Frankfurt, Germany, where Tad got on with his schooling and Mary reveled in the history of the place. But she soon found out that a change of scene involves taking oneself along. She couldn't escape her depression and her growing paranoia, and because the Europeans assumed that the widow of an American president must be a rich lady, they charged her accordingly and all of her worries about money came rushing back. And she was still every bit as alone as she had been back in that Chicago hotel room. The spas near Frankfurt were of no help to her, and the doctors there advised that she might find relief in Italy.

Above: Mary consigned most of her wardrobe to a secondhand dealer in New York in hopes of raising funds, but the public was indifferent to her plight and to the value of her clothes.

She couldn't afford to go to sunny Italy when winter cold drove her from Frankfurt, but she went instead to the South of France and settled in Nice for the season. She and Tad spent the following summer in Scotland, with visits to Paris and London along the way. It is safe to say that Mary was happy traveling. Although Frankfurt was a letdown after that, she had the company of an old friend, Sally Orne, who was taking a grand tour of Europe. Her husband had served in the Lincoln administration and was now even closer to the Washington power structure. Mrs. Orne was appalled at what had become of Mary Lincoln, and she appointed herself a committee of one to do something about it.

There was a bill languishing in Congress to grant Mary a widow's pension "upon the same principles and for like reasons with any other officer who fell in the war," but it was going nowhere. It wasn't easy for the legislators to feel the pain of a woman who wintered in the South of France and summered in the Scottish highlands. But, thanks to Sally Orne and her connections, Congress finally approved a lifetime annual pension of $3,000 for Mrs. Lincoln. The Senate had voted for $5,000, and it was a compromise, but Mary vowed not to "murmur another word on the subject." Some years later, the larger amount was granted, and it became Mary's legacy to subsequent First Ladies.

> *"Only my darling Taddie prevents my taking my life."*
>
> —Mary Lincoln, October 1867

In the midst of it all, war had broken out in Europe, and Mary thought it was time to go home. Robert's wife had just given birth to her first grandchild, the girl she had always wanted, and to make it sweeter, they named the baby for her grandmother. Mary spent time in London and toured Italy before boarding a ship bound for New York.

The reunion with Robert's family in Chicago couldn't have been more perfect. His law practice was thriving, his big new house "charming," and the new baby delightful. But two months after they arrived, Mary's life turned sour again.

Tad came down with a fever that had begun with a cold, exactly as his brother Willie had. Mary, who had always been oversolicitous of her children's health, wrote to a friend that he was "very very dangerously ill," but this time she was quite right. Tad died, three months after his eighteenth birthday, of what

Above: Mary's first home abroad was in Frankfurt, Germany, and it was a far cry from her girlhood home.

the doctors diagnosed as "compression of the heart." Mary managed to summon the courage to go to his funeral, but the burial was beyond her. Once again, she was plunged into deep despair.

She withdrew into herself as never before, even ignoring Robert's family and denying herself the pleasures of being a grandmother. As she had done in the past, she mostly sat in the dark, although she took frequent trips in search of relief from the multiple illnesses, some of them imagined, that she suffered from. She developed a maniacal fear that something would happen to Robert, but in her frequent bouts of hysteria, she accused him of trying to kill her. She was still convinced that she would wind up in a poorhouse somewhere, but she began carrying large amounts of cash and bonds in her pockets and her handbag, and she went on unreasonable shopping sprees, buying things she didn't need—seventeen pairs of gloves on one occasion, and $700 worth of jewelry on another, although she rarely left her room and had no occasion to wear it.

Robert had made it a point to keep his mother at arm's length, but now he had to step in. He was worried not only that she'd spend all of her money, but that some opportunist might easily relieve her of it before she could. He got a court order to take away her personal control over her money, but the only legal ground for that was insanity. A doctor examined Mary and declared her "a fit subject for hospital treatment." And Robert produced enough other witnesses to prove it would be to her own benefit if his mother were confined in a mental institution. It was a painful decision, but Robert was certain it was the only one he could make.

Although the record of Mary's commitment to the Cook County Hospital noted that she had no "homicidal or suicidal tendencies," she felt completely betrayed by her son and she tried to commit suicide that very night. She drank large quantities of laudanum, an opium derivative that was the nineteenth-century equivalent of sleeping pills, but it didn't have any effect, and the following day Robert delivered her to Bellevue Place, a private sanitarium about thirty-five miles outside of Chicago.

It was an unpleasant experience, but not an uncomfortable existence for Mary. She had her own room and freedom to roam the grounds, and she had frequent visitors, among them her sister Betsey Edwards, who had largely ignored her for years. Quite possibly because she felt that Mary's confinement was a black mark on the family's social standing, she was able to have Mary released after four months at Bellevue Place to live in her Springfield home. Five months after that, another legal hearing concluded that Mary was "restored to reason," and she was freed.

She stayed in the Edwards home for about a year, and although her behavior was still a little eccentric, her mental condition seems to have improved. But she wasn't comfortable

"My financial means do not allow me take advantage of the advice [my doctors] have given me, nor can I live in a style becoming to the widow of the Chief Magistrate of a great nation, although I live as economically as I can."

—Mary Lincoln to the U.S. Senate, December 1868

among old friends and old memories, and she abruptly left to take up residence in Paris. Her letters from there show no signs of any mental problems, except homesickness, but her health was clearly deteriorating, and after four years abroad, she sailed back home.

Back in Springfield, Mary patched up her relationship with Robert. He had been criticized for not taking her in, but she defended him by telling a reporter, "His kind heart has urged this many times…. But I did not desire for him to do so, for he had his own brood to look after." The reporter said, "Mentally, Mrs. Lincoln is active and clear, talks with great rapidity, and is pleased to meet her friends who may call to visit her."

Visits to her at the Edwards house may not have been as pleasant as they had been when Mary moved there for the first time more than forty years before. Now she was severely dressed in black, the curtains were drawn tight, and her mind had almost completely shut out the world of the living. She fell into unconsciousness in the darkened room, and she died quietly there on July 16, 1882. She was sixty-three years old.

Mary had once told a friend, "You will rejoice when you know that I have joined my husband and my children," and he echoed what many felt, that "I have mourned with her often and why should I not rejoice

Below: The parlor at the Lincoln home in Springfield.

Visiting the Lincoln Museum and the Lincoln Home

When the Lincoln Museum opened in Springfield, Illinois, in the spring of 2005, The New York Times called it "an astonishing use of technology." Using the latest multimedia techniques, the facility at 212 North Sixth Street offers a unique look at the life and times of Abraham and Mary Todd Lincoln. It is open, for a small admission fee, from 9:00 A.M. to 5:00 P.M. every day except Thanksgiving, December 25, and January 1, and on Wednesdays until 8:30 P.M. For more information, call 217-558-8844, or go to www.alpm.org.

The house where the Lincoln family lived on South Seventh Street in Springfield, Illinois, has been restored to its original appearance in a four-block historic district. It is administered by the National Park Service, and is open from 8:30 A.M. to 5:00 P.M. every day except Thanksgiving, December 25, and January 1. There is no admission charge. The house is furnished with pieces Mary chose for their home. Mary Lincoln is buried alongside her husband and three of their sons nearby at the Lincoln's Tomb State Historic Site, which is open on the same schedule as the home.

Springfield is located two hundred miles southwest of Chicago, and one hundred miles northeast of St. Louis. Interstate 55 provides north-south access to downtown Springfield; use exit 98B (Clear Lake Avenue) from the south, and 92A (Sixth Street) from the north. East-west access is on Interstate 72; use the Clear Lake Avenue exit from the west and Sixth Street (Business I-55) from the east.

The Lincoln Heritage Trail, a 325-mile drive east from Springfield, is a marked route into Indiana and Kentucky that leads to special sites connected with the early life and career of President Lincoln.

Eliza Johnson

Abrupt Change

Eliza Johnson wasn't the type to hold press conferences, but when she arrived at the White House four months after her husband, Andrew, became president in the wake of the Lincoln assassination, it was inevitable that she would be met there by a gaggle of reporters. She gave them a kindly look and said, "My dears, I am an invalid." Then, as if to drive the point home, she slowly turned and started climbing the stairs one step at a time.

She certainly looked like an invalid. Although only in her mid-fifties, Eliza Johnson's hair had turned snow-white and her body seemed to be wasting away. She wore a white shawl over her shoulders even though it was August and Washington was sweltering hot. The recent Civil War had been hard on Eliza Johnson—she had lived with the sound of hostile gunfire—and she had been suffering from tuberculosis for years. The pain of it all was etched on her face, but if any of those reporters had bothered to look a little deeper into her bright eyes, they might have wondered if the new First Lady was as decrepit as she claimed to be.

Had they been able to follow her up the stairs to the residential quarters, they would have had even more to wonder about. The new official family residence was shared with the Johnson daughters: Martha, along with her husband and three children, and the widowed Mary and her two children. Sons Robert and twelve-year-old Andrew, Jr., were moving in, too, and all of them, like Eliza herself, were eager to stake out their own territory in their new home. But all of them deferred to Mother Johnson's strong will, giving her the first choice when she insisted on taking a relatively tiny room for herself directly across the hall from her husband's office, even though she had many better choices. It was a sunny room that overlooked the White House grounds, and she could watch her grandchildren playing on the lawn from there; but it was its proximity to her husband's office that mattered most to her.

---

*Eliza's son Charles was killed during the Civil War,
and so was her son-in-law, daughter Mary's husband,
Daniel Stover. Both were in the Union army.*

Eliza McCardle Johnson

Born
October 4, 1810,
Leesburg, Tennessee

Parents
John McCardle and Sarah
Phillips McCardle

Marriage
May 17, 1827, to Andrew
Johnson (1808-75)

Children
Martha (1828-1901);
Charles (1830-63); Mary
(1832-83); Robert
(1834-69); Andrew, Jr.
(Frank) (1852-69)

Died
January 15, 1876,
Carter Station, Tennessee

Eliza would spend all of her days at the White House in that little room, knitting and reading and listening carefully to everything that was going on just beyond her open door. She frequently crossed the hall to give the president advice, or to calm his often violent temper, but during her nearly four years as First Lady, Eliza only ventured downstairs to appear in the mansion's public rooms on two occasions. Her health was a problem, of course, and that was the excuse that was given for her reclusive behavior. She was far more concerned about Mary Lincoln's tarnished legacy in Washington society, and realizing that truth was less important to them than juicy gossip, she wanted to steer clear of that kind of abuse for herself.

Martha Johnson Patterson's husband, David T. Patterson, was a Tennessee circuit judge. Later, he became a United States senator.

Above: Son-in-law David Patterson served as President Johnson's eyes and ears in Congress during the impeachment debate.

Eliza gave the job of official White House hostess to her oldest daughter, Martha Patterson, who had been a frequent White House guest when her fellow Tennesseean Sarah Polk was First Lady. She was a student in Washington during the time her father was a congressman, and like other Tennessee students away from home, she was invited to spend holidays at the executive mansion. She didn't share Sarah's concept of austere entertaining, but Martha prepared the social set for her style by saying, "We are plain people from the mountains of Tennessee, called here by a national calamity. I trust too much will not be expected of us."

The new president had given Mary Lincoln an extra six weeks to move out of the White House, but when he moved in himself, the public rooms were still draped in black bunting, and souvenir hunters had vandalized them. Pieces had been snipped from wallpaper, curtains, draperies, and carpets; nicks had been gouged out of some of the wooden furniture, and many pieces had been carried off, even some quite heavy ones. The East Room, which had doubled as a wartime barracks, was infested with lice, and the State Dining Room, which Mary Lincoln had closed off long ago, was filled with mold. The other rooms were all filthy, and there were signs of wear and neglect at every turn.

Martha and the rest of the Johnson family didn't arrive in Washington until midsummer, and with Congress out of session and the social season in hiatus, she had time to make the place presentable before she had to present her own face to important guests. Congress appropriated $30,000 to do the job, and Martha personally supervised the spending of every penny of it. Among other things, she brought portraits of former presidents out of storage and gave them prominent positions on the walls of the public rooms. She had slipcovers made for the damaged upholstered furniture, and she bought sheets of muslin to cover the damaged carpets rather than have them replaced. Considering the damage that had been done, it wasn't nearly enough money, certainly not enough to

First Ladies in Fashion

Inaugural Gowns and Other Ceremonial Dresses

Like America's presidents, First Ladies have come from every segment of society. But all of them have had one thing in common: they each established fashion trends that defined their era. From Martha Washington's homespun dresses to Harriet Lane's lace berthas, from Barbara Bush's three strands of pearls to Laura Bush's tailored pantsuits, what the First Lady wears is frequently what women all over the country soon adapt to their own wardrobes.

The First Lady's initial fashion statement, in most cases, is the gown she chooses to wear to her husband's inaugural ball. These inaugural ball gowns hold a place in history as a First Lady's mark on her new position as the nation's first hostess. One of the most popular exhibits at the Smithsonian's National Museum of American History is "First Ladies: Political Role and Public Image," which among other things, includes the inaugural gowns of First Ladies from Dolley Madison to Laura Bush. Others First Lady gowns are displayed at several of the presidential libraries and at the National First Ladies' Library in Canton, Ohio.

The suits and business attire the First Ladies wore at White House official functions and receptions, on good will tours, and other public appearances were sometimes calculated to enhance the president's opinions and policies, while at the same time reflecting the First Lady's own sense for business dress. And when the First Ladies dressed for play or rest, her casual clothes often made a more personal statement on the First Lady and how she chose to present herself when out of the public eye.

Beginning with formal gowns and then showing business attire and casual wear, this portfolio recalls many of those statements made by our First Ladies, from ball gowns to blue jeans, from hairdos to hats, and from sequins to sweatsuits, these are snapshots of the women who America accepted as the standard of elegance and attractiveness for their time.

Right: Ida McKinley's inaugural dress was made of blue velvet, which was her favorite color.

Above: Martha Washington dressed plainly but elegantly and was known for her homespun style.

Above: The Yellow Rose of Texas: Lady Bird Johnson twirled in her A-line inaugural ball gown, which was designed by John Moore.

Left: Sarah Polk's silk inaugural gown was in delicate ivory.

Above: In 1989, Barbara Bush wore a royal blue gown by Arnold Scaasi to her husband's inaugural ball.

Below: Bess Truman's simple gown was a reflection of her Missouri roots.

Right: Elizabeth Monroe's taste in fashion reflected her years in France.

Left: The pattern reflected in Caroline Harrison's 1889 inaugural gown was a motif of Indiana burr oaks.

Right: Laura Bush's 2001 inaugural gown was made of red chantilly lace and silk satin with crystal beading.

Above: Edith Wilson was a wealthy businesswomen by time she became First Lady and that was reflected in her elegant style of dress.

Left: First Lady Rosalynn Carter (here with daughter Amy) was a practical woman: She chose to wear the same gown to her husband's inaugural ball that she had worn to his Georgia gubernatorial celebration.

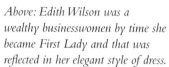

Right: Angelica Van Buren was a regal presence in the White House.

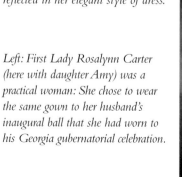

Left: Jacqueline Kennedy was possibly the best dressed of all the First Ladies. She wore this silk dress by Oleg Cassini to a dinner for Nobel Prize winners.

Right: Eleanor Roosevelt wore this pink rayon crepe gown to the 1945 inaugural reception. It was made by Arnold Constable, Fifth Avenue, New York.

Left: Just like Lucy Hayes's personality, her dresses were simple, dignified, and chaste.

Right: Helen Taft was a legendary White House hostess; she wore pink to her husband's inaugural ball.

Above: Elaborate beaded hair combs were central to Louisa Adams's image.

Left: Lucretia Garfield's lavender satin 1881 inaugural gown featured a short lace train.

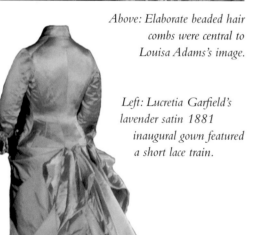

Above: Betty Ford wore a stunning Asian-inspired dress for a White House reception on March 10, 1976.

Right: Mamie Eisenhower's inaugural gown, which was designed by Nettie Rosenstein, was in her favorite color, pink, and embroidered with 2,000 rhinestones.

Above: First Lady Edith Roosevelt was an accomplished society matron and trendsetter; she always wished her gowns to be "absolutely unique."

Above: Julia Tyler's short eight-month tenure as First Lady is still a fashion benchmark.

Right: Florence Harding's 1921 inaugural gown was a flapper-style dress designed by Harry Collins.

Left: In 1969, Pat Nixon's jewel-studded silk satin inaugural dress was adorned with Austrian crystal and was designed by Karen Stark for Harvey Berin.

Left: In 1981, Nancy Reagan wore a gown in her signature red color to one of her husband's official state dinners.

Right: Grace Coolidge's red evening dress was made of chiffon velvet and had a detachable train.

Right: Hillary Clinton's 1993 inaugural gown was designed by Sarah Phillips and featured a blue velvet silk overskirt.

Left: Mary Todd Lincoln was often criticized for extravagance, but her dresses were beautiful. This gown with its black stripes and off-white silk taffeta material was worn for a sitting with Mathew Brady.

do more than just restore what had been trashed, but it is likely that no other woman could have accomplished so much with so little.

In the midst of the refurbishing, Martha did double duty as her father's nurse when an illness brought on by overwork and the nasty Washington heat kept him confined to his room for more than a month. She also took on the job of social secretary to her mother, reading and answering literally tons of mail from people looking for jobs or for war relief. Her sister, Mary, backstopped her when she wasn't looking after their children, but the bulk of the work that was expected of the First Lady fell on Martha's shoulders.

If the White House was made reasonably opulent again, its young mistress was determined not to change her image as a plain person from the mountains of Tennessee. She began her days in the White House basement, skimming milk and supervising the operations of the dairy. Then, following the example of Sarah Polk, she made a daily tour of the house, making sure it was being kept spotlessly clean. When Martha appeared at receptions and dinners, she refused to dress in the low-cut fashions of the time, preferring instead the high-necked style that was popular back home. Fashion-conscious Washington literally stood up and cheered.

Her mother, Eliza, meanwhile, established a daily routine of her own. The president always stopped for a chat with her for a half hour or so on his way to his office, and then she made a tour of the upstairs rooms. It was especially important to her that the president's bedroom was orderly and kept the way he liked, and she made a daily check of his wardrobe to make sure that he was turned out the way she liked. Most days, she met with Martha to discuss the daily menus and to make sure the kitchen staff knew exactly how the president preferred to have his meals prepared. Although her deeply lined face showed that she most likely was the invalid she claimed to be, Eliza's sunny spirits never did. She was always cheerful and happy as she tended to her self-imposed domestic duties.

Eliza doted on the children who lived in the White House: her young son, Andrew, whom the family called Frank, and her five little grandchildren. All of them had the run of the house, as the Lincoln boys had, and it wasn't easy to predict where they might turn up. The president's office wasn't off-limits to them, and he was always delighted to see them. If there happened to be any visitors around when they popped in, he expected them to be as welcoming to the children as he was, which was expecting a great deal indeed. Frank was enrolled in a private school, but tutors came to the White House to teach the younger ones, and their daily routine kept them out of sight during the

Above: Daughter Martha Johnson Patterson was Eliza's official White House hostess, but she was very careful not to let it go to her head.

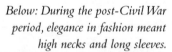

Below: During the post-Civil War period, elegance in fashion meant high necks and long sleeves.

Like some other First Families, the Johnsons brought a pair of cows to the White House to keep the family supplied with fresh milk, cream, and cheese, not to mention keeping the lawn clipped.

Eliza spent part of her day reading newspapers and official reports and highlighting items she thought the president should see. It was a lifelong habit of hers.

morning hours. But the afternoons were their time for roaming, and they most often roamed to Grandma's room, where they knew that she would be waiting for them with hugs and warm smiles.

Eliza once said, "It is all very well for those who like it, [but] I don't like this public life at all. I often wish the time would come when we could return to where we best belong." But she and her husband did sometimes entertain old friends upstairs at the White House. On those occasions she dressed in gowns that, though simple, were made by the best dressmakers from the finest fabrics—she was an accomplished seamstress herself, and she knew how to direct them. But Eliza never dressed to please her guests. It was her husband's eye she wanted to catch, and she was never as pleased as when he complimented her, which he did often.

A Unique Team

Eliza had known Andrew Johnson since he was a teenager and had wandered into her hometown, Greeneville, Tennessee, where he found work in the local tailor shop. She was the daughter of Sarah and John Curdle, the town's shoemaker, and when her father died, Eliza helped her widowed mother make ends meet by crafting crazy quilts and sandals. It's probably not true, but a legend that still survives has it that on her first sight of the Johnson boy, she told her friends, "There goes the man I am going to marry."

Below: Eliza as a young woman.

Andy soon moved on to a different town for a better opportunity, but he kept in touch with Eliza. He went back to Greeneville when the town's only tailor died, and he took it as an even better chance to improve his life. But before he took over the shop, he married Eliza Curdle. He was eighteen and she was sixteen, making her the youngest bride of any of the First Ladies. They were husband and wife for almost fifty years, and although they were frequently apart, everyone who knew them agreed that they were deliriously happy together. "Two souls and minds merged into one," was how one of them put it.

As newlyweds the Johnson's moved into a rented house on Main Street. They lived in the back room and converted the front one into a tailor shop where they worked side by side. Each of the rooms was about twelve feet square. Andy never finished his apprenticeship, running away long before he worked out his obligation, but he had learned enough to be a master at the trade. Before long he was successful enough to hire assistants and to begin investing some of his money. He bought two lots in town as well as two houses and a blacksmith shop, and then he bought a bigger building for his tailor shop.

There is no question that Andy Johnson had a flair for entrepreneurship, but it is also true that he had an excellent business manager in Eliza. It was she who ran his business enterprises. She had been educated at the local academy, where she had mastered reading and writing and discovered that she had a special talent for mathematics. Andy was unschooled, but he had taught himself to read by the time they were married, and Eliza broadened his education by teaching him how to write and how to handle numbers. Although he, too, had a flair for mathematics, she always managed his investments and his finances throughout their life together.

Above: A typical tailor shop of the period. Andy's was more of an open space with room for gathering and gossiping, and Eliza didn't have a sewing machine, which wasn't patented until 1853, the same year Andy became the governor of Tennessee.

Andy was an eager student, although he never managed to develop a notable writing style. But he soon found a better use for words—he was a spellbinding public speaker. Recognizing his talent but not able to hone it herself, Eliza arranged for him to become a member of a local debating society, and before long he became known around town as a man with more important abilities than plying a needle.

A political life seemed inevitable when he was elected to the local Board of Aldermen, and even more so when he was eventually appointed mayor of Greeneville. The board held most of its meetings in Andrew's tailor shop, while Eliza listened quietly in the background. She kept her opinions to herself, but she didn't waste any time in sharing them with her husband when they were alone.

Andy and Eliza weren't ever completely alone at that point in their lives. They had four children by then, and they had traded the back room of the shop for a house of their own big enough to give them all breathing room. Martha was born in 1828, followed two years later by their first son, Charles. Their second daughter, Mary, was born in another two years, and like clockwork, another son, Robert, arrived two years after that. Then the pattern was broken. Their youngest boy, Andrew, Jr., was born eighteen years later.

Below: The Johnsons' youngest son, Andrew Johnson, Jr., was called Frank.

Andy had been away from home for short periods touring with one or another of the several debating societies he had joined. In Tennessee, they were the equivalent of theatrical companies at the time, and their debates were the only contact many people had with the world away from their own farms, except for traveling preachers. Andy's first extended absence from home was when he went to Nashville as a member of the state House of Representatives. Eliza stayed home to watch over the children and take care of the family businesses. Thanks to her, as Andy's political star rose, so did his investments in real estate, since it was Eliza's forte.

He was away from home more and more often as his political career grew, but when Andy Johnson was at home in Greeneville, he was regarded as the town's leading citizen, at least among the common people whom he carefully cultivated as his special constituency. His tailoring business, which he

Above: Andy's tailor shop was Greenville's answer to a general store or a barbershop; it was a place for sharing the local news of the day.

The building that was Andrew Johnson's shop in Greeneville is still standing, and it still has a sign over the door that says, "A. Johnson, Tailor."

would eventually lease to a partner to meet the time demands of a political life, employed half a dozen men. The payroll included the people he hired for fifty cents a day to read newspapers and books to his employees, as had been done for him when he was a young apprentice. His family lived in the big house that he owned in the center of town, and he bought a farm nearby for his mother and stepfather. Andrew also owned several slaves who functioned as house servants to help Eliza with her domestic duties.

When the time came for Martha to go to school, Eliza and Andrew could afford the best that East Tennessee had to offer, and Andy continued his own self-education by devouring the material in his daughter's textbooks and scrutinizing her lessons. He did the same thing when his other children went to school. He never allowed his political cronies into his home—that was what he used the tailor shop was for—and he spent all his hours there enjoying his family.

The Johnson's never indulged their children, but Andrew wasn't harsh with them, either, as many were in those days. But while he had become one of the town's leading citizens, Greeneville had its own social hierarchy, and as far as they were concerned, Andrew Johnson was still just a tailor, and he and Eliza were often snubbed. "Some day I'll show the stuck-up aristocrats who is running the country!" he confided to Eliza. "A cheap purse-proud set they are—not half as good as the man who earns his bread by the sweat of his brow." Needless to say, those purse-proud aristocrats were all Whigs, but Andy had become a Democrat.

Whenever Andy Johnson was called upon to make a formal speech, more often than not it was Eliza who wrote it for him. But he didn't need her help, or anyone else's, when he took to the stump to win his neighbors over with hope for the future, both for themselves and for the Democratic Party. He could talk for hours, and he usually did, without losing anyone's attention even for a moment. Then, with Greene County in Andy's hip pocket, Eliza subscribed to newspapers published in other parts of the state, with an emphasis on the opposition press. She clipped articles from them and pasted them into scrapbooks organized by various political issues, and they became the basis of his talking points for speeches and debates. Over time, they ran out of room in the house for all of the scrapbooks, and Andy had

"Tell it as it is or not at all."

—*Andrew Johnson's first rule for his children*

a shed built in the backyard that Eliza organized into a kind of personal library for him. Nothing escaped her eye; Andy had a natural gift for oratory, and Eliza made sure that he always had something important to say.

His next step was election to the state senate, and although Eliza stayed home again, she kept in close touch with him. He didn't always need her advice, but she was always primed to give it to him when he did. Eventually word of his accomplishments reached former president Andrew Jackson at the Hermitage, and the talk around Nashville was that Andrew Johnson was his true successor.

Unique among the First Ladies up until her time, Eliza Johnson had never had any experience at entertaining while her husband was climbing the political ladder. Andy was sociable, but never social. He was at his best meeting people casually, and he never had time for the kind of parties and receptions that were considered essential to political success. He was always too busy advancing his self-education, and the only company he really enjoyed were the common people, who he believed were the only kind who mattered. He had never become a lawyer, another traditional requisite for a man interested in public service, and he had a lot of catching up to do, considering the books he hadn't yet read.

Methodists and Baptists

Eliza Johnson was a devout churchgoing Methodist, and she made sure that her children were, too. Her husband, a former Baptist, refused to join them in church on Sunday mornings. He didn't have anything against religion particularly, but he confined his faith to daily Bible reading on his own. If Andy had any religion at all, it was the worship of the common man. He repeatedly pointed out that Joseph, the husband of the Virgin Mary, was a carpenter, and so, probably, was Jesus; Moses was a stonecutter, and Saint Paul a former tent-maker, he said. And on a personal level, he couldn't resist reminding people that Adam had been the first tailor, sewing fig leaves together as he did.

When Andrew was elected to Congress in 1843, Eliza once again stayed at home, but their daughter Martha was already in Washington. They had enrolled her in the Catholic Female Seminary in Georgetown, where she was studying along with Harriet Lane, James Buchanan's niece. Harriet had some inkling that she might one day be the hostess at the White House, but nothing could have been further from Martha Johnson's mind. It was far from her father's mind, too, and he made it a point to guide her to courses that would bring her up to the highest levels of the Greeneville elite, while shunning such frills as music, drawing, French, and Latin.

When Andy went home to Greeneville to campaign for a second congressional term in 1847, he found that not all was well with the rest of his family. Eliza was beside herself with worry that Charles, her favorite child, was teetering on the edge of alcoholism, and their youngest, Robert, was having lung problems, which worried her even more. Eliza's own health had begun to fade by then, too; she was going through the early stages of tuberculosis. The Johnsons accepted the new adversities stoically, but when Andy went back to Washington, Eliza became uncharacteristically silent. "I think my family must all be dead," he wrote to a friend, "for I have not heard from them in twenty days." Eliza was too sick to write.

When his congressional career ended after a complicated round of redistricting at home, Andrew left Washington after ten years there hoping to be closer to his family as governor of Tennessee. By the time he was elected Tennessee's chief executive, Andrew Johnson, who ran as a man of the people, had a personal fortune estimated at some $50,000, an impressive amount in those days. He said it had all come through toil and thrift, but although he could never have been accused of avoiding hard work, it was Eliza's thrift that had made him one of the richest men in the state. While Andy was away serving in Congress, she bought an unfinished brick house in the middle of town. The owner hadn't been able to finish building it, but Eliza's family accounts were in good enough order to allow her to buy it from him and call back the carpenters and bricklayers.

Above: The front of the Johnsons' Greenville house is deceptive. A wing about equal in size juts out behind it with a two-story back porch.

The house abutted the sidewalk, but it had a large side lawn and a big backyard filled with fruit trees, where a smaller building housed the kitchen. There were two large rooms on each of the two floors with a wide center hall between them. The Johnsons moved into the house not long before their last son, Frank, was born, and their daughter Mary was married to Daniel Stover, who owned a large farm not far away. Mary's wedding was the only social event at the Johnson house that year. Andy wasn't too fond of spending money, and Eliza was too frugal herself to be bothered with anything as frivolous as a house party, even though her husband was governor and some people expected it of them. He had always wanted to be the equal of the local aristocrats, but he despised them too much to enjoy their company.

After two terms as governor, Andrew Johnson went back to Washington to take a seat in the U.S. Senate. When he came home at the end of the first session, he found that his family had gotten along quite well without him. Mary was expecting her third child, Robert was running for a seat in the state legislature, and Charles appeared to have sworn off drinking. Both Charles and Robert had taken over their mother's investing activities, and the Johnson real estate holdings had grown considerably.

Fortunes of War

During the next session of Congress, Eliza joined Andy in Washington. It was the only time she was ever there until she moved into the White House.

> *"[I] remained at home caring for the children and practicing economy."*
>
> —*Eliza Johnson on her husband's time in Washington*

She had young Frank with her, and they were joined by Robert, who was by then a member of the Tennessee legislature and a rising star among the state's Democrats. He had come to report to his father on the progress of the elder Johnson's plan to run for the presidency—a bid he was doomed to lose. In the meantime, son Charles had started drinking again, but he was prospering in spite of himself as co-owner of a drugstore in Greeneville, and he had become adept at buying and selling stocks, a talent he inherited from his mother.

Eliza never had anything to say about her impressions of Washington, but even though he was tireless in his efforts to have the voters send him there, Andy had a hard time finding good things to say about it himself.

They were there when Abraham Lincoln became president and some Southern states responded by removing themselves from the Union. Andy led the opposition to secession with passionate speeches in the Senate. *The New York Times* said, "His name is in every mouth, and he is frequently applauded as the man of the age." But if Senator Johnson was leading the fight against breaking up the Union, back in Nashville, the governor of Tennessee was pushing for secession. After the president called for troops to defend their country, citizens of the state started calling for secession, too. Andrew was painted as a traitor to his state and to the Democratic party, but most of all to the common people he claimed to represent.

Eliza was still in Washington with him while all this was going on, and even though she was safer there than she would have been back home, she was with her husband when he went home to make his case. Their train was met by protesters at every town they passed through, and after they crossed the border into Tennessee, a mob burst into the car where Andy and Eliza were seated. Andy had a gun and he showed it to them, prompting the conductor to order, "No shooting, gentlemen, please! There are ladies present." The only shot Andrew Johnson fired was a defiant, "I am a Union man!" So, too, was the lady with him.

As they got deeper into the state, the mobs grew more hostile, invariably calling for a lynching. A double hanging surely would have happened at one border town where the protesters had a clear plan to string up the senator and his wife, but a telegraphed order from Confederate president Jefferson Davis prevented the train from stopping there. Davis had no special respect for the Johnsons—he considered them traitors, too—but he knew that if they were to be lynched they would become martyrs to the Union cause, and Tennesseeans might be moved to stay loyal to the Stars and Stripes. Besides, there was always the remote possibility that Andy would see the error of his ways, and it was that hope among many rebels that kept him and Eliza alive.

When they reached Greeneville, Andy set up a two-room office in the hotel he owned, and Eliza went to work furnishing one of them with mementos of Andy's career in public service. But while his past accomplishments were impressive, his future was very much in doubt. It didn't seem to matter to him. He had only one goal in mind by then: to keep his state in the Union.

Above: Matthew Brady's photograph of Andrew was taken during the time of his presidency.

In the meantime, the Confederates were making impressive headway. The governor raised a 55,000-man army and placed it under Jefferson Davis's command. Then he offered to make Nashville the Confederate capital, even though Tennesseeans hadn't yet voted for secession. When the election was scheduled, Andrew Johnson took to the stump again, this time in the company of men who had once been his political enemies. His former Democratic allies completely abandoned him. Although his life was clearly in danger—the word on the street was that he was marked for assassination—he made hundreds of impassioned speeches against secession, but in the end the vote went against his cause. Though the state's voters approved secession by a two-to-one margin, Andrew's own constituency in East Tennessee went two to one the other way. He considered it the greatest victory of his political career; but he was still regarded as a traitor, and leaving Eliza and his family behind, he left the state he had tried to preserve. Eliza refused to join him, even though her own life was in danger, too.

Andy left behind a corner of Tennessee that was claimed by both sides in the war, and it was strategic to each of them. The Johnsons' own property was confiscated by the Confederates—their house was converted into a field hospital—and Eliza and Frank had fled to the safety of the Patterson farm in the next county. Her son-in-law Judge Patterson was in jail, and Robert, Charles, and Mary's husband, Daniel Stover, had gone into the hills as guerilla fighters for the Union cause. Eliza, meanwhile, had no idea where her husband was. Some said he had been murdered, others that he was on his way home at the head of a volunteer army, and some that he had gone back to Washington. The latter was true, and he was speaking out, more than nearly anyone else, about saving the Union and upholding the Constitution.

Word of his family was almost nonexistent for Senator Johnson, until he received a letter from Robert. "Mother is in Carter County," he wrote, "her health very much improved. All the family are well."

Robert turned up in Washington a couple of weeks after his letter arrived, and he was made a captain of militia with orders to sign up some volunteers to follow him back into East Tennessee.

At about the same time, his father headed for Nashville, which had been captured by Union troops. He had been made military governor of Tennessee, and he had also been commissioned a brigadier general in the Union army.

The Confederate army had abandoned most of Tennessee except for pockets in the east, ironically, the same territory that was leaning to the North. The rebels still controlled Greeneville, but Eliza had been allowed to go home in the meantime, and her house was restored to her. After Andrew became military governor, though, his family was once again high on the list of traitors, and an

While the Civil War fighting was taking place, Eliza made forays in all kinds of weather to carry food to men "on the scout" who were hiding out in caves in the nearby mountains.

order was issued to force them out of the territory. But Eliza Johnson wasn't ready to go. She protested that her health was too frail for her to go anywhere, and the provost marshal in charge agreed to postpone her evacuation. It wasn't until six months later that he reviewed the case, and she was driven from her home with ten-year-old Frank at her side late one day in October.

She had a plan to go to Nashville to rejoin her husband. But it was a dangerous trip, and she recruited her son Charles and her daughter Mary and her husband, Daniel, to go with her. They were all high on the list of traitors, too, but even a difficult trip through hostile country seemed better than waiting for a lynch mob to track them down.

They made it as far a Murfreesboro, a little less than fifty miles from their destination, before a rebel leader confronted them and ordered them to board the next eastbound train. But the former governor outranked him and he countermanded the order, giving the Johnson family safe passage the rest of the way into Nashville. Eliza and her husband were reunited there that same day.

Their son Charles formally joined the army after that, but it turned out to be a short career. He was thrown from his horse and died of a skull fracture. Eliza would never completely recover from the shock. Her son Robert was back in the army by then, too, and he was prevailing on his father to make him a brigadier general with authority to raise his own brigade. In the meantime, he got into a fight with another officer over their differing recruiting methods and he was arrested. That matter had no sooner been smoothed over when he started drinking more and began taking long absences away from his men. He was stationed in Cincinnati at the time, and Eliza took it on herself to go there to see if she might talk some sense into him. Her health took a bad turn for the worse while she was there, but her mission was apparently accomplished. Robert managed to raise a regiment and lead it back to Tennessee. When Eliza herself went back, it was confirmed that Frank had tuberculosis, just as she did. It wasn't life-threatening, but it was one more thing for his mother to worry about.

Robert didn't distinguish himself as a military officer, and on the eve of the Battle of Chattanooga, with the fate of all Tennessee in the balance, he suddenly resigned his commission, claiming that his father had asked him to do it. In one of the rare letters that Andrew Johnson ever composed himself, he wrote to his son: "My grief… has been enough without your adding to it at it this time. I have determined that no act of mine should be an excuse for your recent course of conduct and do not now form it. You tender your resignation predicated upon my wish for you to do so, as I obtained the commission for you."

Robert chose to stay on, and he saw action at Chattanooga, although the victory wasn't enough to drive the rebels out of Tennessee, as had been hoped. His father was disappointed, but he was determined to hold on, and he went to great lengths to encourage Mary and Eliza to do the same. As it turned out, they had reservoirs of fortitude that even he didn't know about. He was thoroughly weary, and it is quite likely he wouldn't have survived the war without his wife and daughter at his side.

Robert added to their anxiety by announcing that he was planning to look for a new life in the West, but Eliza talked him out of it, and he agreed to stay closer to home. Taking advantage of a lull in the war, he resigned from the army and joined his father's staff. But along with that good news, the Johnson family got the bad news that their Greeneville house had been ransacked by rebel troops, and every scrap of paper that Eliza had carefully saved and catalogued over the years had been burned or scattered to the winds.

Back in Washington, President Lincoln was already making plans for a second term. His vice president, Hannibal Hamlin, was a New England radical, and Lincoln was interested in replacing him with a War Democrat who could guarantee votes from other parts of the country. His first choice was General Benjamin Butler, who fit the profile, but wasn't interested for a number of reasons, not the least of which was that he was sure Lincoln wouldn't get the nomination and that he himself would make a dandy dark horse candidate. But Lincoln had another horse in his stable, Andrew Johnson.

Above: Andrew is to the left of President Lincoln in this lithograph of a White House reception, and Mary Lincoln is to the right. The president is greeting future First Lady Julia Grant, whose husband General Grant is standing behind her. Eliza missed the party.

When he went to Washington as the vice president-elect, Andrew Johnson left his family behind in Nashville. The war wasn't over yet, and bands of rebel soldiers were still roaming in the area around Greeneville. Eliza didn't want to go to Washington, and that left Nashville as her only option.

Had she gone to Washington with him, Eliza most likely would have saved Andy from himself on the day of his inauguration. His term as Tennessee's military governor had taken a toll on Andy's health, and he was visibly ill when he arrived in the national capital. But he accepted an invitation to a victory party staged by the administration's Democratic wing and stayed far into the night. The next day as he waited to be escorted onto the Senate floor, he fainted and was revived with a shot of whiskey. Then he had another before he was led out for the ceremony.

The press was careful not to report that the new vice president was drunk, but no one else, not even his friends, thought he hadn't had one too many sips of Tennessee's most famous export. President Lincoln put the whole episode behind him a few days later when he said, "I have known Andrew Johnson for many years. He made a bad slip the other day, but you need not be scared. Andy Johnson ain't no drunkard." Not everyone was convinced, but it was the truth. The whole scandal passed quickly. There was too much war news distracting the country's attention, and when the war ended less than a month later, a drink or two sounded like a good idea to just about everybody in Washington.

Had Eliza been at Andy's side, not only might the incident never have happened, but she could have set the record straight quickly. She had done it before. Her husband was no teetotaler, but he wasn't a slave to booze, either, and nobody knew that better than she did.

Eliza wasn't with him when he took the oath of office as president, either, but Martha had written to him that Eliza safe. The letter she wrote when news of the Lincoln assassination reached her reflected the family's worries: "Are you safe and do you feel secure? Poor Mother, she is almost deranged fearing that you will be assassinated."

Martha's letter also reported that Mary had taken Frank to Knoxville, but that Robert had slipped off the wagon again and he still hadn't comprehended what had happened. He didn't yet know that his father had become president, a turn of fate that the rest of the family took as a kind of disaster in itself.

Above: Andrew taking the oath of office as president at Washington's Kirkwood House Hotel after the death of Abraham Lincoln.

A Family United

The new president was slow to gather his family around him, but when they came east from Tennessee, they brought him a kind of happiness he hadn't felt in years. He and Eliza perfectly complemented each other. Although he was one of the great orators of his time, Andrew Johnson was a man of few words in private, and he had a quick temper, and both qualities sometimes led to unfortunate misunderstandings. Eliza, on the other hand, had a gentle way with people in general, and her husband in particular. She was the only one who could calm his rages and encourage him to speak up when he needed to. That was why she stationed herself in the White House in a room where she could keep a close eye on him. Eliza loved her Andy with all her heart, and her pride in him never wavered. He knew it, and he returned her love in kind.

Their son Robert was made a part of the presidential secretarial staff, and he and his mother spent long hours together trying to reconstruct the record of Andy's former life that had been lost in the Greeneville raid late in the war. They were forced to rely on their memories because the written records were lost forever. For an invalid, Eliza Johnson had a very busy life in the White House.

Below: George E. Atzerodt, the killer with cold feet.

Conspiracy

It was natural that Eliza would be worried that her husband's life was in danger after President Lincoln was assassinated, but she didn't know that her fears had a solid foundation. Later investigations revealed that the conspirators had selected a man named George E. Atzerodt to kill Vice President Johnson. On April 14, 1865, Atzerodt checked into the Kirkwood House, which was also Andrew Johnson's hotel, and watched Andrew's movements all day. But on the fateful evening, the would-be assassin left the hotel for an evening of barhopping. When his room was searched, police found a bowie knife hidden in the mattress and a coat belonging to John Wilkes Booth, the Lincoln assassin, hanging in the closet. It was apparent that Azterodt had lost his nerve at the last minute, and Andrew Johnson's life was spared.

Above: Andrew's popularity was never in doubt during the first year of his presidency. White House receptions were well-attended and enthusiastic crowds greeted him when he traveled anywhere outside Washington.

Below: Among the Johnsons' grandchildren were Andrew, Sarah, and Lillie Stover, the children of their daughter Mary.

The first social event of the Johnson administration was the annual New Year's Day reception, seven months after Andy became president. The event had always been well attended, but the 1866 version was easily the most crowded yet. It took guests nearly half an hour to make their way to the White House door from the front gate. Eliza was predictably indisposed, but her daughters, Martha and Mary, took their place at their father's side to welcome the stream of well-wishers.

Martha had done a masterful job of restoring the White House, but the place was still austere. Some of the damaged furniture had been removed, giving the rooms a bare appearance, but she filled the empty spaces with floral arrangements. Because of the large number of people who showed up, there wasn't much empty space to deal with anyway.

The president himself was a perfect host. He had friendly words for everyone who shook his hand, and he set a new precedent by insisting that the children of his guests be presented to him on their own. The Johnson family adored children.

Two years later, it was this love that moved Eliza to come down the stairs for a public appearance. In their last days at the White House, the Johnsons celebrated the president's sixtieth birthday with a kind of ball that Washington had never seen before. Only children were invited. More than three hundred invitations were mailed to the sons and daughters of Washington officials and to the children of the White House servants. The invitations were sent in the name of "the children of the President," and specifically noted that no adults would be welcome.

It wasn't a typical children's party with balloons and paper hats, but a full-blown reception of the kind usually staged for diplomats and the cream of society. A red carpet was stretched over the path leading to the entrance, and the rooms were filled with flowers. The only parents there were the Johnsons themselves and the parents of their grandchildren, the official hosts.

Eliza greeted every guest seated in an armchair, but her husband lavished hugs and kisses on the younger ones, and hearty handshakes for those whose dignity might be offended by such a display of affection. Dancing was to the music of a company of fiddlers recruited from the marine band. Young students from a local dancing academy helped with the unfamiliar steps and staged a demonstration of their own. Of course, ice cream and cake were served during

The five hosts of the Johnsons' children's ball were the Johnson grandchildren: Lillie Stover, thirteen; Sarah Stover, nine; Andrew Johnson Patterson, nine; Belle Patterson, eight; and Andrew Johnson Stover, eight.

the intermission—it was a birthday party, after all. But apart from that, the children's ball was a grown-up affair without a single condescending note.

Andrew Johnson wasn't finding many things to make him happy in those days. Along with the obvious problems of binding up the wounds of a divided nation, he was having trouble with the cabinet he had inherited from President Lincoln. In spite of calls from different quarters that it was in need of reshuffling, he simply said, "I took my cabinet as I found them," and he seemed ready to make the best of a bad thing.

Chief among the men who had become lightning rods for criticism was Secretary of War Edwin M. Stanton, who had built up unprecedented power over the country's defense establishment. Andrew was loyal to him for the help he had given him while he was military governor of Tennessee, but he would have been just as pleased not to have him as an advisor.

Andrew's ideas for reconstruction of the South were widely accepted by the people, but the radical Republicans in Congress thought he was being far too lenient, and they took it upon themselves to undo everything he had managed to accomplish. He vetoed the measures they passed, but they had enough clout to override him. Among those restored bills was a so-called Tenure of Office Act, which prevented the president from dismissing any appointed official. It was a clear challenge for him to fire war secretary Stanton, which he had been planning to do, and he did, declaring the law unconstitutional. Stanton refused to go, and Congress passed a resolution to impeach the president. His Senate trial ended in acquittal by one vote.

Throughout the ordeal, Eliza served as Andy's rock. The outcome had never been in doubt in her mind, and she repeatedly told him that if he would just follow his conscience, he had nothing to be afraid of. After the vote was taken, William Crook, the president's bodyguard, ran all the way from the Capitol with the news. After telling Andy what had happened, he crossed the hall to the room where Eliza was calmly knitting. There were tears of joy in her eyes, and she was smiling broadly. "Crook, I knew he would be acquitted," she said, "I knew it. Thank you for coming to tell me."

In spite of his vindication, Andrew Johnson's political career was over. But if there were insults and annoyances, there was also a new outpouring of affection. The White House drawing rooms and receptions became more popular than they had been in years. Martha was pleased, but she confessed that "Mother is not able to enjoy these entertainments. My daughter, Belle, is too young, and I am indifferent to them, so it is well that they are almost over."

Above: The Senate visitors gallery was busy throughout the Johnson impeachment trial.

Left: Admission tickets to the Johnson impeachment were difficult to find.

Below: Colonel William Crook, the president's bodyguard, took the news of the acquittal to Eliza, who wasn't a bit surprised to hear it.

When they were officially finished with the inauguration of President Ulysses S. Grant, the former president and his First Lady went to stay with friends for a few days while the rest of the family went back to Tennessee. When they boarded a train for home, they followed the same route they had taken when he went home to fight against secession, but this time there were no lynch mobs waiting for them at every station stop. This time, there were parades and receptions and an outpouring of affection that wiped away all of the hate that the politicians had heaped on them. When they arrived in Greeneville, there was a banner above Main Street that said, "Welcome Home Andrew Johnson, Patriot." Somehow, Eliza always knew it would come to this. Her husband had been vindicated.

Mary had made her parents' old house ready for them. Like the White House, it had been vandalized during the war, but she turned it back into a home. She herself was married to a local man right after her parents arrived, and she and her new husband moved into a house across the street, so she could look in on Eliza every day. In the midst of the wedding festivities, Robert died, an apparent suicide. Young Frank, by then a student at Georgetown University, wrote to his mother promising that he would be a comfort to her in her old age, and that he would never let "any kind of intoxicating liquors" muddle his brain.

For his part, the former president decided he'd like to go back to Washington as a senator again, but the legislature, which had the last word, disabused him of that idea by voting against him. He went back to Greeneville, but it didn't make him happy. "It is a dull place and likely to continue so.... It is as lifeless as a graveyard." he said.

Andrew ran for Congress after that, but although he lost, the campaign took him back to the stump again and he was happier there than ever. His next bid was another shot at the U.S. Senate, and this time the legislature gave him what he wanted. "Well, well, well," he said. "I'd rather have this information than to learn I had been elected President of the United States. Thank God for the vindication." Eliza and Martha had both been holding their breath, worrying that a possible defeat would devastate him. But now he had been vindicated, and while Eliza didn't much like the idea of losing her husband to Washington again, she was very pleased

Below: Although for years it would have seemed a good bet that Eliza wouldn't outlive her husband, she was at his side when he died.

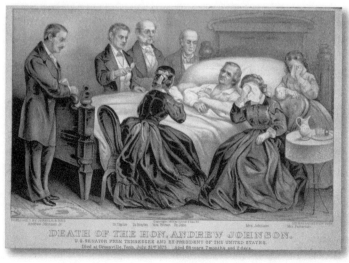

DEATH OF THE HON. ANDREW JOHNSON.
U.S. SENATOR FROM TENNESSEE AND EX-PRESIDENT OF THE UNITED STATES.
Died at Greenville, Tenn. July 31st 1875. Aged 66 years 7 months and 2 days.

when one of his supporters told her that he had said that Andy claimed he owed every success in his life to his wife.

In 1875, when the Senate session ended, he returned home, but the political bug had bitten him again and after a few weeks he set out for Ohio, where there was a campaign in progress. On the way, he planned to stop over at Carter's Station, where Mary was living and where Eliza had gone hoping that the change would improve her health, which had been steadily declining. During his short stay there, Andrew suffered a stroke, and then another one ended his life.

His estate at the time was well over $100,000, but he left no will. He had already given the farm near Greeneville to Martha, and Frank joined his mother at the house in town. Eliza, who had done so much to accumulate the family fortune, took over as administrator of the estate, but less than six months later she had been driven from her home again, this time by illness, back to Mary's farm. Less than six months after her husband died, Eliza, too, was dead, a victim, at age sixty-five, of advanced stages of the tuberculosis that had made her a prisoner in the White House.

Visiting the Johnson Homestead

The Andrew Johnson National Historic Site in Greeneville, Tennessee, includes the Johnson Homestead, another of their houses, and the A. Johnson Tailor Shop. Each of the structures has been restored and furnished to their appearance when Eliza and her family lived there. The home is open every day, 9:00 A.M. to 5:00 P.M., except Thanksgiving, December 25, and January 1. There is no admission charge.

The nearest airport is Tri-Cities, forty-three miles northeast of Greeneville. There is no other public transportation available. By car, use Interstate I-815 to exit 36, to Route 172 South, to Greeneville. From I-81 North, use exit 23 to Route 11E North to Greeneville. The address is 121 Monument Avenue, Greeneville, Tennessee 37743. For more information, call 423-638-3551.

Above: Many of the rooms in the Johnson Homestead have inviting hearths.

Julia Dent Grant

A Charmed Life

In the nineteenth century, many of America's First Ladies preferred to remain in the background while their husbands held center stage. In fact, four of them—Letitia Tyler, Margaret Taylor, Abigail Fillmore, and Eliza Johnson—due to either ill health or temperament, were virtual recluses. Most First Ladies of the nineteenth century were supportive but anonymous figures. However, there were the exceptions who seemed to relish the role. One of these was Julia Dent Grant, who considered her eight years in the White House to be the happiest period of her life. In her memoirs, she would call it "a feast of cleverness and wit."

Julia Dent was born on January 26, 1826, the fifth of the eight children of Frederick and Ellen Dent. The Dents were a prosperous family and owned two homes—one in St. Louis, and a farm called White Haven just outside of St. Louis. Frederick Dent was originally from Maryland and had become wealthy as a merchant in Pittsburgh and St. Louis. Ellen Dent was born in England and educated in Philadelphia. She enjoyed reading and preferred the more sophisticated life of their St. Louis home to the wilds of Pittsburgh.

Julia, however, was born on the farm and, like her father, always preferred the rural lifestyle to city living. She grew up a bit of a tomboy and loved the outdoors. White Haven had woods, gardens, crops, orchards, and animals, including horses for the Dent children to ride. Julia later called her childhood "one long summer of sunshine, flowers, and smiles." The farm also had eighteen slaves. Frederick Dent's strong support of slavery would one day lead to major reservations about his future son-in-law.

When Julia was ten years old, her well-educated mother sent her to the affluent Miss Mauros's boarding school in St. Louis. She remained there for seven years, receiving a well-rounded education uncommon for a woman of that era. It was during these years that her older brother Frederick became good friends with his West Point roommate, Ulysses S. Grant. After graduating from the military academy, Frederick returned home to White Haven while Ulysses was sent to nearby Jefferson Barracks, the largest military base in the United States at the time.

Ulysses visited White Haven often, and the visits increased after Julia returned home from boarding school. They both quickly realized that they had much in common. They both were energetic and loved the outdoors, and they particularly loved horse-back riding together. Some of their differences also

---

Julia Dent Grant

Born
January 26, 1826, near St. Louis, Missouri

Parents
Frederick Dent and Ellen Bray Wrenshall Dent

Marriage
August 22, 1848, to Ulysses S. Grant (1822-85)

Children
Frederick Dent (1850-1912); Ulysses Simpson (Buck), Jr. (1852-1928); Ellen (Nellie) Wrenshall (1855-1922); Jesse Root (1858-1934)

Died
December 14, 1902, Washington, D.C.

Above: Julia Grant, shot in profile, of course.

seemed to unite them. Ulysses could be shy and silent, while Julia was warm and talkative, so she would talk and he would listen. Julia was often self-conscious about her lack of beauty—she was very short and stocky, and had a wandering eye—but Ulysses didn't care; the two were in love and wanted to marry.

But Julia knew there were two huge obstacles to their marriage. The first was her father, who disapproved of his daughter's marrying a soldier, especially one who was an antislavery Northerner (Ulysses was from Ohio). The other problem was that Ulysses's regiment was suddenly transferred to Louisiana. During one of his leaves in the spring of 1844, Ulysses rode back to White Haven to ask Frederick Dent for permission to marry his daughter. Despite Dent's opposition to Ulysses, Julia was his favorite child and he did not want to disappoint her. He told Ulysses that if the couple waited two years, he would approve the marriage. Julia and Ulys, as she called him, were immediately engaged.

Julia Dent Grant was almost always photographed in profile with her left side toward the camera because she was very self-conscious about her disabled right eye. She once considered surgery to correct the problem, but her husband talked her out of it, saying those were the eyes he fell in love with.

Below: Julia Dent and Ulysses Grant were married at her father's town house in St. Louis, Missouri.

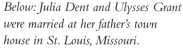

The two years passed, but in April of 1846, Ulysses had to go to Mexico to fight in the Mexican War. After President James Polk tried unsuccessfully to buy the territories of California and New Mexico from the Mexican government, he sent the U.S. army to the disputed border of Texas and Mexico to provoke a war. Three future presidents would distinguish themselves in the Mexican War—Zachary Taylor, the Confederate president Jefferson Davis, and Ulysses S. Grant.

Although Ulysses served well during the conflict and gained valuable battle experience he would use later on, he hated the war. He considered it wholly unjustified and he missed his betrothed, Julia. When Ulysses returned to St. Louis after the war, he and Julia were married immediately on August 22, 1848, at the Dent home. Ulysses was twenty-six years old and Julia was twenty-two. A lifelong conflict between the families of the newlyweds also began that day when Ulysses's abolitionist parents refused to attend the wedding.

Over the next four years, Ulysses was sent to military posts in Detroit and Sackets Harbor, New York. Julia accompanied him and gave birth to their first two children during this period. Julia returned to White Haven to give birth to Frederick on May 30, 1850, and stayed with Ulysses's parents in Bethel, Ohio, for the birth of Ulysses Simpson on July 22, 1852. This son would always be known as Buck.

It was during Julia's pregnancy with Buck that Ulysses was transferred to the Pacific coast. He was first assigned to Fort Vancouver in the Oregon Territory, then to Fort Humboldt in California, the Union's newest state. Julia was unable to accompany Ulysses to his new posts due to her health and the remote location of the assignments. This separation led to a difficult period for the Grants. Julia returned to White Haven with her two children, while Ulysses became despondent and disillusioned over the dull routine of his military life. Ulysses reached the rank of captain, but his feelings of isolation led to heavy drinking and arguing with his superiors. In the spring of 1854, Captain Grant resigned from the army and headed home to Missouri.

The next several years would prove to be the toughest for the Grants as Ulysses struggled to find a successful vocation. He tried farming first, on the sixty acres of land Julia's father had given her as a wedding present. Ulysses cleared the land and built his family a log cabin they called Hardscrabble. With the help of five slaves, the Grants planted crops and raised chickens, but in 1857, their world started to fall apart. The crops failed and Julia's mother died. Then Ulysses fell ill for nearly a year with a chronic cough and fever.

The only bright side for the Grants during the Hardscrabble years was the births of their third and fourth children. Julia gave birth to Ellen, who would always be called Nellie, on July 4, 1855, and to Jesse on February 6, 1858. The newcomers must have been a great joy to the couple, but it also meant two more mouths to feed, and the Grants were just barely surviving.

Above: The Grants called their farm "Hardscrabble," which described the almost untillable land, but suited the log cabin they built there, too.

A Soldiering Life

Later that year, Julia was able to get Ulysses a job with her cousin in the real estate business in St. Louis, but the quiet soldier was no salesman. The partnership broke up a year later, and it seemed like Ulysses had only one option left—to return to Ohio to take a job in his father's leather-goods store in Galena. Before leaving, a humbled Ulysses freed his only slave, refusing to sell him for some desperately needed money. Julia, meanwhile, rented her four slaves out to friends.

The Grants arrived in Galena, Ohio, in April 1860, and Ulysses became a clerk in his father's store. One year later, however, the outbreak of the Civil War would reverse the Grants' prospects forever, as Ulysses had the opportunity to return to the one job he knew he could do well—being a soldier. Just how well would shock everyone, except perhaps for his loyal Julia, who had seen greatness in the man since she first met him.

Ulysses immediately responded to President Abraham Lincoln's call for 75,000 volunteers for the Union army, and in June he was made a colonel and given his own regiment. While Julia stayed in Galena to take care of the children, Ulysses rose quickly in the Union ranks. His decisive capture of Fort Donelson and its 14,000 soldiers in Tennessee in February 1862 was the

Below: General Ulysses S. Grant

Above: Julia with the two youngest of her four children, son Jesse and daughter Nellie.

Below: Julia and her son Jesse are represented in this painting of Grant's winter camp. They are seated by the door of his cottage, the largest in the row of officer's quarters. The general is in the foreground with some of his staff.

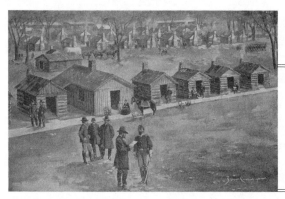

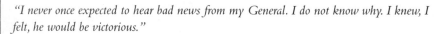

first major Union victory of the war. When the Confederate commander at the fort asked Ulysses for surrender terms, Ulysses replied, "No terms except unconditional and immediate surrender." The victory and the remark made Ulysses a national hero overnight. He gained the nickname of "Unconditional Surrender" Ulysses and a promotion to major general.

As the war dragged on, Julia made more and more trips to be with her husband on the battlefield, sometimes even bringing the children when she thought it was safe. Ulysses loved having Julia with him. She was steady, good-natured, and had common sense. Ulysses was prone to self-doubt and depression, and Julia kept his spirits up. (Later on in the war, President Lincoln would often personally arrange Julia's visits to her husband, knowing the effect they had on him.) Ulysses won decisive victories in Shiloh in April 1862, in Vicksburg in July 1863, and in Chattanooga in November 1863, and Julia was often with him, sometimes caring for the wounded soldiers in the field hospitals.

Julia also traveled back to White Haven to see her father, but their relationship was very strained due to Dent's strong allegiance to the Confederacy. On one trip to visit friends in Mississippi, Julia was nearly captured by Confederate forces. The Confederates had attacked a Union supply house and defeated the local Union troops. They went to the home where they knew Julia was staying, but she had left just before the attack began.

The Grants had one other close call around that time. Their son Frederick was with his father during the battle for Vicksburg and was slightly wounded in the leg. He also contracted dysentery followed by a severe case of pneumonia. As he lay near death back home in St. Louis, Julia rushed to his side, but her son soon made a complete recovery.

By early 1864, it was clear that Ulysses was the Union's best general. President Lincoln promoted him to general-in-chief, only the third military leader to hold that position in the history of the country. He was even being mentioned as a likely presidential candidate after Lincoln left office—all this just four years after being a store clerk in an Ohio tannery. Julia became the center of attention as the great general's wife, a role for which her affluent background left her well prepared.

The last year of the war was a constant series of bloody battles between Ulysses's Union troops and the dwindling Confederate troops led by Robert E. Lee. It became clear it was just a matter of time before the Confederacy would have to surrender. Ulysses set up his headquarters in City Point, Virginia, near the war's late battlefields. Julia moved her home to Burlington, New Jersey, to be as safely close to her husband as possible. Julia continued to visit her husband often, as did President Lincoln and his mercurial wife, Mary Todd Lincoln. Mrs. Lincoln hated Ulysses, referring to him as "that butcher" for his relentless battle style, and she often took her feelings out on Julia. Mrs. Lincoln once derisively said to Julia, "I suppose you think you'll get to the White House yourself, don't you?" Julia shook off the comment, probably confident that she would.

On April 9, 1865, Lee surrendered to Ulysses at Appomattox Court House in Virginia, ending the Civil War and preserving the Union. On April 14, the Lincolns invited the Grants to accompany them to Ford's Theater for a performance of *Our American Cousin*. Julia was tempted to attend but decided instead that she and her husband should take a train home to see their children in New Jersey.

Above: General Robert E. Lee's surrender at Appomattox brought Ulysses's military career to an end, but it also placed him on the road to the White House.

Lincoln was assassinated by John Wilkes Booth that night at the theater and died the following day. It was later revealed that the murder of General Grant was also part of the assassination plot, but it was thwarted when the assassin on board the Grants' train to New Jersey found the door to their private car locked.

> "The General never talked war matters with me at all. He wrote very little about the war, even after the taking of Vicksburg. I don't remember that he wrote me any letter of exultation of joy. He was so sorry for the poor fellows who were opposed to him that he never could exult over any victory. He always felt relieved, of course, and glad that it seemed to promise to shorten the war, but he never exulted over them."
>
> —Julia Grant

After the war, the Grants were lavished with tributes and gifts from a grateful nation. They were given mansions in Galena and Philadelphia. They were also wealthy enough now to maintain a home in Washington, D.C. By 1868, there was only one gift left to give. Ulysses won the Republican nomination for the presidency and won the November election easily despite barely campaigning. Ulysses had little interest in politics, and even fewer plans for the country. He accepted the presidency for the sake of his wife, who craved the role of First Lady as few other presidents' wives ever have. She was ready for her role and she would prove to be one of the precursors for today's active First Ladies.

> "I always knew my husband would rise in the world. I believed he would someday inhabit the highest office in the land. I felt this even when we were newly married and he was making a mere pittance in salary."
>
> — Julia Grant

Life in the White House

The White House was only about fifty years old when the Grants took up residence in March 1869. After the British virtually destroyed the building in the War of 1812, it was reconstructed by the original architect, James Hoban, and completed in 1817. Still, Julia was shocked at its condition. She found cracked, leaking ceilings (one had already caved in); rotting wood in the floors and roof; and damp, worn carpets. She began an elaborate renovation true to the Gilded Age décor that was popular at the time.

Julia added cut-glass chandeliers, gilded wallpaper and woodwork, Grecian columns, and elegant ebony furniture. Julia had an iron fence constructed around the house to give it some privacy, and she made sure the grounds were given constant care. Julia also instructed that the gates to the grounds be kept closed so her two youngest children, Ellen and Jesse, could have the semblance of a home and a yard. By this time, the two older Grant children were away from home—Frederick was at West Point and Buck was at Harvard.

Julia turned the residence into a bustling social setting, both formal and informal. White House staff now had to wear uniforms and gloves. She held regular open houses and receptions in the new Blue Room with the wives of senators and cabinet members. There were also weekly state dinners, usually with thirty guests or more. The dinners were elaborate affairs with twenty or thirty courses prepared by Julia's new Italian chef. The finest china was imported for the White House collection, and Julia would spare no expense for gowns for the festivities.

Below: The Grants' inauguration ball was held in a temporary building built for the occasion. It was a moment Julia had been dreaming of.

Below: This painting shows Ulysses and Julia and their four children in an outdoor setting.

Julia Dent Grant set the standard for White House decoration for the next ninety years with her ornate, extravagant style. The original simplicity of the White House was not restored until First Lady Jacqueline Kennedy redecorated the mansion in the early 1960s.

Some were flowing damask and others were silk velvet. They were often trimmed with her signature black lace and satin, while accessories included flower ornaments, extravagant hats, and diamond jewelry.

Thanks to Julia, the White House had been restored to an object of pride and glamour. Unfortunately, the general did not fare as well as president. His two-term administration was tainted by scandal and corruption. Ulysses's ignorance of politics extended to his political appointments. He appointed friends and business associates to powerful cabinet positions. Some appointees had presented the Grants with gifts after the war, giving the appearance of bribery. Many of his cabinet members had little interest in government except to defraud it for their own financial gain. This atmosphere spread throughout Ulysses's administration, reaching as high as Vice President Schuyler Colfax. To make matters worse, Ulysses continued to support these men even after their crimes were exposed.

The World Tour

The American public still honored the general, but it was clear to everyone that he would have little support for a third term. Ulysses was probably relieved to be leaving Washington, but Julia was devastated. She had loved being First Lady, and she had done her job well. To help ease Julia's sense of loss, Ulysses took her on a two-year world tour starting just two months after they left the White House.

The Grants were accompanied by their son Jesse and a reporter from *The New York Herald*, John Russell Young. Their first stop was England to visit Nellie, who was living near Southampton. England would also set a pattern for the entire trip as the Grants were honored by statesmen and celebrities alike. Both the duke of Wellington and Queen Victoria invited the Grants into their palace homes.

The Grants' itinerary for their tour was impressive. They first visited nearly every country in Europe and then took a U.S. navy ship throughout the Mediterranean Sea. This part of the trip included stops in Egypt and the Holy Land. Their son Fred replaced Jesse for the rest of the trip, which included India, China, Burma, Hong Kong, and Japan.

Above: Julia poses in a photographer's studio. The setting doesn't hold a candle to her own redecorated White House home.

> *"My life in the White House was like a bright and beautiful dream."*
>
> —*Julia Grant*

The adventurous general was ready for more, but Julia had had enough. She wanted to return home to see her children. Julia also had another reason for the timing of their return. The 1880 presidential election was looming, and Julia harbored some hopes of returning to the White House. The Grants returned to the United States in late 1879 and took up residence in their Philadelphia home.

As the election drew near, Ulysses found that he, too, missed the White House and launched a campaign in 1880. Ulysses still had much support within the Republican party and entered the convention as the front-runner. Ballot after ballot, he led in the voting, but he could never get the majority needed for the nomination. The delegates finally chose a compromise candidate, Senator James Garfield, who would go on to win the November election. Julia had expected victory and was once more devastated.

The defeated Grants moved to New York, where grateful friends had built them a mansion and Ulysses joined his son's brokerage firm, Grant and Ward. Julia loved the glamorous life available in New York, attending the theater and socializing with the wealthy, but Ulysses once again showed he had no talent in the business world. Not only did the firm fail, but Ulysses was swindled out of most of his personal fortune by Ferdinand Ward, the firm's co-owner.

Below: Ulysses and Julia stopped long enough to be photographed with other visitors to the Great Pyramids in Egypt. They are third and fourth from the left in the front row of this group.

Above: A day at the beach: Ulysses and Julia relaxing at the Jersey Shore with their son Jesse.

The Gossip Begins

The middle of the nineteenth century saw a tremendous rise in the popularity of the daily newspaper as Americans became eager for news of their developing nation. As more women began to read, newspapers featured more articles on women's lives, particularly those of famous women. Like Mary Lincoln before her, Julia Grant was closely scrutinized; and not surprisingly, the writers were often quite critical. A Philadelphia reporter, pen-named Olivia, once referred to Julia as "fair, fat, and forty." The press went wild when Julia refused to take an undesirable assigned seat at a public ceremony; and when she had an iron fence put around the White House, she was accused of being "too exclusive." Still, most of the coverage was lighthearted, and the good-natured Julia took it all in stride. The public especially enjoyed reading about Julia's youngest child, Jesse, who loved recounting tales about how his two grandfathers, in their old age, still squabbled over their North versus South differences.

By 1884, the general was out of work and Julia found herself in poverty once again. It was America's greatest writer of the era who came to their rescue. Mark Twain had been a friend of the Grants for years and was now a publisher. He offered Ulysses a generous contract for his memoirs. Ulysses went to work on his book, and just when Julia thought the future looked bright again, she received the worst news of all. In October 1884, she learned her husband was dying of throat cancer.

Despite the pain of his disease, Ulysses worked hard on his book, knowing the money from it would make Julia's financial future more secure after his death. In the summer of 1885, concerned friends arranged for the family to move to a cottage at Mount McGregor, near Saratoga, New York. There, Julia would have a nurse, doctor, and maid to help her care for her dying husband. All the Grant children also came to live with their parents that final summer.

Ulysses finished his memoirs in mid-July and died a week later on July 23, 1885, at the age of sixty-three. Julia was so grief-stricken, she couldn't even attend his funeral in New York City two weeks later. Ulysses's death was such a blow that Julia spent the next several years a virtual recluse, living with and seeing only her family. In 1894, she bought a mansion in Washington, D.C., and moved in with Nellie and her three children after Nellie's divorce.

The presence of her grandchildren seemed to restore Julia's interest in life, and she started to see visitors outside her family once again. She also began writing her own memoirs. When they were complete, she submitted her work to publishers, perhaps expecting offers similar to Ulysses's contract with Twain, but the few offers that came were small. Julia decided to shelve her manuscript. Her memoirs would not be published until 1975.

Julia Dent Grant lived out her final years quietly, surrounded by family until her death at the age of 76 on December 14, 1902, in Washington, D.C. A week later, she was entombed with her husband at Grant's Tomb in New York City.

The Personal Memoirs of U. S. Grant *would eventually make over $400,000 in royalties for Julia, an impressive amount for a book in those days.*

Left: Nellie and Algernon Sartoris, the celebrated bride and groom, would eventually divorce. Right: Nellie Grant's wedding in the East Room of the White House was the highlight of the 1874 social season across the country.

A Happy Occasion

The most significant social affair of the Grant presidency was undoubtedly the May 1874 wedding of daughter Nellie, which became a national celebration. Nellie was only eighteen when she met wealthy Englishman Algernon Sartoris on a European tour and was swept away by his apparent sophistication. Despite the president's strong opposition to the marriage, he finally gave his consent and Julia prepared a sumptuous affair.

The wedding was held in the newly renovated East Room, which was packed with fragrant flowers. A marine band played as gifts from the two hundred guests were piled onto several tables and a huge wedding breakfast was served. Julia wore a black silk dress (black because of the recent death of her father), while Nellie donned a white satin dress trimmed with lace, and wore orange blossoms in her hair. Algernon and Nellie exchanged their vows in front of a wedding bell sculpted of roses and baby's breath. It was the social event of the decade, but sadly, the general was right—it would be a difficult marriage that would end in divorce seventeen years later.

Below: Julia's father named her birthplace "White Haven" for his original home in Maryland.

Visiting the Grants

Julia Grant's birthplace, White Haven, has been preserved as the Ulysses S. Grant National Historic Site. It consists of ten acres holding five historic structures—the main house, a stone building, the barn, the chicken house, and the icehouse. The address is: 7400 Grant Road, St. Louis, Missouri 63123. For more information, call 314-842-3298.

Ulysses S. Grant's birthplace in Point Pleasant, Ohio, has been preserved and restored. The one-story, three-room cottage was built in 1817 and stood next to the tannery where Ulysses's father worked. The small cottage is furnished with period items. It is located at 1591 State Route 232, Point Pleasant, Ohio 45153. Telephone: 937-553 4911.

Both Grants are buried in the famous Grant's Tomb. Ulysses was moved into this National Memorial when it was completed in 1897, and Julia Dent Grant joined him in 1902. The original planners of the tomb wanted to build one sarcophagus for both of them, but Julia rejected that idea. She thought her husband should have his own. The tomb is located at Riverside Drive and 122nd Street, New York, New York 10023. For more information, call 212-864-3410.

The Grants' country cottage on Mount McGregor has also been preserved as a museum and the rooms remain just as the family left them, including Ulysses's bedroom, where he died. The clock in the room was stopped at the moment of his death. The address is Mount McGregor, P.O. Box 990, Saratoga Springs, New York 12866. Telephone: 518-587-8277.

Lucy Hayes

Beginnings

When Lucy Webb was a teenager and a part-time student at Ohio Wesleyan University, Sophia Hayes and Maria Webb made a pact that Sophia's son Rutherford and Maria's daughter Lucy would one day be married. It wasn't an arranged marriage in the Old World sense, but an idea that both women thought was worth encouraging, and both of them did, sometimes to the annoyance of their children.

Lucy was from a highly respected family, and her churchgoing habits seemed to be just the thing to bring young Rutherford into line from his backsliding ways, which had his mother worried. Rutherford himself said that he found Lucy "a bright sunny little girl not quite old enough to fall in love with." He added, "And so I didn't." He was nine years older than she was.

Lucy had nothing to say about Rutherford. In fact, she seemed to have developed an interest in a male student at the university. Possibly to separate them, her mother sent her off to Cincinnati, at age sixteen, to become a student at the new Wesleyan Female College there. The school proudly claimed to be the first chartered college for women in the United States, but Mount Holyoke College had been established with a similar program five years earlier, and the Georgia Female College was founded a year earlier than that. The Ohio institution eventually had a better claim to fame than either of those colleges when one of its graduates, the former Lucy Webb, became the first wife of an American president to have a college degree.

Rutherford was establishing himself as a lawyer in Lower Sandusky, the town that would eventually become Fremont, Ohio, but his mother kept him well informed about what Lucy was up to and warned him that if he wasn't careful, some Methodist minister might be likely to carry her off. His sister Fanny Platt was even more persistent. "Lucy Webb has the finest disposition—with perhaps a few exceptions—that woman was ever blessed with—so frank, so joyous, her spirit sheds sunlight on all about her," she wrote to him. "Tolerably good looking, [she] would be handsome only that she freckles. Remarkably intelligent, very much improved in manner since you have seen her."

When he finally did see her again, Rutherford had moved his law office to Cincinnati, but Lucy hadn't been sitting around waiting for him to come back into her life. It was rumored that she was engaged to that fellow back at her former school, and whether it was true or not, she was exchanging love

Lucy Ware Webb Hayes

Born
August 28, 1831,
Chillicothe, Ohio

Parents
Dr. James Webb and
Maria Cook Webb

Marriage
December 30, 1852,
to Rutherford Birchard
Hayes (1822-93)

Children
Birchard Austin
(1853-1926); Webb Cook
(1856-1934); Rutherford
Platt (1858-1927); Joseph
Thompson (1861-63);
George Crook (1864-66);
Fanny (1867-1950); Scott
Russell (1871-1923);
Manning Force (1873-74)

Died
June 25, 1889,
Fremont, Ohio

Above: Lucy and Rutherford on their wedding day, December 30, 1852. They would be together for the next thirty-seven years, until her death.

notes with him. But Rutherford mentioned in his diary that he was looking for a new sweetheart, and as time went by, Lucy's name was turning up more often in its pages. Lucy went on living in Cincinnati after her graduation, and she saw more of the lawyer Hayes. They were engaged in June 1851.

Needless to say, both their mothers were beside themselves with joy, but most pleased of all was Lucy's future sister-in-law Fanny Platt. Lucy found letter writing a chore, but Fanny started bombarding her with letters sharing her strong views on women's rights. In the meantime, Rutherford seemed to be dragging his feet about setting a wedding date, and both families were becoming upset about it. An issue on both their minds was where they should settle down. Lucy leaned toward moving to Chillicothe, Ohio, where she had been born and knew everybody in town, but she was also among friends in Cincinnati. Her fiancé's uncle and chief benefactor, Sardis Birchard, was hoping they'd settle close to him in Fremont, and he offered to build the couple a house if they would agree to live there at least during the summer months. "How say you?" he questioned Lucy, "should I promise? I feel like doing it."

Lucy was noncommittal, and what seemed to be a less than enthusiastic response prompted Uncle Birchard to thunder, "Well, why doesn't the fool marry her? I don't believe she'll have him. If she will and he doesn't marry her soon, I'll get mad and marry some old maid myself." It was a threat that froze Rutherford's heart. He was looking forward to being his rich uncle's only heir. Four months later, with Uncle Birchard picking up the tab, they were married at the Webb home in Cincinnati on December 30, 1852. The couple honeymooned in Columbus, where he was trying a case before the Ohio Supreme Court.

Their plans for a wedding trip to Canada were postponed for eight years because of Lucy's first pregnancy. Their first child, a boy, was born in November 1853. He wasn't given a name, but was known only as "Puds" until the family insisted on something more formal and they named him for Uncle Birchard. But they insisted that he should be called Birchie, in the interest of informality.

After they settled in a new house in downtown Cincinnati, Lucy's new "sister" Fanny Platt began taking her to women's rights rallies and lectures, beginning a short education that lasted until Fanny died, unfortunately only two years later. But the foundation had been laid, and Fanny's lifelong influence over her brother had given him strong beliefs that Lucy had become more easily able to absorb. Lucy developed an interest in politics that bordered on a mania, but because it was impossible for her to have a political career of her own, she transferred her own interest to promoting one for her husband. He was already leaning in that direction, but he needed the gentle push.

The couple's second son, Webb Cook, was delivered by Lucy's brother Joe, who was a doctor. (Joe and his mother lived with Lucy

*Below: The first of Lucy
and Rutherford's eight
children, Birchard Austin Hayes,
was always called Birchie.*

> "The more I love Birchie, the dearer is my dearest Ruddie to me."
>
> —Lucy Hayes on motherhood

and Rutherford.) Two years later, another baby boy, whom they named Rutherford Platt and often called Ruddie, was welcomed into the household.

When the Civil War broke out and President Lincoln issued a call for volunteers, the future president Rutherford Hayes was among the first to respond. As the father of three, and overage at forty, he could easily have sat it out, but with Lucy's strong encouragement, he signed up as a major in the Twenty-Third Ohio Volunteer Infantry. It was the first regiment in the Union army that required its volunteers to stay in the service for three years or for the duration of the war.

Above: The Hayes' son Webb earned the Army's Medal of Honor in the Philippines in 1899.

Rutherford saw his service commanding troops that engaged the enemy often, and he himself was wounded in three different battles. He was promoted several times, finally reaching the rank of brevet major general, and he soon became a famous hero of the war.

Lucy had prepared herself to be a model soldier's wife, but she found it a trial. Her husband arranged for her and little Birch to visit him for a time at camp. but when his unit, which also included her brother Dr. Joe, left for the front in Virginia, she went back home. She was pregnant for the fourth time, and she felt very much alone, even though hardly a day went by that her husband or her brother didn't write. She was especially pleased to hear from others about Rutherford's accomplishments in the field and the admiration he was earning from the troops he led, because it confirmed her belief that he had a talent for leadership that could give him a brilliant career in politics.

Then one day, an urgent telegram arrived from him. He had been wounded in the mountains of Maryland, and it was severe enough that he would have lost his arm if not for the efforts of his doctor brother-in-law. His message was simply, "I am here. Come to me." She was in Washington in less than a week, but Rutherford wasn't where she expected to find him. A mistake in the telegraph transmission had placed him there, but he was actually in Maryland.

> *"I don't know why any man with a happy home wants to leave it."*
>
> —*Sophia Hayes, Lucy's mother-in-law*

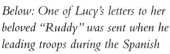

Below: One of Lucy's letters to her beloved "Ruddy" was sent when he leading troops during the Spanish American War.

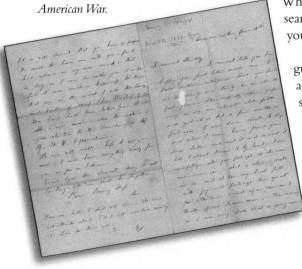

Lucy had never been to Washington before, but she waded into the depths of the bureaucracy and managed to locate every military hospital there, and she found her way to the surgeon general's office as well. But none of them knew of General Hayes. Lucy finally got the information she needed from a soldier in Rutherford's regiment whom she met on the street quite by chance. When she was finally reunited with Rutherford after more than a week of searching, she couldn't see the humor in his greeting, "Well, you thought you would visit Washington when you had the chance, did you?"

After his wound healed, Rutherford's regiment was assigned to guard duty in the mountains of West Virginia, and Lucy took Webb and Birchie to share his quarters until the troops moved on in the spring. She rejoined him in the field again with all four of their sons a few months later, but the visit was cut short by the death of her baby, eighteen-month-old Joseph.

The next time Lucy went into the war zone, she left her boys behind, but when it became apparent it would be a relatively long stay and they were in no particular danger, she rented out her house in Cincinnati and arranged to have her mother join her along with Ruddie and Webb. Lucy became a favorite in camp, partly because of her cheerful disposition and partly for her skills as a seamstress that kept the men's ragged uniforms in good repair.

After the family left for home, the Twenty-Third Regiment headed for Virginia and some of the bloodiest fighting they had seen. In the midst of it, Rutherford was nominated to run for Congress back home, but he begged off, citing his more important duties. Still, his name stayed on the ballot, and he won the election without setting foot in the district he was to represent. He also became a father in absentia when their fifth son was born in September 1864. As usual, the couple were slow to name the baby, but when Lucy suggested that they honor her ancestor Captain Billious Cook, her husband countered with the name of his commander, George Crook.

Within days of the baby's birth, the local newspaper reported that Rutherford had been killed in battle. Lucy's family kept the paper from her,

Among the men who served with her husband, Lucy's favorite was Lieutenant William McKinley, the future president.

though, and by the time she saw it, she already had a telegram from him assuring her that he had been wounded but was still very much alive. She had more anxious moments when he served during the siege of Richmond, but it was all soon over. She went to Washington again, this time *with* her husband rather than searching for him. He was a freshman congressman now, and the political career she had wished for him became a reality.

Lucy didn't like Washington at first, but she was soon swept up in its social life. She preferred to stay home in Ohio, although she made the round-trip several times during Rutherford's two terms in Congress. The trips weren't necessary after he was elected governor of Ohio in 1868. Although Lucy kept up her strong interest in national politics, she blossomed into a model hostess and a friend among local politicians after they moved to Columbus. Her husband, the governor, was most interested in social reform, and Lucy supported him almost to a fault. Throughout his entire political career, she generally stayed in the background, but her influence over him was unmistakable.

Below: A photographic portrait of First Lady Lucy Hayes.

The Lady Gives a Hand

While she was in the White House, Lucy always had a warm, almost motherly, welcome for everyone who came to call. Among them was an aged veteran of the War of 1812 who sent his uniform on ahead intending to wear it for a photograph with the First Lady. When he opened the package, he was reduced to tears because his sergeant's stripes hadn't been sewn to the sleeves. Rather than just consoling him, Lucy brought out her sewing kit and sat down on the floor to attach the stripes for him.

She also doted on her family. Birchie was fourteen, and Webb eleven; Lucy had lost two of her sons, but a new baby, their only daughter, Fanny, was part of the household, along with nine-year-old Ruddie. Their eighth child, Manning Force Hayes, was born in 1873, and died at the age of eighteen months, seemingly of dysentery, on his mother's forty-third birthday.

After he left the governorship, Rutherford ran for Congress again, but though he lost, he was still a tireless campaigner for other candidates, and he was eventually reelected governor. The house Uncle Birchard had promised them, which they called Spiegel Grove, was finally finished, and Lucy would have been content to stay there, but she was once again in the public eye. The *Ohio State Journal* gushed that she was "a perfect queen of a woman and demonstrated as of old that she is equal to any emergency." Rutherford joked that "one would think that it was the 'old lady' who was inaugurated." Some people wished that had been the case.

Rutherford did not stay Ohio's governor for long. The next year he was chosen as the Republican candidate for president, and the election that followed between Rutherford and Democrat Samuel Tilden resulted in claims of a tainted election. The original vote count claimed Tilden the winner and the follow-up count resulted in Rutherford as the winner. It took several sessions of Congress to determine a winner, but in March of 1877 the Hayes family moved into the White House.

The Dry White House

Below: After the inauguration of President Hayes, guests at White House parties and receptions faced the prospect of celebrating without a drink in hand.

After Rutherford and Lucy took up residence at the White House, a tavern around the corner changed its name to "The Last Chance." Mrs. Hayes did not approve of drinking, and the First Family banned all traces of alcohol from their new home, just as they had at their old one back in Ohio. It was quite a dramatic change from the tenure of the previous First Lady, Julia Grant, who had gone so far as to concoct a very potent combination of Champagne and Cointreau that she called Roman punch. There was no pun intended, but it did have a nasty kick to it.

There was a precedent for the drying of the White House. Sarah Polk had banned spirits from her entertainments there. But she made an exception by allowing wine to be served at dinner parties. The Hayeses, though, substituted lemonade with crushed strawberries to make a drink that resembled red wine. That was what led to the First Lady's nickname, Lemonade Lucy.

Lucy took all the blame, and some of the credit, too, but she wasn't the one who ordered the ban. Her husband had done it. Lucy took a temperance pledge when she was a young girl, and she never wavered from the promise she made. But it was a personal matter to her, and she never imposed her belief on others outside her own family. The president was a nondrinker, too, although he was known

to enjoy an occasional beer among his cronies; but the ban had nothing to do with their personal preferences. People who had formerly been passionate about the abolition of slavery had, by and large, taken on the new cause of driving demon rum from American society, and they had formed a new Prohibition political party. It was luring Republicans to its banner in alarming numbers, and President Hayes's no-drinking policy was his way of showing them that Republicans could be just as bluenosed as anybody.

The ban had the potential of creating international incidents. Foreign diplomats expected to be entertained with fine wines, and they were easily offended when they weren't. The issue came to a head even before the ban was announced, when grand dukes

> "Water flowed like champagne in the Hayes White House."
>
> —*Secretary of State William Evarts*

Alexis and Constantine, the sons of the Russian czar, visited Washington and were scheduled to be honored at the first state dinner in the Hayes White House. The secretary of state reminded the president that Russia was a long-standing ally of the United States and it was of great importance to entertain its young representatives in a style they were accustomed to finding in other world capitals. "A dinner without wine would be an annoyance if not an affront," he said. Rutherford was forced to agree, and "just this once," he ordered in a supply of wine for their pleasure.

It was Lucy's debut as White House hostess, and she pulled out all the stops. The table in the center of the State Dining Room had a mirror in the center representing a lake, surrounded by ferns and ivy. Pink azaleas in the center

Afterword

The drying of the White House was an albatross around Lucy's neck, but it was her husband's policy and not hers. As the Hayeses prepared to leave the White House, the president wrote in his diary: "It is said Gen. Garfield will restore wine and liquor to the White House. I hope this is a mistake. I am no fanatic on this subject. I do not sympathize with the methods of the ultra temperance people. I believe that the cause of temperance will be most surely promoted by moral, religious, and educational influences and by the influence of example. I would not use the force of law as an agency for temperance reform. If laws on the subject are enacted, let them be for the security of the community from nuisances and crime. Let the temperance reformer keep to the text influence, argument, example. When Lucy and I came here, we banished liquors from the house because it was right, wise and necessary; because it was due to the large support given me by sincere friends of temperance reform; and because I believed it would strengthen the Republican Party many who would otherwise join the Temperance Party."

Right: Cartoonist Thomas Nast came down on the side of the temperance cause with a representation of a tavern as "the bar of destruction," with death as the bartender.

On her first day in the White House, Lucy was faced with the problem of which of her guests was entitled to use the State Bedroom. She had them draw lots for the honor.

Above: The gown Lucy wore for her first White House reception sent a message that her appearance and personality was going to be intoxicating enough for any of her guests.

Below: Even receptions outside the White House, like this one in New York, stuck to the Hayeses' temperance policy.

suggested an island. The room itself, as had become traditional, was filled with colorful, fragrant flowers.

Lucy had appeared at her husband's inaugural wearing a chaste black silk dress and a matching bonnet, but this time she fit everyone's image of a First Lady. Her cream-and-gold dress, with three-quarter-length sleeves, was of brocaded taffeta, and it had a long train attached to generous strips of satin at her hips. It had a daringly deep neckline, but she filled the space above it with a lace scarf. She wore a single yellow rose in her hair. Lucy's rich black hair was parted severely in the middle and twisted into a bun on the back of her head, as many women wore their hair back then, and even more started doing when Lucy set the example. She never wore a hat, but she loved to wear flowers in her hair.

The dining table was set with six wine glasses for each of the thirty-six guests, and they were put to good use as the fifteen courses were served one by one, and then during the round of toasts that followed. But neither the president nor the First Lady used their glasses for anything but water. At the end of the dinner, he made the solemn announcement that this would be the last time that alcoholic beverages would be served in the Hayes White House.

If he had announced that the United States was declaring war on Russia, it couldn't have caused more of a stir. The Prohibitionists were delighted, but the First Family was generally ridiculed; and many angrily charged that the president and his wife had no right to impose their own morality on guests of the government. "They must follow precedent in dispensing that which they have to do merely as temporary inhabitants of the White House," reflected the common sentiment.

Many said that this was all just a ploy to save money, but money seemed to be no object at Lucy's entertainments, and she was unstinting at scheduling them. As usual, the president was expected to bear the brunt of the expense, and their dinner parties were rarely budgeted at less than $10 per guest. Wine and whiskey would obviously have added a great deal to that cost, but the Hayeses were not as frugal as many of their predecessors had been.

The president stood his ground in spite of the criticism. He had followed a similar policy as governor of Ohio, and he said that in both instances, he had the dignity of his subordinates in mind. Young men do disgraceful things when they have too much wine, he pointed out, and he hated to see "noble minds rendered unfit to be trusted in public office because of drink."

In the end, their uncompromising policy had the positive effect of convincing most of the country that the president and his wife were honest and sincere people. Hayes had come to office under the

First Impression

By the time Lucy Hayes came to Washington, newspapers were assigning reporters to the new beat of First Lady watching. Lucy was praised at the inaugural for her "gentle and winning face [and] bands of smooth dark hair, with that tender light in the eyes which we have come to associate with the Madonna." But one of the ladies of the press couldn't help wondering if her colleagues might not soon be calling for her to "frizz that hair, powder that face, bare those shoulders, and hide John Wesley's discipline out of sight." Of course, Lucy had grown up following the strict disciplines of the founder of the Methodist Church, and she wasn't going to take advice from the fashionistas.

Left: Lucy ignored the suggestions she received from the fashion press. Her image was fine with her.

cloud of a controversial election, and quite unpredictably, sticking to his principles in this way helped him to overcome it.

Lucy's first reception, and the first test of the new ban, was held, appropriately enough, on St. Patrick's Day. Nobody seemed to notice, or care, that there was no green beer available. For this event, and for all the ones that followed, Lucy called on cabinet wives to assist her as hostess. Not having any grown daughters—her only daughter, Fanny, was just ten years old—she also invited her nieces and cousins as well as the daughters of friends to help her, both with entertaining and secretarial services. The result was that there were more attractive young women in the White House while the Hayeses were there than at almost any other time. It made Lucy's entertainments livelier and more popular with single young men, even if all they were offered to drink was lemonade and water.

Lucy dressed well, but she was no fashion plate. Mostly, her relatively austere style brought her praise and was widely copied, but the people who made and sold fashionable gowns weren't at all pleased. One of them said that the wife of a comparatively wealthy man drawing a substantial government salary and living rent-free in a house that they neither had to heat nor furnish, ought to be spending more money on clothes. It would help not only their business but a large segment of the economy as well. They were certain of it. But Lucy wouldn't rise to the bait. She had more important things to think about than playing dress-up.

Below: Lucy's White House staff included Cabinet members' wives as well as relatives and the daughters of her friends.

Among the women Lucy recruited to help her in the White House was future First Lady Ida McKinley, whose husband was serving in Congress at the time.

Among those important things was dressing up the White House. More than any previous First Lady, Lucy was a well-informed student of the mansion's history, and few others had as much love for it. On her first tour of the rooms, she said, "No matter what they build, they will never build rooms like these again!"

Congress wasn't too fond of President Hayes, and they weren't forthcoming with funds for the White House even though it had fallen into disrepair again during the wild and woolly Grant years. Lucy made do. She scoured the attic and basement storage rooms for furniture that she could spruce up, and she strategically placed her finds over holes worn in the rugs that she couldn't afford to repair. Torn draperies were turned to face the other way, or rehung upside down so the damage would be less obvious. She also haunted local auctions hunting for bargains in furniture and accessories that would help make the house more presentable.

It wasn't until well into Rutherford's term that Congress finally came up with an appropriation for repairs and redecorating, but Lucy had a better use for the money. The White House conservatories were connected to the mansion by a billiard room, and she had the billiard table consigned to storage and the space converted into a greenhouse. Not only did getting rid of the pool table satisfy Lucy's Methodist principles, but it opened a pleasing vista from the State Dining Room into the enclosed gardens. She spent fully a quarter of the money Congress gave her to expand the number of greenhouses along the west front—there were now twelve of them—and she put aside more of it to bring in a gardener from Ohio to take care of them. Before she was finished, she had added a staff of ten to tend the plants and flowers, including a woman who specialized in making bouquets and another whose full-time job was delivering White House flowers as gifts to friends and local hospitals. Lucy Hayes loved flowers and she loved sharing them.

Among Lucy's other White House improvements was finishing a project that had been dragging for years: bringing running water into all parts of the house. It can only be imagined how the press dealt with that development. Lucy also made space available for typewriters, a newfangled invention that she thought might be useful, and she had telephones installed after inventor Alexander Graham Bell visited the White House to demonstrate his new invention. She couldn't call anybody outside the house, but she knew that the day wasn't far off when she could. Lucy Hayes was the very model of the "new woman."

Below: Lucy spent most of the money that was appropriated to upgrade the White House on turning its conservatories into showplaces.

Music Wherever She Goes

When Thomas Edison visited Washington to show off his latest invention, the phonograph, to Congress, Lucy invited him to the White House to do the same for her. The entranced congressmen detained him, and he didn't arrive until after eleven at night. Lucy had gone to bed by then, and it took her an hour to dress for the occasion. But the inventor waited for her, and then it was her turn to be enthralled. It was well after three in the morning before she let him go. Needless to say, when Edison brought his phonograph to market, Lucy was one of his first customers. She also bought a good supply of the wax cylinders that brought music into the house, but she never recorded her own voice.

Left: Inventor Thomas Edison found an eager customer for his new phonograph in Lucy.

The New Women

The Hayes presidency began right after the country had marked the first hundred years of its existence with a massive World's Fair in Philadelphia. The Centennial Exposition was more about the future than the past, and chief among its wonders were such laborsaving devices as washing machines and vacuum cleaners, which would once and for all free women from household drudgery and give them, in some cases, an opportunity to find jobs outside their homes. Already, businessmen were casting off their old prejudices and starting to hire women—at lower salaries than men—and industry was beginning to treat them like human beings for the first time. Up until then, women were expected to serve their husbands without complaint and be happy they had one to support them.

Most of the so-called new women regarded Lucy Hayes as their natural role model. No other First Lady had ever graduated from college, and few of them had shown any interest in women's issues, such as they were, until then. Lucy had demonstrated a great deal of concern for such causes as equal pay and higher education for women before she became First Lady, and it wasn't farfetched to assume that she would use her new clout to popularize them.

Among Lucy's most persistent petitioners were members of the National Women Suffrage Association. They had been pushing for ten years to secure the vote based on the Declaration of Independence's guarantee of natural human rights, but now they

Above: Visitors to the Philadelphia Centennial Exposition were dazzled by amazing new machines like the one that turned out rolls of wallpaper.

Lucy was a bit cool on the issue of women's suffrage, but she could get passionate about fighting for sexual equality in wages, although not publicly.

Bloomer Girls

It was usually easy for Lucy to spot the "new women" at her receptions because they frequently appeared wearing bloomer dresses. The costume had been made popular by a reformer named Amelia Bloomer of Seneca Falls, New York, a close associate of women's rights pioneers Susan B. Anthony and Elizabeth Cady Stanton. She published a newspaper called The Lily *that promoted women's suffrage, temperance, and higher education for women. It had a circulation reaching toward half a million.*

Women of the day were expected to wear tight whalebone corsets under heavy layers of clothing even in the heat of the summer, and Ms. Bloomer took up the cause of giving them some relief. She took her cue from another social reformer, Fanny Wright, who had created an outfit with a comfortable loose bodice and a knee-length skirt worn over Turkish-style pantaloons—the fashion ancestor of pedal pushers and pants suits. The getup covered all of a woman's body except her hands, especially her ankles, which were off-limits to male eyes; but it was still regarded as scandalous. The Lily *completely endorsed the new fashion, so much so that the pantaloons became known as bloomers. So did the women who wore them—and thousands of them did. Eventually Amelia abandoned the style herself, saying that it was taking too much attention away from the real issues, but in the meantime it had made her name a household word. She concentrated on the cause of women's suffrage after that, but she didn't live to see it become a reality. Among her descendants was First Lady Betty Ford, who fought harder for women's rights than Amelia Bloomer was ever able to.*

Above: The symbol of the "new woman," the bloomer dress, was amazingly successful.

Below: Elizabeth Cady Stanton, president of the National Women's Suffrage Association, found Lucy a tough nut to crack, although the First Lady believed in rights for women.

were trying a different approach. They wanted nothing less than an amendment to the Constitution that would make it a legal matter and not one of moral persuasion.

They were willing to grasp at any straw of support, and when Rutherford said in a prepresidential speech that he believed equality for all citizens was the cornerstone of democracy, they figured that he was in their corner. But when his first State of the Union address called for helping all sorts of citizens from sailors to Native Americans, but never even mentioned women, the association sent a delegation to his office with a demand that the next time he spoke before Congress, he must at least give a nod to the still-denied rights of the 20 million wives, sisters, and daughters of the republic. He said that he would "consider it."

Before the women left, the president introduced them to Lucy, who talked to them for more than an hour and gave them a tour of the house. Following her own established custom, Lucy didn't commit herself, but it appeared likely that deep down she shared her husband's view that while it was all very well for women to want to vote, the vast majority of them weren't ready for the responsibility. They had too many distractions raising children and pleasing their husbands. Not discouraged, the suffragists sent their president, Elizabeth

Cady Stanton, to have a follow-up talk with Lucy. Ms. Stanton was also a
leading Prohibitionist, and she admired the First Lady's stand on the issue. It
gave her the "respect and admiration of all true women," she said. But as proof
that flattery will get you nowhere, Lucy still wouldn't promise to become a
mouthpiece for the women's suffrage movement, although Ms. Stanton left with
a warm affection for the First Lady. Everybody did. Part of the problem was
that it was considered gauche for a First Lady to have strong opinions about
anything except keeping White
House guests happy.

The Women's Christian
Temperance Union (WCTU)
believed that it might have an
inside track for Lucy's support.
Except for keeping the White
House dry, she hadn't done much
to champion their cause, but the
membership knew she was a sister under the skin. Among the organization's
public efforts for attention was placing drinking fountains in parks all over
the country, and their ultimate goal was to put an elaborate one on the White
House lawn as a special tribute to Lucy.

*The first congressional resolution for a women's suffrage
amendment was introduced in 1869. It didn't become
a reality until 1920, fifty-one years later.*

The president didn't consider that a very good idea. He thought it would
bring more ridicule to the First Family. Instead, he proposed that they hire a
prominent artist to paint Lucy's portrait. The ladies thought that it was a brilliant
idea and they began a national direct mail campaign to raise funds for it. One
of the letters suggested that even a dime would be a welcome contribution, and
when it crossed her desk Lucy decided that it was about time for her to offer her
own opinion on the subject. She
considered begging "painful," but
she also said that she thought her
memory must certainly be worth
more than ten cents. She consoled
herself by saying that they'd never
bring in enough money that
way. She didn't want the portrait
anyway, she said, preferring to be "enshrined in the hearts of the people."

> "I trust I am not a fanatic, but I do want my influence to be always in favor of
> temperance…. [But] I shall not violate the Constitution, which is all that, through my
> husband, I have taken an oath to obey."
>
> —Lucy Hayes's opinion on temperance

The ball was already rolling, though, and William E. Dodge of the Young
Men's Christian Association pushed it along by promising to bring in other
philanthropists like himself to raise the funds. He, too, considered ten cents an
insulting contribution—even a dollar was too little as far as he was concerned.
He called on clergymen to help raise $10,000 for the project, a quarter of which
would pay for the portrait itself and the rest to be used for printing temperance
literature.

The committee hired Daniel Huntington, a well-known Hudson River
School artist who had turned to portrait painting. Before this commission, both
Presidents Lincoln and Van Buren had sat for him. Lucy was captured wearing a

Above: Lucy and Rutherford ordered cufflinks and a brooch with their own cameos as gifts to one another for their silver wedding anniversary.

Below: The National Soldiers Home on the outskirts of Washington was a presidential retreat on the order of today's Camp David. Lucy enjoyed the surroundings and she enjoyed visiting with the disabled war veterans, too.

burgundy dress with generous amounts of lace at the neck and sleeves; a bunch of flowers, which had become her trademark, was pinned to her waist. She was posed in a classical garden setting with a stream running through it, rather than in front of a drinking fountain as had been suggested. But the message was clear enough for the temperance women. The larger-than-life-size portrait was presented to the White House, but the WCTU was denied the pleasure of having the First Lady herself unveil it for them. The gift wasn't formally accepted until after Lucretia Garfield had become First Lady.

Lucy herself had unveiled several White House portraits while she was there. During the White House refurbishing, she commissioned likenesses of all the former presidents who weren't already represented, and she had a full-length portrait of Martha Washington created to hang on the wall opposite the image of the first president.

Lucy had written to one of her sons, "Really and truly I am the same person that led a humble and happy life in Ohio. [It is] natural and easy.... Sometimes my native modesty gives me severe twinges. Without intending to be public, I find myself a quiet mind-her-own-business woman rather than notorious." That may be the reason why she resisted the advances of big national organizations looking for her official support. But along with modesty, Lucy had a native instinct for charity.

Back when her husband was governor of Ohio, she devoted a large amount of her time to working with young and handicapped people. She was especially attentive to improving conditions at a home for the orphans of Civil War veterans, and she regularly volunteered as a teacher at a school for deaf and dumb children.

In her early months as First Lady, Lucy took on a special campaign to finish the Washington Monument. It had stood as little more than a stump for close to half a century. Although it wasn't finished until 1885 and was dedicated by President Chester A. Arthur, it might still be unfinished if Lucy hadn't spurred Congress to get on with the job.

During the Buchanan administration, a large cottage on the grounds of the National Soldiers Home just outside Washington was set aside as a presidential retreat. The only other president who went there, except for Buchanan, was Abraham Lincoln, but the Hayes family thought of it as a heaven on earth, and while the president and his staff commuted to the White House from there each day, Lucy stayed behind. She was happy to get away from the summer heat, and

she found special pleasure there visiting with the disabled veterans, who appreciated her attentions.

Lucy took an active interest in social conditions in Washington itself, and she made improving conditions in the city's slums a personal project. The poor and downtrodden could be found at the White House door every day of the week, and Lucy left orders with the gatekeeper to find out where they lived and then had money sent to them, and she also sent food by the wagonload into their neighborhoods. When she heard about a down-and-out Civil War veteran who was dying, she had furniture and bedding sent to his rooms, and then she took up a collection among her husband's cabinet ministers and was able to include $125 in cash to help the man get back on his feet. In a single month, January 1880, Lucy personally gave nearly $1,000 to help Washington's poor and homeless. It wasn't a typical month, but her generosity never wavered during all four of her years in the White House.

Lucy Hayes was one of the most personally popular of all of America's First Ladies. The press gave her unprecedented attention, and the bulk of the coverage was positive—she was a master at sidestepping controversy—but she was the first president's wife to travel around the country, and people were given a chance to see her close up. She found special delight in visiting historic sites up and down the East Coast, and she made frequent trips back to Ohio to catch up with family and friends. The trip that made the biggest difference, though, was the one she and her husband took across the country in the summer of 1880. No other sitting president had ever done such a thing. The Hayeses had the advantage of being able to travel on the new transcontinental railroad that, although it had been finished eleven years earlier, was still quite a novelty. They stopped many times along the way for sightseeing in the mountains and prairies, usually riding through rough country in army ambulances and wagons. After they reached San Francisco, they toured the California coast by stagecoach with General William Tecumseh Sherman, the commander of the U.S. army, riding shotgun. He was part of an official party that included about twenty people. The tourists ranged from as far north as Vancouver Island, making the return trip to San Francisco by steamer. They were greeted enthusiastically everywhere they went, and the people she met were instantly entranced by the charming First Lady.

Above: The Hayes were the first president and First Lady to visit the West Coast, and the Palace Hotel in San Francisco welcomed them by filling their room with locally grown flowers.

"*[Mrs. Hayes's] strong healthful influence gives the world assurance of what the next century's women will be.*"

—*Newspaper columnist Mary Clemmer Ames on Lucy's influence*

Above: The president with two of his sons, Rutherford (left) and Webb, who also served as members of the presidential staff.

Their cross-country tour lasted for seventy-two days, and although the people they met loved them for it, the Washington establishment grumbled that a president had no business being away from his office for so long. One critic even suggested that it was a plot on Lucy's part to keep people from insulting her husband, which many of his enemies in the capital weren't above doing. But he had already made it clear that he wasn't going to run for a second term, and the man who was taking most of the Democrats' heat was former president Ulysses S. Grant, who was politicking for a return to the White House. He lost in the end, when the Republican nomination went to James A. Garfield, whose victory at the polls was taken as a tribute to the success of the Hayes administration.

In the meantime, the president and Mrs. Hayes were more popular than ever. Their entertainments had become legendary by then, and Lucy didn't scale back when there was no longer any future in it. They also broke precedent by accepting invitations to dinner parties at other people's homes, and they began bringing friends and family, especially the younger ones, from Ohio to enjoy their White House parties and receptions. Their own younger children—Fanny, who was now thirteen, and Scott, ten—had been living at the White House all along, but now they were invited to join in the fun for the first time. Among the Hayeses' older sons, Rutherford and his brother Webb had served on their father's staff and were already veterans of White House entertaining; and the eldest, Birchie, though he lived in Ohio, was a frequent visitor, usually with his young friends in tow. Altogether, it gave a welcome youthful touch to Lucy's entertaining.

Lucy often said that she looked forward to the day when it would be all over. But when the day finally came and she busied herself overseeing the final luncheon welcoming a new president to the White House, she said, "It was well I was so hurried for the goodbyes would have overcome me… I grew to love the house."

> *"I never saw more weeping people call to say good-bye in my thirty-six years at the White House."*
>
> —*Thomas Pendell, chief doorkeeper, on the Hayeses' departure*

A New Life

Even as Lucy was gearing up to become a former First Lady, the organizations that had courted her for support didn't slow down their efforts. Representatives of temperance organizations haunted her home, Spiegel Grove, in Fremont, Ohio, with requests to shower her with the testimonials that had been unwelcome at the White House. They deluged her with friendly petitions, often accompanied with requests for donations; and the national temperance organization made plans for a grand celebration honoring Lucy's contribution to the cause. The assassination of President Garfield gave the Hayeses a convenient excuse to downgrade the round of presentations, and it was politely suggested that the tributes might be mailed to Lucy rather than presented in person with so much ceremony.

Lucy was tactful about it, but she steadfastly refused to lend her name either to the temperance movement or the cause of women's suffrage. She had, however, accepted the presidency of the Women's Home Missionary Society (WHMS). Affiliated with the Methodist Episcopal Church, its goal was to enlist Christian women to go into slums and ghettoes to "enlighten the minds, reform the habits, and purify the minds of the inhabitants." It was a cause that Lucy could relate to, and although with reluctance, she agreed to serve as its president, but in name only. After she retired, she submitted her resignation to the WHMS, but she was lured back on the premise that the organization wouldn't be able to survive without her, even though she had never taken any active role in it beyond allowing her name to be used. Again reluctantly, she agreed to stay on as president of the organization. With that, the board began making plans for expansion from its primary base in Ohio into the northeastern states. Citing poor health, Lucy managed to avoid most direct participation, but when the church agreed to make it a national organization, it seemed to be a miracle cure for whatever might have been ailing her.

Lucy had an aversion to speaking in public, but her "words of encouragement" at the society's annual meetings and occasional regional gatherings made her the first former First Lady to make any kind of speech at all. Her talks were more memorable for what she had to say than for who she was.

Lucy's strong enthusiasm for improving conditions in the home life of "the uninformed, destitute and unfortunate of our own race—those of our own kith and kin," knew no bounds, but before long her basic message began to change. "If our eyes are to be gladdened by the sight of heathen lands rapidly becoming Christian, we must direct our efforts to protect from heathenism our own land. We see the paganism of other lands—of Asia, of Africa, of Europe—which has poured in upon our shores."

After a lifetime of carefully avoiding being painted with any kind of political brush, Lucy Hayes was wading into one of the touchiest issues of the late nineteenth century, the rising tide of foreign immigration, but she couched it as a new Christian crusade. In reality, she was motivated by the competition for financial support from foreign missionary organizations.

Thank You Note

Although she persuaded the temperance people not to make their testimonial presentations in person, Lucy nevertheless appreciated the gesture, and she wrote an open letter to the movement's leaders. "I cannot express the happiness it gives me to be assured that our manner of life in the White House has been approved by so many intelligent people," she said. "Certainly the sentiment is gaining strength that the duties of hospitality can be suitably observed without the temptations and dangers arising from the use of intoxicating drink." But still, even as a private citizen, she didn't show any interest in climbing on the temperance water wagon.

She also identified a threat just as great among African-Americans. "It is represented by conscientious observers," she informed one audience, "that the colored people increase more rapidly than the white in proportion to their numbers, and that the proportion of the ignorant and unchristian does not diminish." She fired similar verbal arrows at the Chinese, Latin Americans, and Mormons, all of whom she said needed a good dose of old-fashioned religion, and perhaps the dedication of a few good female teachers.

It was all very good for the growth of the WHMS, and Lucy was especially gratified to see girls organizing themselves into junior auxiliaries. She wrote to one of them: "I think you have gotten hold of the most certain and promising field of our work. The young people once interested in doing something for the happiness and good of their fellow creatures will grow and strengthen in this work."

Under Lucy's leadership, the society's membership grew to more than 40,000, and it had some 40 missionaries on its payroll. Its influence extended to the West, where it established schools for Native American children, and to the South, where it ran industrial schools and added home economics to the curricula of existing schools. The WHMS also set up an immigration center in New York, and it established reading clubs and ran a popular lecture bureau. Lucy was proud of her involvement in the organization, and it didn't hurt her personal image a bit.

Lucy's retirement years at Spiegel Grove were all that any woman could wish for. She was secure in the respect of her neighbors, her five children were all close enough for frequent visits, and she was active again in the local Methodist Episcopal Church where she taught a Sunday school class and worked on socials and fund-raising projects. It pleased her greatly that her husband, who had avoided church membership until then, joined her there every Sunday morning. She usually joined him at reunions of his old Civil War regiment, as well as other veterans conventions that usually involved traveling, which was one of her greatest pleasures.

Lucy was given only eight years to enjoy her life at Spiegel Grove. In the spring of 1889, she suffered a stroke while sitting in church. She seemed to have recovered when a couple of weeks later, she slumped in her chair while reading a garden catalog. The victim of a second stroke, she slipped into a coma and died quietly on August 28, 1889, sixty days short of her fifty-seventh birthday. A Washington newspaper said, "No death ever before touched the hearts of the American people except that of Abraham Lincoln."

Before her husband himself died of a heart attack three years later, he summed up his own feelings in a speech when he said that his marriage to Lucy was "the most interesting

Below: The First Family relaxed at home at Spiegel Grove after their retirement. From left to right: Birchard; his wife, Mary; the president; Scott; Rutherford; Lucy; Fanny, and Webb.

Farmer's Wife

The Hayes retirement residence was not a farm, but Lucy had plenty of animals for company. Along with a noisy mockingbird, a Siamese cat, and a goat, the family had two dogs in the White House, and the entire menagerie retired to Ohio, too. Lucy's favorite was a greyhound she called Gryme, who followed her everywhere. They had a flock of ducks and another of chickens, dozens of pigeons, and five cows, one of whom Lucy named after herself, as well as the usual complement of horses. The president's faithful horse, "Old Whitey" (a common name for generals' horses, apparently), who was the most famous White House pet, died before they left the White House.

Lucy loved each and every one of the animals, and a letter to her daughter who was away at school was so filled with news about them that her father added a postscript: "Your Mother as usual recalls the brute creation, but omits to give your Father even the 'cold respect of a passing glance.' He nevertheless still lives, and he loves his daughter consumedly."

fact in my life." He said that she had been the "crowning felicity" of his life and that she lavished "happiness on all others." They had been together for nearly forty years.

Right through their time as America's First Family, many believed that it was Lucy who was calling the shots. A newspaper reporting on one of her trips said, "Mr. Hayes will serve as acting president in her absence." But while Lucy always had the president's ear, she never controlled his head. Her greatest talent was supporting her husband without ever dominating him. Lucy Hayes was one of a kind, not just among America's First Ladies, but among American women in general.

Below: Rutherford once wrote, "The best part of the present house is the verandah." Lucy agreed.

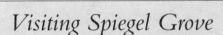

Visiting Spiegel Grove

The Rutherford B. Hayes Presidential Center is located in Fremont, Ohio, just off the Ohio Turnpike between Akron and Toledo. The route from the turnpike to the twenty-five-acre site is well marked.

Spiegel Grove, the house that Uncle Sardis Birchard built for Rutherford and Lucy as a wedding present, is also where the Hayes family lived before and after going to the White House. Both Lucy and Rutherford are buried on its grounds. The massive library on the grounds is the first presidential library in the United States. It contains more than 70,000 volumes, 75,000 photographs, and one million manuscripts.

The mansion is open Monday through Saturday from 9:00 A.M. to 5:00 P.M.; Sundays and holidays, when the library is closed, the mansion is open from noon to 5:00 P.M. The site is closed on Thanksgiving, December 25, and January 1. The fees for admission are $10.50 for adults and $4.00 for children ages six to twelve. Children under six get in free. For more information, call 800-998-7737.

Lucretia Garfield

An Educated Woman

In 1848, Lucretia Mott and Elizabeth Cady Stanton organized the first women's rights convention ever held in the United States. It took place in Seneca Falls, New York, and attracted 250 people, 40 of whom were men. The convention resulted in the Declaration of Sentiments and Resolutions, and it signaled the official beginning of the American women's rights movement. The declaration declared that women were entitled to the same rights as men—the right to vote, the right to hold property, equal status in divorce and custody issues, and equal access to education and employment.

Lucretia Rudolph was just sixteen years old when the convention released its declaration, and she became a strong supporter of the movement. However, most Americans at the time believed that the only role suitable for a woman was as wife and mother. To believe in women's rights was to invite ridicule and suspicion. Such reform was viewed as a threat to the American family and the American way of life in general. As a result, many women in the nineteenth century found themselves submitting to the traditional role of the American woman. This was especially true of any woman married to a man involved in politics. And Lucretia Rudolph would be no different when she would marry a future president of the United States, ten years after the Seneca Falls convention.

Lucretia was born on April 19, 1832, in Garrettsville, Ohio in an area of the state known as the Western Reserve. She was one of four children born to Zebulon Rudolph and Arabella Mason and was often called by her nickname, Crete. Zebulon was a carpenter and he found plenty of work building cabins and barns for all the new settlers in the area. The Rudolphs had strong religious convictions and belonged to the Disciples of Christ Church. The sect believed in total freedom of religious thought and accepted only the Bible as their source of authority. Zebulon became one of the community's religious leaders, often leading the Sunday services.

Pioneer life was difficult and Lucretia's childhood was not a particularly happy one. There were many arduous chores for the Rudolph children, and the harsh Ohio winters were especially tough on Lucretia, who suffered from chronic lung problems. However, Lucretia's parents did encourage her love for reading by having her read stories from the Bible to the family.

Lucretia Rudolph Garfield

Born
April 19, 1832, in Garrettsville, Ohio

Parents
Zebulon Rudolph and Arabella Mason Rudolph

Marriage
November 11, 1858, to James Abram Garfield (1831-81)

Children
Eliza (Trot) Arabella (1860-63); Harry Augustus (1863-1942); James Rudolph (1865-1950); Mary (Mollie) (1867-1947); Irvin McDowell (1870-1951); Abram (1872-1958); Edward (Neddie) (1874-76)

Died
March 14, 1918, South Pasadena, California

Independence

When Lucretia was sixteen, her parents sent her to a boarding school called the Geauga Seminary in nearby Chester, Ohio. The school had some strict religious rules—dancing was forbidden, and Sunday clothes had to be worn every day—but academics were also emphasized. Lucretia received a strong education in English, math, science, speech, and the Latin and Greek classics. It was at Geauga that Lucretia met the first love of her life, Albert Hall. After they both graduated in 1850, she and Hall kept in touch through letters. It was also at Geauga that Lucretia first met another student, James Garfield.

Like most pioneers in America's early history, Zeb Rudolph and the other community leaders had a strong faith in the future. While Lucretia was at Geauga, they were busy building a college in nearby Hiram, just four miles from the Rudolph home. They named it the Western Reserve Eclectic Institute (now Hiram College), known as the Eclectic for short, and it was finished in time for Lucretia to enroll in its first term in 1850. The Eclectic was very unusual in one respect for an American college—it admitted both men and women.

Lucretia enjoyed her studies at the Eclectic very much, and she started the school's Ladies' Literary Society. Her correspondence with Albert Hall would end after she became convinced that he would never become a proper Christian, but by that time another student had his eye on Lucretia. Her former classmate from Geauga, James Garfield, had enrolled in the Eclectic as well, and was working his way through school as the janitor. James was a brilliant student, often filling in for the teachers when they were ill, and by their junior year, he was showing an interest in Lucretia.

Lucretia was not interested at first, but during her senior year, James started writing letters to Lucretia and she would write back. In a courtship typical of the times, the two wrote mostly general thoughts about their lives rather than having any romantic exchanges. James appreciated Lucretia's intelligence but seemed concerned about her apparent support for women's rights. As their relationship developed, Lucretia seemed equally concerned about what marriage might mean to her plans to become a teacher.

After Lucretia's graduation in 1854, any ideas of marriage were delayed when James enrolled in Williams College in faraway Massachusetts to finish his education. While he was gone, they continued their letter writing and Lucretia became a teacher, first at the Eclectic and then at a school in nearby Ravenna, Ohio.

After his graduation from Williams in 1856, James returned to Hiram to teach at the Eclectic. He would soon be promoted to principal, but his relationship with Lucretia seemed to reach an impasse. James had reservations about marriage in general, saying it was like a "lottery." Lucretia enjoyed the independence her teaching position gave her, and she also had discovered that

Above: Lucretia Garfield's portrait as First Lady.

Below: James A. Garfield at the age of sixteen.

James had been involved with another woman while at Williams. Once again, any resolution to their relationship was avoided when Lucretia accepted a new teaching position at the Brownell Street elementary school in Cleveland.

Cleveland was Lucretia's first taste of a big city, and she loved it. She took walks past the mansions and gardens of Cleveland's Millionaire's Row, she attended plays, and she continued her own education by taking courses in art and music. Most of all, she loved teaching.

Though James still had reservations about marriage in general and Lucretia's modern view of womanhood, he finally proposed to her in April 1858, and Lucretia accepted. It is an indication of the societal pressures on women at the time that Lucretia would leave a place she loved, and sacrifice a position that gave her the independence she craved, to become a housewife for a man whose interest in her seemed based more on duty than love.

An Uneasy Relationship

As the November wedding day approached, James grew even more distant from Lucretia. It prompted her to send him a facetious invitation to his own wedding. The couple was married on November 11, 1858, at the Rudolphs' home, but there would be no honeymoon. They moved into a boardinghouse on the Eclectic campus, and James continued his duties as school principal. He also started to think seriously about a career switch to politics and entered his first race as a Republican for a seat in the Ohio state senate. Lucretia accepted the duties of housewife, and by the end of 1859 she was pregnant with her first child.

James won the state senate seat, and in January 1860 he moved to Columbus, the state capital, leaving Lucretia behind. He seldom visited Lucretia, even after the birth of their first child, Eliza, nicknamed Little Trot, in July 1860. It was around this same time that James revealed to Lucretia that he thought their marriage might have been a mistake. The distance between the couple, both physical and emotional, would grow even greater with the outbreak of the Civil War. James was a strong supporter of the Union cause, and he signed up to lead a regiment of Ohio volunteers.

James saw action in several major battles, including Shiloh in Tennessee and Chickamauga in Georgia, over the next two years and rose to the rank of major general. His political career also received an unexpected boost in the 1862 congressional elections, when James was elected to the House of Representatives, a seat he would not be able to assume until the end of 1863 due to the war.

During these years, Lucretia grew increasingly disillusioned about her marriage. James's trips home were so rare, Lucretia estimated that in their first five years of marriage, they had lived together for just twenty weeks. Despite these separations, the couple did have a second child, Harry Augustus, in October 1863.

Above: The future president with his fourth child, Mollie. Lucretia gave birth to seven children.

Below: The Garfield kids who lived into adulthood included Mollie, Harry, James, Irvin, and Abram.

Life in Washington

In December 1863 tragedy struck: Three-year-old Little Trot contracted diphtheria and died. But, sadly, Eliza's death was what it took for James to finally realize that his family needed to be together. He rented a house in Washington where they would live while Congress was in session from November through March. The rest of the year, the Garfields would live in their Hiram home that Lucretia had found and fixed up for them while her husband was in the army.

For the next several years, the Garfields became a real family. Two more children joined the clan—James in 1865 and Mary (nicknamed Mollie) in 1867—and James was reelected to the House two more times. Lucretia also found an outlet for her intellect when she and James joined the local literary society. In 1867, Lucretia and James took a well-deserved vacation, a four-month tour of Europe. Lucretia's years of loneliness and doubts were over. She had finally reaped the rewards of her patience.

In the years after their return from Europe, the Garfields continued to prosper and to grow. Lucretia gave birth to three more children—Irvin in 1870, Abram in 1872, and Edward (nicknamed Ned) 1874. The Garfields were forced to sell their summer home in Hiram because it was now too small, and bought a bigger house in Washington to accommodate the growing family. Lucretia set aside one room in the new Washington home as hers alone. In this room, she privately pursued her reading, painting, and writing.

Lucretia Garfield had more children than any other First Lady except her immediate predecessor, Lucy Hayes. Lucy Hayes was mother to eight, while Lucretia had seven children.

James continued to serve in the House of Representatives, rising to the powerful position of chairman of the Appropriations Committee, which was charged with overseeing how the government spent money. Lucretia and her husband had grown very close by this time, and James sought out her advice on government decisions often. The political climate in America had grown very contentious, especially over the issue of Reconstruction and whether the South should be punished for its role in starting the Civil War.

It was a particularly difficult time for the Republican party. There were accusations that many congressmen were accepting bribes from the railroad companies in return for favorable votes on loans and contracts. The party was also divided over the spoils system of political appointees. The Stalwarts, led by former president Ulysses S. Grant, believed government jobs should be at the discretion of the party leaders, who usually chose their friends and business associates. The Half-Breeds, like President Hayes and James Garfield, believed appointments should be based on the merits of the available candidates. James's stand on this issue would prove very fateful in a few short years.

In 1876, Lucretia and James were faced with yet another tragedy: Ned, who was just two years old, died of whooping cough. To help ease their sorrow, they bought a 160-acre run-down farm in Mentor, Ohio, to be their new summer home. Over the next four years, most of Lucretia's free time was spent fixing up the old farm they called Lawnfield. She supervised the repairmen, bought furniture, and chose paint colors. During the summers, James and his two oldest sons planted crops and fruit trees. By 1880, Lawnfield had become a beautiful farmhouse where Garfield family and friends came to visit often. The farm was one of Lucretia's proudest accomplishments.

> "[Lucretia] is so prudent that I have never been diverted from my work for one minute to take up any mistakes of hers."
>
> —James Garfield on his wife's intelligence and abilities

The Presidency and Tragedy

In January 1880, the Ohio legislature elected James to serve in the U.S. Senate the following term. However, the Republican party had other plans for him. It was a presidential election year, and James strongly supported fellow Ohioan John Sherman. However, the two front-runners were ex-president and Stalwart Grant and Half-Breed James Blaine. The Republican Convention that summer became deadlocked. Ballot after ballot, neither front-runner could garner the majority of the votes needed for the nomination—Sherman held the key votes.

After James rose to give a rousing speech in support of Sherman, many of the delegates started to consider James as a compromise candidate to break the deadlock. Lucretia was ambivalent, preferring her husband be nominated on his merits rather than simply because the delegates were deadlocked. Both Sherman's and Blaine's delegates soon started switching their votes to the new candidate. On the thirty-sixth ballot, a stunned James Garfield was nominated to be the Republican candidate for president, with Stalwart Chester Arthur as his vice presidential running mate.

James conducted most of his 1880 presidential campaigning from the front porch of Lawnfield. Voters came from all around the country to hear the candidate speak, and Lucretia served as the consummate hostess, feeding the visitors and even putting some of them up for the night. When the votes were counted in November,

Below: The dining room at Lawnfield, the Garfield home in Mentor, Ohio, contains the Haviland china Lucretia bought for the White House.

James was ahead by one of the narrowest popular vote margins in presidential election history—only ten thousand votes separated him from the Democratic candidate, Civil War hero General Winfield Hancock. James won the electoral vote easily, however, and was elected the twentieth president of the United States.

After James's inauguration, both he and Lucretia became immediately occupied with their duties. The president set about the impossible task of trying to please both sides of his divided party with his advisors. He followed Lucretia's advice and appointed James Blaine as secretary of state, thereby removing him as a possible opponent in the next election. However, by choosing both Stalwarts and Half-Breeds as his appointees, President Garfield seemed to anger everyone. Lucretia, meanwhile, pleased everyone with her intelligence and charm as hostess at the White House receptions and dinners. She seemed to adapt very quickly to a role for which she had little experience.

For her first major project, Lucretia decided the White House needed some renovation. She researched the history of the mansion and had started to formulate her ideas on redecorating; but in May 1881, she came down with a severe case of malaria, a disease common in Washington at the time because of the capital's still-prevalent swamps.

> *"The vast concourse of people covering all the vast space in front of the Capitol was the grandest human spectacle I have ever seen."*
>
> —*Lucretia Garfield on her husband's inauguration in 1881*

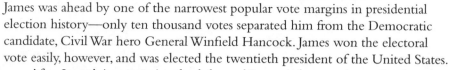

Below: Son James R. Garfield served as Theodore Roosevelt's Interior Secretary.

James postponed his presidential duties and stayed by his wife's side as she lay near death for the next month. After Lucretia improved, the Garfields went to a summer home they owned in the oceanfront town of Elberon, New Jersey, where they thought Lucretia might recover more quickly. In late June, however, James had to return to Washington to catch up on his presidential duties.

On July 2, 1881, President Garfield was headed to his alma mater, Williams College, for a class reunion and to enroll his two sons, Harry and Jim, in the freshman class. As he was waiting in the station for his train, he was shot in the back by a fanatic Stalwart, Charles Guiteau. Guiteau had been an unsuccessful office seeker at the White House for weeks and finally had been barred from it

> *Lucretia Garfield was only the second First Lady to have a college degree. Lucy Hayes was the first.*

after being passed over as the United States consul in Paris. He grew enraged and shot James Garfield so the Stalwart Arthur could become president.

Even though she had her own illness and exhaustion to contend with, Lucretia rushed back to Washington from Elberon to be with her husband, but his condition looked bad from the start. The president was bleeding internally, and medical techniques were still very primitive. What seemed to help James the most was having Lucretia close by. Although still very weak from her bout with malaria, the First Lady stayed by his side the entire time and often prepared some of his favorite meals to keep his spirits up.

Above: Two generations of the Garfield family together at the White House (left to right):

The Inauguration

Before the inauguration, Lucretia went to New York to shop for her gown. To avoid the reporters who had been besieging her since the election, she traveled under the assumed name of "Mrs. Greenfield." Besides visiting dressmakers, Lucretia also served as a liaison between James and his Stalwart antagonist, Roscoe Conkling, to discuss cabinet appointments.

Above: The inaugural ball program, and a scene that depicts the cast of a minstrel show serenading the new president at the Capitol.

The Inaugural Ball was held at the original Smithsonian building, which had just been completed. Lucretia wore a lavender satin gown trimmed with point lace and a long plaited train. (The gown is still at the Smithsonian, displayed as part of the museum's collection of First Lady costumes.) In keeping with the Garfields' religious beliefs, no alcohol was served at the ball, and perhaps also because of their early religious training, the Garfields left the ball at 11 P.M. when the dancing started.

What Really Killed President Garfield

When President Garfield was shot, the practice of sterilization was not yet widespread, nor was it entirely understood by the medical community. As James lay dying from his gunshot wound, doctors probed at him with instruments and even their fingers to find the bullet that was still in his body. The doctors believed the president's chances of survival depended on the removal of the bullet, but they probably did more harm than good and might have even caused the infection that eventually contributed to his death.

At one point, the doctors brought in Alexander Graham Bell, who had recently invented the telephone. The X-ray had not been developed yet, but Bell had also invented a metal detector machine he thought would be able to locate the bullet. However, the effort failed because James's bed had metal springs—a relatively new invention— preventing the machine from giving an accurate reading.

Right: The wounded president was taken to the house in Elberon, where he spent his last days in a room overlooking the Atlantic Ocean.

Above: The Garfield's seaside home at Elberon, New Jersey, was where Lucretia went to recover from a brush with malaria in the summer of 1881.

In August, the stifling heat of the capital grew too much for the president to bear, so he was put on a special train to Elberon so he would be more comfortable. Lucretia nursed him the best she could, and the president lingered for a couple of months, but he finally succumbed to infection and a weak heart on September 19, 1881. James Garfield was just forty-nine years old. He was the fourth president to die in office and the second to be assassinated, a mere sixteen years after the first, Abraham Lincoln, in 1865.

James lay in state in the Capitol until he was taken by train to Cleveland for the funeral. All along the route, Americans lined the tracks to say good-bye to their leader. As her husband was buried in Cleveland's Lake View Cemetery, Lucretia became the first First Lady to attend her husband's funeral. An estimated 250,000 mourners joined her. Several years later, James's body would be transferred to the huge Garfield Monument mausoleum built for him and his family in the same cemetery.

"Oh, why am I made to suffer this cruel wrong?"

—Lucretia Garfield on the death of her husband of twenty-three years

Return to Private Life

Lucretia returned to Lawnfield and set about organizing her husband's documents and letters for a presidential memorial library. The American public also came to the financial aid of Lucretia, raising a huge sum, for then, of $360,000. In 1882, Congress also came to the aid of the four widowed First Ladies still alive at the time—Lucretia, Julia Grant, Mary Lincoln, and Sarah Polk—and granted them each a lifetime $5,000-a-year pension. In 1883, Congress also realized that the process of filling government jobs had gotten out of hand and passed the Pendleton Federal Civil Service Act. Now federal jobs would be filled based on the merit system, a welcome change, but two years too late to help President Garfield.

Lucretia outlived her husband by thirty-seven years, but she continued to have a full life, watching her successful children and grandchildren grow up. She spent most of her time at Lawnfield and wintered with relatives in Pasadena, California. She died in Pasadena on March 14, 1918, at the age of eighty-five. She was returned to Cleveland to be entombed with her husband in the Garfield Monument.

Above: Lucretia spent her summers at Lawnfield surrounded by thirteen of her sixteen grandchildren and fond memories.

Visiting Lawnfield

The Garfield home at Lawnfield is preserved as a National Historic Site at 8095 Mentor Avenue, Mentor, Ohio 44060. Mentor is located off I-90, about twenty-five miles east of Cleveland. Much of the original home and grounds has been either preserved or restored, although all the papers and documents of the original library have been donated to the Library of Congress. For more information, call 440-255-8722.

The Garfield Monument is located in Lake View Cemetery, 12316 Euclid Avenue, Cleveland, Ohio 44106. The building is considered the first true mausoleum built in the country. It serves as both crypt and memorial for James and Lucretia Garfield, and other family members as well. Take I-90 into Cleveland and exit at Eddy Road, then exit to Euclid Avenue. Call 216-421-2665 for more information.

Left: The Garfield home at Mentor, Ohio.

Ellen Arthur

An Irreplaceable Woman

When Chester A. Arthur assumed the presidency after the assassination of James A. Garfield, a New York woman named Julia Sand, who was a stranger to him but frequently offered him her advice, wrote: "What the nation needs most at present is rest. We are all worn out with watching—and when people are very tired, they are apt to be irritable, unreasonable, and ready to quarrel on small provocations. If a doctor could lay his finger on the public pulse, his prescription would be perfect quiet." Chester, or Chet, as he was known, was the third president in a single year, and his predecessor had died a lingering death. It was thoughtful advice.

A kind of quiet was largely what President Arthur gave the people he served during his abbreviated term. If there were any surprises from his administration, it was that he was far more competent than most observers expected. The biggest surprise was his sophisticated White House entertaining, especially considering that he didn't have a wife. When he recruited his youngest sister, Mary Arthur McElroy, to serve as the White House hostess, he refused to make the job an official one, and she declined to relocate to Washington except part of the time. He managed very nicely on his own. Until then, Chet Arthur's life had revolved around parties and he knew quite well how to plan a good one.

Chester Arthur's wife of twenty-one years, Ellen, had died suddenly a year and a half before she would have become First Lady. By all accounts, if she had lived she probably would have been as fondly remembered as her husband has been forgotten.

Chet was already a successful lawyer and a leader of the New York Republican party when he was introduced to Ellen Lewis Herndon by her cousin and his friend, Dabney Herndon, while Ellen was visiting New York with her mother. At nineteen, Nell, as he called her, was frail, but her dark eyes, soft brown hair, wide jaw, and high cheekbones made her one of the prettiest of all the wives of the men who became president. She had a disposition to match, outgoing and cheerful, and her contralto singing voice was regarded as one of the finest in the country. She had trained to become an opera singer, but she put her talents to use giving recitals for charities and as a soloist in several choirs, including the highly respected Mendelssohn Glee Club, an organization of professional musicians. And, of course, she delighted her own guests by

---

Ellen Lewis Herndon Arthur

Born
August 30, 1837,
Culpepper County,
Virginia

Parents
Captain William Lewis
Herndon and Frances
Elizabeth Hansbrough
Herndon

Marriage
October 25, 1859, to
Chester Arthur (1829-86)

Children
William Lewis Herndon
(1860-63); Chester Allan,
II (1864-1937); Ellen
Herndon (1871-1915)

Died
January 12, 1880,
New York, New York

providing most of the entertainment at the constant round of parties she and her husband held after they were married.

Nell became a New Yorker when she married Chet, but she had lived in Washington since she was a young girl. The only daughter of Frances Elizabeth Hansbrough and William Lewis Herndon, Nell moved to the capital with her parents after her father was assigned to help establish the Naval Observatory there. Captain Herndon was already a famous navy man, known for his exploits leading a historic expedition to find the source of the Amazon River; and his wife parlayed her own impressive background among the Virginia aristocracy into becoming a doyenne of Washington society.

Chet and Nell fell in love almost the moment they met, and their engagement would have been short and sweet if disaster hadn't entered her life. In 1858, her father was in command of the SS *Central America,* a steamship that was bound for New York carrying a cargo of gold and a full complement of passengers when she was caught in a storm off Cape Hatteras. The ship began to break apart in the pounding waves, but Captain Herndon managed to save nearly all of his passengers—every woman and child survived thanks to him—and then he went back to his post on the ship's bridge as it slid beneath the waves.

Since Nell was his only child, her fiancé stepped in to take care of her mother's affairs. This meant that Chet would have to go to Virginia to meet the rest of the family. War was in the air at the time, and as a brigadier general in the New York State militia he worried about what sort of reception was in store for him. The Herndons and the Hansbroughs were slaveholders and most decidedly on the other side of the dispute. But in spite of Chet's concerns, they warmly accepted him as a "fine looking young man," and they decided that they all liked him, even if he was a Yankee.

Above: Ellen Arthur died before she was able to make her mark as First Lady.

Nell and Chet were married several months later, on October 25, 1859, at Calvary Episcopal Church in New York City. They moved into the Herndon townhouse around the corner, overlooking Gramercy Park, where they stayed until the spring of 1861, when the Civil War began to change their lives.

Chet's militia unit was mustered into the Union army when the war broke out, and he himself was appointed the state's chief quartermaster, with responsibility for transporting, housing, clothing, and arming not only New York regiments but others that passed through on their way to the front.

An impressive memorial to Ellen's father was erected on the campus of the U.S. Naval Academy in Annapolis, Maryland.

Details, Details

Nell saw very little of her husband during the early years of the war. As quartermaster general, he was called upon to supervise the building of barracks and forts, approve contracts for uniforms, and buy stores of ammunition and food, among other things. He rarely got more than three hours of sleep a night. But it was the little things that brought on the greatest headaches. One of his aides wrote: "One Sunday it was required that the outfit that was to be sent to a regiment in the country to enable it to move to the front the next day was short five dozen pairs of stockings. After consulting with Arthur, I went to the church, got [department store owner] A. T. Stewart out and got him to go with me to his store and get out the stockings. Mr. Stewart used to tell with great glee how he was got out of church one Sunday to make fifteen cents."

Although he was eager to see action in the war, the closest Chet came to it was an inspection tour that took him to the Fredericksburg area in Virginia, where Ellen's family was living in fear of the very troops he was there to inspect. He placed a guard around one of the Herndon homes to keep them safe. His mother-in-law, as could be expected considering her deep Southern roots, was a rabid rebel. But she chose to sit out the war in Europe, so her influence on the Arthur family was negligible. Ellen, on the other hand, didn't need anyone to encourage her sympathies with the South, although she made a conscious effort to keep them to herself. One of her uncles was in command of the defense of the Confederate coast; another uncle, Brodie, who was a doctor, was serving as an officer in the Confederate army, and so were his two sons, Dabney and Brodie, Jr., both of whom were captured and sent to prisoner of war camps in the North.

Her cousin Dabney, who was also Chet's close friend, was being held in a prisoner of war camp on an island in the East River,

"Mr. Arthur is an officer in Lincoln's army. How the people here do abuse him."

—Dr. Brodie Herndon, Ellen Arthur's uncle

and Ellen made frequent trips out there to visit him. Her husband arranged it willingly, although it was an embarrassment to him. He felt close to Dab himself, and Ellen thought of him as a brother.

In the meantime, after the birth of their son William, in 1860, the Arthurs moved to a residential hotel on Broadway, two blocks west of the Herndon townhouse, which had become a target for picketing "patriots." The hotel was elegantly furnished and it gave them more room for entertaining, which both of them loved more than almost anything else. If there were tensions between them over the war, Ellen was doing her best to hide them, and Chet laughed off her sympathies for the other side by referring to her as "my little Rebel wife." He had a rebel sister, too. Malvina Arthur had gone to South Carolina as a teacher, and married a local man who served in the Confederate army. She had no particular attachment to the cause, but she worried constantly about her husband. "I don't want him blown up," she repeated often.

Considering his connections to the South, no matter how vague they might have been, not many people were surprised when General Arthur resigned his commission the day after President Lincoln announced his Emancipation Proclamation. He wasn't strongly either for or against slavery, but he thought that freeing the slaves was only going to prolong the war, and like most New Yorkers, he was sick of the fighting. The war hadn't been going well up until that point, and it seemed as though it was going to drag on forever. Though Chet had been one of the first to become a Republican when the party was established, he was also fed up with its standard-bearer and he said that he "would not vote at all rather than vote for Lincoln as the next President."

Idealism aside, a need for more money was really at the heart of his decision. His military pay was adequate enough for a typical family, but the Arthurs weren't at all typical. During his two years of service as a military official, he had built up an impressive number of important contacts and friends, and that could translate to more legal work with higher fees, and he was ready to start collecting them.

Nell had grown up in a house full of servants, and she was eager to follow in her mother's footsteps as a legendary hostess. For his part, Chet had developed some expensive tastes as well. Fine clothes were among them, and he was tired of wearing a uniform and constantly bumping into other men who were dressed the same way. He was something of a gourmet, too. As one friend put it, "He loved the pleasures of the table and had an extraordinary power of digestion." He also enjoyed fine wines, as his wife did, and he could "carry a great deal of liquor without any manifest effect other than greater vivacity of speech."

Predictably, his law firm flourished, and before long Chet and Nell were affluent enough to be able to move into their own brownstone house a few blocks north on Lexington Avenue. Nell embellished it with the finest furniture and accessories that money could buy, and she hired a staff of Irish immigrant servants to help her step up her lavish entertaining. The Arthurs also became parishioners at the Episcopal Church of the Heavenly Rest on upper Fifth Avenue, the most fashionable house of worship in town. Ellen demanded the

Below: No one was more surprised than Chester A. Arthur when he found out that he had become president of the United States.

affiliation, but like her husband, she was less interested in the Gospel than in the propriety of it all. Chet was the son of a Baptist minister, but to his mother's great distress, he never went to church as an adult until Nell insisted on it.

Chet's father routinely wrote to him advising that he needed to get religion lest he should die without the Lord's saving grace. But when the couple's son, William, died in 1863 at the age of two and a half, neither he nor Nell had the solace of religion. Nell was convinced that she had contributed to the boy's death, which was apparently from an aneurysm in the brain, because she thought she had been too demanding by filling his brain with learning and strict discipline. Their second son, Chester II, who was born the following year, would have no such demands made on him. His mother completely spoiled him, and he grew up with no special interests at all, neither in the worlds of business nor of politics, and he lived his adult life as a playboy.

During the war years, Chet's understanding of military law helped him become one of New York City's most successful lawyers, if not one of the wealthiest. He didn't have to hustle for business, and that left him with the time to begin advancing his political career. He was a good soldier for the conservative wing of the Republican party, known as the Radicals; and he never put his own interests above the leaders he served as he worked tirelessly to collect donations and outright assessments from the city's wealthiest men, most of whom were his friends.

Above: Nell was active in New York's Church of the Heavenly Rest on Fifth Avenue at 90th Street, despite living far downtown; she thought it was a fashionable place to worship.

The house at 123 Lexington Avenue, near East 28th Street in New York City, where Ellen Arthur died and her husband took the oath as president, is still standing, though it is quite run-down compared to the time they lived there.

Nell was his partner in this. It gave her a reason to do what she enjoyed doing most, charming guests at her lavish parties. It was a talent that opened many a wallet for the Radical Republican cause. Chet, meanwhile, was spreading his own wings. He began spending more and more time out of his own house, much to Ellen's annoyance, at party headquarters, where another frequent participant in the discussions there said that he was "always smiling and affectionate in his manner toward his friends." He cultivated new important friends in the likes of J. P. Morgan and the city's most accomplished writers, editors, and educators after he was elected to membership in the exclusive Century Club; and before long, his legal clients included Tiffany & Co. and R. G. Dun & Co., which became Dun & Bradstreet.

But in the postwar years, which became known as the Gilded Age, the best opportunities were in the political world, serving the interests of big business rather than being a part of the business establishment itself. New York City at the time was in the clutches of the Tammany Hall machine headed by "Boss" William M. Tweed who directed graft, honest and otherwise, into the coffers of the Democratic Party; but Chester, a Republican, managed to get the job as counsel to the city's tax commission. It helped the Republicans get their share of the graft, and for some of them to get other city jobs, but except to say that he never collected more than his salary from the job, Chester was silent about his role in it. At any rate, he resigned from the job after a year, and his declared income dropped by more than half. Yet there would be better days ahead.

Chet's big break came in 1871 when President Grant appointed him collector of the port of New York. Nobody was happier about it than Nell. Their only daughter, Ellen, was born the same day the appointment was announced, but having another mouth to feed was the least of her problems. Nell had five servants to clothe, feed, and pay, and her seven-year-old son, who was enrolled in an exclusive private school, had several expensive special tutors, in spite of her resolve to take a relaxed approach to his education. The Arthurs also had become accustomed to taking long, expensive vacations. To make matters worse, the country was in the midst of a recession that was cutting into everyone's lifestyle. Everyone, that is, whom Nell felt the need to cultivate as her social set.

She supported charities and sometimes lent her singing talents to their fund-raisers, usually along with making huge cash contributions. She always had a box seat during the Metropolitan Opera season, and she made sure she was invited to all the best parties. She had more than a just a nodding acquaintance with such families as the Astors, the Vanderbilts, and the Roosevelts. Keeping up with them was obviously expensive.

Few political wives were ever a greater asset to their husbands than Nell Arthur. One of his friends said that she was "one of the best specimens of Southern womanhood…. She visited and kept up his list of friends." One of those friends, Tom Murphy, who was Chet's mentor, said, "I knew her very well, indeed for years. She was almost like a sister to me." Putting the lie to photographic evidence, he added, "She was not a handsome woman, not a large woman in size; she hardly weighed 125 pounds. But she had affection and great fine sense, and Arthur loved and appreciated her."

The most perceptive comment anyone made about Nell was, "Mrs. Arthur was a very ambitious woman. There was no happier woman in the country than she when her husband was made the collector of the port of New York."

The income that came with the post alone would have made any man's wife happy. It was the same $50,000 salary that the president would soon begin earning when he gave himself a raise, and five times that of the vice president and members of the cabinet. This was a time when the average man on the street was

Below: President Arthur with his only daughter, Ellen, who was nine when her mother died.

lucky to be earning $500 a year. The collector's job represented a first-class ticket on the gravy train.

Nell was obviously pleased that his job allowed her to live in a style she had always wanted, but she was so unhappy with Chet's own lifestyle that she seriously considered asking him for a divorce. She might have done it if there hadn't been so many pleasant perks that came with her marriage. It wasn't that she didn't love her husband and that he didn't adore her. It was just that Chet Arthur wasn't as attentive a husband as she could wish for. In most marriages that most likely would have been a sign that there was another woman out there somewhere, but that most assuredly wasn't the case with the Arthurs. When he said that he was going to spend the evening out with the boys, he really meant it.

Almost every night of the week, Chet could be found eating and drinking with his friends and his cronies, smoking Havana cigars and exchanging political gossip until the small hours of the morning. One of those friends recalled, "Arthur was always the last man to go to bed in any company and was fond of sitting down on the front steps at three in the morning and talking with anyone who dared to stay." Nell chose to ignore her isolation, and she resigned herself to going to concerts, the opera, theater, and recitals with friends rather than with her husband.

Sometimes she went out alone. The evening of January 10, 1880, was one of those times. She had gone to a concert and a cold rain was falling while she waited for a carriage to take her home, and the next day she came down with a cold. It quickly developed into pneumonia, and one day after that she was dead.

Her husband, typically, wasn't with her when the illness struck. He had gone to the capitol at Albany for a series of meetings. When word of Nell's condition reached him, it was early on a Sunday morning, and the only way he could get back to New York was on a slow milk train that stopped for unloading at every station along the way. By the time he reached his wife's bedside, she was already in a coma; she never opened her eyes during the nearly twenty-four hours he sat there.

Nell's death completely devastated Chet. He had lost his only true love, but he was also consumed with guilt over how he had neglected their home life for his political one. He himself had only seven more years to live, and they were momentous ones, but nothing could ever compare to the loss he felt and what he knew he could never replace. "Honors to me now," he said ruefully, "are not what they once were."

Above: The Arthur's daughter, Ellen, who was named for her mother, was too young during her father's presidency to serve as his official hostess.

The Gentleman From New York

Less than a year after his wife died, Chester A. Arthur was selected as the vice presidential candidate of the Republican party. It had been a compromise, as such nominations often are, to balance the candidacy of James A. Garfield of Ohio and bring vote-rich New York over to his side.

The only sour note to Chet's triumph was that he knew how much Nell would have reveled in it. When he got home from the convention, his eight-year-old daughter brought a bouquet of flowers to the dinner table to offer her congratulations. He leaned over to kiss her but was overwhelmed with tears. He patted her on the head by way of a thank-you, and he said, sadly, "There is nothing worth having now." But deep as his grief was, only his family was aware of it. To outsiders, and most especially to the voters, he was still the charming, sophisticated gentleman from New York without an obvious care in the world. He never left the state during the entire campaign, and made as few speeches as possible, preferring to do what he did best, raising funds for the campaign. Nobody regarded him as presidential timber, least of all Chet himself, but it was of no particular concern; Garfield was young and in good health, easily able to serve as president for eight years, possibly even longer if all went well.

Chester Arthur was in New York on July 2 when a strange-looking bearded man walked up to President Garfield at the Baltimore and Potomac train station in Washington and fired two bullets into his back. When the assailant was grabbed by a policeman, he said, "All right, I did it and I will go to jail for it. I am a Stalwart and Arthur is President."

Nobody was more surprised than Vice President Arthur, who responded to a reporter's request for an interview: "What can I say? What is there to be said by me? I am overwhelmed with grief over this awful news." At first he refused to go anywhere near Washington until he knew more about the president's condition, but he was eventually persuaded to make the trip, even though Garfield was not dead and would cling to life until the middle of September.

The thought that he might become president completely unnerved him, as it did just about everyone else, no matter what their political persuasion. *The New York Times*, which had been one of his strongest supporters in the past, had

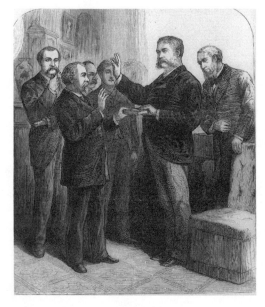

Below: Chester was sworn in at his home—the only president except George Washington to take the oath in New York City.

to admit it felt that as far as the presidency was concerned, "General Arthur is about the last man who would be considered eligible for that position." When the oath of office was administered by a state judge at the Arthur home in New York, there was a large crowd gathered on the street outside, but nobody was cheering. The new president himself was sobbing.

Back in Washington he grew into the office surprisingly quickly. But there was one thing he absolutely refused to do. "I will not live in that house," he said of the White House. The previous two presidents might have said the same thing if they thought they could. The place was dowdy, drafty, and dirty. He gave Lucretia Garfield plenty of time to move out, conducting his presidential business at the home of a friend, and then he called in Louis Comfort Tiffany, the son of his old client the jeweler Charles Tiffany, who was the most celebrated interior decorator in the country.

Work on the White House started immediately, and one of the great pleasures of the new president's life was strolling over after dinner each night to see how the project was coming along and to

Left: Interior designer Louis Comfort Tiffany, son of the founder of the New York City jewelry store, added many touches of his "American Aesthetic" style to the Arthur White House.

Below: The typical Tiffany style included stenciling on the walls and stained glass detailing.

A Touch of Class

Louis Comfort Tiffany, President Arthur's decorator of choice for the White House, was the son of New York's most prominent jeweler. After his father died, he became a vice president of the company and its artistic director, but he had already established himself as an innovative decorator of homes, private clubs, and houses of worship, a career that began when he revolutionized the production of stained glass. His company developed a line of free-form objects of colored glass that he called Favrile, and it soon began producing decorative lighting fixtures, metalwork, enamelware, and ceramics that defined the style of the 1880s. His lamps are valuable collector's items today, and his church windows a great source of pride to the institutions that treasure them.

add his own experienced input. The first stage involved moving out worn furniture, drapes, carpet, and other furnishings that were all sold at public auction. He didn't raise a lot of money that way, but it helped. Largely, he was paying for the job out of his own pocket.

Chester Arthur and Tiffany lavished attention on the mansion. The main hallway was painted in a soft olive color and its niches covered in gold leaf. The frieze was replaced with brass work highlighted with geometric designs in gold and silver, and the ceiling was embellished with a gold-and-silver pattern with sections decorated by the interlocking letters, "U.S.A." The Red Room carried out the patriotic theme with circles of gold and silver stars on the ceiling and a border of stars and stripes. There were similar Tiffany touches in all of the public rooms, but the climax was a jeweled glass screen fifty feet long, held in place by marble columns between the main corridor and the north vestibule. It was not just a thing of remarkable beauty; it also had the practical effect of cutting down drafts.

The work had progressed well enough for the president to condescend to move into the White House in December, a little less than three months after he assumed the presidency. He asked his youngest sister, Mary Arthur McElroy, to serve as "Mistress of the White House," but in deference to the memory of

"When I went to the White House, I was absolutely unfamiliar with the customs and formalities."

—Mary Arthur McElroy on serving as White House hostess

Above: His sister, Mary McElroy, served as his White House hostess, but President Arthur refused to give her the title or the status of First Lady.

his wife, Chester drew the line at giving her the position with any of the responsibilities of protocol; he regarded the job more as that of a servant than a partner.

Mrs. McElroy had a finishing school education, and she was up to the job, but she wasn't interested in moving to Washington. She had been married to a successful insurance executive in Albany, New York, for thirty years; she had four children, and she liked her life exactly as it was. Her brother persuaded her to make it a part-time job, coming down to Washington for four months of the year during the social season.

Before she did anything else, Mary called on former First Lady and fellow New Yorker Julia Tyler for advice. Julia had been retired for nearly forty years, but she accepted the invitation to help receive guests at the White House again. Mary's next call was on Harriet Lane, who had built an enviable reputation for herself as White House hostess when her uncle, James Buchanan, was president, and who had moved back to Washington as a widow. She, too, eagerly accepted the invitation to make a comeback.

Their first White House dinner involved another former First Lady, Julia Grant. It was held in honor of her and her husband, and in spite of the fact that official Washington was still in mourning for President Garfield, it was a glittering affair, and it set the stage for the Arthur style. The State Dining Room was set for thirty-four, and satin-tied bouquets of roses were set at each lady's plate, while the men were given boutonnieres. The fourteen-course dinner was complemented with eight different kinds of wine. Mrs. Grant, dressed in diamonds and lace, was noticeably impressed by the Tiffany touches around her.

The decoration of the White House for the Grant dinner involved lavish displays of flowers. It had become something of a tradition by then. But President Arthur established a new, if temporary one, by having a fresh rose placed in front of a hand-tinted portrait of his late wife every day. Back in New York City, he kept her room exactly as it had been on the day she died, right down to the open book she was reading before she slipped into a coma. And he had fresh flowers placed there every day, too.

In Washington, Chester donated a stained glass window in Nell's memory to St. John's Episcopal Church, where she had sung in the choir for several years. He insisted that it be placed on the south side of the building and lighted at night so that he could see it from his lonely room in the White House across Lafayette Square. But he never spoke of Nell nor his still very real grief to anyone outside the family. When a woman questioned him about it, he snapped, "Madame, I may be President of the United States, but my private life is nobody's damned business."

Mary McElroy was strongly against giving the vote to women. She was president of the Albany Association Opposed to Women's Suffrage.

Entertaining and Legacy

Unlike other chief executives, Chester Arthur never delegated the responsibilities of entertaining. His sister Mary was there to help carry out his orders. One of his first acts upon moving into the White House was developing a plan that would be followed at every affair. It wasn't exactly a one-size-fits-all program, but it was close to it, and it served with only minor variations through several administrations that followed.

If other presidents and First Ladies adopted President Arthur's ideas, few before him had his refined taste, and few others had his sense of style. Since the days of Martha Washington and Dolley Madison, what the First Lady wore and how she carried herself had been a prime topic of conversation, but in this administration, it was the president himself that people loved to watch. A published description of him painted a picture of "the 'city man,' the metropolitan gentleman, the member of clubs, the type that is represented by the well-bred and well-dressed New Yorker; the quiet man who wears a scarf and a pin and prefers a sack coat to the long tailored frock coat that pervades politics, and a derby hat to a slouch hat that seems to be regarded in some quarters of this Union as something no statesman should be without. This is a novel species of president."

He always wore a tuxedo to White House dinners and receptions, as well as to the theater, concerts, and the opera, all frequent destinations. At other times, he wore handwoven tweeds to the office, and contrary to the published report, he wore a black frock coat with a black tie and a gray waistcoat over gray trousers. Everything he wore was custom-made for him in New York.

Chester usually wore a top hat with his frock coat when he went out for drives. His carriage, drawn by a pair of lively matched bays, was quite the most elegant in town. Like President Washington, he had his coat of arms painted on the doors. But unlike Washington, he designed it himself. He also designed the first presidential flag. Most of all, it was Chester Arthur's impeccable manners that impressed most people. And it was Nell, a Southern belle, who had taught him these social graces.

President Arthur was adamant about keeping his family out of the spotlight. Daughter Ellen, who was approaching ten when he became president, was left behind in New York under the care of the family servants. But halfway through his administration, Chester decided to rent the house, and she came to live in the White House. He kept her out of sight, although she was sometimes allowed to put in an appearance at afternoon receptions. Her only public duty was the presidency of the Children's Christmas Club, which raised funds to buy Christmas dinners for poor children in the capital.

The Women's Christian Temperance Union made a strong proposal to ban alcoholic beverages from the White House, but Mary McElroy ignored them.

Below: After the Arthur renovations, the White House's Blue Room, a favorite receiving room of many First Ladies, was given silk wall covering. The room was crimson red until Martin Van Buren's presidency in 1837.

Chester II, called Alan, went off to college at Princeton while his father was still vice president. Like his father, he was a clotheshorse and a party animal, but unlike either his father or his mother, he had very little ambition beyond enjoying himself. He visited the White House several times, but each time he was kept in the background like his little sister.

White House entertaining was subdued in the early months of his administration out of respect for the memory of the assassinated James Garfield and the president's own mourning for his wife. But during the last two years of Chester's White House tenancy, the number of balls, banquets, and receptions grew both in frequency and magnitude. His public receptions always filled all of the available space, and nobody went home without a new affection for the president.

Above: Newport, Rhode Island, was among President Arthur's favorite vacation spots, and he was a popular visitor there.

Among the lures that intrigued the women of Washington was the presence of a president who didn't have a wife. They turned out, literally by the thousands over the years, to see if they might be able to cure him of the affliction, but it was always a case of irresistible forces meeting an immoveable object. None of them could possibly hold a candle to Chet's beloved Nell.

The president was suffering from Bright's disease, a usually fatal kidney ailment, and although he had taken several trips as far south as Florida and as far west as Yellowstone National Park hoping that his health would improve, he grew noticeably weaker. He tried to keep his condition to himself, although it was as plain as the lines in his face; and when it was recommended, he angrily rejected the idea of canceling official parties and banquets. He didn't want his legacy to be less than that of a robust chief executive in an era when manliness was considered a virtue, and he couldn't bring himself to burden people with sympathy for him. A friend put it this way: "He could not bear to have his friend or the public know that the strong man whom they knew in health was slowly fading away." All he could do was keep the parties going.

The last party was held on February 28, 1885, and more than three thousand people came. The president was in a weakened condition, and the well-wishers were hustled past him four abreast so he'd have fewer hands to shake. Mrs. McElroy recruited forty-eight women, daughters of prominent local families, to assist her in making everyone feel welcome even if they didn't get a chance to shake the president's hand.

After his next public appearance, there was a different presidential hand to shake. It was the inauguration of the twenty-second president, another man from the state of New York, named Grover Cleveland.

Chester went back to his old law practice in New York soon afterward, but his strength was gone, and his presence in the office was largely ceremonial. His sister Mary McElroy and another sister, Regina Caw, went to New York to nurse him, and his son, who graduated from Princeton that same year, and daughter Ellen, now fifteen, stayed close to home. On the last day of his life, November 18, 1886, the former president supervised the packing of all his personal and official papers to be taken out and burned. An era was ended and, as far a Chester A. Arthur was concerned, best forgotten.

Above: President Arthur was one of America's most urbane presidents, but he was born a country boy in this tiny house in North Fairfield, Vermont.

Visiting the Arthurs

The home that Chester and Ellen Arthur owned at 123 Lexington Avenue in New York City is still standing, but it has been greatly altered, and not for the better. The original two-story brownstone is now a five-story row house and it's down-at-the-heels. Only a plaque on the facade hints at its significance. Ellen's birthplace in Virginia no longer exists, but Chester's birthplace in North Fairfield, Vermont, has been reconstructed. It is on Route 36, ten miles from Saint Albans. The site is open, with no admission charge, Wednesday through Sunday from mid-June through mid-October. Both the president and Mrs. Arthur are buried in the Rural Cemetery at Albany, New York.

Frances Cleveland

The Early Years

Just as the young and stylish First Lady Jackie Kennedy had captivated the nation with her beauty and glamour and had a particular influence on young women of her era, the nineteenth century also had its First Lady icon of youth and beauty in Frances Folsom Cleveland. Frances became the nation's youngest First Lady ever when she married President Grover Cleveland in the White House on June 2, 1886. She was just twenty-one years old, but she immediately endeared herself to the American public with her wholesome beauty and social grace. Her enormous popularity was probably responsible for President Cleveland's reelection in 1892.

Frances was born Frank Clara Folsom (her name would later be legally changed to Frances, although Grover would continue to call her Frankie) on July 21, 1864, to Oscar Folsom and Emma Harmon in Buffalo, New York. Her father was the friend and law partner of Grover Cleveland, and it was Grover who bought Frances's first baby carriage. The two youthful lawyers had a thriving practice and a lively social life. They loved wild adventures and staying up late in Buffalo's saloons.

Frances had a privileged childhood and, as an only child, had the full attention of her doting parents. She would spend carefree summers at the home of her grandparents in nearby rural Folsomdale. There, she had many cousins to frolic with, and her father would visit on weekends to take her on fast carriage rides. Another frequent visitor to Folsomdale was Grover Cleveland. Known to the children as Uncle Cleve, he was also on the rise in state political circles at this time.

As she grew up, Frances was able to attend the best schools in Buffalo, but her idyllic childhood would receive a severe jolt two days after her eleventh birthday. Her father was killed in Buffalo when his speeding carriage went out of control and he was thrown to the pavement. Oscar Folsom left his family only a $5,000 life insurance policy, but he left his estate in the charge of the very able Grover. Over the years, Grover made shrewd investments on Folsom's $5,000, which enabled Folsom's widow and child to live well, and Frances to continue to attend the best schools. After an ill-fated stay with Emma's sister in St. Paul, Minnesota, the family settled in a new home back in Buffalo.

Frances Folsom Cleveland

Born
July 21, 1864,
Buffalo, New York

Parents
Oscar Folsom and Emma
Harmon Folsom

Marriage
June 2, 1886, to Stephen
Grover Cleveland
(1837-1908)

Remarried
February 10, 1913,
to Thomas J. Preston
(1870-1955)

Children
Ruth Cleveland
(1891-1904); Esther
Cleveland (1893-1980);
Marion Cleveland
(1895-1977); Richard
Folsom Cleveland
(1897-1974); Francis
Grover Cleveland
(1903-95)

Died
October 27, 1947,
Baltimore, Maryland

Above: Frances Folsom was twenty-two when she married President Cleveland. He was forty-nine, and the local gossips had a field day when their engagement was announced.

Throughout her school years, Frances was an excellent student and a favorite of her classmates, especially the boys. As she matured into a young woman, her beauty started to attract many of Buffalo's most eligible bachelors. At seventeen, she became engaged to one Charles Townsend, but less than a year later, Frances broke off the engagement and decided to attend Wells College in Aurora, New York, instead. Wells was a school for women where social training was as important as academics.

In 1884, Frances was leading the quiet life of a college student when she and her mother received a fateful invitation to visit an old friend in Albany. Just one year before, Grover Cleveland began his meteoric rise in politics when he was elected mayor of Buffalo. Now he had just been elected governor of New York and he asked Frances and her mother to visit him at the governor's mansion. When Grover saw what a lovely young woman Frances had become, the forty-seven-year-old bachelor was captivated.

After Frances returned to Wells, Grover started writing her letters and sending her flowers. Frances was flattered and felt very secure with the man who had always taken such good care of her family. She started writing him back, and true to the Victorian influence of the times, a love-letter relationship started to flourish. Frances's mother also approved of the relationship, admiring Grover and trusting that his intentions were honorable. There was one other reason Grover was a good catch: There was already talk that the governor was one of the front-runners for the Democratic nomination to run for the presidency in 1884.

That summer, Grover did receive the nomination, and the campaign against the Republican nominee, James Blaine, became one of the most contentious in American history. Blaine's staff discovered that Grover had a ten-year-old illegitimate son in Buffalo. The Cleveland campaign accused Blaine of accepting bribes from the railroad industry when he served in the House of Representatives in return for securing government aid. Grover offered a very effective solution to all the charges for the voters. He recommended that they vote for him to keep him in public life where he was clearly better qualified than Blaine, and send Blaine back to private life where he was better suited. Grover won a narrow victory in the November election, with New York casting the decisive votes. Little more than a year before, Grover was just the mayor of Buffalo, now he was headed for the White House. But it was not the only big plan he had.

Left: Like James Buchanan, Grover Cleveland moved into the White House as a bachelor.

The First Sister

Grover Cleveland entered the presidency as a bachelor and had his sister Rose Cleveland serve as White House hostess for the first year of his term. Rose was a gracious hostess, but she never felt at ease in the political world. She was an educator and an intellectual who spoke eight languages and with little patience for the small talk of White House dinners. She later admitted that she was so bored in reception lines, she would silently conjugate Greek verbs to pass the time. After her brother's marriage to Frances, she gladly returned to her teaching and writing career in New York.

Many presidents before Grover needed to ask family members to serve as White House hostess in the absence of a First Lady. Some of the presidents' wives were invalids or recluses. Thomas Jefferson, Martin Van Buren, and Andrew Jackson entered the White House as widowers. James Buchanan was the only lifelong bachelor to serve as president. His young niece Harriet Lane served as hostess during his one term in office. But after Grover, all presidents have entered the White House with wives who served as active First Ladies.

Above: Rose Cleveland, the president's sister, served as his White House hostess for a time. She found the job boring, and many guests called her attitude "grim," even "terrifying."

An Invitation to the White House

Right after taking office in March 1885, Grover arranged for a visit from Frances and her mother. During the visit, the couple discussed marriage, although there was no formal proposal. Grover was waiting for Frances to graduate from Wells that summer. Meanwhile, the visit from the Folsoms was stimulating speculation around Washington that the president was considering marriage. Most of the rumors, however, centered on Emma rather than Frances, because she was much closer in age to the president.

After Frances's graduation, Grover sent a formal proposal to her in the Adirondack Mountains in New York, where she was vacationing. Frances immediately accepted, and the date of the wedding was set for June of the following year, but there would be no public announcement of the engagement. Grover valued his privacy and hated the press, particularly the gossip columnists. He swore both families to secrecy, and the Folsom women went on an eight-month tour of Europe.

During the Folsoms' absence, the American press went to town. Their investigators discovered that it was actually the young Frances who was probably the president's betrothed, because an ex-aide of Grover Cleveland had once asked him why he was still a bachelor and Grover replied, "I'm waiting for my wife to grow up." The Folsoms returned to New York on May 27, 1886. The

"LOOK ON THIS PICTURE—

AND ON THIS"—

HOW WE SHALL LOOK WHEN WE GROW OLD.

Right: A cartoonist's view of what an aged Frances might look like. She lived to the age of eighty-three and proved the artist wrong.

Above: The press had many names for Frances, but one of the favorites was "Yum-Yum." Her husband called her "Frankie."

Below: An engraving called "The Mother's Kiss," shows Emma Folsom kissing her daughter the bride.

following day, the president handed out handwritten invitations to his cabinet members for his June 2 wedding to Frances Folsom, to be held in the Blue Room of the White House. It would be the first time a president's wedding would be held at the executive mansion.

With the help of the press, Frances would become a national celebrity overnight. The public started buying pictures of the bride-to-be and hanging them in their windows. Women copied her hairstyle—up, with a bun tied at the back—and her habit of wearing a flower attached to her dress. Her picture was placed on a countless array of advertisements, without her permission, from soap to sewing machines to underwear. Scores of reporters camped outside her New York hotel hoping for a glimpse of the blue-eyed, chestnut-haired beauty.

Early on the morning of June 2, 1886, Frances snuck into the White House to avoid the press, and the Blue Room was decorated with hundreds of roses, pansies, begonias, and orchids. For the ceremony, Frances wore a lace veil and an ivory satin wedding gown with a fifteen-foot train. John Philip Sousa's band played a wedding march. Afterward, there was a twenty-one-gun salute outside the White House, and church bells rang throughout Washington, D.C., to honor the newlyweds.

Grover tried to keep their honeymoon destination, Deer Park in Maryland's Blue Ridge Mountains, a secret, but the press was already there with their binoculars and cameras when the honeymooners arrived. For the next week, they monitored every movement of the couple. The coverage led to a new term for the reporters—"keyhole journalists"—although Grover preferred to call them "ghouls."

Back at the White House, Frances immediately impressed the staff and guests with her social grace. Her youth and beauty helped, but she also attributed her success to the social training she had received at Wells College. Frances made one change to the White House social schedule by adding a public reception on Saturday afternoons so working people could come to see her. Soon thousands of Americans, mostly women, were waiting in line every

To deal with the prolific usage of Frances's image on countless advertisements, President Cleveland tried to get Congress to pass a bill that would prohibit the use of any female's image without her written consent. The bill was introduced but did not pass.

week to shake the hand of the new First Lady. She received so much fan mail, a form letter had to be used so she could reply to them all.

To help deal with the pressures of White House life, Frances and the president set up a second residence they called Oak View just outside Washington and actually spent more time there than at the White House. Like most presidential families of the nineteenth century, the Clevelands escaped the oppressive summer heat of Washington at their summer home, Grey Gables, in Buzzards Bay, Massachusetts.

The second residence helped the Clevelands enjoy some privacy, but the press and the public still could not get enough of Frances. Whenever she traveled outside Washington, usually on trips back to Buffalo to visit her family, a huge entourage of reporters was sure to follow. According to all accounts, she handled the pressure with great aplomb, although there were few quotes from the First Lady—she felt it was improper for women to speak out in public. Whenever Frances had any questions about her duties, she would contact ex-First Ladies Harriet Lane, Julia Tyler, and Julia Grant for advice and suggestions.

A Break From the White House

As the 1888 presidential campaign got under way, the Democrats made good use of Frances's immense popularity, adding her picture to posters of Grover and his running mate, Allen Thurman. The Republicans took advantage of the press's antagonism with the president by spreading rumors that the president beat his wife. Frances responded with a letter condemning the charges as "wicked and heartless lies" calling her husband "kind and affectionate."

In the November election, Grover won the popular vote but lost the electoral vote, and thus the presidency, to his Republican opponent, Benjamin Harrison. Grover and Frances were deeply disappointed. The president took his popular-vote victory as a strong sign of support, however, and immediately started planning another run in 1892. Frances was particularly confident that they would return to the White House.

*Above: President Cleveland greeting
a young admirer at one of his White
House public receptions.*

"I detest him [President Cleveland] so much that I don't even think his wife is beautiful."

—One of Grover Cleveland's political foes

After Grover and Frances left the White House, they moved to New York City, where Grover took a job in a corporate law office. One thing he did not miss was the press. Since he was no longer president, the "ghouls" left him alone and the couple enjoyed what they would later call the happiest years of their marriage. The happiness was also due to the birth of their first child, Ruth, in 1891, who would come to be known as Baby Ruth.

As the 1892 presidential election approached, the country was suffering significant growing pains and the economy was a mess. America had taken the lead in the Industrial Revolution, and immigration was at an all-time high. The East was becoming urbanized with large factories and workers forming unions, while the expanding West was predominantly farmers, ranchers, and miners. The two sides had different needs, and the nation's leaders, particularly the president, were caught in the middle.

The 1892 election once again pitted Grover against the Republican incumbent Benjamin Harrison, but this time, Grover won easily. The Clevelands were back in the White House, much to the delight of the public and the White House staff who had come to adore Frances during Grover's first term. The First Family also once again set up a second residence outside Washington for privacy.

Above: Frances with the first two of her five children, daughters Ruth and Esther. Esther was born in the White House, but Ruth was born in New York between the two Cleveland presidencies.

Candy Bar Controversy

Contrary to popular myth, the Baby Ruth candy bar was not named after Baby Ruth Cleveland. The candy bar made its appearance in 1921, long after Ruth Cleveland was a baby. The Curtiss Candy Company, which first released the candy bar, wanted a catchy name for its new product. The biggest name in the nation at the time was Babe Ruth, the famous baseball player. However, Curtiss did not have permission from Ruth to name its candy bar after him. Ruth had a deal with another candy company. They decided to call their new candy bar Baby Ruth.

Lawsuits were brought against Curtiss for illegally using Babe Ruth's name. However, Curtiss's representatives claimed in court that the Baby Ruth candy bar was in fact named after Baby Ruth Cleveland, and the lawsuits were dismissed. Babe Ruth stayed in the headlines for many years afterward, and the Baby Ruth candy bar flourished. It is still a popular candy bar today.

Tough Times for the Nation

Grover, however, inherited an economy on the verge of a depression and his second term would be a difficult one. Unemployment was high, and banks were failing in record numbers. At one point, America's gold reserves reached their lowest point ever, and Grover had to borrow $65 million from a group of New York financiers led by J. P. Morgan. Grover also had to deal with physical problems when he underwent emergency surgery to remove a malignant tumor from his jaw.

Above: Grover, Frances, and little Ruth, at the start of the second Cleveland presidential term.

As the president struggled with the country's economic problems, Frances remained popular with the American people. A second daughter, Esther, was born to the First Family in 1893, the first baby ever to be born in the White House; another daughter, Marion, joined them in 1895. Many foreign dignitaries visited the White House during Grover's second term, some admittedly to meet the First Lady, whose fame had spread worldwide. Countries that sent ministers included France, Italy, England, China, Japan, Turkey, Korea, Turkey, and Haiti. Frances also continued to hold her receptions for the public, often shaking thousands of hands in a single day. Her image, now as a doting mother in addition to being a beautiful wife, continued to appear on many advertisements.

Frances also had a huge influence on fashion trends of the day. Whenever newspapers would carry a story of a particular fashion she was wearing, American women would usually adopt the style. One time, a zealous reporter made up a story that Frances had stopped wearing the bustle, a piece of padding worn at the back of a dress to support the material. As a result, the bustle went out of style and Frances herself stopped wearing them.

Right: The First Lady surrounded by the wives of her husband's Cabinet ministers. Like most other women, they followed her lead in fashion.

The Clevelands had to close the White House grounds to the public for the protection of their children. The public was so curious about the children, a crowd would gather whenever they were outside. Once, the crowd started passing Baby Ruth around in a hysterical manner. Another time, a woman took out a pair of scissors to cut off a lock of the baby's hair.

By the time the 1896 election approached, Grover knew the Democrats would have no interest in renominating him. Grover did all he could to correct the economy, but it was still struggling and Americans blamed the president. His popularity was at an all-time low. In the November election, the Republican William McKinley defeated the Democrat William Jennings Bryan, and after the inauguration in 1897, the Clevelands left Washington. Frances had loved being the First Lady, but she knew this time, there would be no return. Frances maintained her tremendous popularity until the end—at her final Saturday reception, over 20,000 people showed up at the White House to say good-bye.

Grover Cleveland's Final Years

The Clevelands moved to the college town of Princeton, New Jersey, and settled in a large house they called Westland. For the next twelve years, Frances would be active in Princeton civic causes and Grover would do some writing and lecturing, but mostly they would spend time with their still growing family. Frances gave birth to two sons while living in Princeton—Richard in 1897, and Francis in 1903. The family would also know tragedy in 1904, when Ruth contracted diphtheria and died. She was just twelve years old.

As Frances watched her husband grow older, she was pleased to see that the now prosperous nation was forgetting about the depression of the 1890s and was honoring the ex-president for his long service to his country. When he died in 1908, his final words were, "I have tried so hard to do right." Probably no one knew this more clearly than Frances.

Left: The Cleveland's son, Richard, was born not long after they left the White House and moved to Princeton, New Jersey, where Frances lived for the remainder of her life.

Frances was only forty-four years old when she became a widow in 1908. She would remain in Princeton for her remaining years, keeping busy with educational causes for women. She would serve as a trustee for Wells College and as a member of Princeton University's Women's Club, and help found the New Jersey College for Women. Frances was invited back to the White House in 1913 by President Taft and his wife and took a tour of her old home, including the Blue Room, where she had been married twenty-six years before. She also remarried in 1913 (she was the first First Lady to do so) to a professor of archaeology named Thomas J. Preston. She met Preston while he was a teacher at Wells, but he would later secure a post at Princeton.

Frances lived her final years away from the spotlight that had shone on her so brightly when she was First Lady and that she had handled with such dignity. She died in 1947 while visiting her son, Richard, in Baltimore for his fiftieth birthday. She was eighty-three years old and chose to be buried with "her beloved husband" Grover Cleveland and Baby Ruth in Princeton.

Above: Marion Cleveland, Frances's third child, was born at the White House in 1895, the midpoint of her father's second presidency.

Visiting the Clevelands

Grover Cleveland's birthplace is located at 207 Bloomfield Avenue, Caldwell, New Jersey. The only New Jersey native to serve as president, Grover spent his first four years in this house built for the pastor of Caldwell's First Presbyterian Church, a position his father had taken in 1834. The family later moved to upstate New York. To reach the Grover Cleveland birthplace, take I-280 West from New York to exit 5/Caldwell. For more information, call 973-226-0001.

Frances Folsom Cleveland's gravesite is next to her husband's in the Princeton Cemetery, which at one time was called the "Westminster Abbey of the United States." The First Lady's tombstone is engraved as "Frances Folsom Cleveland Preston." To get there, take the New Jersey Turnpike to exit 8/Route 571 West to Princeton. The cemetery is located at 29 Greenview Avenue, Princeton, New Jersey. Telephone: 609-924-1369.

Right: Grover Cleveland's birthplace at Caldwell, New Jersey, is part of a state park today.

Caroline Harrison

Transplanted Hoosiers

No one knew, least of all Benjamin Harrison, what direction his life might have taken after he left home for college if he hadn't met Caroline Scott. His father, John Scott Harrison, the son of the ninth president, William Henry Harrison, had hoped to be able to send him to Yale University, but he had fallen on hard times and at virtually the last minute he was forced to settle on Ohio's Miami University, which at least was known in those days as the Yale of the West.

Carrie, as she was often called, who was also a freshman there, was the daughter of John Scott, a professor of chemistry and physics, whose home young Ben began visiting frequently. He didn't have any special fascination for science, but he did have a natural attraction to the professor's daughter, and like opposite poles of a magnet, she couldn't resist him either.

Their romance blossomed over that first year, but then Dr. Scott moved on to establish a girls college, the Oxford Female Institute, and Carrie and her sister Lizzie transferred there. Though the new school was in the same neighborhood, the girls were locked in their dormitories from early in the evening and the boys at the university were kept to a rigid schedule that made socializing difficult at best. Carrie, who had strong powers of persuasion, especially with her father, forced a change in the rules to allow for longer visiting hours at the institute, and the most frequent visitor, as she had hoped, was Ben Harrison.

They sat on the front porch when the weather was nice, or they took moonlight carriage rides, and when it turned bad in the winter months, they went for sleigh rides. Ben was a serious young man almost to a fault. He was determined to make something of himself and he was willing to do whatever it might take in the way of work to make it happen. But when he was around Carrie he was a completely different person. She was serious about her studies, too, but she loved a good time, and it was infectious.

Caroline was much more than just a party girl. Her father, a respected educator, was a Presbyterian minister, and her mother, Mary, was well educated

> "[Carrie is] charming and loveable, petite and a little plump, with soft brown eyes and a wealth of beautiful brown hair."
>
> —Benjamin Harrison, age seventeen

Caroline Lavinia Scott Harrison

Born
October 1, 1832,
Oxford, Ohio

Parents
John Witherspoon Scott
and Mary Potts Neal Scott

Married
October 20, 1853, to
Benjamin Harrison
(1833-1901)

Children
Russell Lord (Russell Benjamin) (1854-1936);
Mary (Mamie) Scott (1858-1930); unnamed stillborn child (1861)

Died
October 25, 1892,
Washington, D.C.

Above: Carrie's father, Reverend John W. Scott, was the founder of the Oxford Female Institute in Ohio, where she was one of the first students.

and highly cultured. Their daughter had already shown great talent as a painter, and her skills as a musician seemed to point to a career in music. Contrary to the strict rules of their household, Carrie was a natural dancer and she adored gliding across a dance floor. But she had to do it on the sly, and although Ben's family frowned on dancing, too, the pair often slipped out of town to find parties where a band might be playing.

Miami University was a state institution, but its religious base was strongly Presbyterian, and students were encouraged to accept the denomination as their own. Ben, who had slipped away from his family's church, delighted his father when he joined the Presbyterian church. It was also expected that such a good public speaker as he (he was president of the debating society, after all) was predestined to become a Presbyterian minister. Almost half of his graduating class answered the call, and he was ready to join them himself, but he had another option. He thought he might like to become a lawyer, and he agonized over the choice for months. On one hand, lawyers were generally considered a class of scoundrels; and on the other there was great honor in being what he called God's co-worker. He never said what tipped the balance, although he hinted that he might welcome the opportunity to bring moral excellence and dignity to the legal profession. It was the profession he chose in the end, and it is quite likely that he had supporting a wife in mind when he did. He and Carrie were already secretly engaged long before graduation and his day of decision.

Carrie still had a year of schooling ahead of her when Ben graduated, and he was facing two years of apprenticeship in a Cincinnati law office. It was grueling servitude for him, and Carrie didn't have a moment to call her own, either because on top of her own studies, she was teaching music to freshman girls at the institute.

Her letters were frequent, but not at all frequent enough for the lovesick Ben. There were enough of them, though, to let him to know that Carrie's health was breaking under the strain she was putting herself through, and the need he felt to rescue her led him back to Oxford, where he convinced her parents to let her go to visit relatives in Pennsylvania for a rest. They agreed, even though it would take her farther away from all of them, and the "cure" seemed to work. Ben, who hadn't been able to make up his mind on the matter of setting a wedding date, announced that they would be married within six months, in spite of their age and his immediate prospects. His plan was to join her in Pennsylvania and take a sort of prehoneymoon trip by way of Niagara Falls before going back to Oxford to be married, but not everybody believed it was going to happen that way. There were strong rumors among their friends that he and Carrie were already secretly married that and the trip was a smoke screen.

The rumors weren't true, but Ben was determined to have her drop out of the institute, and an early marriage might help make it happen. Furthermore, the house where he had been boarding in Cincinnati had been sold and he was left without a place to hang his hat or his shingle as a lawyer. Marriage would help solve that problem, too, because it would redefine his housing

Prophetic Advice

Benjamin Harrison and Caroline Scott each had uncommon
intelligence and a firm idea of their future together. But even
they couldn't help worrying that they might be too young to
get married. Ben consulted his old friend John Anderson, who
strongly advised against it, beginning by saying, "You are crazy."
His letter concluded: "This world is not your friend, it is your
enemy and it requires hard labor to defend yourself. Love is
powerful as an incentive, but will it pass current for potatoes and
beef? Coffee and muffins for two are not paid for by affection
existing between the two. Hard cash buys! Where will it come
from?" The couple chose to ignore his advice, but they would soon
have reason to wonder if Anderson might have been right.

*Above: President and
First Lady Benjamin
and Caroline Harrison
in the White House.*

requirements. Thus they were joined together by Caroline's father on October
20, 1853. The bride was twenty-one, the groom a year younger.

The newlyweds started their life together at the Harrison family farm
near North Bend. When Ben was admitted to the bar soon afterward, he and
Carrie decided to move to Indianapolis, where they felt there might be better
opportunities. There was no social ladder to climb in Indianapolis, and the cost
of living was relatively low. They also had a protector out there in the person of
William Sheets, Ben's cousin, who took them in until they could find a home
of their own and helped them get oriented. Sheets was a successful Indianapolis
businessman and he moved in the best circles. That would be important to
a fledgling lawyer, and Ben also had the advantage of being the grandson of
William Henry Harrison, who was still fondly remembered in the capital of the
Hoosier State. Yet he was still a stranger there, and a young one at that, and the
going was rough.

Carrie was soon far enough along in her first pregnancy to need a doctor's
attention, which they couldn't afford, and they decided that she should go back
to Ohio to live with her parents until their first son, Russell, was born. Ben,
meanwhile, stayed behind to try to rustle up a law client or two. Clients weren't
easy to find, and collecting fees from them was often even tougher. As Ben put
it, "A five dollar bill was an event." But he wasn't without some resources, and
before Carrie and the baby were ready to come back to him in Indiana, he had
managed to find shared office space in the courthouse building. It helped him
get to know other lawyers and to
meet potential clients from the
local business community. He
had also been appointed crier, a
kind of master of ceremonies, at
the federal court, collecting $2.50
every day the court was in session.

> "Mrs. Benjamin Harrison belonged to a younger group; she too was a power, her tastes
> were artistic, her creations in needlework lovely and her vitality charming. She laughed
> readily, and her gaiety and intellectual gifts made her delightful to the younger women
> coming into the church."
>
> —Church record from the First Presbyterian Church, Indianapolis

Above: Sewing circles, like the one that kept Caroline busy, turned out new clothes for the poor.

Better than the steady, if meager, income, the job gave him exposure, and trial lawyers began asking him to assist them with their cases. Still, his progress was slow.

Ben's law practice was still providing only a hand-to-mouth existence when William Wallace, one of the most successful lawyers in town, asked him to become his partner. Wallace was the son of a former governor with political ambitions of his own, and he was looking for a partner who could keep his business running while he was out campaigning. He couldn't have made a more perfect choice than Benjamin Harrison. While Wallace was out campaigning, Ben was building their business, and the results surprised both of them. The candidate lost the election, but he kept the partnership going when he settled down to business again. Young Ben's financial worries were behind him at last.

As in most working-class cities in the mid-nineteenth century, religion was the glue that held the Indianapolis community together, and Carrie Harrison quickly became a pillar of the First Presbyterian Church, where Ben's cousin William Sheets was an elder. Even without the connection, though, Carrie stood out. Ben became a deacon and superintendent of the Sunday school, where Carrie took charge of the infants. Carrie was also conspicuously active in the church's chief organization, the Ladies' Sewing Society, which met at least once a week, sometimes more often, for afternoons of sewing for the needy and exchanging gossip. At least once a month, their meetings extended into the evening, and the women's husbands and older children were invited to share a supper and some more gossip. It was about the only kind of social life that Indianapolis had to offer in those years, and Ben and Carrie became its shining stars.

Ben wasn't far past voting age, but apart from religion, politics was a universal passion among his neighbors, especially his fellow lawyers, and it was only natural that he would eventually get the bug. His grandfather had made his reputation in this very place, and his father was a congressman representing an Ohio district in Washington. John Scott Harrison's name was even being mentioned often as a presidential candidate. But the elder Harrisons were both old-fashioned Whigs, and Ben decided that if he was going to have any kind of future in politics, he'd be smart to catch the wave of the future by joining the new Republican party.

Needless to say, his father, the Whig congressman, wasn't too pleased about his son's choice of party, but he was also upset by the fact that he was getting involved at all. He had carefully trained his son in the nuances of politics, but only as an exercise that he hoped would persuade him to rise above the life of a politician, which he said was "a drug which should never be found in a gentleman's library or parlor, fit only to scent a beer house.... None but knaves should ever enter the political arena." But John Scott Harrison wasn't the first father to have his advice ignored.

"Ben was the only Republican in the family and the more shame for him."

—John, Benjamin Harrison's brother

For his part, Ben was determined to provide a comfortable living for his wife and son, and he didn't have the time for a sideline career. As he put it, "Business engagements have crowded me pretty close." His business interests were closely intertwined with his partner Will Wallace, though, and Wallace was, as Ben said, a "devoted politician." Ben's responsibility to the partnership was running the office and dealing with the courts, and he didn't have the time for anything else; yet, when Wallace decided to run for county clerk, he prevailed on his partner to take to the stump for him. It was a heady experience for Ben. He had become a politician, and a Republican one at that. He was the winning candidate for the office of city attorney in the next election, and there was no turning back.

> "I have a good hope that by mutual help and by God's help, we may have the residue of our lives without having our heart's sunshine clouded by a single shade of mistrust or anger. I know it is possible, and I would rather succeed in such an effort than to have the highest honors of earth."
>
> —Benjamin Harrison to his wife, Carrie, on life before entering politics

By 1858, when Carrie gave birth to their daughter, Mary, whom they called Mamie, the proud father had already become secretary to the state Republican central committee, a job that put him in close contact with the party's leaders all over the state. Two years later, he was elected reporter of the state Supreme Court, a job that was not only highly important but also extremely lucrative.

It was the same year that his fellow Republican Abraham Lincoln was elected to the presidency. Indiana had given its votes to him, and Ben Harrison's work for his candidacy across the state was an important factor. He was front and center when the president-elect passed through Indianapolis on his way to Washington, then he settled down to his work, which he had every reason to expect would give him the means to buy a big house for Carrie and the children. When the news of the firing on Fort Sumter reached town, Ben had to decide if he was going to answer the president's call to arms. His son, Russell, was nearly seven years old, daughter Mamie was three, and Carrie was seven months pregnant. Ben was thirty years old with a promising career ahead of him, and his first thought was to stick to the business at hand.

But the business was almost more than he could handle. He still had his law partnership, but the job of Supreme Court reporter could have taxed the energies of several men. He had almost no time for his family; and although Carrie never complained, realizing that the effort he was making was for her and the children, Ben was beginning to wonder if was all worth it. Carrie's own life took a step backward a few months after the war began, when her third child arrived stillborn. Both she and Ben were plunged into deep mourning for a time, but they took solace in the fact that they already had two bright and attractive children. There was a lot to be desired in their home life, and Ben blamed himself. Before he had time to remedy the situation, Ben became a colonel in the Grand Army of the Republic, leading his own regiment of Indiana volunteers in Kentucky.

Below: General Harrison made a name for himself in battlefield action leading Union army troops.

A New Life

Benjamin Harrison went off to war a lawyer with no military experience, and he came back after three years as a brigadier general, an honor that he earned for heroism during the Battle of Atlanta. He was also determined to change his life. He promised Carrie that he would "settle down to a life of quiet usefulness" and make their home "brighter and happier."

Ben had thought of little else while he was away at war, and now that he was home, he worked hard at keeping the promise he made to himself. He bought a buggy, and he and Carrie took evening rides again as they had when they were courting. He went bass fishing with young Russie, and he watched proudly as Mamie painted alongside her mother. Before the war, he had spent his evenings studying and writing, and now he took up gardening. He and Carrie took full advantage of all the social opportunities their church had to offer, and they were often seen at the theater or the opera as well. Ben and Carrie were a real couple for the first time since they were married, and it made them perfectly happy.

Ben was reelected to his old job of Supreme Court reporter, with its lucrative sideline of publishing the proceedings in book form, and he had joined a bigger law partnership than the one he left behind. But while he was earning a better income than before, his priorities had changed and he made time for his family. Carrie couldn't have been more pleased.

He was able to settle his debts and to expand and improve their house, and his two children were enrolled in private schools. They even managed an expensive family vacation in New England. Russie joined his father bird hunting, and his parents busied themselves scouting college opportunities for him. Mamie, a young teenager by then, got a chance to try out the social skills her mother had taught her, and she made an impression among strangers as a "bewitching, handsome, fascinating, and intelligent young girl."

Ben had become a trial lawyer by this point, and his work on high-profile cases made him an even better-known local figure. It was inevitable that the Republicans would come calling, and they encouraged him to run for governor in 1872. Running didn't mean that Ben would have to be far from home. Carrie was pleased with the idea: Because Indianapolis was the state capital, he wouldn't have to leave home at all if he were elected.

A Matter of Opinion

When the diaries of former president John Quincy Adams were published, he was less than kind in his assessment of Ben Harrison's grandfather President William Henry Harrison. He claimed that he had been "absolutely rabid in his thirst for lucrative office," and he went on to charge that President Harrison had "a lively and active, but shallow mind…not without talent, but self-sufficient, vain and indiscreet." Ben's father, the former president's son, was outraged and he prevailed on him to do something about it. "I would travel to Boston and wear out as many horsewhips on his back as the police would allow me to do before an arrest," he said, apparently not realizing that the author was dead by then. But his advanced age prevented such satisfaction in any case, and he insisted that Ben should exact vengeance for the sake of his own wife and children. "The Adams family from the foundation of the government have had the spoon of the U.S. Treasury in their mouths and took care to hold on until choked off by the will of the people," he railed. Ben cooled him down and cautioned against a response or a denial, either one of which he said would be undignified. Benjamin Harrison was a fighter, but he knew how to pick his battles.

As it happened, Ben didn't get the nomination at the party's convention, but the prospect whetted his appetite. It boosted his standing, too, in an odd way, by raising him above petty politics. As a newspaper that had previously opposed him noted, "Honest men like General Harrison are not in demand just now with the plunderers." He campaigned for presidential candidate Ulysses S. Grant, and when the general took the state and the Republicans got control of the legislature, there was another boom for Ben to run for Congress. He refused on the grounds that it would disrupt his home life.

Russell had left home to enroll at the Pennsylvania Military Academy, and the family planned to send him on to Cornell University when he graduated. The house was a lonely place without him, and Ben and Carrie gave their full attention to young Mamie. Very little was denied her. But Ben drew the line when she asked if she could take dancing lessons. That was against his religion.

Carrie solved the problem. Reminding Ben of the good times they had flouting the church rules back in Oxford didn't get her anywhere, so she decided to enlist the women of the church to bend the rule. Quietly conspiring with other mothers of teenage daughters, she convinced them that there was nothing wrong with allowing the girls to dance, as long as they did it in their own homes and not on church property. The problem was that she knew Ben would "never allow an ungodly fiddle in the house," but she was able to solve it by recruiting another less restricted mother to use her home as a dancing academy. They hired a professional instructor, and the girls were happy; so were the local boys. Carrie never bothered to tell Ben what their daughter was up to, in spite of her pride at Mamie's dancing; and even Russie, who spent afternoons when he was home from school twirling the young girls around the secret dance floor, never mentioned it to his father.

The financial panic of 1873 affected Indianapolis more than most other cities. But in the midst of bank failures and lost fortunes, Ben Harrison's law practice flourished with foreclosures and bankruptcy cases, and he was financially secure enough to start work on the new home he had promised Carrie so long ago. He bought a double lot at the edge of town and, following Carrie's specifications, started work on building a two-story brick house with an attic ballroom that would stand far back off the street near the back of the lot. Carrie preferred a big front yard because the back faced another street and she knew she wouldn't have much privacy beyond her back door.

It took nearly a year to build the house, and when they were finished it was a showplace. Ben was especially proud of his large library. He had the bookcases custom-built by an Old World cabinetmaker through a barter arrangement in exchange for legal fees. The room was dominated by a large portrait of his grandfather, the former president, which served as a reminder to visitors that Benjamin Harrison was something more than an average successful lawyer. Building and furnishing the house cost the Harrisons $20,000, which is about $334,000 in today's money.

Below: Carrie was a regal-looking woman, but she had a disarming common touch and a well-developed sense of humor.

Above: Twenty-third president Benjamin Harrison was seven years old when his grandfather, the ninth president, was elected in 1840.

Their new home made it possible for the Harrisons to entertain more frequently, and Carrie added to her already widespread reputation as one of the most gracious hostesses in the city. Their circle consisted mainly of the friends they had made at church, but included most of the elite of Indianapolis. The sewing circle started holding most of its sessions in Carrie's parlor, and the Harrison house took on all the earmarks of an annex to the First Presbyterian Church. Ben and his friends often went off on hunting and fishing trips together, and while they were gone, their wives made the house their second home.

Politics appeared to be in the past for a man with such a busy schedule, but there was a groundswell for Ben to run for governor again, and even the opposition press agreed it was a fine idea. But he turned the honor aside, claiming that his family needed his full attention. But while the Harrison family was away on vacation in Sault Sainte Marie, the Republican state committee nominated him to run for governor. He had already begged off on their first offer, and he wired them that they had better be ready to make a strong case or they'd find themselves without a candidate. The people made their case for them. When the family arrived back home, several thousand were gathered at the train station with a cannon salute and a parade back to their house, which had been decorated with flags and bunting in anticipation. Still, Ben wouldn't commit himself, although the demonstration in his front yard lasted until well after midnight.

The next day was Sunday, and he and Carrie spent it at church while telegrams and other messages urging him to accept the nomination rained down on their house. He kept everyone in suspense until late evening when he finally agreed to run for governor of Indiana. He lost the election, which was held ahead of the national one, but that gave him time to go out and campaign for presidential candidate Hayes as well. Taking daughter Mamie along with him, he stumped throughout the Midwest, and what his speaking skills couldn't accomplish, Mamie's charms often did. It earned Hayes's gratitude and his admiration, and Ben and Carrie were among his first visitors at the White House.

In spite of his defeat at the polls, Ben was now the undisputed leader of the Indiana Republicans, and their home shifted from a church meeting place to a political clubhouse. Russell had gone to college in Ohio rather than Cornell, as had been planned, and he was establishing a new career in Philadelphia at that point. Mamie, now twenty, had become one of the most popular young women in Indianapolis, and her mother couldn't avoid the comparison to herself at that age. They were more like sisters than mother and daughter, and they took frequent short vacation trips together, freeing the house for those serious discussions of politics.

But politics was only part of the stimulation available in the Harrison household. Ben became a charter member of the Indianapolis Literary Club, whose membership included writer Booth Tarkington and poet James Whitcomb Riley. Among her church activities, Carrie had organized a reading club, and through it she discovered a new talent for reading aloud and acting out scenes from popular books. The literary club gave her a new audience, and even authors were impressed by her readings of their work. Both Ben and Carrie were also active in raising funds for a new church building, and they became missionaries to the community, an effort that created a whole new Presbyterian body in a neighborhood where none had existed before. Then, as if Ben didn't have enough to do, President Hayes appointed him to the Mississippi River Commission, which was formed to deal with navigation and flood-control problems. He initially rejected the offer, but during a trip to Washington, the president talked him into it.

President Hayes visited Indianapolis not long afterward, and he spent an evening with the Harrisons. Carrie was proud of the attention it brought her, but she was prouder still of the local reaction to the lawn party she arranged for the president and the First Lady. It made her the talk of the town, but, then, Carrie had already grown quite accustomed to such praise.

Ben had also cultivated a close friendship with James A. Garfield, and he not only delivered Indiana to him when he ran for president, but he stumped the country for him all the way to New York. It seemed to be a foregone conclusion that his efforts would earn him a spot in the Garfield cabinet, but again he demurred. He had set his sights on running for the Senate instead, because it would allow him more time at home to keep an eye on his business and to spend more time with Carrie and Mamie. Garfield was intent on having Ben Harrison in his cabinet, but although it would have been important to his state, Ben resisted a considerable amount of arm-twisting. He arrived in Washington as a senator and not as a cabinet minister.

Carrie was with him, and they turned the occasion into a family reunion, bringing Russell in from Montana, where he had since moved to become a cattle rancher, to join Mamie and his mother and father for the Garfield inauguration. Ben himself was sworn in as a senator the same day, with his wife and children beaming in the visitors gallery. Carrie planned to move to Washington in time for the next congressional session, and she sent Mamie on ahead to find the family a suitable place to live. The Harrisons' daughter was now twenty-four years old and the vivacious belle of Indianapolis, and her friends predicted that she wouldn't find Washington to her liking because there were so few young gentlemen there. She found an available floor in a boardinghouse that had four rooms and a bath. Although both she and her mother were wizards in the kitchen, the best part was that the place had a great reputation for its food. It would give them more time to enjoy Washington society, and Mamie was all for that.

Ben was more than pleased. He missed his family, and he knew that Carrie's charm was going to help him in the obligatory receptions that made the world turn as far as official Washington was concerned. For her part, Mamie wasn't looking forward to socializing with all those practically ancient officials, but she was pleased to know that they were only required to make first calls, and after that she'd be free to chart her own course.

Below: Carrie holding her grandson, Benjamin Harrison McKee, while the child's mother, Mamie, stands proudly in the background as grandfather, Reverend Dr. Scott dandles her daughter, Mary, on his knee.

The Washington winter didn't agree with Carrie at all, and she spent most of it in a sickbed. Mamie served as her nurse as well as her father's companion, but her heart was back in Indiana. She had lost it to a young man there named Bob McKee. Her brother, Russell, was in Washington most of that winter, too. He was smitten with May Saunders, a senator's daughter described as a "stunning blonde," and the most sought-after young woman among the young men Mamie had told herself didn't exist in the capital.

Summer adjournment finally took the Harrisons away from the city. Carrie had been recuperating from her long illness at a Maryland resort, and she was the first to leave, fit enough to hold a round of receptions back home. She went back to Washington again when her husband went there for the next congressional session, but once again her health failed her, and she spent the following summer away from her obligations as a hostess. Although Ben had obligations of his own back in Indianapolis, he took Carrie to a spa in another part of the state. When they got home, there was a message waiting for them from Russell. He had asked May Saunders to marry him, and in spite of all the other offers she was getting from other Washington swains, she accepted.

Carrie and Ben spent the Christmas holidays planning their trip to Omaha to see their son married, but in the midst of their planning and holiday entertaining, another kind of life-changing message arrived. It was from an influential Republican businessman suggesting that Ben ought to consider running for president. His reply didn't say yes and it didn't say no, but between the lines there was an unmistakable maybe.

Carrie was too sick to make the trip to Nebraska for Russell's wedding, but his proud father and his sister were there, and so was Bob McKee, Mamie's new fiancé. The wedding itself was the highlight of the winter of 1884 in Omaha. The fathers of both the bride and the groom were United States senators, and May Saunders's father had been territorial governor in Nebraska for seven years. It was still just a rumor, but people were whispering that the groom's father might be the next president of the United States.

Although the mother of the bridegroom had been too ill to go to the wedding, when the newlyweds arrived in Indianapolis the following day, she had organized a second wedding reception for them and entertained more than five hundred close friends in her home.

Ben had extended the congressional recess by several weeks because of the wedding, and when he went back to Washington, Carrie stayed behind rather than face another Washington winter. He had too much work ahead of him to get involved in socializing anyway. Not only had the enthusiasm for making him a presidential candidate taken a toll on his working hours, but making a good record had become that much more important. But still, the senator was silent about whether he'd accept the nomination anyway. He had a history of walking away from honors the party was willing to give him.

Below: Nebraska Senator Alvin Saunders, Russell Harrison's father-in-law, brought his own political savvy into the Harrison camp.

In fact, when the Republicans met for their national convention that year, Ben Harrison was at home in Indianapolis tending his garden and enjoying his wife's company. The convention nominated James G. Blaine instead; but Ben didn't show any signs of remorse, promising to campaign for Blaine. The fact that the Republican candidate didn't take Indiana didn't appear to faze Ben, though. He had other things on his mind. His daughter, Mamie, the apple of his eye, was married in a lavish wedding the day after the 1884 election that made Grover Cleveland the new president.

Above: Benjamin brought a pledge of independence from political bosses to the 1888 presidential campaign.

Carrie went back to Washington with him for the next Senate session, and when the Christmas recess rolled around, they stayed there. The workaholic senator was too busy, and with both children gone, their Indianapolis house was too empty for Carrie. They went home together in the spring, and while Ben mended political fences and brought his law practice up to speed, Carrie went back to her church work and cultivating her garden. By late spring, they were ready to take a long relaxing trip.

As chairman of the subcommittee on Indian Affairs, Ben arranged a six-week fact-finding tour of the West, and he invited Carrie and Mamie to go along. The women joined the party in St. Paul, Minnesota, and then went on their own to Helena, Montana, for a long visit with Russell and his wife. Mamie headed back east to be with her new husband, and Ben and Carrie set off on what they called their second honeymoon. They went as far west as Portland, Oregon, and then ranged down the coast to California, with a side trip to Yellowstone National Park.

Carrie opted to stay home during Ben's last session in the Senate, and he wrote to her that his evenings hung "very heavy" on him, confessing that he didn't consider himself a "a good hand at making friends," which had never been a problem when Carrie was around. When he went home again, the feeling that the move was going to be a permanent one made the Harrisons all the more lonely. That changed suddenly on March 15, 1887, when Benjamin Harrison McKee, their first grandson, was born.

During the rest of the spring and summer, Ben pushed himself earning legal fees, and he earned several impressive ones, although it left him somewhat exhausted. He obviously needed a vacation, but instead he decided to send Carrie, the baby, and Mamie and her husband off for a few weeks in the Maryland mountains. He went right on working, because "I owe some money and I want to pay it." But at the last minute, he decided to join the family at their vacation house, which was near to some of his old Senate cronies, who were also relaxing and enjoying themselves. Naturally, the talk turned to politics, and once more Ben reiterated that he had dropped any plans to become president. But some of the gossip they shared seemed to indicate that he might still be able to pull it off.

Among the campaign paraphernalia that flooded the Republican convention were fans featuring a portrait of Carrie Harrison over a short but glowing statement of support for her husband, "Little Ben."

Above: The Harrison's Inaugural Ball filled the Pension Building in Washington and set the stage for the coming of the "gay nineties."

Below: The White House was a crowded place in the Harrison years, residents included daughter Mamie McKee and daughter-in-law May Harrison and Carrie's beloved grandchildren.

By the following spring, Indianans were solidly behind a Harrison candidacy, but the possible candidate himself had no confidence in the professional party leaders, and he placed his campaign, such as it was, in the hands of relative amateurs, among them his son-in-law, Bob McKee, who commented, "If any fellow can make heads or tails out of this grand hub-bub of lies, counterclaims, and a few truths that slap him on every side, he is more level-headed than I am." The arrival of Russell Harrison with the Montana delegation did little to enlighten him. But he arrived on the heels of his father-in-law, former Nebraska senator Alvin Saunders, who worked to bring some experience to the politicking.

The Indiana delegation, though enthusiastic, wasn't the only factor in the field. There were no less than nineteen contenders. The bewildered Bob McKee wrote to the folks back home: "The whole race seems like a lot of horses on the track. One runs to the front awhile, then another lays on the whip and forges ahead, but the horses cannot hold the gait clear around the track—so another lays on the whip in turn and comes to the front for a moment, and so it goes." Six days and seven ballots later, the convention unanimously nominated Benjamin Harrison to lead them to the White House.

When the candidate arrived back home, the crowds had dismantled the picket fence around the house, claiming the pieces as souvenirs. At the same time, delegations of supporters came to call, and Ben invited them in. Carrie was having her baptism in presidential politics. Ben began a long series of "neighborly chats" on his front porch, and supporters came by the thousands to hear what he had to say. His most important speech that first day was to more than five thousand of his neighbors, whom he had lived among for more than thirty years.

Back to Washington

Benjamin Harrison was a familiar face around Indianapolis, but many people there, while they respected him, regarded him as cold and aloof. In some ways he was, but Carrie was the direct opposite and now it was up to her to burnish her husband's public image. It was still customary for presidential candidates to stay close to home during campaigns and let others speak for them.

But, still, the voters were curious about him, and newspaper people descended on Indianapolis to file stories about Benjamin Harrison the man. The main thrust of their reports was that he was a family man who spent his evenings at the family fireside enjoying his wife's company or taking long carriage rides and evening strolls with her. Carrie's personality came though in nearly every human interest story that was filed from Indianapolis that summer and fall. It helped that Carrie never seemed to tire of having strangers trooping through her home. It was as though she were auditioning for the role of First Lady, but it was actually her own natural personality at work.

After Ben won the election, the activity in the Harrison home grew even more intense, with advisors, office seekers, and reporters arriving at the front door. Carrie avoided the crunch by taking Mamie to New York for a preinauguration shopping trip. They left for Washington aboard a special train on February 25, 1889.

A New Woman

Carrie's first act as First Lady was to tackle the problem of making the White House presentable. Others had made that their first project, too, but no one had approached it in quite the same way. She held a meeting with the secretary of state to get his cooperation in the effort to make a better impression on foreign dignitaries. Next she called in an architect and scheduled a round of meetings with him to share her ideas. Then she held a press conference to get public support for them, and she lobbied important members of Congress for their support. For good measure, she also involved an enthusiastic Harriet Lane in her planning. Carrie had an impressive plan in mind that included adding new wings, a pair of art galleries, and fountains on the lawn, and the bill to make it all possible passed the Senate with ease. But it was blocked in the House because of a political feud between the president and the Speaker, and in the end, Carrie was left with the same problem other First Ladies had faced: redecorating her new home with limited funds.

Most of all, she needed to improve the presidential living quarters. Russell and May had come there to live, and so had Mamie and Bob, who had two children by then; Carrie's father, John Scott, came along, too, and so did her widowed niece, Mary Lord Dimmick, who would serve as Carrie's social secretary. All in all, it strained the resources of the available living space.

More than many of her predecessors, Carrie took a maternal interest in the mansion. Among the things she discovered in her roof-to-basement tours was the china service other First Ladies had used, and she had it all brought out to be cataloged and put on display. China was one of her passions since the days when she taught ceramic painting to the women in her church back home. She created the design for her own china and conducted classes in the art for Washington wives. She also taught classes in French, and she grew orchids in the greenhouses, making them the corsage of choice for her women guests, and women across the country for that matter. Altogether, Caroline Harrison hadn't changed a bit from her Indianapolis days, and it was even rumored that she cooked the family's meals herself.

But it was soon obvious that Caroline was more than just a homebody. She was an astute politician, although she had been hiding that talent during most of her married life. She acquainted herself with every issue that her husband was dealing with, and if he made what she considered an important speech, she called the press's attention to it. She also discussed those issues with him, and he listened carefully to what she had to say because, he felt, "a woman's intuition is often more valuable in matters of statecraft than a man's logic."

Carrie occasionally came in for press criticism, but it was never quite so damaging as when the millionaire merchant John Wanamaker gave her a twenty-room beach house at Cape May,

Below: Blueprints for renovations to the main floor and second floor of the White House were altered when Congress cut funding and Carrie had to make do with what she had available.

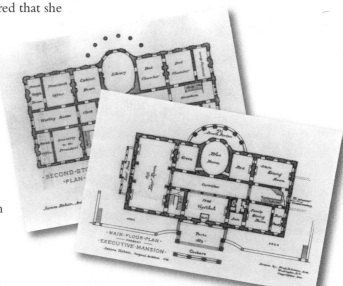

Going Public

No other First Lady had ever delivered a public speech she wrote herself until Caroline Harrison addressed the Daughters of the American Revolution. "We have within ourselves the only element of destruction; our foes are from within, not without," she told them. "It has been said that 'the men to make a country are made by self-denial,' and is it not true, that for the society to live and grow and become what we desire it to be must be composed of self-denying women? Since this society has been organized and so much thought and reading directed to the early struggles of this country, it has been made plain that much of its success was due to the women of that era. The unselfish part they acted constantly commands itself to our admiration and example. If there is no abatement in this element of success in our ranks, I feel sure that their daughters can perpetuate a society worthy the cause and worthy themselves."

Above: Carrie was made president-general of the newly formed Daughters of the American Revolution, which she saw as a powerful political force for women in government.

Below: Mary Harrison, Benjamin's second wife, was Carrie's niece and had once been her social secretary.

New Jersey. It was immediately characterized as a bribe, but the president countered that he had been negotiating to buy the house in the first place. When Carrie and her family moved to Cape May for the summer, the criticism only increased. She was also lambasted in the press for other perceived gaffes, and it didn't please her at all. "What have we done that we should be held up to ridicule by newspapers?" she asked. "Cruelly attacked, made fun of for the country to laugh at. If this is the penalty, I hope the Good Lord will deliver my husband from any further experience."

Carrie redeemed herself in the court of public opinion with her strong support for two prominent, but weak, women's organizations, the Daughters of the American Revolution (DAR) and the Women's Medical Fund for the Johns Hopkins Medical School. Although she had butted heads with the press, she understood how to get publicity, and because of her doggedness, both organizations became respected as fighters for women's rights.

The Women's Medical Fund had been established to raise half a million dollars for the medical school that would be handed over only in return for a promise that the institution would promote education and medical careers for women. Carrie was made head of the national committee and she coordinated the efforts of fifteen local branches. She had an even stronger interest in the DAR, which had recently been formed by female government employees as a "political force for women." She agreed to become its first president, and she began an intense lobbying effort for its goals, using the social schedule of the White House to help get the message across.

Until she became an activist for women's rights, Carrie had suffered by comparison to the youth and vivacity of former First Lady Frances Cleveland.

After Carrie's death, Benjamin Harrison married her niece Mary Lord Dimmick.

>
> *Carrie had electric lights installed in the White House,
> but she was afraid to touch the switches that turned them on.*

Above: The West Sitting Hall at the White House was the first to have electric lights, thanks to Carrie's efforts, but she was afraid of them.

By this stage of her life, she had become heavy, her hair had turned gray, and her illnesses had left her with bags under her eyes. She rose above it by dressing elegantly, and her personality won over even her husband's enemies.

Carrie's sister died in the White House in December 1889, but she went ahead with plans to decorate the first Christmas tree that had ever been seen in the mansion. She also brought dancing back for the first time since Sarah Polk lived there almost forty-five years earlier. That was predictable—few women enjoyed dancing as much as Carrie Harrison, in spite of her strict Presbyterian upbringing.

It all came to an end in the summer of 1892 when Carrie became ill with what was diagnosed as tuberculosis. She spent the summer in the Adirondack Mountains, but it didn't help, and not long after going home to the White House, she slipped into a coma. At one point when she regained consciousness, her husband asked if there was anything he could do. She smiled and answered, "No, dear." A month later she was dead. The presidential election campaign was just getting under way, but both her husband and the opposition candidate, former president Grover Cleveland, made no public appearances out of respect for the woman who was quite likely the most underrated First Lady in the history of the presidency.

Below: The Harrison home in Indianapolis, Indiana, was completely redecorated by the second Mrs. Harrison, but has since been restored to a home that Carrie would easily recognize.

Visiting the Harrison Home

A few years after Caroline Harrison died, Benjamin married her niece Mary Lord Dimmick. Mary completely redecorated the family home, and when the former president died, she sold it and moved to New York. She sold the Indianapolis house in 1937 to a foundation that restored it to its original condition, bringing Carrie's furniture out of storage. The house at 1230 North Delaware Street in Indianapolis is now open Monday through Saturday from 10:00 A.M. to 3:30 P.M.; and on Sundays in July, August, and December from 12:30 P.M. to 3:30 P.M. It is closed on major holidays, and the admission fee is $6.00 for adults.

Ida McKinley

A Life of Privilege

Ida Saxton McKinley, the wife of America's twenty-fifth president, William McKinley, lived almost exactly sixty years. Her life can best be examined in two distinct segments of nearly equal lengths. The first half of her life is best characterized as one of privilege and wealth. Her second three decades were marked by tragedy, illness, and despair.

She was born on June 8, 1847, the eldest daughter of James Saxton and Katherine DeWalt Saxton. Ida had an older brother, George, and a younger sister, Mary. Theirs was a socially prominent and wealthy family in Canton, Ohio. Ida's paternal grandfather, John Saxton, founded the *Ohio Repository*, the first newspaper in Canton. Ida's father, James, was a well-respected banker, and the third wealthiest man in town, and the Saxtons pampered their children with all the accoutrements expected of the progeny of the well-to-do in the late nineteenth century. The children were educated locally in Canton's finest private schools, but also spent time in boarding schools in Delhi, New York, and in Cleveland. Both Saxton girls attended the finishing school at Brooke Academy in Media, Pennsylvania. Ida was a popular student, and when she returned in 1868, she was referred to as the "belle of Canton."

When she returned to Canton following her time in finishing school, Ida became active in a variety of community affairs. These included participating in a performance at Schaefer's Opera House, a fund-raiser to build the new, stone structure that would become the Presbyterian Church. After the March 1868 performance at Schaefer's, she was voted the most popular actress in the play.

But being pretty and popular did not provide sufficient satisfaction to the ambitious Ida. From a young age, Ida was strong and independent, and exhibited talent in financial matters. Her broad-minded father awarded her a position in his Stark County Bank. Starting as a teller, she eventually gained the experience and knowledge to manage the bank when her father left the city. Decades

> **Ida Saxton McKinley**
>
> **Born**
> June 8, 1847,
> Canton, Ohio
>
> **Parents**
> James A. Saxton and
> Katherine DeWalt Saxton
>
> **Marriage**
> January 25, 1871, to
> William McKinley, Jr.
> (1843-1901)
>
> **Children**
> Katherine (1871-75);
> Ida (1873)
>
> **Died**
> May 26, 1907,
> Canton, Ohio

> *"Mrs. McKinley is not adapted to days of handshaking nor to bows from car platforms. She is not only an invalid, but a woman of strongly domestic preferences. . . . In her youth, Ida Saxton was the belle of Canton, O., and the mature graces of Ida McKinley amply bear out this earlier reputation."*
>
> —Seattle Post-Intelligencer, *September 13, 1896*

before the exploits of Susan B. Anthony and the women of the suffragette movement, Ida was an outspoken proponent of women's rights or, at the very least, for women having opportunities equal to men of the day. It was quite unconventional for a young woman from a wealthy family to have a job outside the home, let alone to hold such a position of authority. This eventually gave way to rumors that the family's funds were depleted, to which her father, James replied, "I want her to be able to support herself if trouble comes her way."

Before gaining such prominence in the banking business, Ida had finished her debutante days by embarking on an eight-month-long grand tour of Europe, as many young ladies of the nineteenth century were wont to do. From 1869 to 1870, twenty-two-year-old Ida and her sister, Mary, along with their escort Jeannette Alexander, visited England, Ireland, France, Germany, and Switzerland. Her financial acumen came in handy, managing the funds of their whirlwind tour. Yes, Ida lived a privileged life; however, it was not a sheltered or reclusive one.

Upon her return from Europe, Ida found that her father had purchased her grandparents' house (now the site of the First Ladies' National Historic Site). Also upon returning, Ida built on her relationship with Major William McKinley. She was tall, with very long auburn hair, blue eyes, and a good figure—young Ida had caught his eye at the bank.

"The Major" had served in the Union army during the Civil War, enlisting in the Twenty-Third Ohio Infantry at the age of seventeen, soon after the opening shots were fired at Fort Sumter. He valiantly served the cause of the Union, including fighting on the battlefield at Antietam, the bloodiest battle ever fought on U.S. soil. He returned to Ohio with a record of which any young man might well be proud. In 1867, he moved from his hometown of Niles, Ohio, to Canton to establish a law practice. Ida and he had met a number of times before Ida's European jaunt, first at a church picnic in 1868, following introductions by William's sister Anna. After Ida's return, they began dating seriously and their romance started to blossom.

William was the seventh of eight children, born in 1843 to William and Nancy Alison McKinley. He was hardly a blue blood, though his father did own a small iron foundry. At a young age, William had shown interest in becoming a Methodist minister. He had attended Allegheny College, but his studies were cut short by illness. The postwar era found him studying law in the Poland, Ohio, office of a Judge Charles Glidden, where he was a careful, faithful, industrious, and competent student. He also entered Albany Law School. Records show that in 1867 he passed the bar exam, and then got a job working for Judge George Belden. The judge was so overburdened with work

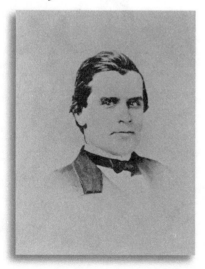

Below: The future President McKinley at the age of nineteen, a year after he joined the Union army and six years before Ida Saxon first noticed him.

that he offered a case to William, who went on to win it. By 1870, he had been elected to his first post, that of prosecuting attorney of Stark County—the first prosecuting attorney to take office in the county's new courthouse.

Shortly after he began his new job, Ida and William were engaged. He was taken with Ida's outgoing personality, charm, and spunk, which seemed to complement William's friendly yet unassuming disposition. While some people found Ida to be strong-willed and opinionated, others thought she was sweet and gentle. Both impressions were probably accurate.

Twenty-seven-year-old William married twenty-three-year-old Ida in a lavish ceremony at the just-opened First Presbyterian Church in Canton on January 25, 1871. Because William was Methodist and Ida was Presbyterian, they had two officiants, one representing each denomination. (Later, Ida became a Methodist.) Refreshments were served in the ballroom of the Saxton House, and the couple departed by train for a honeymoon in New York. The new couple moved into a house the Saxtons gave them as a wedding present. Theirs would be a loving and devoted marriage, and their early years were happy ones. Like any young married couple, they had big dreams for the future, but no way of knowing the tragedies that would soon befall them.

Ida McKinley had complained of severe headaches for many years, but the onset of convulsions and seizures mystified doctors. Historians have since theorized that she suffered from epilepsy, but doctors in the late nineteenth century did not fully understand the malady, and they treated her symptoms, not her illness. She cut her hair short, hoping that by eliminating her heavy braids, her headaches would abate. She took medicine to control the seizures, but that often made her listless, her senses dulled and her eyes struggling to focus. She was also diagnosed with phlebitis, an inflammation of the veins, which would eventually render her a complete invalid.

While still in relatively good health, Ida gave birth to the McKinleys' first child, daughter Katherine, on Christmas of 1871. Baby Katie was just one when Ida's mother, for whom Katie was named, died. A second daughter, Ida, was born in April 1873, following a difficult labor and delivery. By this time mother Ida was seriously ill, and her frail baby died in August of the same year. Then tragedy struck again, in June of 1875. All the love her parents showered her with could not save Katie, and she died of typhoid fever at the age of three. In a three-year period, Ida lost her mother and both of her children. The stress and trauma exacerbated her maladies.

Today we know that a severe trauma can trigger epileptic fits. However, back in 1875, epilepsy was regarded with distaste, or at least, ignorance. As William McKinley continued his political career and rose through the ranks of Ohio Republicans, the public was shielded from the true nature of his wife's illness. Ida was left to descend into a state of depression and confusion from which she could not escape for the rest of her life. William tried to console her

Above: The graves of the McKinley's only two children, Katie, who died at the age of four, and Ida, who lived for just four months, were eventually moved to Canton, Ohio.

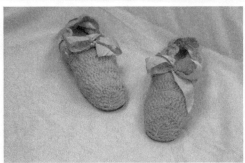

but was overcome with grief himself and became resigned to the tragedies until the end of his days. Because of it, William developed a sense of fatalism, which was obvious to those around him in the White House, even though he appeared open and gregarious in public.

A Commitment to Politics

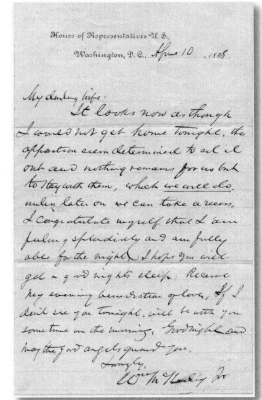

Below: This letter from her husband has a wish for the invalid Ida: "May the good angels guard you."

In 1877, at age thirty-four, William won a seat in Congress. His exemplary character, ambition, and quick intelligence enabled him to rise rapidly in the House. During his fourteen years there, he became the leading Republican tariff expert, supporting higher taxation on foreign goods in order to spark sales of American products. He was also appointed to the powerful Ways and Means Committee. In 1891, he was elected governor of Ohio, serving two terms.

Meanwhile, Ida's condition continued to be a taboo subject, and she was protected by those close to her who knew "the truth." Once, when one of Mrs. McKinley's nieces heard the word "epilepsy" applied to her aunt, she was outraged that the Democrats would "stoop so low as to invent lies about McKinley's wife."

Throughout her husband's career, Ida took an interest in helping when she could, traveling with him whenever her maladies would allow. For example, William's involvement in Canton's temperance movement was due to Ida's interest. He strived to keep Ida close by, just in case she needed him. While William served in Congress, she often had him called out of meetings to answer questions, calm her tantrums, or simply bring her a needed pen or a book. The couple lived in a hotel across from the Capitol, and every morning William tipped his hat to her as she watched from the window. And no matter what, at 3:00 P.M. sharp, he would stop whatever work he was doing, excuse himself, go to the window, and wave his handkerchief at his wife, waiting for her to wave back. Ida spent most of her days in a small Victorian rocking chair that she had owned since childhood, and her husband was never far from her side. He arranged their life to suit her convenience and tirelessly indulged seemingly her every whim.

In 1892 William McKinley chaired the Republican National Convention and was nearly nominated for the presidency. Millionaire industrialist Mark Hanna had unofficially opened a McKinley-for-president headquarters in Minneapolis (the site of the convention), yet this run for the top office was not meant to be. In 1893, William faced a personal crisis that almost sidetracked his political career. He had cosigned bank notes totaling more than $100,000 to help a friend start a business. The business failed, and he was expected to repay the loan. William did not have the money, so Ida put her $92,000 estate at his disposal. His friends, led by Hanna, raised the funds to repay the debt. Nevertheless, the public was sympathetic to William, and his wife's gesture was applauded.

Above: Ida campaigned with her husband in the 1896 campaign although women still couldn't vote.

When William considered his run for president, Mrs. McKinley's health was a concern to many who thought the demands she placed on him would impede his ability to serve. William thought not, and to prove it he gave an enormous party for Ohio Republicans, on the occasion of their silver anniversary. Ida rallied for the cause and received people for more than six hours straight, experiencing no problems. Political pundits turned the seemingly negative into a positive, and a campaign biography was written about her and added to her husband's biography. Wild rumors—such as that Ida was a clandestine English spy—were quelled, and for the first time, a (future) First Lady's image appeared on a campaign pin.

William ran his presidential campaign primarily from Canton, to stay close to Ida. His opponent, William Jennings Bryan, logged 18,000 miles traveling the country to give whistle-stop speeches, while William ran a front-porch campaign. He greeted thousands of guests who arrived by rail, and from his front steps he spoke almost daily. Using the latest in modern technology, including the telegraph and new long-distance telephone services, William was in close touch daily with his campaign manager and with Republican headquarters in New York. Ultimately, more than 750,000 people from nearly every state of the Union visited Canton to hear William speak, and many praised the candidate's patient and loving treatment of his wife. His devotion to her became a major political asset, and he won the election by a substantial margin. The first Republican to be elected by both Northerners and Southerners, he saw his victory as a historic reuniting of the country. "I am no longer called the President of a party," he wrote. "I am now the President of the whole people."

Below: The setting for McKinley's inaugural supper. Ida fainted during the festivities and was carried home without any explanation.

On to Washington

There was little resemblance between the young Ida who married William McKinley in 1871 and the veritable invalid who moved into the White House with him in March 1897. A congressman's wife who visited the White House provided this description of her: "She sat propped up with pillows in a high chair with her back to the light. Her color was ghastly. Her poor relaxed hands, holding some pitiful knitting, rested on her lap as if too weak to lift the weight of diamond earrings.... She shook hands with us lightly but didn't speak."

Ida might have been a dynamic First Lady had fate not stepped in. She was often morose, depressed, and irritable with everyone except her husband, whom she adored. She could pull it together at times, showing strength and determination, but this seemed to cause her to have increased seizures. When she was feeling well, she could be cheerful, kindly, and concerned for those around her. But as time went on, she became more moody and increasingly reliant on her husband. Though he could hardly afford it, William hired a maid to look after his wife, and Ida faithfully received William's attention daily for the rest of their life together. William's devotion to his wife was admired by many. As Margaret Leech writes in her biography, *In the Days of McKinley*, "He was absorbed in the practice of his secondary career of psychiatric nurse."

In 1898, while Congress was in session, Ida went back to Canton without her husband. She had such violent convulsions that the doctors feared for her life. When the president reached his hometown, the doctor told him his wife was unconscious and there was no hope for her. William sat at her bedside, rubbing her hands and caressing her forehead. Sometime later, she opened her eyes, grasped his hands and whispered, "I knew you would come."

In his memoirs, White House physician Dr. Presley Rixey described Ida's condition at the time: "She had been an invalid for years, but a sweet faced, uncomplaining and self-denying one, whose health fluttered constantly and rarely for a few hours remained stationary. It was only by the heroic fortitude of her physicians and the self-effacing devotion of her husband that she enabled ever to endure the shortest journey."

Although she occasionally appeared at state dinners and in receiving lines, Ida's attendance at these functions was sporadic due to the unpredictability of her seizures. In an attempt to calm her and make her appear more stable (and to continue the ruse of Ida's being in good health), her doctors sedated her with powerful narcotics. In a break with tradition, the president insisted that his wife be seated to his immediate right at state dinners, rather than at the other end of the table. This change in protocol was necessitated by the president's need to respond to his wife's possible seizures. Each time she suffered a seizure, William covered her face with a handkerchief to reduce her embarrassment. At the onset of the worst episodes, the president would wheel his wife out of the room.

Because of her alleged phlebitis, Ida often received her guests while seated, holding flowers in her lap so she would not have to shake hands. The president enlisted the aid of Jennie Hobart, the vice president's wife, to ease Ida's social

Below: Although she wasn't always up to the task, Ida refused to let anyone stand in for her as the White House hostess. She had a formidable ego that wouldn't allow it.

responsibilities. Mrs. Hobart stood at her side and urged people along if they took Ida's attention for too long. Jennie became Ida's friend and confidante, calling on the First Lady daily.

When the departing president Grover Cleveland and his wife invited the McKinleys to the White House, Ida declined, so the president-elect ended up dining alone with Mr. and Mrs. Cleveland. Ida attended her husband's inauguration and the ball that followed, but she fainted and had to be escorted home with the new president at her side and the party still going strong. It was a pattern that would repeat throughout the McKinley administration, as the president adjusted White House protocol, his schedule, and his life to monitor and manage his wife's condition. William's devotion and loving attention to her was the talk of the capital. Mark Hanna once remarked, "President McKinley has made it pretty hard for the rest of us husbands here in Washington."

William's devotion to Ida was gratefully received and returned, and perceived by many to be admirable traits. Her wishes and desires became the center of his life, and he never failed in his thoughtfulness for her. Some speculated that she suffered some "attacks" when the president got too distracted talking to someone else, often a female, and did not pay enough attention to her. Regardless of the veracity of her ailments, the attention she required often took a toll on the president. In April 1898, he confided to his friend H. H. Kolsaat, "I have been through a trying period. Mrs. McKinley has been in poorer health than usual. It seems to me I have not slept more than three hours a night for the past two weeks."

Despite her illness, Ida often insisted in playing the part of hostess, and at times she did so successfully. Particularly during 1898, she gave a number of elegant receptions and invited friends from Ohio to attend a series of musicals she organized. Yet while she could be witty and charming one minute, she could also be

Below: As First Lady, Ida appeared with the president when he tended to the ceremonial side of the job with such duties as reviewing parades.

Ida McKinley couldn't stand the color yellow. She banned all yellow things from the White House, and even ordered all the yellow flowers in the garden to be uprooted.

As First Lady, Ida crocheted an estimated one thousand pairs of slippers, which she gave to guests and friends.

shrewish and irrational the next, depending on the medication she was taking. Even when sick, she refused to relinquish the role of presidential hostess to her younger nieces, canceling the entire 1900 social season rather than have someone standing in her place.

It would certainly seem an asset to the president that he had as his wife a strong, intelligent, opinionated woman of high social stature. She did not hesitate to offer the president her political opinions. William took her advice seriously, and Ida's influence seems to be apparent in his adoption of temperance and in some of his government appointments. When Cuba revolted against Spain in 1895, many Americans sided with the rebels and called for intervention against the Spanish; but William refused to get involved amid criticism from cabinet members, including Assistant Secretary of the Navy Theodore Roosevelt. When the United States finally did get involved in the 100 Day War, some reports have it that the Spanish-American War was declared at Ida's urging, but there is little evidence to bolster such a claim. The result of the war was one of the most lopsided war victories in American history. And when the dust settled, the United States controlled Puerto Rico, Guam, and the 7,200 islands of the Philippines. But the profitable outcome of the war was not without criticism. Many people did not approve of America's seizing territory far from its shores, but William, who agonized over the decision, finally approved the takeover.

Below: This campaign poster promoted presidential candidate William McKinley with Ida and his mother, Nancy Allison McKinley.

Planning for the Future

One of Ida's happiest moments came toward the end of the president's first term: In the summer of 1899, William surprised her with the news that he had repurchased the house they had lived in as a young couple on North Market Street in Canton. He had bought the residence outright for $14,500. They spent considerable time making plans for the house they would live in after leaving Washington, referring to the coming days as a second honeymoon. Despite the tragedies that transpired there in the earlier years, the McKinleys were determined to create the home of their dreams, a home in which they would share every moment of their love for, and with, family and friends.

Mr. and Mrs. McKinley were looking forward to leading a quiet life at North Market by themselves, free from public demands and the pressures of the world. William confided to his personal secretary, George Cortelyou, "Now I shall have a home, what I have wanted for so long;

a home I can go to. If I have a place like that I can get away any time, and could take you with all the help we need…we could transact all the executive business there." Indeed, President McKinley was hopeful for an "uninterrupted companionship" as his shared dream with Ida for their future in the North Market home. William told Cortelyou, "Some of the tenderest memories of my life are centered there, and some of the saddest. I am as happy as a child to have it back. It's a fine old place."

Although very much an invalid, Ida was hardly incapacitated. She took short outings alone to New York and Baltimore, and longer trips throughout the country with her husband. In spite of her poor health, Ida often accompanied her husband on his trips whenever possible, including journeys to New Orleans, Boston, New York, Los Angeles, and San Antonio, Texas. In the summer of 1901, William left on a victorious six-week tour across the American continent. Mingling freely with the crowds, he was the last chief executive to do so. "If it is in the mind and heart of anybody to kill me, he will do so," he said, "for plenty of opportunity will be offered him." William McKinley traveled more than any American president up until that time, and he was on the road again as he and his entourage headed for Buffalo, New York, and the Pan-American Exposition in early September 1901.

When the Pan-American Exposition opened in 1901, William McKinley, like any other American, wanted to see the wonders at the fair that he read about in the daily newspapers. He liked world's fairs. They were, he said, "the timekeepers of progress. They record the world's advancement." He had been to the Columbian Exposition in Chicago in 1893, and the Cotton States Exposition in Atlanta two years later. It was an unprecedented time of growth and prosperity in the United States, the beginning of a new century. And William was to be the president to guide the country into its new millennium.

William had hoped to be in Buffalo, then the eighth largest city in the country, for the opening of the exposition in May. However, Ida was ill, and because he didn't travel without her, he postponed the trip. In his place he sent the vice president, Theodore Roosevelt. Upon Roosevelt's return to Washington, William pressed Roosevelt for details, and he raved about it. During the months prior to the presidential visit to the exposition, the newspapers followed the chronically "delicate health" of Ida, because her husband, who loved her greatly and doted on her, would not make the trip unless she was in good health. When the time came to leave, Ida appeared well enough to accompany him, but in reality she did not want to leave their home in Canton, where they were spending the summer.

On September 4, 1901, the First Family arrived in Buffalo by special train from Canton. Little did the McKinleys know that this would be their last trip together. As the train pulled into the Terrace Railroad Station overlooking Lake Erie, it was greeted by a twenty-one-gun salute. In his eagerness to honor this most popular president, the cannoneer—a coast guard officer and veteran of William's Civil War

Above: Although officially described as "an invalid," Ida had more energy than the description suggested. An epileptic, she didn't always show the symptoms of her poor health.

Below: She wasn't an activist, but Ida showed an interest in "womanly independence," and the First Family's visit to Mount Holyoke, a woman's college, was an important one for her.

Secret Service

The Secret Service was established in 1865 to safeguard the nation's currency, and it is best known as the agency responsible for protecting the president. It took on this duty in 1901, after the assassination of William McKinley. Prior to Theodore Roosevelt's administration, presidential safety was an ad hoc mix of private security, local officers, and presidential confidants.

Although two presidents had been assassinated before William McKinley, the White House was still a public place with well-wishers and the curious regularly streaming through three times a week. Only one room on the first floor was off-limits, and William routinely shook hands with visitors. Yet his secretary was concerned by the hate mail that flooded in every day. Some of the messages claimed that "infernal machines" had been planted near the White House. The Intelligence Bureau of the Treasury—the Secret Service—too busy concentrating on foiling counterfeiters and ferreting out Spanish spies, posted no guards at the White House at night. And the suggestion for a presidential bodyguard was laughed at.

Although not yet a year into his second term as president, William McKinley was engaged in a running battle with the Secret Service. Despite proven threats, no matter how hard they argued, he refused to allow his guard to be increased or to change his schedule of appearances.

When William was assassinated in Buffalo, New York, the Secret Service formally became the protector of the president. Today, the Secret Service's mission statement says it is "mandated by statute and executive order to carry out two significant missions: protection and criminal investigations. The Secret Service protects the President and Vice President, their families, heads of state, and other designated individuals."

regiment—had placed the cannon so close to the railroad tracks that when the salvo began, the presidential car shook violently. Although there were no injuries and only minimal damage was done to the train, the presidential party was worried about Mrs. McKinley, who was greatly unhinged by the incident.

Several minutes later, the train pulled into a special platform built at one of the entrances to the exposition grounds. Wearing a black frock coat and a high, black silk hat, President McKinley, his right arm tightly around his wife's waist, stepped from the train. Following a short and ceremonious greeting by John Milburn, the head of the exposition's board of directors, President and Mrs. McKinley, watched by a crowd of more than 60,000, made a quick tour of the exposition grounds. The McKinleys were then driven to the Milburns' home on Delaware Avenue, about one mile south of the exposition. They were scheduled to return to the exposition the next day.

The Milburns were accustomed to entertaining important visitors. Earlier that summer the Roosevelts had stayed with them, as had the French ambassador and his family. But clearly the president was different, and in anticipation of the visit Milburn had completely renovated his large wooden home. The Milburns were concerned about their guests—not the president, an affable, easygoing man who liked nothing more than smoking a cigar (he smoked over twenty per day)—but rather Mrs. McKinley. For in spite of the president's best efforts to hide it from the public (and even his best friends), the Milburns knew, as did the rest of the country, about the First Lady's condition. Although it was not openly discussed, there were constant references in the press to her fortitude, her ability to withstand the rigors of being the nation's First Lady, and endless paeans to the president, whose solicitude of his sickly wife embodied, it was said, the most admirable of husbandly virtues.

But because of Ida's illness, the Milburns were not permitted to entertain as lavishly as they would have liked. There wasn't much time, anyway, because the president wanted to see as much of the exposition as possible, and the wonders it displayed. Of special interest to the president were the Ohio Statehood Building and the Electric Building, ringed by hundreds of illuminated incandescent lights.

The next day, Thursday, September 5, 1901, President William McKinley made his last public appearance at the exposition. By the early morning, the expo was already full of people and there was a feeling of festive excitement building for the president's speech. Of the more than 116,000 people who would go through the turnstiles that day, more than 50,000 would hear William's speech that same afternoon. The exhibitions and sidewalks were full to capacity as at least six different bands played their music to the milling crowds. The president, as always, was eager to go out into the multitude, shaking hands and greeting people face-to-face, although he was strongly discouraged to make such close-up contact.

The president's speech was an enormous success. He spoke of the tremendous prosperity of the nation and its limitless potential for the future. He went on to include topics ranging from the progress of man, the Spanish-American War, and the continuance of industrial growth, which the Pan-Am helped to demonstrate. In attendance that day was Leon Czolgosz (pronounced "cholgosh"), a Detroit-born anarchist of Polish parents, who was prevented by Secret Service agents from approaching the stage where William was speaking.

The president eventually went on a tour of the expo like any other visitor. As he strolled through the various displays, he came within yards of Czolgosz, who was biding his time for a good opportunity. But it was not to be. "I was close to the President when he got to the grounds, but was afraid to attempt the assassination because there were so many men in the bodyguard that watched him. I was not afraid of them…but afraid that I might be seized and that my chance would be gone forever!" *The New York Times* later reported.

The Board of Women Managers of the exposition planned a special luncheon in Ida's honor on September 5. However, Ida chose to return to the Milburn home with her husband without notifying the hosts. They were left to discover this fact and communicate it to the assembled guests in the Women's Building on the exposition grounds.

Below: Ida's health forced a postponement of the president's scheduled appearance at the Pan-American Exposition in Buffalo, New York.

The President's Last Day

The next day, September 6, President McKinley arrived at the exposition at about 3:30 P.M. Complaining of fatigue, Ida took a carriage back to the Milburn house to rest, and the president proceeded to the exposition, where he was scheduled to meet the thousands of people who, in spite of the oppressive heat, were waiting at the Temple of Music.

Once in the hall, the president took his position under a bower of palms, and to his left was Milburn, to his right secretary Cortelyou, and opposite them Secret Service operatives. Along the aisle down which the public must pass were numerous soldiers and guards from the exposition police, but the security detail was arranged to accommodate the well-wishers. It was said that the president was never in a better mood; he was smiling from the moment he stepped into the building, and when he announced that he was ready for the doors to be thrown open, he appeared as though the coming onslaught of handshaking was to be a long-anticipated pleasure.

At 4:00 P.M. the doors to the auditorium were opened and the public flooded in. It was extremely hot in the room—over ninety degrees. William stood in the center of the room as the crowd, in single file, moved past him, shaking hands as they passed. He was sporting a pink carnation in his lapel (when he received guests at the White House, he often wore a pink carnation and presented it as a gift to visitors). At the auditorium that day, just seconds before he was shot, William had removed his carnation and given it to a young girl in the crowd. (After his death, Ohio adopted it as their state flower.)

One of the first to have hurried forward in the reception line was Leon

Below: Even after the president was shot, he instructed his aides on how to break the news to Ida. To everyone's surprise, she took the news calmly and stayed by his side until he died eight days later.

Czolgosz. When he had finally reached the president, Czolgosz did not look into William's face. As the smiling president reached out to take the man's right hand, Czolgosz extended his left hand, pressed it against the president's chest, and fired a gun he was concealing under a handkerchief. At precisely 4:07 P.M. while the organ played a Bach sonata, the president's assassin fired twice before he was tackled and driven to the ground. One bullet bounced harmlessly off a button, the other pierced the president's stomach, went through his colon and kidney, and lodged in the muscles of his back. Czolgosz shouted, "I've done my duty," then the guards wrestled him to the ground and began pounding him in the face. William stopped their assault with the words, "Be easy with him, boys."

Within minutes, an electric-powered ambulance arrived to remove William from the scene. The physical damage to his organs alone was not enough to cause death, but the infection caused by the path of the bullet and the dubious quality of the medical care given to the president would take its toll. Ironically, had the new medical tool of X-rays (which were introduced at the Pan-American Exposition) been available, they would have helped save the dying president. Moreover, if a series of medical mistakes had not been made, his injuries (which developed into gangrene) may not have been fatal.

While Ida was not present when her husband was shot, she stayed by his side virtually the entire time during his struggle to recover. William, even in his critical condition, was concerned for Ida's well-being and hoped that she would receive the proper care.

For a week, President McKinley clung to life, although he drifted in and out of consciousness. Even as his condition worsened, the public was kept optimistic by false reports. A congressman from Buffalo told a crowd of gullible reporters, "It is not true that the physicians are without hope or that those gathered in the house are despondent. Everybody about the house is hopeful."

Early in the evening on September 13, the administration of oxygen brought William back from a comatose condition. "Mrs. McKinley," he slowly whispered, and then closed his eyes in pain. It was apparent to everyone whom he knew that the end was near; the time had come to say his good-byes. When Ida was seated, she took her husband's hand, and they sat in silence for a few moments before the president whispered, "Goodbye, all; good-bye. It is God's way. His will be done." These were the last words William McKinley spoke.

Ida, sobbing pitifully, stood and slowly released her husband's hands and disappeared into her own room. As the evening continued, the president's pulse grew fainter and fainter. At 2:16 A.M., Dr. Rixey put his finger on the president's neck, tears streaming down his face. He slowly raised his head and turned to face the others in the room. "It is over," he said. "The president is no more."

Word of the president's death spread, and the world poured forth thousands of messages of regret, almost overwhelming Ida. Officials had a difficult time reaching Theodore Roosevelt, who was on a hunting exhibition in the Adirondack wilderness. The last he had heard, William was shot but would recover, so it was a shock to discover that he was now president.

The world was in a state of mourning. Nowhere was the pain of Williams's death felt more sharply than in Buffalo, where the funeral was held in the Milburn home. Before the ceremony, Ida was led into the chamber by her physician, and she sat alone with her husband, the man who had supported

Above: A portrait of the assassin, Leon F. Czolgosz, after his arrest for shooting President McKinley.

> "My wife, be careful…how you tell her. Oh, be careful!"
>
> —President William McKinley, after being shot, on how the news should be broken to his wife

Above: Ida went through the ordeal of her husband's funeral and burial without having a single seizure. She never had another, in fact, during the six years she lived afterward.

and comforted her through all the years of wedded life. Her support was gone, but she had not broken down. While other political dignitaries paid their last respects to William, Ida sat alone at the head of the stairs, a wan, white figure in a black gown, listening to every spoken word, to hymns and prayers.

On the morning of September 16, 1901, President McKinley left Buffalo the same way he had arrived—by train. The president's body proceeded to Washington D.C., for two days. His coffin would rest in the White House East Room during a period of intense national mourning. As America's first modern president, he had presided over an era of great international expansion. The new president, Theodore Roosevelt, spoke for the nation when he called him "the most widely loved man in all the United States." Finally, on September 18, William McKinley was buried at Westlawn Cemetery in Canton, Ohio, near his two small children. The public cry for swift justice was loud and intense. The murder trial for the death of the president started barely more than a week after he breathed his last. On October 29, 1901—less than two months after he killed President McKinley—the assassin died in the electric chair.

> *"All a man can hope for during his lifetime [is] to set an example, and, when he's dead, to be an inspiration for history."*
>
> —*William McKinley on his legacy*

Her Final Years

With the First Lady being utterly dependent on the president, many believed Ida would be unable to cope with the assassination of her husband. Yet she surprised almost everyone by her strength and courage. For the eight days that William lingered following the attack, Ida remained at his side, comforting and nursing him. After his death, the new widow accompanied his coffin from Buffalo, the site of the shooting, to Washington, D.C., and attended the funeral without being medicated. The assassination, tragic though it was, appeared to have given Ida the strength to live more independently than when William was attending to her every whim. Having already faced the loss of both of her children, Ida seemed to have finally found some inner resolve. Her last years were spent alone and in seclusion in her hometown of Canton, Ohio, with her sister taking care of her in the North Market Street home William had repurchased for her. That second honeymoon had never come.

Below: During her last years, Ida appeared to be a new woman. She was partial to wearing egret feathers, which became her trademark, much to the dismay of the Audubon Society.

Though she received President Roosevelt when he came to town, she saw very few people except for her sister and her nieces and nephews. She visited her husband's grave almost daily, and spent her last days praying to be at her husband's side.

Ida Saxton McKinley died on May 26, 1907. Her own untimely death occurred just four months before a new mausoleum, now known as the McKinley National Memorial, was dedicated to her husband on September

30, 1907. After the formal dedication of the monument, William McKinley, his wife, Ida, and their two daughters, Katie and Ida, were moved from their respective burial sites in the adjacent Westlawn Cemetery to be interred within the monument.

If the record Ida left is not totally successful, one can still admire both her courage and her determination. Her legacy was not one of success, but one of doing the best job she could while battling crippling and debilitating illnesses.

Below: Ida and William and their two daughters are buried in Canton, Ohio, not far from the president's former home, which was torn down some years ago to build a hospital.

Visiting McKinley Landmarks in Ohio

The McKinley Museum is part of the National McKinley Birthplace Memorial located in Niles, Ohio. It consists of memorabilia from President William McKinley's early life in Niles; Civil War and Spanish-American War artifacts; campaign materials; and presidential items. The memorial is in the center of a complex with two wings. One wing is the McKinley Library, while the other wing houses the museum and an auditorium. The memorial is located at 40 North Main Street, Niles, Ohio 44446. For more information, call 330-652-1704.

The gravesite, McKinley National Memorial, located in Canton, Ohio, is the final resting place of the president and Ida. It is located adjacent to Westlawn Cemetery, where William was placed in a temporary vault near his two baby daughters. Eight years later, a massive mausoleum was constructed and dedicated by President Theodore Roosevelt. William and the children were exhumed and reinterred inside the circular interior. The president was placed in a black polished sarcophagus, one of a pair set on marble pedestals; when Ida died she was buried here. The children are entombed within the rear wall. The First Ladies' National Historic Site is located in the Saxton McKinley House, 331 South Market Avenue, Canton, Ohio 44702. The telephone number is 330-452-0876.

The National First Ladies' Library, in the newly designated First Ladies' National Historic Site, is found in a building with significance as the only residence with direct historical ties to President William McKinley remaining in his hometown of Canton. It was the family home of Ida, and he and his wife lived in the house between 1878 and 1891. The Saxton McKinley House breathes new life as the first-ever facility dedicated to documenting the lives and accomplishments of America's forty-one First Ladies and other important American women in history. The public rooms of the house have been restored to their original splendor, complete with ornate historical wallpaper and period furniture. Great care has been taken to ensure that all design elements, including patterns of wallpaper, carpets, and area rugs, are authentic.

On the second floor is Ida Saxton McKinley's sitting room and adjacent bedroom. The wallpaper for these rooms was hand-screened by Scalamandré to historically represent the wall coverings in favorite rooms at Ida Saxton McKinley's North Market Street residence, according to two original pictures of those rooms.

Edith Roosevelt

Young Edie

The young mother shepherded her four children through the railroad station in Jersey City, New Jersey, toward the train that would take them to Washington, D.C. She was the object of intense interest by everyone in the train station. Men took off their hats and women bowed in respect. The woman, dressed in black and heavily veiled and escorted by the stationmaster to a private car awaiting the family, was forty-year-old Edith Roosevelt. She was on her way to Washington to assume her duties as First Lady of the United States. Her husband, Theodore, had become president two days earlier following the assassination in Buffalo of President William McKinley.

Edith Kermit Carow was born on August 6, 1861, at the home of her maternal grandparents in Norwich, Connecticut. Her father, Charles Carow, came from a distinguished family that traced its origins to France, where the family name was spelled "Quereaus." The Quereaus were Huguenots who, because of persecution at the hands of Catholics, had migrated to the New World in the 1600s, where they anglicized the spelling of their name to "Carow." Edith's mother, Gertrude Tyler, was a descendant of an English family that had also migrated to the Americas in the late 1600s.

Edith was the second child born to Charles and Gertrude Carow. Their first, a boy, was born in 1860 but died a few months later. Another girl, Emily, was born in 1865. The young family moved out of the Tyler home in Connecticut in 1864 and set up their own residence in a house on Livingston Street in lower Manhattan, just off Union Square. Nearby was the mansion of Cornelius Van Schaak Roosevelt. The Roosevelts were a large and prosperous family with branches scattered throughout New York State. Soon, Edith became friendly with Corinne Roosevelt, the youngest grandchild of Cornelius Roosevelt and the sister of Theodore Roosevelt. Through her friendship with Corinne, Edith was a frequent visitor at the Roosevelt home, and she soon became friends with Theodore as well, who was nicknamed Teedie. He called her Edie, and they often played together. One of Edith's earliest memories was as a three-year-old, in April 1865, standing in the window of an upper floor of Cornelius Roosevelt's mansion with Theodore at her side, looking out onto Union Square as the funeral procession of the assassinated president Abraham Lincoln went by. Lincoln's body was on a lengthy trip back to his home in Springfield, Illinois,

---

Edith Kermit Carow Roosevelt

Born
August 6, 1861,
Norwich, Connecticut

Parents
Charles Carow and
Gertrude Tyler

Marriage
December 2, 1886, to
Theodore Roosevelt
(1858-1919)

Children
Theodore, Jr.
(1887-1944); Kermit
(1889-1943); Ethel Carow
(1891-1977); Archibald
Bulloch (1894-1979);
Quentin (1897-1918);
stepdaughter Alice Lee
Roosevelt Longworth
(1884-1980)

Died
September 30, 1948,
Oyster Bay, New York

Above: Theodore Roosevelt's father, also named Theodore Roosevelt, had a summer home at Oyster Bay, Long Island; in this photo he sits with his wife on the verandah. A young Edith Carow and the Roosevelts' daughter Corinne are on the lawn.

Below: Edith predicted that as First Lady, she would "meekly listen" to her husband's official business "as becomes our sex and position."

and was being taken to major cities for Americans to pay respects to their late president.

Shortly thereafter, Theodore Roosevelt, Sr., the father of Teedie and Corinne, bought a house at 28 East 20th Street in Manhattan, about six blocks north of Cornelius Roosevelt's home. When Teedie's mother, Martha (Mittie) Bulloch Roosevelt, noticed how close the friendship was between her son and Edie, she invited the young girl to join the Roosevelt children for tutoring in the house on 20th Street. There, in the second-floor nursery, the children were taught their lessons by Anna Bulloch Gracie, Mittie's sister. Edie loved to read and would often spend time reading aloud to Teedie. Theodore, Sr., was a great believer in physical fitness, and he converted a spare bedroom into an open-air space devoted to exercise. Teedie was severely asthmatic and frail, and his younger brother, Elliott, was often ill with migraine headaches. Their sister Bamie was also a sickly child who was born with a spinal defect. Father Theodore encouraged vigorous exercise for all his children, and over the years, Teedie conquered his physical disabilities and grew into a strong, self-assured young man. Edie, however, had always enjoyed good health and found no need to participate in the exercise regimens at the Roosevelt home. She would go off by herself and read a book.

Even in these young years, before she was ten years old, Edie was a serious, self-possessed child. The happiness Edie enjoyed in the Roosevelt family was not found in her own. In the 1860s, her father's shipping business, Kermit & Carow, began to fail. As it did, her father's drinking increased, and the combination of hard economic realities and a drunken father created heartbreaking tension within the family. They were forced to move often, and after 1867 they never owned a home of their own. As an older woman, Edith took great pains to avoid any discussion of her early childhood.

Childhood Sadness

The stigma of her father's alcoholism and poverty was deeply distressing to Edith, and she avoided talking or writing about those years or allowing anyone else to learn about them. Like many people of her time, she chose to repress unpleasant family memories. But, when Edith was sixteen, she wrote poetry to deal with her pain:

"This my lonely sanctum is; / There I go / When my heart all worn by grief / Sinketh low / Where my baseless hopes do lie / There to find my peace, go I, / Sad and slow."

—Poem written by Edith Carow at age sixteen

Her acceptance in the Roosevelt family was a source of great happiness, and Edie's mother was grateful that the Roosevelt brood accepted her daughter as one of their own. In 1869, the Roosevelts went off for months on a European tour. It was time to close the school and for the children to go on to the next level of their education. Edie and Teedie corresponded frequently over the months, as the young man told of his adventures in Europe and expressed a desire to return home as soon as possible.

In the fall of 1871, Edith's parents enrolled her at Miss Comstock's School, an exclusive finishing school for young ladies located in two brownstones on West 40th Street. The owner of the school, Louise Comstock, was a stern headmistress who believed that well-to-do young women needed a foundation in life centered on religion, morals, and good conduct. All her lessons were based on inspirational themes designed to instill these virtues. Edith's favorite subject was English literature, an interest that remained with her throughout her life. She also developed a passion for music, and although she played no instrument, Edith loved going to concerts and operas. But perhaps the most important influence Miss Comstock had on Edith was to strengthen her deep moral and religious sense.

By the early 1870s, the Roosevelts had moved to a larger town house on West 57th Street in Manhattan. Theodore and his family spent a good part of 1872 in Europe, and when they returned later in the year, Edith resumed her friendship with Theodore, who was now a strong, handsome, and vigorous young man of fourteen. Their friendship continued throughout their teenage years, often at the Roosevelt summerhouse in Oyster Bay, Long Island. In February 1878, Theodore Roosevelt, Sr., died at the age of forty-six. The loss of his father was devastating to young Theodore, by that time a student at Harvard University. Later that year, something happened between Edith and Theodore that derailed their relationship. Neither ever spoke or wrote about it, but some have speculated that Theodore proposed to Edith and that she, for whatever mysterious reason, turned him down. Others believe that that some argument occurred that estranged them.

Whatever the cause, Theodore started to court other young women in Massachusetts, and the name Alice Hathaway Lee began to appear in his letters after 1878. Alice Lee was a beautiful, delicate young woman from a well-to-do family. Theodore proposed to her, and she accepted. Members of the Roosevelt family assumed Edith must have been deeply upset by the news, but if she was, she never showed it. In New York she hosted a dinner for Theodore, and when he and Alice Lee were married in October 1880, Edith went to Massachusetts

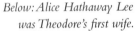

Below: Alice Hathaway Lee was Theodore's first wife.

Edith called her future husband Theodore, and she referred to him by that name throughout their marriage. He was never known as Teddy; his family nickname was Teedie.

to attend the wedding and, in the words of another guest, "danced the soles of her feet off" at the reception. Edith, true to character, never showed her disappointment.

Edith and the new Mr. and Mrs. Roosevelt moved in the same social circles in New York City and often came into contact in the years after the wedding. Everyone seemed to love Alice, but the young woman sensed—and often commented to people—that Edith did not like her. She was mystified as to why she seemed unable to penetrate Edith's cool and distant exterior. They spent time together on the Jersey shore and they also attended Corinne's party when she was formally introduced to society. For Edith, however, there was no coming-out party. During the early 1880s, her father's financial situation worsened. As his fortunes waned, his alcoholism grew more severe. Her family's difficulties made Edith a less attractive marital prospect, and she seemed destined to spend her life as an "old maid."

On March 17, 1883, Charles Carow died. He was only in his fifties, but years of alcohol abuse had finally taken its toll. Edith preferred to remember the good parts about her father: his love of books and nature, which he had passed along to her; his teaching her how to ride horseback; going to the theater together. Alice Lee Roosevelt attended the funeral, but Theodore was unable to do so. He was in Albany: His political career had taken off in the fall of 1881, when he was elected to the New York State Assembly at the age of twenty-three.

But Theodore Roosevelt's life was about to be turned upside down. By the spring of 1883, Alice was pregnant with their first child. As Alice's pregnancy progressed, Theodore divided his time between New York City and Albany, and he looked forward to being a father. Then, on February 14, 1884, disaster struck. At 3:00 A.M. in the house on 57th Street, Theodore's mother died of typhoid fever at the age of forty-nine. Theodore had been summoned from Albany and arrived just a few hours before his mother died. Upstairs, Alice was about to give birth, but she, too, was mortally ill. After his mother died, Theodore climbed the stairs and resumed his vigil at Alice's bedside. She had given birth to a healthy baby girl but was dying of Bright's disease, a kidney ailment. Without regaining consciousness, Alice Roosevelt died at 2:00 P.M., scarcely eleven hours after his mother's death.

Of course, losing both mother and wife in a single day was an almost unbearable tragedy, and Theodore coped by running away and by shutting it out of his memory. For the remainder of his life, he would never discuss Alice or her death, even with close members of his family. His daughter, who was named Alice Lee, never once heard her father speak about her mother. Shortly after Alice Lee died, baby Alice was given over to the care of Theodore's sister Bamie. Theodore then left for the Dakota Territory (the future states of North and South Dakota), where he bought land and hoped to open a new chapter in his life.

> "Edith always seemed deeply detached from the external accidents of life. Her warmth and passion lay far beneath the surface."
>
> —A friend of Edith's commenting on her character

He decided not to run for reelection to the New York Assembly. Instead, he would pursue the life of a rancher and would write books about the West. His lengthy absences from New York meant he had little to do with the raising of his daughter.

From time to time Theodore returned to New York to visit little Alice and to find out what was going on in the Republican party; although he lived in the Dakota Territory, he really never lost his interest in New York politics. During these visits, he and Edith made strenuous efforts to avoid each other. If he went to visit Bamie or Corinne, Edith made sure she was not there. They avoided being at the same social events. Perhaps the memories of their failed romance were still too painful, especially in light of Alice's death. Theodore had also said that he believed a man should marry only once in life. If his wife died, he should honor her memory by not taking a new wife. These were the brave and idealistic assertions of a young man who had suffered a terrible tragedy. Perhaps Theodore sensed that if he and Edith met again, their relationship would be rekindled.

The Second Mrs. Roosevelt

The ballet of avoidance worked for a year and a half. Then one day in September 1885, Theodore arrived at Bamie's home for a visit. Edith had been there earlier in the day and was supposed to have left before he arrived. But she hadn't, and they met on the staircase. They chatted, and soon they began seeing each other. Two months later, on November 17, 1885, he proposed marriage. She accepted, as she knew she would. Some of their friends had always believed that after Theodore's marriage to Alice, Edith decided to simply wait—she knew that one day she would marry Theodore Roosevelt. In later years, Edith, in a characteristically blunt moment, would say that had Theodore's marriage to Alice lasted, he would have been "bored to death."

To some, Theodore and Edith may have seemed an unlikely couple. He was outgoing and filled with passion and enthusiasm. A dynamo that never seemed to sit still, he could be loud and exhausting. In contrast, Edith was reserved and distant. While he reached out as a politician to shake every hand in sight, she avoided human contact by hiding her hands in a muff or a bouquet of flowers. While he never stopped talking, she sat back, eyes downcast, and rarely uttered a word, except perhaps to urge him, gently, to be quiet for a moment. They adored each other. Their character traits, seemingly so opposite, were a bond that held them together. He placed her on a pedestal, like a goddess. She regarded him, at times, as another child—a loving one, but a big baby nonetheless.

Their marriage did not take place immediately. Theodore had decisions to make: Should he be a rancher, write books, or enter politics? Edith, too, had decisions and responsibilities facing her. Her mother and sister had decided to live in Europe, and they were counting on Edith to help them make the move. In the spring of 1886, Edith went with her family to Europe, and Theodore headed back to the Dakota Territory to contemplate his future. Being a rancher

Above: Edith was fashionable but not fashion-conscious. "The wife of the President, it is said, dresses on four hundred dollars a year," sniffed a society matron, "and she looks it."

Theodore and Edith Roosevelt were prolific readers all their lives. He sometimes read two books a day. Although not formally educated at a university, she read widely in English literature.

was exciting, and writing was something he could always do; but Theodore's real passion was politics—precisely in what role, he did not know, although a colleague at his ranch predicted he would one day be president of the United States. Theodore did not disagree, apparently thinking it a distinct possibility.

In July 1886 Theodore returned to New York to prepare for his wedding. But then, in one of those sudden turns that seemed to mark his political life, the Republican party nominated him to run for mayor of New York. He was twenty-eight years old and had no possibility of winning, but he accepted the nomination because he felt it was his duty to answer the call of his party—and because he loved being in a political contest. He came in third in a three-way race, but he was not disappointed, because he had never expected to win.

The mayoral diversion aside, he and Bamie sailed for England a few days after the election. On December 2, 1886, Theodore and Edith were married in St. George's Church, Hanover Square, in London. Theodore's friend Cecil Spring-Rice (who would later serve as the British ambassador to the United States) was the best man, and Edith's sister, Emily, was the maid of honor. The newlyweds left for a honeymoon on the continent. They visited the south of France and stopped in on Edith's mother, who with Emily had settled in Italy, later returning to the United States in the spring of 1887.

One of the first issues the new couple had to confront was what to do with little Alice. Theodore understood that taking Alice from Bamie would be wrenching for both of them—Alice knew no mother other than Bamie, and she scarcely knew her father. But Edith made it clear that she would consider Theodore's child as her own. She welcomed Alice as her daughter and always attempted to treat her as she would her own.

One of Edith's first tasks was to put her stamp on Sagamore Hill—a house that had been built for Alice Lee and would now be presided over by Edith. She wasted no time in bringing in her own family furniture and setting up her own household. Edith gave birth to her first child, a son named Theodore Roosevelt, Jr., at Sagamore Hill on September 13, 1887. She had expected her mother and sister to come from Europe to help her at the birth, but her mother became ill and did not want to travel. As a replacement for her own family, Edith asked Mary Ledwith, a longtime Carow family servant who would follow Theodore and Edith to the White House, to assist her. Significantly, she did not ask Bamie—she wanted to keep a certain distance from Theodore's siblings, probably in an effort to demonstrate that she was now mistress of her

Below: Young Theodore was a rancher and a hunter.

family and capable of making her own choices. It was an unmistakable sign, the kind of distancing that Edith had no trouble with as a young woman and as mistress of the White House.

Other children followed on the heels of Ted, as he was called. Kermit, a second son, was born in 1889. A daughter, Ethel, came in 1891, and Archibald was born in Washington in 1894. Quentin, Edith and Theodore's last son, was born in 1897, in Washington. Edith's five children referred to their stepsister Alice as Auntie Sister, a whimsical nickname that stuck throughout their long lives. Edith had a number of miscarriages over the years, but she and Theodore had produced a large and vibrant family—one that would capture the imagination of the American public.

Washington Years, 1889-95

In November 1888, the Republican presidential candidate, Benjamin Harrison, defeated the incumbent president, Grover Cleveland. As a reward for campaigning for Harrison, Theodore received an appointment as a member of the Civil Service Commission, and the family moved to Washington, D.C.

Theodore and Edith found a small house on Jefferson Place in Washington. Although nowhere near the size of Sagamore Hill, it was adequate as a part-time residence, since during the summer, Edith and the children returned to Oyster Bay. Edith enjoyed the social scene in Washington. She got to know the great writer Henry Adams, a descendant of the presidents John Adams and John Quincy Adams, and he in turn adored her. A literary and social set formed around Adams, and Edith was one of its most enthusiastic members. Through Adams, she met a universe of fascinating people in the arts and in politics. She also made friends on her own with many political wives whose husbands were Theodore's colleagues. The Roosevelts entertained frequently, and their dinner parties were usually populated with writers and philosophers from the United States and Europe.

These early Washington years were filled with the responsibilities facing all young parents. As the family grew, Edith created routines that would be maintained even throughout the White House years. One of these rituals was her daily reading to the children. Usually before dinner, Edith would gather her young brood around her for a reading session. Then Theodore would storm in from work and the household erupted into joyful turmoil as father got down on the floor and joined the children in their games—until Edith put an end to the chaos by calling everyone in for dinner.

In 1892, President Benjamin Harrison was defeated for reelection by his predecessor, the Democrat Grover Cleveland. With the change in administrations, Theodore assumed he would be out of a job and that President Cleveland would want to appoint his own men to the Civil Service Commission. Theodore offered his resignation, but Cleveland refused to accept it and asked Theodore to remain on the commission for another two years. Theodore was delighted, as was Edith, who was not ready to leave Washington.

Above: Daughter Ethel (top) and son Quentin (bottom), each in their element enjoying the outdoors.

Above: Edith with two of her children, Ethel and Archie. She gave birth to five in all.

On February 1, 1894, Edith and Theodore were invited to have dinner at the White House with President and Mrs. Cleveland. Throughout the entire Harrison administration—a Republican administration—they had never been invited for a personal visit to the White House, although they had attended many official functions at the presidential mansion. Now they had an up-front view of many of the rooms in the house that they themselves would soon occupy.

In 1894, another electoral opportunity was offered to Theodore. New York Republicans asked him again to run for mayor. Before making a decision, he consulted Edith, who told him that she was opposed to his running for any office. Theodore declined the offer and decided to head to the West for a few weeks. When Edith soon found out that Theodore had desperately wanted to run and was now very depressed, she was filled with remorse. She wrote to Bamie that she was a poor wife for failing to appreciate Theodore's needs. Bamie assured her otherwise, and the crisis passed, but it created a serious rift in the marriage—and it led to a resolution on Edith's part never to stand in Theodore's way when it came to major political decisions.

The next two years, 1894 and 1895, were difficult ones for the family. The children were often sick—including Alice, who had problems with her legs that required Edith to massage them every day. Edith herself was afflicted with frequent migraine headaches and was exhausted much of the time. Theodore worried about her health and urged her to go off for short vacations, which often revived her. On April 25, 1895, Theodore resigned from the Civil Service Commission. Several weeks later, Edith received a letter from her sister. Their mother, Gertrude Carow, had died in Italy on April 27, 1895. Over the years, Edith had become increasingly estranged from her mother. With her mother gone, Edith now worried—even dreaded—that Emily would return to the United States and ask to move in with her. Throughout her life, Edith always felt more comfortable when Emily was at arm's length.

Politics and War, 1895-98

Upon the family's return to New York in the spring of 1895, Theodore was appointed a member of the police commission of the city of New York. The family had use of an empty house owned by Bamie at 689 Madison Avenue, but Edith and the children spent most of their time at Sagamore Hill. Theodore hurled himself into his job as a police commissioner, roaming the streets at night to see that police officers were doing their jobs and making sure that the law against bars being open on Sunday was enforced. Within six months he was so exhausted and tense from overwork that Edith feared he would have a nervous collapse. She decided to spend more time with him in Manhattan, where

"Alice needs someone to laugh and romp with instead of a sober and staid person like me."

—Edith Roosevelt on her stepdaughter, Alice Roosevelt

the children could also take advantage of all the cultural opportunities the city offered. Ted and Alice took dancing lessons, as Edith had done as a child, and Ted enrolled in a public school, the first in his family to do so.

In November 1896, William McKinley of Ohio, the Republican candidate, was elected president. Once again, a Republican administration was installed in Washington, and Theodore was offered the post of assistant secretary of the navy. Edith welcomed the return to the nation's capital in April 1897. She loved the opportunity once again to join Henry Adams's social set and to renew the friendships made in the early 1890s. Theodore, as usual, thrust himself into his new position with manic energy. The secretary of the navy was John D. Long, but, in fact, Theodore, through the force of personality, ran the department. His objective, clearly enunciated on many occasions, was to expand the navy, especially the battleship division, and to make it an appropriate military force for a powerful country.

Shortly after the birth of Quentin in 1897, Edith began to feel ill. At first Theodore thought she might have typhoid fever. When Edith did not improve, everyone became concerned. In February 1898 she was diagnosed with an abdominal abscess, which required surgery and a lengthy recuperation. For Theodore, Edith's illness came on top of a growing international crisis with Spain. On February 15, 1898, the U.S. battleship *Maine* mysteriously exploded in the harbor of Havana, Cuba, killing more than two hundred American sailors. Cuba at that time was a colony of Spain and was seeking independence, which was supported by the United States. Many people in the United States assumed the *Maine* had been sabotaged by the Spanish, and newspapers across the land called for the United States to avenge the *Maine*. "Remember the *Maine*" was the chant for war, and leading the charge was Theodore Roosevelt. President McKinley was more cautious. He was not so certain that the Spanish had blown up the *Maine*, and investigations tend to support the theory that the explosion on the *Maine* was indeed an accident.

McKinley resisted war for two months, but the pressure on him was relentless, and in April 1898 he gave up and asked Congress for a declaration of war. Edith dreaded this moment. She knew that the moment the United States went to war, Theodore would insist on being in the thick of it. And she was right. He was determined to quit his job, join the military, and go off to Cuba to fight the Spanish. His fellow politicians thought he was insane. His close friend Henry Cabot Lodge believed that Theodore's precipitous actions would ruin his political career. Theodore did not care. He had made up his mind, and no one—not even his beloved wife—would stop him. He had, in fact, a fatalistic, almost cold, view of his fate. If he were killed in battle, he pointed out to a friend, his family would be financially well-off.

On May 6, 1898, Theodore resigned as assistant secretary of the navy, went to the Brooks Brothers clothing store, where he purchased a stylish and expensive uniform, and, on May 12,

Below: Quentin and Archie at Sagamore Hill.

Above: Colonel Roosevelt and his Rough Riders were made heroes after their victory at San Juan Hill in the Spanish-American War.

left for San Antonio, Texas, to join his regiment. His unit, the First U.S. Volunteer Cavalry, became known by its popular name, the Rough Riders. After a short period of training, they were shipped to Tampa, where they would set sail for Cuba. Although still recovering from her surgery, Edith took a train to Tampa to spend one night with Theodore before he left for war. It was a welcome but wrenching interlude. After a day together, she returned to New York to wait and to hope for the best.

In July 1898, Theodore's name became known throughout the United States—and became legendary in American military history—when he bravely led a charge against the Spanish at San Juan Hill. This event thrust Theodore Roosevelt into the national limelight and opened up a new world of political opportunity. While awaiting his return from Cuba, Edith noticed an article in *The New York Sun* recommending that the people of New York elect Theodore Roosevelt governor of their state. Edith clipped the article and mailed it to her husband, perhaps as a warning of things to come.

The war with Spain was over in a matter of weeks. With the U.S. victory assured, the Rough Riders were sent back to the United States, landing at Montauk, on the eastern end of Long Island in New York. Edith and the children visited Theodore in camp shortly before he and his fellow soldiers were discharged. By September 1898, he was home in Sagamore Hill, and within one day of his arrival had met with Senator Tom Platt, the most influential Republican in New York State. Theodore was to be nominated for governor.

The Politician's Wife

Theodore Roosevelt accepted the Republican nomination for governor of New York on the flag-decked stage of Carnegie Hall in New York City on October 5, 1898. In the audience was Edith, who was filled with pride when the audience cheered him wildly. Ten days later, he embarked on a cross-state campaign tour by train, accompanied by a contingent of Rough Riders. Edith remained at Sagamore Hill, assisting Theodore's secretary with his mail.

On November 8, 1898, Theodore Roosevelt was elected governor of New York. In December, Edith went by herself to Albany to have a look at the governor's mansion. She was anxious about her reception in the state capital, but she relaxed after meeting people and seeing the mansion, which was large enough to accommodate what she called her "six bunnies."

Inauguration day, January 1, 1899, found most of the family sick with the flu, but Theodore was healthy and full of energy as he bounded to his swearing-in

> *"Under Edith's management, the atmosphere at Sagamore Hill was one of order and harmony except when Ted got too careless with his pet snakes and toads."*
>
> —*Theodore's secretary, 1898, on life with the Roosevelts*

ceremony in the subfreezing Albany temperatures. Edith attended a reception for more than six thousand people, then went to bed, where she spent most of the week as New York's new First Lady.

One of her first projects was to create a gymnasium in the mansion for Theodore. Several other rooms were turned into bedrooms. Old art was replaced, and the house was refurbished and freshened. When her sister offered to come over from Italy to help, Edith told her, bluntly, not to come.

Edith enjoyed being First Lady of New York. She liked living in the large governor's mansion, and she took pleasure in giving numerous large parties for the political elite of the state. The children loved the house, too, with the exception of Alice, who was now a teenager and wanted to be away from home as much as possible. The children's pets were sometimes a problem, as at one reception during which Edith noticed that the odor from the children's dozens of rabbits, hamsters, snakes, and toads had begun to seep into the public rooms.

Edith hoped that Theodore would stand for reelection in 1900. But the Tom Platt Republicans were now through with Theodore. He had been an attractive and unbeatable candidate in 1898, but he was uncontrollable and would not play their brand of politics. They hatched a plan to get him out of New York State by having him nominated for the vice presidency when President McKinley ran for reelection in 1900. Theodore was noncommittal about this prospect, but Edith was opposed. Not only did she not want to leave Albany, but she believed that the vice presidency was a dead end. The last vice president who had been elected president was Martin Van Buren, in 1836.

She would not get her way. The Republican convention was wildly enthusiastic about Theodore. He was still the hero of San Juan Hill. After seeing the enthusiasm of the convention from her box seat, Edith accepted the inevitable. In November, Theodore was elected vice president of the United States. Inauguration day, March 4, 1901, dawned rainy and cool in Washington. Theodore took the oath of office in the Senate chamber, while McKinley was sworn in outdoors on the eastern front of the Capitol. Edith then took the children to a room over a drugstore on 15th Street and Pennsylvania Avenue. She had rented the space so she and the children could have an unobstructed view of the inaugural parade as it wended its way from the Capitol to the White House.

For a man of Theodore's energy, the vice presidency was torture, but it didn't remain that way for long. In September 1901, President McKinley was shot in Buffalo, New York, while on a receiving line at the Pan-American Exposition. Theodore left immediately for Buffalo, while Edith, who was shocked and fearful, remained at their vacation cottage. After a few days, when President McKinley seemed to be improving, Theodore left Buffalo and joined his family in the Adirondack Mountains. A day after his return, however, they received a telegram saying that McKinley had taken a turn for the worse. On the night of September 13, 1901, Theodore was summoned back to Buffalo. He left immediately, boarding a horse-drawn buckboard that clamored

Below: Kermit and his dog, Jack. As an adult, he served in the British and American armies during World War I and World War II.

Above: The Roosevelts were cramped for space in the White House, but daughter Ethel had her own room.

off into the night. The next morning, Edith received a telegram from Theodore. President McKinley had died at 2:15 in the morning, making Theodore the twenty-sixth president of the United States.

Theodore moved into the White House on September 23, and Edith arrived two days later with a cook and two maids in tow. Mamie came as well, to help with the children. Edith was surprised to discover that the White House was not very comfortable for a large family. In the early 1900s, the president's office was located on the same floor as the family quarters. The president and his staff occupied half the second floor, and there simply wasn't enough room. Archie and Quentin had to double up, while Alice, Kermit, and Ethel were each given their own rooms. Ted had no permanent room because he, at the age of fourteen, was now away at school. Edith said that living in the White House was like living "over the family store."

The country had never seen anything like the Roosevelt family. Theodore, ever the political animal, realized that his young and attractive family was a political asset. Stories and pictures appeared in magazines and newspapers across the nation, and in short order, the country was in love with the Roosevelts. How could one not love this family? The pictures of young Archie and Quentin lining up and saluting the White House police force, or of Archie sitting on his pony on the grounds of the White House, were irresistible. And the antics of seventeen-year-old Alice, which sometimes scandalized her parents—such as when she smoked in public—were endlessly fascinating to the press and public.

Edith and Theodore loved the White House. They began each day with breakfast and a walk in the garden. The older boys were away at school, but Edith still continued her tradition of reading to the younger children before dinner. Edith's comment about living over the family store led to action on the part of Congress, which authorized money for a long-overdue restoration. In 1902, the Roosevelts moved out of the White House for a few months as it was renovated. The old greenhouses to the west of the mansion were torn down and a wing of offices, known as the West Wing, was constructed in their place. The West Wing still houses the president's working office, the Oval Office. The former office space on the second floor was given over exclusively to the family quarters, thus providing much-needed space. The 1902 restoration, undertaken

Below: Apprentice Rough Rider Archie Roosevelt.

White House China Collection

After becoming First Lady, Edith Roosevelt discovered that the White House had enough china to serve no more than eighty people at one time—an inadequate amount given the requirement for large state dinners. Edith purchased a 1,320-piece set of white English Wedgwood, which was enough for 120 place settings, and had the plates decorated with the Great Seal of the United States. She also inventoried all china in the White House, thus founding the White House China Collection, which remains on display to this day.

Above: Edith's choice of china for the White House was from the venerable firm of Wedgwood.

under Edith's strong leadership, was one of her most significant achievements as First Lady.

The White House under the Roosevelts became the center of the social season in Washington. Edith, a woman of sophisticated tastes, introduced French cuisine to the menus of state dinners. The number of formal White House dinners also increased. She was a highly organized First Lady. She held weekly meetings with the wives of cabinet officials in which the women discussed issues of the day. Some of the women were not happy with these formal get-togethers, but no one contradicted Edith. Edith also established the tradition of hanging the portraits of First Ladies in the White House. Today, the White House First Ladies portraits constitute one of the most distinguished collections in Washington.

By 1904, the Roosevelts had been in the White House for three years, and it was an election year. Theodore was the obvious favorite for election to a term of his own, but he remained superstitious and thought he might lose. He didn't, and it wasn't even close. He was elected to a term of his own by the largest landslide in history. On election night, he announced that he would not run for another term as president in 1908. Edith was horrified at the announcement, which seemed to be made off-the-cuff. She didn't necessarily want to stay another eight years in the White House, but she felt her husband had needlessly made himself a lame duck on the very night of his election. As it turned out, Edith's political instincts were accurate. Theodore's premature renunciation was a statement he lived to regret for the remainder of his life.

By the second term, the family had settled into regular seasonal routines. Edith and the children spent summers at Sagamore Hill. Theodore would come up from Washington on weekends, and Edith would meet him at the railroad station in

Below: Like everything the Roosevelts did, their White House receptions were lively affairs.

To accommodate the large numbers of guests at White House dinners, Edith Roosevelt used outside caterers rather than relying on the White House kitchen.

Above: The White House wasn't big enough to contain them, and so sometimes Edith staged her official parties on the lawn outside.

Below: The opening of the Panama Canal was a proud moment for Theodore, and he made the most of it.

Oyster Bay. He traveled like any other passenger, on a regularly scheduled Long Island Railroad train. The fall and winter were spent in Washington, where the social season was in full swing. In 1905, Theodore and Edith bought a small cabin in the woods in Albemarle County, in northern Virginia. The retreat, which they named Pine Knot, was an excellent place to get way from Washington. There, they relaxed, read books, and cooked simple meals. Theodore would usually fry some chicken, and Edith would make tea. Their Secret Service protection remained discreetly apart in the woods surrounding the cabin, thus giving the couple a sense of privacy. In 1906, Theodore and Edith journeyed to Panama to witness the construction being done on the Panama Canal. It was the first time a sitting president and his wife had left the country while he was still in office.

The Roosevelt White House years ended on March 4, 1909, when Theodore's hand-chosen successor, William Howard Taft, was sworn in as president as a raging blizzard blanketed Washington with snow. Before the ceremonies, the family assembled on the portico of the White House for one last photograph. Alice commented that they all looked like they were going to a funeral. Ever the mischievous child (even though she was now a twenty-five-year-old married woman), Alice made faces at spectators as her car drove away from the White House. She said she was doing an irreverent imitation of Mrs. Taft's "hippopotamus face." In later years she also claimed that she and her half brothers had planted a voodoo doll on the grounds of the White House to curse the Tafts. The White House would never see a family like this again.

Retirement

Edith was content to go home and preside over Sagamore Hill; but for Theodore, the postpresidential years were difficult. He was an ex-president at fifty, and he missed being at the center of the action. Within a matter of months, Theodore was in the thick of political controversy as he found more and more to criticize about the Taft administration, which he believed had abandoned his reform policies, especially his dedication to conservation. By 1912, he had decided to seek the presidency again. Edith, as usual, was opposed. Ever the voice of realism, she told him, "You will never be president again," but he was not to be stopped. The problem for his candidacy was that the Taft forces controlled the party machinery, and even though Theodore won primaries in the few states that had them, the Taft people were able to manage the convention. Taft was renominated, and, in an impulsive decision, Theodore and his supporters walked out and formed a third party—the Progressive, or Bull Moose party, so nicknamed because Theodore said he felt as healthy and strong as a bull moose.

Roosevelt Family Weddings

Two weddings highlighted the second term of Theodore Roosevelt. In March 1905, Theodore gave away his niece Eleanor at her wedding to Franklin D. Roosevelt, a distant cousin and a member of the branch of the Roosevelts who lived in Hyde Park, New York. Eleanor was the daughter of Theodore's beloved late brother, Elliott, who had died of alcoholism at a young age. Then, in April 1906, Alice was married in the White House to Congressman Nicholas Longworth of Ohio, who was fifteen years her senior. Edith planned the entire wedding, which received saturation coverage by the media. When Alice came to say good-bye after the wedding, a tired and irritated Edith told her she was glad to see her go, that she had been nothing but trouble. Alice, who was amused by her stepmother's bluntness (probably because she knew she was right), went on to an unhappy marriage. Both she and her husband had numerous extramarital affairs, which were widely known throughout Washington and a source of eternal embarrassment to her family.

The Bull Moose campaign split the Republican party and gave the election to the Democrat, Governor Woodrow Wilson of New Jersey. At the beginning of the campaign, Theodore said he did not expect to win but was making the challenge in order to influence the party for the future. In Milwaukee, in October, while leaving for a speech, Theodore was shot in the chest by a would-be assassin. In typical Roosevelt fashion, he went on with his address, his shirt drenched in blood. The bullet had been slowed by the manuscript of his speech, which was in his coat pocket, but it had penetrated the wall of his chest and damaged a rib. Edith was told of the assassination attempt while attending the opera in New York. She left immediately for Milwaukee, where she joined Theodore in the hospital and stayed with him until his release.

Theodore's third-party candidacy severely damaged his credibility in the Republican party. Had he let Taft go down to defeat in 1912, the party may well have turned to him in 1916, and he most likely would have won against Wilson. But he was now anathema to traditional Republicans, who controlled the party, at least in the short run. As he had done before, he consoled himself with a long trip, this time into the Amazon rain forest of Brazil. Once again, Edith was left alone for months as her husband risked his life.

In 1914, Europe was engulfed in World War I. Theodore, unlike President Wilson, was pro-war and wanted the United States to join the conflict on the side of the Allies against the Germans. In April 1917 the United States entered the conflict, and Theodore's boys, now young men, went off to fight. Theodore

Above: "Princess" Alice was the public's favorite of all the Roosevelt children, and her marriage to Nicholas Longworth was not just a wedding, but a full-blown media event.

Below: Edith was the most athletic of the First Ladies, and more at home in casual clothes. But when the occasion called for it, she could be as elegant as any woman she entertained.

Edith Roosevelt was an avid horseback rider who rode in Washington's Rock Creek Park during her White House years.

had always been an advocate of the "manly" virtues of war, but his words came home to haunt him in the most tragic way. In July 1918, his beloved Quentin, only twenty years old and a pilot fighting for the United States in France in World War I, was shot down and killed. Theodore and Edith were shattered. He never recovered from the death of his dear son. Theodore's health, severely compromised by his trip to Brazil and by his obesity and premature hardening of the arteries, made Theodore an old man at age sixty.

Despite his physical infirmities, he still looked forward to participating in politics, and many Republicans believed he would be the nominee in 1920. Even Edith thought it a possibility. But it was not to be. On the wintry afternoon of January 5, 1919, Theodore sat by a window in Sagamore Hill looking out at the twilight on Long Island Sound. He was in a reflective mood and told Edith now much he loved Sagamore Hill. That night, he retired about 9:00 P.M., tended by his longtime valet. Edith looked in about midnight and made sure not to wake him—he was sleeping soundly. But a few hours later, the valet came to her room and said that Theodore had stopped breathing. She rushed to his room, shook his shoulder and called out, "Theodore, darling!" But he was dead. He was sixty years old.

Theodore Roosevelt's funeral was held on January 8. Following tradition, Edith remained at home and read the simple service that was being held in Christ Church in Oyster Bay. Theodore was buried in Young's Cemetery in Oyster Bay. Among the spectators was former president Taft, who sobbed openly at the grave of the man who had been his friend and who had helped end his presidency in 1912.

Below: A very rare quiet moment in the lives of the Roosevelt family. They were constantly in motion and on the go.

Widowhood and Final Years

Edith, now a fifty-eight-year-old widow, adjusted slowly to Theodore's death. She was by that time a grandmother and enjoyed the company of her large family, but she still relished her times alone. There were frequent trips to Europe, but most of her days were spent at Sagamore Hill and at a house she purchased in Connecticut.

In 1932, she reentered the political arena briefly to campaign *against* another Roosevelt. Franklin D. Roosevelt had been nominated by the Democratic party for president. Edith loved Eleanor and was fond of Franklin, but there was bad blood since the early 1920s, when Eleanor had campaigned against Ted when he ran as the Republican candidate for governor of New York. Edith had wanted Ted to follow in his father's footsteps, but when he lost the 1924 race for governor, his career in active politics ended. Campaigning against Franklin was one way of getting back at the Hyde Park Roosevelts. In reality, however, Edith and the Sagamore Hill Roosevelts believed there was only *one* President Roosevelt, and that was Theodore.

They never accepted Franklin as president, even though in fact, many of his policies were exactly the same as Theodore's later stands on issues.

Franklin went on to be elected president four times, and in many ways eclipsed Theodore. Edith eventually came to like Franklin—even though she refused to vote for him—and she outlived him. Before her own end, however, she suffered two more terrible tragedies. In 1943, in the midst of World War II, her beloved Kermit committed suicide in Alaska while in the military. Like his Uncle Elliott, Kermit was afflicted with alcoholism and depression. He had always been very sensitive, and although he married and had children and seemed to enjoy life, he was, in fact, a deeply disturbed and unhappy person. Cousin Franklin had even made sure that Kermit did not get posted to a combat zone; he did not want Aunt Edith to have to worry about her sons being in combat. Now Kermit had died not by the hands of the enemy but by his own gun.

Edith was never told that Kermit committed suicide. She always believed he had died of heart failure. Then, in July 1944, her firstborn, Ted, died of a heart attack in Normandy, France, where he had participated in the D-day invasion of the continent. He was only fifty-six years old. Ted had not had success in electoral politics, but he turned out to be a prominent general in the army, receiving numerous awards for bravery. His death meant that Edith had now survived three of her five children.

After Ted's passing, Edith's life closed down even more. By this time, she was in her mid-eighties and in frail health. She stopped keeping a diary in 1945, and for the last two years of her life was basically bedridden, tended by nurses and visited by her daughter, Ethel, and son Archie. On the morning of September 30, 1948, she slipped away quietly. She was eighty-seven years old. Edith Roosevelt was laid to rest at Young's Cemetery, next to the only man she had ever loved.

Above: Theodore Roosevelt, Jr. was a general during the D-day operation in World War II. He earned the Medal of Honor, which his father had been denied.

Below: The Queen Anne-style Sagamore Hill house at Oyster Bay, Long Island, served as Theodore's alternate White House. It was the family's favorite spot.

Visiting the Sagamore Hill National Historic Site

The Sagamore Hill National Historic Site consists of eighty-three acres of land on the Long Island Sound near Oyster Bay, New York. It includes Theodore and Edith's home: Queen Anne–style and boasting twenty-three rooms, the brick-and-wood shingled house remains furnished as it was during his lifetime, with a special emphasis on the postpresidential years 1909 through 1919. Also on the grounds are a visitors center, a bookstore, and the Theodore Roosevelt Museum at Old Orchard. The main house is open seven days a week in the spring and summer, and from Wednesday through Sunday during the fall and winter, but it's closed on Thanksgiving Day, December 25, and January 1. Tickets for a forty-five-minute guided tour may be purchased at the visitors center. Admission is $5.00 for adults and free for children sixteen and under.

Sagamore Hill is located some forty-five miles east of New York City and is accessible by car from the Long Island Expressway (I-495) or the Northern State Parkway. The address is Sagamore Hill National Historic Site, 20 Sagamore Hill Road, Oyster Bay, New York 11771. Go to the Web site, www.nps.gov/sahi/, for more information.

Helen Taft

A Privileged Beginning

Every spring, tourists flock to Washington, D.C., to stroll by the Tidal Basin and view the thousands of beautiful cherry blossom trees in bloom. They're able to enjoy the trees thanks to the efforts of First Lady Helen Herron Taft. Brought to the city by Helen in 1909, the cherry blossom trees represent just one of the many enduring legacies of one of the nation's most influential First Ladies. Helen was also a notable example of a president's wife who wanted her husband to be president more than he wanted it. Through William Howard Taft, Helen experienced the political power she was denied because she was a woman. During her term as First Lady, from 1909 to 1913, women were still not even allowed to vote in national elections.

Helen (nicknamed Nellie) Herron was born on June 2, 1861, to John Herron and Harriet Collins Herron of Cincinnati. She was one of eleven children, although three of her siblings died in infancy. The Herron family had a strong intellectual background: John Herron was a lawyer and a state senator; and most of the Herron children were college graduates. Herron also belonged to Cincinnati's Literary Club, which is how he met William Taft's father. As a child, Helen went to the private Miss Nourse's girls school, where she received a well-rounded education, including history, languages, and literature. She had a particular interest in music and practiced piano every day.

When she was seventeen, Helen had an experience that would have a profound effect on the rest of her life. Her father was a longtime friend of the U.S. president at the time, Rutherford B. Hayes. The two had been law partners at Herron's law firm before Hayes started his political rise. In 1878, Helen was invited to spend a week at the White House as a guest of the First Family. She later described the experience as "the climax of human bliss" and she vowed to one day live in the White House.

Even though their fathers knew each other, Helen and William Taft did not meet until 1879, when he was a law student at Cincinnati Law School. They were immediately attracted to one another's curiosity and intellect, and the two became part of a group of friends who gathered together to discuss such issues as politics, literature, the arts, and other cultural matters. In 1880, William graduated law school and started his practice while Helen continued her education at Miami of Ohio University, studying German, literature, history, and the sciences. After college, she continued her music studies at the Cincinnati College of Music.

Helen Herron Taft

Born
June 2, 1861,
Cincinnati, Ohio

Parents
John Williamson Herron
and Harriet Collins
Herron

Marriage
June 19, 1886, to William
Howard Taft (1857-1930)

Children
Robert Alphonso
(1889-1953); Helen
Herron (1891-1987);
Charles Phelps
(1897-1983)

Died
May 22, 1943,
Washington, D.C.

Above: Helen wanted to be First Lady much more than her husband wanted to be president.

The courtship between Helen and William would last for five years. Helen was very interested in women's rights; she was also passionate about literature, music, and politics and wanted to be sure any possible husband would accept her as his equal. William did eventually ask Helen to marry him—twice—but she did not accept. There were other men who also wanted to marry Helen, but she kept them all waiting, asserting her independence and working as a teacher.

During these years of courtship, William was busy building his career. He served as assistant prosecutor, collector of internal revenue, and assistant county solicitor. In 1885, he once again tried to persuade Helen to marry him. This time, she accepted. They were married on June 19, 1886, in her family's home, and they honeymooned for three months in Europe.

Married Life and a Judgeship

In 1887, William reached another milestone in his career: Ohio governor Joseph Foraker appointed him to the Ohio Supreme Court. Two years later, President Benjamin Harrison appointed thirty-two-year-old William to the position of United States solicitor general and the Tafts moved to Washington, D.C. Helen was overjoyed by her husband's success, and she loved living in Washington. It was around this time that the Tafts met Teddy Roosevelt and his wife, Edith. This friendship, and Helen's ambition, would be the two key factors in the Tafts' journey to the White House.

William's stint as solicitor general ended when the Harrison administration came to a close. Although Helen was disappointed, William was happy to return to Cincinnati as a circuit judge; it was the career he had always wanted. William went on to serve as circuit judge for eight years, and it was during this time that the Taft family grew. The Tafts' first child, Robert, was born in September 1889, followed by Helen in August of 1891 and Charles in September 1897. Helen was an excellent mother, inspiring her children to be as intellectually curious as she was and to love music. Helen also found time to head the Cincinnati Orchestra Association and helped found the Cincinnati Symphony Orchestra in 1892.

In 1900, Washington called on William again when President McKinley asked him to head a commission to bring stability to the Philippines. The United States had just acquired the territory from Spain as a result of the

Below: Son Robert Alphonso inherited his mother's reserve, but he had a brilliant public career.

While visiting Hawaii on a stopover before reaching the Philippines, Helen learned the local sport of surfing.

Spanish-American War, and McKinley wanted to establish a civilian government. William was intent on keeping his judgeship, but Helen persuaded him to take the position. She knew it would be a great adventure for her family. She also knew it was one step closer to national recognition and the presidency.

En route to the Philippines, the Tafts stopped in Hawaii, Japan, and China for some sight-seeing before reaching Manila. When he arrived, William immediately found himself in conflict with the head of the American military there, General Arthur MacArthur (father of the famous general Douglas MacArthur). MacArthur believed in harsh treatment of the local Filipinos to control them, while William wanted to help the Filipinos run their own country.

Above: Helen and her husband made the voyage to the Philippines more enjoyable with afternoon card games out on the deck.

William won the battle when MacArthur was removed and William was named civil governor of the islands in 1901. During his three years in charge of the islands, William improved educational and health services and reformed the judicial system, tax structure, and civil service. Helen accompanied her husband on a trip to the Vatican, where he negotiated the purchase of 400,000 acres from the Catholic Church to redistribute among the Filipino people. While at the Vatican, Helen had an audience with Pope Leo XIII.

Besides keeping a close eye on the children and teaching them the local language, Spanish, Helen showed herself to be a gracious hostess at official affairs while in the Philippines. She exhibited a lifelong disdain for racism by inviting Filipinos to all affairs and took a great interest in learning about the country and its people. She learned their dances and occasionally dressed in native costumes. She also explored the countryside, becoming the first White woman to visit the rugged mountain area called the Luzon. Helen advised her husband on all political decisions and started a program to make sure the Filipino children had enough milk to keep them healthy.

Below: As governor of the Philippines, William made great strides in improving living conditions.

William had one bitter disappointment while he was in the Philippines. In 1902, President Roosevelt, who had succeeded President McKinley after he was assassinated, offered him the position of Supreme Court justice. It was the one job William had wanted all his life, but he reluctantly turned it down, feeling he had not yet finished his mission in the Philippines. Helen also advised him against accepting the appointment— she knew that if he accepted the judgeship on the Supreme Court it would end all hopes of his presidency.

By 1904, William felt his job in the Philippines was complete, and he returned to Washington. President Roosevelt offered him the cabinet position of secretary of war. Although, again, William would have preferred a judgeship, Helen and the president persuaded him of the value and importance of the position. During his term as secretary of war, the Tafts visited many countries around the world including Russia, Cuba, Italy, Germany, and, most often, Panama. One of William's main duties was to

Above: When she became First Lady, Helen said that she felt like Cinderella. Her former life had been one long rehearsal for the moment.

Below: Women's suffrage first became a reality in the Wyoming Territory in 1869, but it didn't spread to the entire country until 1920.

oversee the U.S. Army Corps of Engineers, which was charged with building the Panama Canal, Roosevelt's pet project.

The more Roosevelt worked with William, the more he valued his insights and intelligence. The secretary of war soon became the president's most trusted advisor. When Roosevelt traveled away from the White House, he would leave William to run things. The Tafts also became an important part of the Washington social scene, attending all the major events including the marriage of Roosevelt's eldest daughter, Alice, in 1906. Helen attended First Lady Edith Roosevelt's weekly "parlor cabinets" for cabinet members' wives to keep informed on what was going on in Washington and to prepare for her future duties. She also held her own reception once a week for the wives, although she found them "monotonous" and did not continue them once she was First Lady.

Helen's interest in politics deepened in Washington. She kept up on the issues of the day by attending Senate debates and she helped her husband write his speeches. Like many other wives of politicians, Helen was careful not to express many of her opinions in public so her husband wouldn't lose any possible votes; but there was one issue that was an exception—women's rights. Helen made it abundantly clear that she supported a woman's right to equal education and the right to vote. On other issues, Helen held her tongue in public, but she was undoubtedly very involved in private discussions with William.

As the 1908 presidential election approached, the Republican party needed a candidate. President Roosevelt had declined to run again, but he was still

The Women's Vote

It seems incredible to us today that women were not granted the full right to vote until 1920, 144 years after the signing of the Declaration of Independence. In 1848, the first women's rights convention, in Seneca Falls, New York, made the first organized call for a constitutional amendment guaranteeing women's suffrage, but it would be another thirty years before a bill was brought before Congress. It would be introduced, and defeated, every year from 1878 until 1919, when it finally passed and was made law the following year.

During all those years, the usual argument against women's suffrage was that it would be a threat to the family: The belief was that if women had power, they would neglect their family duties and American society would collapse. Even when small gains were made in the struggle—as in 1869, when Wyoming became the first state to grant women the right to vote in local elections—it was not for freedom's sake. It was simply to entice more women settlers to the rugged West, where the men needed wives.

Without the vote, it was also impossible for women to get elected to any office of significance. It was under such a system that intelligent American women like Helen Taft felt they could only experience the power of the political world through their husband.

immensely popular and powerful. It would be up to him to choose the party's candidate, and Helen lobbied intensely on her husband's behalf. Roosevelt liked William very much, but he had concerns over William's indifference to becoming president. Helen decided to meet personally with Roosevelt to persuade him to choose William. Roosevelt found Helen's aggressive attitude offensive and the two strong personalities became bitter enemies. However, whatever she said to him must have relieved his doubts about William and he chose him as the party's nominee. Once again, William wanted to say no and wait for a Supreme Court justice appointment, but Helen had her heart set on being First Lady. She persuaded him to run and, with Roosevelt's endorsement, he won the Republican nomination easily.

William hated campaigning, calling it "one of the most uncomfortable four months of my life." Helen guided him through it, helping him with speeches and advising him not to speak of President Roosevelt too much. The country was very happy with Roosevelt's seven years of Republican leadership, so William won the November election easily over the Democrat William Jennings Bryan. It may not have been William's dream come true, but it was Helen's. It had been thirty years since her "blissful" stay at the White House had changed her life, and now she was thrilled to be moving into the White House as First Lady.

Above: Helen said that riding next to William to his inauguration was her proudest moment because it established a new tradition.

In the White House

On inauguration day, 1908, Helen became the first First Lady to ride in the presidential carriage with her husband. She had probably worked harder for her husband's election than had any other First Lady, and she felt she deserved to be there. From that year on, all First Ladies have accompanied their husbands in the inaugural parade.

In her first weeks in the White House, Helen showed that she planned to be an active and conscientious First Lady. One of her first acts was to hire many African-Americans to White House staff positions. Helen made an arrangement with a car dealer in which the dealer supplied the White House with cars in return for advertising using the First Family's name; the Tafts' 1908 Stanley Steamer was the first presidential auto. Helen decorated the White House with many of the Asian artifacts she had brought back from her visits to the Philippines and Japan.

Below: Pauline, the Taft's cow, was like a member of the family, but she did most of her grazing at the lawn of the State, War, and Navy Building.

❀

The Tafts kept a pet cow named Pauline Wayne on the White House grounds to supply the family with milk. It was allowed to wander the White House lawns during William's entire term.

❀

Above: The Tafts found the Philippines a little primitive at first, but their dining options injected a touch of class to life there.

The People's First Lady

Helen Taft did not want to be First Lady simply for her own satisfaction. Whenever she had the opportunity, she also used the privilege of her position to help others. Besides hiring many African-Americans for her White House staff, she helped many women get jobs in government that they had previously been denied. One woman wrote Helen a letter asking for help to start a kindergarten for African-American children. Helen invited her to the White House and helped her get her funding.

The First Lady also became an advocate for immigrants. When she heard of one immigrant boy who was refused entry into the United States because of a speech problem, Helen intervened and the boy was allowed entry. Her concerns about the working conditions for young immigrant girls in factories across the United States prompted a congressional investigation.

Helen also made a symbolic gesture, far ahead of its time, for her and her husband's twenty-fifth wedding anniversary party at the White House. Among the many guests invited, Helen made sure the leading Catholic priests, Protestant ministers, and Jewish rabbis of the day were all encouraged to attend.

Helen Taft believed the White House should have a more formal and stately atmosphere. She insisted that the staff wear fancy uniforms, and she hired a personal housekeeper to keep the executive mansion running efficiently. Her formal dinners were quite elaborate, and she went to great lengths to make sure the White House chefs were preparing the meals according to her high standards. Helen thought the First Family deserved the kind of royal treatment the Tafts had received in the Philippines. As a result, Helen did not endear herself to the White House staff, and when her husband left office, there would be no traditional farewell speech to the staff.

Helen also initiated a program to beautify the capital city, especially Potomac Park, which was mostly a mosquito-filled swamp. Her first step was to bring in cherry trees. She had fallen in love with the beautiful pink blossoms of the trees during her visit to Japan. When the mayor of Tokyo heard of her desire to fill Washington with cherry blossoms, he sent her more than three thousand trees as a gift to the American people.

Helen was also busy on the political side of White House life. She attended many of the president's meetings and would make a point of taking part in any important conversations she saw him having. She also played a major role in many of his political appointments, including the cabinet. She personally vetoed the appointment of Nick Longworth, Alice Roosevelt's husband, as minister to China.

Helen was such a perfectionist as a First Lady, she earned the nickname "Nervous Nellie," a term still used today for an anxious person.

In her first few weeks in the White House, Helen also hosted countless dinners and parties, entertaining most of the members of Congress and their wives. Helen could often be seen at the dinners speaking to diplomats about political issues of the day, sometimes in their own language. However, some people thought she was going to exhaust herself with the schedule she was trying to maintain—they were right. In May 1909, Helen suffered a serious stroke, losing her ability to speak and the use of her arms. The extent of her illness was kept from the public, and doctors feared she may never recover, but within a little over a year Helen made significant improvement. The Tafts' daughter, Helen, returned from college to nurse her mother back to good health and also to host some White House affairs. Meanwhile, William visited his wife every day and read to her.

It was a bitter disappointment for Helen to spend so much of her time as First Lady in ill health. She had dreamed so long of the opportunity, and when it came, she could perform very few of the duties she wanted. But she was well enough to attend a huge party thrown for the Tafts, held in June 1911: It was to celebrate the Tafts' twenty-fifth wedding anniversary. The entire White House grounds were decorated in lights, and more than three thousand guests attended. It was one of the biggest parties ever to take place at the White House. Luckily, Helen was also able to arrange many musical events at the White House where she and her guests could simply sit and be entertained.

Helen's illness may have also affected William's performance as president. He proved to be indecisive and spent more time out of Washington than any president before him. Many people felt that William had more of a judge's personality than a president's. He liked to listen and let the law determine decisions rather than be a leader and take strong stands himself. Whereas Roosevelt was known for taking a strong stand, William was more deliberative. While Roosevelt often approached the American people for support, President Taft didn't know how to enlist the aid of public opinion. And he could not come close to matching Roosevelt's popularity. Without Helen at his side, he didn't seem to know what to do—without her, he was not a politician. Toward the end of his term, he called the White House "the loneliest place in the world."

Above: Helen Taft and her only daughter, Helen.

Below: Washington's famous cherry trees were a personal gift to Helen Taft from Yukio Ozaki, the mayor of Tokyo. The first two thousand trees arrived diseased, but they were replaced two years later thanks to Helen's persistence.

Home Improvements

Helen had a strong desire to make the White House and the surrounding area more beautiful as an indication of national pride. She was inspired in many ways by a lovely park she had seen in Manila called the Luneta. Planting the Japanese cherry trees around the Tidal Basin was her first project; Helen planted the first two trees herself in March 1912.

Besides politics, music was Helen's greatest interest in life, and her memory of the Luneta also inspired an outdoor performance area on the White House grounds. The area included grandstands and a stage, similar to those in Luneta, where Helen scheduled many musicals and concerts throughout each summer of her brief tenure as First Lady.

Above: William Howard Taft was the heaviest of all the presidents. Six feet tall, he averaged about three hundred pounds.

Below: For the gathering to celebrate the Taft's silver wedding anniversary, Helen mailed announcements to four thousand politically important people across the country.

As the 1912 election approached, William did not want to run again. But despite her illness, Helen wanted another term as First Lady. The Republican party also thought that as an incumbent, William was their strongest candidate. Once again, William bowed to the wishes of others and ran for "the loneliest" job in the world.

Yet the Republican party underwent a costly split during William's term—the conservative faction backed President Taft, but the Progressives who missed Roosevelt's activist approach to government would not support him. The Progressive faction persuaded Roosevelt to run on a third-party platform, splitting the Republican vote and assuring the Democratic candidate Woodrow Wilson's easy victory.

Life After the White House

After his unhappy years at the White House, William was not upset at leaving Washington. He said his first reaction was that he already felt younger. Helen knew her fragile health needed some rest and she adapted well to a quieter life. William secured a teaching position at Yale University as a professor of law. He became a content and popular teacher, while Helen completed her long recovery from her stroke and attended concerts and the theater whenever she could. She also managed to complete her memoirs, *Recollections of Full Years*, in 1914, recounting her experiences as First Lady. She was the first First Lady to have her memoirs published.

William had been a law professor at Yale for eight years when it was finally time for his dream to come true. In 1921, President Warren Harding filled a vacancy on the Supreme Court by appointing William chief justice. The Tafts returned to Washington, and Helen was glad to return, even though her health did not allow her to have the social life she once had there.

William was a hardworking chief justice, and Helen once again became his closest advisor. In their spare time, Helen and her husband enjoyed visits from their children and grandchildren and spent quiet evenings together reading, listening to music, and reminiscing about their long, exciting, and productive lives. They even managed one more trip to England, where they were treated like royalty.

By 1930, William's health was beginning to fail. He had suffered two heart attacks and was forced to resign from his beloved Supreme Court position. He died on March 3, 1930, just one month after his resignation, and was buried at Arlington National Cemetery, the first president honored with a resting place at the cemetery for America's military heroes. Helen was heartbroken over the loss of her companion of forty-four years, one of the first presidents to give his First Lady status as his main advisor and confidante.

After her husband's death, Helen kept as busy as she could for the remainder of her life. She continued to live independently in the Washington home she had shared with William. She traveled extensively and founded the Anna Louis Inn for poor girls. She also became an honorary vice president of the Girl Scouts. She followed the First Ladies' tradition of not taking a stand on controversial political issues, but her daughter, Helen, fulfilled some of the dreams her mother could not. Helen Taft Manning went on to become an outspoken supporter of women's rights and a professor of history. Both Taft sons eventually entered politics: Charles Taft became mayor of Cincinnati, and Robert Taft served in the U.S. Senate from 1939 to 1953.

Eleanor Roosevelt invited Helen back to the White House in 1940 for a final visit. It must have been a bittersweet view of the place that sixty-two years before had filled her with such hopes, and thirty years before had proven to be such a disappointment. At the age of eighty-one, Helen Herron Taft died on May 22, 1943, in Washington. She was buried next to her husband, becoming the first First Lady to be interred in Arlington National Cemetery.

Above: When the tafts visited Glacier National Park, the local Native Americans gave Helen a "sacred wimpuss skin," but they didn't bother to explain what sort of animal a wimpuss might be.

> *"I had always had the satisfaction of knowing almost as much as he [William] about the politics and intricacies of any situation. I think any woman can discuss with her husband topics of national interest. I became familiar with more than politics. It involved real statesmanship."*
>
> —*Helen Taft on life with her president husband*

Below: The Taft family sold the house where he was born in Cincinnati, Ohio, before William became president. It has been restored as the William Howard Taft National Historic Site.

To Visit the Tafts

The best options to trace the history of William and Helen Taft involve a visit to either the William Howard Taft National Historic Site, in Cincinnati, or the burial site at Arlington National Cemetery, in Arlington, Virginia. The William Howard Taft National Historic Site, which is the house that William Howard Taft was born in, has been restored to its original appearance. To get there, take I-71 South to the Taft Road exit, or I-71 North to the Reading and the Florence exit, to Auburn Avenue. The site can be found at 2038 Auburn Avenue, Cincinnati, Ohio 45219. The telephone number is 513-684-3262.

William Howard Taft and Helen Herron Taft are buried side by side in Arlington National Cemetery. A stone monument marks their plot. Take I-95 to I-395 North to the Arlington National Cemetery exit. For more information, call 703-697-2131.

Ellen & Edith Wilson

An American Romance

"You shall never want for wifely love and faith and sympathy, my darling, or for anything that love can give. We shall be one in hopes and plans and anxieties and sorrows and joys." It was with those words that Ellen Louise Axson formally accepted the proposal of marriage from Thomas Woodrow Wilson. For his part, he confessed that he didn't understand how he had deserved the love of this "marvelous woman," but that it moved him to "boundless joy and gratitude," and he said he thought that if any couple was ever ready to be married, it was most certainly he and Ellen.

They were married on June 24, 1885, by her grandfather Isaac Axson and the groom's father, Dr. Joseph Wilson, both Presbyterian ministers, at the manse of Reverend Axson's church in Savannah, Georgia. Ellen had designed her own simple wedding dress, whose long skirt was looped on one side to reveal a shorter lace skirt beneath it, and she wore a lace veil that her late mother had made for her own wedding. The family was still in mourning for Jane Axson, and there were no flowers and no music at her daughter's wedding.

The couple left the same day for a six-week honeymoon in North Carolina with a short stopover at Augusta, Georgia, for a tour of scenes of the bridegroom's boyhood. During their quiet time away, they studied German intensely and worked their way through a pile of books on government and politics. It wasn't everyone's idea of vacation reading, or even what passed for honeymoon diversion, but Ellen and Woodrow had both always been serious students, and they thought of their new life together as a powerful intellectual partnership. Ellen had put aside a promising career as an artist, but as she told him, "It would not be a sacrifice to die for you, how then can it be one to live for you."

They had met nearly three years earlier, after Woodrow, a young lawyer, first saw her during services at the church in Rome, Georgia, where her father was pastor. He was instantly attracted to her, and because her father and his were friends, he knew he would be introduced to her. Ellen was twenty-three years old, and he was twenty-seven. She was five feet, three inches tall with a good figure and dark reddish brown hair piled high in a braided knot; her face was soft and feminine, and her deep-set brown eyes were piercing. Woodrow had the air of an aristocrat, but if Ellen found him attractive, there was no sign of it.

Ellen Louise Axson Wilson

Born
May 15, 1860,
Savannah, Georgia

Parents
Reverend Samuel Axson
and Margaret Jane
Hoyt Axson

Marriage
June 24, 1885, to
Thomas Woodrow
Wilson (1856-1924)

Children
Margaret Woodrow
(1886-1944); Jessie
Woodrow (1887-1933);
Eleanor (Nell) Randolph
(1889-1967)

Death
August 6, 1914,
Washington, D.C.

A Community of Women

When Ellen was a teenager, she abandoned all hope of ever finding a husband, and along with her closest friend, Beth Adams, she began planning to create a home for unmarried women like themselves. Beth would be the manager, and Ellen would support the operation by selling her drawings and paintings. Even after each of them became engaged, the plan was still very much alive in their minds.

She had been courted by just about all of the eligible bachelors in Rome from the time she was sixteen, and she had found all of them wanting. She confided in a friend that if she were ever to fall in love, it would be against her will, and she had become well-known around town as a man hater. It wasn't quite the case, but Ellen Axson had high standards, and she codified them early in her life. To get her interest, she wrote, a man must be "good, nice, handsome, splendid, delightful, intelligent, and interesting." Nobody she met had all of those qualities, and most had none of them. Woodrow Wilson, on the other hand, had enough of them to get her attention. But he had to work for it. Woodrow's legal business took him back to Rome about a month after they met, and he began calling on Ellen. In another month, he wrote to his mother that he had made up his mind to marry her. For her part, Ellen had no such intention. She did agree to write to him, but there was no hint of even latent love in her eyes.

As devout Presbyterians, both Woodrow and Ellen were strong believers in predestination, and they must have interpreted the series of coincidences that followed to be part of God's plan. Ellen decided on the spur of the moment to spend some time with friends in Morganton, North Carolina, unaware that the Wilson family was vacationing nearby. Not only that, but they had changed their plans at the last minute and were even closer than they might have been. By the time Woodrow found out how near they were to each other, though, Ellen had been called home because of a sudden illness that had overtaken her father. She wrote a letter to Woodrow explaining the change in plans, but it didn't reach him until the day she intended to leave. In the meantime, he took a day trip into nearby Asheville, and as fate would have it, that is where Ellen was, too. She had missed her train connection there and checked into a hotel for the long wait for the next one. Woodrow happened to pass the hotel that afternoon, and when he saw her in the window of her second-floor room, he changed his own plans to leave the following day, and took a room in the hotel himself.

He took advantage of the opportunity to drive Ellen to the resort where his family was staying, and she was given an unexpected introduction to his mother, his sister, and his brother. They apparently approved of Woodrow's choice, because he suddenly asked her to marry him as they passed through the hotel lobby on their way to catch their trains the next morning. Ellen knew by then that she loved him, but she didn't know quite what to say. "I was letting those precious moments slip away," she later recalled, but she haltingly said, "yes."

Below: Ellen Axson had established high standards for possible suitors, and Woodrow Wilson met enough of them.

> *"You can call me anything you please except Ellie Lou. I have a decided dislike to that name, indeed to all compound names."*
>
> —*Ellen Axson to her fiancé, Woodrow Wilson*

He left right away for Baltimore to begin his studies at Johns Hopkins University, and she finished her trip home, where the only person she told of what had just happened was her younger brother, Stockton, confiding to him that her new fiancé was "the greatest man in the world." The rest of the family found out about her intentions when a diamond engagement ring arrived in the mail a few weeks later.

Ellen's father died not long afterward, and the small inheritance he left her made it possible for her to enroll at the Art Students League in New York City. She and Woodrow hadn't seen each other during nearly the entire first year of the engagement, and they met along the way, visiting Washington briefly and then going on to New York together. Once she was settled in a women's boardinghouse, he went back to school in Baltimore. Ellen had graduated from the Rome Female College, but the Art Students League was as different from it as a box of crayons is from a palette of oil paints. The students had a say in both the government of the school and the courses it made available. The teachers were mostly young, and though most of them had been trained in Europe, as most successful artists were, they had no patience with the older established American painters. They had their own recipe for success, and Ellen adapted to their pattern perfectly. One of her teachers praised her work for its "great feeling" and her strong but delicate understanding.

New York City itself was her classroom. The Metropolitan Museum of Art had moved into its new building at the edge of Central Park five years earlier, and although its collection was still small, it brought works of art from around the world for special exhibitions, and Ellen never missed one of them. She also haunted the city's galleries and was a frequent visitor to the studios of painters who were members of the league. Ellen was also an avid theatergoer, and she became active in the Episcopalian Church of the Heavenly Rest, which had lured her away from her Presbyterian heritage with its ritual and its choral music, which she said put her in a "rapturous state of mind." She soon went back to her roots, much to the relief of her family and her fiancé, when she joined Scotch Presbyterian on Fourteenth Street near the school; and that led to an offer to teach part-time at the Spring Street Mission School for African-American youngsters.

During that same year, Woodrow finished writing his first book, *Congressional Power,* which established him as a rising young scholar. He inscribed the copy he sent to Ellen: "As your love runs through this, my first book, so it must be the enabling power in all that I write hereafter." He confessed to other thoughts about her that might be out of place in "the public face of a book."

Below: Describing his wife, Ellen, Woodrow reflected that, "No president but myself ever had exactly the right sort of wife."

He also confided in her that his fondest dream was to become a public servant, but since that was beyond his means, he would settle for guiding public policy with his pen. That shocked Ellen. "Of all the world's workers," she said, "those that to my mind take by far the highest rank are the writers of noble books. [But] men of letters are constantly going into public life in England, why not in America, too?" He agreed that there was probably nothing he couldn't accomplish as long as she was at his side.

Ellen had been given the honor of acceptance in the Art Students League's advanced-painting class, a first-class ticket to a satisfying future as a fine artist, but when Woodrow accepted an offer to teach history at Bryn Mawr College near Philadelphia, she left New York right away to go home to Georgia and get ready to marry him.

When they finally arrived at Bryn Mawr four months after they were married, Ellen was already pregnant. Partly because she wanted her baby to be born south of the Mason-Dixon Line and partly because Woodrow couldn't afford the medical expenses, she opted to live with relatives in Georgia until the baby was born. Two days after she arrived there, the new baby arrived, too. She named her first daughter Margaret Woodrow. At about the same time, Woodrow was awarded a Ph.D. from Johns Hopkins University. Ellen was freed of the guilt she felt for having left him alone, because she knew it had given him the quiet time he needed to study for his final exams.

Woodrow joined Ellen and the baby in Georgia, and they spent the summer there. He dreaded going back to Pennsylvania because Bryn Mawr was a girls school, and he would have been happier teaching young men. He also had another book in mind, this time on the subject of the "philosophy of politics." Much of the source material was in German, and Ellen, who already spoke the language, read most of the books for him, separating the wheat from the chaff. She took advanced courses in the language, too, because her husband thought that he should take his family to live in Germany for a year or so while he completed his research. Ellen had nearly $1,500 left of her inheritance, and she offered it to finance the trip.

But the trip was postponed when she became pregnant again, and it seemed to be a permanent postponement when they rented an eleven-room house and furnishing it dipped dangerously into her money. As before, she went to Georgia for her pregnancy, and as before, Woodrow joined her there as soon as he could. This time he welcomed the change in his surroundings to be able to

get on with his writing. He desperately wanted a son, but their second child
was another girl whom they named Jessie Woodrow. When Ellen and her babies
went back to Pennsylvania in the fall, her brother Eddie went along, and so
did Mary Hoyt, one of her oldest friends; Mary hoped she could get a college
education there if she could save the cost of room and board by living with the
Wilsons. The big house was filling up.

Woodrow hated his job, but he got some relief, and welcome extra income,
by giving a series of lectures at Johns Hopkins. By spring, he received an offer
from Wesleyan University in Connecticut to teach political science and history,
with a comfortable increase in salary. He had a contract with Bryn Mawr, but
he broke it on a technicality, and the family, and extended family, moved on to a
better life.

Ellen, who hadn't been particularly social at Bryn Mawr, took her duties of
a professor's wife more seriously in Middletown, Connecticut, their new home.
She made as many as seven social calls in a single day right after they arrived,
and she was always gracious when the calls were returned. By midwinter,
though, she was pregnant again, and like the last time, it left her almost
constantly ill, and that brought her social activities to an abrupt end.

Ellen had severe crying spells when her third child turned out to be a girl,
but her husband had long since made up his mind that a girl would be just
fine with him, as long as he had the assurance that this would be Ellen's last
pregnancy. The baby, Eleanor Randolph, whom they would call Nell, instantly
won both their hearts.

Woodrow was still a lecturer at Johns Hopkins then, and he had published
another book, *The State,* which was accepted as a textbook at Harvard. He was
also at work on his third book, part of a series called *Epochs of American History.*
In the meantime, Wake Forest University had given him an honorary doctorate,
and Williams College offered him a full professorship. He turned down that
offer, however, because the trustees at Princeton University made him a better
one, an unusual unanimous election to the chair of Political Economy and
Jurisprudence. He told Ellen that none of this would have happened without
her.

They rented a house in Princeton, and the owner gave Ellen a free hand to
redecorate it. In the meantime, her brother Eddie went to school in the South,
and his older brother, Stockton, who had also been living with the Wilsons for

Above: Woodrow, Ellen, and their three daughters sat for this photo two years before Ellen's death in 1914.

Parental Pride

Of their three children, Ellen was closest to Jessie, who grew into a beautiful young woman with all the best qualities of both her mother and her father. The youngest, Nell, was Woodrow's favorite because of her playfulness, a quality he himself lacked. Margaret, the eldest, was also well loved by both parents, who—with an affectionate tongue in cheek—characterized her as "proper part of the time, vulgar the rest."

a time, left for graduate school at Johns Hopkins. The family shrunk back to Ellen, Woodrow, and the three girls. The eldest, Margaret was four years old, Jessie was three, and the baby, Nell, had yet to celebrate her first birthday. The girls would grow up in Princeton, where the family lived for nearly twenty-three years.

Professor's Wife

Ellen entertained frequently at their Princeton home. The local elite were rock-solid Presbyterians of the sort she and her husband had been raised among, and the faculty welcomed them, both for Woodrow's accomplishments and for Ellen's easy charm. She also began encouraging students, especially those from the South, to consider her house their second home. It was these visitors who let her in on one of the college's best-kept secrets, that cheating was fairly common there. Ellen was appalled, and she formed an organization of students she trusted to create and work for an honor system for their classmates. She recruited Woodrow to promote the idea among the faculty, and by mid-semester, Princeton had its first code of honor, thanks largely to Ellen Wilson.

The house they had rented was as drafty as a tent, and it was too small for their extended family, which by then included, along with the three girls, Ellen's brother Eddie; Woodrow's nephew George Howe; his cousin Helen Bones; and his aging father, Joseph Ruggles Wilson, who, although he wasn't a permanent resident, was there most of the time. They also entertained a constant round of visiting relatives, and sometimes Woodrow and Ellen were forced to sleep in the nursery. It was clear that they needed a bigger house, and after her husband bought a building lot, Ellen went to work designing one. Ellen's blueprint for her new home went through several changes dictated by costs, but in the end she had created a two-story Tudor house. The half-timbered second floor overhung the first, which had a full basement under it. The third floor was left unfinished, but it could hold more bedrooms if the household grew, which it had a history of doing.

Cost of Living

A few years after the Wilsons were settled in Princeton, the wife of a man who was considering an offer of a professorship wrote to Ellen to find out what it would cost them to live there. She responded that her own household consisted of ten persons: "Two of these are servants, and two are very large and hearty college boys." Their basic monthly expenses, she estimated, were: "food and lights, $100; servants, $29; coal, $12; water, $4." Rent and other costs, she pointed out, depended on an individual family's lifestyle. Her own husband's base salary was $3,000 a year, but he worked hard to generate other income.

Above: Ellen completely redesigned their Princeton home to suit her needs and tastes.

The grueling lecture schedule and the pressures of publishing left Woodrow completely exhausted, and Ellen insisted that he should go to Europe for a vacation. A wealthy neighbor, who realized how important a rested Professor Wilson was to the college, offered to pay for the trip, but Woodrow refused until Ellen talked him into it. In addition to the usual signs of fatigue, he had developed stiffness in his right hand that made it impossible for him to write. He couldn't hold a pen and he could only peck out words on a typewriter, one letter at a time, with his left hand.

Woodrow agreed to deliver a series of lectures and to write a multipart biography of George Washington for Harper's *magazine as a way of paying for their new house.*

He was gone for fifteen weeks, the longest time he and Ellen had ever been separated. She spent the time visiting her family, but she was also inspired to go back to her artwork, which she had not touched in more than ten years. She painted landscapes and portraits, made copies of several paintings in the Princeton collection, and reproductions of several sculptures that she admired. Most of her art, which Woodrow pronounced better than the originals, decorated their home, and some of it would one day hang in the White House.

"The house is nearly finished and it is a dream."

—*Ellen Wilson on her new home*

The land where the president's mansion stood on the Princeton campus had been donated to the college in 1753 by one of Ellen Wilson's ancestors.

During their early years at Princeton, Ellen home-schooled her daughters. By the time she was five, little Nell could read anything a youngster might be expected to comprehend at that age, and Jessie and Margaret were already comprehending the Greek classics, with a marked preference for Plato's dialogues. Their mother also substituted Shakespeare and English poetry for their usual bedtime reading. After three years of learning at their mother's knee, the girls were put under the supervision of a German governess who taught them to speak French and, of course, German; she also helped Ellen gain more ground in her quest for mastery of the language. The tutor eventually took a job teaching at a nearby private school, although she went right on living at the Wilson house, and Ellen enrolled the children at the school, much to the delight of the headmistress, who regarded them as her most accomplished students.

The next big change in the Wilsons' lives came near the end of the school year in 1902 when Woodrow was elected president of Princeton University, the first who wasn't a Presbyterian minister. By the time he formally accepted the honor in the fall, Ellen had already been busy planning the redecoration of Prospect, the president's mansion on campus.

Ellen was only the fifth mistress of Prospect, and she felt a need for a complete redecoration. The university hired Edward J. Holmes, a professional decorator, to handle the job, but Ellen had her own ideas, and they were completely opposed to what he had in mind. "If Mr. Holmes does not agree with me, so much the worse for Mr. Holmes," she said. "He will be dismissed with so much less compunction." She had spent her vacation in New York, Boston, and Philadelphia hunting for antiques, and she intended to use them whether the decorated agreed or not. She ruffled some feathers among the local establishment by having the drawing room done in rose brocade, but she smoothed them down by reminding them that the room was to be used for formal entertaining, and it should be formal right down to the wall covering. She found discarded marble fireplaces and chandeliers in the basement and had them cleaned and reinstalled. She added a second bathroom upstairs and a washroom on the first floor, and she had the place wired for electricity for the first time since the mansion was built. She also completely redesigned the grounds. Where a formal French garden had been, she put in colorful flower beds with a fountain in the center. She added an arbor of climbing roses to one side, and purple wisteria grew up the side of the house.

Among Ellen's contributions to the mansion was an original design for a large stained glass window that was executed by Tiffany & Co.

> "The house is one of the most beautiful in Princeton, a display of Ellen's inerrant taste."
>
> —Woodrow Wilson on the president's mansion at Princeton after Ellen redecorated it

At the end of their first year in the president's mansion, Woodrow began making plans to take Ellen to Europe for a second honeymoon, making up, he said, "for many, many things." Leaving the children with relatives and the rest of the family behind, they arrived in England in early July. After a few days in the Lake District, in homage to Ellen's favorite poet, William Wordsworth, they went up to Edinburgh and then headed for London with lingering stops along the way. London, with its museums and galleries, was a high point for Ellen. An even higher one was the Louvre in Paris. She had never dared dream that she would ever see its art treasures close up. After visiting Switzerland and Italy, they went back to Paris for a few days for a second look before sailing for home. They had been gone for nearly three of the happiest months of Ellen's life.

As president of the university, Woodrow implemented unprecedented change that included adding a law school, a graduate school, and another school specializing in science and electricity. He also worked with the faculty to revise the existing course of study, a task that alone would have completely taxed the energies of a less-driven man.

For her part, Ellen was busier than ever, too. She entertained the faculty at formal dinner parties, handling every detail from the menu to lavish floral decorations. She held an open house for the entire freshman class, and she entertained the trustees during each of their quarterly meetings. Her home was also open to the university's official guests as well as for ministers who arrived each weekend to preach at the chapel. It was a punishing schedule, and she had to admit that the endless round of entertaining bored her as much as it tired her. But Woodrow was also annoyed at having to give up so much of his writing time, and she realized that she needed to put a happy face on the situation. "No use grumbling about it," she said.

As a kind of reward for her faithfulness, Woodrow sent Ellen and Jessie to Italy in the spring. Everything went beautifully until they reached Assisi about a month into a picture-perfect tour, where Jessie contracted diphtheria. A doctor was dispatched from Princeton with a serum that wasn't available in Italy, and in another week, the girl had recovered. But it had been an anxious time for Ellen. Before they left, they had attended the funeral of Ruth Cleveland, the daughter of their friends Frances and Grover Cleveland, who had died of the same disease, and Ellen almost refused to believe that her own daughter wasn't going to meet the same fate. Jessie was admitted to a convent for two weeks of complete rest before leaving for home.

Below: Landscape design was one of Ellen's talents, and she redid the gardens of all her homes.

Above: The gardens at the Vatican were as much an inspiration for Ellen during her trip to Italy as the Sistine Chapel, which awed her.

A Traveler's Impressions

It would be hard to say whether Ellen was more moved by the Vatican than she had been by the Louvre. She made several visits there, and of her last she wrote: "It was hard to turn my back on it forever! I could scarcely keep from crying. It is the only place I have had any such feeling about. But I was fortunate in one respect; one corner of Sistine Chapel had been covered by scaffolding, hiding the Delphian Sibyl—much the most beautiful of all—so that I had given up all hope of seeing her. But yesterday, the scaffolding, which is on great rollers, had been moved along a little, and she stood revealed! —And she is one of the most beautiful creatures in the world!—The Venus of Milo of course being the other.... There is no other face so truly inspired. Beyond any doubt she sees in a vision 'all the glory that shall be.'"

Florence was to have been the pinnacle of their tour, but Ellen resigned herself to missing it. On the other hand, Jessie hadn't. She knew how much it meant to her mother, and she told her that if they didn't go there, it would be "very, very bad" for her still-delicate health. Her doctor agreed that if she weren't indulged, there was no telling what might happen. Ellen was worried about the expense and the fact that she'd miss the university commencement, but Woodrow was understanding on both counts and wired them to get on with their adventure. Florence left her "gasping and overwhelmed." She went on from there alone for a weekend in Venice, which she rated as "perfectly glorious."

Along with her duties as a hostess and her husband's helpmate, Ellen also joined the Ladies' Auxiliary and helped with its fund-raising activities, and she made it a special personal cause to upgrade the university's infirmary, raising enough money to pay for nurses and maids. She also began spending her summer vacations at Old Lyme, Connecticut, an artists' colony at the time,

In Venice, another tourist told Ellen that she had an amazing resemblance to Titian's Flora. Yes, she said, "and Giotto's tower, too."

and she formed friendships with the leaders of the new school of American Impressionists, including Childe Hassam, Willard Leroy Metcalf, Robert Vonnoh, and others whose work she not only admired, but began to emulate. Though they agreed that her work was good enough to be exhibited along with theirs, she preferred to promote the sale of their work because she knew that they needed the income, and she kept her own paintings in the background.

For their twenty-fifth wedding anniversary, in 1910, the Wilsons bought a painting, *Valley of Assisi* by Chauncey Foster Ryder, one of her friends from Old Lyme, for $600. It was more than they could afford, but she told the artist that he should be pleased "that a woman would give up new evening gowns, etc., etc., for two years to possess this painting." But she added, somewhat cryptically, that she would probably end up selling the landscape in another year.

Ellen knew what others only suspected. Four years earlier, a speaker at a testimonial dinner had suggested that Woodrow Wilson run for president of the United States. Everyone laughed it off, especially Woodrow, but friends began to notice that his speeches were starting to take on political overtones. He had become disenchanted with university politics; and when his booster George B. M. Harvey, the editor of *North American Review*, invited himself to dinner at the Wilsons, he offered Woodrow and Ellen what he considered a road map to the White House. It led through Trenton, and he encouraged him to run for governor of New Jersey.

Above: Ellen's second daughter, Jessie.

A Political Life

Harvey had already consulted with the state's Democratic leaders, who hadn't elected a governor in eighteen years, and they found the prospect of having the president of Princeton as their candidate more than just appealing. But the man himself still wasn't convinced. After their summer vacation in Old Lyme, though, quite likely with Ellen's prodding, he agreed to take on the challenge that would change their lives.

The family went back to Princeton in the fall to begin their ninth year in the president's house. The election was still three months away, and Woodrow had hoped to delay his resignation until then. The trustees, however, asked him to sever his ties right away, and to show that there were no hard feelings, they voted to give him an honorary doctor of laws degree and to let the family keep the keys to the president's mansion until after the first of the year.

Ellen had already demonstrated her skills as a hostess, but now the guests at Prospect were no longer intellectuals and Presbyterian ministers but politicians and reporters. "You need the hide of a rhinoceros," to deal with them, she said.

"One of the most interesting things about Woodrow Wilson is his wife."

—Delineator *magazine*

Above: Wherever Ellen lived, she surrounded herself with original art, which often included her own works (note her paintings on the wall).

She resented much of what was being said in the press about her husband, herself, and her daughters, but she also had the disposition of a friendly house cat, and she quietly let the hurtful gossip roll over her.

When the campaign ended in November with an impressive victory, Ellen wrote to George Harvey, "We are a very happy and excited family! Excited chiefly over the size of the majority, of course, yet great as the result, it is not so great as the campaign! I am more proud of that than anything else."

There was no governor's mansion in New Jersey at that time, and with few if any social obligations as the governor's wife, Ellen was able to spend more of her time reading newspapers and journals and educating herself on the issues that made the wheels of politics turn in the Garden State. She also had long conversations with political leaders, one of whom said that he thought she was a much better politician than her husband ever would be.

George Harvey, meanwhile, was setting all the necessary machinery in motion for his real goal, a chance at a Wilson White House, although for his part Woodrow still doggedly denied that such a thing was even remotely part of his plan for the future. Ellen put a stop to his protestations by telling him, "Please don't say again that you 'are not thinking about the presidency.' All who know you well know that it is fundamentally true, but superficially it can't be true, and it gives the cynics an opening which they seize with glee."

When the three-time presidential candidate William Jennings Bryan went to Princeton to deliver a speech, Ellen invited him to have dinner with her and Woodrow. By the time the evening was over, the two men had turned their indifference into friendship, prompting the governor's secretary to tell Ellen that "you have just nominated your husband" as a presidential candidate.

Woodrow's tenure as governor made it a definite possibility. Always a demon for hard work, he managed to push through all of the sweeping reform legislation he had proposed during the campaign. "It has all been so dramatic," Ellen wrote to a relative. "As for Woodrow, his physical strength is not the least

Credit Where It's Due

During one of the interviews Woodrow gave during his speaking tour, a reporter asked him, "Have you been taught mostly by your wife, or by your three daughters?" His answer was, "From Mrs. Wilson, not only have I learned much, but have gained something of a literary reputation. Whenever I need a poetic quotation, she supplies it, and in this way I acquire the fame of possessing a complete anthology of poetry. From my daughters, however, I have learned what every parent knows of himself—that I do not know how to raise children."

wonderful thing about his new development. He keeps us all gasping." He had enough strength in reserve to make a cross-country speaking tour that summer, and there was no longer any doubt in anybody's mind where he intended to end up.

While he was away for the summer, Ellen, Jessie, and Nell moved the family's possessions to a big house in Sea Girt, New Jersey, that had been built as the governor's summer residence. Ellen had her first taste of dealing with the general public there, as New Jerseyans dropped by for a look at the only governor's mansion they had. As they had at Princeton, family members came to call with great regularity, happy to have the nearby beach as a diversion.

The Wilson-for-president bandwagon was rolling at full tilt by the fall, and he had stopped denying his interest in the nomination. But all was not sweetness and light. A conservative wing of the Democratic party, ironically led by his former mentor George Harvey, correctly perceived Woodrow as a Progressive, and had begun quietly working against his candidacy. Ellen herself stanched one of their whispering campaigns with a letter to a Louisville, Kentucky, newspaper that surprised the editor. He said he had never seen such a strong defense written by "a lady." In another letter that refuted charges about their family finances that had been made by *The New York Sun*, she ended her explanation of the real facts by saying, "I don't know what he would do to me if he knew I was writing all this, but I am sure I can trust your discretion."

Ellen went with her husband on campaign swings, and she was a star attraction wherever they went. She confided to a friend that she had no desire whatever to become First Lady, but she believed with all her heart that her husband was the most qualified man in the United States to be president, and the role came with the territory.

When the Democrats met in Baltimore to choose their candidate, there was strong opposition to giving the nomination to Woodrow. When it eventually appeared that he had lost, he wired his backers to withdraw his name, but when Ellen heard of it, she was furious. "What can be gained by a withdrawal?" she fumed. "You must not do it." He took her advice and withdrew his order rather than his candidacy. He got the nomination in the end, but not until after forty-six ballots had been taken. They had decided that if he were to lose the nomination, they would take another trip to England, but now they were going to hit the campaign trail instead. It would be a three-way race with another Progressive, Theodore Roosevelt, running as a third-party candidate against Woodrow and President William Howard Taft. It wasn't going to be easy.

For the first time, Ellen was confronted by rumors in the press about herself and her daughters. She was forced to deny that she approved of women who smoked and that she was extravagant with her wardrobe, among many other silly things. In every case, she wrote her own press releases and grimly handed them to the reporters who were watching her every move, usually reminding them that she wasn't running for anything.

But whether she wanted to or not, Ellen became First Lady in November, when her husband was elected president, and her life was turned upside down.

She spent time each day working with her husband on his cabinet nominations, and among others who would owe their new jobs to her was Secretary of State–designate William Jennings Bryan, who hadn't been her husband's first choice. She also had to buy dresses for the inaugural and for White House entertaining. She had to make arrangements for smoothly replacing the Tafts in the White House, and she had to deal with a new army of reporters with personal questions about things she'd rather have kept to herself.

She and the girls went to New York on a shopping spree. She bought dresses for all of them, and jewelry for Margaret, Jessie, and Nell as "inauguration presents." When her husband found out that she hadn't bought any beads or baubles for herself, he bought her a diamond pendant, which the family called "the crown jewel."

Neither the president-elect nor his wife had ever been inside the White House, and Ellen had only passed by it once in her life, until President Taft and his wife gave them a tour right after they reached Washington for the inauguration. Ellen was familiar with the history of the presidency, and she was happy to find out that the rules had changed considerably by 1913. Running the White House would be much less a strain, financially or physically, than it had been for many other First Ladies. For one thing, except for personal servants, the government paid the salaries of the White House staff, and when they went on vacations, those staff members would go along with them, also at government expense. Their only financial outlays would be personal ones, and the president's salary was now $75,000 a year, with an additional $25,000 for expenses.

The traditional Inaugural Ball was canceled that year because the incoming president considered it a needless expense, so Ellen began her career as First Lady the day after the inauguration with an East Room reception for one thousand well-wishers, and another the day after that for nearly as many. Margaret, Jessie, and Nell, now twenty-seven, twenty-six, and twenty-four, respectively, assisted Ellen in receiving guests at these receptions. Also helping with hostess duties were Woodrow's cousin Helen Bones and his sister Annie Howe.

Ellen inherited an experienced staff from Helen Taft, the previous First Lady. Among them was Belle Hagner, who had served as social secretary for both Mrs. Taft and Edith Roosevelt; she calmly guided the three Wilson daughters, and their mother, too, through what they described as a "mad social whirl." Ellen herself wasn't without the necessary experience after having spent ten years as a university president's and governor's wife. But this was a bigger job than either of those, and Ellen and Woodrow had little time left over for each other. They solved the problem by taking afternoon drives together, and it became a daily habit. They also went to the theater, a long-standing family pleasure, at least once every week.

Theodore Roosevelt had overseen a major renovation of the White House, but Ellen decided to change a few things about it. Seven new bedrooms on the second floor were served by a corridor that she found too dark, so she had the

A Shining Example

Ellen arranged for a meeting of influential Washingtonians to discuss the problems in Washington's African-American neighborhoods, and William Jennings Bryan addressed the group. "The most eloquent speech here tonight," he told them, "is the one that has not been made at all, for actions speak louder than words. The fact that the wife of the president is with her presence here lending support to the movement is enough. As crowded as my life is, I feel that if she can find time out of her busy days to be here and to work for this cause, I can too."

Above: Democratic leader William Jennings Bryan was one of Ellen's staunchest allies.

walls redone and the carpeting replaced. She brought her own furniture and had some of her artwork brought down from Princeton. She also brought back a painting of voluptuous nudes that Helen Taft had banished to the Corcoran Gallery.

Margaret was given a room large enough to accommodate the grand piano she needed for her vocal lessons, and her sisters shared a room, as they had all their lives. Ellen decorated and furnished the family quarters in soft colors and flowered pastels, choosing fabrics, carpeting, and wall covering that was handcrafted by women in the Appalachian Mountains. It created a new national enthusiasm for their work, and Ellen was made president of the Southern Industrial Association to encourage the production and sale of American crafts.

She also became chair of an arm of the National Civic Federation, an organization formed to improve living conditions in Washington's slums, and she often led congressmen by the arm on tours of neighborhoods she believed were "disgraceful." At her urging, the Federation built model housing in slum neighborhoods, and it was always the destination of her eye-opening tours.

Ellen also found time to campaign for better working conditions for government employees. She made unannounced visits to offices that she pronounced "unsanitary." The lighting and fresh air were substandard, but she was especially upset about restrooms for female employees that were few and far between and woefully inadequate.

Above: The prominent sculptor Augustus Saint-Gaudens, and other professional artists, too, regarded Ellen as one of his colleagues.

Her unprecedented whirlwind pace came to a halt as the Wilson presidency went into its second year. On the orders of the family doctor, she was confined to the White House and sent off for a long vacation in the New Hampshire mountains. Although she was there for a rest, Ellen became active in a club for artists, a group that included Kenyon Cox and Maxfield Parrish, along with the architect Augustus Saint-Gaudens. She allowed some of her own paintings to be exhibited, and eventually had a one-woman show of fifty landscapes at a prestigious Philadelphia gallery. Ellen also entertained family and friends as she had

always done, and she was especially pleased to welcome Jessie's new fiancé, Francis Sayre, a Harvard-trained lawyer. Mother, daughter, and fiancé spent long afternoons and evenings planning the wedding.

The wedding was held on November 25, 1914, in the East Room of the White House. Ellen had gone back to Washington in mid-October, refreshed from her prescribed rest, although she tired easily. She presided over a full schedule of receptions and teas, all the while making plans for Jessie's big day. Invitations had been sent to five hundred people, and announcements to as many more.

During the winter that followed, the social activity at the White House increased dramatically, and daughters Nell and Margaret became grist for the Washington rumor mill. Margaret wasn't involved romantically with anyone, but the press and the wagging tongues invented any number of suitors. Nell was secretly engaged to Ben King, an adventurer who was off prospecting for gold in Central America, but no one outside the family was aware of it, and it wasn't a factor when eyebrows were raised over her infatuation with her father's secretary of the treasury, William G. McAdoo. What put Washington in a tizzy was that he was twenty-six years older than she was. Ellen forced Nell to break off her engagement to Ben King and to stay away from McAdoo for a few weeks, hoping that the romance would cool. It didn't, of course, and Nell's engagement to McAdoo was announced before the rumors could get any further out of hand. Ellen's strength was diminishing again by spring, and Nell decided that she wanted a simple wedding. The ceremony was conducted in the Blue Room rather than the more formal East Room. "This is marriage, not a wedding," Nell pointed out.

Above: Ellen's daughter Eleanor set her own ground rules for her wedding, which was a simple affair even though she was part of the First Family, and the groom a Cabinet member.

Among Jessie's wedding gifts was a $5,000 check from her parents "to do with as she wished even if her husband didn't approve."

Ellen's health seemed to have been restored by the time the wedding date rolled around, but people close to her chalked it up to sheer willpower. As she wrote to a friend, "I am still far from well.... Nobody who had not tried can have the least idea of the exactions of life here and of the constant nervous strain of it all,—the *life*, combined with the constant anxiety about Woodrow, his health, the success of his legislative plans etc., etc. If I could only sleep as he does. I could stand twice as much." Her doctor advised another New Hampshire sojourn, but she couldn't bring herself to leave her husband again.

Ellen spent most of her afternoons supervising the planting of the White House rose garden, which she had designed, but she couldn't walk except on a nurse's arm. Her doctor moved into the White House, where he would be constantly on call. He knew what she and her husband did not, that Ellen was in the advanced stages of Bright's disease, a usually fatal kidney condition, and that there was nothing he could do except make her comfortable during what would surely be her last days.

On what was her final day, August 6, 1914, the Senate passed the slum clearance bill that she had proposed, and House leaders sent word that they, too, would pass it the following day. Ellen was still lucid when the news arrived, but then she became unconscious and she died, with a smile on her face, a few hours later. Her husband and her daughters, including Jessie, who was pregnant with the Wilsons first grandchild, were at her side. The president walked to a window overlooking Ellen's unfinished garden and sobbing uncontrollably, said, "Oh my God! What am I to do now?"

Ellen's funeral in the East Room was a simple affair, and her casket was put aboard a special train that would take her home to Georgia. Woodrow sat silently beside the casket, oblivious to the tolling of church bells and the silent crowds that had gathered along the way. She was buried in Myrtle Hill Cemetery in Rome, Georgia. On the journey there from the train station, with a stop at the church where Woodrow had first seen Ellen thirty-three years earlier, they passed a hillside where the local garden club had planted flowers spelling out the words "Welcome Home Ellen," in anticipation of a visit she had planned to make in the fall.

The Bride Wore Black

After his Ellen died, President Wilson went into a period of all-consuming mourning that lasted well into the following spring. "God has stricken me almost beyond what I can bear," he said. When he had become president two springtimes earlier, there were four women in his life: his wife, Ellen, and his three daughters, Margaret, Jessie, and Nell. Margaret, who was twenty-nine when her mother died, gave up the public life she detested and went to New York to get on with her studies for a singing career; Jessie, twenty-eight, had married Frank Sayre and moved with him to Williamstown, Massachusetts; and the youngest, Nell, was married to Treasury Secretary William G. McAdoo and living in his Washington home. The only woman left in the president's household was his cousin Helen Woodrow Bones, who had moved into the White House to serve on the First Lady's secretarial staff and to help with the entertaining. Woodrow asked her to stay on to help him with the obligatory social functions, but there were precious few of those in a White House that was officially in mourning. "No one could offer cousin Woodrow any comfort," Helen said, "because there is no comfort."

If his deep depression wasn't debilitating enough, the president was hardly the picture of health. He suffered from asthma and other respiratory problems; he had arteriosclerosis, too, and he had been slowed down by a series of minor strokes. Added to all that, he had also lost nearly all the vision in his left eye, and he had started wearing the pince-nez glasses that became a kind of trademark with him.

Fortunately, Woodrow had the constant professional services of Dr. Cary T. Grayson, a lieutenant in the navy's medical service. He had been President Theodore Roosevelt's personal physician and stayed on at the White House during the Taft administration, and then President Taft highly recommended him to the Wilson family when his own presidency ended.

Among the orders the doctor gave Woodrow was to get out for a round of golf every day, and he went along on these outings, frequently encouraging the president by letting him win, and over time, they became intimate friends. Woodrow thought of the thirty-five-year-old Grayson as the son he never had. The financier Bernard Baruch, who was a close friend of Woodrow's, said that he was "the President's intellectually compatible friend who wants nothing, represents nobody, whom he can trust implicitly."

But the doctor had other patients as well. Among them was Helen Bones, who he decided needed a friend or two and some relief from the oppressive atmosphere of the White House. His fiancée, Alice Gordon, recommended her

> "Lieutenant Grayson is both a Democrat and a Virginian, neither of which can be helped."
>
> —William Howard Taft on his doctor

Left: Edith Bolling Galt Wilson

Edith Bolling Galt Wilson

Born
October 15, 1872,
Wytheville, Virginia

Parents
William Holcombe
Bolling and
Sallie White Bolling

Marriage
April 30, 1896,
to Norman Galt
(1862-1908)

Widowed
1908

Remarried
December 18, 1915,
to Thomas Woodrow
Wilson (1856-1924)

Children
None

Died
December 28, 1961,
Washington, D.C.

Above: As a teenager, Edith Bolling's future as the wife of a Virginia planter seemed predictable. She did eventually marry a Virginian, but not the traditional kind.

close friend, a Washington gadfly named Edith Bolling Galt. The doctor considered her an attractive woman who would be good company for Helen, and when he introduced them and they discovered that they each had a passion for walking, Dr. Grayson was a happy man. He believed that exercise could cure just about anything that ailed a person, and here he was killing two birds with one stone.

The widowed Mrs. Galt was forty-two years old and both beautiful and charming. She was five feet, nine inches tall with gray-blue eyes and dark hair, and she was described as a "fine figure of a woman." She also had a winning smile and an even more disarming Southern accent.

Edith had grown up in Virginia, a direct descendant of the Native American princess Pocahontas and her husband John Rolfe. After her schooling, which wasn't exceptional, she went to Washington at the age of nineteen for the first of several extended visits with her older sister Gertrude and her husband, Alexander Hunter Galt, who had become the sole owner of the family business, Galt & Bro., the oldest and best-known jewelry and silver store in the capital. It was inevitable that she would meet her brother-in-law's cousin, Norman Galt, the heir apparent to the highly profitable enterprise. It was obvious to everyone that Edith was in town on a husband-hunting expedition, especially to Norman, who thought that he would be the perfect catch for her. But in spite of his promising future, Edith didn't seem to notice him and she kept him, on a string for four years while she played the field.

By the time Norman died in 1908, after they had been married for twelve years, he had inherited the business and Edith was his sole heir. She hired a good manager to run the emporium for twenty-six years before she sold it to her employees in 1934, and she became one of the richest women in Washington, D.C. She took frequent trips abroad, and she bought the first electric automobile in Washington, which made her into a kind of landmark around town, more for the erratic way she drove than for the novelty of the machine.

But when she wasn't frightening horses with her runabout, Edith could be found any day of the week briskly walking beside Helen Bones in Rock Creek Park. After several months of the routine, though, she had still not been introduced to Helen's cousin the president. The women met in the park and ended their jaunts with tea at Edith's house. Woodrow and Dr. Grayson were usually out on the golf course at the times the ladies got together.

Then one day they all got caught in the rain, and the golfers and the hikers made a beeline for the White House where, muddy boots and all, they literally bumped into each other at a turning in a corridor. Recalling the meeting, as she

"I know now that I was still very much of a child, for it did not occur to me that Norman Galt's frequent visits were in any way due to his interest in me. He was about nine years my senior, but he seemed so much older, and I never gave him a thought."

—*Edith Bolling Galt on her first husband*

Edith Wilson's former business is the oldest store in Washington today, and the oldest jewelry store in the country.

often did, Edith wrote that,in spite of the mud she was tracking into the house, "[I was] secretly glad I had worn a smart black tailored suit which Worth had made for me in Paris, and a tricot hat which I thought completed a very good-looking ensemble." Woodrow invited the women to have tea with him and the doctor, and they spent an hour drying out in front of a fire. Edith turned on her charm, and the president was captivated.

Just before Ellen died, she had made Dr. Grayson promise that he would make sure that her husband would get married again, and it is likely that Edith Bolling Galt was his candidate. But Woodrow had been looking around on his own in the meantime. Back in 1907 he had met a woman named Mary Peck on a trip to Bermuda and corresponded with her off and on ever since. There were hints that they may have been having an affair, but there was no perceptible fire to go with the smoke. Still, he wrote to his wife that he found Mary "fine and dear." She had since left her husband, changed her name back to Mary Allen Hulbert, and was living in Boston. Woodrow's letters to her grew more frequent after he was widowed, always hinting that she could help ease his despair if she would come to live at the White House.

Mary didn't take the bait. She was weighed down with personal financial problems and she began making some suggestions of her own that maybe he ought to be helping her with them. Woodrow Wilson was a generous man and time and after time he came to Mary's rescue. But the more help he gave to her, the more she seemed to need—and he started to resent it. He was looking for help himself, but she was too self-absorbed to see it. His letters to her started to become more formal, and then they stopped altogether.

Another woman, Nancy Toy, the daughter of a minister and the wife of a Harvard professor, also began to correspond with Woodrow. He invited her to dinner at the White House, and it was the first time in months that anyone had seen him enjoy himself. Woodrow and Nancy had so much in common that it seemed as though a good friendship, if not a romance, might be blossoming. But then the talk turned to religion, and he quickly found out that Nancy had none. "There are people who believe only so far as they understand," he said. "That seems to me presumptuous and sets their understanding as the standard of the universe.... I am sorry for such people." Nancy Toy was not invited back, and that left the slate clean until Edith Galt came to dinner.

Within a month of their chance meeting, Edith had become an almost nightly dinner guest with the president's official family in his private quarters. He always sent a car to pick her up, and she was usually taken for a drive with her host for a predinner tour of the countryside. The dinners were usually followed by an evening of reading aloud and conversation before the official car took her home again.

There was still very little formal White House entertaining to deal with, but Margaret Wilson had come back from New York to help her father when she was needed. Along with Helen and her mother, the president's sister, and

Above: The President's eldest daughter, Margaret, left the White House to pursue a musical career in New York after her mother died.

Dr. Grayson, she was always on hand when Mrs. Galt came to call. But one evening, they all decided to take a stroll out on the lawn, leaving Woodrow alone with Edith for the first time, Then, as she described it, "Looking at me with those splendid fearless eyes that were unlike any others I have ever seen, he said, 'I asked Margaret and Helen to give me an opportunity to tell you something tonight that I have already told them.' Then he declared his love for me." She protested, "You can't really love me. You don't really know me. And it is less than a year since your wife died." He brushed her protests aside and then he asked her to marry him. She responded that she wasn't sure and needed a little time to think about it.

The president was an unusually busy man at the time. While his wife, Ellen, had been dying, World War I was breaking out in Europe, and on May 8, 1915, a few days after he asked Edith to marry him, the liner *Lusitania* was sunk by a German U-boat. Woodrow's deeply felt hope for neutrality in the war seemed to have died with the 124 Americans who had perished on board.

But still he found time to write to Edith. Sometimes several handwritten notes passed between them every day, and he had a private telephone line set up between her house and his. She also had his confidence in matters of state, and sometimes he asked for her advice. When he showed her the draft of his note to Germany responding to its defense of the *Lusitania* incident, she asked him to rewrite it "for me," because she didn't think he had put enough of his own passion into it. When he took her advice, his secretary of state, William Jennings Bryan, resigned in protest. He had been given the job in the first place thanks to Ellen Wilson's intercession. "Far from being a calamity to have him resign," Edith wrote, "it was a real benefit."

Edith seems to have advised him on other official actions as well. In one of her letters to him, she said, "Thank you… for all the tender little things that

The Princeton Tiger

In order to keep their relationship out of the public eye, Edith and the president saw one another only behind the closed doors of the White House. She wrote, "Almost every day we would keep in touch through faithful little Helen who would come for a walk and bring me a line from 'The Tiger' as she lovingly named him. She said he was so pathetic caged there in the White House, longing to come and go as she did."

made me feel your love, and for the real confidence and sharing of the big ones that make up your busy life." Little by little, he began sending her daily packets of state papers, annotated with his own comments, and she added her own opinions to them before she sent them back.

Although there were very few people in Washington who didn't realize that love had come to the White House, Edith was coy about it. She had, in fact, agreed to marry Woodrow, but not until after he had left the White House because she wanted him, and the world, to know that she loved the man and not the office.

Woodrow soon grew tired of the clandestine love affair and he all but demanded that they should announce their engagement. His daughters and the rest of the family highly approved of Edith, after all. At the same time, his cabinet held a secret meeting to discuss the situation, and all of them agreed that he ought to get married again, but not right away. They were worried that if a wedding were to take place so soon after the president buried his first wife, it might cost him the election in 1916. But as it turned out, none of the cabinet ministers could bring himself to inform the president of their consensus. As one of them pointed out, it would be a mission that "neither my head nor my heart was enlisted... and my official head might suffer decapitation."

In the meantime, Woodrow had loaned money to Mary Allen Hulbert, and his political enemies had gotten wind of it. They apparently had come across a secret letter stating that the loan was really a gift to cover up an affair. Woodrow was informed that it would emerge during the campaign, dragging him through the slime of scandal. He realized that Edith's name would be smeared as well, and after assuring her that none of the charges was true, he broke their engagement to protect her from the lies that he knew were coming.

For her part, Edith reserved judgment, but she let him know that she would stick with him no matter what might happen. She said it in a letter, though, and he wouldn't open it, fearful of what it might contain. A day later he was bedridden with a fearsome malady that Dr. Grayson couldn't identify, except possibly that it was a broken heart. Edith's visit to his bedside brought about a veritable miracle cure.

Below: Home run! Woodrow's new American romance became public knowledge at a World Series game. The fans approved.

The incident only served to draw them closer together, and on October 6, Woodrow wrote a press release announcing that he and Edith were going to be married. The ceremony would take place in another two months, but at Edith's home, not the White House. Public reaction was generally positive, although many Washington society women complained about having a "tradeswoman" leading them. Edith and Woodrow were seen in public for the first time right after the announcement was made, but their first real introduction to the American public as a couple came on the day the president threw out the first ball at a World Series game in Philadelphia while Edith sat beaming in the background.

They started going to the theater together and he became a regular dinner guest at Edith's house. The Secret Service detail, which had become used to having evenings off, hadn't been as busy in years, but they all agreed they were happy that "the boss made good," and old friends and family seconded the sentiment. Even with the war in Europe dragging his spirits down and taking a toll on his strength, there was a new spring in his step and people noticed that he was forever quietly whistling through his teeth the melody of the popular song, "Oh! You Beautiful Doll."

> 'You are the only woman I know who can wear an orchid. On everybody else, the orchid wears the woman."
>
> —Woodrow Wilson to Edith

Their wedding was scheduled for December 18, when the president arrived at Edith's home wearing a cutaway coat and striped trousers. His valet, Brooks, had been trying for years to get him to dress like a president, and this was his moment of victory. Edith, unusual for a bride, wore a plain black velvet gown and a matching hat. Of course, she wore orchids; she always did when there was an occasion for it.

Edith's mother gave the bride away, but Woodrow had no best man. He had asked Colonel Edward M. House, his closest friend and advisor since his days as New Jersey governor, to do the honors, but he was getting ready for a peace mission to Europe, and both men agreed that was more important than showing up for a wedding.

The couple had been plagued by reporters ever since they announced their engagement, and they were determined to give them the slip when they went away for their honeymoon. They planted a rumor that they would leave from Union Station, but as the gentlemen of the press were assembling there, they followed an evasive route in an unmarked car to Alexandria, Virginia, where a train was waiting for them on a siding. Even

Below: Yes, presidents encouraged photo ops as far back as 1915. Even the dignified Woodrow and Edith had to deal with the photographers.

the engineer hadn't been told that they were bound for Hot Springs, also in Virginia. They arrived at the Homestead Hotel in the midst of a snowstorm, and Edith wrote to her mother that "the weather is cold but radiant. And so are we."

Helpmate

Changes were made at the White House while they were away. The president and his first wife, Ellen, had slept in separate bedrooms, but now the immense Lincoln bed had replaced the single bed in Woodrow's room. His daily routine changed, too. When Ellen was First Lady, they breakfasted together at eight in the morning in the dining room. Woodrow and Edith had a light snack in their bedroom at six and then they went out for a round of golf before having a larger breakfast two hours later—also in their bedroom.

When Woodrow went to his office, Edith went along, staying at his side and offering her input as he dictated letters. She left at 10:30, when his official appointments began, but they were back together for lunch at 1:00. After dinner, which was always scheduled for 7:00, they went back to the office for more work together. Some evenings they went to the theater together, but there was little entertaining at the White House during these dark days.

Edith took a strong interest in her husband's diet and his health, and with the eternal gratitude of Brooks, his valet, she made sure that he started dressing better. When they first met, she observed that his suits were made by a "cheap tailor." "They were not smart," she said. She also took charge of the management of the household and of Woodrow's financial affairs, a job she was well prepared for after her years of running a business of her own. Edith also started screening his mail, summarizing some letters, answering others, and discarding the ones she considered frivolous. Out of an average of six hundred letters a day, the president was rarely bothered with more than twenty.

Above: Both Edith and Woodrow enjoyed evenings at vaudeville theaters seeing shows that included everything from trained animals to comedians, singers, and acrobats.

As the election grew closer, the president took to the road again, not only to push his programs that were stalled in Congress, but to find out what his chances for reelection might be. Edith went everywhere with him, and everywhere she went the crowds seemed to adore her. The fearful cabinet had to admit that they had been wrong when they concluded that she'd be more of a liability than an asset.

In the midst of the president's battles with Congress, Colonel House arrived at the White House to report on his European peace mission, and he was taken aback when Edith didn't leave the room. He was surprised, though, at how much she seemed to know about foreign affairs, although he was chagrined that she was thoroughly familiar with the contents of a private drawer in the president's desk. It contained several memos he himself had written in code, but Edith knew how to decode them. House also quickly realized that Edith was more hawkish on the European war than the president was, and he decided that she might be a valuable ally.

Edith was busy at the time trying to read every book in her husband's rather large library so that they could talk together about "permanent things that the present unrest could not disturb." It obviously brought them closer together, and his oldest, most trusted friends, including Colonel House, noticed that he was confiding in them less and less. The Wilson daughters noticed the same thing. Edith and Woodrow had become a team, and he didn't seem to need input from anyone else.

When he was nominated for a second term, Woodrow was hailed as the man "who kept us out of the war," even though he was strongly promoting a program of preparedness. His Republican opponent, Charles Evans Hughes, had a remarkably similar background to Woodrow's. A clergyman's son, he had been a university professor and a governor who stood up to special interests. Their beliefs were similar, too. Both were convinced that what the world needed was a strong international organization. Theodore Roosevelt, who was sitting this one out, called Hughes "Wilson in whiskers."

Because of their similarity, the campaign stooped to mudslinging and outright slander. The rumor that Woodrow had bribed Mary Allen Hulbert came out into the open as a "fact," and she announced that she had been offered thousands more to speak out against the president but chose not to accept it. Edith came in for her share of campaign gossip, too, and it was repeated over and over that she had been having an affair with Woodrow while he was still married to Ellen. A joke that made the rounds asked the question, "What did Mrs. Galt do when Wilson proposed?" and answered, "She fell out of bed."

The president thought it was bad form to campaign from the White House, so he and Edith moved to a rented New Jersey estate to campaign from there. She made the place off-limits to the press, and even forbade the campaign committee to take pictures of them there.

Possibly the largest voter bloc opposing Woodrow was Irish-Americans who believed that the president would take them to war on the side of the hated British. He won them over in a strange way. After he got a letter from

one of them saying that he'd never vote for him, Woodrow answered with a well-publicized telegram. "I would feel deeply mortified to have you or anybody like you vote for me," it said. "Since you have access to many disloyal Americans and I have none, I will ask you to convey this message to them." It was a gamble, but it worked, and the Wilson camp began to fill up with Irish-American supporters. For her part, Edith worked the hustings, shaking hands with and talking to every party leader she could. On the day after the election, it seemed apparent that Hughes had won, and it wasn't until early in the morning of the following day that West Coast returns tipped the balance in Woodrow's favor. Edith and Woodrow were sailing up the Hudson River aboard the presidential yacht at the time. They were on their way to the christening of his new granddaughter Ellen Axson Sayre. Whatever happened, their life together would blissfully go on.

Now that she knew she'd be First Lady for another four years, Edith exerted her power by asking, through her husband of course, the press secretary, Joe Tumulty, to resign. She didn't have a problem with how he was doing his job, but she found him common and coarse, not at all the sort who should be representing her family. Joe had been close to Woodrow almost from the moment he decided to run for New Jersey governor, but Woodrow did as he was told. Tumulty, who knew Woodrow almost better than anyone, managed to save his job, but not their close relationship. It was Edith's first shot across the bow of the ship of state.

During her first year at the White House, Edith entertained cabinet wives once a week as a way of getting to know them better and to get their opinions on current issues. But by the beginning of 1917, she dropped the meetings from her schedule, noting privately that she had grown weary of their attitudes. She

Above: Before she married Woodrow, Edith was the talk of Washington because she had one of the few cars in town. As First Lady, she left the driving to someone else as the couple rode to his second inauguration in an open car.

Above: During World War I, the Wilsons brought a flock of sheep to the White House to clip the grass while the men who usually did it went off to war. Edith had the wool made into yarn to knit socks for the soldiers who needed them.

went on with the obligatory White House social schedule, but she was getting bored with that, too, and she scaled dinners and receptions back to an absolute minimum.

By February, Germany announced that it was lifting restrictions on submarine warfare, and Washington went on a war footing. Citing an old piracy law that was still on the books, it was decided that merchant ships could be armed without congressional authorization, and it was Edith who quietly set the wheels in motion while her husband was confined to his bed with a serious cold. A few days later, he had recovered enough to send a message to Congress for authorization to enter the European war.

Edith was quick to get the spirit. She put the White House on a Spartan budget and stopped buying clothes for herself. It meant a virtual end to official entertaining. She closed off most of the first-floor rooms at the White House to help conserve coal, and on days when other Americans were expected to do the same thing, she shut down the heat altogether. Edith also established a Red Cross unit at the White House, and she dragooned Helen Bones and several of her own female relatives to sew pajamas for the boys going off to war. She had a herd of sheep brought to the White House lawn to replace the grass cutters who had been called up in the military draft, and she ordered that their wool must be used to make socks for soldiers. Edith and her husband carefully followed the government guidelines calling for meatless Tuesdays, and they gave up sugar on designated days, and bread and cereals on others.

Later in the year, Edith volunteered as a Red Cross worker, and spent her days giving food to troops who were leaving for France. Although she wore the same uniform as the other women, she was often recognized, although the publicity about her activities was kept low-key. Her husband often drove out to pick her up at the end of the day, and of course, he was always recognized; and he cheerfully shook hands with as many of the boys as he could. He loved them all like sons, and it showed.

As the war began to turn in the Allies' favor, Edith and Woodrow went to Massachusetts for a vacation at a place that happened to be next door to Colonel House's summer cottage. It was there that the president drafted his Covenant of the League of Nations, and House had a big hand in it. Edith, however, was excluded from their discussions—they were in House's territory,

Edith took up horseback riding during the war because Woodrow's advisors thought that their daily round of golf made them appear elitist and uncaring. She even tried to learn how to ride a bicycle—Woodrow had once toured England on one— but she never could quite get the hang of it.

not the White House—and she never forgave the presidential advisor. She was already disenchanted with him anyway.

By early November, the Allies had ratified most of Woodrow's peace terms—his Fourteen Points—and the Germans followed by asking for a cease-fire. When the armistice was signed, the president and his wife danced and partied through the night. A week later he announced that he would go to Paris to sign the peace treaty. Edith's hand was in this, too. None of the president's advisors thought he should go, because they felt that he would be upstaged by the other world leaders who would be there. Only Edith thought otherwise, and she exerted all the influence she had on her husband to overrule them. She wasn't part of the official delegation, but Edith went along, and so did her social secretary. Dr. Grayson was at the president's side, too, but now he wore an admiral's stripes on his sleeve.

Above: The First Couple were welcomed to London by Britain's King George V and Queen Mary.

That they landed on December 13 didn't faze the president, who, while not superstitious, regarded it as his lucky number—there were thirteen letters in his name. They were housed in a lush Napoleonic palace that Victor Emmanuel, the king of Italy, who was one of their many guests, told them was too grand even for the likes of him. The actual peace sessions were delayed waiting for the arrival of David Lloyd George, the British prime minister, and the Wilsons and the other leaders were feted at a round of parties that went on for nearly a week.

The Wilsons spent the days, including their wedding anniversary, visiting French and American hospitals and consoling the wounded men. When it appeared that the peace negotiations were going to be delayed even longer, Edith and Woodrow took a trip to London where they were received by King George and Queen Mary at Buckingham Palace. They were overwhelmed by the affection of the crowds, but their reception in Italy was even more overwhelming. Woodrow Wilson had become a world hero, hailed as "the best friend of humanity."

Meanwhile, back home, unknown to the president, Senator Henry Cabot Lodge and former president Theodore Roosevelt, who had only days to live, were conspiring to wreck his plan for a League of Nations. They had already sent secret messages to the French premier and the British prime minister informing them that if the idea became part of the peace treaty, the American Senate would reject it. When the treaty negotiations finally got underway in January 1919, Woodrow was taken by surprise when his plans seemed to be ignored. It was a tough time for him, but Edith made it bearable. She insisted that

"On that day we rode on the trains of three heads of state—the King of England's from London to Dover, the President of France's from Calais to Paris, and King Emmanuel's from Paris to Rome."

—*Edith Wilson*, Memoir

> *Edith managed to slip into the conference hall, and she was hiding behind a curtain when her husband presented the League covenant.*

he take long walks with her every morning so he wouldn't miss his exercise. But their conversations didn't turn to his experiences around the negotiating table.

She found out about his disappointment when she took a walk with Henry White, a career diplomat who was part of the negotiating team. He told her that Colonel House was negotiating with some of the delegations on his own, and that he was holding back vital information from the president. He suggested that she must tell her husband, and she did. But still, by mid-February, House had managed to shepherd the League of Nations Constitution through, and if the well had been poisoned, nothing Edith could say would change the president's opinion of his old friend.

Popular support for Woodrow's plan for a world body was strong when they arrived back home, and the Wilsons held a dinner party at the White House to celebrate and to try to persuade Senate leaders that it was an idea whose time had come. Edith sat next to Senator Lodge, and spent much of the evening mocking him and suggesting that the people were behind her husband even if a few stuffy senators were not. Mr. Lodge was not amused. His mind wasn't changed, either. The following day, he took to the floor of the Senate to denounce this "supranational government" that would have American troops marching under foreign flags.

When Woodrow and Edith went back to Paris, where approval of the treaty was lagging, he was told that Colonel House, whom he had trusted, was undermining the effort.

Above: Massachusetts senator Henry Cabot Lodge and Ohio congressman Nicholas Longworth (who was married to Alice Roosevelt) worked tirelessly to sandbag Woodrow's efforts to bring America into the League of Nations.

That was when Edith went to work in earnest. She scanned newspapers for articles that seemed to prove that House was working against her husband, and she never missed a chance to offer her opinion about the man. She said that she did it to keep Woodrow from being hurt any more than he already had been in his relationship with his former close advisor.

While they were in Paris, the president suddenly became ill, and Dr. Grayson's original assessment was that he had been poisoned. Other doctors were of the opinion that he'd had another stroke. He went straight to work after just a day in bed, though, in spite of Edith's strong objections. Then a few days later he announced that they were going home. He was getting nowhere with the Europeans, he said, and he'd had enough. It broke the stalemate, and the modified treaty was signed. Most of the changes that were made smacked of appeasement, and the blame was placed squarely on House's doorstep. Edith felt that it was proven that she had been right about the man all along, and now her husband had been given undeniable proof.

When they got back to Washington, they found out that Woodrow's support was dwindling dangerously in Congress. Woodrow was noticeably weakened from his recent illness, but he made a decision that the only way to save the treaty, and the League of Nations, was to go on a coast-to-coast speaking tour. Edith approved, but only on the condition that his itinerary should include time out for rest. For what may have been the first and only time he overruled the First Lady, he insisted on a whirlwind pace, in spite of his health. "I don't care if I die," he said, as long as the treaty was ratified.

The schedule called for more than one hundred speeches, mostly delivered from the observation car of the special presidential train, which averaged about four hundred miles a day. At every stop, local political leaders boarded the train, but Edith delegated herself to deal with them. Her husband had enough to do. In most places, the crowds were eager to see Edith, but while she put in appearances, she made it a point not to speak, on the theory that nothing should be allowed to dilute the president's message. He made excuses for her, often telling the crowds that Edith was a shy woman.

As the tour progressed all the way to the West Coast, Woodrow's strength seemed to be leaving him, but his speeches seemed to be getting more electrifying. At Pueblo, Colorado, after touring the state fair, he took to the stage, but the words wouldn't come. Edith was beside herself until he recovered and he began to speak, bringing many in the audience to tears. Later that same night, he called Edith to his train compartment. He was ill, he said, and the

Mystery Illness

When Woodrow completely lost his power of speech in Pueblo, Colorado, Edith took control and canceled the trip, whether he approved or not, and the train raced almost nonstop for 1,700 miles back to Washington. By the time it arrived there, Woodrow had recovered enough to walk to his car with a smile on his face and his daughter Margaret on his arm. Dr. Grayson had briefed the press, telling them that the president's attack had come from overwork and the lingering effects of the illness that had struck him in Paris. It wasn't serious, the doctor said, and with rest, he would soon be back at his desk.

Right: A sign that Woodrow had recovered from his illness was resuming his routine of daily drives into the nearby countryside.

doctor was called. He seemed to have recovered by morning, but Edith decided that the rest of the trip ought to be canceled. Once again her husband overruled her, telling her that his enemies would call him a quitter.

Once back in Washington, Woodrow's appointments were canceled for a few days while Edith tried to nurse him back to health. He had completely lost the vision in his left eye, he was plagued by headaches, and he couldn't sleep. Neither could Edith, but she had been an insomniac for years.

The following day, a high-level British intelligence agent requested a meeting with the president. Edith met him at the door and informed him that her husband was too ill to see anyone and that she would take his information and have a response ready in a few hours. In the months ahead, she was often accused of acting as a surrogate president, meddling in official business, but she swore that this was the only time she did.

A few days after that, the president collapsed and Dr. Grayson called in a team of doctors, who confirmed that he'd had a stroke and that he was completely paralyzed on the left side. The medical bulletin said only that he was a "very sick man," and needed complete rest.

The medical bulletins became much more positive right away. The press collared some of the members of the team of doctors, but while they wouldn't say that the president's condition wasn't serious, they all agreed that he would probably recover. Edith was sure of it by now. She had a strong faith in his healing powers, which she had seen before, and along with the others in the White House, she believed that he was the only man capable of leading the country, even if he was incapacitated. Even Vice President Thomas Marshall said that it would be "especially trying" for him to assume the powers of the president.

When the cabinet met, they discussed the legality of the problem. It was pointed out that while President Garfield lay dying for two and a half months, his secretary ran the government and there had been no problems. But these were different times. They called in Dr. Grayson, who told them that while the president's condition was improving, it was much too early to say whether the crush of official business might bring about a relapse. Then he told them that Woodrow had heard about their meeting and wondered how they were able to hold it without his authorization. That changed their minds, and they concluded that the government would go on, just as it had when the president was abroad.

There were clues that the stroke had impaired Woodrow's mental functions, but Edith refused to believe it, and Dr. Grayson backed her up. In the meantime, she began a White House routine that drew everyone into presenting a positive face to the public, who regarded the president as a hero. Edith could nearly always be found at her husband's bedside, but she limited affairs of state to about fifteen minutes a day, spending the rest of the time reading aloud to him, as she had done since they were married, or listening to phonograph records, a pleasure she had introduced him to. Otherwise, the house was kept as quiet as possible. No one outside the doors of the White House knew anything about the president's condition or what caused it. That, of course, led to a wide range of

Defending Herself

While the president was ill, Edith issued an order that all official dispatches should come to her and not to the president. It was her intention to decide what could be acted on without bothering her husband, and to show him only what he absolutely had to see. One of the doctors had explained to her, "Every time you take him a new anxiety or problem, to excite him, you are turning a knife in an open wound." The same doctor told her that the president must not resign because it would remove his will to go on living.

Rumors went though Washington that Edith had unilaterally assumed the powers of the presidency for herself. She characterized it as a "stewardship," though, and after the crisis passed, she wrote: "I studied every paper sent from different Secretaries or Senators, and tried to digest and present in tabloid form the things that, despite my vigilance, had to go to the President. I, myself, never made a single decision regarding the disposition of public affairs. The only decision that was mine was what was important and what was not, and the very important decision of when to present matters to my husband. He asked thousands of questions, and insisted upon knowing everything, particularly about the Treaty.... He would tell me what Senators to send for, and what suggestions he had to make to them. These directions I made notes of so, in transmitting his views, I would make no mistake. I would read them to him before going to the interviews. This method of handling interviews was another suggestion of the doctors. It is always an excitement to one who is ill to see people. The physicians said that if I could convey the messages of Cabinet members and others to the President, he would escape the nervous strain these audiences would entail. Even the necessary little personal conversations that go with an official interview would consume the President's strength."

speculation, but all that Woodrow's doctors would say was that he needed a very long rest, adding that they'd have a statement if his condition became critical.

As Woodrow was convalescing, King Albert and Queen Elisabeth of Belgium paid a visit to Washington and they were intent on seeing the president. They spent about fifteen minutes with him before Edith insisted on distracting them with a tour of the White House. Their descriptions of the scene were the first the press had been able to get from behind the dark windows of the White House. By this point, reporters and congressmen alike were beginning to tire of the dearth of information, and Edith bore the brunt of their frustration. Some said that the United States was being subjected to a "petticoat government," and some referred to the president as "the First Husband."

When Congress defeated the Treaty of Versailles, Edith debated not telling her husband that his greatest dream had been dashed. She believed that the news would kill him, but she knew that she would have to take a chance and tell him. Even she was surprised when he said, "All the more reason I must get well and try again to bring this country to a sense of its great opportunity and greater responsibility."

Woodrow was showing strong signs of recovery by then: His appetite came back, and he started writing notes to his cabinet ministers asking them to put off decisions until he recovered, which he assured them he soon would. He even dictated and edited his annual message to Congress. By the spring of 1920, Woodrow was able to preside over a cabinet meeting for the first time. It was obvious to all the members that he still wasn't back to normal, but the meeting lasted an hour and would have gone on longer if Edith hadn't insisted that they call it quits for the day. He held another meeting the following week, but the men who had been around him for years missed the old spirit that had once made meetings like this lively.

Edith and Woodrow began spending afternoons sitting on the portico watching the sheep who were still there nibbling at the grass, and often enjoying the company of Dr. Grayson's two-year-old son. And while there was still some talk that he should resign, he was beginning to give serious thought to running for a third term so that he might breathe new life into the debate over the League of Nations. A poll among likely Democratic voters favored Woodrow's son-in-law William McAdoo, but he had said he wouldn't run if the president wanted to. As for the president's chances, he finished a close second in the same poll. If Edith had an opinion, she kept it to herself, at least for the time being.

When the Democrats nominated James M. Cox to be their 1920 standard-bearer, Edith was visibly pleased. The Wilsons were close friends of the vice presidential nominee, Franklin D. Roosevelt; Edith had traveled to Europe with his wife. She wasn't so sure about Mr. Cox, but she did know that she didn't like Warren G. Harding, the opposition candidate. His campaign motto was "A Return to Normalcy," and in the light of the year she had just spent helping to promote "normalcy," she was offended. But even when he was elected, she was happy at last. Now the Wilsons could get on with their own lives.

Below: The formal dining room on the second floor of the Woodrow Wilson House was where Woodrow courted Edith and eventually asked her to marry him.

A Private Life

The League of Nations met in Geneva for the first time a few days after the election, and a few weeks later, the Nobel Peace Prize for 1920 was awarded to Woodrow Wilson. In the spring, when Warren G. Harding was inaugurated, the former president arrived for the ceremonies on Edith's arm wearing a cutaway coat and a high hat. Edith was wearing an orchid, of course. She was offended when the new president bounded up the steps of the Capitol, while the former one had to take an elevator.

The Wilsons bought a town house on S Street in Washington, and they moved their memories there, including Ellen Wilson's painting of the Madonna, and a formal portrait of Edith as First Lady. They drove there in a Pierce Arrow touring car that Woodrow had bought from the government and had repainted in orange and black, the Princeton colors. On the orders of Dr. Grayson, who had been given permanent duty with the former First Family, the retired president was limited to one caller a day.

Edith broke her own rule when she hired a relative as their secretary. During her years in the White House, she had forbidden giving jobs to any members of the Bolling family.

Above: Edith with Mrs. Claude Swanson at the unveiling of a statue in Washington.

They hired John Randolph Bolling, one of Edith's relatives, as their secretary, and he took care of fending off well-wishers and answering their mail. Woodrow's daughters were scattered. Nell McAdoo and her husband had moved to California, Jessie was still living in Massachusetts, and Margaret had gone back to New York for another try at a singing career.

Edith enjoyed their new privacy. She liked watching congressional debates and playing cards with her friends, but mostly she enjoyed watching over her husband, a job that had become second nature to her. They started going to the theater again, especially to Keith's Vaudeville House every Saturday. The theater owner had to hire special security guards to keep their admiring fans at bay, but the Wilsons' presence was bringing them in, and many willingly paid extra for seats near the presidential box.

Late in January 1924, Woodrow's health failed him again. Three days after his collapse, he died quietly with Edith at his side. Although she had faced the possibility many times, his death weighed heavily on Edith, and it took months for the reality to set in. She began taking trips to Europe again, and she was pleased by the acclaim she received there, although she knew it honored her husband and not her. She became a grande dame of Washington society and she was well-received in spite of the stigma of her days as a "tradeswoman." She took an active part in researching material for Woodrow's biography, and she wrote her own memoirs. She lived long enough to have a place of honor at the inauguration of John F. Kennedy, although few who were there knew who she was. She died in the house on S Street on December 28, 1961. She was eighty-nine years old.

Below: The Woodrow Wilson House in Washington has been made into a presidential museum.

Visiting the Woodrow Wilson House

The red-brick Georgian town house on Washington's Embassy Row where Edith and Woodrow lived after their White House years is now the only presidential museum in the capital. Edith lived there from 1921 until she died in 1961, and bequeathed it to the National Trust for Historic Preservation. The house is furnished as it was when Edith died and is filled with mementos of the First Family's life together.

The Wilson house is located at 23-40 S Street, SW, Washington, D.C. It is open from 10:00 A.M. to 4:00 P.M., Tuesday through Sunday, and it is closed Mondays and major holidays. Adults are charged an admission fee of $5.00; the student fee is $2.50.

Florence Harding

Development of a Maverick

Florence Mabel Kling was born on August 15, 1860. Her father, Amos Kling, had desperately wanted a son, and he never forgave Florence for denying him one. Even after his wife, Louisa, gave birth to a boy the following year, and another one five years after that, Amos always seemed to carry a grudge against little Florence. The only interest he bothered to take in her was to make sure she was brought up as a boy.

Amos was a wealthy businessman, and he was usually too busy satisfying his lust for making money to supervise his daughter's upbringing anyway. He had migrated from Pennsylvania to Marion, Ohio, a few years before Florence was born, and he took a job as a combination bookkeeper and salesman at the local hardware store. It wasn't long before he had saved enough money to buy the place.

The Civil War broke out when Florence was still a baby, and Amos joined the Republican party because he thought it would be good for his business. He was quite right. Marion, Ohio, became a boomtown during the war, and he used his new connections to corner the market on building supplies, with the Union army as his best customer. The prices of nails, nuts, and bolts were constantly going up because of wartime inflation, and Amos quickly became one of the richest men in town.

But wealth in nineteenth-century Middle America didn't guarantee social status, and Florence grew up mostly on the outside looking in. Her father was a newcomer in town compared to its founders and their descendants, and they still decided who was who.

Although she showed great promise as a pianist, and practiced for seven hours a day, Florence could most often be found in her father's store, even when she was too small to see over the counter. She could see enough to watch the training of his apprentice, though, and she learned the basics of the business faster than he did. She also found time to, as one of her neighbors recalled, "tomboy her way through the games of childhood." Except for the red ribbons she always wore in her hair, Florence was just one of the boys. More significant, she was usually the instigator and the leader of their games and pranks.

When the war ended, Amos decided to move on to bigger things than the hardware business. He invested heavily in real estate and he raised prize cattle and horses, and he became president of the Farmers and Mechanics Bank.

Florence Mabel Kling De Wolfe Harding

Born
August 15, 1860,
Marion, Ohio

Parents
Amos Hall Kling and
Louise Mabel Bouton
Kling

Marriage
March 1880, to Henry
Athenton De Wolfe

Children
Marshall Eugene De
Wolfe (1880-1915)

Divorced
1886

Remarried
July 8, 1891, to Warren
G. Harding (1865-1923)

Died
November 21, 1924,
Marion, Ohio

Then he converted its second floor into quarters for his own building and loan association. The next logical step was to build a mansion worthy of his new station in life, and on a trip to Europe to buy horses, he accumulated furniture, statuary, and other touches of elegance for it. Florence loved the stable behind the mansion, and although she wasn't yet a teenager, she became one of the most accomplished horsewomen in Marion.

As she grew older, Florence's father insisted on teaching her what he himself was learning about the banking business, and he demystified the ins and outs of the real estate business while he was at it. He may not have had any thoughts that Florence might take over his businesses one day—women still didn't do such things—but he was, as she explained it, "obsessed with disgust over the ignorance to the majority of women in business matters," and he wanted no child of his, not even a daughter, not able to understand the power of money.

Florence herself wasn't interested in becoming a businesswoman, but she wasn't interested in mastering the skills of running a house, pleasing a husband, and raising children, either. She was sure that she was going to make her mark as a concert pianist. Her father encouraged her dream, and he even drove her to practice "until her fingers bled." Yet he wouldn't send her to New York City to study, as she wanted, but rather enrolled her in the Cincinnati Conservatory of Music. A career as a concert pianist was all very well, but it was more important to him that she acquire the skills of a music teacher for the day when she might have to earn a living for herself. The conservatory also served as a kind of finishing school, where Florence was schooled in languages and social graces; she learned a good deal about fashion in Cincinnati, too. And the idea swirling among her fellow students that the day wasn't far off when women might be accepted in the world of business intrigued her.

Florence's schooling was cut short when she was called home to take care of her mother, but she went back to Marion a changed young woman. If Amos thought she was still his docile daughter willing to do anything he asked, he had another thing coming. They fought one another almost continually in shouting matches that sometimes went on for hours, and before long she decided the only way she could escape from her father was by getting married.

She had no one in particular in mind, and even though she was a rich girl, and a popular one, not very many young men in Marion were inclined to want to deal with the job of "taming" such a headstrong woman. She wrote in her diary, "Vice often comes in at the door of necessity, not the door of inclination." She was in a position to know. She was pregnant.

Florence's father wanted her to marry well, and it was noticed around town that she was "a prime favorite with men."

The young man who helped her make this bid for freedom from her father possible was Henry De Wolfe, a handsome young man known around town as Pete. He was from one of the oldest families in Marion and a young representative of the town's elite, but there were signs that he was on the road to becoming the town drunk as well. That appealed to the rebel in Florence. What appealed to her even more was that his father, Simon De Wolfe, and Amos Kling despised each other.

Pete De Wolfe wasn't in love with Flossie, as Florence was called, and he even denied that the baby she was carrying was his. It was never quite clear that he actually married her, but they "eloped" to Columbus and then gravitated to the nearby town of Galion, where they lived as husband and wife, whether a justice of the peace had made it legal or not. Either way, common law would have made the match binding. Neither of their families approved, and both Amos and Simon cut the couple adrift. Their child, Marshall De Wolfe, was born less than six months after the couple left Marion, and although Pete still denied that he was the father, he agreed to take on the responsibility of raising the baby.

But in spite of the burden, or possibly because of it, Pete went right on drinking, and then on December 22, 1882, he vanished. Two days later, on Christmas Eve, Florence and her baby made their way home to Marion, where she broke into a house that she knew was empty and she and her baby curled up in a corner and went to sleep.

But Florence was a determined survivor. She had spunk, and she had an entrepreneurial spirit. Within a week of her arrival, she had somehow managed to borrow a piano and she was giving lessons to several youngsters at fifty cents an hour. Simon De Wolfe came forward to take care of her grocery bills, and she was soon able to rent rooms for herself and the baby.

It wasn't until baby Marshall was four years old that Amos relented and offered to let her come home. But when he insisted that she must change her name back to Kling and rename the baby, too, Florence stubbornly stayed where she was.

She eventually grew disenchanted with motherhood. Once he had passed his babyhood, she lost interest in Marshall, although she was still determined to support him alone as a single mother. Then, after she filed for a legal separation from her husband, her father came back to her with another offer. He said that he was willing to adopt her baby and raise him as his own son, and Florence gratefully accepted. She was on her own at last. She sued De Wolfe for divorce, and that made her independence a fact.

Life was far from easy for a young divorced music teacher in a place like Marion. She began spending her evenings at the local skating rink, as she had

> *"That short unhappy period of my life is dead and buried. It was a great mistake."*
>
> —*Florence Harding on her early life*

Above: Young Warren Harding broke a lot of hearts during his early years in Marion, Ohio.

before all her troubles began, and her piano students helped keep her mind off her problems during the day.

One of those students was a girl named Charity Harding. The family had their own piano, and Florence went to their house for the music lessons. One of the members of the household was a handsome young man named Warren Gamaleil Harding, the owner and editor of the *Marion Star*, but she knew him as the cornet player at the skating rink.

There already had been some talk that he and Florence had become involved with one another. Indeed, in responding at the divorce proceedings, Henry De Wolfe claimed that she had been spending most of her days at the printing shop and her evenings at the skating rink, and that she had more than just a casual interest in Mr. Harding.

As for the young man, who was five years younger than Florence, he wasn't exactly a prime catch in the sea of love. He had dropped out of law school out of boredom, and everything he tried seemed to fail. He spent the only real money he had made recently—the commission on an insurance policy for Amos Kling's new downtown hotel—on a new cornet rather than paying off a debt or two, although he had plenty of those. Yes, he owned the local newspaper, but it was floundering and it was mortgaged to the hilt. He also had a reputation as a gambler, and there wasn't a tavern in town where he wasn't greeted by name. More important, Warren was a ladies' man, and he preferred "unmarriageable" ladies. But for all that, and for all her denials, Florence considered Warren Harding a special kind of challenge, and when she began to court him, he didn't fight her off.

Florence and her father were on speaking terms by that time, but when he found out about Warren, the fat was in the fire all over again. He threatened to cut off her inheritance, and when he met the young newspaperman at the courthouse, he assured him that if he married Florence, he would personally shoot him down in the street. Predictably, such threats only served to make Florence more determined. "The very lessons my father had drilled into me of careful thought, self-reliance, self determination, gave me strength to use my own judgment despite his objections," she said.

Before much longer, Florence and Warren were engaged, but it is open to conjecture which one of them actually popped the question. He had obviously given the idea a lot of careful thought, and all of the pieces fit together. For her part, Florence found him "a stationary man," who needed a "progressive woman" like her to get him moving in the right direction. Even before their engagement, she had put together a plan to retire some of the *Star's* debts. When the plan began to work, he found that he had enough money left over to start building a house, which Florence designed. Some of the money they needed came from her mother, who, unlike her husband, completely approved of Warren Harding, and did what she could to see her daughter happy at last.

They were married on July 8, 1891, in their new house, almost as soon as it was finished. More than three hundred guests crowded in to witness the ceremony, but Amos Kling was not among them. In fact, he had sent out word to his friends and associates to boycott the affair. Unknown to anyone but those who were in the back of the room, Louisa Kling, the bride's mother, defied her husband and showed up. No one ever mentioned it, and even Florence didn't know until much later.

Florence was proud to be called Mrs. Warren G. Harding, but she never wore a wedding ring to display her pride. "I don't like badges," she said. She did, however, have a badge of office in mind for her new husband. During her wedding reception, she confided to several friends that this was her first step on the road to making Mr. Harding president of the United States.

> *"I'd rather go hungry than broil a steak or boil potatoes. I love business."*
>
> —Florence Harding on her lack of interest in domestic things

Businesswoman

The first thing Florence did when the Hardings returned from their honeymoon was to abandon her piano students. The second was to take over an empty desk in the office of the *Marion Star*, and make a thorough study of its books and financial records. The paper's circulation was being handled by an outside company that cost more than it brought in, so she canceled its contract and took over distribution herself. In less than a month she managed to turn a loss into $200 worth of income, but that was only the beginning.

Obviously, Warren was happy with the new turn of events, but he was pressured by her demands and the sudden changes they brought, and when it led to stomach trouble, he and Florence moved from their own house into the Harding family home, where his father and mother, both homeopathic doctors, could take care of him. Their accommodations were cramped and uncomfortable, and whenever his medical problems allowed it, Warren began

Below: Warren was a hands-on newspaper publisher. Even while he was running for president, he took the time to help set type for its pages.

Florence sold papers to her newsboys for a penny apiece, and they resold them for two cents.

to travel, leaving Florence to cope on her own. As a newspaper editor, he had free passes on all the railroads, and he used the privilege to make the rounds of meetings of state Republicans, and once he even ranged as far as Washington, D.C. Then, as signs of depression began to set in, he went to the Kellogg sanatorium at Battle Creek, Michigan, and he didn't come home for a year.

The paper's business manager quit while Warren was gone, and Florence replaced him. She kept the job for the next fourteen years. Her first order of business was to build circulation, which in turn would allow her to boost advertising rates. She mapped out routes through local neighborhoods and then she hired schoolboys to make deliveries to homes and businesses. They became known as "Mrs. Harding's boys," and she was like a mother to them, although business being business, she could also be a hard taskmaster.

Little by little, Florence wound up in charge of everything from circulation to advertising sales. She bought the newsprint and she supervised the running of the presses, and she still found time to organize and run what she called a "registration bureau" to personally deal with customer complaints. On top of that, she subscribed to a news service and monitored the Teletype, deciding what national and international news would interest the *Star's* readers.

About all that Florence didn't do was write the editorials and establish official policy. Even if he was away a lot of the time, Warren was still the paper's managing editor.

By the time Warren came back home, Florence's accomplishments with his newspaper left him speechless. His health was still precarious, and she took on the added responsibility of nursing him. But at the office they were clearly a team. The talk around Marion was that she was a nagger, and it is true that she often put his nerves on edge, but she was also a loving wife, and she always managed to bring him back from the brink. "The talk about being boss makes fine conversation," Florence said, "but I can tell you I know when to retreat."

Landmark in Journalism

On the local front, Florence recommended stories for publication that she knew would be of interest to women. Then she went a step further by hiring Jane Dixon as a reporter to generate more of such coverage. She was the first female writer to work on any newspaper in Ohio. The people of the town were scandalized at the idea that Ms. Dixon would do such an "unwomanly" thing, but Florence backed her to the hilt, and eventually readers got over their prejudice. Circulation even went up a bit, and Jane Dixon turned out to be a good reporter.

Freed from business concerns, Warren found time to join every fraternal and civic booster organization in town, but that was good for business, too. Florence did a lot of entertaining in their home, and some of the time the guests were politicians. Her husband had become a force among Ohio Republicans—his newspaper was their mouthpiece—and Florence helped him put his relationships with them on a personal level.

Warren didn't have an enemy for miles around, except Amos Kling. He was determined to destroy his son-in-law, and at one point he bought up and then called in all of Warren's loans. It would have been a masterstroke if Warren's friends didn't bail him out. Beaten but unbowed, Amos invested heavily in a rival newspaper, intending to put the *Star* out of business, and he quietly discouraged his friends from supporting any local causes that Warren Harding was interested in promoting. Warren took it all in stride, and "the Old Gent," as he called Amos, wasn't ever able to get the best of him.

Warren Harding had a roving eye, and their marriage hit a major snag after three years when he got the wife of a local businessman pregnant. There had been rumors of his extramarital exploits almost from the beginning, but this time the woman was not only a respected member of local society but also one of Florence's best friends. Florence was devastated beyond words, but eventually she wrote, "I have become a better wife for all the difficulties I have been through." At the same time, she knew that Warren's wandering eye would probably lead to more of the same. "There is no devotion like a husband's as long as he is far enough out of his wife's sight to do as he pleases," she said. But she needed Warren as much as he needed her, though, and she made up her mind to make the best of a bad thing.

Above: Florence carefully read every letter and telegram that Warren received, but he managed to keep his love letters away from her eyes. There were many, so it wasn't easy.

The Duchess

In the early years of their marriage, Warren called Florence "the boss," but he was an avid reader of a satirical series of stories in The New York Sun *whose main character was called "the duchess." She was described as fussy but cool, with "curves in de brains" and a passion for "runnin' de money." He thought that seemed to describe his wife as well, and Florence became known as "the duchess" for the rest of her life. But she was still the boss. She always called her husband "Wurr'n."*

A Political Wife

Even though Warren reveled in the friendship of politicians, he didn't seem to have any political ambitions of his own until he announced that he was going to run for the state senate in 1899. The scuttlebutt around town was that Florence had imperiously ordered the decision, but considering his personality, it was probably likely that he had made up his own mind. At the time, he was a Republican in a strongly Democratic county. The town of Marion was run by Republicans, but they preferred to run it without the likes of Warren G. Harding, whom they considered a liability in spite of all the comfort his newspaper gave to them. That was most likely because Amos Kling was their leader. In a district that included four counties, Marion County had come up in a rotation to name the candidate that year, and there was enough Republican strength in the other three to make Warren a contender.

Florence was the first to see the possibility, and while she may not have ordered her husband to take a chance at it, it is certain that she persuaded him to. Florence ran his campaign for him, leaving him free to concentrate on preparing the speeches for his appearances, which she arranged herself. In the meantime, Amos Kling was doing all he could to wreck the Harding candidacy, even to the point of going out and making speeches of his own. For his part, Warren became convinced that what the man was saying was true, and he accepted his argument that his candidacy would wreck his business. Florence knew better, and she reminded Warren of her father's motives, which had nothing at all to do with Warren's welfare. That was when he tore up his statement of withdrawal. When it was all over, no one at the victory celebration had a better reason to smile than Florence. She had not only engineered the beginning of her husband's political career, but she had stood up to her father and won again.

During the campaign, a local Republican fixer named Harry Daugherty took note that Warren Harding was going to make a "dandy-looking president," and hitching his wagon to the Harding star, he took the candidate under his wing. Florence was suspicious of him—she wanted that job for herself—but she was impressed by his presidential remark. She thought that her husband could be president if he wanted to, and she certainly wanted him to. She started assembling a new wardrobe in anticipation of soon becoming First Lady, and she began upgrading Warren's closet, too, ordering custom-made suits for him so that he, too, could look more "presidential."

She carefully arranged all of his public appearances after that, and she always made sure that she was with him when he did. Remembering his roving eye, she established a hard-and-fast rule: "Never let a husband travel alone."

It meant that Florence had to turn the day-to-day running of the *Marion Star* over to the staff that she had hired and trained, but she kept in touch as much as she could. When she found out that Warren had ordered his managing editor never to mention his accomplishments in the legislature, she told him, "I am the boss. Forget that order. I'll take the responsibility." After all, what was the

Below: Without Harry Daugherty's political genius, not even Florence, for all her ambition, could have engineered Warren's rise to power.

point of owning a newspaper if you couldn't use it to crow about yourself once in a while?

Considering that the seat he held was traditionally a rotating one, everyone except Florence was surprised when Warren was elected to a second term. It represented a detour from the path Florence wanted him to follow, but Senator Mark Hanna, who ran things in Ohio, nixed his ambition to run for governor. He did, however, allow him to become lieutenant governor. And then the Hardings began to travel, and Warren became more nationally known for his odd but spellbinding speaking style. He never went anywhere without Florence until 1905 when she developed nephritis and was near death. She got better after surgery, but her recovery was slow and she was bedridden for five months, wondering all the while what her Warren might be up to. What he was up was the same old thing. He was having an affair with another one of her old friends. It would be more than thirteen years before she found out about it, and it would come close to wrecking her marriage, because it still hadn't cooled down.

After Florence recovered, she began traveling with Warren again. He was a popular speaker on the Chautauqua circuit and she toured with him. They also took long vacations together, but the most surprising one of all was a six-week grand tour of Europe with no less a person than Amos Kling. The seventy-three-year-old widower had recently married a thirty-five-year-old woman, and she talked him into burying the hatchet with his daughter and son-in-law. He went her one better and named Florence his heir. Not only that, but he happily paid for their European junket.

Amos drew the line at supporting Warren's candidacy for governor, though, but Warren lost the 1910 election anyway, even with Florence's forceful help during the campaign. He had made the mistake of ignoring the political bosses, although he thought that would make him more appealing

Below: Warren ran his presidential campaign from their home, where Florence was able to keep an eye on his flirtatious ways.

Role Model

Florence's first visit to the White House was when she and Warren were invited by President and Mrs. Taft to a party marking their wedding anniversary, and she and First Lady Nellie Taft discovered that they had an uncanny number of things in common: Both had been educated at Ohio music conservatories; both thoroughly understood the workings of the business world; both had supported themselves teaching music; and both were married to comparatively passive men who relied on them to give them a push through the doors of politics when they needed one.

to the voters. More than once during campaign rallies, he told the voters that "I was nominated in spite of the bosses.... I owe allegiance to only one boss." And then, asking Florence to stand, he went on, "She's a mighty good one, too."

The Hardings had taken a second trip to Europe in the meantime, but when they went abroad for the third time in 1911, it was in England that Florence had her first brush with feminism. The folks back home generally assumed that she must already be highly in favor of women's rights, but now she saw the issue through new eyes. "There are certain times and places wherein women must be militant to obtain their proper degree of justice and right," she wrote. "In England, for example, where women were not allowed equality of opportunity in any endeavor, where men refused them partnerships and erected before them the stone wall of petty convention, I understand why women smashed windows and hacked doors." Florence wasn't ready to take to the streets to promote sisterhood, but women who were knew they had an ally.

Warren's interest in politics had cooled somewhat after he lost the gubernatorial election, but it was reborn when he was tapped to place President Taft's name in nomination for his reelection. Florence, meanwhile, was hard at work having his name placed in nomination for United State senator. She got her wish, and after her husband became Senator Warren G. Harding in 1915, they moved to the capital city.

Below: Even when he was a senator, people could help noticing that Warren looked "presidential."

Strangers in a Strange Town

Although Florence had traveled extensively, she was still a small-town girl, and she was dismayed at the coldness she found in Washington. "It is indescribable," she said. Her health began to fail again, but she bought an Embassy Row town house with part of the inheritance from her late father, and the distraction of furnishing it helped restore her, even when her trunk of pills didn't. She also got into the spirit of following the Washington custom of making social calls, although she made few friends when she did. An old friend noted, "She was never at ease, and often on the defensive, but for the sake of her husband's position, she was eager to be liked and anxious to make a good impression."

Florence was a bear for public recognition for herself as well as her husband, and her experience running a newspaper gave her more access to the Washington press corps than the average senator's wife. She used it well then, and later, too. But she wasn't able to take control of Warren's office as she had back in Marion. His professional staff didn't need her help or her advice. Warren still did, though. She almost never missed a Senate debate, and she took her opinions home with her. It was common knowledge that Senator Harding met with important people at home rather than in his office so that his wife could take charge of the discussion without staffers around to overrule her ideas. Another Senate wife noted, "Anyone can play the game who is courageous, ruthless and shrewd, and Florence was all three. He took so seriously what Florence said." Almost no one else did. Most congressional wives simply ignored her, except for the wife of Ohio congressman Nicholas Longworth. The former Alice Roosevelt went out of her way to ridicule Florence.

Alice was especially sarcastic when the subject turned to the close relationship between Florence and her own former best friend, the multimillionaire Evalyn Walsh McLean. Evalyn was a nonconformist, to say the least. She smoked too much, she drank too much, she flirted with men too much, and she indulged in morphine too much. It was all too much for most women who had come to maturity in the genteel 1890s, but not for Florence. She didn't even mind when Evalyn made a big play for Warren.

Above: Evalyn Walsh McLean, one of the most flamboyant Washington society women, took Florence under her wing.

A lifelong horse lover, Florence hated automobiles. Their car was "the only thing we ever owned that she did not have a desire to run," her husband said.

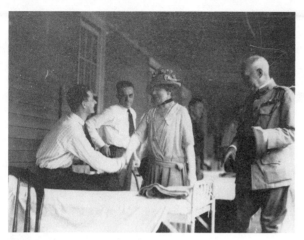

Above: Florence was tireless in her volunteer activities during World War I. She was a familiar face in local hospitals, and she arranged outings for many of her "boys."

Evalyn's father had struck gold in Colorado when she was young, and he moved the family to the ornate Washington mansion where she grew up. One of her great accomplishments as a young woman was snagging newspaper heir, and owner of the *Washington Post*, Edward B. McLean as a husband.

Evalyn and Florence became fast friends, and it was Florence's entrée into the Washington social swim, even if it was often in a backwater of nonconformity. They became like sisters, although Florence was old enough to be Evalyn's mother, and the younger woman transformed Florence's wardrobe from the slightly dowdy dresses that were fine for Marion, Ohio, but out of place in cosmopolitan Washington. Their friendship also had a positive effect on Florence's health, and even Warren had to admit that she hadn't looked better in years. She didn't need the pills her father-in-law sent her any longer, and on the other side of the coin, she never followed Evalyn's lead in taking stronger drugs. She had too much to do to surrender her brain to alcohol and morphine.

When World War I began, Florence volunteered for every patriotic duty she could. She worked to find housing for war workers who were flooding the capital, and she helped set up recreational facilities for the women who were among them. She still hadn't worked up any enthusiasm for nurturing children, but she became an almost constant visitor at nurseries and day-care centers that served working women. And she also volunteered for the Red Cross feeding stations for soldiers headed to France. Evalyn took over a wing of Walter Reed Hospital, and she arranged outings for the men assigned to it. When she visited "her boys," Florence went along, writing letters for the wounded men and distributing gifts to them, and she loved every minute of it. It took her back to her days of nurturing newsboys, even if it didn't bring back memories of her son, who was now dead, but whom she hardly knew.

In the meantime, Warren was up to his old tricks. He'd had thinly disguised affairs with more than half a dozen women. Florence seemed to be aware of most of them, and she knew that they could be dynamite in a national campaign. Whether that was the reason or not, when there was a groundswell to make Warren president, Florence put her foot down. After saying that it would be a terrible mistake for both of them, she told a meeting of his backers that "I am decidedly opposed to it." Warren seconded the motion every time the subject came up.

But when President Wilson proposed his League of Nations, Florence became a virulent enemy of the idea, out of fear that American boys might be sent off to foreign wars without congressional approval, and she felt a strong need to do something about it, up to and including getting Warren elected president. She denied that she had lobbied him to vote against Wilson's plan, but in light of her past history, not very many people believed her. Not many believed that she didn't want him to run for president, either, and the boom went on. Typical of the comments from his supporters was, "Senator and Mrs. Harding will make the best president we have ever had."

Harry Daugherty, of course, believed it more than anybody else, and he knew that only Florence was standing in his way. It wasn't an easy sell, and she held fast until just weeks before the Republican National Convention began. Her decision finally came after a session with a popular Washington clairvoyant, who predicted that her life was going to change and that her future was bright; she added, however, that it would also be "dark." Florence kept it to herself, but Warren made it official a few days later when he threw his hat into the presidential ring.

> "Mrs. Harding is the only candidate's wife who came more than halfway to meet newspaper reporters."
>
> —The New York Times

During the preconvention campaign, the husband of Warren's longtime mistress, Carrie Philips, sent him a blackmail note. He had found all of Warren's love letters to her—fifteen years' worth of them—and he said he would have them published unless he received $25,000 in hush money. Florence had known about the affair for more than two years by then, but she knew that if her husband refused to pay, he'd not only lose the presidency but his Senate seat as well. She advised that he should pay, but not until after he got the nomination and he would be in a position to divert campaign funds to make the payoff. The blackmailer agreed, and Florence never agreed to let Warren withdraw as he still wished to. It is likely that he was thinking about all those other women. He had written torrid letters to every one of them.

No other candidate's wife had ever been more active at a national political convention than Florence was at Chicago. Harry Daugherty was Warren's campaign manager and chief arm-twister, but Florence was the undisputed queen of his campaign headquarters.

Below: Florence was a constant presence at Warren's side during his run for the presidency; they could usually be found on their front porch.

She worked hard at painting a picture of domestic bliss, lamenting that they had no children, because "Warren loves them so." And she made a show of doing needlework, which she claimed pleased him. She didn't march for women's rights, as other delegates' wives did, but she assured an adoring press that, "Yes, I'm a suffragist." Florence didn't shy away from criticizing the other potential candidates, either, and she took stands for attribution that had always been previously reserved for the candidates themselves. Not even Warren had as much to say as she did.

Leaks about her husband's affairs were starting to surface, although nobody could prove that any of them was more than just a rumor. Warren was ready to throw in the towel, and Florence was wavering. But she made him promise to wait.

Her horoscope had told her that the tide would turn after noon on Saturday, and the time had not yet come. The stars were right, as it turned out. Florence told Warren that "destiny has marked you for the man and you are chosen."

Warren chose to conduct an old-fashioned "front porch" campaign from their house in Marion. That brought a horde of reporters to Ohio, and they started nosing around the courthouse and other front porches in town. They came close to uncovering the blackmail plot, and hoping to bury the scandal once and for all, Harry Daugherty passed the hat among well-heeled Republicans to make a final offer of the original $25,000 demand plus a $2,000 monthly payment as long as Warren was in public office. Another of Warren's former mistresses was paid off, too, but not as handsomely. But then, her affair with him had been comparatively short. At least two others asked for money, but they were turned down.

Florence was given a prominent role in the campaign. This would be the first election where women had the vote, and she was up to the job of wooing them, even if the campaign publicity painted her as an ordinary housewife who liked to sew curtains and chat with her neighbors over the back fence. She also engineered photo opportunities, and although she was less than photogenic, she always managed to put her best face forward.

The professional politicians didn't know quite how to handle a campaigning woman, and Florence was generally left to her own devices. She knew exactly how to appeal to voters, though, male or female. At one rally she told them, "I am a politician, my husband is a statesmen." As she always had been, Florence was also the statesman's chief advisor, and he frequently told the official ones that they'd better "ask the duchess" for answers to their hard questions.

Florence was also an innovator. She was the first to use Hollywood movie stars as campaigners. Her friend Evalyn McLean had scores of show business friends, and at Florence's suggestion, she recruited Al Jolson to

Below: Celebrity endorsements were Florence's idea. Stars like Al Jolson and Blanche Ring went to Marion to show their support for Warren.

organize them. One day, a whole trainload of celebrities, including such stars as Mary Pickford, Douglas Fairbanks, and Lillian Gish, arrived in Marion for a wild rally that was recorded for posterity by a bank of newsreel cameras. Party chairman Will Hays, who would soon become the despised Hollywood censor, telegraphed his congratulations and heaped wild praise on Florence for her innovation.

When the candidate and his wife left town on a train of their own for a round of whistle-stop campaigning, Florence was always out on the observation deck with Warren, and no matter who else also happened to be there, he made it a point to introduce her first, and the crowds loved him for it. It was very clear that they adored his wife. As one of the party faithful put it, "If the Democrats had been smart, they'd have nominated a woman for president."

Warren not only won the election, but it was by the biggest margin in a century. Florence told her admirers, "You and I both know that if Warren had been defeated I would have been the most miserable woman in the world this morning instead of being the happiest. I am a regular fraud to say that I am scared out of my happiness by the responsibility, even as great as that responsibility is, for I am not."

> "I shall not be sorry when the campaign is done and I am back in Washington. It is good to be missed."
>
> —Florence Harding on the nasty presidential campaign

Jazz Age White House

Warren put off naming his cabinet until after he and Florence had taken a long vacation. He claimed that he wanted to appoint only the best people so that his place in history would be assured, based on his skill as a judge of men. But at the same time, he wanted men he liked around him, and there were quite a few others who he knew would come around to call in some very important favors. So he did what any man in a position like that might do, he put Florence in charge of screening the potential candidates.

He considered her a shrewd judge of people and a thoroughly professional politician, and he figured that with Florence's input he would be able to put together a cabinet that would be the envy of all the presidents who came before him. But what he didn't figure on was that Florence didn't like some of the men he might have chosen himself, and she wasn't above letting her personal opinions get in the way. She had been keeping a little list for years, and no slight had gone unrecorded. Warren was probably also aware that his campaign had bankrupted the Republican party and it was being kept afloat by four or five men who would certainly be in line for a payoff from the new administration. Even Florence was going to have a hard time keeping them away from the public trough.

One of the names most often mentioned was Harry Daugherty, who expected to be named attorney general. Most Washington insiders regarded him as an out-and-out crook, and they may have been right. But he was close to both Warren and to Florence, and they clearly owed him something. Harry nearly blew his chance when he claimed in public that he had personally "made" the new president, and Florence had a fit. Rebutting that Warren himself, and no one else, not even her, was responsible for his own success, she quietly scratched Harry's name from her list of cabinet recommendations. Harry managed to work his way back into her good graces by telling her, "I want to be in Washington to protect Harding from the crooks. I know how trustful he is, and I know who all the crooks are." Florence certainly couldn't argue with that, and Harry slipped back onto the "recommended" list, even though nobody else but Warren thought it was a wise idea.

In some instances, Florence even surprised the nominees themselves. When she told banker Andrew Mellon that she was looking forward to working with him in Washington, it was the first he heard that she had decided to make him treasury secretary. Florence also involved herself in choices for ambassadorships, and even the new White House gardener was an old family friend of the Klings. Another old friend was named postmaster in Marion even though he had failed the civil service examination. Whoever needed a job knew that Florence was the go-to person in this administration.

People who were close enough to her said that when Warren took the oath of office as president, she whispered every word along with him. She raptly followed every word of his inauguration speech, too. And why not? She had carefully edited every word of it for him. As they were being escorted into the White House that afternoon, Florence turned to her husband and said, "Well, Warren Harding, I have got you the presidency, now what are you going to do with it?"

The first thing he did was to declare the White House open to the public for the first time since the United States went to war against Germany almost three years earlier, and people seemed to come from everywhere to have a look. The Inaugural Ball was held that evening at the sprawling McLean mansion, where Evalyn had, as she put it, "contrived a scene that I found immensely satisfying." Most of the members of the new administration were there, but

Below: Never one to miss an opportunity, Florence became part of the media herself, taking a turn at cranking a newsreel camera when the press gathered on the White House lawn.

Above: The wives of the Philippine commissioners were happy to smile for the newsreel cameras, but the broadest smile of all was on the face of their hostess, the First Lady.

the Hardings stayed home. They had a big day ahead of them.

Warren appeared in the Oval Office almost at the crack of dawn the following day, but Florence was already there. She had her own duties, though. She had let it be known through her finely honed publicity machine that she would personally guide tours of the White House for her guests any time they cared to drop in. She also posed for photographs with many of the visitors when she took her new dog, Laddie Boy, for walks out on the lawn.

Dissenting Voice

As far as the public was concerned, Florence Harding was one of the most popular women ever to have lived in the White House, although many on the staff found her "unconventional" and "unusual." One person who refused to be impressed was Ike Hoover, who had served several presidents as the White House's chief usher. He said: "Mrs. Harding was wild and anxious, but so constituted that she could not be a social success. She made most progress with politicians who came to see the President." The president's valet, Brooks, who had been on the staff nearly as long, called the remark "blasphemous."

When she was putting together her new wardrobe, Florence chose a color that became popular with the public as "Harding blue," and she also used it when she was decorating White House rooms, one of which had its walls covered in Harding blue silk. Most of her decorating harked back to her days in Marion: She covered chairs and sofas with chintz or velvet, and she placed silver-framed photos of their family and friends everywhere that space wasn't taken up by her huge collection of elephant figurines.

Above: "I know what's best for the President," Florence said. "He does well when he listens to me and poorly when he does not." It may have been true. Warren kept his silence.

Florence maintained a dizzying social schedule. Every afternoon she posed for photographs with members of any organization that happened to be meeting in Washington, and later in the day she circulated from room to room chatting with invited guests. Doorman Ike Hoover said that while the president's appointment list was longer than any he could remember, Florence's was always longer still.

Few evenings when no official entertaining was scheduled went by without as many as twenty dinner guests, and the after-dinner entertaining usually stretched on until well after midnight. Every now and then, Warren would take the evening off to play poker with his cronies, or at least that's where he said he was going, and Florence got the evening off, too. But there weren't many of those. She almost never let him out of her sight.

Florence also revived the custom of state dinners and formal receptions, but she broke precedent by turning many conversations among her official guests around to tales from her own life story, which many of them found as refreshing as they were fascinating. She protested that she hated being "dressed up all the time," but others who knew her said that the opposite was the case. Younger women who were calling themselves flappers were showing more and more of their legs, but Florence kept her skirts no higher than eight inches from the floor. Some said it was because she had ugly ankles, but she claimed that it was how she had been brought up, and "it is not for me to dictate to American womanhood." Still, she always wore a black velvet neckband and—rather quickly—so did every fashion-conscious woman in the United States, even the flappers, who called them "Flossie clings."

The times were changing in the United States when the Hardings were in the White House, and the traditions of White House entertaining were changing, too. The old guard of Washington society considered Florence, and all that she stood for, beneath them, but Florence had a new guard solidly behind her, thanks to Evalyn McLean and her pals, who brought a new kind of glitter to the White House. Movie stars, vaudevillians, and other celebrities were frequent guests, and their own public relations people made sure that all the United States noticed. What outsiders were not allowed to see or hear about was that in spite of the constitutional amendment against it, liquor was always plentiful upstairs; and not only was the quality better than the average

Florence was the first First Lady to have a radio brought into the White House, joining three million other Americans who were transforming it from "a passing novelty."

First Dog

After Florence made sure that she was seen walking her dog, Laddie Boy, Airedales became the most popular pet in the United States, and Laddie Boy himself was considered the best of the breed. A dog-food company that obviously knew what it was doing named one of its brands after him, and it is still popular more than eighty years after Laddie Boy himself went to doggie heaven. According to Florence's publicity machine, the dog was part of the family—the child they never had—and when letters arrived addressed to him, they were always promptly answered. The Harding pet was on hand for social events whenever it was practical, and even had a special stool reserved for the times he showed up at cabinet meetings. Not surprisingly, Laddie Boy was known among members of the White House press corps as a "publicity hound."

Below: If the dog world had a king, it would have been Warren's dog, Laddie Boy. All of America fell in love with this wildly popular Airedale.

speakeasy's, but the First Lady herself often handled the bartending chores, usually in the privacy of a bedroom.

Florence worked tirelessly for such causes as women's equality and animal rights—she removed all of Teddy Roosevelt's hunting trophies from the White House—and the plight of disabled veterans brought tears to her eyes. But she still had plenty of time left over to run the political side of the presidency. Every cabinet member kept in constant touch with her, and they relied on her to lobby for them with the president, who was rather casual in his handling of the government's business between rounds of golf and afternoon poker games.

In 1922, Albert Fall, the secretary of the interior, handed over oil-drilling rights in a navy petroleum reserve to his friends Harry Sinclair of the Sinclair Oil Company and Edward Doheny of Pan-American Petroleum. The California site was called Teapot Dome. Fall, who stood to profit hugely from the deal, cautioned that it needed to be kept quiet in the interest of "national security." The president, who wasn't cut in on the windfall, said, "These fellows seem to know what they are doing." Florence, who knew everything that was going on, had nothing to say. She was busy planning for an extended trip to Alaska.

The trip had been postponed the previous year, and now it was postponed again when Florence became desperately ill and seemed on the verge of death. When news of her condition was released, it started a round of prayer meetings and vigils in every corner of the country and even abroad. The White House was inundated with floral tributes, theaters and movie houses called for minutes of silent prayer from their audiences, and newspapers ran editorials and long articles praising her accomplishments almost as though she had already died. It was said that even Warren prayed for her.

Above: Florence took her time saying farewell to her White House staff when she and Warren left for an extended trip.

Then, as if by a miracle, after several weeks of discouraging medical bulletins, Florence began to show signs of recovery. "I knew I wouldn't die," she said. "Warren needs me." Then she ordered the White House open to tourists again. She believed that the country needed her, too, but it would be several months before she began making public appearances. She let it be known that she was solidly behind Harry Daugherty's announcement that her husband would run for a second term, but what she mostly talked about was going to Alaska.

Warren himself had become seriously ill, and his doctors advised against making a 15,000-mile trip that would involve more than seventy major speeches, reviews of dozens of parades, and attendance at an endless round of dinners and receptions. But he said that he had promises to keep and he would make the trip, even if Florence wasn't insisting on it.

After several days of touring the exotic Alaska Territory, the Hardings turned around and headed for home when word came from Washington that the Teapot Dome scandal was beginning to leak out and that Secretary of the Interior Fall and Attorney General Daugherty were about to be exposed for their part in it. The president was torn between an instinct to cover it in whitewash, and a belief that exposing it would not only personally absolve him but give him an air of integrity. Then he went back to his bridge game.

Their ship docked in Vancouver a day or two later, and the Hardings went ashore for a rally, but he skipped a luncheon because he said he wasn't feeling well after eating some crabmeat. Florence, who had shared that same meal, said she'd never felt better in her life. Warren was no better when they reached Seattle, and the next stop was canceled altogether. In San Francisco, he was carried off the train on a stretcher and hidden away in the Palace Hotel downtown. Less than a week later, the president was dead.

One of his doctors was convinced that he'd had a heart attack, and not food poisoning as the others believed. Although he had rarely been left alone since his first attack, Florence seems to have been the only one in the sickroom for a long period before death came, and that led to some rumors that she had poisoned her husband, possibly to rescue him from the scandal that was about to erupt. She didn't help her case when she refused to have a death mask made, as was customary; she also refused to allow an autopsy to be performed, even though the doctors couldn't agree on the cause of death. Florence raised some more eyebrows when she ordered that her husband's body should be removed from San Francisco immediately, and ordered an armed guard posted around it in the meantime. Her own steely personality didn't help, either. Florence Harding never shed a tear for her late husband in public.

Though Florence was eager to have her husband's body removed when he died, she insisted that he should remain where he was overnight so that his spirit would have time to completely leave his mortal bonds.

Few people really believed that Florence had murdered her husband, but fewer still weren't convinced that he hadn't been murdered. The long list of suspects included Harry Daugherty, one of the president's doctors, who the whisperers said was having an affair with Florence, and even future president Herbert Hoover, who had joined the party on the West Coast after the Teapot Dome business began surfacing. The most common belief was that they all had a hand in it and that the death of the president was the result of a convoluted conspiracy.

The trip back east involved the entire country in Warren Harding's death. The bodies of other presidents had been taken from Washington for burial, but this was the first time Americans could pay their respects before the funeral. The windows of the observation car had been removed so that crowds along the route could see the president's flag-draped coffin inside. But Florence was nowhere to be seen. She had taken to a berth in another car and kept the shades drawn. There were rumors about that, too. People said that she'd had a nervous breakdown. People, that is, who didn't know Florence Harding. One of her maids noticed that she "had turned to ice," and her friend Evalyn McLean said that she gave "no sign of weakness or collapse."

The Widow Harding

Tributes to the late president were warm and heartfelt, and added a touch of admiration for Florence. A Boston newspaper said, "If the Constitution permitted, she could take the chair vacated by her adored husband and life pal, and pick up the reins from his lifeless hands and administer the affairs of this great nation with ability, wisdom, and in a statesmanlike manner."

But Florence had a bigger job ahead of her. She was determined to protect her husband's reputation and his place in history. That meant reading through every scrap of paper he left behind, official and private, and destroying what she thought the public should never know. She also had to get rid of some of her own memories, and she gave away most of her clothes and Warren's too. She even gave away her dog, Laddie Boy.

Below: The scandal that rocked the Harding administration was known as "Teapot Dome." This Chinese teapot, one of Florence's favorites, serves as a kind of symbol of the blot on Warren's memory.

On the night before Warren's funeral, Florence spent several hours talking to her husband's corpse, assuring him that "nothing can hurt you now."

When Florence left the White House, she moved into the McLean mansion, where a bonfire burned for days turning incriminating evidence into ashes and smoke. "We must be loyal to Warren and preserve his memory," she told a trusted aide who had come to help her carry boxes and suitcases to the flames. She missed the cache of love letters Warren had hidden in the Oval Office. Harry Daugherty thoughtfully purloined them before she could stumble on them.

Florence also wrote to old friends and associates asking them to return any of Warren's letters to them. She said that she wanted to build an archive for future researchers, but few of them were fooled. Still, most did as she asked. She burned most of them, and she also burned nearly every document she could find about her own early life.

While hearings on the Teapot Dome scandal tarnished the Harding legacy, a Senate investigation of Harry Daugherty's affairs may have been worse. Florence wasn't surprised that Harry managed to wriggle free, but she was blindsided by some of the revelations that came up about Warren's private life. There were some things she hadn't known about, such as a bank account that he maintained to buy off the president's mistresses. Harry kept such things out of the public record when he pleaded the Fifth Amendment, claiming that because he was Warren and Florence's attorney, it was privileged information.

Over the next few months, Warren's reputation teetered on the brink of public scandal, and Florence began to feel the heat as well. She had inherited almost half a million in property, investments, and cash from Warren, and she had investments worth $100,000 in her own name, plus a substantial amount left over from her inheritance from her father. It made her an uncommonly wealthy woman, and her former friends in the Fourth Estate began to wonder if she had come by it honestly.

Florence let it all roll off her back. She bought a house in Washington and entertained close friends both on her own and with Evalyn McLean at her estate nearby. She involved herself in the animal-rights movement again, and Florence seemed like her old self again after a year of widowhood. She was even planning a trip to Europe when her health began to fail again and her doctor ordered her to go home to Marion. She fought like a tiger against it, but finally agreed that she would go there for the summer, but not for retirement. When fall came, she was still there, but making travel plans. But by November, it was obvious that Florence's health was failing. She died of nephritis on November 21, 1924, in Marion. She was sixty-four years old.

The next day, the *Washington Post* carried a tribute apparently written by Evalyn McLean, the owner's wife and Florence's closest friend. "Florence Harding was a good woman," it said, "as good as gold, as true as steel, as brave as a lion, a gentle as a dove, as sweet as the flowers.... Foremost among this remarkable woman's personal qualities were courage and resoluteness, but even those paled before her inflexible fidelity to her friendships and her friends."

Above: After she left the White House, Florence chose not to return to the Hardings' house in Marion, Ohio.

Visiting the Harding Home

The house where Warren and Florence Harding were married and lived for many years is at 380 Mount Vernon Avenue in Marion, Ohio. The two-and-a-half-story Queen Anne–style house has been restored and furnished with pieces Florence originally selected for it by the Harding Memorial Association, which runs it along with the National Park Service. A building in the backyard, built as press headquarters for the 1920 presidential campaign, contains a museum of Harding family memorabilia. Florence and Warren are interred in a mausoleum nearby.

The home is open to the public at no charge Wednesday through Sunday, Memorial Day through Labor Day. Marion, Ohio is located on U.S. Route 23, forty-five miles north of Columbus in north-central Ohio.

Grace Coolidge

Vermont Natives

Grace Goodhue was a twenty-five-year-old teacher at the Clarke School for the Deaf in Northampton, Massachusetts, when she went outside to water flowers on a warm day in the spring of 1904. She was enjoying the sun when she noticed a movement in the second-floor window of an adjoining building. There stood a young man gazing intently into a mirror as he shaved. He was clad in long johns—and he was wearing a hat, apparently to hold an unruly lock of hair in place. He looked so funny that Grace laughed out loud. The young man shaving was a lawyer and aspiring politician named Calvin Coolidge.

Soon after, Calvin arranged for his landlord to introduce him to his neighbor. By coincidence, they were both Vermonters. Grace was a young teacher seven years Calvin's junior who had moved to Northampton to pursue her passion to help the deaf. On the surface, their Vermont origins would have seemed the only thing they had in common. She was lively and outgoing and loved to be around people. He was shy and had difficulty making small talk—and he made little effort to try. But, in one of those mysteries of courtship and marriage that defy easy explanation, they hit it off at once. She liked his shyness and his offbeat sense of humor. He was captivated by her beauty and the warmth of personality that he lacked. They complemented each other. (Calvin's landlord later said that he was happy to introduce Calvin to Grace, because, "Having taught the deaf to hear, Miss Goodhue might cause the mute to speak.")

Calvin Coolidge did not have the personality of a typical politician, for which handshaking, backslapping, and pretending you were interested people were requirements for success. He was taciturn and moody and at times sarcastic. But he was ambitious and had been succeeding in politics. When he met Grace Goodhue, Calvin was the clerk of courts in Northampton, and he had already served a term as a member of the city council and as city solicitor. But the full, almost unbelievable, realization of his ambition would be in the future. On that sunny morning when she glanced up at the window and saw this amusing man in long johns and a hat, Grace Goodhue had no way of knowing that she was about to begin a journey that would take her all the way to the White House.

Grace Anna Goodhue was born on January 3, 1879, in Burlington, Vermont, the only child of Andrew and Lemira Goodhue. Her father, an electrical engineer, worked at the Gates Cotton Mill in Burlington. For the first year of

---

Grace Anna Goodhue Coolidge

Born
January 3, 1879,
Burlington, Vermont

Parents
Andrew Issacher
Goodhue and Lemira
Barrett Goodhue

Marriage
October 4, 1905,
to Calvin Coolidge
(1872-1933)

Children
John (1906-2000);
Calvin, Jr. (1908-24)

Died
July 8, 1957,
Northampton,
Massachusetts

Above: Calvin Coolidge was a quiet man in the midst of the noisy era called the "Roaring Twenties."

Below: Grace Goodhue, the future Mrs. Coolidge, was an only child who grew up in a world of adults.

her parents' marriage, the couple lived in humble mill housing. When Grace was two years old, her father and mother bought a home of their own on Maple Street in Burlington. When she was four, her father was injured in a mill accident—some wood he was cutting at the mill shattered and fragments broke several bones in his face. Because her father needed quiet during his recovery, young Grace was sent to live temporarily with the family of John Lyman Yale. Grace came to love the Yale family, and it was through them that she first met children who were hearing impaired.

Burlington was a town with excellent schools, and Grace was an excellent student. She performed very well in traditional subjects and was also talented in music. In addition, Grace was an outgoing and sociable young woman who clearly reveled in the companionship of other people. She graduated from high school in 1897 but was unable to attend college immediately because of illness. During the year between high school and the start of classes at the University of Vermont, Grace stayed at home and did exercises to overcome scoliosis, commonly called curvature of the spine. When she finally started classes, she once again excelled in her studies and quickly became active in campus social life. The University of Vermont did not have a large female student population in those days, so Grace and her sister students formed close bonds. She joined with a group of women to establish a chapter of the Pi Beta Phi sorority, and the members frequently met at the Goodhue home, where Grace continued to live with her parents.

Andrew and Lemira Goodhue were somewhat surprised when Grace, soon after her graduation from the University of Vermont, applied for a teaching position at the Clarke School for the Deaf in Massachusetts. They had assumed she would continue to live at home and teach in Burlington, but Grace had other ideas. Caroline Yale (of the Yale family, of course), was the principal of Clarke, and she eagerly accepted Grace as a member of the school's teacher-training class.

Life in Northampton was safe and pleasant for a single young woman. It was the site of Smith College, one of the nation's preeminent colleges for women, and much of the town's social life was oriented toward women. Grace resided in Baker Hall, a residence for single women, and she quickly settled into her new life. Teaching the deaf and advocating on behalf of the deaf community were to remain her lifelong interests.

After meeting Calvin in 1904, the two began to correspond. Unfortunately, however, her letters to him do not survive. Whether she or someone else intentionally destroyed them, or whether they were inadvertently lost over the years, is impossible to know. His letters to her, however, survive, and they reveal a passion and intensity of feeling that was rarely, if ever, shown in public. This man, whose public face was often expressionless or even sour, expressed an ardor and infatuation for the dark-haired beauty who lived across the street from him. He pursued her with vigor, and she responded.

But Lemira Goodhue was opposed to the marriage of Grace and Calvin. She did not care for the dour, uncommunicative young man. Her Grace, in Lemira's view, deserved better. When she suggested that Grace was not yet fit to be married because she couldn't bake bread, Calvin said they could buy a loaf. Mrs. Goodhue argued with Calvin, and he responded by trying to win her over to his point of view. The bitterest argument was over the wedding date, which Lemira kept urging that they postpone, probably in the hope that it would never take place. But in the end, Calvin won the day. The Goodhues yielded, and he and Grace were married in their living room on the cold, rainy afternoon of October 4, 1905, before a small group of friends and family.

At the outset, Grace agreed to a traditional marriage. She would stop working, and Calvin would be the sole supporter of the family. He was the "boss" in the marriage—or bossy, as some might have said. He set the tone, provided the direction, and never asked for advice from his wife. When he was cranky and out of sorts, which was often, she soothed him. When he announced a decision, she accepted. Grace did not seem to mind this arrangement. Indeed, something in her nature welcomed it. In her old age, she commented on how she missed his guidance. Their first child, a son named John, was born on September 7, 1906. A second child, whom they named Calvin, Jr., came along on April 13, 1908. By 1908, Calvin Coolidge was a member of the Massachusetts House of Representatives. He needed to be in Boston part of the year for the legislative sessions, leaving Grace to be a part-time single mother. When Calvin was away in Boston, she often relied on the other males in her life—such as the pastor of their church— to help with the boys and to provide a male figure in their lives during the frequent absences of their father.

In later years, Grace fondly remembered the simplicity of their early married life. As a state official, Calvin was not well paid, and he needed to supplement his government salary with income from his law practice. They lived on a tight budget, and for their first home they rented rooms. Although they were not rich, life for Grace was more than just taking care of children. She maintained contacts with her old sorority and became active in Pi Beta Phi affairs, some of which took her on travels across the country. During the years when the boys were young, her husband's political ascent continued. From 1910 to 1911 he was mayor of Northampton, and in 1912 he became a member of the Massachusetts senate. In 1916 he was elected lieutenant governor, and in 1918, he ascended to the office of governor of Massachusetts.

Above: As a teacher of the deaf and the wife of a man who didn't talk much, Grace was a sensitive woman who found joy in the sounds and sights of the world around her.

Below: The Coolidge's son John became a student at Amherst College right after the family moved into the White House.

"I have such faith in Mr. Coolidge's judgment that if he told me I would die tomorrow morning at ten o'clock, I would believe him."

—Grace Coolidge on her husband

Throughout her life, Grace Coolidge was an avid fan of the Boston Red Sox. She collected Red Sox scorecards, and she sat in the Red Sox dugout during the 1925 World Series.

National Prominence

It was during his term as governor of Massachusetts that Calvin Coolidge achieved national fame. When the Boston police went on strike in 1919, Governor Coolidge took a hard line, stating that no one had the right to strike against the public safety anytime, anywhere. This stern warning made him a national figure and a hero in the Republican party overnight. Such was his newfound popularity that Calvin began to think he had a chance to win the Republican presidential nomination in 1920.

But the Republican bosses instead selected Senator Warren G. Harding of Ohio as the party's nominee. But Calvin was so popular that a movement developed at the Republican National Convention to have him named the vice presidential candidate. When he was nominated, Grace was surprised that he was willing to go on the ticket. (True to form, he never discussed it with her.) She knew that the largely ceremonial position of vice president might not appeal to her husband, who enjoyed being in charge as a governor. He accepted anyway, and in November 1920, the Harding-Coolidge ticket swept to victory, defeating the Democratic party's candidates, Governor James M. Cox of Ohio, and Assistant Secretary of the Navy Franklin D. Roosevelt of New York.

With the election won, the Coolidges prepared to move to Washington. During Calvin's public service in Massachusetts, the family had maintained their home at 21 Massasoit Street in Northampton, and they intended to return to it one day. In late February 1921, they received a rousing send-off from friends and neighbors as they left for the nation's capital. Calvin and Grace decided that they could not afford to buy a house in Washington given the low salary ($12,000 a year) paid to the vice president. Instead, they chose to take over the $8-a-day suite of rooms that the outgoing vice president, Thomas Marshall, was vacating at the Willard Hotel. The suite was quite small, consisting of only two bedrooms, a dining room, and a reception room. The boys, who were now fourteen and twelve, were sent away to the Mercersburg Academy, a boarding school in Pennsylvania. The suite at the Willard was adequate for entertaining only a few guests, but Grace and Calvin did not complain. It would be their home for the next two and a half years.

In 1920, Congress refused to provide a separate residence for the vice president. Today, the vice president of the United States has an official residence: a large house on the grounds of the U.S. Naval Observatory in the District of Columbia.

On March 3, 1921, the Coolidges went to Washington's Union Station to greet President Harding and his wife on their arrival from Ohio for the inauguration. The next day, March 4, 1921, Calvin Coolidge was sworn in as vice president in the chamber of the U.S. Senate. The ceremonies then moved outdoors, to the eastern front of the Capitol building, where Harding was sworn in as the twenty-ninth president of the United States. Florence Harding, the new First Lady, was an intelligent, strong-willed woman who had clearly stated likes and dislikes. She proved to be a popular First Lady, who opened up the White House to the public after it had been shut for so long during World War I and the subsequent illness of President Woodrow Wilson. But it was no secret that Florence Harding, for whatever reason, did not like the Coolidges. She rarely showed any courtesy to Calvin and Grace and never invited them to the White House, and she went out of her way to lobby Congress not to create an official residence for the vice president. If these snubs bothered Grace, she never let on. Grace quickly became one of the most popular figures in Washington society. Like her husband, whose principal institutional function was to preside over the U.S. Senate, Grace presided over informal meetings of the wives of senators. It required gentleness and tact, not to mention a sense of humor, and she had all these traits in abundance. Grace and Calvin dined out almost every night. When asked why, given that the vice president did not exactly enjoy mingling with people, Calvin replied, "You have to eat somewhere." Grace liked to stay out late and enjoyed parties, but Calvin always observed his 10:00 P.M. bedtime. And he insisted that she leave a social function with him. Throughout their marriage, he could be a tyrant on matters large and small, but she went along. He was the boss of the family, and from all indications, she was perfectly happy with that arrangement.

Life in Washington was pleasant and uneventful. The boys were tucked off in school, and when Congress was not in session during the summers, Grace and Calvin returned to New England, where the weather was cooler and the pace of life easygoing. The summer of 1923 found them in Plymouth Notch, Vermont, at the home of Calvin's father, Colonel John Coolidge. John, now seventeen, was at a military camp for civilians in Massachusetts, while Calvin, Jr., fifteen years old, had a summer job on a tobacco farm near their hometown of Northampton.

The Coolidges had been concerned about President Harding's health. He seemed pale and depressed and did not look healthy.

Above: Vice President-elect Coolidge and Grace at Warren Harding's inauguration.

Below: Grace was active in support of many organizations, but her favorite job was launching the annual sale of Girl Scout cookies because she got the first taste.

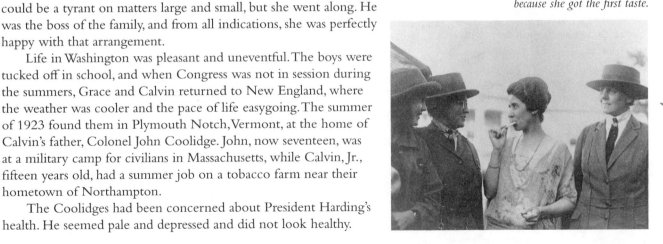

"She [Grace] had a simplicity and charm, seemed thoroughly to enjoy her position as wife of the Vice President, was amused by all the official functions and attentions, and was always absolutely natural and unimpressed by it all."

—*Alice Roosevelt Longworth on Grace Coolidge*

No one knew, of course, that Harding had a serious heart ailment and suffered from high blood pressure and hardening of the arteries. And they had no way of knowing that Harding's health was being compromised by the terrible stress he was under. The president knew that a series of scandals involving corruption in his cabinet was about to be made public.

On the night of August 2, 1923, Calvin and Grace retired to their bedroom in Colonel Coolidge's home after a typical day. Some time after midnight, a car came barreling down the road and screeched to a stop in front of the house. The driver, a newspaper reporter, jumped out and banged on the front door. The reporter was breathless with shocking news. President Harding had died suddenly in a hotel in San Francisco while on a trip to the West. Calvin was now president of the United States.

The Coolidges dressed, said a short prayer, and Calvin immediately dictated a telegram of condolence to Mrs. Harding. In the meantime, the local congressman, Representative Porter Dale, arrived at the house and suggested that Calvin take the oath of office immediately. But who would administer it? Calvin turned to his father, who was a notary public, and asked if he would swear him in as president. Grace, who had been crying, found an oil lamp, which she lit and placed on a small table in the center of the parlor. A copy of the oath was found, and at 2:47 A.M. on August 3, 1923, Calvin Coolidge was sworn in as the thirtieth president of the United States. It was the only time in U.S. history that a father had sworn in his son as president.

Following the taking of the oath, Calvin signed a written copy of it. He and Grace then shook hands with the few people in attendance and went back to bed. It was a simple ceremony and one that was, like Calvin himself, short on words. The following morning, a small group of residents of Plymouth Notch lined the road as Calvin and Grace made their way to the train that would take them back to Washington.

Below: President and First Lady Coolidge relaxed, but still quite formal, on the White House verandah with their sons John and Calvin, Jr.

White House Years

The Coolidges did not move into the White House until August 21, 1923, since the outgoing First Lady, Florence Harding, needed a few weeks to get her affairs in order. The nation welcomed the new first couple. The scandals that had tormented Harding became public in 1923 and 1924, and Calvin was forced to deal with them, particularly the notorious Teapot Dome affair, which involved corruption on the part of Harding's secretary of the interior. The Coolidges, unlike the Hardings, seemed like a happy, uncomplicated family. Mrs. Harding had been popular, but she had been seriously ill much of her time in the White House, and she was often lampooned in the press as a domineering wife, a classic battle-ax to a henpecked husband. When rumors later broke about Harding's extramarital affairs, which occurred even during his presidency, the Coolidges seemed all the more like a more normal, middle-class American family.

Grace Coolidge was in many respects the perfect First Lady. She was young and pretty and was well liked in Washington from her years as wife of the vice president. She had no agenda of her own and was happy to let her husband be the president of the country and the head of their immediate family. Everyone liked her and felt good in her presence. Unlike her husband, who said little or nothing in public, Grace loved to engage people in conversation, which made her the ideal hostess at receptions and state dinners.

Calvin also seemed the perfect president for the times. As was also the case in his personal life, he was frugal with the public's money. He believed in small government and in allowing private enterprise to flourish with minimum interference. His was the philosophy for the 1920s—the era of big government, expensive social programs, and huge defense budgets came later in the face of economic depression and another world war.

The year 1924 was an election year, and there was little doubt that in this prosperous and peaceful time, Calvin Coolidge would be nominated and elected president in his own right. Republican party leaders were delighted to have a scandal-free candidate with an attractive wife and young family. But the excitement of the election was shattered in the summer of 1924 when a terrible tragedy struck the Coolidge family and changed their lives forever.

In July 1924, sixteen-year-old Calvin, Jr., was home from school and spending time at the White House. He enjoyed playing on the White House tennis court, and after a strenuous match one day he developed a blister on his foot. The blister became seriously infected, and the infection quickly turned into septicemia—blood poisoning. He was rushed to the Walter Reed hospital, but in the 1920s there was little that could be done. Antibiotics had not yet been invented, and all the doctors could do was hope that the infection would disappear on its own. Calvin suffered terribly, begging his parents for relief, but he died on July 7, 1924.

The Coolidge family was devastated. Following an emotional service in the East Room of the White House, the boy's body was returned to Vermont for burial. After Calvin, Jr.'s death, Calvin said, "When he died, the glory and power of the presidency went with him." President Coolidge never recovered from his son's death. He was not a particularly robust individual and had always been plagued by indigestion. His son's death cast a pall over his life and seemed to rob him of energy. Even before the tragedy, Calvin had never worked a long day, but now he worked even less, arriving in his office near 10:00 A.M., taking a nap in the afternoon, and returning to the family quarters

Above: Helen Keller, a deaf mute who overcame her handicaps, found a strong advocate in Grace. She read the First Lady's lips with her hands and Grace had a lot to say. She had "talked" to the deaf many times.

Below: Tragedy struck the White House when Calvin, Jr., died suddenly of blood poisoning.

The Coolidge Pets

Calvin and Grace Coolidge were great pet lovers. The most famous of their menagerie was the white collie Rob Roy, who is immortalized in the Howard Chandler Christy portrait of Grace Coolidge that hangs today in the Red Room. Less well-known was the white collie Prudence Prim, who was brought into the White House as a companion to Rob Roy. Prudence Prim sat in a chair next to the president and shared his breakfast cereal every morning. Another favorite was Grace's Chow Chow, Tiny Tim, who was very attached to the First Lady.

Grace was also fond of birds and usually had cages full of canaries around the White House. The most amusing White House bird was a South American troupial named Do-Funny, who would often sit on the president's shoulder and peck his ear.

After Rob Roy, the most well-known White House pet was Rebecca, the raccoon. Rebecca was chained when she was on the White House lawn, but indoors she had the run of the mansion. Many of the staff hated or feared her, because she would tear women's stockings and rip holes in clothing. Rebecca loved to dine on chicken, persimmons, and cream and eggs. Eventually, she became too much to handle in the White House and was donated to a zoo, where she spent the remainder of her life.

Top: Grace's white collie, Rob Roy, was one of the most famous of a long line of White House dogs, but it wasn't only dogs she loved.

Bottom: Her pet raccoon, Rebecca, was almost as familiar to America as Grace herself was.

in the White House by 6:00 P.M. Today he would probably be diagnosed as suffering from depression.

Grace, by contrast, soldiered on despite her loss. She smiled and went about her duties, keeping her pain inside and showing a dignified face to the public. In November 1924, Calvin Coolidge was elected president in his own right. It was an overwhelming victory, a testimony to the popularity of the frugal, crusty New Englander and his much-loved wife. On March 4, 1925, Grace, resplendent in a moonstone-gray duvetyn and a hat trimmed with goose feathers, rode between Calvin and Senator Charles Curtis of Kansas in an open limousine from the White House to Capitol Hill for the inauguration. Along the way, thousands of spectators cheered the First Couple. Grace waved back vigorously; the president stared straight ahead. It was a cloudy, cold day, but the rain held off. The Coolidges preferred a low-key ceremony. They dispensed with the traditional post-inaugural luncheon and instead had sandwiches with a few friends at the White House before venturing outdoors to view the inaugural parade.

In her later years, Grace rarely spoke about the White House, although she always talked about Calvin. The White House years were marked by tragedy, excitement, and opportunity, but they also represented a life that neither she nor her husband had wanted or expected—living under constant public scrutiny and with Secret Service protection. One summer, while vacationing in South Dakota, Grace and her Secret Service agent went for a morning walk in the nearby hills. When she did not return for lunch, the president became frantic. He lived by the clock; lunch was served every day punctually at noon. Anyone who dined with him—including his wife—was expected to be on time and

*Above: Calvin and Grace riding
in an open car to the Capitol
for his inauguration. Calvin wasn't
smiling, but Grace's smile was big
enough for both of them.*

appropriately dressed. The president was certain Grace and her agent had had an accident. In fact, they had gotten lost and showed up two hours late. Calvin was furious, although his anger was never directed at Grace. Instead, he ordered the agent transferred immediately. When rumors began circulating that the president had been jealous of Grace's relationship with her agent, the First Lady was more amused than embarrassed. She was relaxed and able to laugh at herself and her husband.

Calvin Coolidge was a notorious penny-pincher, whether with his own money or the government's. But even he knew when it was time to spend. In 1927, it was apparent that the White House was in need of a major restoration. The last one had been done in 1902 under Theodore Roosevelt, and it was time for another overhaul. Cracks in the walls and ceilings on the upper floors revealed that a significant amount of work needed to be done. Grace thought it was a good opportunity to expand what had been the "attic" floor into a much larger third floor with a solarium. The work was done between March and September 1927. During that time, the Coolidges moved out of the White House into an elegant mansion at 15 DuPont Circle in Washington, which was lent to the First Family during the renovation.

While living in these temporary quarters, Grace and Calvin Coolidge had the pleasure of greeting the aviator Charles A. Lindbergh and his mother. Lindbergh had just made his daring solo flight across the Atlantic and was a national hero. The Coolidges were no different from other Americans in their pride in Lindbergh's achievement. While being honored by the Coolidges, Lindbergh was introduced to Anne Morrow, the woman who would one day become his wife. Grace always felt that she had been a matchmaker between Charles and Anne Lindbergh.

*Below: Among the most honored
guests at the Coolidge White House
was aviator Charles Lindbergh,
who brought his mother, too.*

In August 1927 the Coolidges vacationed again in South Dakota. On the morning of August 3, Calvin turned to Grace and, apropos of nothing, said "I have been president for four years today." She had gotten used to his pronouncements without context. Only later did a newspaperman inform her that Calvin had submitted a one-sentence press release earlier that morning that read, "I choose not to run for president in 1928." Grace had to laugh. It was so like him. One of the most important decisions in his life was made without one word of discussion with his wife, who in turn learned about it from a stranger.

Above: Calvin's father, John, was a frequent White House visitor before he died.

Privately, Grace welcomed Calvin's decision not to seek another term in 1928. Five and a half years were enough. In 1926 the president had suffered another blow, when his eighty-one-year-old father died. He had tried to rush to Vermont as the end approached, but he arrived shortly after Colonel Coolidge's death. He was bitter about not having been at his father's bedside, and he blamed the duties of the presidency for preventing him from doing the things that ordinary mortals do. In addition, Grace worried about his health. His digestive problems had become worse, and his energy levels had declined over the years. Grace herself was frequently ill during 1927 and 1928, so she, too, welcomed the prospect of a quieter life outside of the limelight.

With retirement in sight, the year 1928 passed quickly. In the summer, the Republican party nominated the secretary of commerce, Herbert Hoover, for president. His opponent, Governor Alfred E. Smith of New York, the Democrat, was a popular politician, but he was a Roman Catholic, and no member of the Catholic Church had ever been elected president. But most important, the country was prosperous—some called it "Coolidge prosperity"—and Hoover benefited from the good times and won a landslide election. The Coolidges did not campaign actively for Hoover, but soon after the election, they had the president-elect and his wife to the White House for dinner. Grace and Lou Hoover, the incoming First Lady, liked each other and got along well, so the transition went off without any problems.

On March 4, 1929, Calvin and Grace Coolidge walked out of the White House for the last time. After Hoover's inauguration, they left immediately for the railroad station, where a friendly crowd waved them off as their train took them home to Northampton. Grace, holding her Chow Chow Tiny Tim, waved from the rear platform of the train as it pulled out of the station. They were on their way home.

Retirement in Northampton

Below: The Coolidge retirement home in Massachusetts became a tourist attraction.

The former president and First Lady returned to their old home at 21 Massasoit Street in Northampton. It was small—and it seemed even smaller after so many years in the White House. But they both liked the house and wanted to make it their home once again.

But that proved difficult. Calvin liked to sit in the front porch with Rob Roy at his side, but privacy was impossible. Massasoit Street was soon clogged with automobiles as tourists drove by hoping to catch a glimpse of the former president and First Lady. The Coolidges soon realized that they could not simply return to their old way of life. Having been president and First Lady permanently altered their lives, and privacy was a rare commodity.

After a year in the old house, Calvin and Grace decided to purchase an estate, called the Beeches, a large house near Northampton on eight acres of land and complete with a tennis court and a swimming pool. Most important, it was surrounded by a fence and protected by a large iron gate. The former president could sit on the porch and not been seen from the street. And Grace could walk her dogs through the surrounding meadows away from the prying eyes of tourists.

The first year of retirement was marked by the personal joy of John's marriage to Florence Trumbull, the daughter of the governor of Connecticut. A graduate of Amherst College in 1928, John was a tall, reserved young man who combined the affectionate impulses of his mother with the reserved, dignified demeanor of his father. Now twenty-three years old, he had a job with the New York New Haven & Hartford Railroad. The wedding, on Sept. 24, 1929, took place in the Plainville Congregational Church in Connecticut and was front-page news in all the national newspapers.

Above: There were few pleasures in Calvin's life he enjoyed more than sitting on the front porch with Grace.

In the summer of 1929, Grace was awarded an honorary degree from Smith College. In 1930, her alma mater, the University of Vermont, awarded her another honorary degree. The citation read, in part, "All ours when the schoolgirl lived and worked among us; ours still though not unshared, when the First Lady cast her kindly spell of act and speech and manner over the hearts of a nation; ours now when we honor in her guise the crown of achievement, the art of all arts, the power of grace, the magic of a name." Even out of the White House, the country still loved Grace Coolidge.

Shortly after John's wedding, Grace's mother, Lemira Goodhue, died at the age of eighty-one. She had been ill for years, but she had lived to see her daughter and son-in-law become America's First Family. The loss of her mother was not unexpected, but it added a note of sadness to a year that for Grace had otherwise been a happy one.

At the time of Mrs. Goodhue's death, the nation was shocked by the collapse of the stock market, the first step in the cataclysm of the Great Depression that descended on the country during the 1930s. The stock market crash and the ensuing Depression was a severe blow to Calvin Coolidge, who saw the prosperity identified with his administration evaporate in a few short years. More important, his notion of minimal government, of unregulated free enterprise, was repudiated by the electorate in the elections of 1930 and 1932, which swept the Republican party from power and installed the Democrats in Congress and the White House. The American people did not blame Calvin Coolidge for the Depression. They saved their wrath for the incumbent president, Herbert Hoover, who was defeated for reelection in 1932 by Governor Franklin D. Roosevelt of New York. But Calvin knew that the world had changed. He often said during these years that he did not belong to this era, that his time had passed.

It was a pessimistic, somewhat emotional, assessment from a man not accustomed to sharing his personal feelings. And perhaps his bleak outlook on life had to do with his awareness of his failing health. In 1930, the Coolidges took a long trip across the country, something they had never done before but

In 1929, Grace Coolidge was named one of America's twelve greatest women in a poll in Good Housekeeping *magazine. She was honored for her outstanding place in the nation as a symbol of home and family life.*

could now easily undertake. Everywhere they went, large, enthusiastic crowds greeted them. In California, they stayed at William Randolph Hearst's castle at San Simeon, and in Hollywood, they met many famous movie stars of the day. The trip was a joy for Grace, who always loved to meet people and see new things. But after that trip, Calvin rarely traveled, and he cut back even more on his work hours. He had agreed to write a newspaper column, but ultimately decided that the work was too strenuous.

On July 4, 1932, Calvin Coolidge observed his sixtieth birthday. His physical maladies were becoming worse, especially his indigestion. Some of the self-prescribed remedies probably made matters worse, but the list of foods he could no longer eat grew longer and longer, and the pains associated with this complaint became more intense. His digestive problems were probably the early signs of a heart problem that went undiagnosed by his doctors, who pronounced him to be in generally good health. He knew otherwise.

On the morning of January 5, 1933, Grace left the Beeches to go shopping. Calvin spent the morning in his office in Northampton, then returned to the house for lunch. Grace arrived home from her shopping expedition around noon and found Calvin dead on the floor of his study. He had dressed for lunch and then suffered a fatal heart attack. Grace ran downstairs and told a servant, "My husband is dead."

Grace was deeply shocked, but with her usual fortitude and sense of duty, she went through the funeral rituals and comforted friends and family. Calvin and Grace had decided before his death that he would not have a funeral in Washington, D.C. Instead, a simple service was held at Edwards Congregational Church in Northampton. President and Mrs. Hoover attended the service, as did the incoming First Lady, Eleanor Roosevelt, and her son James, who represented President-elect Franklin D. Roosevelt. A light rain was falling as the motorcade set off for Vermont, where Calvin would be buried next to his parents, his son Calvin, Jr., and five generations of Coolidges. Mrs. Coolidge, pale-faced and with large, sad eyes, listened as the minister said prayers and her husband's casket was lowered into the ground. Then, leaning on John's arm, she left and returned to Northampton. She had been married to Calvin for twenty-seven years and had turned fifty-four just two days before Calvin's death. Her long widowhood had begun.

Widowhood

Widowhood was a difficult adjustment for Grace. She had relied so much on Calvin—for large things as well as small. It took some time for her to discover that she could have experiences of her own and enjoy them, without having to look to her husband for his guidance and approval.

Following Calvin's death, an old friend from the days on Massasoit Street, Florence

"I am just a lost soul. Nobody is going to believe how much I miss being told what to do."

—Grace Coolidge on life after Calvin

Adams, became an important part of Grace's life. An outspoken Democrat, Florence was not hesitant to express her vocal support of Franklin Roosevelt's policies. Grace, a Republican, was

not used to expressing her political views and usually listened to Florence in good-natured silence. But she had no trouble with Florence's politics (Grace was very fond of Eleanor Roosevelt), and she enjoyed her company.

Another small pleasure of widowhood was the ability to travel unrecognized. Often dressed informally, she and Florence Adams would get into a car and take long drives. On one such occasion, in 1934, they were driving through Virginia. Florence had made reservations at an exclusive inn, but before they arrived, they were caught in a rainstorm. When they arrived at the inn, they looked disheveled and rain-soaked. The manager was suspicious about their appearance and told them there were no rooms left, even though they had made reservations. Florence had arranged to have mail delivered at the inn, and when she asked if there were any mail for "Mrs. Adams and Mrs. Calvin Coolidge," the manager almost fainted. Suddenly he found rooms for them, but they declined and moved on.

In 1936, Florence persuaded Grace to go on her first trip to Europe. Grace had never traveled abroad and was reluctant to do so because she feared being recognized. Florence assured her that the two of them could drive anonymously all over Europe and would not be recognized. For the most part they were not. But someone alerted a hotel in Switzerland that a Mrs. Adams and the "wife of a former president" were about to be guests. When Florence and Grace arrived, the hotel management greeted them like royalty, bowing and begging to fulfill their every wish. The hotel manager took Florence aside and asked her to make sure that "Mrs. Lincoln" did not hesitate to ask for anything she needed. Grace laughed at the thought that the hotel staff thought she was Abraham Lincoln's wife.

In 1937, Grace decided to sell the Beeches. The house was just too big for her to live in by herself, so she decided to have a smaller house built on Massasoit Street opposite Florence Adams's home. The new house, called Road Forks, had the unique feature of a living room on the second floor. Grace wanted to be close to the treetops, and with a second-floor living room, she could sit and look out the windows at treetop level. Grace's first grandchild, a girl named Cynthia, had been born in 1933. It was a disappointment for her that Calvin had not lived to see her. A second granddaughter, Lydia, was born in 1939, and both her grandchildren provided great joy to Grace as she aged. Grace's financial situation improved in 1937 when Congress voted to grant her an annual pension of $5,000. Calvin had left his entire estate to her, but she had learned to be frugal and was very cautious when it came to spending money, even on herself.

Throughout her life, and especially in the years of her widowhood, Grace Coolidge maintained a strong connection to issues relating to the deaf. She served as a trustee to the Clarke School until the end of her life. A fellow trustee, Senator John F. Kennedy of Massachusetts, who would one day follow her husband into the White House, came to know and love Grace. In the final years of her life, Grace was the chairperson of a centennial fund-raising campaign for the Clarke School. She knew politicians and philanthropists, and she was well connected with the deaf community, having befriended, for example, the great Helen Keller back in the 1920s.

After the United States entered World War II in 1941, Grace became an active and energetic participant in the war efforts. Even before the U.S. entrance into the war, Grace had raised funds to bring refugee children from Germany to the United States. Unlike the isolationists, she understood that the United States did not live in an insular world. As the war progressed, Grace rented out Road Forks for the use of the Waves, the women's auxiliary organization of the U.S. navy. Smith College in Northampton had been chosen by the navy as the training site for women officers, but off-campus housing was scarce. Grace moved in with Mrs. Adams, across the street, and turned over the house to the Waves for the duration of the war.

With the war over in 1945 and her war work ended, Grace spent more and more time at home. Her passion for baseball continued, but she no longer journeyed to Boston to see Red Sox games but listened to them on the radio. Her love of reading continued, and she always enjoyed being outdoors in the sunshine. As in the early post–White House years, she studiously avoided any publicity. In 1954 she got her first television, which she liked watching, but her first loves were always reading and the radio.

In 1952, Grace's health began to decline. She was clearly suffering from heart failure, although she disliked going to doctors and preferred to keep any discomfort she was feeling to herself. Although she enjoyed doing her own shopping, it became more and more difficult for her to undertake any strenuous activity. In the last years of her life she lived at Road Forks with three other people: Ivah Gale, a friend from her childhood years; Lillian Carver, a young woman who served as housekeeper and occasional cook; and John Bukosky, a chauffeur who had driven the Coolidges for years. She followed politics in the newspapers and was happy when a Republican, Dwight D. Eisenhower, was elected president in 1952. Mrs. Eisenhower invited Grace to the White House to see how it had changed, but she declined the invitation. For one, she no longer had the strength to travel, but she also had no desire to return to the White House. The years she had spent there were her years; now that time had passed and she was content not to relive old experiences.

In February 1957 she was hospitalized for treatment of her heart disease, but when she returned home, it was clear to many of those close to her that her days were limited. As always, she maintained a cheerful demeanor, and in the last letter she ever wrote, in May 1957, she told a friend that she was "gaining strength day by day."

Grace Coolidge died quietly on July 8, 1957. She was laid to rest in Plymouth Notch, next to her husband and dear son. The Coolidge tombstones are among the most simple of all presidential grave markers. They contain only their names and birth and death dates. The only indication on Calvin Coolidge's tombstone that he had been a president of the United States is the presidential seal.

Calvin and Grace Coolidge were enormously popular in their time. Today, they are out of fashion in a world that has moved beyond the simple virtues they represented. As First Lady, Grace belonged to an era in which women were expected to be homemakers and men led their families. It was a role she willingly accepted and one that she embodied in the way she fulfilled her duties as First Lady—as loving wife and mother, with a cheerful and outgoing personality that made visitors feel welcome, and a nonpolitical presence that kept her personal opinions private. She lived through decades of profound change and moments of poignant personal tragedy, but at all times she maintained a steadiness of purpose and a warmth that inspired the love of her countrymen.

Above: Artist Juliette Thompson painted a portrait of Grace to be placed in the White House.

Below: President Coolidge and his First Lady rest in peace in Plymouth Notch, New Hampshire, where he lived most of his life.

Visiting the President Calvin Coolidge State Historic Site

The Calvin Coolidge State Historic Site is located in Plymouth Notch, Vermont, the birthplace and boyhood home of President Coolidge. The site is a complex of buildings that have been preserved in their original appearance. Included are the homes of Calvin Coolidge's family, the community church, the cheese factory, the one-room schoolhouse, and the general store. Calvin and his family are buried in the nearby town cemetery. Plymouth Notch is six miles south of U.S. 4 on Vermont 100A, about midway across the state. The address is Route 100A, Plymouth Notch, Vermont 05056.

The site is open daily from May through October, 9:30 A.M. to 5:00 P.M. It is closed during the winter. The site's office, in Aldrich House, is open weekdays year-round and has exhibits designed for winter visitors. There is an admission fee for both children and adults. For more information, call 802-672-3773 or log on to www.HistoricVermont.org.

Louise Hoover

Equal Opportunity

When Lou Henry was a child, she was given two lessons from her parents that would shape the rest of her life: First, her father taught her that she could do anything a boy could; second, a strong Quaker influence in her religious upbringing instilled in her a strong sense of duty to serve others. Her entire life would reflect these beliefs, and she was one of the most active First Ladies the White House has ever seen.

Lou Henry was born on March 29, 1874, in Waterloo, Iowa. She was the first child of Charles Henry, a banker, and Florence Ward Henry, a schoolteacher. Her father loved outdoor activities and taught Lou fishing, horseback riding, hiking, and camping. During the Iowan winters, Lou continued her love of athletics by becoming an expert ice skater. The harsh winters, however, became too tough on Lou's mother, who suffered from bronchial asthma. In 1887, Charles Henry moved his family, which now also included baby sister Jean, to the new Quaker settlement of Whittier, California. The Henrys were not Quakers, but Charles knew the new town needed a banker. The family often attended Quaker services on Sundays and Lou grew to appreciate the Quaker teachings of simple living and tolerance of others.

Lou and her father continued to pursue the love of hiking together, and the California weather was ideal for them to often walk five miles a day through the surrounding Puente hills. Henry, an amateur naturalist, also taught Lou all about the local plants and animals. Lou discovered she had a particular fascination with rocks, and she started her own collection. The Quaker community also emphasized education, and Lou was an excellent student, studying Latin, geography, and history.

When she was sixteen, Lou had completed all the schooling Whittier, California, had to offer, so her parents sent her to a high school in nearby Los Angeles. During the summers away from school, her camping trips to the high Los Angeles mountain ranges were now long treks on horseback and included hunting and fishing for meals and sleeping in the canyons.

Lou graduated high school in 1893, and then joined her family, who had moved to Monterey, California. Her father had opened a new bank there, and Lou worked for him as a cashier for a while. She also had a teaching job, but neither banking nor teaching fulfilled her ambitions. However, there was a

---

Louise Henry Hoover

Born
March 29, 1874,
Waterloo, Iowa

Parents
Charles Delano Henry
and Florence Ida
Ward Henry

Marriage
February 10, 1899, to
Herbert Clark Hoover
(1874-1964)

Children
Herbert Charles
(1903-69); Allan Henry
(1907-93)

Died
January 7, 1944,
New York, New York

Above: Lou Henry grew up in Waterloo, Iowa.

summer lecture at the new Stanford University in nearby Palo Alto that would change her life.

It was a geology lecture by Stanford professor John Branner, and Lou was overjoyed to discover she could attend Stanford as a geology student. She enrolled in 1894 as the only female geology major in the school. Among the many young men Lou would meet at Stanford was Branner's senior student assistant, Herbert Hoover, a member of the first class of the university when it opened in 1891. At first, Herbert was painfully shy, but the young couple discovered they had much in common. Their love of geology was most obvious, but they were also both originally from Iowa and had a Quaker upbringing. Herbert was an orphan raised by a Quaker uncle in Oregon.

For the rest of the year, the couple dated steadily, and Lou's social skills helped Herbert overcome his shyness. However, Herbert graduated in 1895 and immediately went to work as a mining engineer in California's High Sierra Mountains. This separation lasted several years, and the couple had to rely on letters to maintain their relationship. Lou continued her studies at Stanford, while Herbert was hired by an English engineering firm, Bewick, Moreing, & Co., to explore mines in western Australia.

Lou became the first woman in the United States to receive a bachelor's degree in geology in 1898, but she also found that no firms wanted to hire a female geologist. At the end of the year, she received a letter from Herbert from Australia, telling her he had just accepted a position in China as a consultant with the Chinese Bureau of Mines at a very high salary. In the letter was also a proposal of marriage. Lou accepted and the couple was married at her parents' home in Monterey on February 10, 1899. On February 11, they were on a boat headed to China.

The newlyweds settled in Tianjin, about sixty miles from China's capital city of Beijing, and Herbert began his long travels to distant mines in China's countryside. While he was gone, Lou would study Chinese and immerse herself in the new culture. When Herbert returned from his trips with samples of ore, Lou became his invaluable assistant, cataloging their collection and sending some samples back to John Branner at Stanford for evaluation.

The Hoovers also traveled around the country as often as they could and saw the Great Wall at Lanzhou. When they traveled, however, they had to be accompanied by armed guards for protection. It was a sign of the times. Many foreigners were in China at the time, modernizing the undeveloped country and making a lot of money doing so. The developers were there with the approval

Right: As a teenager, Lou wrote an essay on "Universal Suffrage."

Above: The highlight of a camping trip: Lou rides a burro.

of the Chinese emperor, but many Chinese people hated the foreign influence.

In the spring of 1900, a rebellion began, led by a group calling themselves the "Righteous Harmonious Fists," or Boxers for short. Their goal was to rid China of all the "foreign devils," and one of their first strikes was at Kao Li, just a hundred miles from Tianjin. Eighty people were killed at Kao Li, and the Boxers' next destination was Tianjin. Herbert ordered his entire staff to leave the city, including Lou, but she refused. The Hoovers helped fortify the city the best they could and waited for the attack.

The Boxer Rebellion began on June 19, but a couple of thousand Russian soldiers who had become trapped in the city helped the foreign residents as they took refuge in the center of the city. The attack became a monthlong siege, with Lou serving as cook, nurse, and organizer. She was almost shot twice—once a bullet punctured a tire of the bicycle she was riding, and once shots were fired into the bedroom of their home. American troops finally arrived in mid-July and the Boxers retreated. Despite the end of the siege, China was still a dangerous place for Americans. The Hoovers left the following month for London, where Herbert became a partner in Bewick, Moreing, & Co.

Below: Among Lou's abilities was writing in Chinese.

London, Family, and World War I

For the next several years, the Hoovers' "Red House" residence in London remained home base for the couple, but Herbert's job kept them traveling throughout the world. At different times, Lou found herself living in Japan, Australia, India, Egypt, Russia, and Burma. In each location, Lou continued to serve as her husband's geological assistant and study local cultures, often adapting the dress of the native population. She also wrote articles about her experiences, especially those during the Boxer Rebellion in China. The busy couple also found time to have two children. Herbert Charles arrived in August 1903, and his brother, Allan Henry, arrived in July 1907.

The Hoovers also collaborated on some important writing on mining at this time. Lou helped her husband publish *The Principles of Mining* in 1909. Together, they translated a sixteenth-century Latin book called *De Re Metallica*, which, despite its age, was considered the Bible

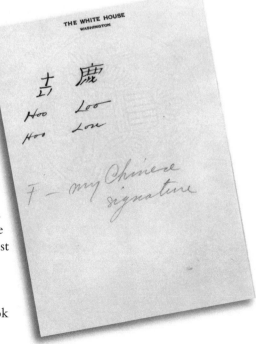

Above: Lou with her first son, Herbert Charles.

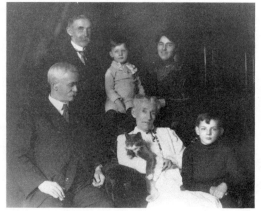
Below: Lou with her family: Allan Herbert, Jr., father Charles Henry, Will Henry, her grandmother Ward, and her sons, Herbert and Allan.

of mining information. The Hoovers spent five years compiling the finest translation ever of the book, clarifying all of its remarkable information for the first time. In 1914 the Mining & Metallurgical Society of America awarded both Hoovers its first gold medal for "Distinguished Contributions to the Literature of Mining."

As the Hoover children grew to school age, Lou decided she wanted her sons to have an American education. The Hoovers rented a house on the Stanford campus and split their time between London and Palo Alto. In London, Lou became very busy with a philanthropic group called the American Women's Club. The group raised scholarship money for poor students and provided housing and food for London's poor. By 1914, Lou was president of the group. Also by 1914, the winds of World War I were blowing in Europe.

It is a great irony that war brings out the best in some people. This was probably true of Lou whose desire to serve was so strong, and it was also a conviction of her Quaker faith; she had converted to her husband's religion after they married. After sending her children home to California, the Hoovers started to grapple with the huge humanitarian concerns of World War I. Thousands of Americans found themselves stranded in London when the war broke out and passage home was nearly impossible to find. The U.S. ambassador asked Herbert to help organize the return of these Americans back to safe land. As head of the Society of American Women, Lou found housing or gave money to thousands of the stranded, particularly to those with children. She also helped establish the American Women's Hospital as sick and wounded soldiers returned from the battlefields in Europe.

However, the Hoovers' greatest effort would come in Belgium, where the German occupation had caused tremendous food shortages. Herbert was named head of the Belgian Relief Commission, which aimed to get food, shelter, and clothing to thousands of Belgians, and Lou worked at his side throughout the effort. She returned to the United States, giving speeches and raising money for the cause. She also secured donations of food and clothing and persuaded the Rockefeller Foundation to provide free shipping of the goods to Belgium.

A Christmas visit to Belgium revealed conditions even worse than Lou expected—the country was on the brink of famine. She wrote articles for American newspapers appealing for donations and even stood in Belgian railway stations handing out sandwiches and coffee. She also led a campaign to help Belgian women, many now on their own because of the war, make their own money by selling Belgian lace. Herbert's Relief Commission provided the thread to the women and Lou helped get the lace exported and sold.

By 1917, the increasing German bombing of London forced the Hoovers to return to California. They would only be there a few months when the United States entered the war and President Woodrow Wilson asked Herbert to head the U.S. Food Administration. Its purpose was to persuade Americans to conserve food and fuel so that the American forces in Europe would be well

Above: The Belgian Relief Commission to help refugees from World War I was a cause the Hoovers were single-minded about.

supplied. With the food shortages in Europe, Wilson believed that conservation and rationing was the key to an Allied victory.

The Hoovers moved to Washington, D.C., and Lou helped her husband spread the word. She offered special recipes through newspaper and magazine articles and encouraged meatless and wheatless days. Lou also worked with the thousands of young women who came to Washington seeking jobs because their husbands had been sent to Europe. Lou started a local Food Administration Club to help feed and house the women, often providing the money out of her own pocket.

It was also at this time that Lou first became involved with the Girl Scouts of America. Scouts were providing countless services to aid the war effort, raising money, making clothes, and baby-sitting for working mothers. The organization had been founded in 1912 by Juliette Gordon Low to encourage responsibility and independence in young girls. It was a controversial organization at the time—women were still not even allowed to vote—but Lou supported the Girl Scouts wholeheartedly, and it would become a lifelong commitment.

After the war ended in 1918, Herbert was named head of the American Relief Administration and sent to Europe to continue relief efforts for civilians still suffering from hunger and disease. Lou stayed at home and helped raise money for the cause. At one benefit dinner in New York, she helped raise $3 million. She also started building the new Hoover family home on San Juan Hill on the Stanford campus, the dream home where she hoped to spend the rest of her life.

The home was completed in 1920, but Washington had another offer for Herbert. President Warren Harding offered Herbert the cabinet post of secretary of commerce, which was the department developed to support American business and encourage economic growth. Herbert had risen from an orphaned childhood to become a self-made millionaire. In his appointed positions, he had always handled limited funds very efficiently, so he seemed a likely choice for the post. Herbert would serve seven years as secretary of

Below: Herbert was what people called a "self-made man." A millionaire many times over, he diverted his skills to public service.

After World War I, King Albert and Queen Elisabeth of Belgium came to America to honor Lou with one of its highest awards, the Cross of Chevalier, for her service to Belgium during the war.

Above: Like Grace Coolidge, seen here in the background in the light dress, Lou (in the middle in uniform) was an ardent supporter of the Girl Scouts. She was sworn in as a troop leader by Juliet Low, the movement's founder, in 1917.

commerce, from 1921 to 1928, under both Harding and President Calvin Coolidge. It was during this time that he would develop his philosophy of the role of government in America's economy. He did not believe in direct government intervention in the economy. Instead, he advocated a system of voluntary cooperation among private citizens and businessmen: They would organize to achieve a goal, but the government would support but not control such organizations. It was a philosophy that would eventually be severely tested.

Back in Washington during Herbert's cabinet years, Lou became deeply involved in the Girl Scouts. In 1922, she was elected national president of the organization. She also maintained her own local troop the entire time she lived in Washington. Even though she was nearing fifty years old, Lou took her troop on frequent hiking and camping trips into the woods, teaching the girls all she had learned from her father about the outdoors when she was young.

> *"Bad men are elected by good women who stay at home from the polls on Election Day."*
>
> *—Lou Hoover encouraging American women to exercise their newly granted right to vote*

Lou also believed strongly in the value of athletics for girls and organized the first National Conference on Athletics and Physical Education for Women and Girls. Under Lou's guidance, the group persuaded many schools, colleges, and the Young Women's Christian Association (YWCA) to organize intramural sports and physical education courses for girls throughout the country.

Below: The Hoover administration spanned the last years of Prohibition, when government agents poured illegal whiskey into sewers.

Teetotaler in the White House

Lou Hoover was a strong supporter of enforcing the country's Prohibition laws on alcoholic drinks. The law had not been enforced since it had been passed, and most Americans who drank before the law were still finding ways to obtain liquor. It was even well-known that President Harding served alcohol in the White House.

Herbert Hoover was a wine connoisseur and had acquired over the years a substantial and impressive wine cellar. Lou's conscience, however, would not allow such a defiance of Prohibition. She insisted that Herbert dump out his entire collection in obedience to the law.

The Presidency

In 1927, President Calvin Coolidge surprised everyone by announcing he would not run for the White House again in 1928. Herbert was very popular among Republican officials as an excellent businessman, a dedicated humanitarian, and an honest politician. A movement began to make him the party's nominee for president. At the Republican Convention in Kansas City in June 1928, Herbert won the nomination on the first ballot.

Lou did not want to campaign with her husband at first. She preferred her own work, which kept her very busy, and would rather have spent the time getting acquainted with her two new grandchildren. However, toward the end of the campaign, she did join her husband on his rail tour of the United States. She publicly said, "I enjoy campaigning, because my husband makes the speeches and I receive the roses," but she was glad when it was over. They were both especially pleased with the results. Herbert easily won the election and became the thirty-first president of the United States.

Lou immediately showed how well prepared she was to be First Lady. She was educated, worldly (she spoke five languages), experienced, and confident. She spruced up the White House décor with many of their own possessions from around the world and restored several of the mansion's historic rooms like the Oval Room, the Monroe Bedroom, and the Lincoln Study. The Hoovers also increased the staff at their own expense—they paid for their own personal secretaries—and President Hoover accepted no salary during his term.

Above: Lou and Herbert's canine companions included a Belgian police dog named King Tut, a schnauzer named Whoopie, and a Gordon setter called Englehurst Gillette.

A Minor Ruffle

At one of her afternoon teas, Lou created a controversy by inviting the wife of Oscar DePriest, the first African-American elected to Congress in thirty years, to attend. Lou knew there would be a problem with her gesture in many parts of a still very segregated United States. In fact, she researched the last time an African-American had been invited to the White House and discovered it was during Teddy Roosevelt's term. President Roosevelt had invited Booker T. Washington to the White House, which resulted in major race riots in several Southern cities.

Lou, however, strongly disapproved of discrimination, and Mrs. DePriest attended a White House tea on June 12, 1931. The tea went off smoothly, but there was a strong condemnation of the First Lady in many Southern newspapers. The Texas state legislature also passed a resolution condemning the First Lady officially. Lou stuck to her beliefs. Later, she also invited the Hampton and Tuskegee choirs to perform at the White House, the first African-American performers to entertain in the presidential home in more than forty years.

Above: A cowboy band from Texas delighted Lou when they arrived to serenade her.

Lou remained very distant from the press during her term as First Lady, not permitting personal interviews or casual photographs.

Lou also entertained often and lavishly, trying to uphold the dignity of the White House tradition. She held afternoon teas daily, and the Hoovers invited guests for breakfast, lunch, and dinner every day, with the number of guests for a meal often in the hundreds. Only the best food was served at dinner, and there were often as many as seven courses. Waiters and all servants in view had to be formally dressed, and Lou worked out a complicated system of signals so that their presence would be as unnoticeable as possible.

Lou was also a close advisor to her husband as he worked on his initial plans for the country. A strong conservationist, Herbert was able to add about three million acres to the national forest system. The president also called Congress into special session to deal with the growing economic problems for American farmers. After World War I, American farmers reaped the profits of the tremendous demand for their products in a starving Europe. They borrowed extensively and increased production, but those markets disappeared as Europe recovered, and prices plummeted.

Farmers spent the 1920s in a depression that the rest of the country was about to experience. Herbert signed the Agricultural Marketing Act of 1929, the first big government system to aid the farmer in peacetime. It set up special loans and ways to buy farm surpluses, but because Herbert did not believe in strong government intervention, it avoided production control, which would later prove to be the key to raising prices.

In October 1929, the stock market crashed and the American economy fell into the Great Depression. Herbert worked hard to end the Depression, but his optimism that volunteerism and American businessmen would turn the economy around was unfounded. He kept assuring the public that "prosperity was just around the corner," but it never was. Unemployment rose from 6 million in 1930 to 12 million in 1931. Volunteer organizations ran out of money, and people lost their homes. Shantytowns were built on the outskirts of many American towns using little more than scrap wood and tin. They soon came to be known as Hoovervilles.

Below: Families driven from their homes by the Great Depression settled in makeshift camps they called "Hoovervilles," blaming the president for their sudden misfortune.

Lou became the first First Lady to talk on the radio, at the dedication of Washington's Constitution Hall in 1929.

Lou was deeply troubled by the criticism her husband received and tried to make her contribution to the recovery. Her regular radio broadcasts called on volunteers, especially those with wealth, to help those less fortunate. She encouraged the Girl Scouts to do all they could to make sure any families they knew with babies had enough milk. White House affairs became much simpler, and Lou tried to help the American cotton industry by wearing cotton evening gowns. She used all her contacts at charity organizations like the Red Cross to lend whatever support she could, even making many anonymous personal contributions when their funds ran out.

In the last year of his term, Herbert finally abandoned his policy of nonintervention and made $2 billion in direct aid available to banks, railroads, farmers, and other failing businesses. It was the type of program President Franklin D. Roosevelt would use with much success later on, but for Herbert, it was too little, too late. The 1932 election was coming, and most of the United States blamed Herbert for not doing enough to help the people during the economic crisis.

But Herbert received the Republican nomination again, and this time, Lou campaigned with him every day. They traveled 12,000 miles throughout the country but were often received with boos and jeers. There were even death threats against the beleaguered president. He lost decisively to Roosevelt in the November election, and the Hoovers left the White House, finally returning to Lou's dream home in Palo Alto. Her term as First Lady had coincided with one of the country's most trying times, and her years in the White House had been a bitter disappointment.

"I majored in geology in college, but I have majored in Herbert Hoover ever since."

—Lou Hoover discussing her admiration for her husband

Above: The Hoover's former home in Palo Alto, California, was given to Stanford University.

Below: Lou left the White House an embittered woman and retired with her husband to New York, where she died eleven years later.

Retirement

Lou was no longer First Lady, but she still had her desire to serve, and she kept busy in her retirement. She was still national president of the Girl Scouts and wrote articles and gave speeches on their behalf. She particularly championed the participation of the handicapped in the Girl Scouts. The Hoovers maintained a second home in New York City, in the Waldorf-Astoria Hotel, and the former First Lady continued to support charity organizations like the Salvation Army and the Red Cross on both coasts.

One of Lou's pet projects in her final years was the preservation of her husband's birthplace in West Branch, Iowa. Lou restored the house to its original appearance and bought extra land to set up a park surrounding the house. She also set up a library and museum and established the Hoover Birthplace Society to preserve the site permanently. Additionally, Lou helped her husband put together the 200,000-volume Hoover Library on War, Revolution, and Peace at Stanford University.

After World War II broke out, the Hoovers again labored hard on relief efforts particularly in support of Finland, which was resisting invasion from the Soviet Union. On January 7, 1944, the Hoovers were staying at their New York City home in the Waldorf-Astoria when Lou was stricken by a heart attack and died. She was sixty-nine years old. More than 1,500 people attended her funeral, including two hundred representatives from the Girl Scouts. She was buried in Palo Alto, and honoring Lou's wishes, the Hoovers' California home was donated to Stanford as the permanent residence for Stanford University's future presidents.

Herbert Hoover died in 1964 at the age of ninety. When he was buried at the Hoover Birthplace Park in West Branch, Iowa, Lou's remains were moved from Palo Alto to West Branch to lie with her husband's.

> *"The ambition to do, to accomplish irrespective of its measure in money of fame, is what should be inculcated. The desire to make the things that are better in a little way with what is at hand—in a big way, if the opportunity comes."*
>
> —*Lou Hoover expressing her belief in service to others in a letter to her children*

*During the Depression, many people wrote to Lou,
often asking for money. She almost always would send them
a check to help them out. When some tried to repay her years later
by sending a check, Lou didn't cash them. After her death,
her husband found hundreds of uncashed checks in her papers.*

*Above: The Herbert Hoover birthplace
in West Branch, Iowa, near Iowa City,
is part of a complex that includes
the Herbert Hoover Presidential
Library & Museum.*

To Visit the Hoovers

*The Herbert Hoover Presidential Library & Museum is
located in Waterloo, Iowa. The site contains the cottage where
Herbert was born, a blacksmith shop similar to the one owned
by his father, West Branch's first one-room schoolhouse, the
Friends meetinghouse where the Hoover family worshipped,
and several homes of the era. Also located on the grounds are
the Hoover Presidential Library Association, the gravesites of
the president and Mrs. Hoover, and an eighty-one-acre park of tall grass prairie. One
of the galleries in the museum's permanent collection focuses on the life of Lou Henry
Hoover. The site is located in West Branch, ten miles east of Iowa City, just off Interstate
80 at exit 254. The telephone number is 319-643-5301.*

*The Hoovers' presidential retreat, Camp Rapidan, is a 164-acre complex once
consisting of thirteen buildings plus a large outdoor stone fireplace, several miles of hiking
trails, a stone fountain, and manmade trout pools. Only four buildings currently remain.
When the Hoovers left office, they donated the complex to Shenandoah National Park
for use by future presidents, but all future presidents used President Roosevelt's more
accessible Camp David instead. Today, Camp Rapidan is managed by the National
Park Service and is listed on the National Register of Historic Places. The camp can
be reached by foot off the park's Skyline Drive via the Mill Prong Trail. The telephone
number is 540-999-3500.*

*The Hoovers' Palo Alto home is still owned by Stanford University and is now known
as the Lou Henry Hoover House. It was designated as a National Historic Site in
1985, and it continues to serve as home of the university's president.*

Eleanor Roosevelt

Ugly Duckling

Eleanor Roosevelt said that her mother was "the most beautiful woman I have ever seen," and there were few in 1880s New York City who wouldn't have agreed. Many would also add that her father was one of the handsomest men about town as well. But their daughter didn't seem to have inherited any of their good looks. She was plain, she was gawky, and because of it she was painfully shy. She had beautiful golden blonde hair, but it rarely brought her any compliments. Her mother called her Granny, because she seemed so old-fashioned. "My mother was troubled by my lack of beauty," Eleanor recalled. "She tried to bring me up well so that my manners would compensate for my looks."

Her father, Elliott, was the centerpiece of Eleanor's universe. Like his brother, future president Theodore Roosevelt, he was an avid sportsman; and as a teenager he had lived at a frontier fort in Texas where he hunted big game and "wild Indians" with equal enthusiasm. When he was in his early twenties, he took a trip around the world, and he was also one of the first Americans to travel to India to hunt tigers from the back of an elephant. Back home, he was a widely admired polo player, fox hunter, and breeder of fine horses; and, although he considered it a bore and he was more interested in social causes than society functions, he was at the very top of New York's gentry, representing one of the city's oldest and wealthiest families.

Eleanor's mother, the former Anna Hall, had a similar pedigree. She was a descendant of the Livingston family, among the biggest landowners and a political force in colonial New York and the Hudson River Valley. Her marriage to Elliott Roosevelt was the highlight of the 1883 social season, uniting as it did two of the most important families in the city.

Eleanor was the first of the Roosevelts' three children, and she was an only child for the first five years of her life. Her brother Elliott died at the age of four, and the youngest, Hall, didn't arrive until she was seven. By that time,

---

Anna Eleanor Roosevelt

Born
October 11, 1884,
New York, New York

Parents
Elliott Roosevelt and
Anna Rebecca Hall
Roosevelt

Marriage
March 17, 1905,
to Franklin Delano
Roosevelt (1882-1945)

Children
Anna Eleanor (1906-75);
James (1907-91); Franklin
Delano, Jr. (1909); Elliott
(1910-90); Franklin
Delano, Jr. (1914-88);
John Spinal (1916-81)

Died
November 7, 1962,
Hyde Park, New York

Anna Roosevelt's ancestor Robert Livingston administered the oath of office at George Washington's inauguration.

little Eleanor had become the center of the family's attention. She had every luxury that might be expected for a little rich girl, including a French nurse. She learned to speak French before she mastered English.

Her father began to drink heavily when Eleanor was about five, and in hopes of finding a cure, the family took an extended tour of Europe. Anna eventually rented a house outside Paris and enrolled Eleanor in a convent school, which soon expelled her for lying, a girlhood habit that she later recalled came from fears that she wanted to hide.

Above: Young Eleanor Roosevelt (middle) with her father, Elliott, her brother Elliott, Jr., and cousin Gracie Hall. Her father and her brother both died when Eleanor was not yet ten years old.

Elliott stayed behind in a French sanitarium when Anna and her children went home, and Eleanor would not see him again until her mother died a year later. The eight-year-old was unmoved when she lost her mother, but secretly happy that it was she her father turned to for solace, even though his stay was brief. He was a patient at a Virginia sanitarium by then. Anna had bequeathed custody of her children to their grandmother Mary Hall, and they moved into her town house, where Eleanor's brother Elliott died soon afterward. Her beloved father died less than a year after that, her third loss in less than a year and a half—and Eleanor was only ten years old. "I knew in my mind that my father was dead," she wrote, "and yet I lived with him more closely than when he was alive."

Eleanor had almost no friends, and her grandmother forbade her to visit her Roosevelt relatives, whom she considered frivolous. It was especially upsetting because Eleanor had developed a special fondness for her father's brother, Uncle Ted, who was the only person who was able to bring her out of her shell. She was allowed, though, to visit Ted's sister Corinne during the Christmas

A Life of Service

While her father was alive, he took little Eleanor along with him when he went to serve Thanksgiving dinners at the Newsboy Clubhouses, part of the Children's Aid Society, a program established by his own father to help street urchins. Her Grandmother Hall encouraged her to make regular visits to handicapped children at the Orthopedic Hospital, another of her grandfather's charities; and her aunts and uncles on the Hall side of the family often took her along with them when they went to sing for the unfortunates at the Bowery Mission. Her uncle took her along when he went to decorate children's Christmas trees in the Hell's Kitchen neighborhood, one of the nastiest in New York City. It was these frequent excursions in an otherwise sheltered life, Eleanor said, that made her "conscious of the fact that there were people around me who suffered in one way or another."

holidays—it was her only exposure to playing with boys, because they weren't welcome in her grandmother's house. But Eleanor was always the wallflower at her aunt's parties. "They were more pain than pleasure," she recalled. Not only was she unusually tall and awkward, but her grandmother dressed her in dowdy clothes that made her mother's characterization of her as "Granny" seem like a prophecy.

One of the boys took pity on her during one of the parties, though, and he asked her to dance with him. It was her distant cousin from the Hyde Park branch of the Roosevelt family. He was two years older than she was. His name was Franklin. They had been introduced once before, but this was the first time that they actually spoke to one another.

Life at Grandmother Hall's house was grim, and dealing with a budding teenager must have been a strain on the woman, too, because at the age of fifteen, Eleanor was packed off to England where she was enrolled in a school called Allenswood that was run by a French refugee named Marie Souvestre. The headmistress took an instant liking to Eleanor, and she went to work helping her overcome her shyness and her very low opinion of herself. Eleanor's education up to that point had been a haphazard kind of thing, but Mademoiselle Souvestre more than made up for lost time, and she quickly discovered that the girl had "an old head on her young body." She was able to recite poetry that she had read only once, and she could repeat dinner conversations nearly verbatim days after listening to them. The Allenswood girls were only allowed to speak French. One word of English brought them a demerit.

Above: Eleanor (third from left, back row) went to a private school in England where all of the students were required to speak French.

Eleanor stayed at Allenswood for three years, which she described as the "happiest of my life." She learned to take care of herself there, to choose her own clothes, to travel independently, and most important of all, to make close friends. She even stopped biting her nails and telling fibs. Eleanor wasn't afraid anymore. "Never again would I be the rigid little person I had been before," was how she put it. Obviously, she was eager to stay on for the fourth year that would complete her education and her transformation, but she was about to turn eighteen, and her grandmother ordered her home to be introduced into society. There was to be no argument about it.

Mademoiselle Souvestre didn't want to lose her. She was proud of Eleanor's transformation from an ugly duckling into a promising young woman, but she thought that Eleanor's special intelligence and her natural sympathy would be diluted in New York's shallow social world. Besides, there was still work to be done. For all the transformation that had taken place, she thought that Eleanor was still not "joyful."

"Mlle. Souvestre shocked me into thinking."

—Eleanor Roosevelt on her education

Socialite

There was little joy to be found at her grandmother's Hudson Valley country house, where she spent the summer. But when fall and her eighteenth birthday rolled around, it was time to get herself ready for her "coming out" during the Assembly Ball at the Waldorf-Astoria Hotel in December. Her mother and her grandmother and all of her aunts had been introduced to society in the same way, but they had each been beautiful belles of the ball, and Eleanor knew that she couldn't possibly measure up to them—after all, her mother had told her so while she was still a toddler.

Eleanor wore a gown that had been made for her in Paris, and her golden hair was arranged at the city's most prestigious salon, but like most girls her age, she dwelled on things about herself that could ruin the whole thing. She thought she was too tall, that her mouth was ugly, and her chin too small. She was afraid she wasn't a very good dancer, either, but that probably didn't matter, because she didn't expect to be asked, and she was right about that. She had been away for so long that she didn't know anyone who was there, except for her own relatives, and she danced very few figures in the cotillion. She left the ball as early as etiquette allowed. "By no stretch of the imagination could I fool myself into thinking that I was a popular debutante," she recalled.

But if Eleanor had been a weed among roses at her debut, she gradually developed a wide circle of friends who admired her for her genuine warmth and her obvious intelligence. She made the rounds of fashionable parties during her first winter as a socialite, but she generally found her fellow partygoers dull and vapid, and now that she had other friends who were more stimulating, she stopped accepting invitations on the social circuit.

As a young society woman, she was a member of the Junior League, which had recently been formed to engage in fund-raising for the less fortunate. A few of the members were interested in going beyond staging parties to raise money, and Eleanor was drawn to them. Among the league's projects at the time was supporting settlement houses that brought educational and recreational

Above: Eleanor was introduced to New York society at her coming-out at the Waldorf-Astoria Hotel. She was a shy and quite unremarkable debutante.

Below: When she traveled to Manhattan's Lower East Side to teach at the settlement house, Eleanor had to thread her way through Bowery breadlines to get there.

Settlement House

The settlement house where Eleanor Roosevelt taught was established in 1889 as a "College Settlement," where "educated women" could live among "working people" for their "mutual benefit and education." The concept came from England, where such institutions had been established in the East London slums, and by the time Eleanor appeared on the scene, there were more than sixty of them on Manhattan's Lower East Side and about twenty in Brooklyn. Her volunteer partner, Jean Reid, went downtown in her own carriage, but Eleanor took the Bowery streetcar and walked through several blocks of mean streets to the school. She admitted that it was a "terrifying experience," but she was fascinated by it, and "the children interested me enormously."

opportunities to poor immigrants on Manhattan's Lower East Side, and Eleanor joined with Jean Reid, the daughter of newspaper publisher Whitelaw Reid, to teach children at the Rivington Street Settlement House. Jean taught the youngsters there how to play the piano, and Eleanor taught them dancing and calisthenics.

Her stints at the settlement house began after the youngsters' normal school day, and Eleanor also found time to become active in the Consumers League, which investigated working conditions in sweatshops and department stores. "It had never occurred to me [until then] that the girls might get tired standing behind counters all day long," she said. "I did not know what the sanitary requirements should be in the dress factories, either for air or for lavatory facilities." She learned a lot from these experiences, but she said later that she was still extremely unworldly and innocent. She had discovered "the less agreeable sides of life," but "they did not seem to make me any more sophisticated."

Marriage

Eleanor said that "it seemed entirely natural" when her fifth cousin Franklin Roosevelt asked her to marry him around the time of her nineteenth birthday. They had become reacquainted more than a year earlier, and he seemed to contrive to be wherever she might be, even showing up occasionally to take her home from her classes down on Rivington Street. She had often gone to Cambridge, where he was a student at Harvard, for proms and parties, and she had even visited him at the family's Hyde Park estate, where she had won the respect of his demanding mother.

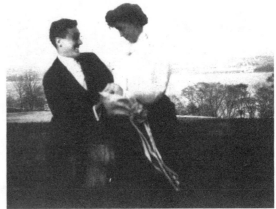

Above: Eleanor and Franklin in a candid shot in 1905 not long after they announced their engagement.

But Sara Delano Roosevelt drew the line at having Eleanor for a daughter-in-law. She had expected Franklin to move back into her house for a few years after he graduated from college, and she resented having her plan interrupted by this "child." She insisted that they keep their engagement secret for at least a year, reminding them that Franklin still had an obligation as a student and editor of *The Harvard Crimson*, and Eleanor had her social work, which Sara found demeaning to the Roosevelt name. She added that they were both still young and needed time to learn more about life. When they agreed, she went to work driving a wedge between them, beginning with a winter-long cruise for Franklin to the West Indies, his studies notwithstanding, leaving Eleanor behind in New York to think things over.

During their courtship, Eleanor and Franklin went to Washington for the inauguration of her Uncle Theodore as president in March 1905, and they had lunch with him at the White House.

A Demanding Mother-in-Law

Franklin's mother, Sara Delano Roosevelt, was the daughter of Warren Delano, who made a great fortune in the tea and opium trade in China. She spent some of her early life in Hong Kong, but most of it at Algonac, the family estate on the Hudson River near Newburgh, New York. A tall and strikingly beautiful young woman, she was pursued by many members of the local gentry, but she surprised everyone when she married James Roosevelt, a wealthy widower who was twice her age, and moved to his estate, Springwood, across the river at Hyde Park. When her son, Franklin, was born, her doctors advised her not to have any more children, and she devoted her life to the one child she did have.

Above: Franklin's mother, Sara, wasn't so sure she approved of the idea of her son marrying Eleanor, but she warmed up in her own way.

Her husband died when her son was eighteen years old, and she became even more single-minded about young Franklin, even to the point of moving to Boston to be near him while he was a student at Harvard. She was strong-willed, controlling, opinionated, and inflexible, and her son couldn't make a move without her input. After Franklin married, over her objections, she manipulated every detail of the newlyweds' lives. She built a town house on New York's Upper East Side that was divided exactly in half, with her on one side and the newlyweds on the other. They couldn't even escape her when they went on vacation: They summered in identical cottages, side by side, on Campobello Island in Canada. When Eleanor and Franklin began to have children, Sara was there to give them advice, which often seemed more like demands. Eleanor didn't seem to resent the interference at first, but as she gained self-confidence, she began to find the dominance of Sara oppressive.

As the couple established themselves as political leaders, they were able to shake off some of Sara's influence over them, but when Franklin was stricken with polio, his mother insisted that they retire to Hyde Park where he could finish his life as a country squire. Eleanor would have none of it, and she encouraged him to get back into a life of politics in spite of his mother's objections. Sara not only despised politics, but she hated anything and everybody outside her own social class, although when the younger Roosevelts became nationally important, she maintained her dignity as the mistress of Springwood, in spite of her strong disapproval. Franklin and Eleanor lived there with her, and when they moved to the White House, she supervised the decorating of the family quarters. After she died, Franklin refused to make any changes either at Hyde Park or Washington that would erase his mother's taste or sensibilities. Eleanor wrote, "There was always a close bond between them in spite of the fact that he had grown away from her in some ways and that in later years they had not often been in sympathy about policies on public affairs." As she had been when her own mother died, Eleanor admitted to being "unmoved" by her mother-in-law's passing.

Their lives went on as before. They still went to parties together, and she went to visit him in Massachusetts just as she had been doing during the previous year. All that changed was that they wrote more letters to each other, but that was private. As far as their friends and family were concerned, they were still just casually dating one another. Eleanor used the year of secrecy about their engagement to try to win over her future mother-in-law, and she seems to have succeeded. They were together almost constantly, shopping, lunching, and going to concerts, the theater, and the opera together. Sara proudly introduced Eleanor into her own tight social circle as a "dear child" whom everyone ought to know.

They finally announced their engagement on December 1, 1904, at the height of the social season and set the wedding date for March 17. It was St. Patrick's Day, but it was also her mother's birthday, and it served as an added convenience for her Uncle Ted, the president. He was scheduled to be in New York to review the parade, and it would save him a special trip to give the bride away. Not that he wouldn't have done it anytime; Eleanor was his favorite niece.

They were married in her cousins' twin houses on East Sixty-Sixth Street off Fifth Avenue, but many of the guests didn't arrive until after the ceremony was over. The St. Patrick's Day parade blocked access on Fifth Avenue and the president's entourage had the Madison Avenue corner clogged. Yet the guest list, which included Vanderbilts, Belmonts, Sloanes, and Van Rensselaers, read like pages from the Social Register.

Eleanor wore a long-sleeve stiff satin dress with shirred tulle at the neck and covered with rose-point Brussels lace that had belonged to her Grandmother Hall. Her veil and long train were of the same lace, and she also wore a necklace of pearls that her mother-in-law gave to her. She carried a bouquet of lilies of the valley, and she wore a diamond-studded gold watch that the bridegroom designed for her. It was suspended from a pin in the form of three feathers from the Roosevelt family crest. She wore it almost constantly for the rest of her life.

Their first home was in an apartment hotel, but when Mrs. Roosevelt went back to Hyde Park for the summer, they moved into her town house. Their honeymoon was delayed while Franklin finished law school, but then they went to Europe, stopping in London and Paris, Milan and Venice, Germany, the South of France, and Scotland. They were away for three months.

The following spring, Eleanor gave birth to her first child, named Anna Eleanor after her mother and grandmother. She was the first of six children

Above: Eleanor's wedding dress was covered with Brussels lace that had belonged to her grandmother. Her uncle Theodore took time out from his presidential duties to give her away.

Below: Their European honeymoon included a sojourn in Venice, where Eleanor had only a book for company on her gondola ride.

During their honeymoon, Franklin did most of the bargaining in France because, although Eleanor had spoken French all her life, he thought that his own mastery of the language was better. In Italy, though, he deferred to her. She spoke Italian well, but he had only absorbed the language through his study of Latin.

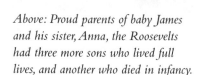

Above: Proud parents of baby James and his sister, Anna, the Roosevelts had three more sons who lived full lives, and another who died in infancy.

born to the Roosevelt family. As Eleanor put it, "For ten years I was always just getting over having a baby or about to have one." One of her babies, Franklin, Jr., died when he was seven months old, and Eleanor blamed herself. She left all her young children in the care of nurses, and she felt that they may have suffered for it.

After their second child, James, was born, and it became apparent that the family was going to grow some more, Franklin's mother had a town house built for them on Manhattan's East Sixty-Fifth Street. But there was a catch. Sara also intended to live there, and although she had the house designed as two separate but equal units, only sliding doors separated them. Eleanor, who knew absolutely nothing about domesticity—she couldn't cook and could barely sew—was happy to be surrounded by servants, but she resented the fact that she was being forced to live in a house that wasn't hers and didn't represent the way she wanted to live. "I was not developing any individual taste or initiative," she said. "I was simply absorbing the personalities of those about me and letting their tastes and interests dominate me."

But as more babies arrived, she got accustomed to the arrangement, and with nurses to tend to the children, she had plenty of time to brush up on her foreign languages, she knitted and did needlepoint, and she became an intense reader. She admitted that while she read everything that was popular at the time, it didn't cover a "wide field." Her taste in reading was confined to what her friends were talking about.

Her horizons were expanded when her husband, by then a successful lawyer, decided to run for the New York state senate as a Democrat in district that had been solidly Republican for more than three decades. He had an unusual approach, though. He visited every village in the district, talked with every farmer, and stopped at every store. Eleanor went with him on some of his tours, and she discovered in her husband a man she hadn't known before and a world that would replace the one she had resigned herself to.

Political Partner

When Franklin won the election, Eleanor was overjoyed. It meant that she would be moving to the state capital at Albany and out from under her mother-in-law's thumb. It also expanded her horizons. "It was a wife's duty to be interested in whatever interested her husband, whether it was politics, books,

When Eleanor became a mother, she stopped working directly among the poor. Her mother-in-law put a stop to it because she was afraid that she'd bring diseases home from the ghettos.

Above: The Roosevelt family during their time in Washington while Franklin was assistant secretary of the U.S. Navy, which might explain why young John and Franklin, Jr., are wearing sailor suits.

or a particular dish for dinner," she wrote. She not only served as hostess for the politicians who gathered in their home, but she visited their wives and local newspapermen, charming them all and expanding Franklin's influence. It was the first time in her life that she socialized with people outside the tight little circle of the friends and relatives back in New York City.

Naturally, topic one in Albany was politics, and Eleanor was soon able to hold her own in any conversation. What she didn't learn from her new friends, she picked up in the visitors gallery listening to debates in the legislature. She was still a housewife and mother, and she reveled in finally becoming domestic now that she was on her own, but she learned to balance her life. During this period, Eleanor became vice principal of a girls school in Manhattan and taught history and English there, along with a current-events program she called "Happenings." It involved tours of courtrooms, police lineups, and the slums of New York City. In her spare time, what there was of it, she also raised funds for the state Democratic party.

During Franklin's second term as a state senator, his support for Woodrow Wilson earned him the position of assistant secretary of the navy in the new administration, and the Roosevelts moved to Washington, where Eleanor's life changed again.

She made calls on wives of congressmen, cabinet ministers, and diplomats, and any shyness she still had wore off quickly as the Roosevelts became the most sought-after couple in town. They were there, however, when World War I began, and it brought their social life to a halt. Instead of partying, Washington women volunteered their time to the war effort, and Eleanor was the most active among them. She joined the Red Cross, the Navy League, and the Navy Relief Society, giving two or three days a week to each of them, and she said, "I loved it!…I simply ate it up."

A Marriage in Trouble

When Eleanor found love letters that had been sent to her husband by Lucy Mercer, her social secretary and close friend, she confronted Franklin and offered him his "freedom" from their thirteen-year marriage. His mother was horrified at the idea of a divorce, which was unheard of in her set, and she threatened to cut her son out of his inheritance if his marriage was broken. Friends pointed out that a divorce would not only end his marriage but his political ambitions as well, and others cautioned Eleanor to think of their six children and her own career, which was beginning to blossom. The couple finally agreed to stay together, but their marriage would never be the same again. It was transformed into a partnership rather than the traditional role, of husband and wife. "I can forgive, but I can never forget," she said years later.

When the war ended, Franklin and Eleanor sailed to Europe so he could supervise the closing of American naval facilities, and they got a firsthand look at the war's destruction, and Eleanor's compassion grew. She spent several days a week at military hospitals at a time when wartime volunteerism had ended. She began to stand up to her mother-in-law, too. "I should be ashamed of myself, but I am not," she said. Their marriage had become strained after a brief affair between Eleanor's husband and her secretary, but it had made Franklin more attentive, and although Eleanor went through dark periods of depression, she made a strong effort to be more relaxed, and for the first time she learned how to be "joyful," the only quality her old teacher had said she lacked.

In 1920, Franklin was nominated to run for vice president. Losing was a foregone conclusion, but it was a chance at national exposure, and he made the most of it, insisting that Eleanor join him on the campaign trail. She did more than stand behind him while he made speeches; she listened to every word and offered suggestions for improving them.

They returned to New York when the campaign was over, and he went back to his law practice. Eleanor went to a business school to learn shorthand and typing, and she volunteered with the new League of Women Voters. She served on a committee that analyzed new legislation, and worked closely with female attorneys, writers, and professors, who gave her a practical education in the world of politics. She characterized the experience, which lasted over several years, as "the intensive education of Eleanor Roosevelt."

Below: Eleanor and Franklin during one of their carefree holidays at Campobello Island.

Crisis

As they had during every summer of their married life, Eleanor and Franklin traveled to their summerhouse at Campobello Island near Bar Harbor, Maine, in the summer of 1921. It would be the visit they would always remember most.

Franklin hadn't had much rest since the campaign. He had gone on a long and strenuous hunting trip as soon as it ended, and restarting his legal career left him little time to relax. This was his first vacation since the war ended, and the whole family was looking forward to it. At the end of the first day, though, he said that he was getting chills and thought he was catching a cold. The next morning he was feverish, but he went ahead with a planned three-day camping trip. By the time he got back, his legs were paralyzed. A medical specialist diagnosed the condition as infantile paralysis. There was no cure available. Eleanor became his around-the-clock nurse until he could be moved back to New York in a private railroad car. He spent a few weeks at Presbyterian Hospital, but once at home, he became Eleanor's responsibility again. "He was tall and heavy to lift," she recalled, "but somehow both of us learned to do whatever was necessary." She also worked at keeping his spirits high, but he was doing a pretty good job of that on his own. "[The therapy] was torture," she recalled, "and he bore it without a single complaint, just as he bore his illness from the very beginning. I never but once heard him say anything bordering on discouragement or bitterness."

As the winter wore on, Eleanor helped him with exercises to stretch his muscles as much as he could, but his mother complained that she was tiring him unnecessarily. She believed that he should lie perfectly still, which Eleanor said "made the discussions of his care somewhat acrimonious." Sara had also resigned herself to the fact that her son would never be active again, and she began making plans for him to retire to the life of a country gentleman at Hyde Park. But her daughter-in-law wouldn't consider it.

With the help of his political mentor, Lewis Howe, Eleanor kept Franklin's business going and his contacts alive. She wanted him to get back to life as he had known it, and she doggedly refused to treat him as an invalid. She wouldn't let anyone else take pity on him either. In the end, she could proudly say, "Franklin's illness proved a blessing in disguise for it gave him strength and courage he had not had before. He had to think out the fundamentals of living and learn the greatest of all lessons—infinite patience and never-ending persistence." She could have made the same observation about herself.

While he was recovering, she kept his name in the public consciousness by involving herself more deeply in politics. She took over the *Women's Democratic News* as editor and publisher, she went to every corner of the state organizing political clubs for women, and she went to the 1924 Democratic National Convention to chair a committee on women's issues for the party platform. Most important, she learned public speaking, a talent she never knew she had, and she built up an entire new circle of friends who would be valuable to her husband when he picked up the pieces of his life again.

Below: Eleanor's closest friends, Nancy Cook and Marion Dickerman, gave her strength during Franklin's illness. Later, they went into business together making and selling Early American reproduction furniture.

A Home of Her Own

In 1924, Eleanor declared her independence from her mother-in-law when she and two friends, Nancy Cook and Marion Dickerman, began building a cottage on Val-Kill Creek, about two miles from the Roosevelt estate at Hyde Park. It was built of fieldstone in the style of the original Dutch houses in the area, and they dammed the creek to form a pool where Franklin could exercise in private. Nancy designed most of the furniture, which was so successful that the three women began to produce Early American reproductions for sale by the Metropolitan Museum in a factory that gave jobs to local people. Although her mother-in-law's house was still her official residence, Eleanor actually lived in the cottage, only appearing at the larger house when there were important guests to entertain.

Above: Franklin, Eleanor, and their son John in Albany, New York, while Franklin served as governor.

That began to happen in 1928 when he ran for governor of New York. By that time, Franklin had a fourteen-pound set of steel braces on each leg and he couldn't stand or walk without crutches or a friendly arm to lean on. But he was otherwise the picture of health, and his cheerfulness had never left him in the first place. He and Eleanor toured the state by car and train and he made several speeches a day, which added up to an eventual victory at the polls. Eleanor was on her way back to Albany again, but this time she was among close friends.

The National Scene

As the state's First Lady, Eleanor resigned her posts in the national party, but she kept her teaching job in Manhattan and commuted back and forth. She filled in as her husband's surrogate at state political functions, and she toured hospitals and prisons to report to him on conditions there. The Great Depression began during his first term, and following Eleanor's advice, Franklin instituted emergency programs to give jobs to the suddenly unemployed and food to the needy, causes that had long been close to her, and it gave him a national reputation.

His popularity in the state led to his reelection to the governor's chair by the biggest margin in history, and that put him out front as the Democrats' choice for president in 1932.

Eleanor had mixed emotions about her husband's election to the presidency. She had worked hard for his election, and her presence had made a difference. She said that she was "happy for him" because she knew that it would make up for the cruel blow that fate had given him. She also knew that he was the right man at the right time to help the country deal with its own cruel blow. But through her smiles, an observant reporter at the victory party noticed that "she looked like a fox surrounded by a pack of baying hounds."

She herself said, "I was deeply troubled. As I saw it, this meant the end of any personal life of my own. I knew what traditionally should lie before me; I had watched Mrs. Theodore Roosevelt and had seen what it meant to be the wife of a president, and I cannot say I was pleased at the prospect. By earning my own money, I had recently enjoyed a certain amount of financial independence and had been able to do things in which I was personally

Forgotten Men

Eleanor didn't think she was doing enough to help the victims of the Depression, the homeless and unemployed that her husband called "forgotten men." Her heart went out to the beggars who crowded the streets of Manhattan, and she handed many of them cards with her address and a message that they could get a meal there. She also hounded state agencies and charities to help people whose stories especially moved her, and her name on a request usually brought results. It was hard to turn Mrs. Roosevelt down.

interested. The turmoil in my heart and mind was rather great that night."

Above: Eleanor resisted Secret Service protection when she became First Lady, but she learned how to protect herself with her own pistol.

On the day after her husband's inauguration, the new First Lady began breaking precedents by announcing that she would begin holding regular press conferences, and then she broke another by adding that they would be open only to women reporters. Over time, news agencies that had closed their doors to women began hiring them because they found themselves scooped by the competition.

Eleanor had a White House limousine assigned to her, but she insisted on driving her own car, a Plymouth convertible roadster with a rumble seat, and she informed the Secret Service that she didn't like being followed around, telling them that "nobody's going to hurt me." She never allowed the Secret Service around her, although she did take their advice and got a gun, and she became an expert at using it.

When veterans marched on Washington demanding their benefits yet another time, she drove to their makeshift camp and spent an hour chatting with them about their problems and what might be done. During the previous administration, federal troops had met a similar group of veterans with tear gas and burned their camp to the ground, and the contrast was a dramatic introduction to Mrs. Roosevelt's style.

In those early days of air travel, Mrs. R, as she had become known, piled up more flight miles than a traveling salesperson. In a sense, that's what she was. She flew to every corner of the country, making unannounced visits to poverty-stricken areas from coal mines in Appalachia to Southern sharecroppers' farms and city slums. She was serving as her husband's "eyes and ears," but her visits brought reassurance

Above: The famous White House Scotty, Fala, retired to Eleanor's care at Val-Kill cottage.

Animal House

When the Roosevelts moved to Washington, D.C., from Hyde Park, they brought along a big German shepherd named Major. He often slept in the corridor outside the typing pool, and if he was there at noon, the women skipped lunch rather than try to walk past him. He was a watchdog and good at defending his territory. He bit the prime minister of Canada, and he tore the seat of the pants of a gardener, but it wasn't until he bit a senator that Eleanor sent the dog home. Another of her dogs, a setter named Winks, had a bad habit of stealing food from formally set tables; and her favorite, an old Scottie named Maggie, bit a reporter one day, and that, as far as Eleanor was concerned, was the end of canine pets in the White House. Her rule was broken in 1942, nine years later, when Franklin's cousin gave him a black Scottie named Big Boy. He changed the dog's name to Fala, after one of his Scottish ancestors, "Murray the Outlaw of Fala Hill."

Above: Eleanor was a proud supporter of her husband's New Deal programs and tirelessly toured facilities like WPA nursery schools.

Eleanor's column, "My Day," appeared six days a week in 180 newspapers. She wrote every word herself, and donated the fees to charity.

to millions that somebody in Washington cared enough about them to meet them on their own ground.

Eleanor not only reported back to the president on these experiences, but she also shared them with his constituents. She had written frequently for magazines and newspapers back in New York and she had even had some success as a broadcaster. Now she began writing a daily syndicated newspaper column that she called "My Day," to share her insights with a wider audience, and she augmented it with monthly magazine articles. She also gave radio talks, and she was active on the lecture circuit, where she handled tough questions from her audiences with disarming aplomb.

Naturally, Eleanor cultivated quite a number of enemies, chief among them rival newspaper columnist Westbrook Pegler, who characterized the new government as "Mrs. Roosevelt's administration." He wrote that she "has been too busy with such undignified trivialities as old-age pension, a ban on child labor, and the protection of the health of mothers and children," to take on the real duties of a First Lady that were required by custom and protocol.

She rarely responded to Pegler's barbs, but in that instance she probably took it as a compliment. Eleanor didn't shy away from the required receptions and dinners, and she handled herself with all the dignity that was expected of her—it was a role she grew up with. But she had to admit that she didn't see the value of standing for long hours greeting people she didn't know. She made it all more interesting for everyone concerned by changing White House functions from controlled social affairs by inviting student groups, representatives of women's organizations, and even on one occasion African-American girls from a reform school, to rub elbows with a surprised Washington elite. Reporters began comparing the White House to a settlement house.

Eleanor made sure she had a competent household staff, and she left the day-to-day details of the social side of White House life to them. "I never had to seat a formal dinner table," she recalled. Although she found receptions tiring—"my arms ached, my shoulders ached, and my back ached, and my knees and feet seemed to belong to someone else"—she scheduled three of them every week. Her husband found standing for long hours in his leg braces

"It was hard for me to remember that I was not just 'Eleanor Roosevelt' but the 'wife of the President.'"

—Eleanor Roosevelt on life in the White House

an ordeal, but he, too, thought it was necessary and worthwhile, although he insisted that the guest lists be kept under a thousand.

When she moved into the White House, Eleanor had made up her mind to stay in the background, but that simply wasn't in her nature. It was her duty, she believed, to help people understand what her husband was doing to help a nation crippled by the Great Depression. Some pundits believed that his New Deal programs sprang from Eleanor's ideas, but she was careful not to shape administration policies. Her job, as she saw it, was to sell those policies, and she was a master salesperson, although some of her husband's enemies accused her of being a "traitor to her class." In a sense they were right. There wasn't an issue that Eleanor didn't have an opinion about, but all of her opinions were centered on the rights of common people, with a strong emphasis on women, young people, and minorities.

But not everything she did worked out according to plan. She started a program to build a model community outside Morgantown, West Virginia, which would involve industries helping unemployed coal miners to get off relief, and to become home-owners with enough land to grow their own food. It was to be established with funds from the Department of Agriculture, which would run it as a "subsistence homestead project," and it would be the model for similar developments in

Below: One of the First Lady's pet projects, the planned community of Arthurdale in Preston County, West Virginia, brought her grief when it failed.

"*Oh Lord, please make Eleanor tired.*"

—*Franklin Roosevelt on his wife's unstoppable energy*

other depressed areas. It was called Arthurdale, after the original owner of the 1,200-acre site.

Arthurdale was perfect on paper, although some called it a "Communistic" scheme, but it was a fiasco from the start. Fifty prefabricated cottages were built, but when they arrived at the site they didn't fit the foundations that had already been laid, and they had to be rebuilt at great expense. The wells that had been dug produced nothing but brackish water, the houses had no insulation, and no one had planned for any storage space. Government employees ran the project with little or no experience in construction, and the would-be home-owners insisted on having their own input, which slowed progress even more. Among other things, they demanded that a cow should be included with each house, which the Department of Agriculture agreed to provide. Eleanor commented, "They wanted cows tied to their back fences. They trusted nobody, not even themselves. They had an eye out all the time to see who was going to cheat them next."

Although all this was beyond her control, Arthurdale was well-known as the First Lady's pet project, and it was she who took the heat. It didn't help when a government press release boasted that by Thanksgiving of 1933, the residents of the model community would be enjoying their own turkey in their own home. But there were no residents and no town until almost a year later, and by then the cost of each house had escalated to an unaffordable $12,000.

Still, Eleanor kept her faith in the project, and other less troublesome projects were built later. She suggested that the first factory at Arthurdale might make post office boxes; but the manufacturer who had a government monopoly on them accused her of undermining the free enterprise system, and the House of

Above: Eleanor's unqualified support of Marian Anderson prompted an African-American newspaper to note: "She broke another shackle in the chain which binds our country in bigotry."

Racial Justice

Eleanor Roosevelt had strong opinions about a lot of things, but the issue of racial equality may have been the one that affected her most. "We have poverty which enslaves," she once said, "and racial prejudice which does the same." When she went to a meeting in Birmingham, Alabama, with the African-American educator Mary McLeod Bethune, the police informed her that Blacks and Whites were not allowed to sit together at public gatherings in the city, and they were directed to opposite sides of the hall. When Eleanor refused to do as she was told, she was threatened with arrest. She compromised by having a chair placed for her in the dividing center aisle. Not long after that, when the Daughters of the American Revolution refused to allow the Black singer Marian Anderson to sing in their auditorium, Constitution Hall, the First Lady immediately resigned from the organization in protest. She had already invited Miss Anderson to sing at the White House, and later she requested opening the steps of the Lincoln Memorial for the canceled concert. Approximately 75,000 people showed up.

Representatives cut off funding after holding hearings that soundly denounced the First Lady for being at the cutting edge of a socialist plot.

It was the first time that any strong official criticism had been leveled at Mrs. Roosevelt, but it opened the door to more of the same, and congressional backbiting dogged her as long as she was First Lady. She found it difficult to believe that some people were opposed to helping other people in need, but she knew that the ones she wanted to help understood her and appreciated what she was doing. That was all that mattered to her. Still, she faced criticism and nastiness that would make an ordinary woman give up. "It is easy to think that Washington is the country," she once said, "and forget that it is a small place."

Her husband never attempted to restrain her. He thoroughly agreed with her concept of social justice, but letting her take the lead protected him politically. Besides, he knew better than to try holding her back.

Above: Eleanor handed over the reins of the Office of Civilian Defense to New York's Fiorello LaGuardia. Typically, he took to the job like a dog with a bone. James Landis, dean of the Harvard Law School, heartily approved.

Eleanor was a pacifist all of her life, and her trip to France on the heels of the First World War turned her into an activist pacifist. She supported antiwar groups and spoke out often about disarmament. But war was on her doorstep. Japan attacked China in 1937, Germany annexed Austria the following year, and the year after that the Nazis took over Czechoslovakia; also Fascist troops backed by Germany and Italy overthrew the government of Spain, starting a bloody civil war.

The United States stayed neutral, but its First Lady was never neutral about anything. "I believe in democracy," she said, "and the right of people to choose their own government without having it imposed on them." She fought hard for emergency legislation to allow war refugees to immigrate to America, but she was overruled by a conservative Congress that believed immigration quotas should be tightened and not expanded.

Meanwhile, the threat of war kept growing. France fell to the German onslaught in 1940, and the Nazis immediately turned to bombing Great Britain into submission. Franklin Roosevelt's second term was coming to an end, and Eleanor encouraged him to retire, but little by little she came to the conclusion that with war seemingly imminent, "no one else had the prestige and the knowledge to carry on in a crisis." He ran, and he won his third term by nearly five million votes.

Although he had promised the voters that "your boys are not going to be sent into foreign wars," and all four of their own sons had been called to active military duty, he formed a new agency called the Office of Civilian Defense to prepare for the possibility that the United States would soon be at war. He made his wife codirector of the agency with New York mayor Fiorello LaGuardia as her partner. It was the only official post Eleanor ever held in her husband's administration.

When war finally came after the Japanese attack on Pearl Harbor, Franklin became a wartime president with a certain amount of immunity from criticism,

Above: Eleanor with her son John and his wife admiring her grandson, John Roosevelt, Jr.

and his political enemies turned on his wife. She was a public official now, and that opened her to official attacks that she had previously been immune to. "I realized how unwise it was for a vulnerable person like myself to try a government job," she said, and she resigned from the post after just a few months.

But that didn't mean she was going to sit on the sidelines. In 1942, she flew to London, again serving as her husband's eyes and ears. Her own eyes were opened by women who were working in factories and serving in the military, and she went home with the opinion that American women could do the same. The following year, as a Red Cross volunteer, she toured Australia, New Zealand, and dozens of islands in the South Pacific war zone, including Guadalcanal, which, like the other islands, was under almost constant air attack after having been the scene of one of the bloodiest battles of the war. Of course, she was criticized for these trips as a gadfly who flew at government expense and only got in the way. But Admiral "Bull" Halsey, who was a skeptic himself at first, said that "she alone accomplished more good than any other person, or any group of civilians who had passed through my area." The Red Cross confirmed that she had inspired more than 400,000 GIs in hospitals and military bases, including many she had met before under different circumstances on her tours of the United States. Because of her knack for remembering faces, she surprised some of them by recalling those earlier encounters.

The president's health was fading visibly, but Eleanor kept encouraging him to soldier on with his strong sense of urgency. With the end of the war in sight, she stood behind his decision to run for a fourth term in 1944, but she said, "I dread another campaign and even more another four years in Washington, but since he's running for the good of the country, I hope he wins." In spite of his haggard appearance and an opposition that never passed up an opportunity to call attention to it, he did win the election by a margin of more than three and a half million votes.

Before the election, he had gone to Teheran, Iran, for a "Big Three" summit meeting with Great Britain's prime minister Winston Churchill and Soviet premier Josef Stalin. At the same time, Eleanor left for a 13,000-mile tour of the Caribbean in an encore to her Pacific trip. The president himself had mapped out her itinerary to visit troops on reconnaissance duty there, but it had been forgotten because of the war news. Even the USO had neglected them. Among the GIs she saw there was her son John, when his ship passed through the Panama Canal. When she visited the outpost in the Galapagos Islands, she and her entourage were the first women ever seen there.

Right after his fourth inauguration, the president went to the Russian city of Yalta for another Big Three meeting, and then after delivering a report on the conference to Congress, he went to Warm Springs, Georgia, to the spa he had bought after his battle with polio, and where he had always found relief. It was there, less than fourteen weeks after his inauguration and a little more than twelve years into his presidency, Franklin D. Roosevelt died of a cerebral hemorrhage. Eleanor was on her own.

A New Life

After her husband died, Eleanor lamented that she "did not want to cease feeling useful in some way." It was Eleanor who broke the news of Franklin's death to Harry S Truman. As the new president, he frequently called on her for advice, and she was visited by a steady stream of foreign dignitaries who made pilgrimages to Hyde Park. All in all, Eleanor was leading a busier life than the average sixty-one-year-old, but she wasn't feeling particularly "useful."

After the war ended with the Japanese surrender in the summer of 1945, President Truman asked Mrs. Roosevelt to serve as a delegate to the first session of the United Nations

Above: President Harry S Truman gave Eleanor a new lease on life by naming her a delegate to the new United Nations.

Getting the Job

When Mrs. Roosevelt's name was put on the list of delegates to the first United Nations session, she faced strong opposition. During her Senate confirmation hearings, Senator Theodore Bilbo of Mississippi denounced her as "pro-Negro," and Senator J. William Fulbright of Arkansas claimed that her appointment would send a message to the world that the United States wasn't taking the organization seriously. Some of her fellow nominees didn't think much of her appointment, either, partly because of who she was, but mostly because she was a woman. She wrote that one of them, John Foster Dulles, "felt the whole world was coming to an end when he heard I was joining the delegation." President Truman, on the other hand, strongly believed that Eleanor would become a great world leader. "Your country needs you," he told her. "Indeed, this troubled world needs you."

that was scheduled to take place in London near the beginning of the new year. She herself had been strongly supporting the idea of such a world organization for years, and it was one of Franklin's most passionate dreams. But she seriously considered turning down the offer because she didn't think she had enough experience in foreign affairs and knew little or nothing about parliamentary procedure. She did accept, though, because she believed that the United Nations would be her husband's most important legacy, and her presence at its birth would be a tribute to him.

Eleanor had expected to be an inconspicuous participant, in the London sessions, but even if her fame hadn't preceded her, she stood out as the only woman in the delegation. There was a great deal of rancor in the gathering as each of the fifty-one delegations jockeyed for position as first among equals, and she was often sought out for advice. It was apparent to everyone that alone among them, she had no personal ambition and no political axes to grind. "She simply moved in as a super mother," one reporter said, "presiding over a large family of often noisy, sometimes unruly, but basically good-hearted boys who now and then needed firmly to be put in their places."

Her shining moment came near the end of the session. The Soviet delegate, Andrei Vishinsky, had been working all along to drive a wedge between the Communist and non-Communist nations, and the last straw as far as Eleanor was concerned was his resolution demanding that war refugees in Germany must be returned to their native countries whether they wanted to go or not, and that they should be denied their freedom of speech. The meeting went into chaos. No one was willing to stand up to Vishinsky, but someone had to, and Eleanor was the only person who was willing to stare him down. "We here in the United Nations are trying to frame things which will consider first the rights of man and what makes men more free—not governments, but men." Her fellow delegate John Connolly said that "it was her presence that saved the day. She was the only person with enough stature in everyone's eyes to squelch him."

After his proposal was voted down, Vishinsky told her, "I admire your fighting qualities." "Why, thank you," she said, "Perhaps next time you might try using *your* fighting abilities on the right side."

By the time the sessions were over, Eleanor had carved out a new niche for herself. She was no longer just the widow of the American president but an important player on the world stage in her own right. She served as a delegate to the United Nations for all the years of the Truman administration.

When the king and queen of England invited Eleanor to Buckingham Palace, she declined because she had committee meetings to attend.

In 1946, she was elected to the chair of the United Nations' Human Rights Commission, charged with drafting an international bill of rights. When the document was presented to the General Assembly in 1948, it was approved with almost no dissenting votes, and she was honored as the only delegate ever to be given a standing ovation; no other delegate has received one since.

During the more than two years while her eighteen-member commission was often working fourteen-hour days drafting the Universal Declaration of Human Rights, she was also a delegate to the U.N. General Assembly, and she still managed to find time to write her newspaper column and magazine articles, and to deliver more than a hundred lectures a year. She also hosted a weekly television program, the first interview show ever seen on TV, and she made a daily radio broadcast. She also worked on her autobiography.

Eleanor had an apartment on the north side of Manhattan's Washington Square, and she converted the old Val-Kill furniture factory near Hyde Park, and near her smaller cottage, into a country home where she could entertain her children and grandchildren—she had twenty-three grandchildren and great-grandchildren. It also served as a place to entertain friends and unwind from the pressures of her schedule. She never let a special occasion pass unnoticed, and if others in the family forgot birthdays or anniversaries, she made it a point to remind them. She deeply believed that family and friends were more important than anything else that competed for her attention.

Eleanor had flown thousands of miles around the United States while her husband was president, and now all of her frequent trips were to other places around the world where she traveled as a goodwill ambassador for the State Department. Her most famous trip was to India in 1952 when she met

Above: Franklin and Eleanor proudly show off their thirteen grandchildren in 1945.

Although Eleanor was not a college graduate, she had several Phi Beta Kappa keys. She also had many honorary degrees, including ones from the University of Utrecht in Holland and Oxford in England. She lectured at the Sorbonne in Paris, and in addition to lecturing at Brandeis University, she served on its Board of Trustees.

with militant students at Allahabad over the strong objection of the family of Indian prime minister Jawaharlal Nehru. They had come to denounce Yankee imperialism, and although she didn't change their minds, she changed their attitude with her answers to their questions.

She had decided that she wanted to devote the rest of her life to the United Nations, but Dwight D. Eisenhower replaced her as delegate when he became president in 1953. Without skipping a beat, she volunteered to work with the American Association for the United Nations, an organization dedicated to promoting support for the United Nations with the American public. Without the demands of her former job, she was able to step up her travel, virtually circling the globe every year. On her seventieth birthday in 1954, she was proud to say that she hadn't slowed her pace, but she admitted that she probably would someday. "Everybody does," she said. But Eleanor Roosevelt wasn't "everybody."

When she was seventy-five years old, Mrs. Roosevelt started a new job as a guest lecturer at Brandeis University and she launched a new television series for the Public Broadcasting Service, with Dr. Martin Luther King, Jr., as her first guest. She cut her newspaper column to three times a week instead of six, but that was the only sign that she might be slowing down.

When John F. Kennedy became president in 1961, he reappointed her as a delegate to the United Nations; he also made her a member of the Advisory Council of the Peace Corps, and chair of the President's Commission on the Status of Women. It was a grueling schedule, but she was accustomed to that.

She began to have down days, which she wasn't used to, but she ignored her aches and pains. "If you pay too much attention to them," she said, "the next thing you know you are an invalid." She was soon hospitalized with an incurable blood disease, and after just a few weeks she died

Below: Among the dignitaries at Eleanor's funeral at Hyde Park in 1962 were President John F. Kennedy, former presidents Harry S Truman and Dwight D. Eisenhower, and then-Vice President Lyndon B. Johnson.

at home of a stroke on November 7, 1962. She was buried next to her husband and their little dog Fala in the rose garden at Springwood, the former Roosevelt estate at Hyde Park. At her funeral, which was attended by President Kennedy and former presidents Truman and Eisenhower, as well as future president Lyndon Johnson, it was Harry Truman who paid her the ultimate compliment. "She was the First Lady of the World," he said.

Visiting Hyde Park and Val-Kill Cottage

The Eleanor Roosevelt National Historic Site is the only site dedicated to the memory of a First Lady. Along with Springwood, the nearby Roosevelt estate in Hyde Park, New York, the site is run by the National Park Service. The cottage is furnished as it was when Mrs. Roosevelt lived there during most of the years of her later life. The grounds are open free of charge, but entry to the house is available on guided tours with a two-day pass that costs $8.00:

It is open every day April through October and Thursday through Monday in November and March. It is closed between December and February. Reservations are suggested during October, when the fall foliage makes it the most popular time for a visit. For more information, call 800-967-2283.

The main Roosevelt Mansion, where Eleanor and Franklin are buried in the rose garden, is a short distance away in Hyde Park, which is located a few miles north of Poughkeepsie, New York. From New York City, take the Henry Hudson Parkway to the Sawmill River Parkway and then the Taconic Parkway, northbound, to Route 55 West (Poughkeepsie) and Route 9 North, the Albany Post Road. From the New York Thruway (I-87), exit at Route 299 East, to 9-W southbound to the Mid-Hudson Bridge and exit at Route 9 North.

*Above: Springwood,
the Roosevelt estate at Hyde Park,
New York, is a few miles north
of Poughkeepsie, New York.*

Bess Truman

Growing Up Together

The story is well known. Harry Truman first set eyes on Elizabeth (or Bess, as she was known) Wallace at the First Presbyterian Church Sunday school when he was six and she was five. Later in life he recalled the incident and described walking in and seeing "a little blue-eyed golden-haired girl." He insisted that he fell in love with Bess on the spot, and that he never stopped loving her for the rest of his life. Throughout their years together, Harry was also known to remark that her blue eyes were still as lovely as the day he first saw them. The lightning bolt of love may, indeed, have struck young Harry Truman in the heart that fateful morning in Sunday school, but it would be a very long time before he would be able to call Bess his wife.

Harry and Bess did not marry until twenty-nine years later, in 1919, when Harry was thirty-six and Bess was thirty-five. They had courted for nine years and been engaged for six, meaning that Harry loved Bess from afar, unrequited, until he was nineteen and she then began to respond to his overtures. There were many reasons for Bess's delayed interest, including Harry's business ventures, political career, family obligations, and military engagement, as well as Bess's responsibilities, in particular her mother. In addition, it probably did not help matters that Bess's mother, the dour Margaret Wallace, made things difficult for the two to evolve into a happy couple. She never changed her opinion—even after her son-in-law became president of the United States—that Harry was not good enough for her daughter.

Bess Wallace was born in a house on Ruby Street in Independence, Missouri, on Friday, February 13, 1885. She was christened Elizabeth Virginia, but her mother called her Bessie, in honor of her close friend Bessie Madge Andrews. Independence back then was a small community with a population that was only a tiny percentage of today's population, and the majority of the town's citizens seemed to be related to one another in some way. Such places are often insular, and usually closely knit, and Independence was no exception. It is not surprising that Bess's eventual life partner grew up two blocks away from her childhood home.

Bess was born into wealth. She was the daughter of David Willock Wallace, a local politician considered the handsomest man in Independence, and Margaret Gates Wallace, known as Madge to her friends and family. In 1887, when Bess was two, her father moved the family to 608 North Delaware Street.

Elizabeth Virginia Wallace Truman

Born
February 13, 1885,
Independence, Missouri

Parents
David Willock Wallace
and Margaret Gates
Wallace

Marriage
June 28, 1919, to Harry S
Truman (1884-1972)

Children
Mary Margaret (1924-)

Died
October 18, 1982,
Independence, Missouri

Above: As a little girl, Bess Wallace lived a life of relative luxury in Independence, Missouri.

Below: Young Bess could dress like a proper lady, but under that bonnet was an irrepressible tomboy who loved sports.

Their new Victorian house was one of the nicest homes on one of the nicest streets in one of the nicest areas of Independence, Missouri. The house was two blocks away from the mansion Madge Wallace's father had built and where, as a child, Bess spent a great deal of time, being fussed over by her aunts and uncles.

As a child, Bess was an accomplished athlete. She was a talented ice skater and swimmer, and played softball and tennis with skill. She was also a gifted horsewoman and enjoyed track-and-field sports, excelling particularly at the shot put. Bess attended Independence High School, where she enjoyed her studies and was an excellent student. She graduated in 1901, with Harry Truman in her graduating class. Bess enjoyed a mostly halcyon childhood on North Delaware, and it wasn't until she was in her teens that she began to understand her father had problems.

David Willock Wallace was an accomplished man and a pillar of Independence society. He was married to the daughter of the richest man in town. He was active in his local church, and he was popular and

One of Bess's favorite First Ladies was James Monroe's wife, Elizabeth, because she so admired Elizabeth's success at what Bess's daughter, Margaret, described as "virtually disappearing from the White House for most of her husband's two terms."

well known around Independence. He was also a respected government official: He served as the deputy U.S. surveyor of customs out of the Kansas City office.

However, perceptions and outward appearances are not always reality. Wallace had serious financial difficulties and his businesses had failed. It was expected of him that his wife would be provided for in the same custom in which she had been raised, one of extraordinary affluence. His wife was apparently adamant that she live in the same style as a married woman as she had when she was the single daughter of a very wealthy father. Madge also believed in the idea of leaving full responsibility for the family's finances to her husband. This rigid standard resulted in Madge's also remaining silent on matters other than finances. When her husband's drinking was in full swing, David would often be carried home and deposited on the front porch of the house by chivalrous friends. Madge never spoke of these incidents, nor chastised her husband for his indulgence, believing it would be "unseemly" for her to comment in such a manner.

David's stress spurred his alcohol use; the alcohol fed the depression; the depression fed his feelings of hopelessness; and his hopelessness was, ultimately, his fatal flaw. In a letter written around this time, he wrote, "To be frank with you, I get pretty *blue* [his italics], over matters. I do the very best that I can but it seems that little good results." In another letter, he again referred to his depression: "I try to look on the bright side of things, but even then it is dark." But David could not overcome his pain and, on June 18, 1903, he took his own life with a single bullet to the head.

Bess and her family had been in the house asleep while her father committed suicide sitting in the bathtub in the bathroom of her childhood home. She was just eighteen. She never talked about the incident afterward, and this event was a major catalyst for her intense desire for privacy, a trait that remained with her for the rest of her life. The local newspapers covered her father's suicide on their front pages, and Bess was horrified by having her family's personal tragedy displayed for everyone to see.

Bess seemed unable to accept that her mother's love for her father was insufficient to dissuade him from taking his own life. Madge's love notwithstanding, David had demands placed upon him that he simply could not satisfy. Bess's befuddlement over the underlying causes of her father's suicide, and her difficulty in understanding why her mother could not have prevented it, surprisingly did not result in her blaming her mother, a reaction that would have unquestionably caused a subsequent estrangement. In fact, the exact opposite happened. David Wallace's suicide resulted in what was once described as "an intense, lifelong bond" between Bess and her mother.

After the death of her father, Bess found herself in the position of having to take care of her mother. She cared for Madge's prosaic, day-to-day needs, but also tried to deal with her mother's emotional problems concerning the suicide of her husband. This reversal of roles would continue for the rest of Madge Wallace's life, with daughter caring for mother.

A Life Together

After Bess's father's suicide, her mother took Bess and her three siblings to Colorado Springs to live for a year. They then moved back to Missouri and lived with Madge's parents, Grandmother and Grandfather Gates, at another Victorian manse in Independence. During this time, Bess decided to take a few years off to help her mother and learn the art of housekeeping, although the most important reason for her not immediately enrolling in college was

> "Why had his wife's love failed to sustain him?"
>
> —Margaret Truman on the suicide of her grandfather David Willock Wallace

Above: Bess and Harry Truman graduated from high school together in 1901. She is at the far right in the second row of their class picture; he is third from the right in the back row.

Below: Bess and her brother George Wallace grew up in this house in Independence, Missouri.

Above: At the age of sixteen, Bess had developed into the belle of the ball, and Harry noticed.

Below: Harry lived on a farm and Bess in town, and their courtship was frequently by mail. He never stopped writing to her even when they were married and living together.

the family's financial problems. Later, however, in 1905, with her grandfather's assistance, Bess enrolled in the Barstow School in Kansas City, a prep school for girls in their teens and twenties. Barstow prepared young women for college, with an emphasis on securing their acceptance to elite East Coast schools like Radcliffe and Vassar. Bess spent a year at Barstow and, according to her daughter, Margaret, she enjoyed it. Her grades were excellent, but she did not proceed on to college. Instead, she returned home to help her mother when her schooling concluded.

During these years, Harry Truman worked on his father's farm and wrote regularly to Bess. It was a long-distance, handwritten courtship, but he tried to visit her whenever he could. Harry soon knew he wanted to marry Bess and he first proposed to her in a letter. She was twenty-six, he was twenty-seven, and they had known each other a lifetime, yet Harry was still nervous about his proposal. He first broached the subject by mentioning diamonds in one letter to her. It was his roundabout way of bringing up the subject of engagement. But he quickly opted for a more direct approach, writing, "Would you wear a solitaire on your left hand should I get it?" he asked. He went on to promise Bess that someday maybe he would "amount to something." Harry had sent the most important letter of his life to Bess and after two weeks, he still did not have a reply from her. He thought for certain he had offended her and so he wrote to her saying, "If being in love with you is any offense, I am sorry but it can't be helped you know."

A day later, Harry had his answer from Bess. It was "no." As heartbroken as he was, Harry was relieved to finally have an answer. He wrote back to Bess and even thanked her for seriously considering his proposal and for "not mak[ing] fun of me anyway." According to her daughter, Margaret, Bess "did not know what to make of this incredibly honest farmer, who was asking her to marry him and simultaneously admitting that he was probably going to be a financial failure." Considering Bess's upbringing—the duality of having an extraordinarily wealthy extended family and a financial failure of a father—it is not surprising that one of her concerns was being adequately provided for. She did not want to duplicate her mother's troubles. Harry's offhanded remark in one letter that "it is a family failing of ours to be poor financiers" must have been quite disquieting to Bess.

It took more than two years for Bess to change her mind about Harry and, on November 2, 1913, during one of their regular Sunday walks, she confided to him that her feelings for him had changed. Harry was ecstatic, and his next letter to her expressed his joy as well as his heartfelt willingness to put Bess on a pedestal. He wrote her a sincere letter expressing joy that she could finally return his feeling. "It doesn't

"I thought that they would never get married. I think Bess wanted to…but Mrs. Wallace…. Nobody was ever good enough for her."

—Janey Chiles, Independence schoolteacher

First Ladies in Fashion

Suits and Business Attire

Right: Eleanor Roosevelt was always well dressed, but she was not known as fashion trendsetter. She is shown here meeting with China's Mme. Chiang Kai-shek, a frequent visitor to the White House.

Left: Laura Bush became known for wearing pantsuits; here she meets Jay Leno, but she also wore this suit to meet dignitaries from the Philippines.

Lower left: Even while doing official business, Nancy Reagan was most often seen in wearing her favorite color, red.

Below: Lucy Hayes was the first First Lady to make publicized tours of hospitals and she was careful to dress for the part.

Above: Rosalynn Carter, here with First Ladies Betty Ford and Lady Bird Johnson, was a leader in the fight for equal rights for women.

Left: Barbara Bush and her husband rarely went anywhere—even official business trips—without First Dog Millie.

Below: When Abigail Adams moved into the unfinished White House, she hung her laundry to dry in the East Room; she also oversaw a large staff and ran her family business.

*Above: Mamie Eisenhower was
the very model of a 1950s matron.*

*Below: Betty Ford, shown here with her family,
called this light blue suit one of her favorites.*

*Above: Hillary Clinton was the first First Lady to wear pantsuits,
but during the time she spent working on healthcare reform, she often
wore feminine suits and her infamous headband.*

*Right: Jackie
Kennedy was
elegantly dressed in
this red suit when
she appeared on
television to give a
tour of the newly
refurbished White
House.*

Casual Attire

Above: Frances Cleveland was, even in casual moments, considered the most beautiful First Lady up until her time.

Above: Even a First Lady has to deal with the family Christmas preparations; here Lady Bird Johnson is decked out in her favorite colors of pink and green.

Left: Like any Texan, Laura Bush is most at home outdoors wearing jeans and sneakers.

Above left: Rosalynn and Jimmy Carter never put on airs or lost sight of their Georgia roots.

Above: Bess Truman's daughter Margaret said that her mother's public facade was "unvaringly sedate."

Left: Hillary Clinton claimed to not be interested in clothes, but she still looked elegant—even in her casual moments.

Left: Gerald and Betty Ford spent the first ten days of his presidency at their suburban house among old friends.

Below: The Kennedy family made frequent getaways to Cape Cod, but they were never out of the spotlight.

Below: George and Barbara Bush's preppy look reflects the influence of their Kennebunkport, Maine summer home.

Right: Mamie Eisenhower's bangs may have been outdated in a fashion sense, but she kept them because Ike liked them.

Below: Nancy Reagan loved beautiful clothes, but she most loved dressing down during visits to the family ranch.

Above: Pat Nixon managed to look attractive even when it was raining.

Left: Dolley Madison's casual clothes reflected her preference for the empire waistline that was trendy during her time.

Above: Harry and Bess were married in 1919 after he returned from the war.

seem real that you should care for me. I have always hoped you would but some way feared very much you wouldn't," he wrote. "When it comes to the best girl in the world in all the universe caring for an ordinary gink like me—well, you'll have to let me get used to it."

For the next several years, Harry continued to work on his father's farm and his responsibilities grew even greater following his father's death in 1914. Two years later, Harry was sworn into the regular army as a member of the 129th Field Artillery regiment. Bess was ready to get married, but Harry's military service became his first priority. Two years after that, in 1918, Harry was sent to Brest, France, following the United States' entry into World War I. While in France, Harry continued to write to Bess, even penning a letter on the USS *George Washington* on his way overseas. Thirteen months later Harry was discharged from the army, and he and Bess could finally wed.

The Trinity Episcopal Church was tiny and the day—Saturday, June 28, 1919—was about as hot as a summer day in Missouri could get. Harry S Truman waited at the altar wearing a custom-made gray suit. His best man was Ted Marks, who had served with him in the 129th. Bess arrived at the church at four in the afternoon wearing a white gown, a white faille hat, and a bouquet of Aaron Ward yellow tea roses. Her brother Frank Wallace escorted her down the aisle and gave her away. Reverend John Plunkett performed the ceremony and, after a reception, the newlyweds headed for Chicago for their honeymoon. Upon their return, Harry and Bess took up residence with Bess's mother at 219 North Delaware Street in Independence.

In November 1919, five months after he and Bess were married, Harry scraped together $15,000 and opened a men's clothing store with his former canteen sergeant, Eddie Jacobson. Truman & Jacobson, Men's Furnishers of Kansas City, did very well for a few years until the business recession of 1921-1922. The store went bankrupt and, when Eddie Jacobson himself declared personal bankruptcy, Harry assumed the responsibility of paying back all of the store's outstanding debts. He refused to file bankruptcy, and it was many years before he was free from debt.

During these years, Bess remained at home, but worked very hard keeping the store's books, often poring over double-entry ledgers until past midnight. Business was excellent in the beginning, however, so Bess never minded the work. In fact, the Trumans' finances were healthy enough for the couple to live quite comfortably, and Bess was happy to have an ever-expanding role in the Independence social scene.

Below: The Trumans' only child, daughter Margaret, was born five years after they were married.

Margaret Truman, daughter of Bess and Harry, had a brief career as a concert soprano. She performed well enough to garner many positive reviews from critics.

However, Bess's delight over her husband's success as a businessman was dampened by a great personal sorrow. Bess had a miscarriage during that first year of marriage and, because she was thirty-five, she worried terribly that she had waited too long to have children. She would suffer through another miscarriage before their daughter Margaret was born in 1924.

Then, ominously, sales at the store began to plummet. The decline in Truman & Jacobson's fortunes did not abate, and in 1922 Harry and Eddie closed their doors for good.

Wife of a Politician

Following the demise of his store, Harry Truman decided to run for a judgeship in Missouri. In 1922, he was elected eastern judge on the Jackson County Court and, while presiding over his court, he also found the time over the next two years to attend the Kansas City School of Law.

During his term, Bess was fully supportive of Harry's new venture, but did not accompany him on his countless visits to townships and political rallies. His position as eastern judge required him to perform the duties of a commissioner of public works. He began receiving phone calls and visits from constituents, labor leaders, and other politicians, and while his wife Bess was fine with this new endeavor, his mother-in-law was not. Harry would sometimes see people at home (they were still living with Bess's mother) and this did not go over well with the elder Wallace.

Harry had been nominated for the commissioner post by political boss Tom Pendergast. Pendergast had mob connections and was later convicted of tax evasion. Harry considered his association with Pendergast the "price to pay" for being in politics, but the brush of Pendergast's reputation also tainted Harry Truman, diminishing, at least to some, and at least temporarily, Harry's reputation for honesty and integrity. In 1924, Harry did not win reelection and his mother-in-law was not the least bit displeased with that particular turn of events. This would ultimately be the only election in his life that Harry Truman ever lost.

Above: Little Margaret was the apple of her father's eye. He doted on her all of his life.

"A woman's place in public is to sit beside her husband, be silent and be sure his hat is on straight."

—*Bess Truman*

In 1926, Harry campaigned widely and was soon elected presiding judge of the Jackson Country Court. During this time, Bess remained at home, caring for her mother and her daughter in what Margaret Truman described as the "Wallace compound." However, Bess kept her eye on her husband's campaign, and even pulled some strings behind the scenes to manipulate the media and the other candidates. Harry's win gratified Bess and, at the time, she was more than happy in her role as a professional politician's wife.

Harry Truman served two four-year terms as judge and then, in 1934, ran for U.S. senator as a Democrat. This time around, Bess made some campaign appearances with her husband, but she found the experience unpleasant. The verbal assaults, mudslinging, innuendoes, and betrayals were far more vitriolic than when Harry ran for judge and she disliked being around it. Nevertheless, Harry Truman defeated his Republican opponent, won the Senate seat by 262,000 votes, and was sworn in, with Bess and Margaret watching from the Senate gallery, on Thursday, January 3, 1935.

Bess's happiness about the win aside, she did not take to the idea of living in Washington six months out of the year. But she accepted her new responsibility, moved into a hotel temporarily, and then found a four-room apartment on Connecticut Avenue for the

Harry admitted that when he was a senator, he had never once issued a report or given a speech that had not first been carefully edited by Bess.

outrageous rent of $150 a month. Senator Truman would be earning $10,000 a year before taxes, and $1,800 a year in rent expenses was a big chunk of the family's income. Bess enrolled Margaret, then ten years old, in Gunston Hall, a private school that reminded Bess of Barstow, and the new senator's wife began to settle into Washington life.

For someone who initially was a bit distraught about being away from life in Independence, Bess Truman quickly adapted to the Washington, D.C., lifestyle, even to the point of enjoying the traditional Thursday afternoon teas with the other senators' wives. She also began exerting her influence over her husband's staff, paying especially close attention to his assistants' personal lives (which must have greatly endeared her to them), always with an eye on the public image of her husband. It was around this time that her humorous nickname "the boss" became entrenched as more of a trait than an affectionate pet name.

In 1940, Harry Truman ran for reelection and won. In 1941, he hired Bess for his staff at an annual salary of $2,400. This caused quite a controversy, yet Bess dismissed the criticism by stating, quite bluntly, that the family needed the extra money. This the public understood, and the hullabaloo cooled.

In 1944, Harry Truman was voted one of the ten most useful politicians in Washington and, in 1944, he was nominated for the vice presidential slot on the Democratic ticket. Franklin Delano Roosevelt was elected that year to his third term as president and, on April 12, 1945, Harry Truman was sworn in

> *"My mother did not want my father to become President—especially through the 'back door,' as he himself called it—moving up from Vice President."*
>
> —*Margaret Truman on Bess*

as vice president of the United States. Harry and Bess Truman were, indeed, a long way from Independence, Missouri.

Bess Truman's life in her first few months as wife of the vice president of the United States was, in many ways, less stressful than when her husband had been a senator or a judge. The main reason was that, other than the presidency, her husband had reached the highest level of United States politics and there was nothing else to run for except president, but that decision was years away, or so they thought.

Making a Splash

As First Lady, Bess Truman was dutiful and dignified, but she hated being in the spotlight and avoided public spectacle whenever she could. There were certain duties required of the First Lady, however, that were impossible for her to evade. Christening airplanes was one of those duties.

A few weeks after her husband's inauguration, Bess was called upon to launch two new navy hospital planes in the traditional, time-honored manner: by smashing a bottle of Champagne against each plane's nose before its first official flight. The new First Lady was handed a bottle of Champagne and she swung it in a way that she hoped was ladylike (no garish windups for Bess), yet would still be forceful enough to break the bottle. It was not.

In full view of the assembled military and media, Bess went on to strike the bottle against the plane's nose eight more times; but, to her chagrin, none of these blows was a smashing success. She then turned to a military aide standing by, handed him the bottle, and he, too, swung away, only to meet with similar failure.

Bess, although a bit nonplussed, moved on to the next plane and, this time, the bottle not only broke on her first swing, it also gave her a humiliating Champagne shower.

Bess's problems that day were due to too little and too much scoring on the bottle. It seems that Champagne bottles need to have deep lines cut in them before smashing them against a plane or boat, and the first bottle had not been prepared in this manner before it was handed to Bess. Thus, it wouldn't shatter. The second bottle, on the other hand, had been scored too much, and it essentially exploded rather than breaking in half, as these bottles are supposed to do. Bess maintained an amused attitude but was seething inside. Her husband later tried to make light of the incident by kidding her about her arm not having the strength it boasted in her youth, when she had been a tennis champ.

Below: Bess was given the honor of christening the battleship USS Missouri. The "Mighty Mo" made history when the treaty that ended the war with Japan was signed on her open deck.

As for Harry, we now know that his job as vice president often kept him on the sidelines. He was kept in the dark by President Roosevelt on a great many things—including the development of the atomic bomb.

Eighty-two days after Harry Truman had taken the vice presidential oath, on April 12, 1945, President Roosevelt was having his portrait sketched at his home in Warm Springs, Georgia. While sitting for the artist, he suddenly complained of a terrible headache, and then collapsed. President Roosevelt would be declared dead just two hours later, having suffered a massive cerebral hemorrhage. Less than three hours later, Harry called Bess with the news, telling her that he was at the White House and he was sending for her and Margaret immediately. "I want you here when I'm sworn in," he said.

Above: Harry, with Bess at his side, took the oath of office after the death of Franklin D. Roosevelt on April 12, 1945. Eleanor Roosevelt (far left) was among the witnesses.

New First Lady

One of the questions from one of the 348 reporters at Harry Truman's first press conference as president was about Bess, the new First Lady. Eleanor Roosevelt had participated in regular press conferences during her tenure as First Lady and the Washington press wanted to know if Mrs. Truman would be doing likewise. President Truman dodged the question, reminding them all that Mrs. Roosevelt was still living in the White House and that she would soon be holding a final press conference. This satisfied the press temporarily, but the eventual answer from the *new* First Lady was met with immediate outrage: There would be no press conferences.

The Gravy Train

After his election, President Truman enlisted his old friend Eddie McKim, an insurance executive by trade, to be his White House chief of staff. McKim may have been a terrific insurance executive, but his judgment quickly went awry after being thrust into the maelstrom that is the White House. One day, an especially harried McKim rushed into the White House press office and demanded an account of everyone's activities. At that time, two secretaries were writing thoughtful replies to the thousands of condolence letters that had come in to the White House to Eleanor Roosevelt following the death of Franklin. McKim became furious, shouted, "Mrs. Roosevelt is no longer riding the gravy train!" and heartlessly fired the two secretaries. When Bess Truman was told of this, she not only immediately rehired the two secretaries, but also informed her husband that he would need a new chief of staff. All of the letters to Mrs. Roosevelt were ultimately answered.

Bess Wallace Truman did not like reporters and she did not trust them. The trauma of seeing her father's tragic suicide splashed across the front pages of newspapers, combined with her horror at how her husband had been written about during his senatorial campaigns, strengthened her resistance and hardened her stance. One of her biggest worries was that the story of her father's suicide would be resurrected now that her husband was in the White House, and she simply would not have it.

After the departure of Mrs. Roosevelt from the White House (the new president and his family had moved into Blair House, telling Eleanor Roosevelt that she could remain in the White House as long as she needed), the Trumans finally had a chance to take a closer look at their new home. On April 19, 1945, Margaret and Bess toured the White House.

The experience for Bess and Margaret of seeing the White House—this time as the place that would be their residence for the next four years—was both joyful and disconcerting. The downstairs rooms were glorious! Everything was clean and polished, and the lower level's appearance did justice to the great history of the house and to its role as the home of the most powerful man in the world. However, the same could not be said for the upstairs quarters, the part of the house known as the residence. This would be where the First Family would live, and it was a shabby place, cluttered with dingy, old furniture, and framed by dull, white walls that had not been painted in twelve years. Margaret Truman later wrote in her diary, "The White House upstairs is a mess…I was so depressed when I saw it."

Her mother, Bess, may not have been depressed, but she was certainly not pleased. She felt it was unacceptable for her and her family to live in a place

Shared Wisdom

For Bess Truman, one of the most memorable moments of the early days of her stewardship as First Lady was receiving a personal letter from Grace Coolidge, President Calvin Coolidge's widow. Calvin Coolidge had succeeded to the presidency upon the death of President Harding, as Harry Truman did upon the death of Roosevelt, and Grace Coolidge had suddenly—in the middle of the night, actually—become the First Lady of the United States, a scenario almost identical to that of Bess Truman's.

Mrs. Coolidge expressed her best wishes to Bess and her husband and wrote that she hoped they would have the three things necessary to survive in the White House: "strength, good courage and abounding health." Bess Truman was moved by the warmth of Mrs. Coolidge's letter and took comfort in the fact that she had her support.

Bess was a stickler for cleanliness. When Harry was a senator and he and his family lived in a small apartment in Washington, Bess never found a D.C. laundry that pleased her. The family's dirty laundry was, thus, sent to Kansas City to an establishment that did the kind of work she demanded.

in such a state of disrepair, and she decided immediately that they would most certainly *not* move in until a major renovation and redecoration of the First Family's living quarters had been completed. She decided that they would all remain at Blair House until the rooms had been refurbished to her satisfaction.

Bess gave very specific instructions as to how she wanted the residence redone. She specified the color scheme for the president and First Lady's suite—lavender and gray—and allowed Margaret to select her own colors for her private suite—Wedgwood blue walls and rust-red sofas. She insisted that the rooms be suitable for a president and his family.

Above: After the 1949 White House renovation, Bess selected this cheery bedroom as her own.

The painters, carpenters, and others assigned to whip the residence into shape worked quickly. Furniture was bought and delivered, walls were painted, a bathroom was installed in Margaret's suite and, within two weeks, everything was ready. The Trumans finally moved into the White House on Monday, May 7, 1945. Their immediate plans were to celebrate Harry Truman's sixty-first birthday there the following day, but Germany officially surrendered on May 7, and this historic event drew everyone's attention, outshining the enthusiasm for Harry's birthday. Harry was unruffled, however, and wrote to his mother and sister, instead, about the day's events, exclaiming joyfully, "Isn't that some birthday present?"

Bess herself was a considerate and kind mistress and the staff found her to be the polar opposite of the frosty matron that the press and the public saw. She was approachable and good-humored in the White House; however, she promptly made some changes and laid down some new rules that both charmed and rankled the White House workers. (One particularly galling decision by Bess was forbidding the White House staff from eating breakfast at work, a practice that had somehow become entrenched during the Roosevelt years. No more free breakfasts, she decreed, and the multitude of mansion workers suddenly had to find another way of obtaining their morning sustenance.)

"Harry and I have been sweethearts and married more than forty years—and no matter where I was, when I put out my hand Harry's was there to grasp it."

—Bess Truman

Above: Harry's Victorian summer White House in Independence was Bess's last home.

Bess's aforementioned attention to her husband's Senate staff's personal lives (which, while well-intentioned and carried out for the sole purpose of keeping an eye on her husband's reputation, was, nevertheless, irritating) probably continued in the White House. But she also insisted that White House maids and housekeepers take Sundays off to be with their families, and she was not above turning down the beds and pitching in to help with the routine cleaning and laundry. She also implemented breaks during the workday, allowing the staff time to rest between tasks. Bess was also known to be thoughtful and considerate toward guests, and, on occasion, would take notice of someone's cold symptoms and offer her own personal homemade remedy.

In early June of that year, Bess moved back to Independence with their daughter, Margaret. The official reasons were to supervise the remodeling of their family home to bring it up to presidential security standards, and to care for her mother, but these reasons were, as Margaret Truman put it, "essentially rationalizations for Bess's retreat from the White House, the presidency, the whole rigmarole of playing First Lady." And whether in Washington or Missouri, "playing First Lady" often required dealing with difficult underlings.

One White House staff member with whom Mrs. Truman did not have a positive relationship was the housekeeper, Henrietta Nesbitt. Mrs. Nesbitt had been Eleanor Roosevelt's housekeeper and had long created and supervised the menus for the First Family. In the early days of Harry's administration, during one of the times when Bess was out of town, there was an incident that illustrated dramatically how it was oftentimes necessary (and wise) for new presidents to hire new staff.

Mrs. Nesbitt stayed on at the White House after Roosevelt's death and she continued to decide what the First Family would eat. One evening, Harry Truman was served brussels sprouts, a vegetable he loathed. Margaret Truman immediately went to Mrs. Nesbitt and asked her to please not serve her father brussels sprouts, seeing as how he did not like them and absolutely refused to eat them.

Food Fit for a President?

Was banished White House housekeeper Henrietta Nesbitt's food as bad as one might imagine, considering the Trumans' swift encouragement of her retirement? A Nesbitt menu from a 1941 luncheon for the Roosevelts survives and was approved by Franklin and Eleanor, who both seemed to like her taste. It was a buffet lunch of tomato soup, salad, ham, beef, and tongue, cake, ice cream, and coffee. In addition, we know that for Roosevelt's final inaugural lunch, he requested from Mrs. Nesbitt chicken à la king. She balked, explaining to the president that she would not be able to keep it hot for two thousand guests, so she substituted chicken salad instead. Perhaps Roosevelt also liked brussels sprouts?

The following three nights, the president was served brussels sprouts despite repeated requests to banish them from the menu. Margaret made a desperate and angry call to her mother, who told her to remain silent and not to do anything more until she returned to the White House. As soon as Bess returned to Washington, the White House staff learned that Mrs. Nesbitt would soon be retiring. Harry Truman was never served brussels sprouts again.

Although she was now First Lady and her husband would have preferred she remain full-time in Washington, early in Harry's term Bess spent a great deal of time back home in Independence, as well as in Denver where her brother Fred Wallace lived. One reason she was away so often was because her brother had developed a serious drinking problem that others in the family could not deal with; another was that she intensely disliked the ceaseless attention paid her by the press when she was in Washington. In fact, this exasperation with being watched extended to her Secret Service protection. She understood the need for security measures while in Washington, but she adamantly insisted that she would not allow Secret Service agents to follow her all over Independence as she went shopping or visited friends. Her bodyguards were reluctant to give in to her demands, yet in the end, they had no choice. (Interestingly, when Harry Truman left the White House, ex-presidents and their families were not provided with lifetime Secret Service protection. John F. Kennedy's assassination spurred Congress to pass legislation allowing such protection, but it took a personal phone call from Lyndon Johnson to persuade Bess to allow agents to watch her and her ex-president husband.)

When Bess was in Washington, she was regularly pestered by the press for pictures and interviews, and yet she was virtually unknown by the public at large. After her husband had been president for nine months, Bess insisted on doing her own Christmas shopping and doing it alone. She went unrecognized in the stores she visited. Insistent on maintaining as normal a lifestyle as possible in a place that was, undeniably, the antithesis of routine and ordinary, Bess refused the press's requests and even canceled many formal White House occasions as she reinvented the role of First Lady—and also redefined her role as Harry Truman's wife.

Back home in Independence, Bess had belonged to a bridge club and, in spring 1946, decided that she would invite all its members to Washington for a weekend visit. The ten women arrived on Friday, April 12—they were met at the airport by reporters who treated them like movie stars—and they immediately began enjoying Washington to the fullest. Bess escorted them on tours of the Smithsonian and Congress, and they had dinner each night with the president. Bess also took them to a circus that was in town, but that excursion was, as Margaret Truman described it, "the only sour note in the whole weekend." Why? Because a clown sat on Bess Truman's lap. This did not sit well with the very dignified First Lady—or with her Secret Service agents.

Below: Even as an adult, Bess was an avid sports fan, and she and Harry were often on hand for football games and other sporting events.

The bridge club's visit served more than one purpose. It gave Bess some time with her friends, but it was also the kind of down-to-earth, personal interest story about the First Lady that the press had been pining for, and they certainly made the most of it. Stories about the Independence ladies made all the papers, and *Life* magazine did an eight-page feature on the visit.

One particular event in the first year of Harry's presidency that rankled Bess was her husband's decision to drop the atomic bomb on Hiroshima in August 1945. Harry had made the decision without consulting Bess, who had, by then, assumed that she was a top advisor to her husband. Bess certainly knew about the existence of the bomb, but did not know that it would be used. Margaret Truman does not think her mother would have tried to talk her father out of using it, but it was not being part of the decision that upset Bess.

The bomb was dropped on August 6, 1945, as Harry was on his way home from the Potsdam Conference, where he had told an indifferent Joseph Stalin about the bomb. Harry had consulted with his military and political advisors and with Winston Churchill about using the bomb to quickly end the war, but not with Bess. "She was forced to face a very unpleasant fact," Margaret Truman wrote of her mother. "She had become a spectator rather than a partner in Harry Truman's presidency. That made her very, very angry."

At the end of 1946, Harry Truman created the Committee on Civil Rights (CCR). He had come to realize that equality for all races in America was not only just, but overdue. The CCR was put in place to deal with racial prejudice and to sustain the advances African-Americans had made during the Great Depression and World War II. Then, in July 1948, continuing his support of civil rights, Harry desegregated the U.S. armed forces.

Bess Truman was supportive of Harry's civil rights efforts, yet once refused to boycott a Daughters of the American Revolution (DAR) dinner at which she was to be honored that was being held in Constitution Hall. Congressman Adam Clayton Powell had asked Bess not to attend because his wife, pianist Hazel Scott, had once been forbidden to play in the hall because of her race. The soprano Marian Anderson had been similarly banned from Constitution Hall (which had prompted Eleanor Roosevelt to resign from the DAR). Bess Truman wrote to Powell that she had no intention of not attending, regardless of the DAR's segregationist policies, because she was "not a crusader." But she also told him that what had happened with his wife had not been right and assured him, "I deplore any action which denies artistic talent an opportunity to express itself because of prejudice against race origin."

Above: The mushroom cloud of an atomic bomb became the symbol of a new age after President Truman authorized the weapon's first use.

Undecided? Hardly.

Bess Truman did not respond well to inquiries from reporters that she considered too personal. When a reporter once asked her secretary what Mrs. Truman would be wearing to a reception, Bess's answer was "Tell her it's none of her business." The secretary wisely (and diplomatically) did not follow that particular order, instead responding that, at the moment, Mrs. Truman was still undecided as to what she would be wearing. That was one smart secretary.

Back to Blair House

The first phase of the Truman family's time actually living in the White House after Harry assumed the presidency was relatively short-lived—only about two years or so. In November 1948, the family had to pack up and move back into Blair House while the White House underwent a major renovation.

Although there had been periodic repairs and remodelings done to the White House since the early nineteenth century (after the British almost burned it to the ground in 1814), there had been no major rebuilding and, by 1947, the White House was, as one architect described it, "crumbling." Harry Truman ordered a comprehensive review of the place and the news was not good.

The foundation was sinking, ceilings and floors were on the verge of collapsing, and the plumbing and electrical systems were dangerously out of date. One day in the summer of 1948, Margaret Truman's piano actually broke through the floor of her sitting room—which was directly above the family dining room. Harry Truman later wrote in his diary, "How very lucky we are that the thing did not break when Margie and Annette Wright were playing two-piano duets."

One of Bess's quirky (yet generous!) habits while living in the White House was to give the president's old clothes to visitors and White House staff.

Experts concluded that the entire building had to be either leveled and a new one built, or completely gutted and rebuilt from the ground up. The exterior walls—which were brick beneath the white paint—could remain, but everything else had to go. Bess played a major role in persuading her husband that no matter how much interior gutting was required, the exterior should remain—both for historical reasons, as well as to maintain continuity in the iconic legacy of the American president.

In November of that year, the Trumans began living, once again, in Blair House. The first thing Bess Truman did was cancel the formal Washington social calendar. Blair House, even with its neighbor Lee House, was unable to accommodate the number of people who might attend a White House dinner or reception. Since Bess had never been all that fond of large social events, one cannot help but suspect that she perceived the hiatus from the White House as a blessing in disguise.

Bess continued to host smaller gatherings, especially for wounded servicemen, but never inviting more than one hundred guests, and she always allowed the guests the run of Blair House, much to the dismay of the staff. They sat on the antique furniture, played the piano, and wandered throughout the house, all with Bess's approval. Because most of these guests were wounded and retired military, security was not a worry, and Bess probably would not have altered her permissive attitude even if the Secret Service had voiced concern. However, on November 1, 1950, Bess's attitude toward protection changed dramatically. That was the day she and her husband were almost killed by two Puerto Rican nationalists during a failed assassination attempt.

On the afternoon of Wednesday, November 1, 1950, Harry and Bess Truman were in Blair House. Harry was napping—a practice he had come to find necessary to contend with the extremely long presidential days—and Bess was chatting with her eighty-eight-year-old mother in Mrs. Wallace's bedroom. Bess was dressing for a trip to Arlington National Cemetery when suddenly gunfire exploded outside the building. She rushed to a window only to see three members of the Trumans' protective detail lying on the ground wounded, one fatally, and two assassins lying in pools of blood.

President Truman later remarked, "A president has to expect such things." Neither he nor Bess showed any outward distress over what had happened that day. But from that point on, Bess was much more willing to accept protection and was cordially accommodating to the agents assigned to her detail.

During the Trumans' time in Blair House, President Truman decided to run for a second term, believing he could be elected in his own right, even though his poll ratings, as Margaret Truman put it, "had sunk so low you needed a wet suit and a few tanks of oxygen to find them." Harry Truman wanted the endorsement of the American people and he was determined to try to win them over on his own. Bess, however, not only did not want him to run, she also did not think he could win. If it had been up to her, they would have handed the reins over to another Democrat, boarded a train back to Independence, and lived out the rest of their lives in quiet retirement.

However, it *was not* up to her, and as soon as Harry made the decision to run, she never uttered another word against it. She whistle-stopped the United States aboard the armor-plated railroad car the *Ferdinand Magellan* alongside her husband, and was the perfect candidate's wife.

It wasn't only Bess who did not think Harry could win a second term. All the polls had Thomas E. Dewey winning by a landslide, but the Truman family's six weeks on the road traveling across America swayed voters and, at 10:14 A.M. the morning after Election Day, Dewey conceded to the president.

Below: As a girl, Bess never dreamed she'd ever be First Lady, nor meet world leaders like Pakistan's Prime Minister Ali Kahn and his wife.

Life After the White House

The renovation of the White House had been expected to take three years. However, the work went smoothly and, twenty-seven months later, on March 27, 1952, the Trumans left Blair House for the last time and moved back to the White House, living there until the end of President Truman's second term in office on January 20, 1953.

Although she shunned the spotlight, ultimately Mrs. Truman did recognize and acknowledge the responsibilities of being First Lady. During her husband's tenure, she oversaw many of the White House social events, and acted as a gracious, albeit reserved hostess. She also saw a great many visitors at the White House as First Lady and enjoyed the Washington, D.C., social scene, having had the opportunity to get to know the area and the people in the political world during Harry's time as senator, and then vice president.

When Harry Truman was president and Bess Truman was his First Lady, Bess managed to manifest a dignified, albeit distant persona to the American people, but it was common knowledge that one of the happiest moments of her life was when she and Harry moved back to Independence in 1953. They were very happy for the next two decades, but then, in 1972, on the day after Christmas, Bess lost her best friend. Harry Truman died at the age of eighty-eight.

Bess lived another decade, always maintaining her dignity and, of course, her privacy, and serving as a quiet sentinel watching over her beloved Harry's legacy. She died in 1982 at the age of ninety-seven. She is buried next to Harry in the courtyard of the Truman Library and Museum in Independence. Before he died, Harry Truman told Bess what he wanted engraved on her tombstone: "First Lady, the United States of America."

> ✿
>
> *Bess shook so many hands in her capacity as First Lady that by the time she left the White House in 1953, her glove size had risen from a six to a six and a half.*
>
> ✿

Above: Bess's official White House portrait was painted by Greta Kempton in 1952.

Visiting the Harry S Truman Library and Museum

The Truman Library and Museum in Independence, Missouri, is one of the most popular presidential libraries in the United States. While he was alive, Harry Truman had very specific ideas about the purpose of this beloved place, and Bess Truman helped fulfill his wishes. According to the mission statement of the library and museum, "The museum exhibits were focused, at Harry Truman's insistence, not on him, but on the presidency and on American history."

The Harry S Truman Library & Museum is located at 500 West U.S. Highway 24, Independence, Missouri 64050-1798. It is open Monday through Saturday from 9:00 A.M. to 5:00 P.M., until 9:00 P.M. on Thursdays, and on Sunday from noon to 5:00 P.M. For more information, call 800-833-1225 or log on to www.trumanlibrary.org.

Below: The Harry S Truman Library is in Independence, Missouri.

Mamie Eisenhower

Growing Up Privileged

The November 1955 issue of *Family Circle* magazine had a line on its cover that perfectly summed up the essence of Mamie Eisenhower. It read "Mamie Eisenhower: First Lady—But Wife First."

Mrs. Ike was happy to define herself as Dwight D. Eisenhower's wife, and she believed her purpose in life was to be a companion and support to him. She once told reporters that she was "thankful for the privilege of tagging along by Ike's side." That said, though, it must be acknowledged that (as was many times the case with pre-feminism women) Mamie was also independently minded and wielded a strong influence on her husband, never hesitating to speak her mind to him when she felt it was warranted.

The façade of passive submissiveness, though, was one of the accepted mores of Mamie Eisenhower's times. The 1966 founding of the National Organization for Women (NOW) set the stage for a change in the perception of women's roles in the United States but, during the Eisenhower years, the public paradigm of the stay-at-home wife was embraced positively—by both Mamie and the public—rather than begrudgingly carried out for political purposes.

Mary Geneva Doud, known as Mamie, was born in Boone, Iowa, on November 14, 1896, the second of four daughters to John "Pupah" Sheldon Doud, and Elivera Mathilda "Nana" Carlson Doud.

Mamie's father's family had immigrated to the United States from Guilford, England, in 1639; Mamie's maternal grandfather was from Sweden; Mamie's mother was born in Boone. Mamie's father, John, moved to Boone in the early 1890s.

Mamie's time in Boone was short-lived, however. When she was but nine months old, her father moved the family to Cedar Rapids, Iowa, where he was very successful in the meatpacking business, managing to accumulate quite a fortune. A few years later, while still in his mid-thirties, he had become wealthy enough to semi-retire. He again moved the family, this time to Pueblo, Colorado. Mamie's sister Eleanor suffered from heart and respiratory troubles and this factored into the family's decision to move to a warmer climate. After that, the family moved quickly to Colorado Springs, and then settled in Denver in 1905.

Mamie's childhood in Denver was privileged, as befitting the daughter of one of the town's most prominent businessmen. The family was close-knit and

---

Mary Geneva Doud Eisenhower

Born
November 14, 1896,
Boone, Iowa

Parents
John Sheldon Doud and
Elivera Mathilda Carlson
Doud

Marriage
July 1, 1916, to
Dwight David Eisenhower
(1890-1969)

Children
Doud Dwight (1917–21);
John Sheldon Doud
(1922–)

Died
November 1, 1979,
Washington, D.C.

Above: At seventeen, Mamie was a rising young star on the Denver social scene.

loving, and her father unabashedly indulged Mamie. Travel, jewelry, clothes, and other luxuries were commonplace during her upbringing. Granted, she attended Denver public schools—Jackson, Coronna, and Mulholland elementary schools—but she also prepared at Miss Wolcott's School for Girls, an exclusive finishing academy for young women from families of means, and she took dance at Miss Hayden's School. In addition, Mamie was a common fixture on the *Denver Post*'s society pages, and there were frequent photos of and articles about the winsome debutante known around town as Miss Doud.

When Mamie was eighteen, her family rented a home in San Antonio for the winter. While visiting friends at the military post Fort Sam Houston in San Antonio, Mamie was introduced to Second Lieutenant Dwight Eisenhower, a handsome young man who had recently graduated from West Point. (Interestingly, Ike, as Dwight was known, graduated 115 out of a class of 164—not a particularly notable ranking for a man who would one day be praised as one of the greatest generals in American history.)

Ike was immediately smitten by Mamie, later recalling his first impression of her as a "vivacious and attractive girl, smaller than average, saucy in the look about her face and in her whole attitude." And it seems as though the attraction was mutual. Mamie had been eagerly sought after by suitors from a young age. Her style, sophistication, charm, and poise were irresistible to many of the young men who crossed her path, but there was something special about this dashing second lieutenant. Mamie recalled Ike as "the spiffiest looking man I'd ever talked to in my whole life."

Courtship, Marriage, and War

It wasn't long after Ike and Mamie met that their courtship began. At this time, Second Lieutenant Eisenhower was earning a monthly salary of $141.67. This necessitated that the new couple seek out more humble amusements, as it was incumbent upon the gentleman during these times to assume the financial responsibility for outings. One favorite dining spot of the two was a local Mexican restaurant called the Original. It was there that they would feast on chili and enchiladas for two for a total cost of $1.25.

Below: West Point cadet Dwight D. Eisenhower.

Mamie's favorite colors were pink, yellow, and green. She not only wore these colors regularly, but also used them in her decorating schemes.

Mamie's engagement ring from Ike was a miniature of his West Point class ring.

Above: Ike and Mamie met in San Antonio, Texas, where he was assigned to Fort Sam Houston and her family was vacationing. It was the start of a whirlwind romance and they were seen together everywhere around the city.

For several months the two courted, and then, on Valentine's Day of 1916, Ike, twenty-five, proposed and Mamie, nineteen, accepted. The proud lieutenant offered as an engagement ring a gold-and-amethyst miniature reproduction of his West Point class ring.

The Doud family loved Ike. They thought him polite, respectful, hardworking, and responsible. Yet following the announcement of their engagement, Mamie's father had a heart-to-heart talk with his daughter, who had her head in the clouds over her engagement. He wanted her to know what being an army wife actually entailed. He discussed with her the cramped quarters they would likely occupy, the low pay, and the frequent moves. John Doud knew quite well how his daughter had lived before meeting Ike. Even Mamie herself laughingly admitted that she was a tad spoiled.

Ironically, Mamie's experience growing up with household staff and watching her father manage budgets and keep things running smoothly would serve her well later in the White House but, for now, John Doud was worried about his daughter's ability to perform even the simplest of household duties like cooking and sewing. He knew that, in theory, she would be able to manage a household, but everyday tasks had always been done for her. None of her father's cautionary tales or concern changed Mamie's mind, though. She was in love, and that was all that mattered.

During the young couple's engagement, Mr. Doud also had a talk with Ike. Doud, although not thrilled that Ike was a military man, insisted that Ike remain in the army corps, rather than join the air corps, which was actually Ike's preference. Ike deferred to his future father-in-law and remained in the army corps.

On July 1, 1916, five months after they were engaged, Mamie and Ike wed. The ceremony and reception were held in the Doud family home in Denver, and the day was notable for another important event: Dwight Eisenhower received his first military promotion the same day.

After a few days in Colorado, the newlyweds spent the remainder of their honeymoon visiting the Eisenhower family in Abilene, Kansas. They certainly must have made quite an impression upon arrival in Abilene: the dashing military man in uniform with the elegant society woman—his pretty new bride—on his arm. They spent some time with Ike's parents, and then boarded a train for Manhattan, Kansas, to visit his brother Milton Eisenhower.

Upon their return to Texas, the happy couple moved into Ike's two-room quarters in the officers' barracks at Fort Sam Houston. His promotion to first lieutenant had come with a raise—to $161.67 a month—and Mamie made

Above: Their first child, Doud, who they called Icky, was born in 1917. He died at an early age.

every penny count. This was to be the first of an astonishing thirty-three homes the Eisenhowers would share over the next fifty-three years—only one of which they would actually own.

What a culture shock moving into Ike's two rooms must have been for Mamie! From a fully appointed house, complete with an attentive staff, she suddenly found herself living in two small rooms, with a "kitchen" that consisted of a coffeepot, a hot plate, a chafing dish, and other portable appliances—all of which were hidden away after using. Moreover, it is probably safe to assume that her father's words resonated in her head when she realized that her culinary skills consisted of the ability to make precisely two things: mayonnaise from scratch, and fudge. Ever resourceful, her new husband came to the rescue, however, and taught her how to cook. One of his specialties was vegetable soup. (Ike also excelled at other homemaking skills. When Mamie was pregnant, it was Ike who let out her dresses.)

The Eisenhowers settled into their new home, and it was at Fort Sam Houston that Ike and Mamie's first child was born. On September 24, 1917, Doud Dwight Eisenhower arrived and was immediately nicknamed Icky (this charming nickname was reportedly inspired by the condition of the lad's diapers). Suddenly, the new parents' two rooms were even more cramped, but their stay in Texas would soon be over. A few months after they were married, Ike was transferred to Camp Colt at Gettysburg, Pennsylvania, where he assumed the position of commander of the U.S. army's first tank corps. He excelled as a commander and instructor and was quickly transferred to Fort Meade in Maryland. The army felt him too valuable to ship overseas for combat duty and he remained stateside during World War I.

The new parents were ecstatic about the new addition to the family. Ike, especially, delighted in having a son. During trips away from home with the army, Ike would call home several times a week and would always start the conversation with questions about Icky. Mamie was good-humored about his enthrallment with his son, but did occasionally interrupt him, interjecting, "How about asking how your wife is?" Ike (probably reluctantly) would stop talking about Icky—but only momentarily—and eventually Mamie simply indulged him and, during their many phone calls when Ike was away from home, willingly talked with him mostly about their boy.

During their stay in Maryland, in the fall of 1920, the Eisenhowers hired a local sixteen-year-old girl to work as a maid and help Mamie with Icky. This decision would ultimately become one of the biggest regrets of their lives. Neither Ike nor Mamie extensively questioned the girl about her recent past. If they had, they likely would have learned that she had only recently recovered from scarlet fever, which is a streptococcus infection and, with a little research, would have also learned that, in all likelihood, she was still contagious at the time that they hired her. Because the girl had successfully weathered the illness, she manifested none of the telltale signs of the disease—the red facial rash, the fever, the sore throat with its resultant hoarseness—all clues that would have alerted and certainly alarmed the Eisenhowers and spurred them to more comprehensive pre-employment questioning.

Two-year-old Icky contracted scarlet fever from the maid. At first, his symptoms were probably no more than a sore throat and perhaps a fever, and his mother doubtless thought he had a cold. By the time the scarlet rash appeared, it was then too late for the child. Scarlet fever runs its course in adolescents and adults, but in children, it can be fatal if not treated with antibiotics. Unfortunately, Icky got sick in 1920—eight years before the development and availability of penicillin.

When his symptoms worsened, a specialist from nearby John Hopkins Hospital was hurriedly summoned to the military base, but there was nothing that could be done for the boy. Icky Eisenhower died on Sunday, January 2, 1921. It was a grim start to the new year for the Eisenhowers.

Icky's body was transported to Denver, where he was buried in the Fairmont Cemetery on January 7, 1921. Every September 24 from then on—Icky's birthday—Ike sent Mamie flowers. Forty-five years later, in 1966, three years before Ike's death, Icky's body was removed from the Denver cemetery and buried in a chapel on the grounds of the Eisenhower Center in Abilene, Kansas. Ike stood silently and watched the recommittal alone. In 1967, Ike spoke of Icky's death, describing it as "the greatest disappointment and disaster of my life, the one I have never been able to forget completely."

Icky's death staggered the young couple—and threatened their marriage. Feelings of guilt overwhelmed them, and they found it difficult not to blame each other for the loss of their son. They managed to stay together by suppressing the deepest emotions affecting them, but the loss wounded them both, and left a psychological scar that never completely healed. Mamie later said, "For a long time, it was as if a shining light had gone out in Ike's life.... Throughout all the years that followed, the memory of those bleak days was a deep inner pain that never seemed to diminish much." It was around this time that Mamie began to cut her hair in the style that became known as "Mamie bangs." It is believed she began wearing bangs to conceal a high forehead, but it is psychologically interesting that she made a major change in her appearance during a period of great emotional upheaval.

Mamie would visit Denver when she became depressed and Ike was not around to comfort her. Yet, her new husband had made it very clear to her what

Above: Little Icky contracted scarlet fever and died in 1921. Neither Ike nor Mamie ever forgot the joy he brought to them.

Ike and Mamie's first child, Doud Dwight, or "Icky," died unexpectedly at the age of three, a tragedy that Mamie always said was the worst heartbreak of her life. For the rest of his life, Ike sent Mamie flowers on Icky's birthday.

Above: Their second son, John, became a general like his father, and he was a strong presence in the Eisenhower White House.

were his priorities. Once during these early years, when Mamie became very upset that he would, yet again, be leaving her on assignment, he told her bluntly, "Mamie, there is one thing you must understand. My country comes first and always will. You come second."

The Eisenhowers' marriage managed to survive and, in 1922, a second child was born, a son they named John Sheldon Doud Eisenhower.

For the next several years, Ike's military career continued to keep him away from home, and Mamie continued to retreat to her childhood home when being a "single mother" got to be too much for her.

One of their longest separations was in the mid-1930s, when Ike spent a year in the Philippines as special assistant to General Douglas MacArthur, and then as MacArthur's chief of staff. Mamie would not accompany her husband to his post there because she did not like the heat. Also, by this time the future First Lady had begun to suffer from a range of physical ailments, including headaches, insomnia, rapid heartbeat, palpitations, and dizziness from Ménière's disease, an inner ear disorder. She spent a great deal of time in bed, as well as a great deal of time in Denver, regardless of which of the many homes she and her husband were living in at the time.

During these years, Ike's military career was relatively undistinguished and, by 1941, he was contemplating retirement and a move to the private sector. He had attained the rank of colonel, but had served mostly in peacetime and there had been little opportunity for him to exhibit his underlying leadership skills. He had worked as a recruiter and served on various committees, but his mundane duties never dissuaded him from continuing to study his chosen career and expand his knowledge of all things military. In 1941, following the Japanese attack on Pearl Harbor, Hawaii, Ike was summoned to Washington to serve under General George Marshall. His many years of preparation would soon be serving him well.

Ike excelled in his wartime duties and, by 1944, was named supreme commander of the Allied forces and was posted in London. Mamie remained in Washington, where they were officially living at the time. Ultimately, Ike's time in Europe would be a period of great personal dismay for Mamie.

"Ike was my career."

—Mamie Eisenhower on her marriage

As soon as Ike landed in Prestwick, Scotland, for his transport to London, he was met by the young woman who was to be his full-time driver, Kay Summersby. Kay was smart, fit, and attractive. She had been born in Ireland, but was a British subject and possessed what has been described as an encyclopedic knowledge of London. It is a fact that Ike was quickly smitten by this charming young woman—and was somewhat indiscreet about his attraction. In a letter to Mamie around this time, he wrote of Summersby: "She is also very pretty. Irish and slender and I think in the process of getting a divorce, which is all that worries me."

Fortunately for Ike, the letter containing these sentiments—comments that would have certainly alarmed Mamie—was never mailed. Ike's aide Harry Butcher forgot to mail it, and Butcher wrote in his diary around that time that Ike had also spoken openly about his new driver's sexiness and appeal.

Throughout the years of the war, Ike wrote Mamie hundreds of letters, many of which can be described as love letters, yet he was undeniably infatuated with Kay Summersby during this period. She was his constant companion and, back in Washington, Mamie began to hear rumors of something going on between the general and a woman young enough to be his daughter. "Upset" is too small a word to describe Mamie's reaction to these rumblings. She became emotionally distraught almost to the point of a breakdown. Around this time, during one of Ike's infrequent visits home, during a three-day stay in White Sulphur Springs in the Napa Valley, Ike slipped twice and accidentally addressed Mamie as Kay. Ike quickly apologized, and tried to assure Mamie that there was nothing going on between him and the winsome Irish lass. "Kay's the only woman I ever see," Ike explained. "She's the only woman I'm ever around, it was just a slip of the tongue."

Kay Summersby ultimately wrote two books about her years with Ike. The first, *Eisenhower Was My Boss*, was written in 1947 and made no mention of a love affair. This book is now accepted as a bowdlerized version of the truth, and the fact that Mamie was a visible presence in Ike's life certainly had a great deal to do with the discretion Summersby exercised in her memoirs. In 1977, however, Summersby published her second book, *Past Forgetting: My Love Affair with Dwight D. Eisenhower*, in which she publicly admitted to passionate kisses and embraces, and an intense mutual infatuation between her and Ike, but revealed that their relationship was never physically consummated because Ike was impotent. The final truth was known, of course, only to the principals, but what is most important in terms of Ike's relationship with Mamie is that he never divorced her and, after the war, he severed all contact with Summersby.

Above: Some say that Kay Summersby, General Eisenhower's driver, became his love interest as well.

Throughout her entire life, Mamie never had a job at which she earned a paycheck.

Above: Ike and Mamie flew to Washington in 1945 for a White House ceremony when he was awarded the Distinguished Service Medal for leadership.

Below: The Eisenhowers went to Chicago for the convention that gave him the presidential nomination; they kept up with the unfolding drama on television in their hotel suite.

After the War

Although the war was over, Ike did not retire from the military. He served as army chief of staff from November 1945 until February 1948. During this time, he wrote a best-selling book about his World War II duty called *Crusade in Europe*, and his reputation as a national hero soared. He and Mamie continued to live in Washington until 1948, when they purchased a farm at Gettysburg, Pennsylvania. Although they lived in dozens of places throughout their life together, their Gettysburg farm was the only home they ever owned.

In 1948, Ike retired from the military and took a position as president of Columbia University. He later wrote that the two and a half years he spent as Columbia University's president were "satisfying occupationally and were personally most enjoyable." During this time, Mamie was busy with their new home and social activities and kept a low profile. Apparently, she was happy to have Ike back in the United States, as Ike later wrote, "My wife and I were happy with my new career." Mamie also is on record as admitting, "I never got used to him being gone. He was my husband. He was my whole life."

In December 1950, however, the living situation for the Eisenhowers changed yet again when Ike received a phone call from President Harry Truman, asking him to accept the position of commander of NATO (North Atlantic Treaty Organization) forces in Europe. In early 1951, Ike took a leave of absence from Columbia and headed to his new post in Brussels. This time, however, Mamie went with him. In his diary, Ike wrote, "Mamie and I discussed this long and soberly, and she was personally so bitterly disappointed that for a while she considered remaining in the United States while I went over to Europe. Once we got to Europe, Mamie liked her house and her circle of friends and had a nice time."

In 1952, Ike and Mamie decided that Ike should answer the burgeoning call to run for president. Mamie knew this would uproot them again, at least until the election was over, but she fully supported the decision and campaigned willingly for her husband.

On November 5, 1952, Dwight David Eisenhower was elected president of the United States, defeating Democratic governor Adlai Stevenson of Illinois. Mamie Eisenhower was now the new First Lady.

> *"I'd like to be a homebody, but I'm really just a movebody."*
>
> —*Mamie Eisenhower on her life as a military wife*

The Residences of Ike and Mamie

A woman who marries a military man must quickly become adept at packing. Mamie's father warned her that the life of a military wife would not be an easy one, and Mamie's life (and that of her son John) was one of constant upheaval. This is a look at the places Ike and Mamie lived from when they were first married until their retirement.

September 1915–May 1917: Fort Sam Houston, Texas
June–September 1917: Leon Springs, Texas (Mamie remained at Fort Sam Houston)
September–December 1917: Fort Oglethorpe, Georgia (Mamie remained at Fort Sam Houston)
January 1917–February 1918: Fort Leavenworth, Kansas (Mamie remained at Fort Sam Houston)
March 1918: Mrs. Ray's Boarding House, Laurel, Maryland; Halverson's Boarding House, Laurel, Maryland
March–November 1918: Gettysburg, Pennsylvania
November–December 1918: Camp Dix, Georgia (Mamie mostly stayed in Denver, Colorado)
January–March 1919: Fort Benning, Georgia (Mamie remained in Denver, Colorado)
April 1919–January 1922: Fort Meade, Maryland (Mamie stayed in San Antonio, Texas, from November to December 1919, and in Denver, Colorado, from May to August 1920)
February 1922–September 1924: Camp Gaillard, Canal Zone, Panama
October–December 1924: Baltimore, Maryland
January–August 1925: Fort Logan, Colorado
September 1925–July 1926: Fort Leavenworth, Kansas
August 1926–January 1927: Fort Benning, Georgia
February 1927–June 1928: The Wyoming Apartments, Washington, D.C.
July 1928–November 1929: Paris, France
November 1928–September 1935: The Wyoming Apartments, Washington, D.C.
October 1935–December 1939: The Philippines
January 1940–1941: The Presidio of San Francisco
February 1940–June 1941: Fort Lewis, Washington
July 1941–February 1942: Fort Sam Houston, Texas
March–June 1942: Fort Meyer, Virginia
July 1942–November 1945: The Wardman Park Hotel, Washington, D.C. (Mamie only); London
November 1945–February 1948: Fort Meyer, Virginia
June 1948–March 1951: Columbia University, New York City, New York
April 1951–May 1952: North Atlantic Treaty Organization, Marns LaCoquette, France
January 1953–January 1961: The White House, Washington, D.C.
1950–1979: Eisenhower Farm, Gettysburg, Pennsylvania
The Eisenhowers' Vacation Homes:
Augusta National Golf Club (Mamie's Cabin), Augusta, Georgia
Newport, Rhode Island
Cochran/Odlum Estate, Indio, California
Axel Neilson's Colorado Estate
Cuzlean Castle, Scotland

Above: While the future president was assigned to the tank corps at Fort Meade, Maryland, Mamie sat out the tour back in San Antonio.

The White House Years

The Eisenhowers' eight-year tenure in the White House would be the longest the couple lived in one place until their retirement, when they would spend almost twenty years enjoying life at their farm in Gettysburg, Pennsylvania.

Mamie felt right at home in the White House. She immediately took to the protocol, the routines, and the nonstop demands for her attention and time. Suddenly, she was back in a structured living situation in which she was catered to, as well as being in charge. Her personal traits—sincerity, compassion, and honest warmth toward people—served her well, and she thrived in the hustle-bustle pressure cooker of life in the White House.

Like the American people, the staff loved the always-effervescent Mamie, although they knew she was a stern mistress when it came to doing things correctly. As First Lady, Mamie always slept until ten and then worked from her bed until noon, or early in the afternoon. She worked reposed for the entire morning, and even met with people like her and Ike's tax advisor, Walter, while lying in bed in her nightgown.

Mamie was noted for saying what she thought, albeit only in private. During one White House white-tie dinner to which Walter and his wife were invited, Mamie greeted them delightedly in the receiving line and said, "Oh, Walter, it's so good to see you. This is the first time I've ever seen you when I wasn't in bed." Although this ingenuous comment raised the eyebrows of those within earshot (including, probably, Walter's wife), Mamie thought nothing of it, and did not consider it the least bit inappropriate.

Above: Ike and Mamie charmed guests at their inaugural ball. The picture on the wall is of Vice President Richard Nixon.

The First Lady from Colorado held meetings with the household staff almost every morning—this marshaling of the troops became a tradition with her and was something she felt strongly about—and she became known for her "white glove" inspections. Mamie was a hands-on First Lady, in some ways like Bess Truman, but dissimilar in that Mamie would delegate the laundry and cleaning duties, while Bess often would jump in and lend a hand. Mamie also became known for her insistence that the White House be gloriously bestrewn with flowers, including her personal favorite, pink sweetheart roses. The Eisenhower years may have been the White House's most colorful period. And when the flower arrangements and centerpieces were changed, the replaced flowers were sent to local hospitals.

Mamie also set her mind to a major project that had been neglected by previous First Ladies: cataloging the White House china. Mamie considered the task important and saw to it that a Smithsonian Institution curator took the time to research, catalog, and rearrange the tableware in the White House China Room.

Mamie had to be creative when it came to adding her personal touch to the White House. Because the building had recently been completely renovated during the Truman administration, Congress decided that the Eisenhowers did not need the $50,000 granted to all incoming presidents and First Ladies for redecorating and new furniture. Mamie made do with what she had to work with and managed to distinguish the Eisenhower White House from

Mamie Eisenhower's "Million Dollar" Fudge

Ike loved Mamie's fudge and it's a good thing he did—this is one of only two recipes Mamie knew how to make when she first married Ike (the other was for mayonnaise!). Ike christened the dessert Mamie's "Million Dollar" fudge. Ike ended up doing most of the cooking in their marriage, but Mamie certainly could make this delightful confection, her specialty. (It was the marshmallow cream that made it so creamy.)

INGREDIENTS

12 ounces semisweet chocolate bits
12 ounces milk chocolate, broken into pieces
7 ounces marshmallow cream
1½ cups chopped walnuts
2 teaspoons vanilla
4 cups sugar
1 can (12 ounces) evaporated skim milk
2 tablespoons butter
Pinch of salt

DIRECTIONS

In a large bowl, combine the semisweet chocolate, milk chocolate, marshmallow cream, walnuts, and vanilla. Reserve. In a saucepan, over medium heat, combine the sugar, evaporated milk, butter, and salt. Bring to a boil, stirring constantly. Cook, stirring continuously, for six to seven minutes. Pour the boiling milk and sugar mixture over the reserved chocolate-nut mixture and beat until the chocolate is melted and the fudge is creamy. Pour the fudge mixture into a foil-lined, buttered nine-by-nine-inch pan, and let it cool at room temperature for a few hours, before cutting into squares. Makes about four pounds of fudge. (Note: Store the fudge in an airtight container.)

Mamie believed in keeping her life and her husband's presidency separate. In the eight years that Ike was president, Mamie only entered the Oval Office four times—and each time was at the invitation of Ike.

the Truman White House. Mamie was also responsible for the creation of the White House Vermeil Room in 1958. As First Lady, Mamie accepted a gift of a beautiful and valuable collection of gilded silver from Mrs. Margaret Thompson Biddle in 1956, and decided the pieces needed their own room.

The Eisenhower administration years in the United States—1953 to 1961—were a study in paradox. America was experiencing a halcyon postwar period in which a booming economy, the increasing prevalence of television, second cars, and the introduction of convenience consumer goods like TV dinners made for a comfortable homeland. Yet the world outside America's shores was changing, and at home, things were not as placid as they seemed on the surface.

Ike had to contend with a myriad potpourri of worries and problems. In 1957, Russia launched *Sputnik,* the first satellite, which terrified Americans with the notion that the "Commies" were spying on them. Senator Joe McCarthy's Communist paranoia led to hearings, blacklists, and Cold War hysteria in the early 1950s. Julius and Ethel Rosenberg's execution for giving atomic secrets to the Soviets, which took place shortly after Ike's inauguration, made things worse. In addition, the groundswell for civil rights for African-Americans took center stage when Rosa Parks was arrested for refusing to give up her seat on a bus to a White man. Add to all this the Russian downing of a U2 spy plane, the liberal Warren Supreme Court, the need to call in federal troops to assure an Arkansas school would be integrated, and a massive, unprecedented plan to construct an interstate highway system, and it is obvious that Ike had his hands full.

Mamie knew this, and she saw to it that Ike's home life (such as it can be when you're president of the United States) and his professional life were two distinct and separate parts of his life. The President is, of course, the president twenty-fours a day, and Mamie knew this, yet the moment Ike stepped into the residence at the end of the workday, she saw to it that he was afforded as stress-free an environment as possible. The most powerful man on earth and his wife would dine on snack tables in front of the television—like countless of his constituents who probably did the exact same thing several nights a week.

Mamie did not like paranoid Communist-hunter Senator Joe McCarthy and saw to it that his name was not on any White House invitation lists.

After dinner, they would both work until around ten or so—Ike on Oval Office matters, Mamie on the voluminous First Lady correspondence she was always trying to keep up with. Then, when the day's work was done, Ike would take up his beloved brush and oils and paint for an hour before he and Mamie would read in bed until they fell asleep. (Mamie loved mysteries; Ike preferred Westerns.)

Ike and Mamie's image while living in the White House was an archetype of the perfect prefeminism couple, and a precise representation of the domestic lifestyle of the fifties. The husband worked, while the wife entertained and made the house beautiful. The husband earned the money; the wife spent it. The husband made the decisions; the wife remained offstage, quiet and out of the spotlight. Mamie was beloved by the American people and her public persona had a lot to do with her being consistently ranked one of America's most-admired women. People knew that presidents and First Ladies often slept in separate beds. Yet, even though Ike and Mamie did have their own bedrooms in the White house residence, it was widely known that they slept together in the same bed, every night—just like millions of other American couples. In fact, Mamie even commented publicly on their sleeping arrangements, admitting that when she awakened in the middle of the night, she liked to "pat Ike on his old bald head anytime I want to."

Mamie reveled in her femininity, as well as in her subservient role to her husband. She willingly posed for White House reporters in a robe and curlers, and she was more interested in the fashion industry than in U.S. industry. Her aforementioned affection for pink extended even to some of the gowns she selected for White House events—pink strapless gowns that one biographer noted would not have been out of place on a teenage girl at her prom. She said she hated what she described as "old lady clothes," and frequently visited Arizona spas to maintain her youthful appearance. Mamie also delighted in the many press accounts about her in which it was mentioned that she looked younger than her years. Concurring with this opinion, she believed

*Above: First Lady Mamie
Eisenhower at the White House in
1954, early in Ike's presidency.*

Mamie epitomized social graciousness. She insisted that every person who wrote to her should receive a personal reply. As First Lady, she received seven hundred letters a month and had a staff of fifteen to help her respond to every one of them.

she looked too young to be a grandmother and insisted her grandchildren call her Mimi.

One sour note in the love affair the United States and the press had with Mamie was the frequent speculation that she had a drinking problem. In fact, some pundits publicly mused that her frequent visits to spas were actually "drying out" sessions. The truth was that Mamie had serious problems with her equilibrium and her balance due to the Ménière's disease she had had since early in her life. Ike was asked about this in 1952 and admitted that he had heard the rumors, but said that, at that time, Mamie had not had a drink for at least a year and a half.

Mamie enjoyed their private life and did what she could to make Ike comfortable, but there was more to her insistence on Ike having some stress-free time than just a love of quiet domesticity. Mamie knew of the toll the presidency was taking on her husband's health. Ike had long suffered from high blood pressure and Crohn's disease, and his ailments, combined with smoking two to three packs of cigarettes a day, made Ike a perfect candidate for serious health problems. In September 1955, during their summer vacation, Mamie's concern for Ike's well-being proved valid when he had his first serious heart attack.

Ike and Mamie were in Denver for a summer vacation. Ike spent a lot of time playing golf, while Mamie saw family and friends. On the morning of September 27, Ike played golf, but he did not feel well. His stomach was bothering him, yet he still sat down for a lunch of hamburgers with onions. During the afternoon, his stomach spasms and cramping worsened and, at 2:30 A.M., Mamie became worried enough to summon Ike's physician Dr. Snider, who immediately ordered the president admitted to Fitzsimmons General Hospital in Denver for a complete diagnostic workup. Mamie never left his side, and was with him when they learned the truth: Ike had suffered a heart attack.

Ike ultimately spent nineteen days in the hospital—as did Mamie. She made herself at home in his hospital suite, even going so far as to have the toilet seat in Ike's room's bathroom replaced with, yes, a pink one. Ike recovered from this first heart attack, but he would suffer a bowel obstruction requiring surgery less than a year later, and a stroke in November 1957.

"As an American woman I have always valued my right to pretty clothes."

—*Mamie Eisenhower on her fashion sense*

When Ike had a heart attack in 1955, Mamie spent nineteen days at the hospital with him, and later signed every one of the responses to the 11,000 people who had written to her and the president expressing their best wishes for his speedy recovery.

During Ike's recuperation from his first heart attack, one question echoed across the United States: Would he run for a second term? Ike was a staggeringly popular president and the common wisdom was, if he ran, he would win. Mamie loved being First Lady, but she loved Ike more. She was very worried that Ike's cardiac troubles and his continual gastrointestinal problems—both of which were aggravated by stress—would kill him if he experienced the pressures of a second term. Mamie did not want Ike to run and would have preferred that they retire to their Gettysburg farm and live out their lives quietly. That dream of Mamie's would eventually be realized—but not yet.

After Ike's cardiologist declared him fit and fully recovered, the president announced on February 29, 1956, that he would be seeking a second term. Even with his health problems, Ike wanted four more years in the White House, and he picked Richard Nixon as his vice presidential running mate. The Democratic strategy during the election—Adlai Stevenson was again the Democratic candidate—was to subtly emphasize Ike's health issues by reminding voters that if they reelected Ike, they could, in essence, be putting Richard Nixon in the White House.

Above: Mamie is interviewed on Air Force One by television broadcaster Walter Cronkite.

The American people were not to be swayed, however, and the Eisenhower campaign slogan—"I Like Ike"—proved again to be an honest representation of the national feelings toward Ike. Ike was elected to a second term by a huge margin and entered his final four years in the White House determined and confident, yet in less than perfect health. With Mamie's help, he survived his second term, tackling domestic and foreign issues, and garnering high approval ratings.

Campaign Duties

During the presidential campaign of 1960, Ike wondered why his vice president, Richard Nixon, had not asked him to campaign for him. The real reason was that Mamie had reached out to Nixon's wife, Pat, and expressed her concern about what a campaign schedule might do to her husband, who had, in the recent past, undergone abdominal surgery and suffered a stroke. Pat asked her husband to not impose on Ike and Nixon complied. Nixon was defeated by John F. Kennedy, and we'll never know if Ike's campaigning may have saved the election for Nixon.

Retirement

Ike left office in 1961 and, in his farewell address, cautioned Americans against putting too much power in the hands of what he called "the military-industrial complex," the first time that term had ever been used to describe the growing alliance between the U.S. military and defense contractors.

One of the traditions of the change in presidential administrations is that the outgoing First Lady gives the incoming First Lady a tour of the White House. In his memoir, *Upstairs at the White House*, chief usher J. S. West recalled the day Mamie showed Jackie Kennedy her new home. The incident illustrates the high regard for Mamie everyone—including Jackie—felt, and emphasizes how easy it was to be overwhelmed by the grandeur of the White House (which was built specifically to intimidate foreign leaders).

There was concern among the White House staff about Jackie's ability to endure a full walking tour of the White House. Jackie had recently delivered John F. Kennedy, Jr., by cesarean section and was still recovering. Mamie was to conduct the tour alone and, at the age of sixty-four, obviously was not going to push Jackie around in a wheelchair. West decided to have a wheelchair and an attendant at the ready and within a close proximity of the two First Ladies in case Mrs. Kennedy became too tired to continue the tour on her feet. Jackie never requested the chair and the tour went off as planned.

Months later, Jackie mentioned to West that Mamie's walking tour had so exhausted her she had had to retire to her bed to recover when she returned home. Mr. West was aghast, and told her that they had had a wheelchair awaiting her request and that all she had had to do was ask for it. Jackie laughed and replied, "I was too scared of Mrs. Eisenhower to ask."

After leaving Washington, D.C., the Eisenhowers moved to their farm in Gettysburg, Pennsylvania, where they lived a life of peaceful retirement. Over their years together, Mamie and Ike were constant companions and she supported him during all his illnesses and incapacitations. Mamie was also with him when he died of congestive heart failure in Walter Reed Hospital in March 1969.

Above: In retirement, Mamie kept in touch with old friends in Washington and remained interested in politics. She was affectionately known as the "Sweetheart of the GOP."

After Gerald Ford's defeat in 1976, Mamie sent the outgoing First Couple a handwritten note. It read, "Words are inadequate from your friends but you can always say: 'God, I have done my best.' Amen."

Ike went out like the general he was. On Friday, March 28, 1969, as Ike lay in bed in the room where had spent the past nine months of his life, he called Mamie, his son John, and his grandson David—the lad for whom Camp David had been named—to his side. He asked them to lower the window shade and help him sit up in bed. He then grasped his beloved Mamie's hand, and said, "I want to go. God take me." Then he died.

Mamie lived alone on the Gettysburg farm for the next ten years, delighting in her grandchildren, and making occasional appearances in support of favored causes. Once a year, faithfully, she traveled to Abilene to visit Ike and Doud's graves, describing the trip as a "journey of love."

On Tuesday, September 25, 1979, Mamie suffered a stroke and was rushed to Walter Reed Hospital, the same place she had spent so many weeks and months in attendance at the bedside of her husband. Mamie spent the remainder of September and the entire month of October hospitalized. On Wednesday, October 31, Mamie told her granddaughter Mary that it was time for her to go, and that she would die the following day. Mamie went to sleep that night and never awakened, dying in her sleep in the early hours of November 1, 1979.

Above: Ike and Mamie are buried nearby the Eisenhower Presidential Library in Abilene, Kansas.

Visiting the Dwight D. Eisenhower Library and Eisenhower Center

The Dwight D. Eisenhower Library and Eisenhower Center, which was dedicated in May 1962, consists of five buildings on twenty-two acres and includes the Eisenhower family home; the Eisenhower Museum; the Eisenhower Library; the Eisenhower Place of Meditation (which is the final resting place of Dwight D. Eisenhower, Mamie Eisenhower, and their son Dwight Doud Eisenhower); the visitors center; and the eleven-foot "Ike Statue."

The library is located at 200 Southeast 4th Street, Abilene, Kansas 67410-2900. For more information, call 877-RING-IKE or log on to www.eisenhower.utexas.edu.

All buildings at the center are handicapped-accessible and open daily from 9 A.M. until 4:45 P.M. From Memorial Day until mid-August, the museum and visitors center are open from 8:00 A.M. until 5:45 P.M. All buildings are closed Thanksgiving, Christmas, and New Year's Day. A small fee is charged for the museum only.

Jacqueline Kennedy

A World of Privilege

In New York City, just about anybody who is anybody, or wants to be, makes it a point to show up in the section of Long Island's south shore known as the Hamptons at least once during the summer. Jacqueline Bouvier was born there. She arrived fashionably late during the summer of 1929 at Southampton, but her family's summer place was in East Hampton, about fifteen miles farther out toward the end of the island. Her father, John Bouvier III, who was known as Jack, named her Jacqueline for himself.

Her twenty-two-year-old mother, the former Janet Lee, a descendant of Irish immigrants, was a rising star in New York society, described by a friend as "highly ambitious, smart, aggressive as hell, a daredevil horseback rider who believed in hard work and self-reliance." Her husband, Jack Bouvier, had been considered one of New York's most eligible bachelors before he married Janet a year before Jacqueline was born. Jack was tall and muscular with a perpetual suntan and a pencil-thin mustache, but what people remembered most about him was his hair. "He must have used axle grease on his hair because it was just about as slick and flat as you could get it," according to a caddie at his golf club. More memorable than his appearance, though, was his personality. "He was divinely decadent," said one of his cousins, who added that "he never grew up." He drove fast cars, he gambled recklessly, he thumbed his nose at the Prohibition amendment, and he shamelessly chased beautiful women who usually called him "Black Jack" and "fluttered around him like love-hungry moths."

A descendant of a French cabinetmaker, Jack's father was among New York's most successful lawyers and stockbrokers, and his sons followed him into the business. Jack was a big success himself, although he always managed to spend more than he earned.

Janet Lee's family approved of her marriage in spite of Jack Bouvier's reputation and the fact that he was sixteen years older than she was, because

Her father always called her Jackie, but Jacqueline Kennedy was annoyed when anyone else called her by that name.

Jacqueline Lee Bouvier Kennedy

Born
July 28, 1929,
Southampton, New York

Parents
John Vernon Bouvier III
and Janet Norton Lee
Bouvier (Auchincloss)

Marriage
September 12, 1953, to
John Fitzgerald Kennedy
(1917-63)

Children
Caroline Bouvier (1957-);
John Fitzgerald, Jr.
(1960-99); Patrick
Bouvier (1963-63)

Widowed
1963

Remarried
October 20, 1968,
to Aristotle Onassis
(1906-75)

Died
May 19, 1994,
New York, New York

Above: Jackie Bouvier lived an ideal life at the age of four; she spent summers by the sea, and winters in a luxury apartment on Manhattan's Park Avenue.

they welcomed the social connections it would bring them. They were descended from fairly recent Irish immigrants, but the Lees were no longer lace-curtain Irish by any stretch of the imagination. James T. Lee, Janet's father, was president and board chairman of the New York Central Savings Bank, and "tycoon" is the only word that fairly describes his real estate ventures. He developed and operated several luxury apartment buildings on Manhattan's Park and Fifth Avenues.

Jacqueline was three months old when the stock market crashed in 1929 and the Great Depression began, but of course she didn't know that. Her family hardly noticed, either.

The Depression would seem to have been a tragedy for a man like Jack Bouvier whose business was selling stocks and, in fact, his income dropped frighteningly. He had a guardian angel, though, in the person of his father-in-law. The value of his own portfolio had been cut in half, but it was still worth $4 million, and he wanted to see his daughter and granddaughter comfortable. Instead of money, though, he gave them an eleven-room apartment in one of his Park Avenue buildings. But Jack still had plenty of friends who could lend him money, and he hit them for enough to redecorate the place, adding a gym and new bathrooms with gold-plated fixtures as well as carving out rooms for an expanded staff of servants that included an English nanny to look after baby Jacqueline.

Jacqueline lived in that luxurious apartment until she was nine years old, although she was away in the Hamptons from May through October. Her sister, Caroline Lee, was born when she was three and a half, and Jacqueline was given a room of her own that was crammed full of toys and stuffed animals from FAO Schwarz. The next step was enrollment at the highly rated Miss Chapin's School, where her teachers complained that she was a "problem child." Her mother explained that the problem was that "her intellectual age ran ahead of her chronological age." She could read before kindergarten and, according to her mother, "Her problem at Chapin was sheer boredom. Jackie would finish her classroom lessons before any of the other children and, lacking things to do, she would make a nuisance of herself. She could be audacious and demanding, even show-offy—a handful."

Below: Jackie's early years at the posh Miss Chapin's school were a trial for most of her teachers.

Attitude Adjustment

The headmistress at Miss Chapin's took advantage of young Jacqueline Bouvier's love for horses to deal with her unruliness. "You are like a thoroughbred," she told her. "You can run fast. You have staying power. You are well built and you have brains. But if you're not properly broken and well-trained, you'll be good for nothing." She went on to tell her that the most beautiful horse in the world was only good enough to pull a milk wagon if it weren't properly trained. The message got through and Jacqueline became a changed little girl.

Like most youngsters, Jacqueline didn't like going to school very much and, like most, she eagerly looked forward to summer vacations. But her vacations weren't like many others. She spent them at East Hampton, surrounded by servants and elegant houseguests at Wildmoor, a six-bedroom house on ten acres down the road from her grandfather Bouvier's estate. The family had seven horses, and when Jacqueline was as young as five, she competed on the circuit of Long Island horse shows. Her mother, who was a master of the local fox hunt, gave her a show horse named Danseuse and she worked long hours training and grooming the animal, which paid off for her in the form of an impressive collection of blue ribbons. She loved competition, and she loved the attention, too. The larger the crowd, the better she did.

But the high life was expensive and Jackie's father was living on borrowed money. He was also still an unrepentant womanizer and by the summer of 1936, when Jackie was seven, Janet had had enough and she filed for divorce. They agreed to a trial separation, and Jack moved from the Manhattan apartment into a hotel. He saw his daughters only on weekends, with the predictable effect on the girls and, like other children of divorce, it didn't take them long to learn how to manipulate their parents. They discovered, as a cousin put it, "That with a little charm and a little cunning, you could get almost anything you wanted." Her parents' problems were also at the root of Jackie's problems at school and when she became a teenager, she became tightly reserved and painfully shy in contrast to the boisterous girl she had been before.

> "Jackie, you never have to worry about keeping up with the Joneses because we are the Joneses."
>
> —Jack Bouvier on his family's social status

Her mother was very concerned about appearances, and as she brought her daughters up she constantly reminded them that being a real lady depended entirely on making an impression of refinement and polish with a cultivated style. She also believed that without money there was no way of creating an impression like that, and she worried constantly that her own funds were running low.

The Bouviers' separation ended with another summer on Long Island, although in a much smaller house, but Jack and Janet were further apart than ever. She managed to stay out of the house as much as she could, and he took advantage of the time alone with them to get closer to his daughters. But they were never to be a family again. The divorce proceedings began in earnest as soon as they went back to New York City in the fall, and the girls were left to their own devices while their mother went about husband hunting and their father went back to his hotel room and his stable of mistresses.

Jackie threw herself into her schoolwork and after she reached the top of her class she stayed there. At home, she became a surrogate mother to her little sister, who was called Lee, and she read novels and became a dedicated movie fan. Although they had been living rent-free in her grandfather's Park Avenue building, their mother moved the girls to a smaller, but no less luxurious, one on Gracie Square across from the mayor's mansion and closer to the Chapin School where little Lee had also become a student. But Jackie interpreted the move as a way of separating her from her father, and she despised her mother for it. Any closeness there had been between them disappeared.

They visited Washington, D.C., together during the Easter break in 1941 and Jackie got her first look at the White House as a tourist. She was not impressed. The National Gallery, though, fascinated her and she said, "My love of art was born there." The trip wasn't the average tourist pilgrimage. The girls' mother had recently met Hugh Dudley Auchincloss, Jr., a wealthy investment banker. She had thoughtfully included a maid on their trip and it left her free to go visiting on her own—always to the Auchincloss estate across the river in Mclean, Virginia.

"Hughdie" Auchincloss had been married twice and he had three children, but he was single at the moment, and he was exactly what Janet had been looking for. He was heir to one of America's great fortunes, worth more than the Lees and the Bouviers put together, and he was at the very top of the Social Register. Not only that, but he was respectable and he was sober, everything that Jack Bouvier was not.

They were married the following spring and eventually they had two children, Jackie's half sister, Janet, and half brother, Jamie. Jackie and Lee moved with their mother to the Auchincloss estate, Merrywood, in Virginia and they lived there for almost all of the 1940s. It was the most elegant place they had ever seen, let alone lived in, even compared with their opulent Park Avenue duplex and her grandfather's palatial estate in the Hamptons. The writer Gore Vidal, whose mother was one of Hughdie's former wives, wrote of its "heavenly ambiance," and he said that everyone who, like himself, had lived there has tried to re-create its atmosphere in their own homes.

It was hard to do. Merrywood was a Georgian-style ivy-covered brick mansion set on forty-six acres along the banks of the Potomac River directly across from the capital. It had an Olympic-size swimming pool and two stables with a network of riding trails. Its four-car garage included a car wash. The kitchen was big enough to serve three hundred guests, and its public rooms could accommodate hundreds more. There were eight bedrooms in the house, and Jackie chose one on the third floor, significantly away from the others, where she could hear the sounds of the river flowing over the rocks below.

Naturally, Jackie's mother took it upon herself to redecorate the place, and by all accounts she did a good job of it, transforming a kind of Victorian interior into something airier and more modern. She did the same for the other Auchincloss estate, Hammersmith Farm in Newport, Rhode Island. Merrywood had been built in 1920, but the Newport farm had been in the family since 1887, and it was the last remaining working farm in a town filled with marble palaces that were the textbook definition of the nineteenth century's Gilded Age. But if Hammersmith Farm was out of town, it wasn't outclassed by the elaborate cottages of the superrich by a long shot. The main house had twenty-eight rooms and thirteen fireplaces and it was set on ninety-seven acres overlooking Narragansett Bay. The gardens had been laid out by Frederick Law Olmsted, the co-creator of New York's Central Park. There were separate stables for workhorses and riding ponies, and barns for Auchincloss's herd of prize Black Angus cattle and others for herds of sheep and flocks of chickens.

When Jackie arrived there for the first time in the summer of 1943, she picked out a third-floor bedroom with a view of the bay, and her mother decorated it in yellow with cane furniture. The farm supplied the nearby navy base with milk and eggs and produce, and to help overcame the wartime manpower shortage, Jackie and the other young people were dragooned into chores that included feeding the chickens, milking cows, and harvesting crops. She also found time to lavish affection on the horses, but not enough to win any blue ribbons with her riding skill. But she didn't mind; 1943 was the happiest summer she had seen in all of her fourteen years.

Jackie had been a student at the exclusive Holton-Arms School in Washington, D.C., but she spent the last three years of high school at Miss Porter's School in Farmington, Connecticut, near Hartford. She could have chosen several schools that would have kept her in the Washington area, but she chose Farmington mainly to put some distance between herself and the Auchinclosses. She was alienated from her mother, and while her mother's husband treated her like one of his own children, she was painfully aware that he was not her father. He was not the Jack Bouvier whom she adored but she believed had let her down. She was uncomfortable with all of them, and preferred solitude.

Farmington was a finishing school in the old-fashioned sense of the term. In the words of a family friend who had graduated from there, "You were bred with deportment and elocution—how to move, how to speak, how to behave." But it was also strong on academic subjects—Latin was Jackie's favorite—and its standards were high. She had no trouble maintaining an A- average during her years there, but she did have a problem with the way she dressed. There was no dress code beyond neatness and good taste, but she refused to follow the trends that the other girls accepted as fashionable. There were a half dozen prestigious boys' prep schools nearby, and she often went to parties at Choate, Groton, and the others, but none of the boys seemed to interest her. "I just know that no one will ever marry me," she said ruefully. It wasn't that she wasn't pretty and charming, far from it, but her mind had matured faster than those prep school boys and they had little in common.

She was busy with her studies, too, and she was a member of the drama club and a contributor to the school newspaper. Most of all, she was a very active member of the riding club.

Below: Jackie's family might be called a dysfunctional one today, but they had a great many pleasant moments in spite of it all.

When Jackie turned eighteen, it was time for her introduction into society. The celebration was held at the old Clambake Club at Newport where she received several hundred of her mother's friends and Hugh Auchincloss's business associates who had gathered for Tennis Week, the high point of the Newport social season. Her mother had bought her a custom-made Christian Dior dress, but she picked out her own from a New York department store that cost less than $60. It was an off-the-shoulder floor-length dress in white tulle that complemented her coloring. Jackie made a gorgeous debutante. She was tall, about five feet, seven inches, and she weighed approximately 125 pounds. She wore her hair long at the time, and it was still curly. Her eyelashes were long, and her eyes were striking. Her smile was captivating, her posture unself-consciously perfect, and her manner elegant. In other words, the woman the world would come to adore had already emerged at the age of eighteen.

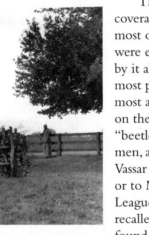

Above: Jackie rode her horse Sardar at Long Island horse shows when she was a young girl.

The following year, she went off to Vassar College. Press coverage of her debut had make Jackie a kind of celebrity, and most of the other freshmen, many of them socialites themselves, were either jealous or awestruck. For her part, she was unaffected by it all and when the novelty wore off, she became one of the most popular of Vassar's undergraduates. She was also one of the most accomplished academically; her name appeared repeatedly on the dean's list. Although she had found prep school boys "beetle-browed bores," they became more interesting as college men, and it was a rare weekend that Jackie could be found on the Vassar campus. She was off to Harvard and Yale for football parties or to Manhattan for nights on the town with scores of young Ivy Leaguers. "She treated dating like a game of skill," one of them recalled, "a means of sharpening her social abilities." While she found the men charming, she wasn't especially interested in any of them as a lifetime partner, "not because of them but because of their lives."

She broke her pattern of summer activities in 1948 when she sailed for Europe with three friends and a chaperone aboard the liner *Queen Mary.* They began their two-month adventure in London with a garden party at Buckingham Palace where Jackie shook hands not only with King George VI and Queen Mary, but Prime Minister Winston Churchill, too. They went from there to Paris and on to the Riviera, Italy, and the Alps. When she got home, Jackie told her mother, "I've had a glimpse. Next time I want to soak it all up."

"Next time" came when she enrolled in Smith College's junior year abroad program, and she went back to Europe for a year that began with six weeks of language arts training at the University of Grenoble. By the time she entered the Sorbonne in Paris, her conversational French was so good that she boarded with a French family rather than live in a dormitory where English was spoken.

Jackie had very nearly not made the trip at all. She had become bored with Vassar, and not long into her sophomore year she decided to quit and become a photographer's model. She'd been modeling frequently in fashion shows, and had even been paid for some pictures of her that were published in *Life* magazine. She had also become romantically involved with Colonel Serge Obolensky, a Russian prince and self-styled arbiter of New York society. She was nineteen and he was in his mid-sixties, and that scandalized her father, even though his own current romantic interest was Jackie's age.

The prospect of a year in Paris cooled Jackie's ardor for the Russian prince, and it was more appealing than posing under hot lights wearing the latest fashions. It was a decision she never regretted. She tasted every aspect of Parisian life, from cocktails at the Ritz to wine at underground cafes and jazz clubs. She went to the opera, the theater, and the ballet; she spent hour after hour at the Louvre and many afternoons visiting artists' studios. She rode around the city on a friend's motorcycle, and she could navigate the Métro like a native. It was the first time in her life that she had been completely on her own. There were no servants, not even central heating; food was rationed, and even a hot bath was a luxury.

When she went home again, it was to George Washington University in Washington, where she majored in French literature and eased back into a life of luxury at Merrywood. During that final college year, she entered *Vogue* magazine's Prix de Paris writing contest, and hers was the wining entry out of 1,280 that were submitted. The prize was a year's internship in *Vogue*'s editorial offices in New York and in Paris. Hugh Auchincloss had reservations about it, fearing that another extended stay in Paris would turn her into a permanent

Prix de Paris

Jackie Bouvier was in her final year of college when she entered and won a Vogue *magazine competition that required her to submit four technical essays on fashion, a personal profile, and a blueprint for an entire issue of* Vogue. *At its heart was an essay on "People I Wish I Had Known" in the world of art, literature, music, or ballet who were no longer living. Jackie chose Sergei Diaghilev, Charles Baudelaire, and Oscar Wilde. The prize was a one-year training program at the magazine, six months in its Paris office, and six in New York. The effort, in addition to the intensive research, included a course in typing, which Jackie had never bothered to learn.*

expatriate. But she put up a good argument, and Hugh gave his approval. He offered to pay her bills and to allow her sister, Lee, to go along for the summer. It was a graduation present for both of them; Jackie had earned her bachelor's degree from George Washington, and Lee had finished her high school education at Miss Porter's.

A New Love

When Jackie completed her year in Paris, she faced the problem of what to do with the rest of her life. Her father insisted that she live with him in New York and work in his brokerage firm, but her mother was just as insistent that she live in Washington and promised to find her a good job if she did. It was a difficult decision—Jackie and her father had a distant, sometimes stormy relationship—but she spent the summer at Newport thinking it over.

It was Hugh Auchincloss who gave her a reason to go to Washington. He suggested journalism as a career, and he had enough contacts in Washington, D.C., to make it possible. He arranged an interview for her with the editor of the *Washington Times-Herald*, and she started to work there early in 1952 as what was called a copyboy in those days, and she was soon promoted to receptionist. When the paper's "Inquiring Photographer" was promoted, Jackie volunteered for the job. It wasn't a plum assignment as newspaper jobs go, and Jackie wasn't a starry-eyed wannabe journalist, but she did her best. She had her own byline, and she had good ideas.

She was engaged at the time to John Husted, a solid citizen and a banker who everyone agreed would make her a good husband, although everyone also agreed that Jackie wasn't exactly head-over-heels in love with him. She started dating other men before long. Both she and Husted were invited to a dinner party at the home of reporter Charles Bartlett and his wife, but Jackie's fiancé was tied up in New York, and she spent the evening in the company of a congressman from Massachusetts named Jack Kennedy. They were instantly attracted to each other, although she noted that "here was a man who did not want to marry." At the end of the evening he invited her to go out with him for a drink, but when they reached her car they found John Husted behind the wheel. He had arrived from New York too late for the party, but then he had come anyway to drive Jackie home. The congressman backed off and that was the end of the spark between Jack and Jackie—for now.

Soon after, Jackie drove Husted to the airport for a trip to New York. She slipped his engagement ring off her finger and dropped it into his pocket without a word. She was no longer engaged.

It was almost a year later when the Barletts, "shameless in the matchmaking," according to Jackie, invited her and Jack to another dinner party. This time he suggested a more proper follow-up date: dinner and dancing at the Shoreham Hotel. It was followed by others, including evenings at the movies with Jack's brother Bobby and his wife Ethel.

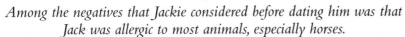

> *Among the negatives that Jackie considered before dating him was that Jack was allergic to most animals, especially horses.*

Over the next several months, Jackie immersed herself in the history of the Kennedy family, and she liked what she learned. More important, she realized that she loved Jack Kennedy. They liked each other's sense of humor, and she liked the things he believed in. It didn't hurt that his income came from a $10 million trust fund—she had been brought up to believe that money matters a great deal—but she also admired Jack's casual attitude about it. Money was a convenience to him and nothing more, and that was what Jackie believed as well. All that worried her was his family's expectations for him and his reputation around Washington as a ladies' man. It was something she could relate to considering her father's activities in that arena, and she saw disappointment and heartbreak on the horizon, but she said that "just as swiftly I determined that such heartbreak would be worth the pain."

Jack and Jackie became an item in the gossip columns after they went together to President Eisenhower's Inaugural Ball, but there was never any hint of an imminent marriage. As far as anyone could tell, Jackie was just one more of Jack's women, a sorority that ran the gamut from movie stars to working girls. He found a kindred spirit in Jackie, and it pleased him to be seen with such a well-dressed attractive woman, but there were plenty of other women whose company he enjoyed just as much.

What was necessary was to begin a campaign to win him completely over, and Jackie went right to work. Jack was a senator by then, and she started interviewing men on the Hill along with the man on the street for her "Inquiring Photographer" feature. Senator Kennedy was her first stop, but she also included Vice President Nixon, several congressmen, and a few congressional pages on her assignment list. It's hard to conceal one's motives on Capitol Hill, and she got several offers of help with her campaign to win Jack's heart, along with a lot of advice to forget about it.

She knew that Jack read her column and she began including such questions as, "Can you give any reason why a confirmed bachelor shouldn't get married?" "Are men as inclined to fall for a line as women are?" and even "Was Sean O'Faolain right when he said that the Irish are deficient in the art of love?"

She also knew that Jack carried his lunch to work in a brown paper bag and she started dropping by with hot take-out lunches for two. Over time, she began to help him edit position papers, and she translated several books from French for him. She also carried his briefcase when his back bothered him, and she went to political dinners with him, even though up until that time she had been a Republican; she helped him shop for clothes, which had never interested him before. She relaxed with him at the movies, too, although he insisted on action-adventure films that she found boring.

Jack still didn't seem to get the message, but she knew that she had at least dented his resolve when he invited her to spend the long Fourth of July weekend with his family at Hyannisport on Cape Cod. She wasn't too eager to join their endless games of touch football or cutthroat tennis—"Just watching them wore me out," she said. "It wasn't necessary for me to be the best." But "best" was a requirement at the Kennedy Compound. Jack's father, Joseph P. Kennedy, made that clear when he said, "We don't want any losers around here." The result was that Jackie got off on the wrong foot. Jack's brothers and sisters wrote her off as "delicate," a description that didn't square at all with the family's image of itself. For what it was worth, Jackie was one of the first of Jack's female friends that was ever invited to the family retreat.

"How can I explain these people? They are like carbonated water."

—Jackie Bouvier on the Kennedy family

Jack may have already known what his father told him that weekend: that he couldn't have a political future if he didn't have a wife to help him create an image of family solidarity. He added that he thought that this girl, Jacqueline Bouvier, would fill the bill perfectly; she was pretty, she was well educated, she was fashionable, and she came from one of the leading families in the Social Register. Most important of all, she was a Roman Catholic.

It was the year that Jack ran for Senate for the first time, and they didn't see much of each other while he—and the rest of the family—barnstormed Massachusetts for the remaining summer and fall. Jack showed more interest in Jackie after he went back to Washington, but although she realized that he might finally be getting serious about her, she said "we didn't talk about it much."

She had moved into phase two of her campaign to win him by then, and her tactics became subtler. When his attention showed signs of flagging, she stopped returning his phone calls, and sometimes she took off on weekend trips without letting him know where she had gone. For a man like Jack Kennedy who wasn't used to being ignored, it was a perfect strategy.

He asked her to marry him in the spring of 1953, but she left him dangling. She had other fish to fry at the moment. Her editor had assigned her to cover the coronation of Queen Elizabeth II, and she was on her way to London. They were in touch while she was gone, but she was away a frustratingly long time. Not only did she choose to go abroad by ship, but after two weeks in London, she took a spur-of-the-moment side trip to Paris for another two weeks.

She gave Jack her answer when he met her at the airport upon her return and it was "yes." She quit her newspaper job the following day and settled into the life of a bride-to-be. One of the first events was an engagement party at Hyannisport that turned out to be a media circus. *Life* magazine was the most prominent presence and its cover story, "*Life* Goes to the Courting of a US Senator," introduced the American public to the famous Kennedy "charisma." Jackie confided to one of the magazine's reporters that "we hardly ever talk politics." Nobody believed it, but it was the truth.

As is usually customary, Jackie's mother expected that she would choreograph her daughter's wedding, and she invited Jack's parents, Joe and Rose Kennedy, to Newport to talk it over. What she had in mind was a quiet, dignified affair with only a few close family friends on hand, but Jack himself put that idea to rest right away. "Your daughter is marrying a political figure," he told her, and press coverage was unavoidable. "The idea is to show Jackie to the best advantage." Then the Kennedy family took over, and Janet Auchincloss wasn't at all pleased. She thought that their plans were "gauche," but Joe Kennedy wasn't pleased with her, either, or the whole Newport scene, for that matter. "Their wealth is from a bygone era," he huffed. "They don't know the first thing about living up there." While the negotiations were going on, Jack took off with a few of his buddies for a two-week Mediterranean cruise, leaving the entire business for Jackie to deal with.

The wedding ceremony, which took place at Newport's Saint Mary's Catholic Church on September 12, 1953, was conducted by Richard Cushing, the archbishop of Boston. About three thousand spectators gathered outside as though it were a Hollywood awards

Above: Jackie's Newport wedding to Jack Kennedy made society page headlines from one end of the country to the other. Among the invited guests was the entire United States Senate.

An Expensive Toast

Just before the wedding of Jackie and Jack, Hugh Auchincloss hosted a bachelor party for Jack Kennedy at the Newport Clambake Club. It was a local custom to toss the Champagne glasses into the fireplace after a toast, and Jack went along with it, inviting his eighteen guests to smash their glasses after drinking to his future bride. Then he did it again. "Maybe this isn't the custom, but to express my love for the girl I'm going to marry, another toast to the bride!" Another eighteen glasses were smashed. Everyone enjoyed the ceremony except the host. Those crystal Champagne flutes had been priceless family heirlooms.

ceremony, and the church was filled beyond capacity. The bride's gown, made of fifty yards of ivory silk chiffon, had been created, along with the bridesmaids' dresses, by a Harlem dressmaker.

Jackie's father had come to town to give the bride away, but her mother had seen to it that he wasn't invited to any of the parties leading up to the wedding. He was even disinvited to the ceremony—many said that he was drunk in his hotel room, although it is just as likely that his ex-wife had threatened him into staying away. Hugh Auchincloss gave the bride away.

The reception at Hammersmith Farm was as much a media photo-op as a social affair. It took more than two hours for the guests to move through the receiving line. In addition to the entire membership of the U.S. Senate, the guest list included scores of Irish Democratic politicians from Boston, and scores more of Hugh Auchincloss's Waspish Republican cronies from New York and Washington, as well as representatives of Newport society—and, of course, a very large crowd of reporters and press photographers.

By the time the young couple settled into a rented house in the Georgetown section of Washington, Jack and Jackie had become the best-known couple in town. She was the youngest wife of a senator, and although she had spent more than a decade living just across the river in the Virginia suburbs, Jackie was totally without experience in the world of politics. She quickly became immersed in it by staging cocktail parties and dinners, but she still didn't like it.

Jackie had always resisted the very thought of ever becoming a suburban housewife, and she was as unfamiliar with domestic chores as she was with politics. She was almost proud of the fact that she couldn't even boil an egg, but that all eventually changed. She soon hired a cook, and she also went to cooking school.

Jackie had grown up with gourmet tastes, though, but there had always been servants around to help her indulge them. She educated herself about fine wines, and Jack learned along with her. She also had impeccable taste in clothes, but he was casual about his appearance almost to a fault, and she took it on herself to upgrade his wardrobe. "I brought a certain amount of order to Jack's life," she said. "We had good food in our house—not merely the bare staples he used to have. He no longer went out in the morning with one black and one brown shoe on. His clothes got pressed, and he made it to the airport without a mad rush because I packed for him."

Jackie knew that it would be nearly suicidal to try sharing the spotlight with her ambitious

Bride in the Kitchen

Like most young brides of her era, Jackie Kennedy was determined to become a good housewife. But she created a disaster every once in a while. She wrote of one of them: "I'd heard those silly stories about the bride burning things, but I just knew everything was going right when suddenly, I don't know what went wrong, you couldn't see the place for smoke. When I tried to pull the chops out of the oven, the door seemed to collapse. The pan slid out and the fat splattered. One of the chops fell on the floor but I put it on the plate anyway. The chocolate sauce was burning and exploding. What a smell!!! I couldn't get the spoon out of the chocolate. It was like a rock. The coffee had all boiled away. I burned my arm and it turned purple. It looked horrible. Then Jack came home and took me out to dinner."

husband—she was too shy anyway—but she made it her mission
to support him. Along with enrolling for courses at Georgetown
University's foreign service school, she joined the Red Cross and
folded bandages; she played bridge and poured tea with other Senate
wives, and she even joined them in the Senate gallery to listen to the
debates. Her husband was far from the best orator there, and she took
it on herself to share with him the lessons she had learned back at
school. He talked too fast and she slowed him down, his posture was
bad and she straightened him up; she reminded him of the importance
of the right gestures, and she taught him restraint, which had been an
alien concept in his energetic life until she came into it.

Jack had been plagued with back pain since the war, and in
spite of spinal surgery, he became a semi-invalid in the second year
of their marriage. He needed crutches to get around, and he wore
a heavy brace, but his doctors said that without more complicated
and dangerous surgery, he was doomed to spend the rest of his life
in a wheelchair. There was only a fifty-fifty chance that he would
survive the operation, but he checked in at the New York Hospital for
Special Surgery, and Jackie went along. She was at his bedside day and
night, feeding him and bathing him and reading to him. Within two
weeks, he was placed on the critical list, and a priest was called in to
administer the last rites of the Catholic Church.

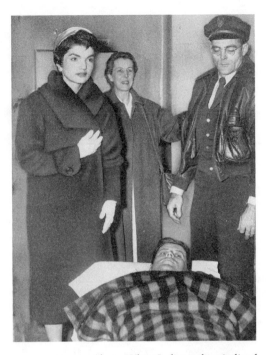

*Above: When Jack was hospitalized
for back surgery, Jackie stayed at his
side for the three months that he
hovered close to death.*

Jack was in the hospital from early October through mid-December, all
the while close to death. When his doctors released him to go to the Kennedy
retreat in Palm Beach, Florida, they told Jackie that there was almost no hope
that he would survive the trip. They also told her that the dressings on his eight-
inch open wound from the surgery would have to be changed every few hours
and they showed her how to do it.

Jack did survive the journey, and thanks to what his mother characterized as
Jackie's skill, gentleness, and calmness, he survived the winter, too. By the middle
of February, he was back in the hospital again for a bone graft on his spine.

During the whole long ordeal, Jackie served as a liaison between his
hospital bed and his Senate office. She also came up with an idea that
researching a book on political leaders who had taken strong risks for the
public's benefit might be good therapy for him. She surrounded him with books
and articles and she edited his notes that would be sent to the team of writers
who would actually produce the manuscript for the book that was called *Profiles
in Courage.* He was obviously too incapacitated to do all of the actual writing,
but he did write parts of the book and rewrote the rest. He wrote in the
preface, "This book would not have been possible without the encouragement,
assistance, and criticisms offered by my wife Jacqueline, whose help during all
the days of my convalescence I cannot ever acknowledge." The book was not
only a best-seller, but it won the Pulitzer Prize for biography.

After he was released from the hospital, Jack was still in nearly constant
pain, and he began making regular trips to New York for special treatments, a

routine that he followed for the rest of his life. In the periods between those trips, it fell to Jackie to supervise his life. He needed regular medication at home and his diet had to be monitored; and she kept track of his important exercise schedule. But her most important job was guarding Jack's secret, that he was a virtual cripple. He never used crutches in public, although he needed them, and his wheelchair was kept well out of sight. Pain or no, Jack Kennedy had political ambitions, and the public must never know about his physical problems.

Jack went back to Capitol Hill with as much bounce in his step as he could possibly muster, and he celebrated his return with a lavish party for nearly a thousand people at Hyannisport. Only close Kennedy watchers noticed that he hung on Jackie's arm during the entire affair, the others found it endearing and quite a good sign for his political future.

To keep the suggestion of a complete recovery alive, the Kennedys took a two-month trip to Europe that was billed as a working vacation. Jackie boosted her own image by serving as Jack's official interpreter; she was thoroughly comfortable in French, the language of diplomacy, but he was not.

Close Encounter

While they were Europe, the Kennedys were invited to a lavish party aboard Aristotle Onassis's yacht, and Jack was especially eager to go because Sir Winston Churchill had also been invited. He was intrigued by the former British prime minister, and he put on a white dinner jacket, something he usually avoided, to make a good impression. But Sir Winston didn't have any time for the young senator, and Jack was visibly hurt by the snub. As they were leaving, Jackie smoothed his feelings when she pointed to his white jacket and said, "Maybe he thought you were a waiter, Jack."

After they returned from Europe, the Kennedys moved into Hickory Hill, a Georgian estate in suburban Virginia not far from Merrywood. It wasn't as large as the Auchincloss estate, but it had stables and bridle paths for Jackie and a swimming pool where Jack could keep up his rigid exercise routine out of the public eye. Jackie took on the job of redecorating the place with special attention paid to Jack's special needs, such as drawers he wouldn't have to bend over to open. She also set aside space for a nursery—she was pregnant. But she was quietly worried about the future of her marriage. In spite of his condition, her husband was still chasing women, and he was talking about running for president, and she wasn't at all sure that she was ready for the responsibility. She had already gone through a miscarriage, but this time she was full of hope that she'd be able to have a child after all, and that it would change everything in both their lives.

Her own life tilted in the direction of politics when, although eight months pregnant, she went to Chicago for the 1956 Democratic National Convention. Some said that she seemed like "a little girl at a grown-up party," and she herself admitted that she didn't know what the shouting was all about. But she got into the spirit of the thing, even to the point of writing a memorable endorsement of Jack's former rival Adlai Stevenson, which he read verbatim from her handwritten text when he endorsed Stevenson's nomination.

After the convention, Jack went off to the Riviera, and Jackie went up to Hammersmith Farm. Tragedy struck when her baby arrived stillborn, and it was compounded by Jack's indifference to the matter. He didn't come home until more than three weeks later. Their marriage had reached its lowest ebb. They sold Hickory Hill to his brother Bobby, and moved into a rented town house in Georgetown where Jackie became a recluse, convinced that after a miscarriage and a stillbirth that she would never be able to have children. Jack, meanwhile, had his political career to think about and he was away most of the time keeping his name alive to an adoring public.

The situation began to change in the spring. Jackie was pregnant again, and though fearful, she was hopeful, and she and Jack bought a house of their own, which she set about redecorating. It was the first time that she had been visibly happy in months. Her happiness grew in November, the day after Thanksgiving, when her first child, Caroline Bouvier Kennedy, was born. Jack was on hand this time, and he was also on hand for the move into their new house, just in time for Christmas. But after the first of the year, he seemed to be everywhere except home. He hadn't yet declared his presidential candidacy, but in 1958, he made more then two hundred speeches in every corner of the country, only flitting back to Washington when he was needed in the Senate. He was needed at home, too, but as Caroline's nanny recalled, "The Senator was not often to be seen." Jackie was happy, though. She had her house, still a work in progress, and she had baby Caroline.

Above: Jack and Jackie relaxing at Hammersmith Farm in Newport with four year-old Caroline and her baby brother John.

Jackie had always stayed aloof from politics and she had avoided being absorbed by the Kennedy clan, but in the fall of 1958, she joined with the family to help Jack get elected for another Senate term. It wasn't like traditional campaigns of the past: There was still a lot of handshaking and backslapping and plenty of enthusiasm, but the Kennedys were establishing themselves as a kind of American royal family, and Jackie's presence on the campaign trail was the icing on the cake. Like a queen, she could be warm and friendly and aloof at the same time; she could impress people with her sophisticated charm, and she also had a natural common touch. There was nothing phony about Jackie, and she was simple and elegant at the same time. She could talk to crowds in perfect Italian in Boston's North End, and when the audience spoke Spanish, she came close to convincing them that she had grown up in Latin America. But she never talked down to any of them.

Jackie didn't make a lot of speeches—she was too shy for that and it wasn't why the family had invited her to take part in the campaign in the first place. It was her presence they wanted—Jack and Jackie were a handsome, appealing couple. A smile, a nod, a wave from Jackie was enough to let people conclude that she was someone they would enjoy knowing. She also had a greater value that was overlooked at first; she was an excellent judge of people and she shared her insight with Jack. Thanks to her unemotional assessments, he was better able to judge the commitment of people who might be important to him. "She breathes all the political gasses that flow around us," he said admiringly, "but she never seems to inhale them."

She didn't inhale any of the contagion of campaigning, either, and when he started his run-up to the presidency in 1959, she decided to stay home with Caroline. Except for brief visits home, and many trips to the tailor to get his wardrobe up to speed, she didn't catch up with Jack again until he formally announced his candidacy in January 1960 and she realized that history had caught up with her, and that their lives were taking what to her was an unwelcome turn. But as she put it, "If Jack didn't run for the presidency he'd be like a tiger in a cage."

Like it or not, Jackie plunged herself into the presidential campaign, and she was as tireless as the candidate himself. She had a way of speaking that convinced people that she shared her husband's goals for the United States, and her sincerity and conviction made it perfectly clear. When they worked crowds together, Jack was awestruck. "Jackie's drawing more people than I am, as usual," he said. It didn't really matter. It was the numbers that counted, and they grew dramatically almost by the day.

Above: Jack and Jackie watched the 1962 America's Cup Race aboard a Navy destroyer that was named for his brother Joe. The winning yacht was from Australia.

Jackie made it a point never to talk about things she didn't understand, she refused to turn her biting wit on the opposition, and she adamantly refused invitations to political cocktail parties and fund-raisers. She still hated politics and she didn't have much patience for chitchat.

It was unpredictable, but the high point of the campaign for Jackie was the time the couple spent in West Virginia. She had led a sheltered life and had never seen real poverty before, and she was visibly moved. "In all the places we

> *"I think it's so unfair of people to be against Jack because he's a Catholic. He's such a poor Catholic. Now, if it were Bobby, I could understand."*
>
> *—Jackie Kennedy on her husband's religious practice*

campaigned, those are the people who touched me most," she said. She went into miners' shacks and stayed far longer than her schedule allowed, and she walked picket lines with striking workers to share their point of view. "I can't believe it," Jack told an aide, "I'm so proud of Jackie." Then he fired off a memo to his staff to promote her more.

They would have to do it without her presence, though. Jackie was pregnant again and she dropped out of the campaign to spend the summer at Hyannisport. She was not present when her husband won the nomination at the Democratic National Convention in Los Angeles, but she was there in spirit. As the campaign got under way in earnest, she began writing a syndicated newspaper column called "Campaign Wife," addressing topics of special interest to women with an occasional nod to her husband, who by inference was going to do something about them.

She and Jack were interviewed at home for the CBS television program *Person to Person* in the fall, a broadcast that was seen around the world. A few weeks later, Jack won the presidency, and although she was in the eighth month of her pregnancy, Jackie went to New York for a ticker tape parade up the entire length of Manhattan Island and beyond to the northern suburbs and then back again. More than a million people cheered them along the unprecedented thirty-mile route.

American Idol

A few weeks after Jack won the presidency, Jackie won America's heart when she gave birth to a son, John F. Kennedy, Jr. She had already been under the media spotlight, but now the press became relentless in its coverage of her not only as a new First Lady but also as a new mother.

It was predictable. Most Americans couldn't recall a First Lady who wasn't a grandmother, and Jackie was not only young but she was also beautiful and glamorous. She had star quality, and even people with different political views were eagerly looking forward to some interesting changes in the social life of the White House after the quiet, understated Eisenhower years. Jackie had already announced that she planned to completely revamp the entertainment schedule, adding coyly that it was going to be "experimental" at first, and that intrigued the press corps all the more. One of them said that "after eight years of feeling older then we should have," a breath of fresh air had come to Washington. Jackie also dropped broad hints that she was going to change the appearance of the White House itself. She said that she found it "cold and

Above: Jackie and her baby, John, Jr., shared the kind of moments that every mother treasures.

> "I feel as though I have just been turned into a piece of public property. It's really frightening to lose your anonymity at thirty-one."
>
> —Jackie Kennedy on her sudden fame

dreary," and it looked like "a hotel that had been decorated by a wholesale furniture store during a January clearance." The outgoing First Lady, Mamie Eisenhower, whose home it was, could only say, "Well, she's awfully young."

That was exactly the point. This was the beginning of the 1960s, and Americans, who like their history expressed in terms of decades, were ready for a change. The ultimate legacy of the 1960s would be the emergence of young people as the arbiters of society's rules, and the Kennedys were on the cutting edge.

It was natural that the First Family would dominate the newspapers and the news magazines, but television was still new enough to be a novelty and it had become the focus of most people's lives, and the networks climbed on the bandwagon. Even viewers who weren't especially interested in what was going on in Washington found images of Jack and Jackie in their living rooms night after night and they were impressed, especially by the First Lady, who reminded them of a movie star. Magazines that had considered Hollywood glamour their own exclusive turf were looking for new subjects now that the collapse of the Hollywood studio system had deprived them of a publicity machine as well as recognizable stars, and Jackie came along at exactly the right moment. All through the Kennedy administration, she appeared on the covers of fan magazines as often as Elizabeth Taylor and Debbie Reynolds had before, and circulation always went up when she did. Jackie had developed an almost unprecedented fan base, and they were all eager for more stories on the First Lady.

Like most other First Ladies, Jackie's formal introduction to Washington society was her husband's Inaugural Ball. She was expected at five of the balls, but she quit after the third and went home alone. It had been a long day and she

Below: Oleg Cassini created this azure blue silk crepe dress that Jackie wore on a trip to Mexico.

The Jackie Look

If Jackie Kennedy had a vice, it was a passion for stylish clothes. The dress she chose for her husband's inauguration was made for her at Bergdorf-Goodman in New York, but she knew from the start that she needed to have her own couturier. It would have to be an American, to be sure, but she was especially fond of her old friend Oleg Cassini because of his continental manners and his European fashion sense. Fortunately he had been an American citizen for almost thirty years, and that put him in the running. She requested that he dress her "like the wife of the President of France," and that he should "make sure no one has exactly the same dress as I do. I want all mine to be original and no fat little women hopping around in the same gown." She also insisted on pre-approving his publicity releases and she asked him to protect her from the advice of fashion and beauty editors because, "I am mercilessly exposed and don't know how to cope with it." For travel, Jackie chose Givenchy and Balenciaga, the creators of the "Audrey Hepburn look," and at home she wore suits and coats by Ben Zuckerman and Norman Norell. But for formal occasions, it was Oleg Cassini hands down. His creations photographed well, and they best expressed what became known as the Jackie look.

Above: Jackie's first public appearance as First Lady was at her husband's inaugural ball in 1961.

had become annoyed with Jack's flirting, which was on display more than usual that night.

Jackie wasn't too happy about the press presence in her life. She accepted it as inevitable for Jack, but she resented any part of it in her own life and especially her children's. She made it a rule that her press office should be polite but tight-lipped, and she refused to endure interviews or pose for photographs.

As a way of protecting herself, she insisted that Jack rent a retreat for her where she and the children could escape for weekends when they weren't traveling. To her mind a weekend extended from Thursday afternoon until Tuesday morning. His choice was Glen Ora, near Middleburg, Virginia, about an hour outside of Washington. The four-hundred-acre estate included a French-inspired manor house and plenty of space for Jackie to indulge her passion for horses. When the lease expired, Jack bought acreage on a nearby mountaintop and built a mansion that he called Wexford, where Jackie's part-time First Ladyship went on as before, although the job would be taken away from her after only four of her long weekends there.

Jackie spent most of her early days as mistress of the White

Jackie insisted that the White House staff call her Mrs. Kennedy. She detested the title of First Lady. The Secret Service name for her was Lace.

House attempting to bring some her own taste to her surroundings. "I intend to make this a grand house," she said. A lot of things she didn't like; Victorian mirrors and "Grand Rapids furniture," for instance, found their way to the dump, but while she roamed the corridors weeding out "horrors," she also found some treasures, furniture and rugs that hadn't seen the light of day since Theodore Roosevelt turned the place over to William Howard Taft.

Her first emphasis was on the family living quarters, and she exhausted the budget in a month. But she had wealthy friends who were willing to help, and she used her undeniable charm to get whatever else she needed from a smitten Congress. She also arranged to have paintings sent over from the Smithsonian to enhance her decor.

She gave lavish dinner parties prepared by a chef she had brought over from Paris, and

Jackie liked to take afternoon naps, and she insisted that the sheets be changed each time she did.

Above: The First Lady became a popular figure on the world stage when she traveled with Jack and outshone him in many ways.

every occasion had a theme. One night her guests might be learning the new dance craze, the twist, and the next they'd be engaged in dignified conversation at a formal black-tie affair. Her guest lists were eclectic, too, ranging from Igor Stravinsky to Tennessee Ernie Ford, and she often arranged to have her guests entertained by symphony orchestras or jazz combos, and Shakespearean actors and poets were often asked to perform as well. Even people with no interest in the arts became familiar with such names as Pablo Casals and Mikhail Baryshnikov, Leonard Bernstein, and Aaron Copland.

Jackie became an international sensation in the spring of 1961, when she and Jack went on their first international tour together to Ottawa, Paris, and Vienna. News reports from Canada barely mentioned Jack's diplomatic accomplishments; the reporters were far more interested in his wife. By the time they reached Paris, where they were welcomed by President Charles De Gaulle with a 101-gun salute, the woman whom the press was calling the "Gothic Madonna" upstaged the ceremony as well as the dignitaries involved. Parisians by the thousand had turned up at the airport and all that interested them was *la belle* "Jah-kee." When the president reached the microphone, he said, "I do not think it is entirely appropriate for me to introduce myself. I am the man who accompanied Jacqueline Kennedy to Paris—and I have enjoyed it." He could hardly be heard above the cheering and it hardly stopped as long as they were in France. Jackie also charmed the testy French president, who confided to Jack, "Your wife knows more French history than most French women," to which Jack replied, "and men."

In Vienna, Jack had a summit meeting with Soviet premier Nikita Khrushchev. They were not impressed with one another and the meeting was a standoff, but Khrushchev was instantly attracted to Jackie, just as the Viennese crowds were. During the state banquet, the crowds shouting "Jah-kee, Jah-kee!" outside had to be dispersed so that the participants could hear each other. The Soviet leader didn't mind—it gave him an excuse to move his chair closer to hers. "They seem to admire you," he said, obviously echoing his own sentiments. Their conversation turned to horses and the arts in the Ukraine, and Jackie was also interested in the dogs that the Soviets were sending into space at the time. He promised to send her one, and he did. At the end of the dinner, a photographer asked him to pose with the president and he said, "I'd rather pose with his wife."

They stopped over in London on the way home for the christening of Lee Radziwill's daughter, Jackie's niece, and she stayed behind for a week's vacation in Greece with her sister and brother-in-law. There, too, she was followed everywhere she went by cheering admirers. By the end of the year, Jackie was named "Woman of the Year" by more than one hundred foreign newspapers, and one of them ranked her along with Pope John XXIII as the two outstanding models for the world.

If Jackie had become America's number-one goodwill ambassador, she was not, like other First Ladies, interested in good works. "I will never be a club woman or a committee woman," she said, "because I am not a joiner." She also said, "I don't want to go down into coal mines or be a symbol of elegance, either." She was, however, interested in raising the American consciousness to be the best they could be without sinking to the lowest common denominator, which had almost become an obsession in the political sector at least.

She put that belief in practice by making her "cause" the restoration of the White House. It ought to be, she said, a place of pride in America's cultural tradition and not just the scene of official parties and receptions. She began by doing her homework, beginning with a personal inspection of thousands of discarded objects in the White House attic and basement and touring warehouses where the detritus of thirty-four presidents was gathering dust. She also put together several committees, including the White House Historical Association and the Fine Arts Committee, which she called "my Politburo"; she also created a new White House staff position, a permanent curator who catalogued everything and would keep track of new acquisitions in the future.

Six months into the project, Jackie decided to recreate the mansion in the French Empire style that had been introduced by Dolley Madison when the present house was new. To make it "authentic," she hired a decorator from Paris, Stephanie Boudin, to oversee the project with her. It soon became obvious that while his French taste was indisputable, he didn't have any sensitivity to American adaptations of it, nor of American history, which was supposed to be the point. Jackie stuck by her decision in spite of the opposition of the authorities who were serving on her blue-ribbon committees, even when he shocked them by insisting that the Blue Room should be painted white, and the Green Room chartreuse. Jackie insisted that the changes were historically accurate and when no one agreed, she pointed out it would cost too much to return the rooms to their original colors.

Money was indeed a problem. Costs were running into the tens of millions and there were fears of a public backlash. Jackie proposed the creation of an illustrated guidebook that could be sold to White House visitors. Close to two million people a year were taking tours of the house without paying an admission fee, and if the souvenir book could be made affordable, sales would go a long way to paying for the project. Once the considerable hurdles were overcome, she jumped into the book's production with the same enthusiasm she had for the project itself, supervising the photography, editing the text, and even suggesting typefaces. The book, which went on sale on July 4, 1962, sold out its first printing in three months, and it is still selling briskly all these years later.

Jackie also went after well-heeled Americans to help. She appointed potential donors to special committees, and she gently twisted their arms when they showed up for meetings. Some were asked for large cash grants, others to donate significant pieces from their own personal collections. Sometimes the donors were surprised to find out how much she knew about their holdings, but they were usually much more surprised at how easily she was able to talk them into parting with them, even when they were determined not to. Jackie Kennedy was as charming as she was gracious and she knew how to get what she wanted.

Below: Jackie was given many impressive gifts for her White House restoration project, including a beautiful antique silver pitcher.

Above: Jackie visited virtually every corner of the world on goodwill missions. One of the highlights was a tour of India's Taj Mahal.

Although she normally hated publicity, she agreed to write several articles about the project for national magazines. Reader response uncovered artifacts that had escaped her eye, and the knowledge of what she was doing earned more public support for her project. She was reluctant to agree when CBS approached with an idea to tape an hour-long tour of the restored house with its reporter Charles Collingwood because she didn't want to be pegged as "a decorator," and she distrusted television anyway. After she was talked into it, she even suggested that her husband might be persuaded to put in an appearance as though he were as shy as she was.

She also suggested that she could do introductions in French and Spanish for international syndication, and the program was eventually seen in 106 countries. The initial broadcast reached more than 46 million Americans, and millions more bought the book that was produced to recreate the tour.

At the same time that she was renovating the White House, Jackie also worked tirelessly on the creation of the National Cultural Center—later to be known as the John F. Kennedy Center for the Performing Arts—which had been set in motion during the Eisenhower administration and seemed to be languishing. She was also passionate about saving Abu Simbel, an ancient Egyptian monument that was threatened by the construction of a dam. She lobbied Congress for funds and she solicited private donations, but her biggest coup was arranging to have the treasure of Tutankhamen brought to the United States for public display. She called for $50 million in donations to save Abu Simbel after Americans had been dazzled by the Egyptian antiquities, and she raised nearly all of it.

Jackie also took several trips abroad on her own—to Latin America, to India, and Europe—on goodwill tours, and with each of them, her star rose even higher. She cut back at the beginning of 1963 when she found out that she was pregnant again, but her White House entertaining and the job of charming visiting kings and queens, dukes, and duchesses went on without a break, although she left the day-to-day details to her staff. She found time to escalate her war with the press, too. She had always insisted on approving any photographs of herself or her children, but now she extended it to every picture taken in the White House no matter who was in front of the camera. And while she had lost her temper many times with her staff, her outbursts were developing into stormy tantrums. She even fired her social secretary, Tish Baldridge, an old friend who had been at her side since Jack's last campaign for the Senate.

Below: Soviet Premier Nikita Khrushchev gave Jackie a pair of puppies that had been born to the first dogs in space. They became part of the Kennedy menagerie, which already included four others.

Weeks before her tenth wedding anniversary, Jackie's baby arrived five weeks early while she was vacationing in Hyannisport. Their third child, Patrick Bouvier Kennedy, was in an incubator for three days before he died, and something in Jackie died with him.

She recovered on an extended visit to Greece with her sister, but when she got back she only touched base at the White House before moving on to her weekend retreat in Virginia. But she was back in time to go with Jack on a political fence-mending trip to Texas. She made her first formal White House appearance after her baby's death at a reception for Supreme Court justices on November 20, 1963, and they were on their way to Texas the next morning.

Above: Jack and Jackie ride into downtown Dallas, and into history, with Texas Governor and Mrs. John Connally on November 22, 1963.

After stops in San Antonio and Houston, Jack and Jackie arrived at a Fort Worth hotel in the small hours of the morning. The next morning, November 22, they went on to Dallas and destiny. A motorcade was arranged to bring the president and Texas governor John Connally to their speaking engagement. The president was seated next to Jackie in the back of their open limousine when three bullets tore through his skull, as their car steered into downtown Dallas. Jackie wasn't hurt, but Jack was on the brink of death.

Her pink wool suit and her pillbox hat were covered with blood and gore, but she refused to even think of changing. She regarded it as a badge of her husband's courage. "Let them see what they've done," she said. "I want them to see."

Jackie was with him in the hospital trauma room when Jack died an hour after the shots rang out. Not knowing whether or not this might be part of a larger plot, the Secret Service ordered the new president, Lyndon Johnson, and Jackie, too, back to the airport and the safety of the presidential aircraft, *Air Force One*. In spite of the possible risk, Jackie insisted on riding in the white hearse with her husband's body.

Jack's close friend Ken O'Donnell was at Jackie's side during the trip back to Washington, and he recalled, "I don't think I have ever experienced the kind of courage she demonstrated, first at the hospital in Dallas and on the plane to Washington, and then during the funeral.... She acquitted herself magnificently and became a symbol for all of us, of great nobility and character in an age of general impoverishment of the soul." In the week that followed, it would have been impossible to find an American who didn't agree.

Jackie was very sensitive about her husband's place in history, but she despaired that "only bitter old men write history." When journalist Theodore White, who was writing an assessment of the assassination for *Life* magazine, interviewed her, he said that she told him, "Jack's life had more to do with myth, magic, saga, and story than political theory....

Before her husband's casket was closed, Jackie placed her bloodstained wedding ring on his finger.

Below: Possibly one of the most moving images of Jackie was when she stood at the swearing-in ceremony of Lyndon B. Johnson while wearing her bloodstained pink suit.

To spare Jackie more pain, the White House nanny was delegated to tell six-year-old Caroline about her father's death. Three-year-old John, Jr., wasn't told.

History belongs to heroes, and heroes must not be forgotten."

It was then that she told him about Jack's apparent fascination with the Broadway musical *Camelot,* especially the song that includes the line, "Don't let it be forgot, that once there was a spot, for one brief shining moment, that was known as Camelot." White was so taken by her passion in telling the story that, although he believed it was rewriting history, he agreed to put it in his article, and it turned out to be exactly the right touch. "So the epitaph of the Kennedy administration became Camelot," he wrote, "a magic moment in American history, when gallant men danced with beautiful women, when great deeds were done and when the White House became the center of the universe." It was the image that Jackie had wanted to create. That it had existed for only a thousand days made the loss all the more tragic.

After Camelot

A few days after the funeral, Jackie wrote to a White House staff member that, "First I didn't want in, now I can't seem to leave." She moved to a borrowed house on N Street in nearby Georgetown, and President Johnson arranged for her to have federal office space and a small staff. But apart from winding down her husband's affairs, Jackie had no idea at all what was going to come next.

She politely turned down invitations to White House functions, and she refused several offers of government positions. In the meantime, she was still the focus of attention in Washington. People crowded both sides of the street for a glimpse of her or a chance to reach out and touch little Caroline and John-John, and tour buses made the house a more important part of their routes than the White House itself. The police and Secret Service had to carve paths through the crowds so that Jackie and the kids could come and go. She didn't lack for company, but her guests found her a distracted hostess, deep in denial and grief.

She bought her own Georgetown house, and decorating it was good therapy for her, although her heart wasn't really in it. "Can anyone understand how it is to have lived in the White House and then, suddenly, to be living alone as the President's widow?" she asked. "There's something final about it." But at thirty-four, "final" was hardly acceptable.

She took several short vacations to get away from the memories that were around every corner in Washington, but the trip that made her feel "like a human being again" was a long weekend in New York. It was soon followed by another, even longer one, and then she decided to sell her house as well as the one in the mountains of Virginia, and bought a fifteen-room co-op apartment on Fifth Avenue across from Central Park.

Below: Caroline and John, Jr. with their mother after a tribute to the fallen president at the Capitol. Behind them are Jack's brother, Robert F. Kennedy, and his sister Jean Kennedy Smith.

People who knew her were amazed at the transformation the move made in Jackie. She had always been at home in New York City, and she liked being able to "walk the streets without being singled out." Her old zest came back, and she jumped into the effort to organize the John F. Kennedy Memorial Library in the Boston area. She made selections from her husband's memorabilia for display there, and she began a massive one-woman telephone blitz to raise money for it. She was always available for fund-raising luncheons, dinners, and cocktail parties, and she traveled anywhere she had to tracking down and interviewing architects for the project. The assignment eventually went to I. M. Pei, who years later would be rumored to be in the running to marry Jackie.

She found time to put in an appearance at the 1964 Democratic National Convention, which many political professionals believed went a long way to assuring that President Johnson would win a term of his own. Then she went back to New York to campaign for Bobby Kennedy, who was running for the Senate there. She privately told Bobby that he shouldn't expect her to show up at the polls. "I'm not going to vote for any other person because this vote would have been his," she told him.

She enrolled Caroline in the prestigious Convent School of the Sacred Heart, and John-John at the equally respected Saint David's School. She took them to the world's fair, to the circus, and for long afternoons in Central Park. She coached John-John's introduction to horseback riding, and she encouraged Caroline to enter competitions with her own horse, Macaroni. Caroline didn't win as many blue ribbons as her mother had at that age, but even Jackie had to admit that her child was a more gracious loser than she had been.

Jackie was also often seen at the opera and she indulged her love for the ballet, and she was the undisputed star at the grand opening of both the Metropolitan Opera House and Philharmonic Hall at Lincoln Center. She never lacked for a notable escort, and the tabloids couldn't resist looking for romantic attachments to them, even though they were wrong every time. Jackie received a steady stream of VIP visitors at her Fifth Avenue apartment, from President Johnson to Adlai Stevenson and Haile Selassie, not to mention a Greek shipping tycoon named Aristotle Onassis, and she was on every New York hostess's A-list.

Her social schedule kept her in Manhattan from Monday through Friday, but she frequently spent weekends and holidays in the New Jersey hunt country, where she had become a member of the Essex Fox Hounds Hunt Club and bought an estate at Bernardsville, the unofficial capital of America's horsey set.

Gradually, Jackie's outlook became international again and she took frequent "sentimental journeys" abroad both alone and with her children.

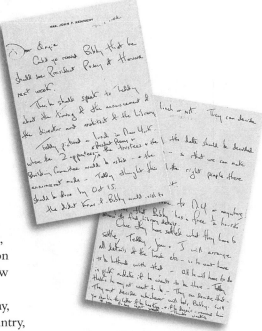

Above: A handwritten note from Jackie to an aide about plans for the John F. Kennedy Memorial Library.

Although the ever-present paparazzi took careful note of her encounters with Aristotle Onassis whenever she went to Europe, they thought nothing of it. He was involved with soprano Maria Callas at the time, and that made better copy. Besides, the Greek billionaire and Jackie had an arm's-length relationship that was almost cold. But it began to heat up little by little, and although he said that he couldn't stand her friends and she asserted that she couldn't abide his business associates, they were seen together more and more often, both in New York and the Greek islands. It was even an open secret that Ari, as everyone called him, was augmenting Jackie's $30,000 monthly allowance.

Jackie O.

Jackie still hated reporters and photographers, but she had an adoring public who couldn't get enough of her. Like it or not, she had star quality. She had soon had enough of it, and she made a decision that she would marry Aristotle Onassis as a way of getting out of the country, even if he himself didn't seem interested. After the Robert Kennedy assassination, she said, "I wanted to go away. They were killing Kennedys and I didn't want them to harm my children. I wanted to go off. I wanted to be somewhere safe."

Onassis was a reluctant fiancé until the very end, and they managed to keep their engagement a secret, largely because they themselves didn't know where it was going to lead. Even the forty-carat diamond ring on her finger didn't attract any press attention. It finally became public knowledge when the *Boston Herald* put the story on its front page, and Jackie and her wedding party were on a plane bound for Greece two days later. When news broke of her sudden departure, it started a firestorm in the press and most Americans felt betrayed. But it was too late to do anything about it; their Jackie had run away.

The wedding took place in Skorpios on October 20, 1968, a month shy of the fifth anniversary of Jack Kennedy's assassination. They honeymooned in Athens and took a cruise to the island of Rhodes aboard his palatial yacht, *Christina*. They traveled often, but their home was on the relatively isolated island of Skorpios, where Jackie, typically, completely redecorated Ari's house to suit her own taste. She made attempts to upgrade her new husband's wardrobe, too, but he put his foot down.

Ari didn't protest his bride's spending and strange behavior very often, but their marriage began to show cracks almost from the start. She was bored, she didn't care for Greek food, and her husband's business associates still hadn't improved in her estimation.

Caught by the Paparazzi

The problem of ubiquitous photographers seemed to have been solved when Aristotle Onassis financed Jackie's lawsuit against Ron Galella, one of the most aggressive of them. The result was that Galella was enjoined from coming within less than twenty-five feet of Jackie and thirty feet of her children. A similar suit sent a Greek photographer to jail for four months. But while Jackie and Ari were vacationing on the island of Skorpios, ten photographers in diving suits and armed with telescopic lenses on underwater cameras snapped an eighteen-page portfolio of them sunbathing in the nude. After the pictures were published, Jackie brushed it off in public, but she suggested that her lawyers should file suit against all the publishers who had bought them, but there were so many of them that it was impossible. All Ari had to say was, "It happens that sometimes I take off my pants to put on my bathing suit. Anything's possible."

She didn't care much for his family, either. If she had had a problem being absorbed by the Kennedy family, that was child's play compared to becoming an Onassis.

Ari decided to bring the whole thing to an end. "I've had it up to here with her," he told a lawyer. "I cannot understand her. All she does is spend, spend, spend—and she's never in the same place I am. If I'm in Paris, she's in New York. If I go to Skorpios, she goes to London.... She's never with me. We socialize in different circles." He hired private detectives to shadow her and he had her telephones tapped, and he rewrote his will. He even romanced newspaper columnists to drive a wedge into her image, which had recovered in the United States by then in spite of her perceived betrayal. The planned divorce never took place. At the beginning of 1975, Ari collapsed with chest pains and was flown to Paris for treatment. Jackie flew to New York, and she was skiing in New Hampshire when her husband died on March 15, 1975.

Above: Aristotle Onassis and his new bride aboard his yacht near the island of Skorpios, where they went to live in near-palatial splendor.

After a nasty court fight over Ari's will, Jackie ended up with $26 million plus another $20 million to cover taxes and legal fees. Back in New York, she settled into the quiet life of a rich widow, entertaining little and shopping less than she had recently. After a while of what to her was a listless existence, she took a job with publisher Viking Press as an editor. It was a part-time job—she only worked four days a week—and the $10,000 salary was less than her budget for hairdressers, but now Jackie O., as people were beginning to call her, had become a career woman. She had no experience as a book editor, except possibly for her work on the White House guidebook, but she was an eager learner. After contributing to the publishing of several books, she took on *In the Russian Style,* an illustrated book on the Imperial Court in the eighteenth and nineteenth centuries tied in with an exhibition at the Metropolitan Museum's Costume Institute. The reviews were mixed, but it established her as a professional. She eventually quit the Viking job, but moved to Doubleday, and broadened her horizons from art books to books by and about celebrities. After all, it takes one to know one.

What Jackie longed for most was privacy, and to keep John, Jr., and Caroline completely out of the limelight. In that regard, she was masterful. She also avoided, as much as she could, any involvement with the Kennedy family. She had never felt particularly close to Jack's sisters, and except for Bobby, who was now dead, and Ted, who watched out for her, Jackie kept the extended family at arm's length, and she avoided contact between their children and hers so that Caroline and John wouldn't take a backseat to them or become involved in their "unstructured" lives.

Jackie was less successful at preserving her own privacy. She was a boldface name in countless gossip columns, photographers followed her everywhere, and she never went out in public without being mobbed by her adoring and curious fans. There was nothing

Jackie refused to eat with Ari because she thought that his table manners were atrocious.

she could do about it, but she never got used to it. She never lacked for gentlemen friends and escorts, but with one or two exceptions, they were only platonic relationships.

Her only serious romance seems to have been with Maurice Templesman, who was a constant visitor to the house she had built on Martha's Vineyard. He was a wealthy diamond dealer and longtime friend who some carped was "a poor man's Aristotle Onassis." A short, portly, older man who smoked expensive cigars, Templesman was anything but poor. Like Onassis, he had a golden touch when it came to making money and, like Ari, he showered Jackie with expensive gifts. He also owned an impressive yacht. It wasn't the *Christina*, but it was good enough for them to use for long luxurious cruises together.

In spite of widespread rumors that he might become Jackie's third husband, that was out of the question. Maurice was already married and his orthodox Jewish wife didn't believe in divorce, although she did kick him out of their house. Jackie understood. "You don't have to be married to be together," he said. And she had been independent for too long to want to tie herself down again, anyway.

In her fifties, Jackie began to tone down her jet-set image, and she became an activist New York gadfly. Among many other causes, she led the fight to have Grand Central Terminal declared a landmark, New York's first, so that developers couldn't desecrate it, and later she fought against the removal of landmark status from St. Bartholomew's Church so a high-rise building could be constructed over part of its property. She also occasionally traveled abroad in support of arts and culture.

Jackie became a grandmother—and she had someone new to shop for—in 1988 when Caroline, now Mrs. Ed Schlossberg, gave birth to a girl she named Rose after her own grandmother Kennedy. At the same time, John, Jr., began his career as an associate in a prestigious law firm, on his way to becoming an assistant prosecutor in the Manhattan district attorney's office after he finished law school. John also introduced his Uncle Ted at the 1988 Democratic National Convention, and *People* magazine hailed him as "The Sexiest Man Alive."

Jackie entered the third act of her life when she turned sixty in 1989. With Templesman's help, she was able to have her Onassis settlement raised to $104 million, and she never had to think about money again. The following spring, Caroline had another daughter, Tatiana Cecilia Kennedy Schlossberg, and Jackie was a grandmother twice over, and then again in 1993 when her third grandchild, John Bouvier Kennedy Schlossberg, was born. The press and public stopped badgering her—she was still recognized, but people kept a respectful distance—and she slipped into a life out of the spotlight, which is what she claimed she had wanted all along. She went to book parties and receptions for causes she supported, and she dug into her duties as a Doubleday editor with a new enthusiasm. Ironically, although she

"She wasn't merely a celebrity, but a legend; no, not a legend but a myth—no, not just a myth, rather a historical archetype, virtually a demiurge. I don't know, do you even address a demiurge?"

—Norman Mailer on Jackie Kennedy's legacy

claimed to despise being in the public eye, she was fascinated by the celebrities who had become her stock in trade.

Most of all, Jackie enjoyed being a grandmother and she was with the Schlossberg children nearly every day—they called her "grandmere" most of the time, but she was just as often called "Grand Jackie" and that suited her at this stage of her life.

At the end of 1993, Jackie was diagnosed with non-Hodgkin's Lymphoma, and she began receiving chemotherapy treatments. The effects were hard to disguise, but she waved off comments by saying that she had the flu. She also executed a living will so that there wouldn't be any question of prolonging her life if the disease progressed.

By spring, it wasn't possible for her to disguise her condition any longer. She was wearing a wig to hide her hair loss, and she had dropped more than forty pounds. When an official announcement was finally made, she was undergoing radiation treatments. She still showed up for work and outwardly she was as cheerful as ever. Maurice Templesman moved into her apartment and he was with her night and day as her condition slowly deteriorated, and he was at her side, along with Caroline and John, through every waking moment of the ordeal. In the meantime, she received visitors, family members, or close friends, one or two at a time. She died on May 19, 1994, at the age of sixty-four.

As she had made certain that she would be allowed to die with dignity, Jackie also had outlined the details of how she wanted her funeral and burial handled. The service took place at the Church of St. Ignatius Loyola, where she had been baptized, and her body was flown to Washington for a private burial ceremony as she was laid to rest next to her husband Jack. She bequeathed her personal papers to her children with the suggestion that they should not be published. Jackie finally had the privacy that she had longed for all her life.

> *"And now the journey is over. Too short, alas, too short. It was filled with adventure and wisdom, laughter and love, gallantry and grace."*
>
> —*Maurice Templesman on Jackie Kennedy's death*

Below: The building that houses the John F. Kennedy Memorial Library and Museum was designed by I.M. Pei.

Visiting the John F. Kennedy Memorial Library and Museum

In the last years of her life, Jacqueline Kennedy devoted countless hours and energy to the creation of the Kennedy Library, which is not only a repository of the president's papers but also a museum with twenty-one permanent exhibits, including a special one on the First Lady.

It is located on Columbia Point in Boston, near I-93, and is open from 9:00 A.M. to 5:00 P.M. every day except Thanksgiving, December 25, and January 1. There is a small admission charge for visits to the museum, but access to the research rooms, which are open on weekdays (except federal holidays), is free, although they are not open for general browsing but restricted to researchers.

To reach the library from the south or north use I-93 (Southwest Expressway) to Dorchester, exit 14, and follow signs to the University of Massachusetts or the library. From the west, exit from the Massachusetts Turnpike (I-90) to "Expressway South" and then to exit 15. Public transportation is available on the MBTA Rapid Transit Red Line to the JFK/UMASS station, where shuttle buses are available. For more information, call 617-514-1960 or 866-JFK-1960.

Lady Bird Johnson

Country Girl

When Claudia Taylor was two years old, her nurse, Alice Tittle, said that she was "purty as a lady bird," and it was true. What she might have said was "ladybug" because she was referring to the nursery rhyme, "Ladybug, ladybug, fly away home." But the red insects were known as lady *birds* in those parts of Texas, and from that time forward, so was Claudia Taylor.

Her father had migrated from Alabama in the late 1880s and settled down about eighteen miles west of the Louisiana border in a little east Texas town called Karnack. It looked a lot like home, except that the land there was better for cotton farming. Better still was its location near Caddo Lake, the only natural lake in all of Texas, which made it cheap and easy to ship the crop by steamboat to Shreveport and then on to New Orleans.

Thomas Jefferson Taylor, who was known as T.J. and was later called "Cap'n" by folks who owed him their living, invested nearly all of the money he had, $500, in a piece of land at the intersection of two old hunting trails and then he became a sharecropper. It wasn't very long before he had accumulated enough money to do what he'd had in mind all along—build a country store. He put his name over the entrance and billed himself as a "dealer in everything." Within a year he was on his way back to Alabama flushed with success and ready to ask Minnie Lee Pattillo to marry him.

Minnie Lee's parents, each from a long line of successful cotton planters, thought that T.J. was "white trash," but Minnie didn't, and although they refused to go to her wedding, she was soon "gone to Texas" as Mrs. Taylor. She had several crates of books in the back of the buckboard, mostly biographies and histories salted with novels and poetry and many books dealing with philosophy, spiritual theories, and mysticism. "She dipped into the occult and beyond the fringe," said Lady Bird, who grew up with her mother's little library.

Before he left to marry Minnie, T.J. had built a house for his bride that was one of the best in town. It was next door to his general store so that he could tend to business any hour of the day. He had bought a cotton gin by then and

Claudia Alta Taylor Johnson

Born
December 22, 1912, Karnack, Texas

Parents
Thomas Jefferson Taylor and Minnie Lee Pattillo Taylor

Marriage
November 17, 1934, to Lyndon Baines Johnson (1905-73)

Children
Lynda Bird (1944-); Lucy (Luci) Baines (1947-)

> *"If I had known the position in the world I was going to hold, I'd have changed two things: my name and my nose."*
>
> —*Lady Bird Johnson on her perceived shortcomings*

Above: Nurse Alice Tittle said that baby Claudia Taylor was "purty as a lady bird." Everyone agreed and the name stuck.

Below: Lady Bird was a baby when her mother died and she went to live with her grandmother.

the local farmers depended on him at odd times. They depended on him for advances of seed money in the spring, too, and most of them planted it on land that he rented to them, much of it acquired through foreclosure on unpaid debts. Cap'n Taylor soon became the biggest landowner in Harrison County, and before long he owned more than 15,000 acres. Much of it produced cotton at the rate of a five-hundred-pound bale every year and the rest was planted in corn and other cash crops. Taylor was the richest man in the county, too, and to be sure that everyone noticed, he built a seventeen-room mansion on a bluff outside of town that became known locally as the Brick House. It had a pair of white columns thirty feet high out front and it would have been a showplace back in Alabama in the days before the war.

The Taylors needed a bigger house for more than making a statement. Their first child, Thomas, had been born in 1901, and their second, Antonio, came along three years later. But Minnie and her boys didn't move into the new house when it was finished. She had gone home to her family in Alabama— some said it was because T.J. had taken up with another woman, but she herself cited poor health. She was gone more than five years, some of the time traveling with her sister Effie, to Battle Creek, Michigan, to soak up W. K. Kellogg's health and nutrition philosophies at his famous sanitarium. After she went back to the big house in Karnack, Minnie suffered two miscarriages, but then in December 1912, when she was forty-four years old, she gave birth to a daughter she named Claudia for her brother Claud.

In spite of Kellogg's regimen, which Minnie followed slavishly, she was still in delicate health. She didn't feel up to raising three children, and she sent eleven-year-old Tommy and eight-year-old Antonio off to a boarding school in New York's Catskill Mountains, and then she began making inquiries about schools for her baby daughter.

When Minnie was fifty and pregnant again, she tripped and fell down a set of stairs, losing the baby she was carrying. A few days later, she lost her own life as well. Her two sons, away at school, weren't told of their mother's death for nearly a year, but little Lady Bird was at her mother's side when she died. It is the only clear memory she ever had of her.

Lady Bird's father shipped her off to her mother's family in Alabama, but she arrived back in the care of her Aunt Effie in time to start school. It was a one-room school where seven grades were taught together, although there were rarely more than a dozen youngsters gathered around the potbellied stove at any one time. There was no love lost between T.J. and Effie, and she regarded Lady Bird as an orphan who had become her sole responsibility.

When Lady Bird was eleven, Aunt Effie took her along when she went back to the Kellogg sanitarium for a refresher course and help for her "nervous condition." It was the first time that the girl had been served dinner on a starched tablecloth and she wore her Sunday best every evening. The fare was strictly vegetarian, which struck her as a bit odd, but she loved every bit of it. She enjoyed the exercise classes and she looked forward to the massages and mineral baths, but most of all she luxuriated in the attention she got as the only

When Lady Bird went to high school in Marshall, Texas, her father had one of his employees drive her there in his pickup truck, but she had him drop her off a few blocks away to avoid the indignity.

youngster in the place. She picked up ideas about nutrition and exercise there that would stay with her throughout the rest of her life.

Aunt Effie had truly become a second mother to Lady Bird. T.J. had remarried, but his new wife wasn't part of the household, and Lady Bird liked that just fine. She found the woman, the former Beulah Wisdom, "pretty, but in a coarse and crude kind of way," and she shed no tears when the marriage eventually ended in divorce.

Still, Beulah had served as a kind of role model for Lady Bird. They weren't far apart in age and her stepmother was an east Texas version of a Jazz Age flapper. Except for her teacher, who became her tutor in the seventh grade after the school closed down, the only other woman she could relate to was Aunt Effie who, although sweet and caring, was "sickly" and needed more attention than she gave.

Lady Bird was a straight-A student at the high school in Marshall, the county seat, but she was relieved when the final grades were posted and she had come in third in her class. It meant that she wouldn't have to make a graduation speech in front of her entire class. It was enough to have been able to graduate high school at the age of fifteen!

With that behind her, Lady Bird went off to summer school at the University of Alabama to study history and journalism. But she missed Texas and in the fall she enrolled at St. Mary's Episcopal School for Girls, a Dallas junior college, which led to her becoming an Episcopalian. Her father objected to her college career—it was considered wasteful for a girl to study beyond high school—but he bought her a new Buick, and he gave her a large monthly allowance and lines of credit in the local stores anyway. She was at the top of her class, too, studying French and discovering dramatics. For her second two years of college, Lady Bird enrolled at the University of Texas at Austin. She graduated from there with honors in 1933, and she stayed on for another two years of journalism studies and graduated cum laude at the age of twenty-one. Lady Bird was determined to become a newspaper reporter; it suited her personality as well as her abilities, and she had "taken up" with David Dawson, the Austin correspondent of the *Dallas Morning News.* "Just to be on the safe side," as she put it, she also earned a teacher's certificate and she learned typing and shorthand so that she might be able to get a job as a secretary as an opening into the business world, even though well-raised young Texas women weren't expected do such things in those days.

Above: As a girl, Lady Bird was dedicated to keeping fit and she shared her enthusiasm with friends. Her interest in exercise and nutrition stayed with her all through her life.

Above: Lady Bird graduated from the University of Texas at Austin in 1934, and returned to graduate school for a degree in journalism.

Campus Opportunities

Lady Bird decided to attend the University of Texas because it was a coeducational institution at a time when there were few of them to choose from. Male students outnumbered coeds there by four to one, and as one of them put it, "Most girls at UT were majoring in a Mrs." Lady Bird was not one of them. It was the variety of social options that appealed to her after two years in a girls' junior college, and she was more serious about learning than even most of the boys. But she had more spending money than most of her friends, and she was one of the few on campus who had her own car, so it was inevitable that even without her natural charm and pleasing appearance she would become one of the most popular students at UT. She never lacked for dates, and she never missed a campus dance or party. But she never "went steady" with anyone until her last two years there, when she met reporter David Dawson. The romance ended with her graduation.

New Worlds

As a graduation present, Lady Bird's father paid for a trip to New York and Washington, D.C., for her and her roommate, Cecile Harrison. Before they left, another friend, Gene Boehringer, who worked in the Texas government, told her to look up a friend of hers when she got to the capital. He was a congressman's secretary, and he knew his way around. But that was what worried her. She wasn't interested in phoning a total stranger, especially one who "knew his way around."

Lyndon Baines Johnson was a stranger no more when Lady Bird met him in Gene's office back in Austin a few weeks later. "He was excessively thin," she recalled, "but very very good looking, with lots of black wavy hair, and the most outspoken, straightforward, determined manner I had ever encountered. I knew that I had met someone quite remarkable, but I didn't know quite what." Lyndon Johnson had that effect on just about everybody he met.

He already had a date for that evening, but he invited her to have breakfast with him the next morning. Lyndon was not one to waste time or miss an opportunity. Lady Bird had an early-morning appointment with an architect to talk about restoring the Brick House back in Karnack and she stood him up, or at least she nearly did. Anyone else might not have waited an hour for her, but Lyndon did, and after breakfast he drove her down into the Hill Country where his roots were. On the way, he told her everything she might want to know about himself, and some things she might not, even how much life insurance he had. "He told me all sort of things that I thought were extraordinary for a first date," she said, and she surprised herself by how much she revealed about her own life and dreams.

The next day he drove her to meet his mother, and the day after that they went to the King ranch to meet his boss, Representative Richard Kleberg, whose family was a part owner of the place. It was the biggest ranch in the country, and it was even bigger than some states.

When the time came for Lyndon to go back to Washington, they had become inseparable and he suggested that because it was on his way, he'd drive her home to Karnack. He stayed overnight, giving her father a chance to size him up, and she said, "I could see that Daddy was impressed right away." She was sure of it when T.J. whispered to her, "You've been bringing home a lot of boys. This time you've brought a man." Although they had known each other for only a week, Lyndon knew what he wanted and it was Lady Bird Taylor. Before he left, he asked her to marry him. Lady Bird might have seen it coming, but she didn't know what to say except that she needed time to think about it.

Then the phone calls began; a day didn't pass without several of them. Seven weeks went by with no acceptance, and so Lyndon went back to Karnack, not only to ask her again but to suggest that they should get married "not next year…but about two weeks from now—or a month from now—or right away." But Lady Bird wasn't ready to make such a decision until she had talked it over with her Aunt Effie, who was in a hospital back in Alabama.

Lyndon explained what happened next. "Bird went to see her Aunt Effie who had raised her, and asked her whether she should marry me. Aunt Effie told her not to, and Bird went back to Texas and told her father and me. Her father said the aunt would never agree, and for her to go ahead. We drove to San Antonio, and she still hadn't said yes until we got there. I sent a friend over to buy a ring, and we were married at the Episcopal Church on the square." He was twenty-six years old; she was not quite twenty-two.

Lady Bird had lived a life of comfort up until then. Her father was rich, and he was more than generous as far as she was concerned. But now she went to Washington to live on Lyndon's $267-a-month salary. It wasn't easy, and it was made worse by a nearly steady stream of family and friends who had always had a hankering to see Washington and used their one-bedroom apartment as a base when they did. Aunt Effie visited and she stayed a month; others didn't stay as long, but the sofa bed in the living room was pulled out nearly every night, and so was the roll-away bed that they had to buy.

Lady Bird had never had to learn how to take care of a house, and now she had to scrub, sweep, vacuum, dust, make beds, and wash dishes. Most of all, she needed to learn how to cook, so she bought a cookbook and taught herself. There wasn't much else she had to do, though—it was a small apartment after all—and she used the time she had left over to read books, magazines, and newspapers and mark off passages she thought

Below: Lyndon and Lady Bird began their married life in Washington, D.C., where he was a member of Congress. Moving from Texas was only one of the adjustments she had to make.

Lyndon didn't like Lady Bird's taste in clothes, and starting buying her a new wardrobe. She didn't like his taste, either, but she went along with it.

Lyndon ought to see. Mostly she had to verbalize them for him because he preferred learning by listening to actually reading.

Lyndon was a busy man in those days. He desperately wanted to get ahead in his career. After they had been married for nine months, he quit his job to take another as the Texas administrator for the National Youth Administration (NYA), one of President Roosevelt's New Deal programs created to get young people off the streets and into part-time jobs and back to school. It meant that they would have to move back to Austin and that Lyndon would be working harder than ever—but so would Lady Bird. Their house became the unofficial headquarters of the NYA and it fell to her to cook for his new associates and to clean up after them. Fortunately, she had figured it all out by then; her graciousness was built in.

About a year and a half after they went back to Texas, the local congressman died and a special election was held. Naturally, Lyndon wanted to run, but he wasn't well known outside his own county and it was the smallest in the district. Ten candidates had already announced their intentions and, besides, he didn't have any money to finance a campaign.

Lady Bird took a long walk with a state senator and learned that out of the field of ten rivals Lyndon could beat four or maybe five of them, and that it would cost $10,000 to find out. A fifty-fifty chance was good enough for Lady Bird. She put in a call to her father. "Daddy," she said, "do you suppose you could put ten thousand dollars in the bank for me? Lyndon wants to run for Congress." He could, he did, and Lyndon threw his hat into the ring the very next day.

Lady Bird was proud of the way he campaigned. "He was never as young, never so vigorous, and never so wonderful." Much as she wanted to, she didn't make speeches for him because, "in 1937, it simply wasn't done in Texas." But he won without her physical presence and he won with a no-holds-barred defense of the New Deal. That impressed the president and so did the young congressman after they met. Before long, Lyndon found himself a member of the House Naval Affairs Committee, one of the most important in Roosevelt's eyes. He also found himself invited to frequent White House breakfasts, and the association was so potent that no one opposed him when he ran for reelection in 1938 and then again in 1940.

The day after the start of World War II, Lyndon went into the navy, and Lady Bird took over his congressional office. She had plenty of respect for his staff, but she believed it was important for him to have someone as close to him as his wife help his constituents understand that he hadn't lost touch with them. It also helped her understand the pressures and the challenges of his job. "I have always been much more interested in politics since then," she said. For his part, Lyndon said, "The Tenth District would have elected her over me if she had run." But she didn't run, he did. And he won even though he was thousands of miles away in the South Pacific.

He was back in his office in 1942 after less than a year away when he found out that an Austin radio station, KTBC, was for sale. It was tiny, with only 250 watts of power, and it didn't broadcast at night. It had only nine employees and an astronomical debt, but the Johnsons were both interested anyway. Both had flirted with the idea of a career in journalism and they dreamed of buying a newspaper one day, and this could be a much less expensive substitute.

Lady Bird's mother had left her a tidy inheritance and her father had invested it well, but he had remarried again and he wanted to get out from under the responsibility. Surrendering the money would solve his problem and Lady Bird really had her heart set on the small radio station. The deal was done, and Lady Bird took up residence in Austin to turn it into a going concern. She eventually succeeded, but it took her seven months. When it turned its first profit—$18—she flew back to Washington to pick up where she'd left off. Less than twenty years later, KTBC had become a multimillion-dollar radio and television enterprise with no debt and a hundred employees. For a variety of reasons, not the least of which was that it was bought with her money and built with her business sense, Lady Bird Johnson was its majority stockholder. She had also inherited a large tract of land from her Alabama kin, and she seeded it in pine trees to be used in making pulp, and she became the most successful tree farmer in the state.

In the meantime, Lady Bird was a congressional wife, and she took the job seriously, although money was tight and wartime rationing made life a chore for everyone. One of her greatest delights was conducting tours of Washington for visiting constituents, and in those days many of them were more than just casual tourists. The war effort had brought businessmen and industrialists there and her contacts with their families went a long way toward boosting Lyndon's reputation where it really counted.

Through it all, the Johnsons lived in ten different apartments in five years between Austin and Washington. Aunt Effie had become a permanent guest by then, and she felt the strain of packing and repacking, too, finally suggesting that she might loan Lady Bird the down payment on a house—out of her future inheritance, of course. Lady Bird found a two-story, eight-room house

Social Whirl

Like all other congressional wives, Lady Bird bought copies of the annual Green Guide *to Washington society and she used it to cut through the maze of people she needed to visit. She had calling cards printed, and every day she dressed up in a hat, a fashionable dress, and white gloves before setting out. "It was like running a business," she said. Mondays were reserved for the wives of Supreme Court justices and Tuesdays for other congressional wives. On Wednesdays she called on cabinet wives, Thursdays the wives of senators, and Fridays the diplomatic corps. She interrupted the routine whenever she was invited to the White House. "I usually made the calls between four and six in the afternoon," she said, "and I hoped the ladies weren't in so I wouldn't have to stay. Most of them weren't, thank heaven." But she always left her card to show that she had fulfilled that part of her social obligation.*

Congressman Johnson didn't approve of owning a house in Washington because he believed it would make him appear less a Texan to the voters.

in northwest Washington, but Lyndon took the wind out of her sails when he couldn't find time to listen to her breathless description of it. She was furious at him for the first time in their married life. "I have nothing to look forward to but another election," she shouted. It shocked him into agreeing to buy the place, but not until he had renegotiated the price and convinced himself that it had been his idea in the first place.

But a house of their own didn't solve the packing and moving problem. They still had to live in his congressional district when Congress wasn't in session, and their economic situation dictated that the Washington house had to be rented when they were away. It wasn't hard to do considering the housing shortage in wartime Washington, but the family still had to put their things in storage, which wasn't much less effort than moving it all to Austin. But Lady Bird coped with it. She was thrilled to have her own house. "I had desperately wanted a nest," she confided to a friend.

Above: Daughters Lynda and Luci were an asset, along with Lady Bird, to Lyndon's campaign for the Senate in 1948. It was close, but he won, and their lives changed again.

She credited having a nest with increasing her lifelong desire to have a family, and after several miscarriages, she finally gave birth to a daughter in March 1944. Lyndon's mother, Rebekah, came to Washington to help her and she suggested that they name the baby Lynda after her father, and that her middle name should be Bird for her mother. Lady Bird, who had been trying to escape that name all her life, reluctantly agreed and her delighted husband pointed out that they were a "one suitcase family," all three of them had the same initials, LBJ.

They made it a quartet three years later when their second daughter was born and they named her Lucy Baines, after Lyndon's youngest sister, Lucia. Baines was her Grandmother Johnson's maiden name. (When she was a teenager, Lucy changed the spelling of her name to Luci, which was a more accurate reflection of its origin.)

Lady Bird was pregnant again when Lucy was two, but it ended in a miscarriage, her fourth, and she never had the son she wanted. When Lucy was a year old, Lyndon ran for a seat in the U.S. Senate, and Lady Bird made her

Lady Bird bought a large duplex in Austin, Texas, in 1943 so the Johnsons would have a permanent home there.

Campaigning by car, Lady Bird never put more than five gallons of gas at a time into the tank so she'd have to make more unscheduled stops in small towns.

first political speeches, crisscrossing the state and sparking several rallies a day. She also formed a women's division of the campaign and set up a phone bank in her backyard. The election was a squeaker, and the outcome was challenged in court, but Lyndon was able to declare victory after a month of counting and recounting, and he picked up an ironic new nickname, Landslide Lyndon, along the way.

Two years after the election, Lady Bird expanded her broadcast holdings by opening a television station in Austin. Few people had television sets in 1951, and to make the business succeed, she also had to become an electronics wholesaler as a way of making them available. On the heels of that investment, Lyndon asked her to buy a piece of land in the Hill Country between the tiny towns of Hyde and Stonewall near where he had been born. The 243-acre ranch on the Pedernales River belonged to his elderly aunt, who lived there in a two-story fieldstone house.

Lady Bird was not impressed. She took one look at the ramshackle, bat-infested house and shouted at Lyndon, "How could you do this to me! How simply could you?" But she calmed down and agreed to pay $20,000 for it—her third real estate buy in less than ten years.

The ranch was an easy drive from Austin, and Lady Bird began living there so she could keep up with the house's reconstruction with one eye and the new TV station with the other. It was like camping out. A few months into it, the worst floods anyone could remember swept through. Eight-year-old Lynda was enrolled at the school in nearby Johnson City, but when the bridge across the Pedernales washed away, she couldn't get home and her mother and her five-year-old sister, Lucy, couldn't get anywhere. In the meantime, the river, which wasn't very far beyond her front door, rose by fifteen feet. Power was out, the telephone dead, and most of the trees outside were washed away. "I thought it was great fun," Lucy remembered, but Lady Bird didn't. "Lucy and I sat in the house," she recalled, "and watched the topsoil from our neighbor's farm float on by, right on out to the Gulf of Mexico, and livestock—cattle and horses—were swept away, too." They were eventually rescued by one of their neighbors who arrived on horseback and drove them to higher ground in her car. It was as close as Lady Bird ever came to a pioneer experience, and it had a profound effect on her.

Lyndon was elected Senate majority leader in 1955. He had also suffered a major heart attack, but it didn't slow him down, although it made Lady Bird's life a lot more frantic. She had to look after his health, and she had a new role to play as the wife of one of the most important members of the Senate. The strain was intensified when he had another even worse heart attack but came through more eager than ever to run for president. He encouraged his press office to put out the word that he was a "miracle man," fully recovered and ready for action. He wasn't, but it would fall to Lady Bird to keep the image alive.

After President Eisenhower was elected to his second term, Lyndon had emerged as one of the most powerful Democrats in the country, and as the 1960 election approached, he formally announced that he was running to succeed him. But the nod went to John F. Kennedy instead, and although Lady Bird was visibly disappointed, she privately admitted that she hadn't wanted him to run in the first place. She was less pleased when Kennedy asked him to accept the vice presidential nomination. "She looked like the survivor of a plane crash," said her friend Phil Graham of the *Washington Post*—but Lady Bird was a trooper and when Lyndon's place on the ticket was made official, she looked like a kid opening Christmas presents.

Public Woman

After twenty-three years of marriage, Lady Bird knew everything there was to know—both good and bad—about her husband. "He was my lover, my friend, my identity," she said looking back on those days. She had expected to be her husband's support system during the presidential race, just as she had been in the others, but early in the campaign she had a call from Jack Kennedy. His wife, Jackie, was pregnant, and he was worried about her having a miscarriage, so he wanted her to be relieved from campaigning. He asked if Lady Bird would fill in for Jackie. Without any hesitation, she answered with a single word, "certainly." It may have made a bigger difference than anyone realized. Jackie had a patrician manner that was hard for Middle America to grasp, but Lady Bird was a down-to-earth woman and she treated strangers like neighbors talking over the back fence.

On the other hand, she looked the part almost to a fault. She had always dressed to please her husband—plain, conservative, and often just plain dowdy. Stanley Marcus of Dallas's Neiman Marcus took her under his wing and she began appearing in more stylish and colorful outfits. She was no Jackie Kennedy, but she wasn't the old Lady Bird, either. The very idea annoyed her, though, because "I just didn't want to spend that much time or money on clothes, but it was really important to Lyndon." Still, she put herself and her daughters on a tight budget, and even if she liked something she'd reject it if she thought it was too expensive. It seemed odd to many because she had been raised in a fairly wealthy family, and her broadcasting company alone was valued at $3 million and she personally owned 52 percent of it. She didn't mind at all if Lyndon bought her clothes and accessories, no matter what they might cost, and he often did, but she had grown up in the Great Depression and,

Below: Lady Bird, third from left at this rally, made her first speech during the Senate campaign.

like most others of her generation, Lady Bird didn't approve of spending money on appearances.

The Kennedys had perfected a campaign strategy of staging "ladies tea parties" with the women of the family pouring and courting women voters. Now they wanted Lady Bird to do the same in Texas in the company of Jack's mother and two of his sisters. She felt a bit out of their league, and she asked her friend Liz Carpenter, who ran a Washington news service with her husband but lived close to Austin, for help and advice. Liz was a flamboyant woman who could shine even among the Kennedys, and she was the perfect opposite of Lady Bird's native shyness. She signed on not just for the tea parties but for the whole campaign. It sounded like fun to her and, as it turned out, it was for both of them. She not only went along as Lady Bird's cheerleader but also coached her on how to handle press conferences and advised her on her speeches, and virtually orchestrated all of Lady Bird's political activities. It was her job, as she put it, to be able to teach Mrs. Johnson to be able to do more than "stand up and say 'howdy' at the barbecues."

As a Roman Catholic, Jack Kennedy was persona non grata in the Texas Bible Belt, and the main thrust of Lady Bird's assignment was to show that whatever his religion, his heart was in Texas. She knew that she was in trouble

When Lady Bird asked her friend Liz Carpenter to assist her with the Kennedy-Johnson campaign in Texas, it took Liz five days to make up her mind. She was terrified of flying and she knew that there would be a lot of it. Her twelve-year-old son brought her around when he told her, "There never has been a bird that crash-landed, and you'll be flying with Lady Bird."

The Mink Coat Mob

One of the most miserable incidents of the Kennedy-Johnson campaign happened in Dallas. Four days before the election, Lyndon and Lady Bird met there for a speech at the grand old Adolphus Hotel, but about four hundred women got there ahead of them. Liz Carpenter called them the Mink Coat Mob, because they were all smartly dressed wives and daughters of the city's most prominent businessmen. They had come to protest what they perceived was Lyndon's sellout to the eastern establishment and to support the Republican presidential candidate, Richard Nixon. One of them hit Lady Bird on the head with a sign that said "Let's Ground Lady Bird" and then she spat in her face. It took the couple half an hour to cross the street through the pushing and shoving crowd, but they kept their cool if for no better reason than that the whole tawdry business was being taped for broadcast on national television. When they finally reached the ballroom for Lyndon's speech, he began it by saying, "If the time has come when I can't walk with my lady through the corridors of the hotels of Dallas, then I want to know about it." Then he smiled to himself. He took the broaching of the bonds of decency as a sign that the Nixon camp was running scared.

Above: Lady Bird and Lyndon covered every square mile of Texas during their campaigns, but the spot they liked best was on the Pedernales River near where he grew up.

when the Kennedy ladies arrived and absolutely refused to wear cowboy hats. It got worse when news reports quoted Jackie Kennedy calling her husband's running mate "Senator Cornpone." It may have gotten a laugh in Massachusetts, but those were fighting words in Texas, and Lady Bird had to pull the irons from the fire.

The tea parties were a resounding success, thanks to Lady Bird, who understood the audience better than her co-hostesses did. She also knew that just winning Texas wouldn't be enough. Before the campaign was over, she traveled more than 35,000 miles and made appearances on her own in eleven states, and she was smiling at her husband's side when he made 150 speeches across the country.

When the votes were counted, the Kennedy-Johnson ticket took the electoral votes of seven Southern states, including Texas, largely thanks to Lady Bird. When they went back to Washington, the new vice president bought an elegant French-inspired mansion called "The Elms" on the outskirts of the city, and his wife began a heavy round of entertaining. Lady Bird enjoyed her own parties, but Lyndon wasn't enjoying his new job. He missed the rough-and-tumble of his Senate days and the job of presiding over the Senate without participating only made it harder to bear. That it was about all he was expected to do made it impossible for him to adjust.

His black moods made her life miserable, but Lady Bird rose above them as she always did. She was suddenly an unexpectedly busy woman. Traditionally, a vice president's wife had no specific duties beyond entertaining, and Lady Bird had become used to that as a senator's wife. But Mrs. Kennedy sloughed off routine assignments to her, things like posing with poster children and hosting luncheons for charity groups. Before long, Jackie Kennedy was calling Lady Bird the "best pinch-hitter in town," and in less than a year, she had gone to bat for her more than fifty times. If she resented it, it never showed. Lady Bird admired the First Lady, and they each regarded themselves as good friends in spite of the difference in their ages and their backgrounds. Still, Lady Bird had to concede "the two of us lived in different worlds."

Below: No real Texan would think of dining outdoors without a plate of barbecue, but Lady Bird made an exception at a Maine clambake, although she required a bit of instruction.

But there were a few sour notes. Protocol mandated that the vice president and his wife should be invited to White House dinners, but their names were repeatedly left off the guest lists. Usually they were reinserted at the last minute by the president himself, who knew more about political reality than his wife or her social staff. Like most of the rest of the White House staff, they regarded the Johnsons as "vulgar hicks."

Destiny

On the morning of November 22, 1963, the kitchen at the Johnsons' Hill Country ranch was a beehive of activity. Eighteen loaves of bread had just come out of the ovens, and there were twenty pecan pies cooling on the counter. Several pots of Texas red sauce were simmering on the stove, a fire had been built outside in the roasting pit, and women were busy arranging centerpieces of fresh flowers.

The Johnson spread in Texas was officially called the LBJ Ranch. It was assumed it was named for Lyndon, but they were also Lady Bird's initials, and her name was on the deed to the ranch.

There was a Texas-style barbecue scheduled for the next morning and the guest of honor was to be the president of the United States and his wife. They were touring Texas at the time, and Lady Bird and Lyndon were scheduled to arrive in Dallas with them that morning.

The barbecue would never take place. Lyndon and Lady Bird were with the president and First Lady in a motorcade working its way though Dallas when the president was shot. The Johnsons were just two cars behind them. President Kennedy was assassinated, Vice President Johnson had succeeded him, and Lady Bird Johnson had become First Lady. The Johnsons were soon on a plane back to Washington far, far away from their Texas ranch.

No one in America knew quite how to assess the sudden change, least of all Lady Bird. But she knew she was going to need all of her strength to move on. She had convinced herself that it was going to be a temporary situation. But during their first night back at The Elms, Lyndon held a meeting in their bedroom with Horace Busby, one of his closest advisors. The conversation was about his chances in the 1964 election and the one beyond that four years afterward. Lady Bird had already counted the days until the next election campaign began and she had told herself that she'd only have to be First Lady for nine months. It was more than she had bargained for, but she knew that she'd be able to hang on that long. What she was hearing, though, added up to what could turn out to be a nine-*year* sentence. She put plugs in her ears and a mask over her eyes and rolled over to lose the thought in sleep.

The next few days were frantic. Lady Bird had to arrange to sell The Elms and figure out what to do about its furnishings. She also had to plan their move into the White House. Lucy was at school in Washington, but Lynda was a student at the University of Texas in Austin, and her mother arranged for her to transfer to George Washington University in Washington. It would make life easier for the Secret Service people assigned to protect her, but Lady Bird needed her to help with her new job as First Lady as well.

Lady Bird also had to be a sounding board for the widowed Mrs. Kennedy, she had to deal with her husband's health and his habits, and she had to smooth feathers when he ruffled them among his staff and others. At the same time she had to establish herself as the new First Lady of the land. She was nothing at all like her popular predecessor. It was the same sort of problem that Bess Truman had faced when she stepped into Eleanor Roosevelt's shoes; but she was no Bess Truman, either.

Above: Lady Bird's beautification programs weren't just about making neighborhoods prettier, but also about improving people's lives.

Lyndon was stepping into the shoes of a popular president, too, and he depended on Lady Bird's strength and her candor when his steps took him out of bounds with the public and the press. That may have been the toughest job of all, but it came with the territory and she had plenty of experience.

In 1964, Lyndon's amazing talent for dealing with Congress came into play as he fought an uphill battle for passage of his Civil Rights Act. Lady Bird supported the idea completely, but somebody had to venture into the South to get the idea across to people who still didn't realize that the Civil War was over, and that the time had come to bury racism with the dead past.

Lady Bird was a Southerner born and bred, and she said that there were some things that shouldn't be changed, like "keeping up with your kinfolk, of long Sunday dinners after church, of a special brand of courtesy…[but] I knew the Civil Rights Act was right and I didn't mind saying so, but I also loved the South and didn't want it used as the whipping boy for the Democratic party."

With that, she left on a 1,628-mile train trip through eight states, including stops in many places that were hotbeds of racism and that the Secret Service insisted she should skip in the interest of her own safety. She ignored their warnings and went on with her "journey of the heart" on her own terms. Lady Bird knew something about the South that Northerners didn't: that women like her—soft, loyal, and "gracious"—were put on a pedestal as symbols of Southern virtue. By using the pedestal as a soapbox, she managed to get her message across. Still, it was a courageous thing for her to do. Passions were running high in the South of the 1960s, but Lady Bird waded in, smiling all the while.

The bill passed and it had given Lyndon a firm grip on the government by the time the Democrats met to name their presidential candidate. His nomination should have been a shoo-in, but the president was filled with doubt. He didn't believe that a White Southerner, even himself, could rally the country. It was Lady Bird who assured him that he could. "You are as brave a man as Harry Truman—or FDR—or Lincoln," she said in a personal letter. "I honor you for it. So does the rest of the country…. I can't carry any of the burdens you talked of—I know it's only your choice. But I know you are as brave as any of the thirty-five [previous presidents]."

Lyndon valued his wife's opinion as much as he had his mother's—they were the only two people in his life whose ideas could trump his own. He accepted the nomination in spite of his own misgivings, and he won the election, too. But like so many other things in his life he owed a big share of his success to Lady Bird.

During the convention, the First Lady came up with a plan to hold rallies in the statehouses of all the Southern states. But the governors of those states, all Democrats, shied away from the idea. Because of the Civil Rights Act, the Republicans were cracking the tradition of a "Solid South" among Democrats, and in their opinion, her presence might associate them with the hated law and cost them their own jobs. Lady Bird had to accept their wisdom, but she still knew that her presence was needed in those states—precisely because of the emergence of the opposition party.

She had made a whistle-stop campaign before, and now she decided to do it again, only this time longer, bigger, and better. No First Lady had ever campaigned *alone* for her husband before, and selling the idea was tough. Party leaders thought it would be a waste of time and money, and even Lyndon wouldn't sign off on it. With no support forthcoming, Lady Bird went ahead on her own and put together her own volunteer staff, personally supervising the ordering of buttons, paper hats, and other campaign paraphernalia, and she mapped the route. The national campaign organizers, who would ordinarily be expected to be involved, looked the other way.

Above: Lady Bird's own whistle-stop campaign was far more successful than any of the experts had predicted.

Her nineteen-car red, white, and blue train, which she called the Lady Bird Special, carried fifteen media people along with a flock of designated hostesses, wives of senators and congressmen, and Lady Bird's staff. She made certain that the fare in the dining cars was not just Southern but regional in all the states that they passed through, and she handed out her own recipe for pecan pie at every stop they made. If all that wasn't enough, before the trip was announced in the first place, Lady Bird spent eleven hours on the phone calling the governors and members of the congressional delegations of each of the eight states she planned to hit. Her plans were already set, but she told them that she was "thinking about it," and she asked for their opinion and their advice on how she should proceed. There were a few governors she missed, like Alabama governor George Wallace, who was an outspoken racist, but most of the others were as pleased to help as she had hoped they would be. As for Wallace, when the train reached Alabama, it had become obvious that Lady Bird was a force to reckon with, and although he didn't get aboard the Lady Bird Special himself, he did send her a large bouquet of roses.

Early in the tour, hecklers supporting Barry Goldwater, the Republican candidate, appeared carrying picket signs. She shamed them by beginning her speeches with an appeal to vote for "both Johnsons," and the protesters, Southern gentlemen at heart, quieted down out of respect for the lady. The First Lady made as many as fifteen speeches a day during the tour, and the local press kept the momentum going long after the train pulled out of the depot. In most towns, well-wishers brought her bouquets and small gifts, and she had them delivered to hospitals and orphanages at the next stop, always with a handwritten note from her. The television networks sent camera crews along, and each day's events reached a national audience on the evening news night after night. The thrust of their reports usually compared Lady Bird to Eleanor Roosevelt, and nothing could have pleased her more. She had gone back to her rural roots, but her appeal extended to the big cities as well.

Before the tour was over, Lady Bird had traveled 1,600 miles through eight states and she made forty-seven formal speeches as

"I got up this morning at three o'clock in the morning and milked twenty cows so I could be here."

—*A woman in the audience on her eagerness to see Lady Bird Johnson in person*

Above: The First Lady often traveled to depressed rural areas to see what could be done and to encourage people there to work for change.

well as several impromptu ones to audiences that added up to half a million people.

The Johnsons' new term in the White House began a few days before their thirtieth wedding anniversary, and Lady Bird was ready for a fresh start. She had become saddened by the decay and deterioration in parts of the country she had visited during her two long train excursions, and she had a feeling that if anybody was going to be able to do something about it, it was probably her. Lyndon encouraged her to take it on as a cause, but he made the mistake of always calling it "beautification," a term she considered "prissy and slight," and she decided to table the idea for a while.

In the meantime, she was still living in Jackie Kennedy's shadow. It was like the comparison of apples and oranges, but it happened all the time, and Lady Bird was always the loser when it did. Rather than trying to fight it, Lady Bird made an end run around it. She got rid of the old East Wing staff and replaced it with her own people, and she established a press office of her own along with scheduling regular press conferences. She fired the French chef and replaced him with an old family friend who understood Lyndon's health needs better anyway, but also brought a Southern touch to the menus at state dinners. Classical musicians and composers were invited less and less often to the White House, and the accent shifted to people associated with Broadway musicals and country and western personalities.

When the Smithsonian asked Lady Bird for one of her dresses for its First Ladies collection, she sent one over with the stipulation that she could borrow it back for special occasions.

Below: Beautification begins with the planting of a single flower, and Lady Bird enthusiastically planted them by the thousands in her travels.

Typically, the First Lady put the White House on a tight budget—both she and Lyndon made an effort to turn off lights in empty rooms—and she did much of her personal shopping at discount department stores. She pushed Jackie's still unfinished White House restoration forward, but she insisted that new purchases should be American-made.

Finally, early in 1965, Lady Bird turned her attention to the environment. Her crusade began with an experimental campaign to improve the appearance of Washington, D.C., a project that many other First Ladies had approached with varying degrees of success. She took a leaf from the book of civil rights and antiwar protesters and organized young people into groups that would march in picket lines exhorting others to pick up trash, plant flowers, and otherwise make the streets more hospitable, even to

At Lady Bird's insistence, the National Park Service planted more than two million daffodil bulbs (her favorite flower) in Washington. It was the biggest landscaping project in history.

the protesters themselves. Her goal was to export the movement to other cities and encourage volunteers to follow its guidelines for landscaping, burying utility lines, eliminating trash, and making their own properties more presentable. She raised money from corporations and solicited their help in a nationwide anti-litter campaign.

Her husband was spending his political capital on his Great Society, transforming American into a place without poverty, illiteracy, or racism, and Lady Bird gave it another dimension. She called for nation that would have a sense of pride in its surroundings, and she moved her campaign out of the cities pushing for better-designed highways with views of something other than billboards and junkyards, and for more parks and playgrounds. At every step of the way, she preached the gospel of more flowers and shrubs and less litter everywhere.

Eleanor Roosevelt, who was fondly remembered as an activist First Lady, always championed her husband's causes, but Lady Bird made this program that she called "conservation" all her own. The president was promoting a better society, but she was determined to create a better place to live for the people he helped. The culmination of her campaign was the sweeping Highway Beautification Bill, which passed Congress in spite of bitter opposition in 1965. The controversy prompted Lady Bird to pull back and rely on public support for her project rather than going to Congress for any more help.

In the meantime, the president's escalating of the Vietnam War cast a pall over his administration, and Lady Bird concentrated on her role as a wife, building a wall around him to protect him from the effects of what was going on outside. It was what she had always done for him in times of crisis. This crisis sometimes emerged in her own White House entertainments when guests brought their war protests though the White House doors, and she dealt with the embarrassment by issuing comments that she "can't handle the war in Vietnam. I am not big enough."

She also shared criticism with her husband over the burgeoning civil rights problem and the administration's efforts to pass a voting rights bill, and she began talking longingly of the next presidential election. "I am counting the months until March 1968," she said, "when like Truman it will be possible to say, 'I don't want this office, this responsibility, any longer, even if you want me. Find the strongest and most able man and God bless you.'"

Above: Lady Bird and interior secretary Stewart Udall float down the Snake River past the magnificent Grand Tetons in Wyoming.

"Keep America beautiful. Plant a tree, a shrub, or a bush."

—Lady Bird Johnson's call to beautify America

The Johnson Daughters

The Johnson girls, Luci and Lynda, were about as different from each other as two sisters could be. Lynda was like her mother, introverted and tightfisted, and Luci, whom her father called "the pretty one," had a teenager's zest for life that often embarrassed her mother. Lynda patterned herself after the young Lady Bird: She made good grades and carefully followed the rules. On her eighteenth birthday, Luci converted to Roman Catholicism, and her parents took it in stride, but her sister, who like her had been raised in the Episcopal Church, was mortified. At around the same time, Luci announced her engagement to Pat Nugent, and she married him, at the age of nineteen, in a showy wedding soon afterward. For her part, Lynda was having a romance with George Hamilton, the Hollywood actor known for his suntans. If nothing else, it brought her out of her shell, and she began taking an interest in her appearance for the first time. Luci presented the Johnsons with their first grandchild, Patrick Lyndon Nugent, in 1967 and at about the same time her sister announced her intention to marry Chuck Robb, a marine officer who led the White House color guard. Their wedding was the first held in the White House in fifty-three years.

Top: Lyndon, a proud grandfather, with daughter Luci and her son, Patrick Lyndon Nugent in 1967.

Bottom: The White House hosted the wedding of Lynda Bird Johnson and Captain Charles Robb in 1967.

Lyndon shied away from discussions of running for another election, but Lady Bird tipped the balance the other way. Although he had not yet decided to retire, and didn't seem to have such an idea in his head, Lady Bird began making plans for the day when he would step down, even though she knew he would be like a fish out of water when he did.

Lyndon, typically, vacillated about making a decision to retire, but finally in March 1968, he ended a televised speech announcing the relaxation of bombing in North Vietnam by saying, "I will not seek—and I will not accept—the nomination of my party for another term as your President." Lady Bird had personally inserted the sentence into the text. No one was more relieved than she was. Her work as First Lady was over.

She knew that she was going to face another kind of nightmare when Lyndon lit a cigarette on the plane that took them home to Texas. His doctors had put him on a strict diet and had completely forbidden smoking because after his history of heart attacks, they said it would surely kill him. But Lyndon retorted that he was retired now and it was time to enjoy life, not prolong it. For the first time in their married life, Lady Bird found herself without any influence over her husband. He scrapped the diet, too, and he gained forty pounds.

Lyndon spent most of his time postpresidency touring his ranch, but he produced a draft for a book on his White House years and he gave full attention to plans for his presidential library in Austin, where his political career had begun. Lady Bird devoted a great deal of her time to the library, too, but she spent long hours editing her own White House diary for publication. She was also appointed to the University of Texas Board of Regents.

> *The First Lady is an unpaid public servant elected by one person—her husband.*
>
> *—Lady Bird Johnson on her position as First Lady*

A month after the Johnson Library opened in 1972, the former president had another heart attack. He survived it, but his doctors didn't give him much more time to live. "Lady Bird will soon be the prettiest and richest widow in the State of Texas," Lyndon said. When he died, in January 1973, Lynda said, "The Lord knew what he was doing when he took daddy first, because I don't think daddy could have gotten along without mother. I really don't think he could have lived without mother. He depended on her too much."

A "rich and pretty" widow, Lady Bird didn't drop out of sight. She went to work on a campaign to beautify Austin with a program like the one she had pushed in Washington, and she traveled a great deal to all parts of the world to learn more about plants, which had become a passion with her, and she worked tirelessly for the creation of the National Wildflower Center, which was named for her on her seventieth birthday.

Her love for wildflowers is evident along every major highway in Texas, where she encouraged the planting of bluebonnets and Indian paintbrush and other colorful native plants to replace the junkyards and billboards that were once there. She also encouraged her fellow Texans to keep the landscape litter-free with the enduring slogan, "Don't Mess With Texas." And almost no one does.

Above: Thanks to Lady Bird, wildflowers are cultivated everywhere in Texas. She was a picture of beauty in a field full of bluebonnets.

Visiting the LBJ Ranch and Museum

Lady Bird Johnson donated the family's ranch near Stonewall, Texas, to the National Park Service, and it is open to the public every day except Thanksgiving, December 25, and January 1 from 8:45 A.M. to 5:00 P.M.; bus tours are scheduled from the visitors center from 10:00 A.M. to 4:00 P.M. It is still a working cattle ranch, and it has been expanded to 1,570 acres. The ranch house, which Lady Bird restored and expanded, is furnished as it was in the 1960s. Tours are also available of Lyndon's boyhood home in nearby Johnson City. The admission fee is $3.00 for the elderly and children, and $6.00 for adults between eighteen and sixty-one.

To get to the ranch from Austin, follow Highway 290, westbound, to the visitors center in Johnson City; from San Antonio, use Highway 281, northbound, to Highway 290; from Fredericksburg, follow Highway 290, eastbound. The ranch is fourteen miles west of Johnson City.

The LBJ Library and Museum is at 2313 Red River Street in Austin. In addition to housing the president's papers and histories of his administration, the museum's exhibits include a gallery devoted to the First Lady. Admission is free.

Right: The Lyndon B. Johnson Library and Museum in Austin, Texas, dedicates an entire section to Lady Bird.

Pat Nixon

St. Patrick's Babe

Will Ryan's third child and only daughter was born just before midnight on March 16, but he didn't get home from his job in an eastern Utah silver mine until an hour later, and because it was already St. Patrick's Day, he decided that would be her birthday. Her mother called her Thelma, but to Will she was his "St. Patrick's babe in the morning." He called her Babe for the rest of his life, and so did her two older brothers, but when she went to school, her friends began calling her Buddy. She didn't mind because she never had really felt like a girl who might be called Thelma. She buried the name when she enrolled at Fullerton Junior College as Patricia Ryan, and she almost never admitted to having any different name after that.

Her father, Will, had gone to sea aboard a whaling ship as a teenager, and he worked as a surveyor in the Philippines before prospecting for gold in the Klondike and the Black Hills of South Dakota when he met and married Kate Halberstaat Bender, a widow with two children. With his new family in tow, he moved on to try striking it rich in the Comstock lode in Nevada, but he never did find his pot of gold, and he finally decided to try a different line of work.

His Babe was just a year old when he moved his family to Artesia, California, a town of four hundred about eighteen miles southwest of Los Angeles, where he bought a ten-and-a-half-acre truck farm. He had become a farmer, but he thought of himself as a rancher and he called his little spread a ranch, although all it produced was corn and potatoes, cauliflower, cabbages, grapes, and watermelons.

The ranch included a five-room house where his daughter grew up. There was no electricity and no indoor bathroom—no running water at all, in fact—but it did come with an old out-of-tune upright piano left behind by a former owner, although no one in the family ever learned to play it. They were all too busy. The little farm was a family affair with even little Babe pitching in almost as soon as she could stand. The biggest job was pumping water into the tank out back to keep the crops from withering in the dry, hot summers.

When she was six, Babe had developed into a pretty girl with red-gold hair and almond-shaped brown eyes that sometimes appeared to be green or gray and gave an impression of depth. Her father, who was well read and had a local reputation as the sage of Artesia, said that Babe was "smart as a whip," and her teachers agreed. The school's principal recalled, "She was quietly equal to anything. If something needed to be done, she did it. Life didn't bowl her over."

Thelma Catherine Ryan Nixon

Born
March 16, 1912,
Ely, Nevada

Parents
William Ryan and
Katherina Halberstaat
Bender Ryan

Marriage
June 21, 1940, to Richard
Milhous Nixon (1913-94)

Children
Patricia (1946-);
Julie (1948-)

Died
June 22, 1993,
Yorba Linda, California

Above: A farmer's daughter, Pat took on the responsibilities of caring for her father and her brothers after her mother died. She worked on the farm, too, while she went to school.

She had an unusual talent for recitation, and even as a first-grader she was often invited to speak at local clubs. Thelma, as her teachers and her mother—if no one else—called her, was qualified to skip second grade, and in the process, she caught up with her brother Tom, who was two years older, and she graduated from grade school a year ahead of him. She was three years younger than her brother Bill, but all three of the Ryan kids were in the same graduating class.

When Babe was thirteen, her half sister, Neva, graduated from high school and went to nearby Fullerton Junior College. It left Babe as the only female help her mother had with the housekeeping. At the same time Kate Ryan became ill with Bright's disease, a kidney ailment, and then she was diagnosed with cancer of the liver. She spent her final months in a doctor's house that doubled as a hospital, and Babe and her brothers drew closer together than they ever had been. All three were also in the same class at Excelsior High School in nearby Norwalk, but by then Babe had the added chore of running the Ryan household, keeping it "scrub clean" as her father demanded, and cooking for the family, as well as keeping all their clothes clean, pressed, and mended.

In spite of her responsibilities at home, Babe was a straight-A student and she was active in the student government as well. Both of her brothers were on the football team, but she didn't have the time for athletics, even though she had an aptitude for it. There was one activity that allowed her to be home in time to cook dinner, though—she became a star of the debating team. She was also an actor in the school plays, most often as the lead.

During her senior year, her father developed tuberculosis, a result of the oceans of dust he had inhaled during his years as a miner. His three children had already agreed that when he died, they would postpone the settling of his affairs until Bill, the oldest, turned twenty-one so that they wouldn't come under the care of a court-appointed guardian. In the meantime, all three had college scholarships, but considering the family finances, only one of them could go. Tom was selected and he went on to the University of Southern California, while Bill stayed behind to look after the ranch and Babe agreed to nurse their

Legacy

On her deathbed, Kate Ryan told her daughter that there was money in her coat pocket that she had saved from selling eggs, and she wanted Babe to have it. She swore her to secrecy. The money was hers and no one else should know about it. It was a meager amount, but her mother left her a larger legacy. Her brother Tom recognized it in his mother's outlook on life: "She had a big heart. She sacrificed and did things without complaining."

father. She had gone to night school to learn typing and shorthand, but she was much too busy to put the training to use. When her father was admitted to a sanatorium, she took a part-time job at the local bank as a cleaning woman and substitute teller. At the same time, she enrolled at Fullerton Junior College—it was there she became Pat and left her birth name behind—and added a heavy load of studies to her already overloaded schedule. When their father eventually died, Bill went to Los Angeles to join his brother and work his way through college. He left his sister alone to run the family farm.

She made her getaway, as it were, in 1931 when, at the age of eighteen, an elderly couple from Connecticut who had been wintering in California hired her to drive them back home in their Packard touring car. The fee was tiny, but the deal included her expenses and a bus ticket home, and then there was the adventure of it all. There were problems along the way, breakdowns and endless flat tires, but otherwise it was a dream trip for a young woman who had never before been more than a hundred miles from home. "I was driver, nurse, mechanic—and scared," she recalled. When she got to the New York area, she took a job as a secretary at Seton Hospital in the Bronx, and she took courses at Columbia University that qualified her as an X-ray technician. It got her a better job, and she stayed at the hospital for two years. She had developed into a beautiful young woman and she never lacked for a date. She led an active social life, but none of the young men especially appealed to her, and she was homesick for California.

In 1933, Pat used her bus ticket to go home and on to college where she hoped to get a degree and become a department store buyer. Back in Los Angeles, she took all sorts of part-time jobs to earn her tuition as a University of Southern California marketing major, but the one she enjoyed most was being an extra at the movie studios. She appeared in the background in several dozen movies over the next three years.

Pat graduated cum laude in 1937 with a bachelor's degree in marketing and a teaching certificate. It was the latter that led to her first post-college job, teaching at Whittier High School in Whittier, California. A graduate of the school named Richard Nixon had moved back to Whittier to join a law firm in town just before Pat moved there.

Pat got her first job in New York at Seton Hospital through her father's sister Kate, a Roman Catholic nun who was head of the X-ray department there.

New Direction

Pat was the youngest teacher at Whittier High. But her students, who expected her to be a pushover, quickly discovered that she was also the strictest. She confined her social life to weekends, when she drove to Los Angeles to stay with her half sister, Neva, far from Whittier's prying eyes. Among the demands that the school placed on its faculty was that they should participate in community affairs, and at the beginning of her second year in the job, Pat gravitated to an amateur theatrical group called the Whittier Community Players, and it was there that she met Richard Nixon.

He couldn't take his eyes off her, and when they left after meeting during their auditions, he told her, "You may not believe this, but I am going to marry you someday." They got the parts they were after, incidentally, and during the weeks of rehearsal, she learned more about him, most of all that he was anything but impulsive, and that made his opening line all the more intriguing. She also learned how much they had in common, and she wasn't at all surprised when he invited her to meet his parents.

Even though Hannah and Frank Nixon approved of everything they saw about her except her "fragile" appearance, Pat wasn't ready to even think about marrying their son, or anyone else. She started avoiding Dick, but he wouldn't let her ignore him. When she said that she was busy with her schoolwork, he showed up to lend a hand. When she pretended not to be at home, he slipped notes under her door, and when she told him she didn't love him, which was often (whether it was the truth or not), he sat down and wrote long letters to her suggesting otherwise.

They still continued dating in spite of the bumps along the way, but they kept their romance a secret for nearly two years. Only their closest friends had any idea they had more than just a nodding acquaintance. Over time, of course, it became far more than that. Pat not only spent more and more time with Dick, but she became a frequent visitor to his parents' house, and during the summer she even showed up in Hannah Nixon's kitchen at 5:00 A.M. to help her turn out the fifty homemade pies that she sold every day in her husband's grocery store. Pat liked Frank Nixon and she enjoyed his good-

Below: Young Pat was filled with wanderlust, and at the first opportunity, she left California for New York City.

natured teasing, but she didn't have much in common with the dour Quaker, Hannah.

Predictably, Pat began to realize that she was falling in love with Dick, and she missed him when they were apart. They were most happy together walking along the beach, and they had discovered their own special place a long drive away from Whittier: San Clemente, where they had three miles of isolated shorefront all to themselves. Dick drove her there in March 1940 and she was ready to say yes when he asked her to marry him.

It was a quiet wedding at the Mission Inn in Riverside. Pat wore a short French blue lace suit with an A-line skirt, and there were crystal buttons on her short jacket. She wore a close-fitting hat in what the department store described as an "ashes of rose" color, and it was trimmed with blue roses. She wore her first orchid pinned to her shoulder. The newlyweds pooled their resources for a honeymoon trip to Mexico, and then went home to a one-bedroom furnished apartment in Long Beach, moving twice before coming to rest in their first real home, an apartment in Whittier.

They had promised themselves that they would travel while they were still young, and they began keeping the promise with a Caribbean cruise on their first anniversary. When they got back, there was a letter waiting asking Dick to accept a job as an attorney for the new Office of Price Administration (OPA). The $3,200 salary was half what they were earning together in Whittier, and it meant moving to Washington, D.C., but Pat agreed that it was the right thing for them to do. As they were packing to leave, the United States declared war on Japan, Germany, and Italy in the wake of the attack on Pearl Harbor and they found themselves specks in a sea of Americans headed to the capital to join the war effort.

The Nixons arrived in Washington after a cross-country car trip on January 29, 1942, which was Dick's twenty-ninth birthday. It didn't take him long to realize that he was but one of thousands of lawyers in wartime Washington, and not making much of a contribution to the war effort itself, and Pat wholeheartedly agreed with his decision to sign up for active duty as a naval officer. After his training period, he was assigned to the naval air station in Ottumwa, Iowa, and Pat went there with him and got a job as a bookkeeper for his former employer, the OPA, which had offices all over the country to issue and track ration stamps. After six months and still thousands of miles from the war, Dick applied for sea duty, and when he was shipped to San Francisco, Pat went west, too. She decided to stay after he shipped out, and took another OPA job, this time as a price analyst at the same salary her husband had been collecting back in Washington.

Lieutenant-Commander Nixon's tour of duty in the South Pacific lasted fourteen months. After a few more months, he was sent back east, and the couple was living in New York when Pat discovered she was pregnant. The only other thing they knew about their future was that Dick wouldn't extend

Above: Pat and Dick found pleasure walking along the beach in San Clemente. He proposed to her there, and they eventually lived there.

Below: The early years of the Nixons' marriage were interrupted when he became a naval officer.

his naval career. They had no idea where they'd be living when the baby came, except that they had made up their minds that it wouldn't be Whittier. That would have been suffocating after all the other places they had lived except, possibly, in the middle of the Great Plains.

But a group of conservative Republicans back in Whittier had advertised in the local newspaper searching for "a young man, resident of the District, preferably a veteran, fair education, no political strings or obligations" to run for Congress. They might have had Dick's resume in front of them when they wrote it. At least that was what one of his friends thought when he wrote to him about it. Naturally, Dick was interested. Even though there was a baby on the way, both he and Pat had a strong sense of adventure, and it appeared they had just been handed an opportunity for one. They had saved money for a house, but now they'd use it for living expenses until campaign funds kicked in after the June primaries, seven months later. A house would have to wait. Their first expense was their move back to Whittier, and their first child, Patricia, known as Tricia, was born a month after they arrived, with the primary and the prospect of any income still four months off.

The campaign was run on a shoestring, and Pat contributed her own shoe leather, ringing doorbells part of the day and working in the office the rest. She also made a thorough study of the incumbent congressman's record for Dick to attack; and she hosted meetings in local homes to sound out voter attitudes and assess the advice they offered. She also gave up smoking for the duration of the campaign to create a good impression for herself. Her mother-in-law cared for the baby during the day, and Pat took over in the evenings and nights.

Pat sought out volunteers and she decided on the best jobs for them, and before the campaign had progressed very far, she and Dick were characterized as a "team," a rare concept back in 1946, when candidates' wives stayed in the background. It was an image they carried together during their entire political life. About the only thing Pat didn't do was make speeches for her husband. She had shown promise as a debater since she was in first grade, and she loved acting, but she had little confidence in her public speaking abilities, and she begged off by saying that she believed there should be but one voice on campaign issues, the candidate's.

After Dick won the nomination, the election itself was shrouded in doubt. He was running against Jerry Voorhis, a veteran of ten years in Congress, and the handwriting seemed to be on the wall when the primary total gave Voorhis 7,500 more votes than Dick polled.

Dick's big break came when he outshone his opponent in a town meeting debate and immediately called for another. In all, there were three more, and

Pat's only prior political experience had been as a high school volunteer during Al Smith's presidential campaign—as a Democrat.

Dick "won" each of them. In the end, Voorhis lamented that "this fellow has a silver tongue." Dick also had his facts straight, and he owed that to Pat. In the meantime, he toured the large district, making six or seven speeches a day with his wife at his side. He always spoke without notes as a way of showing his grasp of the issues in spite of his inexperience, and he relied on Pat as a one-woman "truth squad" to make sure that he was saying the right things.

When it was all over and he had won, he said, "I think today that my greatest satisfaction over the results of this election is not for myself, but for my wife...."

They turned the drive to Washington into a sight-seeing trip and a chance to relax after the campaign, and when they got there, there wasn't a house or an apartment available. The war was over but the housing shortage had lingered on. They finally settled on a garden apartment in the Virginia suburbs, and for the next four years, Dick had a half-hour commute to the Capitol. Apart from helping with the mail in Dick's office, Pat found herself with little to do. There was no entertaining required of her, and the intricacies of Washington society remained a mystery. They socialized with the families of other freshman congressmen, but they, too, were just feeling their way. The fact that Pat was a suburban housewife kept her distanced from the loop, and as for Dick, he was regarded as the "greenest Congressman in town."

He learned quickly, and when the time came to run for a second term, he was already gaining a national reputation as an anticommunist, and he ran without any opposition in 1948. That meant there was no campaigning to do, and that was fine with Pat. She hated politics. But she had involved herself on the Washington scene by then, and her life had become as busy as it would have been on any campaign trial. Just before the election, their second daughter, Julie, was born and she added baby care to her duties, which also included keeping up with Tricia, who was still a toddler.

In the meantime, Dick's success in the prosecution of Alger Hiss and Whittaker Chambers on charges of passing secrets to the Soviets made him a kind of national hero, and he parlayed it into a run for the U.S. Senate. It was a tough, almost hurtful, campaign, but Pat rode with him across California in an old wood-paneled station wagon, working the crowd while he made speech after speech from the tailgate. They claimed to have driven more than ten thousand miles before it was over. When Dick won the election, his salary increased and the Nixons moved from their tiny apartment into a house in northwest Washington, the first they ever owned. It wasn't elegant, but it had a yard for the girls, and space enough for the whole family. Pat made it homey by sewing curtains and making slipcovers. Her wardrobe was beginning to look a little threadbare, but Dick would one day turn that to their advantage when he pointed out that in Washington's sea of minks and sables, Pat wore "a respectable Republican cloth coat."

His win, which was impressive, made Dick a serious contender for the Republican vice presidential nomination in 1952. He was the youngest member of the Senate and apparently popular in population-rich California and the nomination was his if he wanted it. He did, but Pat wasn't so sure. She'd had enough campaigning to last a lifetime over the past six years, and she dreaded a national tour that would take her away from six-year-old Tricia and four-year-old Julie. The girls were already showing the emotional effects of frequent separations. But the excitement of the Chicago convention, Pat's first, and the elation that came when candidate Dwight D. Eisenhower chose her husband to run alongside him, pushed all of her doubts into the background.

The American public got its first look at Pat during the televised convention proceedings, but they hadn't seen anything yet. She promised reporters that she would be active in the campaign because "Dick and I always work as a team," and she kept the promise. But it got off to a bad start.

The day after the kickoff in California, a newspaper reported that candidate Nixon had accepted a donation of $18,000 to cover his political expenses from a group of California businessmen. Contributions at the time were limited to $500 and were only legal from individuals, not businesses. It caused a furor in the press, but still the Nixon campaign train kept chugging along. It was derailed when follow-up stories began suggesting that Dick ought to resign, and he himself made up his mind that he should. Apart from his top advisors, who had their own futures to consider, only Pat, who would have preferred life as a senator's wife, advised against it. Candidate Eisenhower himself was leaning in favor of resignation, but he agreed to defer his decision until Dick could make his own case on national television and let the people decide. Pat was opposed to that, too. "Why do we have to tell people how little we have and how much we owe?" she pleaded.

It turned out to be one of the most famous speeches in American political history. What is often forgotten about it is that Pat was at Dick's side when he delivered it. A California newspaper reported, "Mrs. Nixon said not a word. She was shown only briefly on four or five occasions during the broadcast. One could hardly detect a movement in her face as she sat on a divan near the Senator's table, her eyes on him. But the character in her face, the picture of her backing up her husband in the greatest test of his life, the feeling of emotion held in restraint which the views of Mrs. Nixon conveyed, made her a vital factor in the success of the appeal."

Among the things that he pointed out during the course of the speech was that, unlike many congressional wives, Pat was not on the government payroll, but what stuck in most viewers' memories was his revelation that his daughter, Tricia, had a black-and-white cocker spaniel named "Checkers" that had been a gift from a Texan in response to an interview Pat had given

Below: Dick was able to spread good will among the press corps when he and Pat took a historic goodwill tour of the Far East.

mentioning that she was planning to buy a dog for her children. The speech, forever remembered as the "Checkers speech," turned the tide dramatically. They had their first inkling of it when they left the TV studio and were met

After the Checkers speech, Dick, thinking he had failed, wrote his resignation from the campaign. Pat talked him out of submitting it.

by hundreds of cheering people. Dick turned to Pat and said, "Well, at least we have the dog vote."

Dick had saved his spot on the ticket, but there were still six weeks to go before the election, and he and Pat crisscrossed the country to the point of exhaustion. It fell to Pat to not only keep his spirits high but to keep a sharp eye out for missteps at the end after fatigue dulled their senses. The final outcome was a landslide vote and Richard Nixon became vice president at the age of forty.

Second Lady

Before the inauguration, the Washington *Star* turned its attention to Pat's immediate future. "The only thing that is clearly expected [of her] is to preside over the Senate Ladies Luncheon Club, a group of wives, daughters, and other assorted relatives of present and past members of the Senate who meet every Tuesday in the Senate office building to roll bandages and perform other chores for the American Red Cross." The rulebook for First Ladies is vague about the requirements of the job, but for Second Ladies there are only blank pages. Pat Nixon was left to play it by ear.

By custom, wives of other administration officials and the diplomatic corps were duty-bound to call on the vice president's wife, and her days were busy. When she made calls of her own, she usually drove herself even though there was an official car and driver at her disposal. And she made it a point to leave parties and receptions early so she could get home in time to put her daughters to bed.

The routine changed abruptly at the beginning of the summer when things might be expected to slow down. The president asked Dick to make a ten-week goodwill tour to Asia and the Far East and insisted that he take Pat along. She had never been away from her children for more than two weeks before, and although she had misgivings, it was the answer to a lifelong dream of seeing the world. This part of the world had never seen an American president or vice president before, and so they made up the rules as they went along. They got a thorough introduction to the art of diplomacy, often learning from their own mistakes. For her part, Pat opted to skip the usual teas and shopping excursions in favor of visiting schools and hospitals—common practice today, but revolutionary in 1952—and they both made a practice of what one reporter called "folksy handshaking."

Below: The Nixon's Asian trip took them to India, where they visited the Taj Mahal. Pat had always dreamed of travel, and this trip was just the beginning of a worldwide odyssey.

A postmortem of the trip in *U.S. News & World Report* said, "Thousands of Asians—workers, storekeepers, school children—will remember for a long time the sight of an American Vice President who was neither afraid nor reluctant to make the simplest gesture of shaking hands with them." In another report, the International News Service wrote, "Perhaps the smartest assignment of President Eisenhower to date was his insistence that Pat Nixon accompany the Vice President on his current Far Eastern tour. Blond, attractive Mrs. Nixon is a hit overseas."

Back home, Pat was usually characterized as "wifely," and although she had a great deal more depth than the label implies, she was content to let it go at that. She didn't like being in the spotlight, and she didn't find any pleasure in sitting for interviews. She traveled with her husband on campaign swings, and she was at his side during the endless round of visits by foreign dignitaries, which had become his responsibility. She mostly enjoyed it, but she resented the time it took away from her daughters.

In 1954, the Nixons were off on another goodwill tour, this time to Central America. As she had in Asia, Pat followed her own schedule, visiting housing projects, orphanages, hospitals, and schools. As one report put it, she went "anywhere she could earn friends for the U.S." In Panama, she was the first foreign dignitary ever to visit a leper colony.

Their own world seemed to crash around them in the fall when President Eisenhower suffered a major heart attack. At the very least, it meant that the Nixons had to step up their busy schedule, and eighteen-hour days became routine. Her hometown newspaper in Whittier said that its correspondents were "marvelling at the way Pat Nixon manages to stretch an already crammed schedule to take on extra duties and yet stay unruffled and serene." Reports from other parts of the country were just as positive.

Eisenhower's recovery was slow, and when he was back at his desk, he advised Dick to resign and take a cabinet post to get experience for the possibility of becoming president himself. The president hadn't yet announced that he'd run for a second term, and when he finally did, he deferred judgment on who his running mate might be. The press hinted that there was a "dump Nixon" plot afoot, and even when thousands of voters in the New Hampshire primary wrote Dick's name on their ballots, the president remained coy. Pat and Dick were in the limbo of uncertainty, and they would be for six weeks until the convention would make its decision.

Pat had already made her own decision. Although back at the beginning she had advised Dick to limit his vice presidency to one term, now she was saying, "No one is going to push us off the ticket." A close friend remarked, "Any time you pressured Pat, her Irish came out."

Dick's ego had been bruised, and he seriously considered stepping down, but Pat talked him out of it. The wind had shifted by then, too, and Eisenhower proudly

> *"Pat…has aroused my admiration as an able campaigner. There is no question but that she is the most charming of the lot."*
>
> —*President Dwight Eisenhower on Pat Nixon*

Above: As the wife of the vice president, Pat took on many of the social obligations of First Lady.

announced that as far as he was concerned, Dick was his choice, as though there had never been any question of it. In the fall, the Nixons were together on the campaign trail again.

Pat knew very well that her second term as Second Lady was going to be more frantic than the first. Mamie Eisenhower was slowing down, and she had let it be known that she intended to call on Pat frequently as a substitute First Lady. "She is like the Rock of Gibraltar," Mamie said.

Except for her command performances at the White House, Pat did most of her entertaining in local hotels. It put a heavy strain on their budget, and they bought a larger house with more space for entertaining. It was a grand English Tudor mansion overlooking Washington's Rock Creek Park, closer to the center of the action. Often it *was* the center of the action. Guests there ranged from England's Queen Elizabeth II to Soviet leader Nikita Khrushchev.

At the beginning of their second term in the number-two spot, Pat and Dick went on another successful goodwill tour, this time to Ghana, and a year later, they set out to show the flag in South America. It started off badly in Peru, when they were harassed by anti-American demonstrations. They ignored the protest and went on with their visit, but when they reached Colombia and then Venezuela, the situation only grew worse, and the Secret Service learned that there was a very real plot to assassinate the vice president. On their arrival in Caracas, they were spat upon—"It looked like snowflakes," Pat recalled—but they still kept to their mission of bringing goodwill to a place that needed some. Shouting mobs blocked their way into the city, and near the end of the route they were stopped in their tracks by a barricade of empty cars. When about five hundred demonstrators rushed toward them with baseball bats and lead pipes, their Venezuelan police escort abandoned them to their own Secret Service detail. The mob smashed all the windows both in Pat's car and Dick's and then they started rocking them, attempting to turn them over. Pat was terrified, but she kept cool, and one of her bodyguards, who had seen service in two wars, said later that she had "more guts than any man I have ever seen."

The ordeal seemed to last a lifetime, but it was only twelve minutes before a big press truck cleared a path for them in the opposite lane of traffic and the motorcade was able to make a U-turn and beat a retreat. They scrapped their planned schedule and went directly to the American embassy, where they found out that a cache of Molotov cocktails had been found close to their next scheduled stop.

In the meantime, communications had been cut off and President Eisenhower dispatched two companies of marines and another two of paratroopers to stand by off the coast. The Venezuelan government filed a strong protest, claiming that their country was being invaded by American "bullies."

A year later, in 1959, the vice president and Second Lady flew to Moscow for the opening of an American national exhibition there. There were no angry mobs at the airport this time, but there were no brass bands or little girls bestowing bouquets of flowers, either. There were no crowds at all, in fact, only a small party of suspicious government officials.

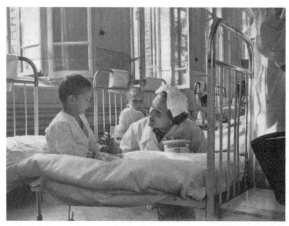

It was during this visit that Dick challenged Nikita Khrushchev to the famous "kitchen debate," an exchange at an exhibit of a modern American kitchen, comparing life in the Soviet Union to life in the United States. Pat was his one-person cheering section.

When Dick began his final year in the office, *Time* magazine reported that Pat's "stamina and courage, her drive and control have made her into one of America's most remarkable women—not just a showpiece Second Lady, not merely a part of the best-known team in American politics, but a public figure in her own right." There was more to be heard from Pat Nixon in the years ahead.

Above: Pat traveled to fifty-three countries as the wife of the vice president, and she visited hospitals and schools in every one of them.

Long Road

When her husband accepted the Republican nomination for the presidency in 1960, Pat and he were inseparable as a political team, and as one of her aides put it, "When you elect a President, you are also electing a First Lady whose job is more than glamour." It was a swipe at Jackie Kennedy, the Democratic candidate's wife, but many saw the simple truth in it.

In his acceptance speech, Dick promised to visit all fifty states between then and November. He and Pat had already hit twenty-five of them, and now they stepped up their pace, pausing only to go back to Washington for four nationally televised debates with candidate Kennedy. As it happened, Dick's televised image was less appealing than his face-to-face encounters with the voters, and they were forced to step up what had already become a grueling pace. But it was all over days before the polls opened, and although he had lost by only two-tenths of a percent of the popular vote, Dick Nixon was on his way to becoming nothing more than a retired vice president.

After the election, the Nixons went home to California, where they built a new house in Beverly Hills. Between his law practice and his writing, Dick was more financially secure than he had ever been, and Pat reveled in gardening and having uninterrupted fun with their daughters, who were teenagers by then. After a summer of contemplation, Dick agreed to run for governor of California,

and for Pat it was déjà vu all over again. She was opposed to the idea, not because she dreaded campaigning, but she wasn't at all sure what his chances were. Opinion polls were in his favor, but Pat completely understood politics and she was worried about deep divisions within the Republican party itself, and she couldn't face another defeat. She finally relented because, as she had often said, it was his career and not hers. Once the decision was made, she took to the hustings again, and scheduled more events than she had in any previous campaign, including the presidential one. Thousands of people lined up for a chance to meet her and shake her hand, and her rallies routinely outdrew the Democratic candidate himself.

In the last weeks of the contest, the Cuban missile crisis pushed everything else off the front page including the gubernatorial campaign, and in the end the election went to incumbent governor Pat Brown. Pat Nixon's secret fears had been realized. Newspapers were writing Dick's political obituary, and he himself thought his career in politics was dead and buried.

The Nixons decided to leave California and they went to New York City where he became a partner in a successful Wall Street law firm, and bought a large apartment on Fifth Avenue overlooking the Plaza Hotel. His political adversary Nelson Rockefeller lived in the same building, but he didn't roll out the welcome wagon. He and other New York Republican leaders pointedly kept the former vice president out of the loop, and it was apparent that his political career was dead, indeed. In the meantime, Pat became a regular at the Nixon, Mudge law firm, where she handled his mail and answered the telephone as "Miss Ryan."

Except for a few appearances for the Republican candidate, Barry Goldwater, during the 1964 election and lengthy fund-raising tours, Dick stayed generally aloof from politics until 1965 when he began to actively campaign for congressional candidates. Although she often complained about having nothing to do, Pat begged off on his new round of travels.

But Pat liked challenges, and by 1967, when her husband's national star seemed to be rising and he was dead even with Lyndon Johnson in presidential preference polls, she gave in to pressure to help Dick redeem himself because she believed that he was the only man capable of solving the host of problems that were facing the country. She would have preferred to give the rest of her life to her daughters, but Julie had already become engaged to David Eisenhower, the former president's grandson, and it was reasonable to assume that Tricia wouldn't be long in leaving the nest. Meanwhile Dick himself began to wonder if he had the heart to try for the presidency,

Julie Nixon was enrolled at Miss Chapin's School in New York City, where the future Jacqueline Kennedy studied as a girl.

but by the end of the year, he had decided to make the run, and Pat climbed aboard to help.

Washington Again

Pat went into the 1968 election campaign without any illusions. She knew that her husband's defeat in the previous election was a serious liability. As unsure as she was, she supported him through the primaries and into the convention and the race beyond. It was her eighth campaign. One of the differences this time was that Julie and Tricia joined her, and they were as good as their mother at drawing enthusiastic crowds.

The outcome, as before, was agonizingly close, but this time it was Dick who beat Hubert Humphrey to become president. When Pat finally moved into the White House, she was surprised how much it had changed in the eight years since she had been there, but one thing that hadn't changed was press speculation about what she'd choose to be her "cause," which many, although certainly not all, of her predecessors had done. She responded that "my only claim to fame both at home and abroad is Dick's life." It was all she ever had aspired to and her role, as she saw it, was to be part of the team they had developed together so many years before. As the wife of the vice president, Pat had visited fifty-three countries in eight years; as First Lady, she would travel to seventy-eight in five and a half years—more than any of her predecessors.

Pat dove into a full schedule of White House entertaining, and her twenty-three-year-old daughter, Tricia, filled in for her when she was away, which was frequently enough for Tricia to be called the "Assistant First Lady." Pat also supervised the redecorating of the White House, which had become a standard part of the First Lady's job. Lady Bird Johnson had been living with the color choices Jackie Kennedy had made, but Pat had the rooms in the family quarters repainted and decorated them with paintings on loan from the Metropolitan Museum in New York. She had most of the television sets removed (there had been as many as three in some rooms) and some of the telephones as well—they were virtually everywhere. The changes were constant throughout the entire mansion as historic pieces of furniture were acquired or brought out of storage. For the most part, Pat kept her changes unpublicized because she didn't want to upstage the contributions of her predecessors, especially Mrs. Kennedy.

After her first five months, Pat found her "cause" in volunteerism, and she toured the country to promote the idea of

Below: The Nixon's daughter, Julie, was very active in the White House; she welcomed many groups like these Girl Scouts.

> *"She'll never be traipsing along behind the President, she'll never be in front of him, but she'll always be at his side."*
>
> —*Roy Day, campaign aide, on Pat Nixon's place with her husband*

Above: One of the happiest days in the Nixon White House was when daughter Tricia married Edward Cox.

more personal involvement by Americans toward one another. She included college campuses in her tours, even though she faced demonstrations by students who were protesting the president's war policies. But although she found the effort satisfying, she steadfastly refused to call it her only project. She felt that her role in opening the White House to more visitors and honoring them for their achievements was actually more important, and she told anyone who would listen that "people are my project." She built on that idea by scheduling Sunday church services in the White House that in some ways enhanced the old tradition of First Ladies' drawing rooms. It brought noted speakers, and it also drew a cross section of society from Supreme Court justices to switchboard operators, and their children as well. Dick had been raised a Quaker and she a Methodist, but they were no longer part of either denomination, and the ecumenical spirit that characterized the White House prayer services attracted speakers as far apart theologically as Dr. Norman Vincent Peale and the Roman Catholic cardinal of New York.

Pat's official entertaining schedule was staggering. In her first year as First Lady, she had welcomed an unprecedented 45,313 people to the White House, hosted 64 state dinners and 116 receptions, as well as teas that drew people into her world at an average rate of 26,000 a year.

The world outside her door seemed to be turning into a war zone, with young people protesting the Vietnam War, and Black militants demonstrating for rights that were still being withheld from them. Both the president and the First Lady received dozens of death threats, and they were constantly criticized for hanging on to "old values" while the rest of the world seemed to be throwing them aside. But their steadfast resistance to accept change for the sake of change was taken by many as a sign that the country might not be going down the drain after all. Columnist David Broder noted that their efforts seemed to prove that "the violence-wracked America of the late 1960s was capable of being governed after all." No one could deny Pat's influence in demonstrating it.

The rage against the White House intensified after the Vietnam War was escalated into Cambodia and protesting students were shot at Kent State University in Ohio. The blame was placed squarely at the president's doorstep.

About the only bright spot in 1971 came in June, when Tricia married Ed Cox, who was working for consumer activist

Above: Among the dignitaries Pat welcomed to the White House was every child's favorite, Big Bird, who dropped by from Sesame Street.

Below: On her trip to the People's Republic of China, Pat characteristically mingled with the people.

Ralph Nader while he was finishing Harvard Law School. The ceremony took place in the White House Rose Garden, and Pat and Dick were more completely relaxed and happy than they had been since they first moved in.

Early the following year, the president made an unprecedented trip to China, and Pat was received there as the wife of "an imperialist running dog." But she'd heard things like that back in Washington from her own people and it didn't get her down. Because Dick and his advisors were behind closed doors most of the time, the reporters who went along concentrated on Pat, and the Western world discovered China through her eyes. The *Chicago Tribune* noted, "We are starting to wonder whether future historians, commenting on President and Mrs. Nixon's trip to China, won't take the view that in official discussions the President talked business and politics with Chinese leaders while his wife did the important work…. She is establishing direct and friendly contact with the Chinese people on a normal human level where children and families, food and health, and service are the most important things." She had read things like that before, too, over her career. About the only thing she had done differently on this trip abroad was to take her hairdresser along.

Four months after they came back, and had gone to Moscow in the meantime, news leaked that someone had broken into the Democratic party's office in Washington's Watergate complex. The news simmered almost unnoticed, and when the Republicans met to name their candidate for 1972, it was still just a footnote to the campaign, and the president was nominated to run for a second term.

Pat and the girls took on their strongest roles yet when they ran as a family in the campaign that followed. Pat herself was called on to make more speeches than she ever had, speaking to three or four gatherings in every city she hit.

In the meantime, stories on the Watergate affair in the *Washington Post* were appearing more and more frequently. Pat was disturbed, but her husband assured her that they were all exaggerations and that it was just another example of a long-standing press vendetta against him. The allegations were damaging, but Pat was most concerned about the antiwar drumbeat and accusations that the Nixons were indifferent to the death and destruction in Vietnam and Cambodia.

But in spite of the well-organized opposition and riots that dogged the president everywhere he went, on Pat's own independent tour, none of her rallies was interrupted by rioters or hecklers. In the end many of the pundits said that he owed his election to his wife's popularity, which he apparently didn't share himself.

At Pat's suggestion, Premier Chou En-lai had two giant pandas sent to Washington's national zoo. They were the first giant pandas to live in America.

In any event, he took every state except Massachusetts and the District of Columbia.

Right after the first of the year, the war issue faded a bit with a breakthrough in the peace negotiations. The bombing stopped on January 15, and a peace agreement was signed six days later. But the Watergate scandal just kept growing.

Not long before the second Nixon inaugural, Congress voted to open a full investigation of Watergate and other Republican "dirty tricks" during the campaign. As more and more revelations came to light, the president began to distance himself both from his staff and his family. He had always made it a point to cheer Pat when things seemed to be going wrong, but this time around, Pat was beginning to feel like a stranger. But her faith wasn't shaken. She believed in her husband, in his presidency, and she was convinced that he was just the victim of a witch-hunt. As time went by and damaging bombshells exploded around her over the next fifteen months, Pat steadfastly stuck by her husband—they were still a team, after all. The social life of the White House went on interrupted. Pat made sure of that.

Above: During campaign swings, Pat loved to greet the young children.

The biggest dinner ever held at the White House took place in May, when prisoners of war who had come home from Vietnam and their families were invited to the White House. All the public rooms were put to use, and the overflow filled a huge tent out on the lawn. The party went on until four in the morning and the electricity in the air was almost palpable.

During the spring, the president had asked his wife and daughters repeatedly if he should step down, and each time they rallied strongly against the idea. But meanwhile, testimony at the Senate hearings seemed to be suggesting otherwise. Another storm broke near the end of June, when former White House counsel John Dean began testifying before the Senate committee. Pat called the hearings "a snake about to devour people," but as far as the public was concerned they were turning over rocks to drive the snakes out. Dean's testimony, along with others, went on for more than a month, with television cameras catching every bead of sweat. Pat refused to watch most of it because she regarded it as political infighting and little more, and she stopped reading newspapers, too, opting to keep up with the news through White House summaries.

Below: The Nixon family marked Election Day in 1972 with a quiet dinner party. Dick won with an Electoral College landslide in spite of the burgeoning Watergate controversy.

The hearings dragged on into the new year, and by January 1974, Congress was beginning to talk of impeaching the president. Pat became the press's window on the White

Former president Lyndon Johnson died on January 22, 1973, the same day the Vietnam peace agreement was signed.

Above: During their 1974 visit to Egypt, Dick and Pat toured the Great Pyramids with Egypt's President Anwar el-Sadat and his wife.

House, but she had been in public life far too long to be drawn into the controversy. Her most often repeated comment was, "I love him dearly and I have great faith."

After several key Nixon aides, including Attorney General John Mitchell, were sentenced to prison for their part in the Watergate conspiracy, the Nixons attempted to get their lives back on an even keel. White House functions went on as before, and the president and First Lady went on an official trip to Europe and the Middle East before turning right around and going off to Moscow for another summit meeting. But when they finally got back to Washington in July, they found that the Watergate scandal hadn't gone away. In fact, the wheels had been set in motion for an impeachment trial in the House of Representatives. Pat, who had seemed to many people, even her family, to be a fragile woman, suddenly became a tower of strength. But the president could find no other reserve, and on August 8, he told the American people, through a televised address, that he was leaving the presidency. At noon the next day, Pat and Dick boarded a helicopter for the first leg of their long, sad trip back home to California.

Retirement

In his 1962 memoir *Six Crises,* Dick had written that great danger comes not during a battle but afterward, and he was living proof of that when he and Pat retired to La Casa Pacifica, their house at San Clemente overlooking the beach where they had courted.

Dick's spirits were the lowest Pat had ever seen, and that was a signal for her to sustain him as she had always done. But her heart wasn't in it, either. In September, he was felled by a blood clot in his leg, and went to the hospital for treatment. He was bedridden even after his discharge, and Pat became his nurse. Surgery followed a few weeks later, and he was an invalid for nearly all of his first year in retirement.

Below: Pat hated this picture of Tricia and Edward Cox, Dick, Pat, and Julie and David Eisenhower on their final day in the White House. "Our hearts were breaking and there we are smiling," she said.

"I don't know how you keep going," she told him, and he answered, "I just get up in the morning to confound my enemies," and he added, "How do *you* survive?" The secret for both of them had been well known for years: They were a team, and they survived with each other's support.

Pat put away all of her Washington memories, the good ones, too, and she built a private life for herself and Dick. She was a homemaker again—she really never had wanted to be anything else. She tended her garden and filled the house with flowers. She read an average of five books a week, mostly new fiction and biographies. The world was heating up beyond their private beach—the Vietnam War had flickered to life again and thousands more were dying—but that situation was out of their hands now. It even went largely unnoticed when Chairman Mao

Tse-tung invited the Nixons to make a return trip to China and they accepted.

Pat was quite happy not to be the center of attention anymore, and she was surprised when, after she was hospitalized with a minor stroke, more than 200,000 letters and telegrams poured into San Clemente. She thought she had been forgotten.

Pat didn't leave the house much. She even retired the Secret Service agent who was assigned to her because she never saw anyone but close friends and family. Her family started to grow when her first grandchild, Jennie Eisenhower, Julie's daughter, was born, followed a few months later by Christopher Cox, Tricia's son.

But the new grandchildren were back east, and in February 1980, five and half years after they arrived, the Nixons left San Clemente and moved to New York. "We were just dying here slowly," she said.

They moved into a town house on Manhattan's Upper East Side, but Pat missed the openness of her California home and in another year, they moved to an estate in Saddle River, New Jersey. Dick went back to work at his old law firm, but he spent most of his time writing books. Pat's health was failing and she rarely left the new house. She had four grandchildren by then, and no reason go anywhere.

Pat eventually added lung cancer to a long list of her ailments and she died at her New Jersey home on June 22, 1993. She is buried at the Nixon Library at Yorba Linda, California. Her husband joined her there after he died the following year. Just before they were married, he had said, "You have the finest ideals of anyone I have ever known." Nothing she did ever changed his mind.

Visiting the Nixon Library

The Richard M. Nixon Library, where both Dick and Pat are buried, is in Yorba Linda, California, a short distance from downtown Los Angeles. It is one of the largest of America's presidential libraries and one of the most impressive exhibits in the museum portion is the "Ambassador of Good Will" gallery, devoted to the life of Pat Nixon.

The library is open daily from 10:00 A.M. to 5:00 P.M. and on Sundays from 11:00 A.M.; it is closed on Thanksgiving and Christmas. The admission fee is $7.95 for adults over twelve and $3.00 for children. To get there from downtown Los Angeles, use Interstate 5 to Highway 91, east to Highway 57, north to Yorba Linda Boulevard. From San Diego, use Interstate 5 to Highway 57 north to Yorba Linda Boulevard. From Riverside and San Bernardino, use Highway 91 to Imperial Highway (Highway 90) and proceed to Yorba Linda Boulevard. The Library is located at 18001 Yorba Linda Boulevard. The telephone number is 714-993-3393.

Below: The Richard M. Nixon Library in Yorba Linda, California, is where both Nixons are buried.

Betty Ford

A Breath of Fresh Air

Betty Ford single-handedly transformed the country's perception of what it meant to be the First Lady of the United States. Not only did she expand the definition of that role but she also dramatically redefined the way the country talked about such personal matters as breast cancer and drug addiction.

Betty's immediate predecessor, Pat Nixon, had been her polar opposite. Where Pat had been restrained and somewhat rigid, Betty was spontaneous. Where Pat had been reserved and distant, Betty was open and sociable. Where Pat had been strict (or at least formal) in her dealings with White House staff, Betty was adamant that all the workers in the executive mansion speak freely to her and the president. Where Pat had adhered to the traditional subservient (or at least deferential) role of women, Betty passionately championed the passage of the Equal Rights Amendment (ERA) and praised the Supreme Court's ruling legalizing abortion.

When Betty learned she had a cancerous lump in her breast and was told she would need a mastectomy, she conveyed this private information to the American people. When she realized (with the help and mediation of her family) that she was addicted to painkillers and alcohol and needed to go into treatment for her addictions, she told the American people about it. When Betty was asked what her feelings would be if she learned her daughter was having an affair, her unexpected response was that she would not be surprised, because her daughter was, after all, a normal human being. When Betty was asked about marijuana, she bluntly admitted that all her children had tried it and that *she, too,* would have indulged in it had she grown up in the 1970s. In the fall of 1975, in what might have been her most startling remark, Betty told *McCall's* magazine that she wanted to have sex "as often as possible."

The United States had never known such candidness from a First Lady before. Many people suggested that Betty Ford was the most outspoken First Lady since Eleanor Roosevelt. When one considers the public personas of

---

Elizabeth Ann Bloomer Warren Ford

Born
April 8, 1918,
Chicago, Illinois

Parents
William Stephenson Bloomer and Hortense Neahr Bloomer

Marriage
1942 to
William G. Warren

Divorced
1947

Remarried
October 15, 1948, to
Gerald R. Ford (1913-)

Children
Michael Gerald (1950-);
John Gardner (1952-);
Steven Meigs (1956-);
Susan Elizabeth (1957-)

"I am indebted to no man, and only to one woman, my dear wife… [My most valued advice is] that which comes from my wife."

—*Gerald Ford on his wife Betty*

Above: Betty was three when her family moved from Chicago to Grand Rapids, Michigan, to start a new life.

Below: As a teenager, Betty was an ebullient young woman, and she never lost her joyful attitude.

Although a passionate supporter of women's rights, including equal pay, Betty, like countless women of her generation, never worked a single day at a paying job after she was married.

her forerunners—Pat Nixon, Lady Bird Johnson, Jackie Kennedy, Mamie Eisenhower, and Bess Truman—that notion has some validity.

Elizabeth Ann Bloomer was born on Monday, April 8, 1918, in Chicago to William Bloomer and Hortense Neahr Bloomer. Her parents called her Betty. Her father was a salesman; her mother, a homemaker; and Betty was the only daughter of three children. When Betty was two, her father moved the family to Grand Rapids, Michigan. She attended public schools in Grand Rapids and, when she was eight, she began taking dance lessons. From her first lessons, Betty Bloomer was captivated by the art of dance. She continued to study and practice through grammar and high school and even started teaching dance to other students to earn money to pay for her own lessons. She earned a dance certificate from the Calla Travis Dance Studio in 1935.

After her graduation from Grand Rapids Central High School in 1936, Betty attended the Bennington School of Dance at Bennington College in Vermont for two summers. The dance school had been founded two years earlier by Martha Graham and her partners, and it would ultimately evolve into the renowned American Dance Festival. Martha Graham was an enormous influence on Betty, and the future First Lady was thrilled when she was accepted into Graham's newly formed New York City dance group. Betty moved to the West Side of Manhattan in her early twenties to study and dance with Graham as an auxiliary with the troupe. To supplement her income, the very attractive Betty worked as a fashion model for the John Robert Powers Agency while living in New York City.

Betty's decision to live in Manhattan was difficult for her family back in Michigan. The Bloomer family was close-knit, and Betty's mother, in particular, was not happy about her daughter's living in New York and being so far away. Ultimately, the physical and emotional distance took its toll and, after a couple of years in the Big Apple, Betty returned to Grand Rapids.

Betty's experiences with both dancing and modeling served her well back home, and she quickly found work as a fashion coordinator, window designer, and buyer for a department store, and also as a part-time dance

"[Betty Ford] is the most refreshing character we've had in public life for some time."

—Photographer Ansel Adams, during the ceremony naming Betty Ford a Fellow of the National Academy of Design

Above: At the age of twenty, Betty was the center of attention as an accomplished dancer.

instructor for disabled children. It was during this period that Betty first married.

In 1942, when she was twenty-four, Betty met William G. Warren, a Grand Rapids salesman. They married the same year and their union lasted five years. The two divorced in 1947 and Betty has rarely spoken in detail about the marriage, claiming that she has little memory of the years she spent with Warren. Some sources offer a range of speculations as to why the marriage failed— including Warren's drinking—but as is always the case with affairs of the heart, only the two people involved know the conclusive truth. Betty has stated on more than one occasion that her first marriage ended amicably. The Warrens had no children during their five years together, and the official petition for divorce claimed incompatibility as the cause for the split.

During this time, Jerry Ford, a 1941 graduate of Yale Law School—he was in the top third of his class—was immersed in his law career in his hometown of Grand Rapids. By late 1947, at the age of thirty-four, he had become a partner in the local law firm of Butterfield, Keeney, and Amberg. Jerry was a University of Michigan football hero, and a charming, dashing, athletic man-about-town whom Betty once described as "the most eligible bachelor in Grand Rapids." The two met shortly after Betty's divorce and quickly fell in love. Jerry proposed to Betty in February 1948, but told her they could not marry until the fall of that year at the earliest—and he was secretive as to the reason why. Betty happily accepted his proposal, yet did not learn until later that Jerry's big secret was that, upon the recommendation of his stepfather, who was the Republican county chairman, he had decided to run for the United States House of Representatives. Perhaps Jerry was apprehensive that Betty would not accept his proposal if a move to Washington, D.C., was included as part of the deal. After all, he probably knew she had moved back to Michigan from New York so she would no longer have to be separated from her family.

Betty later joked that Jerry proposed to her and announced his candidacy on the same day, yet he conveniently forgot to mention the candidacy part when he asked her to marry him. It is understandable why the future president did not reveal his plans to his intended. Aside from the aforementioned concerns about Betty's willingness to live in Washington, there was also the real possibility he would lose the election, thus rendering any discussion of a possible move to Washington moot.

Below: Betty became a part of the Martha Graham Dance Company in New York and worked as a part-time model to keep her dream alive.

Above: Betty and Jerry pose with their parents at their wedding in 1948: (from left to right) Gerald Ford, Sr., Dorothy Gardner Ford, the bride and the groom, Hortense Bloomer Godwin, and Arthur Godwin.

On Friday, October 15, 1948, Jerry and Betty Ford were married at Grace Episcopal Church in Grand Rapids. Jerry Ford was late for the ceremony. He had spent the earlier part of the day glad-handing voters and simply was not able to make it to the church on time. After the ceremony and reception were over, the newlyweds, rather than stealing away to some remote romantic hideaway for their honeymoon, instead attended a political rally for presidential candidate Thomas Dewey. Betty Ford spent her wedding night listening to campaign speeches! It was immediately obvious to Betty how important politics were to her new husband, and perhaps she could foresee her inevitable, ultimate "politician's wife" reality—that her husband's career would always come first.

Three weeks later, in November 1948, Jerry won the congressional election and was elected to the U.S. House of Representatives for Michigan's fifth congressional district. He won by 61 percent of the vote and this political victory marked the beginning of his rise to the presidency, and the start of Betty Ford's life as one of the aforementioned political wives.

The Politician and Mrs. Ford

Suddenly, at the age of thirty, Betty was the wife of a newly elected congressman, living in a new home in Washington, D.C., while also maintaining a home in Grand Rapids.

Betty was taken somewhat unawares by Jerry's political aspirations (after all, he was, for the most part, a nice local Grand Rapids lawyer in her eyes); the move to Washington in 1948 was obviously unexpected. By the middle of 1949, she was pregnant with their first child, Michael, who was born in Washington in March 1950. By the middle of 1951, she was pregnant with their second child, Jack, who was born in 1952. Two more children, Steven and Susan, followed in 1956 and 1957, and as the Ford family grew and the demands on Betty increased, so did the responsibilities of Congressman Ford, who was away from his wife and family more and more, usually getting home late and leaving early the following morning. Betty once joked that she had made so many solo

When Betty accompanied her husband to China and was seen dancing with Chinese children, The New York Times *ran an article titled "Not a Robot at All."*

trips to the emergency room for her sons' many childhood injuries that the car probably knew the way on its own.

Congressman Ford's job was all-consuming and his private life paid a price. Betty ran the Ford household, cared for the children, and also worked for her husband when needed. The pressures on her were enormous and she has admitted that she felt anxious and exhausted during this period, especially when the children were small and her husband's political career was in its earliest stages. During these years, the seeds were sown for her later battles with addictions—she became addicted to alcohol and pharmaceuticals—as well as her triumph over them and her subsequent founding of the rehabilitation clinic that bears her name.

Added to the demands of being the mother of four small children, Betty also had to play the role of wife and ardent supporter of a popular, outgoing, and ambitious politician. Gerald Ford routinely entertained constituents and fellow politicians, and this oftentimes required Betty to serve as hostess and accompany her husband to countless fund-raising dinners and political events. In addition, ironically, considering the impact his career had on his wife and family, Jerry did not keep his professional and personal life separate. The story is often told of the time a reporter asked him if he could call him at some point to set up an interview. Jerry scribbled a phone number on a piece of paper and handed it to the reporter. The journalist looked at it and, assuming it was an office number, requested the name of the person he should ask for when he called. Jerry replied, "Just ask for me," and told the surprised reporter it was his home number. This was typical for Jerry, and it required Betty to always be "on," because she never knew who would be calling when their home phone rang.

Below: Betty, here with baby, Jack, and toddler, Michael, did much of the child rearing by herself while Jerry was a Congressman.

Betty obligingly played her role, however, tending to their young children while also taking on the other responsibilities expected of a busy congressman's wife. She joined all the appropriate Washington wives' clubs, she taught Sunday school, and she tried to keep heart and mind together. Social activities and duties were part and parcel of Betty's life as the wife of a politician. The social obligations required her to be charming, and always dutiful to her husband's career. For Betty, this was not always easy.

Above: Betty, Jerry, their daughter, Susan, and their three sons Steven, John, and Michael.

The Ford Children

In a 1978 interview with McCall's magazine that was published after her husband lost the White House to Jimmy Carter in 1976, Betty Ford remembered back to those early days in Washington, and talked about what it was like to be a de facto single parent. When asked who she felt had had the most influence on her, she responded that it was her mother. But then she opined that her own children would probably answer the same question similarly since, when they were growing up, their father was always away. Still, with all the pressures of growing up in the glare of the public spotlight and with an absentee father, the Ford children have all gone on to reflect well on the Ford family name.

Michael Ford studied at Wake Forest University in Winston-Salem, North Carolina, and then became an ordained minister. In 1977 he joined the ministerial staff of the Coalition for Christian Outreach at the University of Pittsburgh; in 1981 he was appointed student affairs director at Wake Forest; today he is the director of student development there. He and his wife, Gayle, have three daughters: Sarah, Rebekah, and Hannah.

Jack Ford is cofounder of California Info Tech, a company that supplies electronic information kiosks to shopping malls. He was executive director of the host committee of the 1996 San Diego Republican Convention and is married to Juliann Felando. They have two sons, and live in California.

Steven Ford worked as a cowboy team roper on the professional rodeo circuit when he was a teenager and is now an established actor. He has appeared in the movies Armageddon, Black Hawk Down, Contact, Starship Troopers, *and* When Harry Met Sally, *and on many TV series in guest roles; he was a regular on the soap opera* The Young and the Restless. *He now owns a ranch in San Luis Obispo and has bred thoroughbred racehorses. He serves on the board of directors of the Gerald R. Ford Museum and is single with no children.*

Susan Ford Bales is the Fords' only daughter. She's a photographer who studied under Ansel Adams and her photo credits include Newsweek, Ladies' Home Journal, *and the Associated Press. She's the author of two novels,* Double Exposure *and* Sharp Focus, *both "First Daughter" mysteries; a board member of the Betty Ford Center; and a past national spokesperson for National Breast Cancer Awareness Month. She lives in the Southwest with her husband, Vaden Bales, and their two daughters.*

Below: When Betty's oldest son, Michael, left home, he was bound for Wake Forest University in North Carolina.

Betty knew that her husband had lofty political aspirations (although the presidency was apparently never in his sights). In 1964, he was appointed minority leader and it was then that he began focusing on what he considered to be his ultimate political goal, Speaker of the House. Jerry's new congressional responsibilities came with a staggering itinerary. At one point, he was making more than two hundred political appearances a year, traveling all over the country, as well as keeping up with his Washington-based work as minority leader, all of which he undertook alone. Betty, for the most part, stayed home. After all, Jerry wasn't actually running for anything, thus his speeches and appearances were all in support of his party and its agenda, so there was no need for his wife to always appear by his side—a paradigm that is absolutely required when a politician becomes a candidate for office and must project a wholesome, family man persona.

Above: Betty had a busy life as the wife of a Congressman; she often entertained guests from back home and elsewhere.

However, as we've come to learn, these were not happy years for Betty and, by the end of the 1960s, she was on the verge of a nervous breakdown. Her physical pain from a pinched nerve and arthritis, combined with what she perceived to be a deterioration of both her marriage and her family life, led her to treat herself with an ongoing regimen of painkillers, liberally augmented with alcohol. In 1970, Betty sought psychiatric therapy for her problems and was able to regain some semblance of her former self. She emerged from this period feeling mentally healthier and happier, although she was still depending on medication and she was still drinking.

Jerry never rose to the position of Speaker of the House and, in fact, he and Betty discussed his retiring from politics when his congressional term ended. However, one day in late 1973, President Nixon called Jerry and asked him to come visit him at the White House. Jerry did not know why he was being summoned, but he, of course, went and the two men chatted and reminisced. In 1949, Richard Nixon had been one of the first politicians to warmly welcome Jerry to Congress and, during their informal late 1973 meeting, they talked about their shared history. Jerry admitted later that he had had no idea of the purpose of the meeting until later, when he heard that Vice President Spiro Agnew had resigned, and President Nixon then asked him to consider a nomination for the vice presidency, which, after discussing with Betty, he accepted.

Below: Betty waits patiently to help Jerry reel in a big one on a Caribbean deep sea fishing trip.

On December 6, 1973, following what has been described as the most comprehensive background check ever conducted by the FBI, Gerald Ford was sworn in as vice president of the United States. However, his position as Richard Nixon's vice president did not automatically confer on him a role as one of the president's chief advisors.

For the next nine months, Jerry watched more or less from the sidelines as the Watergate scandal unfolded. Jerry has admitted that during this time he was often

During the Ford administration, sixty-six women filled government positions requiring Senate approval, the highest in history to that point. Many historians credit Betty's influence as being responsible for this groundbreaking number of female appointees.

at odds with some of the people giving President Nixon advice, people like Bob Haldeman, John Ehrlichman, and Chuck Colson. Betty was supportive and encouraging during the period of Jerry's vice presidency, and worked diligently to be a visible presence to the American people as the vice president's wife, always gracious, always dignified. Yet it was difficult to always put on a smile and radiate optimism as the significance of the Watergate scandal swelled exponentially, and tainted all things political with uncertainty, suspicion, and shock.

On August 1, 1974, Jerry—who had yet to move into the Blair House, the vice president's Washington residence—received a phone call from the White House chief of staff Alexander Haig, a phone call that would change his and Betty's lives, and that would also change the United States for all time. Haig told a quickly stunned Jerry that an audiotape would soon be released that would be seen as incredibly damning to the president; smoking gun evidence that Richard Nixon, while president, had intentionally covered up the Watergate break-in. Haig told Jerry that it was becoming obvious that the president would either be impeached and possibly forcibly removed from office, or that he would resign the presidency beforehand. Haig then advised Jerry to prepare himself for the possibility that he would soon be president of the United States. Jerry reportedly hung up the phone, turned to his wife, and said, "Betty, I don't think we're ever going to live in the vice president's house."

The Accidental First Lady

After twelve successful reelections and twenty-five years in Congress representing his Michigan district, followed by an unexpected few months as vice president, Gerald Ford was suddenly president of the United States, and Betty was the new First Lady.

Throughout their years in Washington, Betty suffered from osteoarthritis and a pinched nerve, as well as ongoing nervous anxiety. She routinely medicated her stress with alcohol and tranquilizers, and treated her physical ailments with painkillers. Betty continued her drinking and drug use throughout her years in the White House. When her husband was vice president, she had once admitted to a reporter that her occasional drowsiness in public was due to the fact that she took a Valium every day. The United States was stunned. A vice president's wife not only admitted she took tranquilizers but mentioned the drug by name!

As First Lady, Betty was outspoken and honest. She discussed topics publicly that still

"Our long national nightmare is over."

—Gerald Ford, following his swearing-in as president after Richard Nixon's resignation

Above: Betty characterized her role of First Lady as "a twenty-four hour-a-day volunteer job," and she was on call at all hours of the day and night dealing with the responsibility.

retained a taboo aura—premarital sex, abortion, and birth control. It is possible that her drug use and drinking "loosened her tongue," both figuratively and literally. Would Betty have been more restrained when asked questions about sex and marijuana use had she been completely sober? Regardless of the answer to that question, the reality is that Betty did, indeed, answer openly those kinds of questions and was almost immediately embraced by the American people as being, ironically, a voice of sober lucidity; a modern woman who insisted on speaking her mind about the real world she and everyone else were living in.

When Jerry became president, he inherited a slew of monumental challenges, not the least of which was the "Nixon problem." Following Nixon's resignation, the government and the American people were fixated on what would happen next. Would there be indictments? Would a former president of the United States be put on public trial for malfeasance and dereliction of duty? Moreover, if this did happen, and Nixon was ultimately found guilty of felonious behavior while president, would the day come in America when a former chief executive would be sentenced for his crimes and actually imprisoned?

In addition to the Nixon question, President Ford also had to contend with a horrible economy. In 1974, the unemployment rate hit 7 percent, consumer interest rates skyrocketed to 12 percent, the Dow Jones fell a staggering 28 percent, automobile sales fell 23 percent, oil prices were on the rise, and real economic growth was a *negative* 5 percent. Jerry knew that his focus—as well as that of the American people and the Congress and Senate—had to be on restoring economic health to the nation. Yet following Nixon's resignation, Jerry estimated that a full 25 percent of the government's time was being spent on the possible fate of Richard Nixon.

Faced with what Jerry perceived to be a possibly catastrophic drift on a national scale, he turned to Betty to discuss the notion of pardoning Richard Nixon. At this time, Betty knew two things: The first was that her husband had an overwhelmingly positive reputation as an honest politician; the second was that the American people, emotionally bloodied by the revelations of corruption and dishonesty at the highest levels of government, were demanding more honesty from their elected officials. She also agreed with her husband that the attention on the resolution of the Nixon issue was hurting the nation. The distraction was destructive. Betty knew the American people expected her husband to do the "right thing," and she encouraged him to pardon Nixon and put an end to the country's shared national nightmare. She had her eye on the well-being of America, as did her husband, and it made sense to both of them that a decision that would ultimately be for the good of the country would be recognized as such, and be well received by Americans. It would instill support for the new president and move the country forward.

Ironically, this decision did the opposite, in that it, in the end, hurt Jerry's presidency and hampered his ability to govern. There have long been rumors that Jerry was coerced into pardoning Richard Nixon. It has been rumored that Jerry was threatened with a smear campaign; that he would be publicly besmirched by stories that he cut a deal with Nixon to ascend to the presidency on the condition that he would unequivocally pardon the disgraced president. This has never been proven, and the president and Betty have always stated that the decision to pardon Nixon was Jerry's, and that no one compelled his actions.

In retrospect, with all the tumult of an administration change and nonstop talk of corruption, it is easy to see why, in the early months of the Ford administration, times in the Ford household were tense. And soon, health concerns would be added to the mix. On September 8, 1974, Gerald Ford pardoned Richard Nixon. On September 28, 1974, Betty Ford underwent a mastectomy for malignant breast cancer.

Telling the Truth

Jerry and Betty knew that previous First Ladies had concealed from the American people information about their health. Sometimes, many years after leaving the White House, details about a First Lady's health and health problems would surface, but no First Lady had ever gone public with specifics about her personal health while her husband was president. The health of the president, on the other hand, is public information—the details of his annual physicals are released to the press and pored over in newspapers and on TV. But First Ladies

Below: Although he never planned to become president, Jerry characteristically took the job in stride.

Image vs. Reality

During his presidency, an image of Gerald Ford as being boring, clumsy, and clueless took hold in the American consciousness, due in large part to some inadvertent public stumbles and falls by Jerry, which prompted some good-natured mockery by Chevy Chase on Saturday Night Live, *as well as the fact that Jerry did not win election to the presidency but rather inherited it in an "accidental presidency" scenario. The truth, however, as it often is, was different. Jerry's well-known integrity, his boundless gregariousness, and his oftentimes uncanny ability to remember names and faces not only served him well in politics in general and in Congress in particular (and later in the White House), but added additional burdens on Betty who was held to those same standards. (It should also be noted that Jerry was, without question, the most successfully athletic president in American history.)*

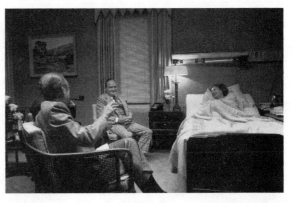

Above: Jerry took comedian Bob Hope to help cheer Betty after her cancer surgery.

aren't required to discuss their health, and most did not, until Betty came along.

Immediately after her breast cancer surgery, Betty released a statement detailing the specifics of her illness, the details of her surgery, and her doctors' plan for her subsequent follow-up treatment. The entire nation suddenly knew about the removal of her breast, her chemotherapy, and her prognosis. She was forthcoming, she was honest, and, perhaps most important, she was unashamed and unabashed about revealing personal details about her body to the American people.

The time, apparently, was right for such openness. Betty's candor was embraced, and it launched what can justifiably be described as a new era of public awareness about breast cancer. Suddenly, the previously taboo topic was written about openly in magazines and newspapers, discussed on TV, and lectured about at seminars. Millions of women went for breast exams, and it is a certainty that Betty's decision to speak out saved many lives. Her decision to simply tell the truth was rooted in her character and personality, yet she knew full well the response her forthrightness generated. "I felt people were asking whenever I appeared in public," she once good-naturedly admitted, "'Which one did she lose?' But I got over it by reminding myself how much good I'd accomplished."

As First Lady, Betty was also open and vocal about other issues that were important to her, specifically a woman's right to choose and the Supreme Court's *Roe v. Wade* decision, and the ERA. She strongly supported both, and admitted so publicly on many occasions. She rankled a great many conservatives by her outspokenness on abortion and equal rights for women, but she never tempered her comments in an attempt to placate. *This is what I believe* is the message she sent out to the nation, and she did so with the full support of her husband, who often admitted that his wife was one of his most influential advisors.

Betty was a social and cultural female firebrand, the likes of which had never before been seen in the White House. Aside from her breast cancer revelation, if there was another single event that can be viewed as iconic of everything that Betty stood for, it would have to be her August 1975 interview with Morley Safer on the CBS news program *60 Minutes*.

Betty—who had not expected to be asked controversial questions when she agreed to the interview, but nonetheless responded to them when Safer asked them—said things during this interview that had never before been said by a First Lady. She talked openly about sex, marijuana, abortion, and other volatile issues, never hedging, never taking offense at a question. Her husband

Above: Betty joined hands with her successor, Rosalynn Carter, to show her support for the Equal Rights Amendment.

Below: On her last day as First Lady, Betty danced on the table in the usually formal Cabinet Room.

E.R.A. R.I.P.?

When Betty was First Lady, she assembled a staff whose sole responsibility was to write congressmen and encourage them to vote for the passage of the Equal Rights Amendment (which was first introduced into Congress in 1923).

During her personal ERA calling campaign, Betty had a separate phone installed in her name in the White House for her calls, so as not to undertake political lobbying on the taxpayers' dime. Betty's efforts for the ERA were not widely approved. At one point, letters were three to one against her and protesters marched in front of the White House carrying "Stop the ERA" signs.

As of 2005, fifteen states have not yet ratified the Equal Rights Amendment, the passage of which continues to be a very important cause to Betty. The fifteen non-ratifying states are Alabama, Arizona, Arkansas, Florida, Georgia, Illinois, Louisiana, Mississippi, Missouri, Nevada, North Carolina, Oklahoma, South Carolina, Utah, and Virginia. According to the Web site equalrightsamendment.org, fifty-seven national organizations and associations have endorsed the ERA (the complete list can be found on their site).

the president was, at first, bemused by her appearance, commenting good-naturedly to her that she had probably lost him ten million votes by her comments. However, as has been noted in many books and articles about the Fords, some of Betty's *60 Minutes* comments were later reprinted out of context and controversy flared. President Ford later revised his lost-votes estimate to twenty million after reading Betty's words in the press.

Twenty-eight thousand negative letters poured into the White House and every letter was answered with a personally written missive from Betty. This would seem to be a possibly fatal blow to her image and standing with the American people, but the backlash was small, and ultimately short-lived. Following her *60 Minutes* interview, Betty's poll numbers skyrocketed—women especially were overwhelmingly supportive—and she was ultimately christened Woman of the Year by *Time* magazine.

"There was even some demonstrating in front of the White House against me as an immoral woman—and how can the First Lady of the land have such immoral ideas? At that time it was pretty shocking."

—Betty Ford on the controversy over her comment that she would not have been surprised if her daughter told her she was having an affair

One month after Betty's notable *60 Minutes* appearance, two assassination attempts were made against President Ford. Both assailants were women, both were captured, and Jerry was unhurt. It is likely that these failed assassination attempts engendered sympathy and compassion toward Betty, especially by American women, as they watched as she stood by her husband, calm and composed, grateful he had been uninjured.

New Challenges

In 1976, President Ford garnered the Republican party's nomination for reelection, and First Lady Betty Ford was one of his most powerful assets during the campaign. She fully agreed with her husband's decision to run, and she did what she could to ensure four more years in the White House. She made public appearances, she gave speeches, she schmoozed with voters, and she gave interviews. Jerry was running against Democrat Jimmy Carter, an unlikely candidate who rose from being a virtual unknown to the American

Betty Ford's Letter to 60 Minutes

One of the most difficult episodes in the first year of Gerald Ford's presidency was Betty Ford's appearance on 60 Minutes *and the resultant explosion of controversy over some of her remarks. The conservative religious right was furious about a handful of comments by Betty. In response to the thousands of negative letters that flooded into the White House, Betty drafted and sent the following letter, which served to reverse her plummeting poll numbers and quiet the angry Americans, many of whom, after her interview, perceived her as a debaucher of youth and a moral degenerate:*

"Thank you for writing about my appearance on the 60 Minutes *interview. The concern which inspired you to share your views is appreciated. I wish it were possible for us to sit down and talk, one to another. I consider myself a responsible parent. I know I am a loving one. We have raised our four children in a home that believes in and practices the enduring values of morality and personal integrity.*

As every mother and father knows, these are not easy times to be a parent. Our convictions are constantly being tested by the fads and fancies of the moment. I believe our values to be eternal and I hope I have instilled them in our children.

We have come to this sharing of outlook through communication, not coercion. I want my children to know that their concerns— their doubts and difficulties—whatever they may be, can be discussed with the two people in the world who care the most—their mother and father.

On 60 Minutes *the emotion of my words spoke to the need of this communication, rather than the specific issues discussed.*

My husband and I have lived twenty-six years of faithfulness in marriage. I do not believe in premarital relations, but I realize that many in today's generation do not share my views. However, this must never cause us to withdraw the love, the counseling and the understanding that they may need now, more than ever before.

This is the essence of my responsible parenthood. It is difficult to express one's personal convictions in a fifteen-minute interview. I hope our lives will say more than words about our dedication to honor, to integrity, to humanity and to God. You and I, they and I, have no quarrels."

people to the standard-bearer and candidate for president for his party. Carter's support from the electorate was questionable and Betty had enormous confidence in her husband's winning the election and, after his abbreviated first term, serving a full four-year term in the White House as the legitimately elected choice of the American people.

Jerry had tremendous support from his party, but the Nixon pardon still haunted his reputation and there was concern in some corners of the Republican camp that this would hurt his chances for winning the election. There were questions, mainly among Democrats, about Jerry's integrity.

Apparently, however, this undercurrent of suspicion did not sway the majority of Republican voters and the election was incredibly close. Gerald Ford ultimately lost to Jimmy Carter by a mere 2.1 percent of the popular vote and only fifty-seven electoral votes. Jerry was gracious in defeat, but Betty was privately devastated by the loss. She had grown to love being First Lady. "I had thought I would hate being First Lady," she once said. "[But] I loved it."

Following President Ford's defeat, the former First Couple retired to Rancho Mirage, California. Betty, likely still reeling from the shock of the defeat, continued to use, and ultimately abuse, prescription drugs and alcohol. Her family became increasingly concerned about her addictions and, in 1978, they persuaded her to enter a treatment facility in Long Beach, California. This was the beginning of her lifelong recovery, as well as the genesis of the achievement for which Betty will likely be best remembered, the founding of the Betty Ford Center.

When Betty was in treatment, she came to the conclusion that rehabilitation therapy should be gender specific—men should undergo therapy with men and women with women. That is one of the guiding principles of the Betty Ford Center. Jerry believed that triumph over addictions could be hampered, or possibly prevented, by mixed-gender therapy.

In 1982, Betty cofounded the Betty Ford Center with her friend Leonard Firestone and it quickly became a very popular rehabilitation destination for men, women, and families battling addictions and, today, the Betty

Below: After his nomination for a full term, Jerry and Betty began their first and only national election campaign. Jerry had never run for any office except in Congressional races in Michigan.

During President Ford's 1976 campaign (which he lost) many supporters, hoping to capitalize on the First Lady's popularity, sported "Betty's Husband for President" buttons.

Ford Center is considered, hands down, the leading treatment facility in the United States.

In October 1999, President and Mrs. Ford were awarded the Congressional Gold Medal, Congress's highest honor. The two were praised for their "dedicated public service and outstanding humanitarian contributions." In their retirement, Mrs. Ford continues to serve as chairman of the board of directors of the Betty Ford Center, and is a highly sought after public speaker. She is also the author of two best-selling books. Her first is a 1978 autobiography titled *The Times of My Life*, in which she told her life story through the end of her years as First Lady. In 1987, her second book, *Betty: A Glad Awakening*, was published, in which she discussed her recovery from drug addiction and alcoholism. Her interests and focus remain the same as when she was First Lady: breast cancer awareness, women's rights, handicapped children, the arts, and the battle against crippling arthritis.

> *"My makeup wasn't smeared, I wasn't disheveled, I behaved politely, and I never finished off a bottle, so how could I be alcoholic?"*
>
> —Betty Ford on her own assessment of her drinking problem

Above: The Ford family: Steve, Susan, Jack and his wife, Gayle, and Mike, with Jerry and Betty, after they retired to California.

> *"[I hope I'm remembered] in a very kind way as a constructive wife of the president."*
>
> —Betty Ford on her legacy

Below: The Gerald R. Ford Museum in Grand Rapids, Michigan, traces the lives of the First Family.

Visiting the Gerald R. Ford Library and Museum

The Gerald R. Ford Library is located in Ann Arbor, Michigan, on the grounds of the University of Michigan. The Gerald R. Ford Museum is a separate facility in Grand Rapids, Michigan.

The Ford Library promotes popular interest and scholarly research in U.S. history during the post–World War II era, especially the Ford presidency from 1974 to 1977. The library collects and preserves the archival record, and aids public access.

The Ford Museum presents an ambitious program of exhibits and special events, including the permanent exhibits A 1970s Gallery, The Young Jerry Ford, Constitution in Crisis, and At Work in the Oval Office.

The Ford Library is located at 1000 Beal Avenue, Ann Arbor, Michigan 48109. The library's hours are Monday through Friday, from 8:45 A.M. to 4:45 P.M., excluding federal holidays. The telephone number is 734-205-0555.

The Ford Museum is located at 303 Pearl Street NW, Grand Rapids, Michigan 49504. The telephone number is 616-254-0400. The museum is open daily from 9:00 A.M. to 5:00 P.M., and closed January 1, Thanksgiving Day, and Christmas Day. Admission is $5.00 for adults, $4.00 for senior citizens, and free for children under the age of sixteen. Free parking is available.

Rosalynn Carter

Where Everyone Knows Your Name

When Rosalynn Smith was a schoolgirl in the tiny town of Plains, Georgia, she never missed the school bus. Her father was the bus driver, and to him every day was "Take Your Daughter to Work" day. That wasn't his only job, however. He worked in the general store on weekends and he tended a farm just outside of town, but his real line of work was running Plains's only car-repair garage, and he kept his neighbors' cars, trucks, and tractors purring along. He wasn't poor by local standards, although he wasn't well-off by anybody's measure, and the Smith family always had a car (even if he had rescued them from the junk heap), which was a sign of status in 1920s Georgia.

Edgar Smith met his wife, the former Allie Murray, when she was in ninth grade and he was driving the school bus. Such things weren't considered unusual in the rural South, and she accepted his marriage proposal, but she wouldn't set a wedding date until after she had graduated from college with a teacher's diploma. Their first child was born a year afterward, on August 18, 1927, and they named her Eleanor Rosalynn, after Allie's mother, Rosa. Rosalynn's first brother, Jerry, was born two years later, and eventually the family grew to include another brother, Murray, and their sister, Allethra.

There were no other little girls in their neighborhood, and during her preschool years, Rosalynn played with her brothers and their friends. But playtime was scarce. They all had work to do, helping their father on the farm, where they grew their own food, and their mother with the housework. Rosalynn and her mother also made all of the family's clothes, and she had her father drive her to Americus, the nearest town that could pass for a city, to sketch clothes on display in store windows that her mother could duplicate for her. By the time Rosalynn went to school, she was one of the best-dressed girls there.

Plains had a population of less than six hundred people and they all knew one another. There was no such thing as privacy, but no one was ever alone in times of trouble, either. It was Plains against the world and they all stuck together. There was no movie theater in town, and no library, or any place else where people could gather except the churches, and there were three of those. Rosalynn's Grandmother Murray was a Lutheran and her husband a Baptist, and her parents belonged to the Methodist Church, and so Rosalynn went to all three, "every time the doors opened." She went to the regular church services and stayed on for Sunday school and afternoon prayer meetings. She

Eleanor Rosalynn Smith Carter

Born
August 18, 1927,
Botsford, Georgia

Parents
Wilburn Edgar Smith
and Frances Allethra
Murray Smith

Marriage
July 7, 1946, to James Earl
Carter, Jr. (1924-)

Children
John William (Jack)
(1947-); James Earl (Chip)
(1950 -); Donnel Jeffrey
(1952-); Amy Lynn
(1967-)

was practically a fixture in the Methodist League, the Baptist Girls' Auxiliary, and the Lutheran Bible School. The Smith family never missed family nights and suppers at any of the three churches and, as if their souls might still need saving, they were on hand for every meeting—usually two a day—when the revivalists pitched their tents in Plains every summer.

When Rosalynn started school, she earned straight As in first grade and she never ever broke the pattern, finally graduating as the class valedictorian. In third grade, she was assigned to help teach mathematics to the younger students. "I knew I wasn't perfect," she said, "but I didn't want my daddy to know." He thought she was unusually bright—and he was probably right—and she worked hard not to let him down, even after he died.

Her father died when Rosalynn was thirteen. Less than a year after that, her grandmother also died and her grandfather moved into town to live with his daughter and her four children. Allie coped by becoming a seamstress and Rosalynn helped her; she also eked out a small income selling milk and butter produced by the family cow, and she leased out her late husband's farm to help keep the family going. She eventually took a job at the local post office, and taking care of the family fell to Rosalynn. At a time in her life when she might have been living the life of a frivolous teenager, she was forced to become a responsible adult.

She wasn't without a social life, though. She dated on weekends, and she played on the high school basketball team. She also developed a close friendship with Ruth Carter, the most popular girl in school. Ruth had a brother named Jimmy, but the Carters lived out in the country and Rosalynn had never met him except in passing. The only other member of the family she knew was their mother, Miss Lillian, the local visiting nurse, who had come to the Smith house often when Rosalynn's father was dying.

After she graduated from high school in 1944, Rosalyn went to Georgia Southwestern Junior College in Americus, ten miles away. She lived at home and commuted there, although it had been her dream to get out of Plains and have a look at the world outside. The world outside, as far as she was concerned, was Ruth Carter's house and Rosalynn had developed a crush on Ruth's brother Jimmy, or at least the photograph of him that was in the living room. He was three years older than she was, and he had been away at school for four years, so he wasn't aware that Rosalynn Smith even existed,

It became a game between the two girls to change that. Whenever he was home from school, Ruth invited Rosalynn to visit, hoping that Jimmy would be at the house when she arrived. Most of the time he wasn't, but finally she got them together. He was friendly enough, but there was no spark there as far as Rosalynn could see and she gave up until he met her

Below: At the young age of seventeen, Rosalynn was shouldering adult responsibilities.

in church a few days afterward and asked her on a double date with his little sister.

They met again when he was leaving to go back to school and Rosalynn became a part of the family farewell at the train station. That had been Jimmy's own idea. He made Rosalynn promise to write and then he left for his first year at the U.S. Naval Academy in Annapolis, Maryland. She kept the promise, and so did he, and by the time he came home for Christmas, a full-blown romance had blossomed. He proposed before he left, but she turned him down.

She was planning to go on to Georgia State College for Women, where her mother had earned her own degree, and they had finally figured out how to get the money together to pay for it. Jimmy understood and his letters kept coming. Then when Rosalynn went to visit him during Washington's Birthday weekend in February, he asked her again if she would marry him and she said that she would. Wild horses couldn't have dragged her away from the idea by then.

It wasn't that Jimmy's father, Mr. Earl, didn't try. He liked Rosalynn well enough, but he didn't like the idea of his son getting married. He had bigger plans for him than having him saddled with a nineteen-year-old girl from town. Ruth wasn't too happy, either. For all of her plotting and scheming, she was jealous of anyone who might come between her and her brother, even if it was her best friend. Only Jimmy's mother, Miss Lillian, was pleased with the match.

The opposition notwithstanding, Rosalynn and Jimmy were married at Annapolis on July 7, 1946. It was a small private ceremony, but the Carter family was there in spite of their reservations. The newlyweds moved to Norfolk, Virginia, where Jimmy, a naval lieutenant, had been assigned. But Rosalynn found herself alone nearly all the time. Jimmy was at sea from Monday through Thursday, sometimes Friday, every week, and he was on duty aboard the ship one of the nights that they were in port. She had never lived anywhere except in Plains, and although she had been her mother's right hand back there, she hadn't learned to cook. She taught herself rather quickly, and she learned how to deal with a landlord, to balance a checkbook, and to keep up with the bills. Jimmy, who somehow had learned all those things somewhere along the way, supported her, and he encouraged her to learn on her own.

She would soon have other skills to learn. Their first child, Jack, was born a few days before their first wedding anniversary. Rosalynn had helped raise her brothers and her sister, but they weren't babies when she started, and there was always someone around to help her when she needed it. Now she was alone with her baby, who "slept little and cried a lot," and a constant round of washing, ironing, cleaning, and mopping. But as she said

Above: Jimmy was a midshipman at the U.S. Naval Academy in Annapolis, Maryland.

Below: Jimmy and Rosalynn were married in 1946 right after his graduation from the Naval Academy.

of little Jack, "I loved him so much (as happened with all my babies) I thought my heart would burst," and she was "more content than I had been in years."

Their lives changed in 1948 when Jimmy was selected for submarine school and they moved to New London, Connecticut. Rosalynn had close contact with all the other navy wives on the base, who swapped baby-sitting chores and shared tips on coping. Better still, Jimmy kept regular hours and he was home every night. Rosalynn felt free and she wasn't lonely anymore.

From there the Carters went to Pearl Harbor, Hawaii, where his submarine was based; their second son, Chip, was born during their year and a half there. When the Korean War broke out, Jimmy's ship, which was due for an overhaul, was sent to San Diego, and Rosalynn, along with three-year-old Jack and four-month-old Chip, flew back to meet it. Before long the Carter family was back in New London. Jimmy had been assigned to a new ship that was still being built and once again, he was home every night. Their third son, Jeff, was born in 1952 on his mother's birthday, August 18.

Soon afterward, Jimmy applied for duty in the nuclear submarine program, and the family moved to Schenectady, New York, where the sub's reactor was being built, and he studied nuclear physics and reactor technology at Union College. The future seemed bright for this young navy family.

Their future took a different turn, though, when Jimmy's father died and he decided to resign from the navy and return to Plains to take over the family farms. Rosalynn was appalled. She had moved away from all that, and she didn't want her children to grow up there. But Jimmy made it clear that she had no choice. He had to do this, and she might as well make the best of it, even though she was pretty sure that she never could.

Back to the Future

"How you gonna keep 'em down on the farm?" the song says, "After they've seen Paree." The Carters hadn't been to Paris, but they had every reason to believe that they would go there one day, and even New London had been a step up from the red-dirt Georgia farm country.

The patterns of Rosalynn's life had changed during the time she had been away, and she now found little things to be a big annoyance, such as cooking the biggest meal of the day in the morning rather than late afternoon because Jimmy had fallen into the habit of inviting customers home for lunch. That meant she also had to finish all her housework in the morning, too.

Rosalynn had become too "citified" for Plains, and she all but ignored the other young women in town, most of whom she had grown up with. She knew that they gossiped about her strange new ways, but it didn't bother her and she went right on making herself miserable until her mother talked her into being more sociable. She had even stopped going to church, but when she started up again, she started smiling more often, too.

When Rosalynn and Jimmy returned to Plains, Georgia, after his time in the navy, they couldn't find a place to live and they moved into a government housing project.

For his part, Jimmy was single-minded about the Carter family business. He drew up plans for a new peanut warehouse and made designs for seed cleaners and dryers, and his enthusiasm for building them was contagious. When Rosalynn caught the bug, she willingly became his partner in the business. She started by going over to his office one afternoon a week to answer the phone, tidy the place, and free him to make sales calls on local farmers who bought seed and fertilizer from him. Before long, Rosalynn was there two afternoons a week, then three, and finally she was there every day, children in tow. Jimmy found little jobs for the boys to keep them busy and out of the way, and in every way the Carter warehouse was a family affair. The family extended to Jimmy's mother, Miss Lillian, his business partner, and his brother, Billy, who was just out of high school.

Rosalynn took over the financial side of the business, keeping the books, sending out bills, recording payments, and paying the bills. During their first year, a drought ruined local crops and business couldn't have been worse. Their net profit for a year of work was $200, and every dime they had been able to save during their navy days was gone. Then, in 1954, the rains came and peanuts poured into the warehouse by the ton. The Carters bought most of the crop and shipped it off to market.

Their success made it possible to rent a big house at the edge of town, and they finally had room to stretch their wings. It was old and drafty, but they loved it. As soon as they were settled, Miss Lillian took a job as a housemother at a fraternity house at Auburn University in Alabama, and Billy joined the marine corps. Free to make his own decisions, Jimmy made big ones and the business never seemed to stop growing.

Like his father before him, he became a leader in civic organizations like the Lions' Club, and he worked on projects to spruce up the old town. His projects ranged from getting the dirt streets paved to designing and helping to build a community swimming pool. He also organized the building of a health clinic, and helped locate a doctor willing to move to Plains. Rosalynn organized bake sales, car washes, and barbecues to help raise money for his projects.

The Carters joined the Baptist Church and both of them became Sunday school teachers, and she became active in the PTA and the garden club, and she was also a Cub Scout den mother, even though she was a full-time, if unpaid, employee at the peanut warehouse.

Jimmy was looking beyond Plains by then. He became state chairman of the March of Dimes and president of the Georgia Crop Improvement Association. At the same time, the couple played golf, went fishing and camping, took dancing lessons, and even mastered speed-reading. For all of her trepidation about going home to Plains, Rosalynn had to admit that she was enjoying life immensely.

Things changed in 1954 when the Supreme Court declared school segregation unconstitutional. It was roundly denounced all across Georgia, and Plains was no bright spot. Quite simply, the attitude was that it wasn't going to happen

Above: The initials, ILYTG, on a compact that Jimmy gave to Rosalynn stand for his sentiment "I Love You the Goodest."

there. A White Citizens Council was formed and the only White male in town who refused to join was Jimmy Carter. Local farmers threatened to boycott his business, but he still wouldn't budge.

In spite of their new unpopularity, the Carter business grew and it prospered. They added a corn mill, and pioneered the development of high-quality seed, which they demonstrated on farms of their own and became growers as well as middlemen.

Jimmy had become a member of the school board, and he pushed for the creation of a central high school that could offer better opportunities for slow learners and gifted kids. It would also have a school band and more sports, but most voters saw it as a Trojan horse for integration, and it was a virtually impossible idea to sell. Partly because of the frustration, Jimmy announced on his thirty-eighth birthday that he was running for the state senate.

Rosalynn was wholeheartedly in favor of the idea even though it meant that she'd be running the warehouse single-handedly during the time he'd be in Atlanta. But she was up to the challenge and she was up for the job of campaigning, too. She worked the phones, personally calling nearly everyone on the voting rolls, she addressed letters to most of the rest, and she went door-to-door in Plains asking for votes. She also bucked the local political machine, but that was a lost cause and, as it turned out, so was the primary election.

Jimmy contested the results, but it seemed to be impossible, too. The county was controlled by the local political boss, and in spite of threats to burn down their warehouse, Rosalynn and Jimmy took him on, looking for proof that he had stolen yet another election. They found plenty of it, and an independent judge declared Jimmy the winner based on their evidence. But a less than independent judge reversed the decision, and it took an order from the secretary of state to get Jimmy's name back on the ballot. It seemed like an empty victory—the general election was only days away and the ballots had already been printed. Rosalynn and Jimmy and a team of volunteers went to all the courthouses in the seven-county district and stamped his name on all of them. But it wasn't over yet. Another order came down that this was going to be strictly a write-in election and all the preprinted ballots were destroyed. In spite of it all, Jimmy won the election by 850 votes. It had been a rough couple of months for Rosalynn and Jimmy, and they might well have given up almost anywhere along the way, but they didn't and they never would again. The Carters had become partners in more than just the peanut business.

Rosalynn didn't go with Jimmy when he went to Atlanta as state senator, although she campaigned for him when he ran for a second term and won. But she considered herself a political wife and she liked the sound of it. She learned to cope with the nastiness when she heard unkind comments about her husband, some of which hurt her and others that made her angry. As Jimmy told

Below: Jimmy jumped into politics as a candidate for the Georgia state senate. Getting the office took a whole lot of doing and a lesser man might have given up. Fortunately, he didn't.

her, "If you don't think I'm doing the best job I can possibly do, then worry about the criticisms. But if you think I'm doing my best, then just relax." It became Rosalynn's political philosophy.

During these years, the race issue was tilting the balance of power from the Democrats to the Republicans all over the South, and in 1964, Georgia gave its electoral votes to the Republican presidential candidate for the first time since the Civil War. Jimmy Carter was not only a Democrat but also a strong supporter of racial integration and that made him a prophet without honor in his own home territory. Yet he decided that he was going to run for Congress.

The campaign got off to a strong start. Both Jimmy and Rosalynn had taken a memory course, and they had the ability to remember the names of people they met and to memorize a few facts about them, too. They were also better organized this time. But in the middle of the effort, the Democratic candidate for governor had a heart attack and withdrew. Jimmy's opponent, who had seemed to be a threat, switched to a run for governor as a Republican, and that left the congressional race wide open for Jimmy. But the Democrats were talking about nominating Lester Maddox, an openly racist restaurateur who met African-American customers at the door with a pistol and an axe handle. There was no way Jimmy couldn't oppose him in the race for governor.

The Carters blitzed the state as a family to beat the better-known Maddox. Jeff, who was fourteen, traveled with Rosalynn, but Jimmy and their two other sons, Jack and Chip, followed their own separate routes, and his mother, Miss Lillian, had her own as well. When any of them arrived in a town they visited the newspaper office and the local radio and television station and announced, "I'm here, interview me." Then they went out and shook hands with everyone they could find on the street. They had gotten off to a late start, but they made up for the lost time, and by Election Day, one or another of the Carter family had visited every town and city in the state of Georgia. But in spite of it, they lost a spot in the runoff election, and Lester Maddox squeaked into the governor's chair.

The next election was four years away, but Jimmy and Rosalynn started running the very next day. She sent off letters to people they had met, and she devised a code so that no one would get the same one twice. She researched issues for Jimmy, and when he wrote speeches, she coded them, too, so that he could deliver them with only a few notes. She even worked out numerical triggers for the jokes he told.

They involved the rest of the family in the effort again, but they lost the help of Miss Lillian when she joined the Peace Corps at the ripe old age of sixty-eight, and Rosalynn was forced to slow down because she was pregnant again at the age of forty. She and Jimmy had been married for twenty-one years, and the youngest of her other three children was fifteen. Amy Lynn Carter was born on October 19, 1967. Not long afterward, while Rosalynn stayed home to take care of the baby, the family's electioneering team lost another member when Jack joined the navy and was shipped to Vietnam.

Below: Rosalynn with her three sons, Jeff, Jack, and Chip. Jeff, the youngest, was only fourteen, when their father ran for governor, but they were all old enough to campaign for him, and the Carter family became a formidable team.

Jimmy's second run for the governor's office went into high gear in the spring of 1970. Baby Amy was two by then, and Rosalynn was free to help, although she hated the idea of leaving her; Jeff was at school in Atlanta and close to the campaign headquarters; and Chip took a year off from college to hit the road with the family again. Miss Lillian, who returned from her Peace Corps service in India, signed on, too, although she was seventy-six years old. But the time had come to expand the staff beyond the family, and young people from all over the state volunteered, many of whom would stick by the Carters through the rest of their political career. They called it their "Hi Neighbor" campaign, but before long, they would be calling themselves the Peanut Brigade.

For her part, Rosalynn recreated the whirlwind tour of the previous race, but there was more time for this one, and she stopped long enough in each town to tour stores and factories and give more people a chance to know her better. She never missed a fair, a livestock sale, a car race, or rodeo anywhere along her prescribed route, which she assessed and changed every weekend. Jimmy and the rest of the family did the same thing, but they almost never traveled together in their effort to shake every hand in Georgia.

Rosalynn was perfection itself in one-on-one conversations, and she actually liked giving interviews, but she was terrified at the idea of making a speech. She was forced into it at one point, but not at all pleased with the result. To make sure it wouldn't happen again, she wrote a speech for herself and looked for opportunities to practice talking in front of an audience. It took some time, but she eventually got good at it, even though she was too proud—even at the start—ever to use notes. Before long she was being invited to rallies that his advisors thought might be a waste of Jimmy's own time.

It was a long campaign, and there never was enough money, but their friends from Jimmy's business and from the other campaigns were asked to let them stay in their homes to avoid the cost of hotel and motel rooms. Each of their campaign offices kept a list of such people and before any overnight visits, phone calls went out, "Rosalynn is coming to town. Can she stay with you?" They drove in borrowed cars, too, and to save more money, volunteers were asked to pick up discarded campaign brochures for recycling into more receptive hands. They learned that mall shoppers usually left theirs in phone booths and tables under message boards and before leaving one, members of the team went around and scooped them up. It wasn't standard practice in most political campaigns, but a Carter campaign went by its own standards.

The odds had been against them right up until Election Day, but he won in spite of them, and Jimmy and Rosalynn moved into the governor's mansion in January 1971. Jack had been discharged from the navy and was a student at Georgia Tech at the time, Jeff had transferred to Georgia State University where Chip was also studying, and all three of them were back in the family fold. With three-year-old Amy, too, the entire family was living in the mansion. The prize, this one anyway, had been won.

Rosalynn's experiences as the First Lady of Georgia weren't a lot different from being the First Lady of the United States. The governor's mansion was furnished with rare antiques and had a museumlike quality about it, with the resulting stream of visitors and sight-seers. She had to deal with a full schedule of receptions and banquets, too. They often entertained foreign dignitaries and they made several goodwill trips abroad—to Europe, to Central and South America, and to Israel. Rosalynn also found time to chair the newly formed committee on mental health, the Special Olympics, and a highway beautification program modeled on the one Lady Bird Johnson had started in Texas.

Naturally, the heavy schedule of entertaining called for building a wardrobe, but Rosalynn found a perfect solution. Jack had gotten married and his wife, Caron, and her mother, as well as Jeff's girlfriend, Annette, all served together as official hostesses with her. All five of them were exactly the same size, and their taste was similar, so they pooled their gowns. Rosalynn had the first preference, but she was pleased to know that any clothes she bought would see quadruple duty. She may have been Georgia's First Lady, but she was still the same frugal woman from Plains.

After her first year as the governor's wife, Rosalynn went to work to learn everything she could about mental health problems and their solutions, an issue that had absorbed her for several years. She volunteered one day a week to work at the Georgia Regional Hospital in Atlanta, and she toured similar institutions around the state. The toughest part of her self-appointed job was holding back tears as she worked with mentally retarded children until a doctor pointed out to her that most of them

Below: When Jimmy became Georgia's governor in 1971, no one was prouder than Rosalynn, and their inaugural ball was the first step in what became a rewarding experience for her.

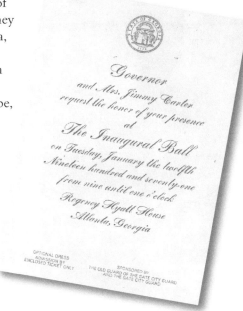

were happy and didn't know they were supposed to be sad. It was his final words, "You've got to get over your tears…we need you," that changed her outlook.

Following Rosalynn's recommendation, the state shifted its emphasis on large hospitals to smaller institutions scattered to be within easy reach of anyone who needed them. The change was dramatic and it was one of Jimmy's great legacies from his term as governor, but he knew, and didn't mind saying so, that the accomplishment had been Rosalynn's.

The Carters were limited to a single term as governor and state First Lady, but Jimmy had a plan for the future. Their work in Georgia had earned national attention for him, and in 1972, at the very beginning of his term, he confided to Rosalynn that he wanted to run for president in the 1976 election. Two years into it, he was tapped by the Democratic National Committee to recruit and coach candidates for the midterm elections, and as he traveled across the country, Rosalynn knew very well where the road was leading.

The Peanut Brigade Goes National

The election was still eighteen months away when Rosalynn made her first campaign swing outside of Georgia. When she went to Florida and started knocking on doors, the reaction was generally the same. "I'm Rosalynn Carter," she'd say, "My husband is running for President." "President of what?" they'd ask, and she'd explain, "President of the United States." The reaction would inevitably be, "You've got to be kidding." She considered it a step up from her first campaign all those years before when the reaction would be "Jimmy who?"

She would hear that question a lot over the next year as she traveled into other states. Even reporters asked it. She used her old technique of visiting newspaper offices and radio and television stations in every town and asking to be interviewed. She found many local reporters at a loss for words, so she carried a list of half a dozen questions for them to ask as a way of getting the ball rolling. Her interviews, especially on the radio, not only spread the word but brought volunteers into their camp.

The Carters had always known how to put volunteers to good use. They made them feel like part of the family and as the volunteer lists grew, their supporters involved their own families as well. It was a long-standing tradition that campaign workers would be individuals, either men or women, but no candidate had ever thought of signing on husbands and wives together as teams, and certainly not encouraging them to involve their children as well. But Rosalynn and Jimmy, and their children as well, were in it together, and it seemed perfectly natural.

During the primary campaign and then the general election, Rosalynn visited forty-two states on her own and she toured several of them time after time. She and Jimmy, who had his own separate schedule, returned to Plains for weekends together with each other, and with Amy. It was also a time for her to share with Jimmy complaints about Washington that she'd heard, and she heard plenty of those.

Her three sons had heavy travel schedules, too, and following the family tradition, their wives were involved as well. Jack's wife, Judy, took time out to have a baby—Jason, the Carters' first grandchild—in August, but Rosalynn's mother took care of the baby so Rosalynn could get out and campaign. Miss Lillian took care of Amy for them, but even she occasionally went on the road as the drive to the presidency heated up. Jimmy's brother, Billy, and his wife ran the Carter business for the duration.

Political professionals scoffed at the idea, but the Carters' secret weapon was their Peanut Brigade. It had been effective when Jimmy ran for governor, but nobody thought that a group of enthusiastic Georgians could spread out across the country. They proved that they might during the New Hampshire primary when they chartered a plane and fanned out across the state talking to anybody whom they could find at home and leaving notes behind for those they couldn't. They went national after that, and they seemed to be everywhere, not just knocking on doors but appearing on interview programs, and always getting the message out that "You might not know Jimmy Carter, but we do, and we know that once you do, too, you'll vote for him." Many people they reached were so impressed that they volunteered to work for him, too.

The run-up to November was all but a blur, but in the end Jimmy had become president. Neither Rosalynn nor he had ever seen the inside of the White House before and now they were going to live there together (and work together, too).

Above: Amy was ten when the Carters moved into the White House and they built a tree house for her that she shared with her nephew, Jason, and the other Carter grandchildren who lived in the big house.

Change of Address

The first change Rosalynn made when she moved into the White House was moving her own office to the East Wing. Other First Ladies had kept theirs in the living quarters, although their staffs worked in the wing that also housed the security, the military, and the visitors office. She wanted to make the living quarters completely private and a place where the family could relax. In addition to the president and First Lady, Amy, Jeff, and Chip and their wives and their children moved into the third floor.

The tone of the Carter White House was as informal as protocol would allow. When guests arrived for their first state

Below: The Carters broke precedent by proudly walking to the Capitol for Jimmy's inauguration.

dinner, Jimmy greeted them by saying, "Hi, everybody! Come on in." They hosted hundreds of these "suppers," as Jimmy called them, and the menus always leaned to traditional, heavily Southern-accented fare. Their parties always began promptly at 7:30 P.M., and Jimmy and Rosalynn left promptly at 11:00 P.M. It had been customary to announce the arrival of the president and his guests with a trumpet fanfare, but Rosalynn retired the trumpeters and she limited the playing of "Hail to the Chief" to just the first few bars.

"Casual dress" began appearing on invitations more and more often. Rosalynn enjoyed dressing up as much as any other woman, but to the dismay of the fashion designers, she preferred to buy party dresses off the rack in department stores, and she made frequent excursions to New York to refresh her wardrobe. Her selections were usually high-necked and long-sleeved and never flamboyant. Showy jewelry wasn't her style, either. Rosalynn preferred to be neat and comfortable, and pretty, and her only hard-and-fast rule about her clothes was that they should be American-made.

Rosalynn started to receive criticism when she began attending cabinet meetings, but it didn't stop her from doing so. She saw the meeting as the easiest and best way for her to understand what was going on, and she felt that she needed to know. The same people who criticized her expected that of her as well.

Rosalynn's fund of knowledge was put to the test in 1977 when Jimmy sent her to Latin America as his personal representative. She was expected to bring more than just a smiling presence to the assignment, but also a thorough understanding of foreign policy. She had to conduct meetings with foreign leaders on matters that ranged from human rights to nuclear nonproliferation and democratization—not to mention the problem with Cuba—as though she were the president himself. She was also expected to handle press conferences wherever she went and to handle herself like a professional diplomat. She did all

Below: Amy was Rosalynn's only little girl. The youngest of her three sons, Jeff, was fifteen when Amy was born.

Daughter Amy

The crown jewel of the Carter White House was their daughter, Amy, the apple of their eyes, who was ten when her father became president. The press adored her and so did the public. She went to a public school, and she was a good student, they reported, as well as an accomplished reader. She herself reported, "I can sew, cook, play the piano, and roller skate. And I can hang for ten minutes from a tree upside down." She found the White House a great adventure. There was that soda fountain that President Johnson had installed in the solarium, and a bowling alley, a billiard table, a swimming pool, and a private movie theater. Her father even had a tree house built for her outside, and as other White House children had discovered, the roof was anything that an active imagination could transform it into. Amy was often invited to state dinners because, her mother said, "We like to have her with us," and she always took a book along because she got "fidgety" with nothing else to do.

of those things. She started by doing her homework and brushing up on her Spanish, and it paid off. She was taken quite seriously everywhere she went right from the beginning, and when the mission was accomplished, she had earned new friends, not just for the United States but for herself as well. Her trip also confirmed that human rights would become the administration's signature issue.

Long before the election, Jimmy had decided that peace in the Middle East was his top priority, and in 1978, he and Rosalynn went to the presidential retreat at Camp David for peace talks between Egyptian president Anwar Sadat and Prime Minister Menachem Begin of Israel. Jimmy had expected the talks to be strained, and he softened the atmosphere by insisting that both men should have their wives along and that Rosalynn should join them, too. Neither he nor Rosalynn offered anything more than moral support, but her presence at Camp David was key to keeping the atmosphere relaxing and friendly, just as the president had known it would. The talks went on for twelve tense days before they finally reached an agreement.

Above: Rosalynn mended strained relations between America and Brazil when she visited there and was warmly welcomed by the people.

Beyond the cause of peace and human rights, Rosalynn had gone to Washington with a well-developed cause of her own—helping the mentally ill. There had been some national interest in the problem since the end of World War II, but nothing serious had been done about it since President Kennedy had conducted a study back in 1961. President Carter formed a new Commission on Mental Health and although nepotism rules kept him from appointing Rosalynn to serve on it, he could, and did, make her its honorary chairperson. She went right to work.

The commission held public hearings in every corner of the country, and it established more than thirty task forces to deal with specific facets of the problem. They promoted the need for more volunteerism and, as Rosalynn had discovered in Georgia, the need to decentralize from large hospitals to smaller scattered institutions. They called for better research and programs for prevention, and they pushed medical insurance companies to include mental disorders in their coverage. Most of all, they were responsible for the acceptance and tolerance of mental disorders by the American public.

Below: Jimmy and Rosalynn welcomed Egyptian President Anwar el-Sadat and his wife, Jihan, to Camp David.

Rosalynn was the most visible participant in the effort, and she turned it into a nearly full-time job. She invited groups of interested people to White House luncheons to encourage them to lobby for a new mental health law, and she even testified before a Senate committee after the bill was introduced. It was the first time that a First Lady had appeared before Congress since Eleanor Roosevelt, and with that one exception, the only time. The law they worked for was passed in September 1980, but the Reagan administration that followed Carter's refused to fund it. There were, however, other reforms and other funding programs that could be implemented without congressional approval, and Rosalynn's four years of hard work wasn't a total waste. She was instrumental in focusing

Above: Rosalynn traveled the country attending meetings on mental health problems.

public awareness on the mental health problem, too, and she's still working hard to find better solutions through her work with the Carter Center Mental Health Task Force, which she and her husband created together in 1982 and which is still her first priority.

Another cause that she championed, passage of the Equal Rights Amendment, failed during her tenure as First Lady. She made speeches, she wrote letters, she lobbied state legislatures, she held meetings, and she even invited former First Ladies Betty Ford and Lady Bird Johnson to join with her. But for all the effort and support, the amendment wasn't ratified during the Carter years, as she had expected it would.

Meanwhile, public attention shifted as the world was watching in horror while millions of refugees began pouring into Thailand out of Cambodia, where a corrupt government had slaughtered half the population. Like the Vietnam War, the events were played out on national television and people were moved to want to help. Rosalynn was sent to Thailand to find out just what might be done, and the scene of misery that she found there was heartbreaking.

Like her mission to Latin America, Rosalynn went to Southeast Asia as a qualified representative of the president and not just his wife. After touring the area, she called on the king of Thailand, who had been planning to close his country's borders because no other country had seemed interested in helping. But now the United States was. Rosalynn met with officials of international relief organizations, and they agreed to work together under a single coordinator after Rosalynn gave them the suggestion. Back in the United States, she held a meeting with the United Nations secretary-general to plead with him to appoint someone to act as that coordinator.

Her next step was to form a National Cambodian Crisis Committee to help raise private funds. She made several speeches, appeared on national television interview programs, and even recorded television ads to call attention to the problem. The response was overwhelming, and in less than a year, the crisis was declared over.

A new crisis put a dark cloud over the Carter White House during the time Rosalynn was in Thailand. Iranian militants had overrun the U.S. embassy in Tehran and took hostage everyone inside. The hostages were imprisoned for 444 days, right up to the last day of the Carter presidency. The standoff kept Jimmy close to the White House—the Russians were making hostile moves in Afghanistan at the same time—and as the next presidential election grew closer, Rosalynn and the rest of the family took to the road to campaign for Jimmy as his stand-ins. Rosalynn soldiered on through the primaries, and although the polls put Ronald Reagan, the Republican candidate, far ahead after the conventions, the gap was slowly narrowing. Jimmy was able to get out and campaign himself, but his participation was limited and Rosalynn bore the brunt of it, prompting press comment that the president was "hiding in the Rose Garden."

Below: Amy went along with Rosalynn on a trip to Nigeria to help solve the problems plaguing little children there.

All things considered, the Carters weren't surprised when Jimmy lost the election. They went home to Plains, but not to obscurity. Both Rosalynn and Jimmy wrote their memoirs, but they also worked hard at creating the Carter Center at Emory University in Atlanta and raising the money to get it off the ground. They run the center together, and in the years since 1982 when it was created, they have continued with the unfinished business of the government, especially in the area of human rights. Their work has had a direct effect on conditions in more than sixty-five countries. Members of its staff, and the Carters themselves, work side by side with the poor and forgotten in those countries, and Jimmy and Rosalynn use their considerable influence with the heads of those states. Their work ranges from monitoring free elections to resolving conflicts, fighting disease to improving farm production.

For her part, Rosalynn also chairs the Carter Center's Mental Health Task Force, and each year she hosts the Rosalynn Carter Symposium on Mental Health Policy. Both she and Jimmy are also active volunteers for Habitat for Humanity, lending their own hard work to building homes for people who couldn't otherwise afford a piece of the American Dream except by contributing this "sweat equity."

It would be an understatement to say that Rosalynn Carter is busier as a private citizen than she ever was when she was First Lady. But it is quite clear that neither she nor Jimmy ever intend to retire.

Above: Rosalynn and Jimmy in 1979, seven months before the Iranian Hostage Crisis began and his presidency unraveled.

Below: The Jimmy Carter Library and Museum in Atlanta.

Visiting the Carters

The Carters still live in their old hometown of Plains, Georgia, part of which has become a historic site maintained by the National Park Service. The Carters' home is not open to the public, but his boyhood home just outside of town can be visited, as can the local railroad depot. The high school that Rosalynn and Jimmy graduated from is used as a visitors center and museum. The Carter farm and the other sites are open from 9:00 A.M. to 4:30 P.M. every day. There are no admission charges.

The Jimmy Carter Museum and Library in Atlanta is an official presidential library, operated by the National Archives and Records Administration, and contains his presidential papers as well as references on his administration. The museum, which contains mementos related to the Carter presidency, is open from 9:00 A.M. to 4:45 P.M. every day and Sundays from noon. Adult admission is $7.00; for seniors, military, and students, it's $5.00. It is located at 441 Freedom Parkway in Atlanta. The telephone number is 404-865-7100.

Nancy Reagan

Life on Many Stages

Married for over fifty-two years and separated only by death, Nancy Reagan was not merely Ronald Reagan's partner and protector, but in his words, his favorite roommate. Her commitment to and affection for her husband was legendary, matched only by the unwavering devotion he had for her.

Nancy Reagan held three unique and distinct careers in her lifetime, all thriving in the glare of the spotlight. Her first was as an actress, the second was a political wife, and the third was First Lady to the fortieth president of the United States, Ronald Reagan. Now in the twilight years of her life, Nancy has been a staunch advocate for the sick and elderly, specifically working to eradicate the Alzheimer's disease that ultimately took away her beloved husband.

Born in New York City on July 6, 1921, it appears that Anne Frances Robbins was the only happy product of an unhappy marriage, a union that ended soon after she was born. Given the nickname Nancy by her mother, she used that name throughout her life. Her father, Kenneth Seymour Robbins, was an automobile dealer, and her mother, Edith Luckett Robbins, was an actress during the silent film era. Kenneth and Edith separated when Nancy was an infant. Kenneth literally abandoned the family, whereupon Edith immediately resumed her acting career, leaving Nancy in the care of her mother's sister, Virginia Galraith, in Bethesda, Maryland. Because her mother traveled a great deal in pursuit of her next acting gig, Nancy saw little of her over the next five years, and had no contact at all with her father. Her parents finally formally divorced in 1928, while Nancy was entering grammar school.

In 1929, when her mother married Loyal Davis, a wealthy Chicago neurosurgeon, little Nancy was transplanted again, leaving Maryland for

---

Anne Frances Robbins

Born
July 6, 1921,
New York, New York

Parents
Kenneth Seymour Robbins and Edith Luckett Robbins

Marriage
March 4, 1952, to Ronald Reagan (1911-2004)

Children
Patricia Ann (1952-);
Ronald Prescott (1958-);
stepdaughter Maureen Elizabeth (1941-2001);
stepson Michael Edward (1945-)

In light of Nancy's eventual fame as the proponent of the "Just Say No" campaign, it's interesting to note that one of her mother's biggest films was The Spirit of the Poppy, *a 1914 cautionary melodrama about drugs. Edith Luckett plays a woman who becomes addicted to heroin after a nefarious doctor injects her against her will.*

Above: Nancy met First Lady Grace Coolidge when she attended the annual Easter Egg Roll at the White House when she was a youngster.

Illinois to live with her mother, her new father, and Loyal's son from a previous marriage. Loyal Davis was well respected in the medical field. He wrote the definitive book on neurosurgery (*Principles of Neurological Surgery*, 1963), was chair of the Department of Surgery at Northwestern University, and for decades edited the professional publication *The Journal of the American College of Surgeons*. From the age of eight on, Nancy came to know and love Loyal as her father, and he officially adopted her when she was fourteen. For the first time in her life, she was able to settle down and enjoy a happy life of wealth and privilege, including private school, summer camp, tennis, swimming, and dancing lessons. Dr. Davis was also an ultraconservative Republican, and his political leanings not only shaped Nancy, but facilitated her first visit to the White House—she participated in an Easter Egg Roll on the White House lawn, and although she didn't get to meet President Calvin Coolidge, she did shake hands with one of her predecessors, First Lady Grace Coolidge.

Upon graduation from the Chicago Latin School for Girls, Nancy enrolled at Smith College in Northampton, Massachusetts, majoring in drama. (She narrowly missed being a schoolmate of fellow First Lady Barbara Bush, as the latter enrolled three months after Nancy graduated.) On school breaks, her mother's theater friends, including Clark Gable and Spencer Tracy, often visited the Davis household in Chicago, regaling Nancy with exciting tales of life in the spotlight, thus sparking Nancy's interest in the stage. After graduation in 1943 and a brief stint working at a department store in Chicago, Nancy turned to acting. Her mother's contacts helped her get started. (Nancy's godmother was also a thespian influence. She was the legendary Russian and American star of stage and screen, Alla Nazimova. Nazimova's most famous film is the ultra-campy 1923 silent *Salome*.)

Nancy Davis became a professional actress, joining Zasu Pitts's traveling company, doing live theater on and off Broadway, even trying a stint at modeling. She soon landed a role on Broadway in the hit musical *Lute Song*, starring Mary Martin. With her stage performances enabling her to hone her craft, an agent from MGM Studios suggested that Nancy head to Hollywood for a screen test. Nancy appeared in eleven B-level films from 1949 to 1956 as a contract player for the studio and received many favorable notices. Her first screen role was uncredited in the 1948 film *Portrait of Jennie*. Other releases included *East Side, West Side* (1949), *Shadow on the Wall* (1950), and *The Next Voice You Hear* (1950). In her last movie, a World War II submarine drama for

As a teenager, Nancy tracked down her biological father—not seeking to bond with him but simply to inform him that Dr. Davis wanted to adopt her. Basically, the conversation was: If you ever decide you care about me, look for the name "Nancy Davis," not "Anne Robbins."

Above: Ron earned his first experience as the "Great Communicator" when he was a radio announcer.

Columbia Pictures, *Hellcats of the Navy* (1957), she was paired romantically on the screen with her husband, Ronald Reagan.

Ronald Reagan had started his career in radio, and then went on to Hollywood as a contract player in B movies. Self-deprecatingly, he referred to himself as the Errol Flynn of the B pictures. By the time he and Nancy met, soon after her arrival in California, he had already been a popular actor for a decade, appearing in such films as *Knute Rockne—All American* and a variety of World War II–themed pictures. Nancy had contacted Ron thinking that in his position of prominence with the Screen Actors Guild (SAG) he could help her with a problem. She had discovered that an actress with the same name had appeared on the Communist blacklist. Such name confusion threatened to put her employment as a SAG actress at risk.

The tall, dark, and handsome president of SAG soon fell for the pretty, petite young actress. They began to date on and off, and their paths crossed for several months while each dated others. Ron was not looking to rush into anything permanent—he had just recently divorced his first wife, actress Jane Wyman. So how did their relationship flourish? As Ronald Reagan told the story in his autobiography *An American Life*: "I found myself booked for a speech to the Junior League Convention at the Del Coronado Hotel in San Diego. I wanted to share the ride with someone and wondered who I should ask to join me. Then it suddenly occurred to me there was really only one person I wanted to share it with—Nancy Davis…. Pretty soon, Nancy was the only one I was calling for dates. And one night over dinner as we sat at a table for two, I said, 'Let's get married.' She deserved a more romantic proposal than that, but—bless her—she put her hand on mine, looked into my eyes, and said, 'Let's.'"

Below: Ron and Nancy shared acting careers but both of them gave it up for a different kind of glamour out on the political stage.

Nancy and Ronald were married on March 4, 1952, in a simple ceremony in the Little Brown Church in North Hollywood. She was nearly thirty-one and he was ten years her senior and a father of two from his previous marriage—Maureen, born in 1941, and Michael, born in 1945. Nancy was also three months pregnant, and their oldest child, Patricia Ann, was born on October 22, 1952. Their son, Ronald Prescott, arrived on May 28, 1958.

In 1958, concerned about balancing motherhood and a glamorous Hollywood career, Nancy determined that her new role was to raise the Reagan children and to support her husband's political ambitions. "I knew that being his wife was the role I wanted to play," she said. She added, "A woman's real happiness and real fulfillment come from within the home with her husband and children."

Above: The Reagans were married in 1952 at the home of their close friend and fellow actor William Holden at Toluca Lake, California.

Below: Ron and Nancy with their one-year-old son, Ron, and eight year-old daughter, Patti.

Although Nancy and Ronald did not appear in any movies together after Hellcats of the Navy, *they did share the small screen in several episodes of TV's* GE Theater, *an anthology he hosted and occasionally acted in. One of their shared GE efforts was called* A Turkey for the President.

Accidental Politician

On behalf of the Screen Actors Guild, Ron was often asked to "say a few words," and his speeches gradually became more and more political in tone. Ron was a staunch Democrat at the time he met Nancy, while she was at the opposite end of the political spectrum. Under the influence of his conservative father-in-law, and with Nancy playing a major role in persuading him to switch loyalties, Ron's outlook gradually and significantly changed from that of a liberal Democrat to a conservative Republican. While still a Democrat, Ron started voting Republican, supporting the presidential candidacies of Dwight D. Eisenhower in 1952 and 1956, and Richard Nixon in 1960. Nancy loved to hear Ron talking politics; she was his sounding board early on. After officially switching his party affiliation to Republican in 1962, he became cochair of the California Republicans for Barry Goldwater in 1964.

With his silver screen star ebbing, Ron was hardly looking to start a new career at age fifty-four, but he got involved in California politics in the 1960s almost reluctantly. At speaking engagements up and down the coast of the Golden State, he was asked time and time again to run for governor. Finally, he consented and defeated incumbent governor Edmund G. Brown, Sr., by a sizable one million votes. Nancy recast herself as the consummate political wife, and in 1966 she became First Lady of California. During her eight years as the governor's wife, Nancy developed the skills that later served her in the White House, but she also incited controversy. She was publicly criticized for her circle of glamorous friends and her expensive, stylish clothing. She frequently conflicted with journalists who wrote negatively about Ron. She also banged heads with staff members when she felt they overscheduled him.

"Nancy moved into my heart and replaced an emptiness that I'd been trying to ignore for a long time. Coming home to her is like coming out of the cold into a warm, fire-lit room. I miss her if she just steps out of the room."

—Ronald Reagan on his love for Nancy

During her tenure as First Lady of California, Nancy sought to support worthwhile causes. She paid visits to wounded Vietnam veterans and became active in projects concerning prisoners of war and servicemen missing in action. During the war, she wrote a syndicated newspaper column, donating her salary to charity. Nancy also made regular visits to hospitals and homes for the elderly, as well as schools for physically and emotionally handicapped children. During one of these hospital visits in 1967, she observed the Foster Grandparent Program in action, which brings together senior citizens and handicapped children, and she soon became the organization's champion. Later, as First Lady of the United States, Nancy continued to help expand the program on a national level. With Jane Wilkie, she coauthored a book, *To Love a Child*, and a song by the same title was written and dedicated to her.

Above: When Ron was governor of California, Nancy became a political personality as well and she supported her own worthwhile causes.

Governor Ronald Reagan was good for California. After two terms, he left Sacramento in 1974 with the California budget showing a $550 million surplus. Despite the fact that he was nearing many people's retirement age, he was a force to be reckoned with in Republican party politics and he was ready for a national stage.

A Standard of Living

Nancy raised eyebrows again as she moved into—and quickly out of—the decaying 1877 governor's mansion in Sacramento. She considered the house a firetrap—and the Sacramento fire department backed this opinion. Not wanting to live in the outdated manse, Nancy moved her family to an exclusive suburb, where they rented a luxury apartment for $1,250 a month. While Nancy reasoned the move was out of concern for her family's safety, many Californians declared snobbery. The Reagans silenced their critics by taking them through the ancient mansion so they could see its decaying condition for themselves.

Right: By 1967, Ron was serving as governor and so the Reagan family moved to Sacramento.

From California to D.C.

Above: The Reagans made the White House all their own after they moved there.

On November 20, 1975, Ronald Reagan announced his candidacy for the 1976 presidential election. Gerald Ford was eventually nominated, but Ron's strong showing in the primaries laid the groundwork for his future presidential bid. Until then, however, and with his term as governor over, the Reagans retired to Rancho del Cielo, the 688-acre California ranch they bought in 1974 shortly before Ron completed his second term as governor. The couple's private retreat overlooks the Santa Ynez Valley and the Pacific Ocean.

In 1980 the Reagans geared back up for another run at the White House. During that campaign, Ron was the tenth and last Republican to enter the race. He defeated Jimmy Carter, and on inauguration day, January 20, 1981, the fifty-two hostages that had been held in Iran for 444 days were freed. The United States seemed optimistic and back on the right track.

Nancy's first year in the White House was marked with image battling, activism, and a violent assassination attempt. The United States had just lived through the down-home, country charm of the Carter family. With the Reagans, glamour not seen since the Kennedy years returned to Washington, but that image change came with a price. Unfairly or not, it seemed that the press perceived Nancy as being a snob and her obvious "champagne tastes" didn't go far to dispel this notion. Right from the lavish first Inaugural Ball, some saw her as "Queen Nancy." Nancy felt her main purpose was to protect and care for her husband, and in so doing she could be unforgiving with those she perceived to be a threat. Nancy was routinely skewered by the press, yet in countless public polls during her entire eight years in the White House, Nancy was considered one of the world's most admired women.

Since Jacqueline Kennedy's renovations of the early 1960s, the White House had fallen into disrepair. Nancy believed the nation (and of course, she and her husband) needed a more suitable First Family home, and she began redecorating immediately following move-in day. Although the White House, indeed, was in need of a face-lift, Nancy was criticized for spending frivolously while the country was in the middle of a recession. She hired Letitia Baldrige, a Kennedy staff member, to assist her in the project. In the Reagans' first year in Washington, Nancy directed a major renovation of the second- and third-

Nancy learned that to deflate critics, she could use humor. In 1982 she appeared at the Press Gridiron Dinner dressed as a bag lady singing "Second Hand Rose." She ended the skit by ceremoniously smashing a red dish representing the Reagans' new White House china.

floor quarters. She encouraged private donations, which eventually exceeded $800,000 and included $200,000 for new china. In addition, Nancy put her love of the arts on display by bringing performers to the White House for the PBS television series *In Performance at the White House.*

Nancy's wardrobe engendered further criticism. Designers donated fashions in exchange for the exposure she afforded them, but the public balked. The Reagans were accused of not caring that many Americans were having trouble making ends meet, while they lived and entertained lavishly, surrounded by well-heeled friends. At times, there was a feeling that the Republican party had been a haven for the rich, with the haves leading the have-nots (Democrats). Nancy came under even heavier scrutiny when she hinted at writing the gowns off on her taxes. She tried to defuse the critics by expanding her work on charitable causes.

Nancy resented criticisms of extravagance. To improve her image, advisors suggested that she associate herself with a serious cause, which prompted her to begin an antidrug campaign. "Just Say No" did much to improve her image, but there was much more to the program than mere image building. Drug use in young people decreased markedly while Nancy championed this cause, one that allowed her to channel her no-nonsense public persona.

Some derided the "Just Say No" campaign as simplistic— liberal Abbie Hoffmann likened the campaign to "the equivalent of telling manic depressives to 'just cheer up'"—but most gave her credit for raising drug awareness to a new level. She worked tirelessly to spotlight the problem: Nancy's antidrug crusade took her to sixty-five cities in thirty-three states, the Vatican, and eight other foreign countries. She appeared on television talk shows, taped public service announcements, and visited prevention programs and rehabilitation centers across the country to talk with young people and their parents. In an interview with *Good Morning America* in November 1981, Nancy said her "best role is to try to bring public awareness, particularly parental awareness, to the problems of drug abuse" because "understanding what drugs can do to your children, understanding peer pressure and understanding why they turn to drugs is…the first step in solving the problem."

Above: Nancy's answer to the growing drug problem was disarmingly simple. "Just Say No," she advised. In spite of criticism, many gave her credit for raising awareness of the problem.

"As I've said many times, drug abuse knows no boundaries. It crosses all lines— geographical, racial, political, economic. There is no one here today whose country isn't affected by the inevitable sorrow and tragedy drug abuse causes.…We must act now, not tomorrow, or the next day."

—Nancy Reagan at the Second International Drug Conference, held at the United Nations in 1985

In April 1985 Nancy expanded her drug awareness campaign internationally by inviting First Ladies from around the world to attend a two-day briefing on the subject of youth drug abuse. It coincided with the fortieth anniversary of the United Nations. Nancy was also the first American First Lady to address the Third Committee of the United Nations General Assembly, whose meeting she attended in October 1988.

The President's Advisor

Above: Always worried about her husband's health, Nancy encouraged him to take frequent trips to their California getaway, Rancho del Cielo.

When Ronald won the presidency in 1980, it was generally agreed that Nancy was one of his most trusted advisors, influencing her husband on personnel matters and on important issues such as arms control and relations with the Soviet Union. When television cameras caught Nancy whispering into the president's ear while reporters asked him questions, speculation increased about her role. Truth be told: The president was growing hard of hearing and she was relaying to him some of what he had missed. While Ronald convalesced after major surgery in 1985 to have polyps removed from his colon, *The New York Times* concluded that a triumvirate was in charge at the White House: the president, his chief of staff, and the First Lady. A year later, the paper described how she had "expanded the role of First Lady into a sort of Associate Presidency."

Although she largely left policy to the Reagan men, Nancy was deeply involved in selecting who those men were. Nancy was reportedly instrumental in the shift from hard-line conservatives to foreign policy moderates which began with the replacement of Judge William Clark as national security advisor and Alexander Haig as secretary of state by Robert McFarlane and George Shultz, respectively, midway into Ron's first term. And in the wake of the Iran-Contra hearings, Nancy became even more cautious of those who worked with her husband.

Nancy Reagan's backstage handling became fodder for late-night monologues and a national concern in 1987, following the publication of former chief of staff Donald Regan's book *For the Record*. In a startling revelation, Regan disclosed that the First Lady regularly dictated the president's schedule after consulting her personal astrologer. In her own memoir, *My Turn*, Nancy attributed her reliance on astrology to her fear that her husband would be shot again. She admitted that she had influence on her husband—and how could she not? "For eight years I was sleeping with the president, and if that doesn't give you special access,

"When she gets her hackles up, she can be a dragon."

—*Former Reagan chief of staff Howard Baker on Nancy Reagan*

I don't know what does." Nancy went on to insist that Regan had exaggerated her influence: "Believe me, if I really were the dragon lady that [Regan] described in his book, he would have been out the door many months earlier." Through it all, Nancy maintained a good sense of humor and could laugh at herself. If crossed, however, she could be unforgiving.

Ron's presidency marked the end of the Cold War. One could sense that by the time the Berlin Wall fell, American president Reagan and Soviet president Mikhail Gorbachev had a deep respect for each other, if not friendship. However, the press tried to paint the relationship between Nancy and Raisa Gorbachev as being as cold as ice. True, they were both strong-minded and powerful women, but only the First Ladies themselves know how contentious their relationship might have been.

Above: Nancy's influence sparked Ron's friendship with Soviet leader Mikhail Gorbachev and his wife, Raisa.

Close Calls

Only sixty-nine days after taking office, Ron narrowly survived an assassination attempt. John Hinckley, a crazed fan of actress Jodie Foster, shot the president with a small-caliber pistol. The bullet ricocheted off the president's car and entered his body under his left armpit. The bullet lodged in Ron's lung, an inch from his heart. Such a wound—and the surgery to remove the bullet—could have been devastating to anyone, much less a man who had just turned seventy. Nancy immediately went to the hospital but was not allowed to be at his side. In her memoir, *My Turn*, she recalls begging assistant Mike Deaver to get her in. "Mike," she pleaded, "they don't know how it is with us. He has to know I'm here."

In his autobiography, Ron recounted the assassination and more important, his bond with Nancy: "Seeing Nancy in the hospital gave me an enormous lift. As long as I live I will never forget the thought that rushed into my head as I looked up into her face." While Ron recovered from the shooting, photos were taken of him in the hospital, looking none the worse for wear just days later. It was said that Ron's overall fitness and good health played a key role in his survival and quick return to duties. Nancy worked diligently to nurse her husband through his recovery and present an ongoing image of vitality and competence. Both handled the assassination attempt with strength and dignity.

"Honey, I forgot to duck."

—*Ron Reagan to Nancy after the assassination attempt on his life*

Right: Nancy was the most important visitor Ron had during the time that he was hospitalized after the attempt to assassinate him.

Above: On the day that the new president was inaugurated, Ron and Nancy went straight from the ceremony to a waiting helicopter that whisked them off on the journey home.

Behind the scenes, concerned about Ron's health following the attempt, Nancy began more closely overseeing his schedule, reducing it item by item if she deemed it too full. If she determined that any staff members were being difficult or unwilling to follow her directives, she relieved them of their duties. Ron thrived on Nancy's attention, and he recognized her as being a shrewd judge of character.

In October 1987 Nancy was diagnosed with breast cancer. Incredibly, even her decision to have a mastectomy instead of a lumpectomy was criticized. She faced her mastectomy with courage and with the same openness as Betty Ford did, allowing the American public to know the details in the hope that her story would inspire, encourage, and motivate others.

As Ron's final days serving as president drew to a close, it became apparent that while the United States adored him, the country merely tolerated Nancy. This pained her, but all that really mattered to Nancy was Ron and his happiness, and she supplied that in full.

After the Republican baton was passed and George H.W. Bush took office, the Reagans returned to their California ranch. Nancy kept busy by writing her memoirs, serving on the board of Revlon, and continuing with her "Just Say No" antidrug program under the auspices of the newly formed Nancy Reagan Foundation. Nancy continued to travel domestically and internationally, speaking out on the harmful effects of drugs and alcohol. Ron wrote the occasional memoir and embarked on a high-priced speaking and consulting tour. They were prepared to enjoy their retirement years together, but that was not to be the case.

The Final Years

Five years after completing his presidency, at the age of eighty-three, Ronald Reagan announced in his famous letter to the American people that he had Alzheimer's disease. Again, with the hope that such news might help others, the Reagans made the information public. Ron shared: "I only wish there was some way I could spare Nancy from this painful experience. When the time comes, I am confident that with your help she will face it with faith and courage." And she did. Nancy devoted herself to his care.

> *"She's the one who wakes up with it every morning and goes to sleep with it every night. You know, I think in that moment before you wake up, I think for a moment she almost forgets, and then of course (she) realizes that we are where we are."*
>
> —*Maureen Reagan on Nancy in her role as caregiver*

As a former First Lady and a very wealthy woman, Nancy could easily have entrusted Ron's care to the best in-home nurses in the world. Instead, she spent day after day with him in their Bel Air home. At first, the signs of the president's worsening condition were not readily apparent, and the realization of his illness brought the Reagan family together. Even infamous Reagan family "wild child" Patti Davis had an opportunity to reconcile with her father. They did not always agree on much while he was president—some think she uses her mother's name as a symbolic gesture of denouncing her father and what he stood for. In later years, though, as her father's disease worsened, Patti sought to be seen standing with her family, instead of against them. Reports said she'd had an "emotional reconciliation with her mother."

Above: The entire family was gathered to welcome the Reagans back to California.

When Maureen Reagan died in August 2001 from malignant melanoma, Nancy chose not to inform Ron of her death, in order to spare him any further hardships beyond his battle with Alzheimer's. "Like all fathers and daughters, there was a unique bond between them," Nancy said about her husband and stepdaughter. "Maureen had his gift of communication, his love of politics, and when she believed in a cause, she was not afraid to fight hard for it."

For the most part, the Reagans lived away from the public eye, although Nancy did appear on an interview with Diane Sawyer in 2002 and at the occasional charitable function to benefit the Nancy Reagan Foundation and the Reagan Library. She nearly came out of acting retirement when director, writer, and actor Albert Brooks asked her to play the part of his mother in his 1996 film *Mother*. Nancy declined because she couldn't bear to be away from her husband.

Nancy admitted that as time wore on, conversations with Ron were impossible, and she had given up showing her husband videos from his political days because he did not remember any of it. When asked why she continued to sacrifice her "golden years" to care for a man who no longer knew her, she simply said, "I know he would do it for me." When a news story reported that Nancy has forbidden Ron's old friends and political associates from coming to visit him, she said it was because it upset him that he could no longer recall the names of the people with whom he had so closely worked.

"What can you say about a man who on Mother's Day sends flowers to his mother-in-law, with a note thanking her for making him the happiest man on Earth?"

—Nancy Reagan on Ron's thoughtful nature

Above: Ron and Nancy were happiest in California, right back where they had started.

Ronald Reagan spent his last few years bedridden, wheelchair-bound, and not knowing anyone—not even the greatest love of his life who stood beside him and oversaw his care. Ron died on June 5, 2004, from pneumonia.

Throughout the pageantry and events of the Reagan funerals and tributes, Nancy stayed close to her husband, just as she did in life. She looked frail and slow in step, with the last ten years as her husband's caretaker having clearly taken a toll on her. Several times the cameras saw her rest her head on the flag-draped coffin, rest her cheek on it, and whisper "I love you." The former First Lady was surrounded by her crying children, who tried to console her and share the burden of her pain. After the service, a tearful Nancy kissed and stroked her husband's coffin while clutching the American flag that had once flown over the nuclear aircraft carrier USS *Ronald Reagan*. She was still reluctant to leave his side.

Life without Ron will never be the same for Nancy Reagan. In recent years, she has devoted her time to projects related to the Ronald Reagan Presidential Library, where she serves on the board of the Ronald Reagan Presidential Foundation, a nonprofit, nonpartisan organization dedicated to developing and fostering President Reagan's Four Pillars of Freedom: preserving individual liberty, promoting economic opportunity, advancing democracy around the world, and instilling pride in our national heritage. Nancy nixed the idea of enthusiastic millionaires who wanted to start "Ronald Reagan University," and expressed her disapproval of the idea of replacing Franklin D. Roosevelt with her husband's face on the American dime.

After Ron's death, Nancy's dedication to him continues in the form of her subsequent fight for stem cell research and the search for a cure for Alzheimer's disease. In the fall of 2004, Nancy and her son Ron thrust themselves into a political battle with George W. Bush and others over the funding of stem cell research, which is opposed by antiabortion activists and the Bush administration. This fight has also helped to soften Nancy's image and perhaps reshape her legacy.

Visiting the Ronald Reagan Presidential Library, Museum, and Gravesite

Situated on one hundred acres overlooking Simi Valley and the Pacific Ocean, the Ronald Reagan Presidential Library and Museum has welcomed more than one million visitors since opening in 1991. It's at once a sightseer's museum and a serious research facility and one of the most modern and extensive presidential libraries in America. Among the holdings are millions of pages of documents chronicling the Reagan presidency and governorship, millions of photographs, a half million feet of motion picture film, and tens of thousands of audio and videotapes, including many of Nancy and Ron's speeches and appearances on television's GE Theater. In addition, there is an extensive collection of Nancy Reagan memorabilia, personal correspondence, speeches, and more. The library's Web site is a vast storehouse of free information, as well as an e-commerce Web site offering the opportunity to buy videos and transcripts, photos, and memorabilia, including books and photos signed by Nancy.

The library is located at 40 Presidential Drive in Simi Valley, which is approximately forty-five minutes from downtown Los Angeles. For more information call 800-410-8354 or 805-577-4000; or log on to www.reaganlibrary.com.

The facilities are open from 10:00 A.M. until 5:00 P.M. every day of the week, except Thanksgiving, Christmas Day, and New Year's Day. There is a small admission charge.

Below: The Ronald Reagan Presidential Library and Museum is in Simi Valley, California.

Barbara Bush

To the Manor Born

Rye, New York, where Barbara Pierce grew up, was, and still is, considered one of New York City's most exclusive suburbs, and the Pierce family was at its upper level of society. Barbara's father was an executive, and later president, of the McCall Publishing Corporation. She went to dancing school before it was time for her to start at the local public school, and after sixth grade she was enrolled at the private Rye Country Day School, as was expected of the children of the town's leading families. After that, she was sent off to Ashley Hall in Charleston, South Carolina, for three years of high school. It was during the 1941 Christmas vacation from there that Barbara met George Bush at a dance in nearby Greenwich, Connecticut. He called himself Poppy, she called him "interesting."

George showed up in Rye the night after he met Barbara, and the night after that as well, until he finally met the Pierce family. To Barbara's relief, they found young George "nice," and that was enough for her. He was, after all, the son of a wealthy Connecticut investment banker. They wrote to each other when he went back to school at Phillips Academy in Andover, Massachusetts, and she to her studies in Charleston, and she saw him again in the spring when he invited her to his senior prom.

The country had entered World War II by then, and as soon as he graduated, George joined the navy. He graduated from flight school the same year Barbara finished high school, and he became, at eighteen, the navy's youngest pilot. They had become secretly engaged by the time she went off to Smith College in the fall, but no one in either family was very surprised when they were let in on the secret. What did surprise everyone was that they planned to get married during his scheduled leave at the end of 1944 and then he expected go back to finish his enlistment while Barbara went back to Smith to get her degree.

George was named for his grandfather George Herbert Walker. His sons called him Pops, and they started calling their nephew Little Pops, which got shortened to Poppy.

Barbara Pierce Bush

Born
June 8, 1925,
New York, New York

Parents
Marvin Pierce and
Pauline Robinson Pierce

Marriage
January 6, 1945, to
George Herbert Walker
Bush (1925-)

Children
George Walker (1946-);
Robin (1949-1953);
John Ellis (Jeb) (1953-);
Neil Mallon (1955-);
Marvin Pierce (1956-);
Dorothy Walker (1959-)

Above: Barbara at the age of seven.

Below: In her teens, Barbara was a private school student in her upscale hometown of Rye, New York.

George and Barbara were married in Rye on January 6, 1945. It was three weeks later than they had planned because George's leave had been delayed. Barbara altered her own plan by scrapping the rest of her college career in favor of following George's squadron around the country. It was the beginning of a lifetime on the move—over the years from their early marriage until their retirement, they lived in twenty-nine different homes.

Because of his earlier combat experience, George was discharged from the service right after the Japanese surrendered in August 1945. The couple's next move was to New Haven, Connecticut, where he had been accepted at Yale University as part of the first group to go to college under the GI Bill. Barbara decided not to go back to college herself because, as she put it, "I chose to have a big family instead." She started right away. Her first child, a baby boy they named George Walker Bush, was born while they were still living in students' barracks on the Yale campus.

Nearly all of the men in George's family were in the investment-banking business. His father was a partner in Brown Brothers Harriman, and his mother's father had founded the highly regarded G. H. Walker and Company. It was a foregone conclusion that he would follow in the family tradition, but he had decided that he didn't like the idea of dealing with intangibles, and he set out to find a product he could develop a feeling for. Besides, he wanted to be his own man.

George found his direction from an old family friend who was the head of a holding company called Dresser Industries that controlled several oil-related operations. He suggested that if there was anything you could feel and touch and make barrels of money with at the same time, it was the oil business. George couldn't have agreed more, and he signed on as a Dresser trainee, which would expose him to the workings of all the companies it controlled.

He left for Odessa, Texas, in a little red Studebaker one day after he graduated from Yale. When he got there, he was put to work sweeping warehouse floors and painting oil rigs, while Barbara and little Georgie went up to Maine to the Bush family's summer place in Kennebunkport. They joined George in Texas themselves after he found a "sorry little house" for them to live in. It wasn't exactly a house, but a two-room apartment with a shared bath, but then, they hadn't exactly been living in palatial spaces between the Yale campus and the navy bases either. It took a while for these Yanks to get accustomed to west Texas itself, and the rough-and-tumble blue-collar

> "I married the first man I ever kissed. When I tell this to my children, they just about throw up."
>
> —*Barbara Bush on her lifelong romance with her husband*

town of Odessa in particular. It was nothing like Greenwich, or even Rye. Barbara's family had been scandalized when she took a part-time job in a factory during the war years. They were relieved that at least the factory was far away from them in Texas.

After less than a year, the Bush family moved to California where, among other jobs, George worked as a salesman for a Dresser company that made drill bits. They settled in the town of Compton where their second child, Robin, was born a few days before Christmas in 1949. They were sent back to west Texas in the spring, this time to the white-collar town of Midland where George made sales calls on oil companies whose headquarters were there. They bought a tract house in a section of town favored by displaced easterners like themselves. But the town also had a mix of people from other parts of Texas and from Oklahoma. What they all had in common was that they were strangers in Midland. But no one is ever a stranger in Texas for long, and the Bushes had no problem blending in with their neighbors, all of whom had small children. They rotated backyard barbecues and they shared baby-sitting chores. George became an elder at the First Presbyterian Church, and both he and Barbara taught Sunday school there. They were active in the local theater group and the YMCA, and she volunteered at the local hospital. They were more at home in Midland than anywhere else either of them had ever lived at any point in their lives. They had become Texans with eastern accents.

George was ready to spread his wings again and with financial support from his uncle, he went into the oil-exploration business with his neighbor John Overbey. They named their new company Zapata after the Marlon Brando movie *Viva Zapata,* which they had both just seen.

The family grew again with the birth of John Ellis Bush in 1953. They called him Jeb. A few weeks after Jeb was born, his little sister, Robin, who was four, was diagnosed with leukemia and there was no cure. George and Barbara took her to New York City, where George's uncle Dr. John Walker was on the staff of Memorial Sloan-Kettering Hospital and a leading expert on cancers such as leukemia, but eight months later, Robin was dead. Barbara's grief was inconsolable, but she eventually healed, and in 1955 she gave birth to another son, Neil, followed in less than two years by Marvin, their fifth child.

In the meantime, Zapata Petroleum had grown big enough to spin off a subsidiary, Zapata Offshore, and George became its president and CEO. In 1959, with five rigs operating in the Gulf of Mexico, the company went independent and the Bushes moved from Midland to Houston to be closer to the coast and to his potential customers. Not only was Barbara upset about leaving the place that had become a home she loved, but she was pregnant again, and she didn't want to look for a new doctor at the same time she was getting to know a new neighborhood. She would also have to find new schools for Georgie and

Above: Barbara was just twenty on her wedding day.

Below: Barbara's mother, Pauline Pierce, was a frequent visitor when her first grandson George Walker Bush was born.

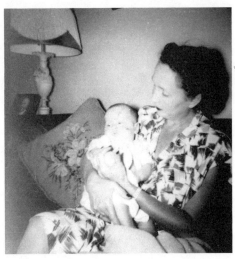

Above: The Bush family in 1956. Barbara holds baby Marvin, and George hefts Neil, while George W. and Jeb pose at their side.

Jebbie, who were quite content where they were. They built a new house in Houston and it was finished at about the same time the new baby was born—a girl they named Dorothy for George's mother and called Doro.

For the next ten years, Barbara Bush was a classic example of a typical American mother, dealing with childhood diseases and occasional forays to the hospital emergency room, keeping dentist appointments, and shuttling the boys to Little League and after-school activities. The Bushes' backyard, with its swimming pool and trees to climb, was a gathering place for other youngsters from the neighborhood, and it all kept Barbara running in place, but contented.

By 1952, George's father, Prescott Bush, was a United States senator from Connecticut, and George himself had been active in Republican affairs back in Midland, so it didn't come as a surprise when he told Barbara that he wanted to be chairman of the local county Republicans. But what did surprise Barbara, for some reason, was that he was going to have to work for the job. She was also surprised that she was expected to go along with him when he made his pitch at party meetings in more than two hundred precincts. It was a repetitive experience, and to ward off boredom, Barbara took up needlepoint. After he got the job, there were even more meetings for them to attend. "They were like a circus," Barbara recalled, "and George was the ringmaster." Slowly, she developed a grudging affection for politics, but George had become completely hooked.

Soon after, George decided to run for the U.S. Senate, and it was Barbara's introduction to the nastier side of politics. George was painted as an "eastern liberal," and she as an heiress who was more at home on the beach at Cape Cod than down at Padre Island in Texas. She still visited the Bush family retreat on the coast of Maine, although not Cape Cod where the Kennedys relaxed,

Above: Barbara's desire to promote literacy started when her sons were young, and it continued to be her work once she was First Lady as well.

Reality Check

When little Neil Bush came down with chicken pox, Barbara tried to amuse him by inviting him to read to her. But he couldn't identify a single word on the page even though he was a straight-A student. When Barbara met with his teacher, she was told that she must be mistaken because Neil was the best reader in the class. To prove it, she had all the children read a line or two, but when she got to Neil, another youngster prompted him with the first word and the teacher with the next one. The boy had been faking it and easily hiding the fact that he couldn't read from a reading teacher who never noticed. The conclusion was made that Neil was dyslexic, and Barbara transferred him to a different school where the reading teacher was more observant and helpful. Barbara also sent Marvin and Jebby there, too. It was a private school that offered a discount for three children, but it still it meant that the Bush budget was stretched thin. On the other hand, the experience was worthwhile in making Barbara a lifelong proponent of literacy.

and whenever she did go back east, she was told that George had become too conservative for their families. In realty, he wasn't at either extreme. As he put it, "Labels are for cans."

In spite of the dirt that was thrown on him, George won the primary, and during the election campaign itself, he and Barbara stumped the state in a bus labeled the "Bush Bandwagon." In many places they visited, even Houstonians like them were regarded as too liberal to be true Texans, and Barbara made it a point not to identify herself as the candidate's wife but just an enthusiastic volunteer supporter. The trick didn't work. Bush lost the election and they went home to Houston to get on with their lives.

But by then their lives were in the world of politics, and George took advantage of an opportunity to run for a newly created seat in the U.S. House of Representatives. When he won, their lives were thrown upside-down again. He had already resigned from the day-to-day operation of the oil company, and the Bushes decided to sell their big house and buy a smaller one as a local base; they took the kids out of school and set out for a new adventure, life in Washington, D.C.

A Political Life

Their son George was a student at Yale by the time George and Barbara moved to Washington, and Jeb stayed behind in Houston to finish high school, but Neil, Marvin, and Doro went along with them. The boys were accepted at the St. Albans School, and eventually went to Andover, as their father had done, and Doro went on to Miss Porter's in Connecticut, where Barbara had been a student at the same age.

Like most freshman congressmen, George had a busy breaking-in period, and so did Barbara as she worked her way through the intricacies of Washington society. He was appointed to the powerful Ways and Means Committee during those first weeks, and they immediately found themselves on everyone's preferred invitation list. It was hard for her to know which were the most important, so Barbara decided to "try everything once." She was able to set priorities before long, but in the meantime she had an unusually thorough introduction to life in Washington. And being social by nature, Barbara cultivated warm friendships that have lasted a lifetime.

During George's second term (he served two terms in the House), Barbara shared her Washington life with the folks back home through a newspaper column called "Washington Scene" that she wrote for the Houston newspapers. She also spent a large part of the summer of 1970 back there in person as George campaigned for the Senate and she took to the road for him, proudly revealing her identity as Mrs. Bush this time. George lost the election, and when he decided not to run for a third term in the House, that left them with an uncertain future.

Below: During George's campaign for senator, Barbara found time in her own busy schedule to make a needlepoint bag promoting him.

George, however, had acquired some influence among Washington Republicans, and he had a very good idea what he wanted to do next. He wanted to be the ambassador to the United Nations. It looked as though his dream might be sidetracked when President Nixon offered to make him a special assistant to the president, and he accepted the offer but suggested that he'd be much happier if he were going to New York. It was the first that Nixon had heard of his preference, although George had brought it up with several members of the administration staff; an hour after he left the White House thinking that he'd soon be back there to report for duty, the president phoned and told him that the U.N. post was his.

After he was confirmed and sworn in, the Bushes went on a tour of U.N. agencies in Europe, and then they went to New York and moved into the ambassador's residence, a five-bedroom apartment at the Waldorf Towers. Barbara's first assignment was furnishing it. She had the rooms painted in soft colors, and she filled the place with potted plants and fresh flowers, then she arranged for the Metropolitan Museum of Art to loan them paintings that she would hang in every room. The museum people were appalled at her apparent lack of taste when she rejected two Monets, until she explained that only American art would do. "When the French start hanging American artists," she explained, "then I'll start thinking about hanging French paintings." The front foyer held several Gilbert Stuart portraits of George Washington. "It seemed like there were hundreds of them," she recalled. "He must have turned them out like rabbits."

Barbara never went to George's office at the U.N. Mission, but she was a regular presence at General Assembly sessions where she could be found in the delegates' gallery intent on her needlework, but absorbing everything that was going on. And two days a week, she visited the Sloan-Kettering Hospital, where daughter Robin had been treated, to work as a volunteer.

What kept her busiest, though, was the entertaining that came with the job. Not only were they expected to receive the ambassadors of the other member nations, but the suite was also where George's boss, Secretary of State William Rogers, held his own luncheons and parties when he was in town. His wife served as the hostess at those times, but Barbara was expected to be smiling in the background.

George loved his job, and what he liked best about it was the entertaining. He often invited other ambassadors and their wives to the Bush getaway in Kennebunkport and to the family home in Greenwich. Barbara frequently invited groups of her Washington friends for parties in the Waldorf apartment, and she couldn't have been happier. "I would pay to have this job," she told a friend. "It is like being taken around the world to meet people from 128 countries and yet never having to pack a bag or sleep in a strange bed."

The Bushes were in New York from 1971 until the beginning of 1973, when President Nixon started his second term. They were probably thanking their lucky stars that George wasn't on the presidential staff while the Watergate affair was coming to light, but they were about to be thrown into the midst of it. Although the Republicans had won the presidential election in spite of the scandal, it was a bad time to be a Republican in Washington, and the president wanted someone the public could trust to head up the Republican National Committee. George Bush was his choice, and he and Barbara reluctantly packed their bags for Washington, D.C., and jumped into the maelstrom.

They were happy to go back to the capital, though. Doro, who had lived in New York with them, was glad to get back to her old school and Neil, who was still a St. Albans student, was able to move back in with the family. Jeb was at the University of Texas and George W. at the Harvard Business School at the time, but Marvin was close by at school in Virginia.

Barbara picked up where she had left off, entertaining often, volunteering at a nearby nursing home, and working for the Republican party. George was away a lot—he logged nearly 100,000 miles in his first eleven months in the new job. He gave speeches, held press conferences, and worked at keeping the party together in the fallout from Watergate. Most difficult of all was raising funds, which was at the heart of the job, but it was like digging for water in the Sahara. "It was a very unpleasant time for everyone," Barbara said. "My tennis foursomes were down to two of us, we couldn't find two more who didn't think President Nixon was lying." It wasn't easy to find anyone who didn't think so, but it was George's job to stand by his party's standard-bearer, and he stayed loyal right up until the end when it became obvious that the only choice the president had left was to resign or be impeached.

George felt that he deserved a reward after President Nixon resigned and Gerald Ford replaced him. He expected that it would be the vice presidency, but that job went to Nelson Rockefeller instead, and as a kind of consolation prize, he was offered an ambassadorship, with the choice of whether it would be to London or to Paris left up to him. But either job would have been largely ceremonial with a lot of expensive entertaining and little challenge, which was what George Bush was looking for. Much as he and Barbara loved entertaining, they'd had quite enough of it during their post at the United Nations, and George held out for the most challenging post on the State Department roster; he wanted to be sent to China. Barbara was solidly behind him, even when the

"Dealing with Watergate was like dealing with a centipede. The other shoe kept dropping."

—George Bush on the Watergate scandal

president told them that they would have to stay there for at least two years. The United States didn't have formal diplomatic ties with the People's Republic of China, so technically there was no ambassadorship post to be filled. But there was a liaison office and George would be at its head.

Gone to China

Leaving their children behind was a special problem for Barbara, but with Doro enrolled in a boarding school, all five had already left the nest. But there was one member of the family she just couldn't leave behind. She had a new dog—there was always a dog in Barbara's life—a blond cocker spaniel named C. Fred, and George had told her that the dog would have to stay home. But the State Department people, and China's representatives in Washington, told her that there was no reason why she couldn't take him along as far as they were concerned, so she bought a small truckload of dog food to take along. Stunned by the investment, George relented and the three of them left for Beijing and the great adventure of their lives in October 1974.

There was a small staff waiting for the Bushes when they arrived in China and they had all been there long enough to be able to guide them through their adjustment to a completely different way of life than they had known before. Barbara had taken a basic course in Chinese, but her household staff didn't speak any English and she wasn't fluent enough in their language to understand what was going on. She found out very quickly that they didn't know how to cook in the Western style, and the Bushes learned to like Chinese food, although they didn't always know what they were eating.

Below: While they were in China, George and Barbara followed the example of the locals and navigated the streets of Beijing on bicycles.

They explored the city on bicycles, and either George or Barbara walked the dog twice a day. They had been told there were dogs in China, but there turned out to be very few of them, and there were certainly no other blond cocker spaniels anywhere in the country. This turned C. Fred into a local curiosity. Most people thought that the Bushes were walking a cat. Barbara herself was a strange sight to most of them too. Her hair had turned gray at the age of twenty-eight and although she dyed it at first, she had given that up years before and so she was one of the few women in Beijing with snow-white hair. She couldn't help wondering why none of the Chinese people she saw on the street had gray hair until a hairdresser confided that most of them dyed it, and that black was the only color available. "Thank heavens!" Barbara said, "They were human."

The Bushes never lacked for company in Beijing. Everyone wanted to visit China, it seemed, and the only way to do it at the time was with a formal invitation from the Bushes to stay in their residence. Barbara served as their tour guide through Beijing's attractions, from the Forbidden City to the Great Wall and literally hundreds of other exotic sites, museums, and ancient tombs in the

Rules of Engagement

While the Bushes were in China, George insisted that they should socialize as much as they could and he broke precedent by attending every National Day reception in the diplomatic community. They quickly learned that every one of these receptions followed exactly the same rigid form. Barbara described them as a series of waves. During wave one, sixteen chairs—always the same number—remained empty until the Chinese officials arrived, and when they did, the hosts immediately left the receiving line and sat down, alternating with the eight Chinese guests. Huge amounts of food were served before the second wave began when ambassadors and senior diplomats were welcomed, and then came lesser diplomats like the Bushes in wave number three. These two groups stood off to the side, eating standing up, and usually taking mental notes on the level of Chinese officials present as an indication of the government's esteem for the hosts. Barbara called the fourth wave, "rent a crowd." It consisted of lesser Chinese officials who sat down to eat in the back of the room without saying a word to anyone, as though there was no one else there. The pattern never varied from one reception to the next. Even the Bush receptions followed the same rules of engagement.

city and the countryside beyond. They were limited in their travels to a twenty-mile radius.

Barbara took thousands of pictures of the places she visited, and then she culled them down into a slide show that she gave often to civic groups around the country after they returned to the United States. She had done the same thing on tours of Washington during her early years there, and her shows were in great demand, usually serving as popular fund-raisers.

The Bushes had been told that they were expected to stay in China for two years, and they would have been delighted to stay much longer. But the adventure came to an early end in November 1975 with an official cable requesting that George go back to Washington to take over the Central Intelligence Agency. Their last duty in China was as hosts for a state visit by President Ford and his wife, Betty. It was Barbara's first experience with the logistics of a presidential trip, and she was happy to be going home where she wouldn't have to be involved with such a thing again.

The Call of Duty

Although both he and Barbara were sad to leave China, George was pleased to have a new challenge with the CIA. He wrote to his family, "It's a graveyard for politics, and it is perhaps the toughest job in government right now…it's not always a clean and lovely business [but] I am convinced it is important."

Barbara returned to her volunteer activities when she went home to Washington, but for the first time in their married life, she wasn't able to interact with George's job. Even though she had more friends than she could count and her children visited her often, she felt an emptiness that led to a form of depression and she couldn't shake it. It never occurred to her to ask anyone for help because she lived by a personal "code" that she shouldn't live for herself but for others. Her malaise disappeared as suddenly as it came on after about six months, but it left her a changed person with more sympathy for others and more openness about herself.

Barbara was forced to sit out the 1976 presidential election campaign because George's job had removed him from politics. When the Republicans lost to Jimmy Carter, though, he sent Barbara to Houston to find them a place to live. He may not have had a "political" job, but a change in the political climate was going to take it away. She found a dream house for them, and they went home to Texas again.

The Bushes missed Washington, but this was a place they loved, and they weren't there long before a new kind of love came into their lives: They became grandparents for the first time with the birth of George P. Bush in 1976 and then Noelle Bush the following summer. Both were the children of Jeb and his wife, Columba, who were living in Houston, too.

Barbara busied herself traveling around the country with her China slide show, raising money for a host of charities, and George became a bank executive as well as a member of several corporate boards. Most of the time, though, he traveled, too, since his political life wasn't completely behind him. Less than two years into his retirement, it was obvious that he was planning to run for president. Barbara wrote to a friend that he was "the right person at the right time for the job."

They were back on the campaign trail together early in 1979, an experience Barbara described as "exhausting." But it was invigorating, too. The most frequently asked question at her press conferences was what her "cause" might be if she became First Lady. Although it wasn't a requirement, it had become a tradition by then, and it would be unthinkable for a candidate's wife not to have anything more in mind than simply being her husband's helpmate.

Barbara gave it a lot of thought. Rosalynn Carter was involved in mental health causes; Betty Ford in arthritis; Pat Nixon promoted volunteerism; and Lady Bird Johnson worked to beautify the landscape. Barbara herself had been volunteering in hospitals and nursing homes for years, and she would have been content to expand that role, but she thought that she ought to look for something that affected a bigger part of the population, that wouldn't cost the government a lot of money, and wouldn't saddle the president with a controversy he didn't need.

Barbara was concerned about a lot of issues: homelessness, hunger, teenage pregnancies, and other similar things that needed attention. "Sad to say," she wrote, "there were plenty of problems.... [then] I realized that everything I worried about would be far better if more people could read, write, and comprehend. More people would stay in school and get an education, meaning that fewer people would turn to the

Below: Youngsters who visited the Bush White House experienced a change in tradition, with story hours presided over by the First Lady.

streets and get involved with crime or drugs…. It seemed that simple. I had found my cause."

The campaign summed it up in a single word, "literacy," but she had to admit that she didn't know anything at all about how to accomplish it. But she was able to learn quickly by asking educators she met during campaign swings what they would do, and they weren't shy with their answers.

The campaign brought the family back together, too. Neil and Marvin took time off from college to travel for their father; Doro took a course at Katherine Gibbs secretarial school to help him with work behind the scenes; Jeb came home from Venezuela where he had been a bank manager; and George W., fresh from the campaign trail himself—he had recently lost an attempt to become a congressman from Texas—went on the road again. Relatives from both George's and Barbara's family joined them, and Barbara herself outran them all.

The biggest problem she faced was a perception that she was a woman of the 1940s in a 1980s world. She met the problem head-on, refusing to color her hair, change her style, or even lose weight. She was what she was, and that's all she was, and to the surprise of her political advisors, the public seemed to like what it saw.

By the end of the primary season, it had become obvious that George wasn't going to be the presidential candidate this time around, and they worked to persuade the delegates committed to them to switch their support to front-runner Ronald Reagan. Most did in the interest of party solidarity, but it still came as a surprise when George was nominated for the vice presidency. The Bush family was back on the campaign trail once again.

Barbara knew next to nothing about candidate Reagan, but she had been campaigning for George all of her adult life, and as long as people didn't ask her what Ronald Reagan might do as president, she was a strong asset to the campaign, making speeches and covering as much ground as her time allowed. When the Reagan–Bush ticket won the election, she said, "In May, we had bowed out of politics forever; six months later, I was the wife of the Vice-President-elect of the United States…. It seemed so sudden."

When Nelson Rockefeller became vice president during the Ford administration, he was the first to use the official vice president's residence at the Naval Observatory. Prior to that, vice presidents were expected to provide their own housing and entertaining venues.

Their new Bush home was the former admiral's quarters at the Naval Observatory, which had become the official residence of the vice president in 1974. Barbara loved the house, but it needed work, and that became her first priority when she went back to Washington yet again.

When the work was finished, Barbara was proud to report, "The rooms say, 'Please come in and sit down,' rather than 'Please stay out.'" It would be her home for eight years, the longest Barbara and George had ever lived in a single place. They were also the busiest years of Barbara's life. She traveled to sixty-five different foreign countries, many more than once, and to all fifty states. She entertained frequently at home and she was on hand for hundreds of other functions around Washington. It was also during this time that the Bushes bought Walker Point, the Bush family retreat in Kennebunkport, Maine, and sold their house in Houston.

Barbara began her deep involvement in the literacy campaign while she was Second Lady. She wrote a book with her dog called *C. Fred's Story,* and raised more than $100,000 for the Literacy Volunteers of America and the Laubach Literacy Organization. She also began appearing at book parties to raise funds for libraries, and she went on book tours, not just to promote sales but also to raise awareness for the importance of parents volunteering in their children's schools. Many states were establishing literacy councils by then, and Public Broadcasting and ABC television joined together to form Project Literacy USA (PLUS) to follow Barbara's lead. She also lent her support to reading programs in senior citizen homes, and English-as-a-second-language programs within immigrant groups.

Also during the vice presidential years, eight new grandchildren were added to Barbara's Christmas list. George, who had spent a lifetime trying to live down the nickname Poppy, was now proudly calling himself "Gampy."

As the 1988 presidential campaign approached, George seemed to be the heir apparent to Ronald Reagan, but it wasn't a foregone conclusion. The vice presidency had evolved into a full-time job as George had taken on more and more responsibility within the administration, and Barbara had taken on a heavy schedule for herself. Neither of them had the time to do justice to a presidential campaign, although the competition for the actual nomination was fierce. There were no less than eight major Democratic candidates at the beginning of the primary season, and six serious Republican contenders. George was the front-runner, but that made him a target for the others. Barbara mostly campaigned on her own, but she hated the negative things she was hearing about her husband, and she made George promise that she wouldn't have to sit in on meetings or watch television. After her days of campaign events, she curled up in the evening with what she called "no think" books. Still, she kept up a steady round of rallies and fund-raisers by day. It was just that she wasn't

Below: George and Barbara arrive at one of his inaugural balls. "My mail tells me a lot of fat, white-haired, wrinkled ladies are tickled pink," Barbara joked about her appearance.

interested in hearing what the opposition had to say about George.

In the end, George was nominated to run for the presidency and Barbara put away her no-think books and began a nine-week whirlwind tour at George's side. She went off on her own campaign tour once in a while, and the couple dropped back to Washington occasionally to keep their jobs running, but for the most part they were together crisscrossing the country day in and day out from Labor Day through Election Day. On that day, George became president of the United States and Barbara the First Lady.

Above: Barbara's White House chefs were sometimes caught flatfooted with sudden changes in schedules that even Barbara herself had a problem dealing with. But they all managed to handle their jobs with relaxed aplomb.

New Challenge

A week after the election, Barbara was the guest of honor at a previously planned literary conference that included the announcement of the formation of the Barbara Bush Foundation for Family Literacy. Its focus is on the entire family, and getting every generation involved in reading. The foundation still exists, and its work continues.

There were fourteen balls for the Bush inaugural, and when they were over, Barbara said "every inch of my body ached." Her dress was a blue velvet with a satin skirt designed by Arnold Scaasi. Her shoes were dyed to match and she said that because she knew she'd wear them just once, she bought the cheapest pair that she could find. Big mistake. She paid the price of sore feet after the marathon of dancing. To make matters worse, the dye came off on her feet and she carried the blue stains for weeks.

All five of the Bush children and their spouses were on hand for the public reception the following day, and so were all ten of their grandchildren. They had a family luncheon during their first weekend in the White House, and 250 guests showed up even though the grandchildren had been asked not to bring their girlfriends or boyfriends, just fiancés. When Barbara told George about the rule, he said "You are going to cause a great many engagements." She might have, but this was already a very big family.

Entertaining was raised to new heights in the Bush White House. George loved it, and he often scheduled dinners and parties on literally a moment's notice. The staff took some time to get used to turning on a dime, but Barbara was used to it by then. On their first Thanksgiving together after they were

*George's final inaugural party was the Young People's Ball. "Lots of fun,"
said Barbara. "It was like being at an aerobics class."*

Above: Barbara followed a fairly strict exercise routine, with tennis being one of her favorites activities.

married, he surprised her by inviting ten of his college buddies to share it with them. The pattern never changed.

Barbara wasted no time getting involved in local charities, but the one that drew the most attention was her visits to a clinic for babies with AIDS. At the time, most people assumed that the virus was spread by contact, and they were scandalized when she was photographed holding those babies, and maybe a little mystified when she didn't contract AIDS herself. But Barbara always did what she thought was right. She spoke her own mind, too, and many times she was quoted as opposing some of the president's views. She knew that they were in agreement just about all of the time, and so did he, and she went right on giving her own press conferences, oblivious to the fallout.

She moved the First Lady's office up from the East Wing to a room in the residential quarters that Pat Nixon had converted into a beauty parlor. Nancy Reagan had used it for that purpose, too, and so did Barbara, but in her case it doubled as an office. She spent several hours a day there on paperwork, and she bought a laptop computer to make it all easier. Just like everyone else, she found the break-in period a lesson in patience, but soon the love-hate relationship with the position of First Lady became all love.

Barbara also took advantage of the White House pool and swam a mile every day, although she was in her mid-sixties by then. She played tennis outside, too, several days a week. Her health never seemed better, but she had developed a thyroid condition called Graves' disease that affected her eyes. Treatment brought it under control, but the First Lady's health is almost as closely watched as the president's, and it became a major news story. Barbara was upset by the attention, but she was secretly pleased that newspapers carefully described the ailment and she knew that it would be helpful to other people who had been diagnosed with it. Her quick recovery made it all the more reassuring that in spite of its ominous name, Graves' disease can be treated.

Barbara was able to demonstrate her good health at a steady round of White House events. During their first one hundred days there, she hosted eighteen receptions, sixteen dinners, twenty-four teas, nineteen luncheons, and two breakfasts, and she entertained fifty-one overnight guests. She still found time to travel to four countries and to nine states, to participate in twenty-four press interviews, and attend eighty-three special events outside the White House. The pace wouldn't slow a bit over the rest of their term. And during the summers when they were officially on vacation, her hosting duties continued

Midway through her term as First Lady, Barbara received an honorary degree from Smith College, the school from which she had never graduated. "I did not earn it," she said, "nor did I deserve it. But I was thrilled."

while at Kennebunkport. She said that "every single day was interesting, rewarding, and sometimes just plain fun."

Like other First Ladies before her, Barbara was a trendsetter. She constantly wore a three-strand set of fake pearls that she had bought for $95, and suddenly women all over the United States were wearing them, too. The fashion designers were happy as well. Her favorite, Arnold Scaasi, said, "Having Barbara as First Lady means that women who weren't buying a new dress because they were a little overweight are buying new dresses now. It means that you don't have to try to look like your daughter any more." Wrinkles were "in," too, and needlepoint became the pastime of choice. Even people who disagreed with her husband's stands on issues admired Barbara's approach. The director of the National Abortion Rights League said, for instance, "She's why politicians should trust women to make decisions for themselves. She's thoughtful, caring, concerned and compassionate, not only about children's lives and the quality of the family, but about the role of women in society."

Above: Barbara and her dogs, Millie and Ranger, dressed in matching jumpsuit outfits.

Barbara also found time to write a book with her dog, Millie, just as she had with her friend C. Fred. *Millie's Book* became a *New York Times* best-seller, and raised more than $1 million for the Barbara Bush Foundation for Family Literacy. George couldn't help commenting, "I am President of the United States and my dog makes more money than I do." She also began a series of radio broadcasts called "Mrs. Bush's Story Time," which was later sold as sets of tapes with a how-to book to help parents read to their children.

Barbara's efforts, which were considerable all through her White House career, culminated with the signing of the National Literary Act in 1991. It was the first law of its kind, and still the only one, intended to ensure that every American adult gets the basic literary skills they need. The signing was Barbara's proudest moment.

When the primaries got under way for the 1992 presidential election, Barbara closed her ears to personal attacks on George again and went to work for him. As she had the last time around, she refused to watch television or sit in on strategy meetings and she read a lot of books instead.

Fortunately, Barbara didn't follow the polls, which would have been more discouraging than the Bush bashing she was trying to avoid. The Democratic candidate, Bill Clinton, came out of the convention twenty-five points ahead. The gap had closed by the time George and Barbara left the Republican convention, but the election was still nearly three months away and they knew

The Bushes' daughter, Doro, was married for the second time during the second presidential campaign. When the bridegroom, Bobby Koch, knelt for the blessing, there were Bush-Quayle stickers on the soles of his shoes.

Above: The First Lady wrote a best-selling book with her Springer spaniel, Millie. George said that he may be president but the dog made more money than he did.

that they had their work cut out for them. This time around, they went their own separate ways, and the whole Bush family fanned out as well.

Barbara started her work at every destination with a big rally and then a series of luncheons and dinners more geared to raising funds than asking for votes. She made the rounds of shopping malls where the most voters were to be found, and she invariably sought out the bookstore to sell some books and make some money for her literacy program. Her "cause" had become her signature, but she was criticized by some campaign experts for seeking out children, because they couldn't vote. "Ridiculous!" she huffed. In one week alone, during September, she worked in eleven cities in seven states. But there was still a long way to go. By mid-October, she had become convinced that they were going to lose. But she kept plugging away, although she quietly began looking forward to going home to Houston and living closer to her children and friends as a private citizen again. What hurt most was the often repeated charge that "George Bush doesn't care about people." Barbara knew otherwise, but too many people seemed to believe it in spite of the evidence to the contrary.

Both Barbara and George strongly believed that would win by then, but Election Day proved them wrong. Barbara was philosophical about it. "The people really wanted a change," she said. The biggest change that happened was in their lives.

Home Again to Houston

As was the case with all presidents, the Bushes' last weeks in the White House were one long good-bye. They had accumulated an incredible number of close friends during the years they were there. Then they moved into a small rented house in Houston. "There is life after politics. Hurrah!" Barbara said.

Below: George and Barbara celebrated their fiftieth wedding anniversary at the White House surrounded by their children and grandchildren.

As far as Houstonians were concerned, they had never been away. But they had been living a life of privilege for a dozen years, and Barbara had to make a few adjustments. She had to get used to driving her own car again, and she had to relearn how to do the household shopping, something she had never done much of before. Her biggest problem was cooking. "I never loved cooking," she said, "just eating."

Determined to live a normal life, Barbara is still besieged by well-meaning people all the time. When someone asks, "Aren't you Barbara Bush?" her standard reply is, "No. She's much older than I am."

They find eating out, which is pretty much a necessity considering Barbara's culinary skills, a trying experience, too. But they do it often, anyway, usually as a way of maintaining their social contacts. And they still travel frequently, sometimes abroad. Both of them were busy writing books during the early years of her retirement and both were involved in the building of a new house down the street from their rented one in Houston. Barbara became a member of the board of the Mayo Foundation in Minnesota and of the Cancer Hospital in Houston. She also became ambassador at large for AmeriCares and, naturally, she still works for the Barbara Bush Foundation for Family Literacy.

At the end of their first year back home, Barbara reminded George of the time when they were first married when she said, "I can't wait for you to retire." "I can't imagine anything worse," he answered, "and I hope I never will." As far as the history books are concerned, he finally was, but nobody has noticed yet. Both George and Barbara were busier than ever as they settled in on their new life, and their sons Jeb and George W. were getting ready to take them back into the political arena, Jeb as governor of Florida and George as governor of Texas. Not long afterward, George and Barbara would be the parents of the forty-third president of the United States.

Above: The George Bush Presidential Library and Museum at Texas A&M University in College Station.

Visiting the George Bush Presidential Library and Museum

The Bush Library on the campus of Texas A&M University in College Station, Texas, is operated by the National Archives and Records Administration. The museum portion contains artifacts and mementos of the former president's life and career, and includes a special large section devoted to his wife, Barbara, which also has a classroom for visiting school groups.

The museum is open Monday through Saturday from 9:30 A.M. to 5:00 P.M. and on Sundays from noon. Admission is $7.00 for adults and $3.00 for students. To get to the museum from Dallas, travel south on I-15 and exit to Highway 21, going east. From Waco, go north on Highway 6.

Hillary Clinton

Baby Boomer

The United States was looking for a fresh start when World War II ended in 1945. People who had been brought up in the Great Depression and then survived the war were ready to start building new lives and new families, and the country experienced a spike in population growth that has been called the baby boom. Hillary Rodham was part of it and the label baby boomer has followed her all of her life.

The label fits. Her parents' values, which she acquired, were a result of having lived through the Depression. Both had known hard times and they believed in self-reliance and the rewards of hard work. They were solidly middle-class and thoroughly Midwestern. Hillary's mother, Dorothy, was the daughter of a Chicago firefighter and, like most other women of her generation, she was a proudly frugal housewife. Her husband, Hugh, came from a working-class family in Scranton, Pennsylvania. He had graduated from Penn State University with a degree in physical education that turned out to be useless in 1935, and he joined a group of wanderers searching for greener pastures by hopping freight trains with no clue where they might be going. In his case he landed in Chicago and he was lucky enough to find a job there as a traveling salesman peddling drapery fabric around the Midwest.

He soon met Dorothy Howell, who was working as a typist for the same company. They were eventually married not long after the United States entered World War II and they settled in Chicago. The war gave Hugh an opportunity to use his college training when he joined the navy and was assigned to boot camp at the Great Lakes Naval Station not far from their home.

After the war, Hugh established his own fabric business in downtown Chicago, and before long he was able to move his family—Hillary was three and her brother, Hugh, a newborn—to Park Ridge, Illinois, a suburb just north of the city, and this was where Hillary grew up. She had a typical 1950s

Hillary Dianne Rodham Clinton

Born
October 26, 1947,
Chicago, Illinois

Parents
Hugh Ellsworth Rodham
and Dorothy Howell
Rodham

Marriage
October 11, 1975, to
William Jefferson Clinton
(1946-)

Children
Chelsea Victoria (1980-)

*When the Rodhams moved to the suburbs of Chicago in 1950,
the baby boom was in full swing. There were
forty-seven children on their block alone.*

Above: Hillary Rodham was a bona-fide baby boomer, born in 1947, and the daughter of a veteran in a big city suburban community.

Below: Growing up, Hillary led a typical 1950s life, from Girl Scout activities to student government at school.

girlhood that ranged from earning merit badges in the Girl Scouts and starring in the girls softball league to being active in her church and taking dance classes.

Hillary did well through her school years: She became involved in the Young Republicans, was elected to the student council, and was named to the National Honor Society. Debating was her first love, and she would challenge anyone with an opinion on anything at all to take her on, and she usually won. Through her activities at the local Methodist church, she began to develop her strong views on social responsibility. Also, it was there she became inspired to read the classics and develop an appreciation for fine art through its active youth organization. Its goal was to open young people's minds to the world beyond Park Ridge, and in Hillary's case it did the job quite well.

Ranging beyond Park Ridge became a reality when Hillary chose to attend Wellesley College in Massachusetts rather than staying in the Midwest. But Hillary was like a fish out of water at Wellesley at first. Most of her fellow students had gone to boarding schools, and they had already traveled abroad. Most of them spoke a foreign language, too, but Hillary was just a simple girl from a Midwestern suburb who didn't share their previous experiences. She did share her father's conservative political outlook, very much the opposite of almost all of the rest of the freshman class, and she was sure she didn't belong in this liberal women's college, which was often regarded as a "girls' school" until the attitudes of the 1960s changed all that.

Quite unlike the girls in Park Ridge, whose only ambition was to marry well and raise big families, there was a sense of destiny in the air at Wellesley at the time. It pointed upward to the role of women as active participants in society, and Hillary eventually got caught up in it. There was a strong movement to reform life at the college itself, and she led the way toward doing away with curfews and other restrictions that she and others believed were putting a curb on their independence. By the time the rules were suspended, Hillary had become president of the college government. Her next successful crusade was to eliminate the basic curriculum requirements.

Among the first things Hillary did during her freshman year was to join the Young Republicans and she became the club's president. But with a growing interest in what was happening in Vietnam and in the battle for civil rights, she soon parted ways with many of her Republican beliefs and she became a dedicated antiwar activist and Democrat.

Hillary was a junior when Eugene McCarthy opposed President Johnson in the primary election campaign, and she drove north to New Hampshire to campaign for McCarthy. Back on campus, she joined in the only protest that was held at Wellesley during the 1960s, a hunger strike by African-American students for more recognition. In her senior year, she went to Washington, D.C., with Wellesley's internship program, and although she had ideological differences with the party, she was assigned to spend nine weeks as an intern with the House Republican Conference. It was headed at the time by Majority Leader Gerald Ford, who became her political mentor. That led to an invitation for her to go to the Republican National Convention as an aide to Nelson Rockefeller's campaign. It was her introduction to politics on a national scale, and she found it "unreal and unsettling." She was back home by the time the Democrats met for their convention in Chicago, and she had her first experience with a demonstrating mob during the Grant Park riots that were the most violent of all the protests of the 1960s. Hillary didn't like what she saw from the protesters, but she wasn't ready to align with the Republican party, either.

After her graduation from Wellesley, Hillary was accepted at both the Harvard and Yale law schools, and she chose the latter. Near the end of her first year at Yale, key members of the Black Panthers went on trial for murder in New Haven and the Yale campus became the focal point of demonstrations supporting them. Then the protests grew larger when President Nixon sent troops into Cambodia, and the campus was shut down. A few days later, protesting students were shot dead by National Guard troops at Kent State University in Ohio. Meanwhile, Hillary had gained national attention with her graduation speech at Wellesley and she was regularly being invited to give others. That week she was on her way to address the League of Women Voters in Washington, and she caused a stir there when she appeared wearing a black armband. She also caused some raised eyebrows when she defended a national student strike among three hundred schools including her own.

Hillary's trip to Washington also led to a grant that allowed her to join the Washington Research Project, an antipoverty organization, during the summer of 1970. Her special assignment was a study of the education and health of migrant children, and when she went back to Yale in the fall, she decided to concentrate on ways the law affects youngsters across the spectrum of society. She donated her spare time to the New Haven Legal Services office, and she worked with the Yale–New Haven Hospital to draft a policy for child abuse cases. Growing up in Park Ridge, she'd had no exposure to such things. She also had no idea that her life was about to change again, even more dramatically than it already had.

Above: By the time she graduated from high school, Hillary was active in the Young Republicans.

Below: As a college intern, Hillary went to Washington to join the staff of the House Republican Conference headed by Representative Gerald Ford.

Irresistible Attraction

Hillary had often seen Bill Clinton around the Yale campus after he arrived at the Yale Law School in 1970. She liked what she saw, too, but she didn't think much of it until he approached her one night in the school's law library. He was staring at her, and it made her nervous, so she walked up to him and said, "If you're going to keep looking at me, and I'm going to keep looking back, we might as well be introduced. I'm Hillary Rodham." That was the end of the conversation, and the only one they had, until the end of classes in 1971 when their paths crossed again as

Above: Hillary met Bill Clinton when they were fellow students at the Yale Law School.

they stood in line to register for the next semester. They spent the entire wait chatting until they reached the end of the line and the registrar said, "What are you doing here, Bill? You're already registered." Then he turned and asked Hillary for a date.

It was no ordinary date. He invited her to see an exhibit at the Yale Art Museum, which they both knew was closed at the time because of a labor dispute. Bill calmly started picking up trash in the courtyard and he invited Hillary to do the same while he convinced the guards that they were volunteer workers. They had the galleries to themselves.

She had regarded him as an Arkansas country bumpkin, but her opinion began to change that night and even more as she got to know him over the next several weeks. "He could converse about anything," she said, "from African politics to country and western music." Hillary already had a boyfriend at the moment, but it wasn't long before he was history.

Hillary and Bill began spending more and more time together, driving around the Connecticut countryside in his old station wagon and hanging out at the beach house on Long Island Sound where he roomed with some other students. It was there that they talked about the future. Most of their fellow students, Hillary included, had only vague plans, but Bill knew for sure that he was going to go home to Arkansas after graduation and run for public office.

He had already agreed to spend the summer organizing the South for Democrat George McGovern's presidential campaign, and he was looking forward to it. But when Hillary told him that she was going to clerk in a California law office, he announced that he was going to go there with her. "Why would you give up a chance to be on the ground floor in a presidential campaign?" she asked, and he said, "For someone I love, that's why." They left for Oakland in June.

They moved into an apartment there together, and while she was working in the law office, Bill was exploring San Francisco and sharing his discoveries with her. He also read almost constantly and shared the things he was learning with her, too. They found an apartment to share when they went back to New Haven in the fall and they furnished it with odds and ends from the Salvation Army store.

They both worked to support themselves and chip away at their student loans, but Bill found the time to open a McGovern-for-president headquarters in New Haven, and to round up a corps of volunteers, which eventually eclipsed the regular Democratic organization and swallowed it up.

In the spring, Bill took a full-time job with the McGovern campaign and Hillary went to Washington to rejoin the Washington Research Project, this time concentrating on gathering information on "private" all-White schools in the South that were being given tax-exempt status, and even public funds, in spite of court-ordered integration. In midsummer, Bill was asked to go to Texas to run George McGovern's 1972 campaign against Richard Nixon in the state. After he accepted the assignment, he asked Hillary to go along, and she was put in charge of a voter-registration drive. It wasn't an easy job. As she put it, "Hispanics in South Texas were, understandably, wary of a blonde girl from Chicago who didn't speak a word of Spanish." But she assembled a solid team, and her own natural enthusiasm carried the day. When the registration period ended a month before the election, she was sent to San Antonio to help get out the vote there. It was a doomed effort from the start, but it was their baptism to politics and both Bill and Hillary came away from Texas with a long list of things *not* to do when campaigning.

After they both graduated from law school in 1973, Bill took Hillary to England to visit the places he had discovered when he was a Rhodes scholar at Oxford. While they were exploring the Lake District, he took advantage of the romantic moment and asked her to marry him. To his surprise, and even a little to her own, she said she needed time to think about it. His answer to that was that he wasn't going to ask her again and if she ever decided she wanted to marry him, she'd have to be the one who did the asking.

Not long after they got home, he invited her to meet him at his hometown in Arkansas. She had already met his mother, Virginia, who had been put off by Hillary's way of dressing in work shirts and jeans. She was a little perplexed by her northern accent, too, and she wasn't sure she liked some of the political ideas Hillary had picked up in Yankee-land.

It took a while, but Hillary and Virginia finally bonded with each other. As Hillary described it, "We figured out that we both loved the same man." But although he was expecting her to, Hillary still wasn't ready to ask Bill to marry her. He was starting a new job as a law professor at the University of Arkansas, and she had to get back to Massachusetts where she had taken a job with the Children's Defense Fund (CDF). It didn't seem as though she would have time to marry Bill soon. Her work with CDF contributed to the congressional passage of the Education for All Handicapped Children Act, mandating that youngsters with any kind of handicap, mental or physical, should be educated in public schools.

Through it all, she missed Bill; she took the Arkansas state bar exam. When she passed and began making plans to move there, Bill had already decided he was going to run for Congress. Before she could give much thought to settling down in Arkansas, she was on her way to Washington as a staff member of a House committee that had been formed to investigate the possibility of impeaching President Nixon. They worked long hours every day, seven days a week under tight secrecy. There were forty-four lawyers involved in the inquiry, but they were nearly all men, all with broad experience; Hillary was only twenty-six years old, but every bit their equal. She called the experience "the most intense and significant experience of my life."

Six months passed before they presented their findings in the form of articles of impeachment, and the Judiciary Committee approved three of them. The

> "Don't worry about Virginia. She just has to get used to the idea. It's hard for two strong women to get along."
>
> —Jeff Dwyer, Bill Clinton's mother's third husband, on her reaction to Hillary

Above: Hillary and Bill on their wedding day at the house he had bought for her in Fayetteville.

Below: Chelsea Victoria was born after Hillary and Bill had been married for five years.

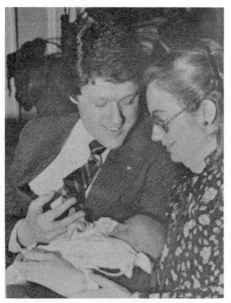

president resigned before the full House could vote on them and the trial itself held in the Senate, and Hillary found herself without a job. She considered becoming a trial lawyer, but her heart told her to go to Arkansas instead. She had been offered a job at the university where she would be teaching criminal law and running the legal aid clinic. But, of course, there was another lure.

Bill had won the congressional primary and the runoff that followed it. Hillary hadn't been much involved in his campaign, but her father, still a staunch Republican, and her younger brother, Tony, showed up to help, a sign to Hillary that her family agreed with her impressions of Bill Clinton. Bill lost the election, but it was obvious that he was just getting started, and among the items of unfinished business was that old marriage proposal. After he bought a house in Fayetteville, Arkansas, he told her, "Now you'd better marry me because I can't live in it myself." This time she said she would, and they were married in their new house on October 11, 1975.

Bill was eventually elected attorney general of Arkansas at the same time Jimmy Carter was elected to the presidency. He was running unopposed and so he had time to take charge of the Carter campaign in Arkansas, and Hillary, still a new bride, went to Indiana to coordinate the campaign there. After the election was over, they gave up their home in Fayetteville and moved to the capital in Little Rock for Bill's new job. It was too far for Hillary to commute to the university, so Hillary gave up hers. The young couple bought a new house in Little Rock, and she took a job with the Rose Law Firm. Hillary had avoided representing private clients until then, but with her husband as the attorney general, she couldn't work in a public capacity without causing a stir. Hillary continued her interest in children's rights and she helped form the Arkansas Advocates for Children and Families, working for reforms in the child-welfare system. She also took on child-advocacy cases *pro bono*, outside the framework of the law firm.

Bill was elected governor of Arkansas in 1978, and when they moved into the governor's mansion, Hillary became its official hostess. He also made her chair of the Rural Health Advisory Committee, and she was still deeply involved in the Children's Defense Fund, which took her to Washington several times a year to preside over its board meetings. President Carter had appointed her to the board of the Legal Services Corporation, a program that funds legal assistance for the poor, and that called for more travel, too. It was during this time she was made a full partner in the Rose Law Firm. It the midst of it all, she became pregnant. Their daughter, Chelsea, was born on February 27, 1980.

The Rose Law Firm didn't have a policy on parental leave, but Hillary was given four months off, and she wasn't earning legal fees during that time. (It's worth noting that when Bill became president, the first law he signed was the Family and Medical Leave Act to help parents and caregivers who don't have the advantage of the support system that he and Hillary had.) Bill was never particularly interested in money, but Hillary's parents, the Depression survivors, had made her aware of building a nest egg for the family, and it become especially important now that they had become a family. Hillary

Chelsea was named for Judy Collins's version of Joni Mitchell's song "Chelsea Morning," which Bill and Hillary had heard while walking around the Chelsea section of London.

knew, though, that building a family savings would have to be her responsibility, and she began looking for investment advice.

The advice she got was to put what money she had into commodities, buying "futures" in things like cattle and wheat and collecting a profit when they were sold, hopefully at a higher price. It's about as risky a business as playing roulette or poker, but in those days of rising prices, the odds were terrific. Hillary did well in this investment game before she lost her nerve, and by the time she quit, she had made $100,000. It would come back to haunt her when she became First Lady, but her investment in a housing development called Whitewater Estates not only wiped out her savings but also resulted in an investigation that stretched out through the entire Clinton presidency.

When Bill ran for a second term as governor in 1980, his popularity had faded with the state of the economy, and he was charged with being "out of touch." The campaign blew up in his face when a surge of Cuban refugees spilled over into a resettlement camp in Arkansas. When the refugees eventually rioted and hundreds of them began roaming the countryside, Governor Clinton sent out the National Guard to help round them up. Then the federal government sent more refugees into the overcrowded camp, although there weren't any federal funds or military assistance to prevent any more riots. It cost Bill the election and the Clintons had to leave the governor's mansion.

Unbowed, the Clintons bought a new house in Little Rock and he joined a law firm in the city, all the while planning to recapture the governor's mansion. Hillary, as it turned out, had been a liability to him. Many of his constituents were suspicious of her independence and her openly liberal views. It didn't help that even as the wife of the governor, she never used her married name but continued to call herself Hillary Rodham. It had seemed perfectly natural to her, considering that she had her own career, and many women of the era were beginning to keep their maiden names or at least use hyphenated names. But that was not the case in Arkansas. When Bill announced his candidacy for a second term as governor in 1982, Hillary quietly changed her name to Hillary Rodham Clinton. Then she packed Chelsea into the car and began touring the state asking for votes.

Hillary became a more active state First Lady after Bill won his election and was governor again. He gave her the touchy assignment of educational reform. It would mean a call for better testing, and Hillary pushed it a step further by recommending the testing of teachers as well as students. That put the teachers against her as well as some civil rights groups. Although both were important to the Democratic party in the state, Hillary stuck to her principles. She pleaded her case directly to the legislature, and eventually she took on the teachers' union in court. But in the end, the reform package was approved, and Hillary could take the credit. More important, in spite of all the acrimony along the way, Bill was reelected to an unprecedented fourth term as governor.

There had been a mild groundswell among national Democrats for Bill to try for the presidency in the 1988 election, and he seriously considered it, choosing in the end to stay in Arkansas. What tipped the balance was the realization that the job would separate him from Chelsea, which was the last thing he wanted. He felt that he had been ignoring her too much already.

Chelsea was six when her father ran for governor again. She had traveled with her mother during the previous campaign, but this time she could read, and she had a fairly good idea of what was going on. It was her first exposure to the nastiness of attack-style campaigning, and she couldn't quite understand why people were saying all those bad things about her mother and father. She hadn't seen anything yet, but she learned how to deal with it at a young age.

In spite of what his opponents had to say, Bill's political star kept rising in national circles. He had been working hard as chairman of the National Governors' Association, and Hillary herself was getting high visibility for her own work on the issues of health and education. It seemed inevitable to most Democrats that Bill Clinton was the perfect choice to take on President Bush in the next election. The president was being characterized as "out of touch"; Bill and Hillary had heard that before.

Up From Arkansas

When Bill announced in October 1991 that he was a candidate for the presidency, the media didn't offer him a lot of hope. He had the required charisma, but he didn't have the right kind of experience, they said. He was an obscure governor from a state most Americans couldn't find on a map, and he was only forty-six years old. But when Bill began campaigning in the primaries, the voters seemed to think otherwise. In spite of her already impressive resume, Hillary was an unknown quantity, too, and she was only forty-four.

Bill and Hillary each recruited campaign staffs that helped turn the age issue into a positive one. The staff members were mostly young, and they all had a youthful enthusiasm that reminded many of the Kennedy campaign. They avoided making

Below: The pressure cooker in the foreground is an appropriate symbol of Bill's early political campaigns.

the comparison themselves, but the country had been longing for a replay of "Camelot" for years, and the youthful Clinton family was appealing. Chelsea was eleven by then and she could, and did, speak for herself. They made it a rule, though, that she was never to be interviewed and that rule stuck throughout their political lives. Hillary could speak for herself, too. She had plenty to say, and people listened. Before long, Bill was telling audiences that when they voted for him, it was a case of "Buy one, get one free." Of course, national campaigns being what they are, the opposition called for caution, telling the voters that they were being asked to vote for Hillary as the "copresident."

No less a person than former president Nixon weighed in with a remark that, "If the wife comes through as being too strong or too intelligent, it makes the husband look like a wimp." It was obvious that Bill Clinton was anything but a wimp, and Hillary wrote it off as resentment over her work on Nixon's impeachment committee. She continued to campaign, looking strong and intelligent. She was clearly both, and there was no point in hiding it.

Bill's nomination was assured by the first week in June when he won the primaries in California, New Jersey, and Ohio, but he was still running third behind his opponents, President Bush and Ross Perot. He and Hillary began campaigning as a family, taking Chelsea with them as they toured the country, but still holding fast to their rule of not allowing the press to interview her or run feature stories about her. "Most Americans didn't even know I had a child until the campaign began," she said. But she thought it was important people understood how seriously she took her role as a mother. "If people didn't know that, they certainly couldn't understand us," she said.

The day after Bill's nomination was made official at the Democratic Convention in New York City, the Clintons and Al Gore, the vice presidential candidate, and his wife, Tipper, set out on the first of a series of bus tours they called their "excellent adventure." It was tough to hold to a schedule of any kind because whenever he spotted a crowd, Bill shouted "stop the bus," no matter

Above: Hillary, Bill, and Chelsea celebrate his nomination as a presidential candidate.

The First Scandal

The 1992 presidential campaign brought on more personal attacks than had ever been raised in any other. The press generally steered clear of rumors, but there was something new in their ranks this election, the so-called supermarket tabloids. When word reached Bill Clinton that one of them was about to publish a "confession" by an Arkansas woman named Gennifer Flowers that she'd had a twelve-year affair with him, he phoned Hillary and told her it wasn't true. Then Hillary got on the phone herself and made a conference call to the campaign staff telling them that she believed in him, and to "get back to work." But the story didn't die. It leaped from the tabloids to the mainstream press and it began to overshadow all the real issues.

Hillary agreed to appear with Bill on the television show 60 Minutes, *which had a large lead-in audience from the Super Bowl that week. She ended a tough interview by saying, "You know, I'm not sitting here, some little woman standing by my man like Tammy Wynette. I'm sitting here because I love him and I respect him, and I honor what he's been through and what we've been through together. And, you know, if that's not enough for people, then, heck, don't vote for him." A few weeks later, Bill made a strong second-place win in the New Hampshire primary and he became known as the "Comeback Kid."*

where they were or what time it was. They didn't make their first scheduled stop until two in the morning, several hours late, but there was a good-size crowd waiting for them. It was a good sign.

The campaign was run from a "war room" in a Little Rock office building, and the section devoted to her campaign effort was called Hillaryland. Although the watchword of the campaign was "It's the economy, stupid," the thrust of Hillary's own speeches was the problem of health care, and the response she was getting made it Bill's special issue, too. In a real way, of course, the inadequacies of health-care insurance and onerous medical costs was the economic issue that affected more families than any other.

Like all presidential campaigns, it was a draining experience, but for the Clintons it was a successful one: Bill Clinton was elected the forty-second president of the United States. It was then that the difficult transition to the White House began. In addition to working with Bill to create an administration team, Hillary had to pack everything they owned to move to Washington. The governor's mansion in Arkansas was the only home they had, and there was no place for anything they owned except the White House, and it happened to be occupied at the time. Hillary also had to find a school for Chelsea, but most of all, she had to decide what role she would play as First Lady. Nepotism laws prevented her from being named to any official position, but Bill and Hillary had developed a close working partnership, and an election, even to the presidency, couldn't change that.

Hot Seat

At Hillary's suggestion, the Clintons rode the last 120 miles of their trip to Washington on a bus from Charlottesville, Virginia. The bus was a reminder of the campaign, but the route was the same one Thomas Jefferson had taken on the way to his own inauguration. It seemed appropriate to Hillary that William Jefferson Clinton should follow in his namesake's footsteps.

There were eleven balls scheduled on the evening of the inauguration, and the new president insisted that he and Hillary show up at all of them. It had become customary for First Families to drop by for five minutes or so at each ball to wave, shake a few hands, and move on, but not Bill Clinton. He treated each ball as if it were the only place they had to go that night, and they didn't leave the last of them until the band started packing up. It was past two in the morning by the time they returned home for their first night in the White House.

Above: The new president and First Lady savor the moment at one of the eleven inaugural balls.

> *"After seventeen years of marriage, Bill and I were each other's biggest cheerleaders, toughest critics, and best friends."*
>
> —Hillary Clinton on the status of her marriage after Bill was elected to the presidency

The Clintons were the youngest First Family most people could remember. No one could recall a workaholic president who labored around the clock, even when there was no crisis, either. The last youngster to live in the White House had been Amy Carter, and the now teenage Chelsea Clinton was going to help turn it into a different kind of place. For starters, the house that nearly always had a dog or two now had a cat, Chelsea's friend, Socks.

On their first full day at the White House, the Clintons held an open house and thousands came. There were so many people, in fact, that Bill and Hillary had to move outside to the lawn to greet them all in the bitter January cold after it became obvious that they couldn't all squeeze inside.

Hillary had put together a staff of about twenty, and she moved some of them into the West Wing where the president's staff offices are. She herself took an office on the second floor above the Oval Office, and the Office of the First Lady, Hillaryland, moved into a suite in the Old Executive Office Building across the drive where the rest of the White House staff was quartered. Hillary's social secretary and her correspondence office stayed in the East Wing. The idea was to integrate the staffs of the president and First Lady, something that had never been done, or even considered, before. Hillary's chief of staff became an assistant to the president as well, and she sat in on the daily senior staff meeting with the president's advisors. Hillary also had a domestic-policy assistant assigned to her office as well as a presidential speechwriter and a press secretary.

Even with her large and extended staff, Hillary had problems adjusting to life in the White House, but she had a mentor. Not long into the term, she traveled to New York to accept an award and visit a public school that was experimenting with volunteer tutoring, and she took an afternoon to visit with former First Lady Jacqueline Kennedy Onassis. Jackie had long since abandoned the world of politics by then, but she admired Hillary , and Hillary admired her. They had talked several times during the campaign, especially about protecting her children from the White House spotlight, and Jackie's advice was already being taken. She also added advice on how Chelsea ought to deal with the Secret Service people, which was an annoying intrusion for a teenager who wanted her privacy.

Jackie also counseled "caution" for Bill who, as a charismatic man like her husband had been, created strong feelings in people both for him and against him. She told Hillary that, because they didn't have a family retreat of their own, they should go to Camp David often or visit friends who lived in secluded places. It was the only way to avoid well-meaning admirers and especially the paparazzi. Jackie had a lot of experience to share with the Clintons. The two women kept in frequent contact by phone from that day until Jackie died sixteen months later.

Above: They acquired a dog named Buddy later, but for most of the Clinton years, the First Pet was Chelsea's cat Socks.

After Chelsea entered Stanford University in 1997, Bill and Hillary got a chocolate Labrador puppy they named Buddy.

Above: Hillary and Bill tried their best to shield Chelsea from the nasty side of political life.

The Secret Service code names for the Clintons were Eagle for Bill, Evergreen for Hillary, and Energy for Chelsea.

The First Lady was expected to be first and foremost the White House hostess, and Hillary took that part of the job seriously. But she also had a serious commitment to social issues, and the press had a problem squaring the two. How could a woman be worried about centerpieces for White House dinners, and at the same time worry about a national health-care plan? It seemed to be a paradox, but thousands of women across the country were able to balance their social and professional lives, and this was how Hillary had been leading her own life all along. Gender roles were changing, and Hillary was at the leading edge. Still, the press didn't get it, and she found herself a target. She was going to have to get used to it.

Five days after his inauguration, Bill asked Hillary to chair a task force on health care. He also asked her to have a plan ready to present to Congress during his first hundred days. He appointed Ira Magaziner, one of his senior planning advisors and a former business consultant with health-care experience, to actually run the task force. Both he and Hillary knew they had an uphill battle ahead, but both of them knew that the problem was already affecting hundreds of millions of Americans and, as the president told them, "We have to try. We have to make it work." Other presidents had tried and failed to deal with the health-care issue—Theodore Roosevelt was the first; Franklin D. Roosevelt had tried to make universal health-care coverage part of his New Deal; Harry Truman tried again with his Fair Deal; and even Richard Nixon had tried and failed. But in every case, the concept had been shot down by lobbyists for the American Medical Association who were certain that its doctor members would be controlled by the government. In Truman's case, the opposition charged that the plan smacked of communism. Lyndon Johnson managed to institute Medicare for retirees and Medicaid for the poor as part of his Great Society program, but that was not without tough opposition. But Hillary, Ira Magaziner, and the other members of the task force were willing to try again and get a plan in place in less than one hundred days.

There were other things competing for Hillary's attention at the same time, though. Hillary's father died, first of all, and

Below: Hillary's first major initiative was pushing for universal health care, but the health industry lobbied strongly against it.

"You have to be you, or you'll wind up wearing someone else's idea of who you are and how you should look."

—*Jackie Kennedy's advice to Hillary Clinton on how to avoid fashion disasters as First Lady*

then after a casual remark she had made, there was an audit of the White House Travel Office that uncovered a host of irregularities and the staff was replaced. The problem was that the replacements included one of Bill's relatives, and that led to charges of cronyism. An investigation showed that no one was guilty of anything except poor judgment and that the original concerns had been justified. That was the first investigation. There were seven separate ones in all, and Hillary found herself at the eye of the storm. The real victim in the "Travelgate" investigation was Vincent Foster, a Tennessee lawyer on the White House staff, who became despondent over what he perceived as letting down the president and committed suicide. In the opinion of many editorialists, the First Lady was not without blame; Vince had been one of her closest friends. The last thing Foster wrote was, "I was not meant for the job in the spotlight of public life in Washington. Here ruining people is considered sport."

The health-care task force continued its work, held meetings with congressional leaders, and organized a team of health-care experts as advisors, a group that at one point included six hundred people. By March, the group realized it was going to take more time than they had to put together a proposal the Congress would consider, and they dropped back to reorganize. They had been dealt a blow when the health-care industry sued them on charges that the First Lady was not a government employee and could not attend task force meetings because she represented "private interests." The task force was eventually disbanded and went into limbo, although Hillary and Ira Magaziner kept up its work. During a tour of the country gathering support for the president's economic policies, Hillary met hundreds of people who needed medical care but couldn't afford it. By September, they felt that the plan had jelled enough that the president could outline it in a nationally televised address, and that it could go to Congress in October. In the meantime, though, the health-care industry organized a massive campaign to roadblock it. Their television ads, a series of vignettes featuring a couple named Harry and Louise, who appeared to believe that affordable health care would ruin their lives, were misleading and even false. They hammered away at the theme that government "bureaucrats" were going to force their own no-choice health-care plan down their throats. Not said, but implied, was that Hillary Clinton was that bureaucrat.

Above: Hillary went to California to meet with victims of the Northridge Earthquake in 1994. Damage came to $25 million and seventy-two lives were lost.

After the plan was submitted, Hillary was the administration's chief witness before the congressional committees, and she spent hours before three of them in the House and two in the Senate. Both Eleanor Roosevelt and Rosalynn Carter had testified before Congress as First Ladies, but neither of them had spoken at such length. Her testimony impressed the conferees, and the public as well. But it was a red flag to the Republicans, who realized that if the bill was passed, they'd be facing another four years with a Democrat as president, and they aimed their fire not at the president but at the First Lady.

The bill that was introduced near the end of October was more than 1,300 pages long. But before anyone even attempted to read it, the opposition dropped the other shoe. An investigation was begun into the business affairs of Jim and Susan McDougal and an Arkansas savings and loan association that they ran. They had been Hillary's partners in her long-lost investment in the Whitewater development. One had nothing to do with the other, but it was also charged that the savings and loan association had made illegal campaign contributions to local candidates, including Bill Clinton. It was the first salvo in a political war that carried on through the two terms of Bill's presidency. Having never even seen the Whitewater property and losing money on it to boot, Bill and Hillary weren't too concerned. But in January, Republican leaders Senator Bob Dole and Congressman Newt Gingrich called for an independent counsel to take over the investigation, and the Clintons realized that they needed to cooperate or risk having their presidential agenda swamped.

Meanwhile, the Clintons got on with their lives. After a trip to Russia, Hillary was asked to lead the American delegation to the 1994 Winter Olympics in Norway, and she and Chelsea eagerly accepted the invitation. It was her first of many official trips abroad without Bill.

When Hillary got back to the White House, the Whitewater investigation was taking on a life of its own, and she held a long press conference to tell her own side of the story, which helped to clear the air. Later on, when the first investigations exonerated the Clintons, it cleared even more. But then another, different kind of story broke. During the annual convention of the Conservative Political Action Committee, a woman named Paula Jones held a press conference to reveal that she had been recruited by an Arkansas state trooper to meet Bill Clinton in a hotel room and had become his "regular girlfriend." The committee labeled it "Troopergate," and started a drive to raise funds to keep the story alive. Jones's next step was to sue the president for $700,000 for sexual harassment.

It was obvious to most that the Clintons were in the middle of a well-organized political battle. Except for the four years of the Carter administration, the Republicans had controlled the White House since the end of Lyndon Johnson's presidency twenty-four years earlier, and they didn't like being out of power. They had money, they had strong organization, and although they called the media their enemy, they knew very well how to control it.

One of the Republican party's many committees, the Project for the Republican Future, went on record with a memo to congressional leaders that health-care reform was a serious political threat to the party and must be killed. The advice was eventually taken. In the meantime, radio talk show hosts worked furiously to discredit the health proposal and the First Lady's association with it, and when Hillary went around the country on a bus tour she called the Health Security Express, to counter the message, it was the first time in history that the Secret Service ordered a First Lady to wear a bulletproof vest. It was obvious by then that her health-care plan was dead in the water, but she kept right on fighting for it.

After the Republicans took control of Congress in the midterm election, Bill and Hillary decided to regroup. She was said to have imaginary conversations with Eleanor Roosevelt, and the advice she came away with this time around was that there was no point in agonizing over day-to-day setbacks, but to press on and do what you could in spite of them. Her response was to take advantage of the wide circle of friends she had made, and she began gathering women together for weekly freewheeling discussions she called "Chix Meetings." At the first of them, she said that she was seriously considering backing away from politics and policy so her husband could get on with his job and had, in fact, had already made plans to skip a forum on First Ladies scheduled that same evening at George Washington University. She was very quickly, and not so gently, talked out of that idea. The consensus was that there were too many women and young people counting on her to be actively involved, if not for herself then for them. Hillary kept her evening appointment and she charged ahead. As her old role model, Mrs. Roosevelt, had said, "When I feel depressed, I go to work."

Above: Women's issues were always high on Hillary's agenda. In this speech, she addressed small businesswomen.

Chagrined by an opposition proposal to put children of welfare mothers into orphanages to help cut welfare costs, Hillary got out her soapbox again. She wrote a long article for *Newsweek* magazine and followed it up with a book about raising children in the modern world called *It Takes a Village*.

In 1995, she took an extended tour of South Asia, and she became an advocate of maintaining U.S.-funded development programs abroad. Congress was debating big cuts in them at the time. Along the way, Hillary became more deeply committed to the cause of women's rights. The issue had always been important to her, but now it was at the top of her mind. At around the same time, Hillary began writing a weekly newspaper column called "Talking It Over" that gave her a new forum for causes that were important to her. Among those at this point were children's health, breast cancer research, public television funding, legal aid, and the arts. She also founded the Medicare Mammography Awareness Campaign to encourage older women to look for signs of breast cancer, which very few were doing up until then.

In spite of the hints of scandal and dealing with a hostile Congress during his first term, Bill Clinton beat Senator Bob Dole in the presidential election in 1996 by a margin of eight percentage points, and both he and Hillary felt vindicated. They may have acquired some enemies, but the majority of the American people were behind them. Hillary had been more active than almost any of her predecessors during the first term, but she had to do it in a private

"The failure was principally political and policy driven, there were many interests that weren't at all happy about losing their financial stake in a way that the system currently operates, but I think I became a lightning rod for some of that criticism."

—*Hillary Clinton on health-care reform*

way. Now she was determined to speak out more, particularly on issues affecting children and families and, of course, health care. The United States was materially better off than it had been, but these were still all unresolved issues, and she intended to do something about them.

Hillary started by organizing two White House task forces, one on early-childhood development and the other on child care. The result was the president's first proposal of the second term, a $20 billion program to improve child care for working families and after-school programs for older kids. Hillary worked for the passage of these and related programs with a full round of speeches and endless conferences with legislators and organizations. She also lobbied for better child-support laws and financial equality for women, and stepped up her visits abroad.

Through it all the investigations into the First Family kept up. Kenneth Starr had become the special prosecutor investigating the Clintons, and after four years of trying, he hadn't been able to uncover anything incriminating. But he was determined to keep on turning over stones to see if anything was lurking under one of them. The effort continued right up until the Clintons' last day in the White House, when they were accused of taking government property with them. That investigation went on for months into the new Bush administration, but all it proved was that there was no truth to the rumor.

Impeachable Offenses

Funded by a right-wing fundamentalist organization, the Paula Jones lawsuit against the president kept dragging on. Hillary had advised against settling out of court because it would put the chief executive in the position of paying money to avoid a frivolous lawsuit, a precedent that ought to be avoided. She admitted later that it had been a tactical mistake.

Less than a week after Bill gave a deposition to the Jones attorneys, he told Hillary about news reports that he'd had an affair with a White House intern, whom he asked to lie to those attorneys for him. In response, Special Prosecutor Starr had received permission to expand his investigation and bring criminal charges against the president. He had found what appeared to the right stone at last.

Bill initially denied any improper behavior to Hillary, but he eventually told her the truth. In the meantime, though, the bigger problem was that he might have been trapped into committing perjury in the Jones deposition, and if adultery was not an impeachable offense, perjury was. Almost nobody knew that better than Hillary, who had made an exhaustive study of the process during the Nixon investigation. She went through a rough couple of days, but there was nothing to do but forgive her husband and forge ahead. She knew that Bill had been the

*Below: Hillary took her message of
equality to women around the world.*

victim of a sucker punch by Starr and that made her all the more eager to defend him. Her standard answer to press queries became, "There has been a concerted effort to undermine his legitimacy as President, to undo much of what he has been able to accomplish, to attack him personally when he could not be defeated politically." Meanwhile, they went on with their work in spite of the feeding frenzy that was going on around them. It included state visits to Africa and to China.

Not long afterward, the Jones case was thrown out of court because the judge couldn't find any factual or legal reason for it to continue. The press began reporting on improprieties in Starr's office, but the counsel soldiered on. He arranged to have the White House intern, Monica Lewinski, appear before his special Whitewater Grand Jury—as it was still called even though the Whitewater issue had been long since dead and buried. Then Ken Starr called the president himself to appear. He opted to videotape his testimony in the White House instead.

Hillary had felt deeply betrayed by Bill's behavior, but she realized it was a private matter, for which he had apologized over and over again. He hadn't betrayed his country and she made up her mind to defend him. When the Starr office sent a petition to impeach the president to the House Judiciary Committee, he also posted his petition on the Internet, clearly illegal, and it backfired on him. Bill Clinton's standing in opinion polls rose steadily, and Hillary's went up even faster, reaching beyond 70 percent. It was she who was selected to carry the ball for the Democrats in the impending off-year election, and she took to the road for dozens of congressional candidates. When it was over, the Democratic party had gained five seats in the House in spite of press predictions that they would surely lose ground.

Almost immediately after the election, New York state senator Daniel Patrick Moynihan announced his retirement, and New York Democrats urged Hillary to run as his replacement. The idea had come up before, but she still thought it was an absurd one.

The House committee rushed through their deliberations on the impeachment so that a vote could be taken before the Republican majority was reduced in January. President Clinton was indicted on two of the articles, perjury and obstruction of justice. The next step would be a trial in the Senate. Hillary had met with Bill's lawyers, advising them on strategy, but she was forced to sit on the sidelines during the trial itself, which dragged on for five weeks before he was finally acquitted. Hillary spent the time listening to arguments by New York Democrats begging her to run for the state's open Senate seat. She still didn't agree with them, mostly because they had several good options right in their own backyard. She also wasn't too sure that she could beat the probable Republican candidate, New York City mayor Rudolph Guiliani, but that was the point. The New York Democrats were convinced that she was the only one who could do it.

Above: Hillary wrote a book pointing out that it "takes a village" to raise children in the world's new order, and she showed the way.

Below: Bill and Hillary sharing an intimate public moment. They were a formidable team when they worked together.

Becoming a New Yorker

Above: The First Lady visits a school and shelter during a visit to Puerto Rico in 1998.

Hillary had done a lot of things as First Lady that no other First Lady had ever done, the most impressive of which may have been her progression from First Lady to U.S. senator from New York. Most remarkable was that she was still the First Lady when she made the announcement. Most of her closest advisors tried to steer her away from considering it, pointing out to her that life as a senator couldn't possibly be as interesting as being the wife of a former president, or carry as much influence. In spite of the arguments against running, Hillary announced that she was "considering it." The Clinton administration would come to an end the following January, Bill himself couldn't run for a third term, and she wouldn't have to worry about having two jobs at the same time. Still, it raised a lot of eyebrows around Washington.

In the meantime, Hillary had a lot of work to do, and it had nothing to do with her White House duties. The ball started rolling in earnest when former senator Moynihan took her under his wing. "Her magnificent young, bright, able Illinois-Arkansas enthusiasm" will make her a hit with New Yorkers and New York, he said. "She'd be welcome and she'd win." But Hillary didn't take Pat Moynihan's word for it. She made the rounds of dozens of state party leaders, including the recently elected senator Chuck Schumer, who was fresh from the campaign trail himself. They all agreed that it was a step she ought to take.

Hillary was also well aware that she could have a good future working on international causes that she was passionate about without becoming a politician. And she knew that getting involved in New York politics in particular would be like walking into a hornet's nest. She was determined to keep up her White House activities whether she was a senatorial candidate or not, and she was concerned that her effectiveness as a spokeswoman for the United States in foreign countries, which had been one of her big pluses as First Lady, might be compromised, not only in Washington, but in New York where she would be expected to give her full attention to local matters. She and Bill had patched up their personal problems by then, and where she had spent most of her life as his advisor and sounding board, now the situation was reversed. She still couldn't make up her mind, but the push she needed came from an unexpected source.

She had been invited to host a kickoff for an HBO movie about women's sports called *Dare to Compete,* and the captain of a girls basketball team, who introduced her, whispered in her ear, "Dare to Compete, Mrs. Clinton. Dare to Compete." She herself had made hundreds of speeches encouraging women to get involved in government, and now she realized that the time had come for her to put her money where her mouth was. But money was part of the problem. She had finally decided she could win, but first she would have to raise $25 million to mount a campaign.

By June, she had formed an exploratory committee and begun hiring a campaign staff, and she was ready to go house hunting. She and Bill had not been home-owners for more than twenty years, and the search was complicated by Secret Service requirements for a former president's family. She settled on a farmhouse and barn in Chappaqua, a northern suburb of New York City in Westchester County. Then she spent the summer on a "listening tour" of the state, and she found out that she liked these New Yorkers, and they liked her, too. She formally declared her candidacy in February 2000. Chelsea took off the first half of her senior year at Stanford, and returned home to take over her mother's White House social obligations, and she found time to campaign with her, too. Both women were old experienced campaigners and it showed.

Hillary's competitor, Mayor Giuliani, was running a negative campaign, calling Hillary a carpetbagger and even holding fund-raisers in Arkansas, but his popularity was never strong in upstate New York, and his record on race relations in the city itself was costing him support there, too. Then midway into the campaign, he was diagnosed with prostate cancer and that, combined with a sordid divorce, forced him to resign from the race. In a way, it was a blow to Hillary, who had mapped out a campaign of a clear choice between them, and now she had to rethink her strategy. To her relief, the substitute candidate, Congressman Rick Lazio, played to his suburban base and positioned himself as the "anti-Hillary" candidate with a negative campaign. In the end, Hillary won the New York senate seat in November. On election night, she told her campaign workers, "Sixty-two counties, sixteen months, three debates, two opponents, and six black pantsuits later, because of you, we are here!" Bill Clinton was on his way to New York and Hillary was on her way to Washington. Even before she arrived, the pundits were predicting that one day in the future, she would be going to Washington as the president-elect.

Below: The William J. Clinton Presidential Library and Center in Little Rock, Arkansas, opened in November 2004.

Visiting the Clinton Presidential Library and Center

The William J. Clinton Presidential Library and Center was opened in Little Rock, Arkansas, in November 2004. It is the largest of the official presidential libraries, including two floors of exhibit space that contain exhibits detailing life in the White House, such as "State Events—Welcoming the World" and "Making the House a Home." It is open Monday through Saturday from 9:00 A.M. to 5:00 P.M. and Sundays from 1:00 P.M. It is closed on Thanksgiving Day, December 25, and January 1. The admission fee is $7.00 for adults, $5.00 for seniors and students, and $3.00 for children.

To get to the Clinton Center, which is close to downtown Little Rock, take Interstate 30. The center is located ten minutes from Little Rock National Airport on I-30.

Laura Bush

Fortunate Daughter

Calling Laura Welch's girlhood sheltered may seem to be a contradiction in terms for a girl who grew up in the wide-open spaces of west Texas, but the description is fairly accurate. She was one of those youngsters that people in the 1950s sometimes called "fortunate daughters." She was an only child in an upper-middle-class family in the small oil-rich town of Midland, where life revolved around the family unit and the local churches. It was a place, as the song says, "where seldom is heard a discouraging word."

Laura's father, Harold Welch, was a homebuilder in a postwar market where houses couldn't be built fast enough to meet the demand. Her mother, Jenna, helped him as a bookkeeper, but she insisted on doing the work at home so that she could be there when Laura came home from school. It also gave her time to become a Girl Scout leader and an active member of the Midland Naturalist Group, with a special interest in local birds and wildflowers.

Like many little girls in those days, Laura started taking ballet lessons at the age of five, and swimming lessons, too. She joined the choir at the First Methodist Church at about the same time and she sang with them until she was in eighth grade. She went to the public school in Midland and, like all the other kids, she walked to and from there every day, mornings and afternoons, and at lunchtime as well. Unlike most of her classmates, Laura knew from second grade what she wanted to do when she grew up. Inspired by her teacher, she decided that she wanted to follow in her footsteps, and all through grade school, her favorite thing was to have friends over to play "school." Laura's friends continued to visit all through high school, and the Welch house became a second home to Laura's big circle of friends. They enjoyed her father's sense of humor and his contagious laugh, and they found her mother a warm and welcoming woman who took an interest in them and what they had to say.

George and Barbara Bush also lived in Midland at about this time, but their son, George W., was not part of Laura's crowd. Except for seventh grade, they

Laura Welch Bush
Born
November 4, 1946, Midland, Texas
Parents
Harold Bruce Welch and Jenna Hawkins Welch
Marriage
November 5, 1977, to George Walker Bush (1946-)
Children
Barbara Pierce (1981-); Jenna Welch (1981-)

> "To understand Laura and me, you must understand Midland. All that we are, all the things we believe in, come from that one place."
>
> —George W. Bush on Midland, Texas, where he and Laura were raised

Midland, Texas

The west Texas town of Midland was established in the 1880s at the halfway point on the Texas and Pacific Railroad that was built to transport cattle between El Paso and Fort Worth. It became the biggest cattle-shipping point in Texas, and those days are still remembered there with the Annual World Championship Rodeo. But a new industry came to town in 1926 when the Gulf oil company made its headquarters there to take advantage of a huge oil strike in the nearby Permian Basin, and other petroleum giants followed, to share in the underground sea of oil that covered 100,000 square miles. Most of them pulled out in the wake of the Depression in the 1930s for the even richer oil fields in east Texas, but another strike just south of Midland in the late 1940s brought them back, along with more than 11,000 new residents.

Above: Where cattle once grazed, oil company tanks now dominate the landscape at Midland.

During World War II, the army air corps established a bombardier school just outside of town, the biggest military base in the world at the time, and more than six thousand GIs and their families flooded Midland. Midland is a quieter place these days, but it is still the home of several oil giants and the companies that serve them, and it has kept its reputation as a nice place to live and to be from.

went to different schools and their paths never crossed during that year, or if they did, neither of them can remember it.

When Laura started high school, she worked on the yearbook staff and she was enrolled in the honors program, but she never involved herself in the student government or anything that seemed political. "I preferred to work quietly behind the scenes," she said. She never seemed to be without a date for the school dances that were scheduled every couple of weeks, and she was the center of attention at the local drive-in most weekend evenings. Laura started driving at fourteen, which was the legal age in rural Texas back then, and like the other girls she crammed into the family car, she developed a taste for Kent cigarettes at about the same age.

Midway through high school, Laura and some of her friends spent the summer in Monterrey, Mexico, where they learned Spanish and studied Mexican culture. Except for brief stays at a Girl Scout camp, it was the first time in her life that she had been separated from her family, and she didn't find it easy to go so far away.

During her senior year, just after her seventeenth birthday, tragedy came into Laura's life one evening when she drove through a stop sign and broadsided another car, throwing its driver onto the pavement and killing him. The victim was a boy named Michael Douglas, whom she had dated several times. "I grieved a lot," she recalled. "It was a horrible, horrible tragedy—it's a terrible feeling to be responsible for an accident, and it was horrible for all of us to lose him, especially since he was so young. But at some point I had to accept that death is a part of life, and as tragic as losing Mike was, there was nothing anyone could do to change that. It was a comeuppance for me. At that age, you think you're immortal, invincible. You never expect to lose anybody you love when you're so young. For all of us, it was a shock. It was a sign of the preciousness of life and how fleeting it can be." The incident was eventually forgotten; there were no charges brought against her and, like all wounds, the sad memory healed over time.

Laura had loved books from the time even before she could read since her mother and father read to her every day. As a teenager she returned the favor by reading to her mother during the 300-mile drive to visit her grandparents in El Paso or to her dad's parents in Lubbock, a 120-mile trip. Long drives are a way of life in Texas, but for the Welch family, the books they took along brought them closer together as they counted off the miles. One of the books Laura read as a young girl, *Doak Walker: Three-Time All-American,* gave her the inspiration to go to Southern Methodist University (SMU) just as the football player had. There had never been any question that she would go to college somewhere, her father insisted on that, but as surely as she knew she was going to be a teacher, Laura knew from an early age just where she would be trained for the profession.

She started at SMU in Dallas in 1964, a time when anti–Vietnam War protests were dominating college campuses across the country. But the protests never reached the SMU campus, not then and not during her four years there. There were no rallies, no riots, and no flag burnings, only quiet discussions. As far as Southern Methodist was concerned, it was still the 1950s. The girls wore dresses and the boys got their hair cut every two weeks. The only change from their lives back home was that they drank an occasional beer and they smoked out in the open. Other than that, they played bridge—Laura was the best bridge player on campus—and they listened to records. Laura had one of the biggest collections, and one of the few that included Beatles albums. She was regarded as "reserved," but she was an excellent conversationalist, and she had a quirky sense of humor like her father's that attracted people to her. She was also an outstanding student. True to her girlhood ambition, she majored in education, and she took extra courses in childhood growth and development and elementary school education, and she earned As in all her courses. She also became qualified to teach math, social studies, science, and languages.

After she graduated in 1968, she took a trip to Europe with members of her family and visited several different countries. She was told that there were no teacher openings in Dallas, so she went to work as a clerk in an insurance company and kept trying. With persistence, she finally found a job teaching third grade in a Dallas public school. A year later, she moved south to Houston for a job teaching second grade at the John F. Kennedy Elementary School in a predominantly African-American neighborhood. She was so popular with her stu-

The Laura Bush Promenade at Southern Methodist University was donated by her husband as a Christmas gift to his wife

dents that they asked her to move up to third grade when they did.

During the two years she was in Houston, Laura lived in an apartment complex that catered to singles, and wild parties were the order of the day, or night. The quiet schoolteacher lived on what was known as the "sedate" side of the complex. She dated occasionally, but never seriously, and she spent most of her spare time reading or sunning by one of the swimming pools.

Then one day, a jet jockey from the Air National Guard base moved into the "crazy" side of the complex. George W. Bush swaggered a lot, smirked a good deal, and organized parties that gave a new meaning to the word "wild." The apartment complex was filled with airline stewardesses, young secretaries, and female students from Rice University, and nearly all of them wanted to meet George, who also had a cool Triumph sports car. Everyone knew George and knew he was the "congressman's son," except for one of the single women in the complex—Laura Welch.

Career Change

The congressman's son George was on the relationship rebound in those days. He had been engaged to Cathy Wolfman, a popular member of the Houston preppy elite, but he had broken off the engagement a few weeks before their planned wedding date. Then he cast his eye on Christina Cassini, the daughter of fashion designer Oleg Cassini and movie star Gene Tierney. Her mother had remarried a Texas oil millionaire, and Tina had become Houston's most desirable debutante. She and George were an item for all of the summer, but then she went to Europe for school, and he was transferred to Georgia for flight training. For the moment he had returned to Houston to join his father in his campaign for the Senate. But in the meantime, George W. had plenty of time for parties and dating.

He eventually left town to go to the Harvard Business School, and Laura gave up life among the party people to go to Austin to get a degree in library sciences from the University of Texas Graduate School. She got her master's degree in 1972 and then returned to Houston to take a job as a children's librarian in the city's public library system. She had hoped that living and working downtown would give a boost to her social life, but it didn't happen and she moved back to Austin to take a job as a librarian at the Mollie Dawson Elementary School in a Hispanic neighborhood. She was already fluent in Spanish, but the experience broadened her skill with the language. Most important, she was back in a setting she had come to love; she felt at home in Austin. But Midland was the home she loved best, and she drove up there most weekends, even though it was nearly five hundred miles away. It was on one of those trips during the summer of 1977 that she was invited to a backyard barbecue and, as fate would have it, so was George W. Bush.

Opposites Attract

Back in 1948, George's father had become a millionaire during an oil boom in Midland, and when another boom emerged in the 1970s, his oldest son had come to town to see if the family history might repeat itself. His chances were even better than his father's had been. Because of a petroleum shortage, the price of oil went up 800 percent during the 1970s, and George W. was on his way to financial riches.

Laura's invitation to that backyard barbecue had been a calculated case of match-making by her former college roommate Jan O'Neill, although she was well aware that all she and George had in common was that they were both single and both over thirty. Laura was almost a stereotype of a school librarian, quiet, reserved, and bookish. George was what the Texans called a "good ole' boy," still wild and not too serious about much of anything except making lots of money. He had announced his intention to run for Congress, and that was another point of difference between them. Laura didn't have much use for good ole' boys, but she despised politics even more.

Laura knew very well what Jan was up to, and she repeatedly turned down her friend's invitations before she finally gave in. She was sure that all of her friends were eager to get her and George together because they were the last two people in their circle who hadn't gotten married by then, and that was practically un-American.

Even the party hosts were taken by surprise with George and Laura's reaction to one another. They didn't stop talking to each other and they stayed in the backyard until midnight. For all his partying instincts, George always cut out at around nine o'clock so he could get home to bed, but in this case he made an exception, and it didn't go unnoticed. What had made the difference? Laura was a good listener and George was a tireless talker. In spite of her misgivings, "I thought he was really cute," she said. "He's also slightly outrageous once in a while…and I found that a lot of fun." His sense of humor reminded her of her father, and that alone was enough to hook Laura.

Below: During his campaign swings as a candidate for Congress, George discovered a different side of the oil business when he talked to roughnecks working on the big rigs.

Oil Entrepreneur

When George went back to Midland, he became what was known as a landsman, securing leases on property that would allow companies to drill on it. It involved long hours in courthouses looking for deeds that had been granted on various parcels to find out who owned the mineral rights, as opposed to the rights to the land itself, and then getting in touch with those owners to offer them royalty deals for drilling. It was a way of becoming completely familiar with the oil and gas business and to make close friends of the men who ran the companies. Eventually, he formed a company himself and called it Arbusto Energy (arbusto means "bush" in Spanish). He expanded it into an exploration company, but it never sank a profitable well, and he merged it into an established company called Spectrum 7, which owned close to two hundred oil wells, and became its chairman. The local oil market crashed in the 1980s, and the company was sold to Harken Energy, which elected George to its board of directors, made him a consultant, and gave him hundreds of thousands of shares of its stock.

Above: George and Laura do the Texas two-step during their brief, but happy, courtship.

Meeting the Family

When George W. took Laura to meet his family, there was another guest at the Bush home—his grandmother Dorothy Bush, the undisputed head of the family. Laura won her over with a naturally sedate manner that made her a perfect fit with the Connecticut society life that Mrs. Bush led. But they were in Texas now and, as often happens there, the conversation turned to sports. Mrs. Bush leaned over and quietly asked Laura, "What sport do you do, my dear?" "I read," Laura answered. As George's mother, Barbara, recalled, "Mrs. Bush darn near collapsed!" But it was a pleasant surprise, and Laura had earned the acceptance she needed.

The conversation, or rather monologue, continued the following evening over a game of miniature golf. She left to go back to Austin the next day, but the following weekend she found George at her doorstep. He was there the weekend after that, too, and he made the trip often. He even skipped the annual family vacation at their compound in Kennebunkport, Maine, to visit Laura.

In October, George took Laura to Houston to meet his family and he announced to them that he intended to make Laura a part of it. All of the family heartily approved of the idea, but George W.'s brothers couldn't help wondering how Laura was going to fit in with this highly active, sports-oriented family. "It was like Audrey Hepburn walking into *Animal House*," his brother Marvin pointed out. But they all agreed that she would bring a kind of peace into a chaotic family, and that seemed to them to be a pretty good thing.

The couple set the wedding date for November 5, which was slightly less than four months after the night they first met. Laura had always been suspicious of guys who came on too strong, too fast, but this time, she said, "It was almost like we'd known each other forever." It was the most impulsive thing that she ever did.

It was a simple wedding as it turned out, especially considering the willingness of both families to pull out all the stops, but it was the way Laura wanted it. It took place in the diminutive chapel at the First United Methodist Church in Midland, rather than in the larger sanctuary. As the mother of the bride pointed out, "The people who were there were very close to them. They wanted their friends, not their family's friends." The next day the local paper said, "The bride wore a street-length dress of candlelight crepe de Chine. It was styled with a long-sleeved, tucked blouson bodice and a pleated skirt. She had a corsage of white gardenias at the waistline."

Below: Far from Texas, the young couple visits the Bush family retreat in Kennebunkport, Maine.

"Laura is a very special person, and I thought that being an only child with few cousins, she was amused by us."

—*Barbara Bush on Laura's reaction to the Bush family*

Laura and George have the same nickname for each other: "Bushie."

After a very short honeymoon in Mexico, the couple moved into George's house in Midland, but George was running in the congressional primary by then, and they hit the campaign trail right away. It was a special challenge for Laura because she had never liked politics and she had no experience whatsoever. Besides, she had always voted for Democrats and she considered herself to be one. "I'm a Republican by marriage," she said. Her mother-in-law, Barbara, had been a campaigner all of her own married life, but the only advice she had to offer was, "Don't ever criticize his speeches."

Very much to her surprise, Laura enjoyed campaigning because of the time in gave her and George together in the car going from one campaign stop to another. In Texas, those stretches are usually long ones, and they had plenty of time to get to know each other with hours of conversation. One of the first things she told George when they started making wedding plans was that she didn't ever want to make public speeches, or even appear in public if it could be avoided. He agreed without a second thought, and he promised her that he'd never ask it of her since he enjoyed both things quite enough for the two of them.

Above: George and Laura took their congressional campaign straight to the people in the back of a pickup truck.

He broke his promise two months into the campaign when he asked her to make a speech for him at the courthouse in Muleshoe, Texas. It was not Laura's finest hour, and she hasn't forgotten it to this day. She managed to get off to a strong start, but she ran out of ideas fairly quickly, and toward the end she found herself reduced to almost incoherent mumbling. She had never spoken to more than thirty people at one time, and they had all been elementary school kids. She worked on her speaking style after the Muleshoe disaster, and she could speak publicly with the best of them before much longer.

George won the primary, but the heat was turned up during the general election when he was characterized as a preppy from the Northeast who didn't know anything, or even care, about Texans and their needs. It wasn't quite true, but it cost him the election anyway, and he and Laura went home to Midland to get on with their lives. George had an oil business to run. Laura had given up her job as a school librarian and she became a housewife, filling out her time with volunteer work. But what the Bushes both wanted was children to raise, and they set the wheels in motion to adopt one. But before that could happen, Laura discovered that she was pregnant, after they had been married for three years.

Laura was thirty-five years old by then, and when the doctor found out that she was carrying twins, he ordered her to stay close to home and get as much rest as she could. By her sixth month, her doctor ordered her to stay in bed.

Then, with seven weeks to go to her due date, she developed toxemia and she was flown to a Dallas hospital. Her condition worsened there, and her babies were delivered by cesarean section five weeks early. They were both girls, and they were named for their grandmothers. Baby Barbara arrived first, weighing five pounds, four ounces; and then Jenna, at four pounds, twelve ounces. Laura's toxemia was cured by the delivery and the girls were strong and healthy. Although incubators had been readied, they weren't needed. As the twins were growing, Laura, a confident public speaker by then, told an audience, "Before George and I were married, we had a couple of theories on raising kids. Now we've got a couple of kids and no theories."

George and Laura's life together was idyllic after the twins arrived. The girls brought the couple even closer together and Laura thoroughly enjoyed life with her extended family, the Bushes. George still had a wild streak in him, and he had a tendency to drink too much, which often exasperated her, although it never quite reached crisis proportions. They went to Colorado Springs with friends to celebrate their fortieth birthdays and, after a night of a little too much celebrating, George decided that drinking took away too much of the energy he needed for his exercise program, and he made up his mind to stop. It is the kind of vow many people can't quite keep, but the same discipline that sent him on a three-mile jog every morning, no matter how he felt, made it easier for him. Not long afterward, with the help of the evangelist Reverend Dr. Billy Graham, an old friend of the Bush family, George became more active than he had already been in the church.

The following year, 1987, Laura and George and the girls moved to Washington, D.C., so they could be closer to the center of George H.'s presidential campaign. It brought Laura even closer to the rest of the family than she had already become. But not long after they settled down in Washington, George got a call from one of his old partners back in Midland. The Texas Rangers baseball team was for sale, he said, and he thought it would be a perfect business opportunity for them. George couldn't have agreed more, and the family moved to Dallas, where he could round up more partners and investors. That done, he became the managing partner, taking care of all of the team's public relations and acting as the spokesman for the other owners, who stayed in the background and ran the business. Once a new stadium was in place, *Financial World* magazine rated the Rangers the most profitable franchise in major league baseball. And George was having the time of his life.

Laura had never been what one would call a baseball fan, but she came to love the game when she went out to the ballpark with George. "It was fun," she said. "Baseball's so slow, you can daydream. It's a very relaxing thing."

The Eyes of Texas Are Upon You

Living in Dallas was like going home for Laura. She had graduated from college about a mile from their new home, her daughters had been born there, and she had scores of friends there. They moved into a trendy enclave beyond the city limits called Preston Hollow that was insulated and peaceful, although she and her friends often ventured out for charity fund-raisers and glittering parties downtown. As the daughter-in-law of the president of the United States, and the wife of the man who had rescued the Texas Rangers, Laura was on every Dallas hostess's Rolodex, and she rarely had an evening to herself unless she wanted one.

Above: George, Laura, and their young daughters relax in Kennebunkport, Maine.

After the Bushes had lived in the Dallas area for five years, George asked Laura what she thought of the idea of moving to Austin—as First Lady of Texas. She didn't think much of it at all. Barbara and Jenna were twelve years old, and she didn't want to see them exposed to the personal attacks on their father that she knew were going to be inevitable. Even if he won, she wasn't so sure that she wanted them growing up in the spotlight, a thing she didn't particularly want for herself, either.

George's father had just lost his bid for a second term as president, and she had been horrified at the things that were said about him during the campaign. She certainly didn't want to wish that on her husband, whose loyalty to Texas was well established by then, but whose eastern roots were still a liability. She was not concerned that it might cost him the election, but that it would hurt his dignity.

Still, she knew what running meant to him, and she supported him all the way. Laura remained shy about stumping the state, but she did appear for speeches at dozens of women's Republican clubs, encouraging their members to help get out the vote. She made some other speeches, too, calling attention to her husband's promises to upgrade education in Texas. It was a problem that needed fixing, and a cause she believed in even more than vote getting.

After George was elected governor, Laura went to Austin with the self-described philosophy, "You can either like it or not, so you might as well like it." She apparently did, and it showed when she became the most popular First Lady in Texas history.

George gave Laura a free hand and she chose to take on programs that reflected her background in books and reading. Her first initiative was to invite prominent Texas writers to give readings from their works at the capitol as part of the inauguration activities. Many of them were not only Democrats but also liberal Democrats at that, so it was a sign of hope to them that a Bush governorship might not be just a matter of politics as usual. Later in the term, Laura made the readings an annual event, the Texas Book

"As a librarian, Laura's idea of a speech is saying 'shhh!' to children."

—George W. Bush on his wife

Above: As First Lady of Texas, Laura started the Texas Book Festival to raise money for libraries in the state.

Festival which is still a highlight of the Austin year and has raised more than $1 million for libraries across the state.

During their second term, Laura's alma mater, Southern Methodist University, gave her a distinguished-alumna award and dedicated a tree-lined walkway outside the library as the Laura Bush Promenade. Also around the midpoint of her tenure, she created the First Lady's Family Literature Initiative, which resulted in legislation to promote early-childhood reading, and she raised funds for several new programs, including "Take Time for Kids," and "Ready to Read." She stressed the idea that a large number of adults were only barely literate, and she pushed to break what she called "this cycle of illiteracy." On that note, Laura quoted the writer James Baldwin: "Children have never been good at listening to their elders, but they have never failed to imitate them." With that in mind, she established a program to encourage senior citizens to volunteer as reading tutors with organizations like the Boy Scouts and the Girl Scouts.

To help caseworkers in their work with abused children and their families, she encouraged the establishment of centers she called Rainbow Rooms, where volunteers would help provide the necessities of life for them. In other areas, she worked in promoting breast cancer awareness programs and fund-raising for cancer research.

At the time she moved into the governor's mansion, Texas ranked dead last among all the states in funding for the arts, and Laura went to work to change the situation. She started by encouraging George's appreciation of art, especially paintings and sculpture, related to Texas and the West. At Laura's urging, the state nearly doubled the funding of the Texas Commission on the Arts during her first year alone. And she began rotating exhibitions of Texas art in both the capitol and the governor's mansion, turning both of them into virtual art galleries.

Laura wasn't as enthusiastic about elegant entertaining, though. There wasn't a single black-tie event held at the governor's mansion during Bush's two terms there. Instead, Laura favored earthier events, frequently featuring Texas-style barbecue, and she usually spiced them with her own homemade chili.

During his campaign for a second term, George said, "There are many reasons I want people to reelect me as governor of Texas. The most important one may be to keep Laura Bush as our First Lady." After Laura made a speech at the Republican National Convention, George took note of the enthusiastic response by saying, "The same thing that has happened to my old man has happened to me. Both our wives are far more popular than we are."

On the Road Again

Laura had become accustomed to life in a fishbowl by the time her husband decided to try for the presidency in 2000, but the thought of a long campaign disturbed her. In spite of her fears, she made speaking tours to thirty cities on her own and as many more at George's side. It began with a major speech at the nominating convention that set the stage for what was to come. Laura had just packed Barbara and Jenna off to college at the time, and she told the national television audience, "Parents often have to get out of the house when their kids go off to college because it seems so lonely. Everyone deals with it in different ways, but I told George I thought running for president was a little extreme." Later in her speech, she said, "George's opponent has been visiting schools lately and when he does, he spends the night before in the home of a teacher. Well, George spends every night with a teacher." She hit her stride that night, and she never broke it.

Even before the convention was over, polls showed that support for Republicans among married couples had soared from a deficit to a six-point lead, and analysts were convinced that it was Laura who had made the difference. Not bad for a woman who could honestly say she was unaccustomed to public speaking.

Home on the Ranch

When George ran for a second term as governor of Texas, it was a stage-setter for the eventual presidential campaign, and he and Laura decided they needed a sanctuary away from the campaign, and the White House, if it came to that. They paid $1.3 million for a 1,500-acre pig farm outside the tiny town of Crawford, about twenty-five miles west of Waco and a two-hour drive from Austin. It was flat, it was dusty, it was lonely, and it was unbelievably hot in the summer, but it had a carpet of Texas wildflowers, old pecan and oak trees, and a river that ran through a spectacular gorge. They hired an architect, and Laura met him frequently on the property to decide on a site for the house that had the best view—although to anyone but a native-born Texan it appeared to be the same in every direction. She had the four-thousand-square-foot house designed to be long and narrow, with the best way to get from room to room a covered porch that runs the length of the low-slung structure. They built a ten-acre pond and stocked it with five thousand bass. They put in a swimming pool as an afterthought when the twins insisted on it. The rest of the design was based on things Laura insisted on. George was busy anyway, and he had said that all he wanted was "room for a king-size bed and a good shower," and a place where he could "invite people over for beans and hamburgers."

Below: The Bushes lead a tour of their ranch in Crawford, Texas; it's now their retreat from life in Washington, D.C.

Although Al Gore was his opponent and not President Bill Clinton, George ran his campaign against the Clinton record, both personal and presidential. And at his father's insistence, he played up the difference between Laura and Hillary Clinton. Barbara Bush weighed in right at the beginning by saying that her daughter-in-law would be a different kind of First Lady because "she would not get into foreign affairs or controversial subjects." Then she went on, "I'm not criticizing Mrs. Clinton, but it's like oil and water. We're talking about two different subjects. They're two different people. I think Laura thinks of others." It was a message with a certain amount of resonance. Even at the beginning of the twenty-first century, a great many women still deeply believed that their place was in the home, and that careers like law, which Mrs. Clinton was actively involved in, should be left to men. As a teacher and a school librarian, Laura posed no threat to that point of view.

Laura made it a point to appear apolitical. In a television interview early in the campaign, she said she never gave George much advice, "except to sit up straight." "We talk about issues, of course. Um. I don't give him a lot of advice. I don't think George wants a lot of advice from me." When she took to the campaign trail, she avoided questions on policy, demurely pointing out, "I am not the candidate." She did, apparently, have strong feelings favoring a woman's right to choose, but she kept them to herself until after the election, when she said that she had asked George not to campaign on the issue, even though he personally supported the antiabortion stance. Because he respected Laura's opinion, and his mother's, incidentally, he kept the issue in the background.

George took Laura's quiet advice on other issues, especially on appealing to women voters. She was an asset on the campaign trail, too, keeping her husband's spirits up, and calming him down when his temper got the better of him, with stern advice that usually began with the words, "Now, Bushie...." and sometimes "Rein it in, Bubba...." She also cringed when he mangled the language, as he often did, but although she tried, there wasn't much she could do about it. He wasn't one of her students, and she quietly accepted the wisdom that you can't teach an old dog new tricks.

Among Laura's contributions to the campaign was the coining of the catchphrase "compassionate conservatism." She was also the deciding voice in the selection of Dick Cheney as George's running mate. Many names had been put forward, but except for General Colin Powell, who refused the offer, George wasn't comfortable with any of them. The key consideration, as Laura saw it, was to pick someone who could complement her husband's personality, and after considering the possibilities, she concluded that it ought to be Cheney, who got along well with George and would also bring much-needed substance and maturity to the ticket. Some of his advisors were against the idea, but Laura fought for it, and she won.

Below: Laura was often at her husband's side during his briefings, but until deep into his second term, she kept her opinions to herself.

Laura vetted his cabinet choices, and most of his staff selections, too, although she agreed with most of them as soon as he chose them. Her husband was in awe of her ability to size people up, and he knew that her judgment was always sound.

Except for her well-received speech at the Republican National Convention, Laura kept her own participation in the campaign low-key. She traveled on bus tours, called "W. Stands for Women," and she often appeared at George's side as he toured the country. She was busy overseeing the final stages of construction of their new ranch house at Crawford, and busier still furnishing it. Her daughters, Jenna and Barbara, college freshmen that year, didn't get involved in the campaign at all.

The outcome of the election hung in the balance for an incredible thirty-six days while votes were counted and recounted in Florida. Three days into it, Laura presided over the opening of the annual Texas Book Festival in Austin with a coolness that amazed everyone. Then she and George traveled to the ranch, where she hadn't yet bothered to include a television set in her decorating scheme. Laura used the time to catch up on her reading and her decorating while George cleared weeds, chopped firewood, and roared over the dirt roads in his pickup truck. Occasionally they took long hikes together. All they would say about the suspenseful vote count was that they would accept the will of the voters no matter how it all turned out.

The Bushes were back at the governor's mansion in Austin on December 12 when the Supreme Court ruled in George's favor, and he found out that his election to the presidency had been confirmed. "It's not over," Laura said. "It's only beginning."

Above: Laura tours the Giza pyramids during a visit to Cairo in 2005.

First Lady and First Reader

When a new administration moves into Washington, it is always preceded by endless speculation about what is going to happen next. In the case of Laura Bush, there was no need for anyone to wonder. Her life's work was between the covers of books. On the day before the inauguration, she hosted a "Salute to America's Authors" in Washington, and in every one of her interviews during those weeks, the subject always came around to books. She talked about her

When her husband was elected President of the United States, Laura Bush said that the title of First Lady was too lofty and not an authentic description of her.

reading as a child, and her habit as an adult of reading in bed every night for "thirty or forty minutes at least," no matter how late it might be. She said that her all-time favorite book is Dostoyevsky's *The Brothers Karamazov,* and that she, and George, too, have read "millions of mysteries," especially by the well-known British mystery writers. She revealed that she is an avid reader of newspaper book reviews, too, and she said that she buys books based on them. She also told interviewers that she digests four newspapers every day, although the president subsequently said that he himself doesn't read any of them.

In the summer of 2001, Laura organized a National Book Fair at the Library of Congress in Washington, D.C., patterned after her popular Texas Book Festival. While the events in Austin are intended to raise funds for Texas libraries, this one called attention to the Library of Congress and invited the public inside to explore its collections and buildings while being entertained by children's book characters, musicians, and well-known authors. It began the day before with a special preview for fourth-graders from local schools who listened to special readings by the First Lady herself. She also used the occasion to announce the formation of the Laura Bush Foundation for America's Libraries to raise funds for the support of school libraries across the country.

A First Lady can't spend all of her time with her nose in a book, though. During the previous administration, *The New York Times* noted that Hillary Clinton had brought about "the official end of an era when Presidents' wives pretended to know less than they did and to be advising less than they were." By that standard, Laura Bush was the first representative of a new era. But although the subject had come up several times during the presidential campaign, she always brushed it aside by saying. "I am going to be Laura Bush."

"As America gets to know her, they will love her as I do."

—*George W. Bush on his wife*

After the inauguration, Laura supervised the move from the Austin mansion to the one in Washington. She moved the First Lady's office out of the West Wing and back into the East Wing, and then she went home to the Crawford ranch for two weeks. The traditional round of parties and receptions would have to wait, because Laura had a family to attend to. The message was quite clear that she had meant what she said when she promised to be "just Laura Bush."

Laura's first major initiative was a summit on early-childhood learning she called "Ready to Read, Ready to Learn," which brought four hundred educators and leaders of community programs together in Washington to discuss ways of preparing preschoolers for their future education. She worked on creating other education programs, too, from finding ways to recruit new teachers and to encourage more parental support for them to helping retired military personnel take their technological skills into the classroom. Eight months into the Bush presidency, Laura's poll numbers were higher than her husband's and higher than the previous First Lady's, too.

Unlike some of her predecessors, and many of her husband's constituents, Laura hates to shop, and she doesn't have much interest in clothes. She buys her makeup off the shelf at the local drugstore, but she doesn't really need it—she has her own natural glow. When Laura became First Lady, she recognized the need for a fashion consultant and, although she still bought most of her clothes straight off the rack, for special occasions she placed herself in the hands of designer Michael Faircloth, who had seen her through her years as First Lady of Texas. His signature slim pantsuits became her signature, too. Naturally, he was pleased to have such a visible client, but he had hundreds of others in Texas, too, including the Dallas Cowboys Cheerleaders. Faircloth has revealed that Laura is a "curvaceous size eight," and has been for as long as he's known her. "She maintains her weight beautifully," he once said. "There is no fat closet or skinny closet." Laura had always leaned toward wearing subdued colors, but they aren't television-friendly, and as First Lady she has switched to brighter shades. She had to switch to shorter jackets, too, so she wouldn't gather wrinkles when sitting for long stretches before making a speech.

Below: A former teacher, Laura's heart has never left the classroom and the joys of guiding youngsters.

Challenge

The morning after the terrorist attacks on New York City's World Trade Center and the Pentagon in Washington, D.C., on September 11, 2001, the whole world had changed, and so did the lives of George and Laura Bush.

Laura toured the local blood-donation centers and visited Walter Reed Hospital, where she talked with three of the injured survivors. Then she held a press conference. "All of us as Americans have the opportunity to show our compassion, our resilience, and our courage.... That's what these members

Above: On one of her frequent trips abroad, Laura greets a woman in Afghanistan.

of the team behind me showed America yesterday as they rushed to the Pentagon to save people. It also gives us all the chance as Americans to do what we can for our fellow Americans, to donate blood in cities where they need an adequate supply." She went on to say, "This is a good time for us to think about the message our children are getting; let them know that most people in the world are good and this is a rare and tragic happening, but let them know that they are safe and are loved all over the country."

Later that afternoon, Laura wrote an open letter to all the elementary school children across the United States. It said, in part, "When sad or frightening things happen, all of us have an opportunity to become better people by thinking about others. We can show them we care by saying so and by doing nice things for them. Helping others will make you feel better, too." She sent a similar message to middle and high school students, as well.

Laura was at the president's side when he addressed the nation the following day, and then she went to work to organize a televised prayer service and call for a National Day of Prayer on the fourth day after the tragedy. Before much longer, the press had begun calling Laura "Comforter in Chief." She deserved the title. While the president was busy working out plans for the country's next steps, the First Lady was just as busy framing words of comfort and reassurance for a wounded nation.

She appeared at a memorial service in Pennsylvania for victims of the crash of a hijacked airplane that was apparently on the way to destroy the White House. And she appeared on early-morning television broadcasts urging parents to hug their children and make them feel secure. She took the same message to the popular Oprah Winfrey show, in an interview centered on the idea of "How to Talk to Children about America Under Attack," and she visited youngsters in New York City whose school had been evacuated during the World Trade Center attack. Her calm erupted in tears at a Pentagon memorial, but she composed herself and said, "I'm not usually teary. That's a Bush family characteristic. I married that." She was far from the only person there who wept that day. Through all of her appearances, Laura became a tower of strength and

The Bush's daughter Jenna is following in her mother's footsteps as a teacher in a Washington, D.C., public school.

calmness with a natural ease and sincere compassion, prompting the press to give her yet another admiring title, "First Mother."

Later that fall, Laura delivered the weekly White House radio address in place of the president. She had taken on a new role, and an activist position, possibly for the first time in her life, against brutality against women and children by the regime in Afghanistan. Her shyness had vanished, her primness was gone, and she was speaking out for women's rights everywhere. Once she found her voice, she never lost it through the rest of her first term in the White House, nor in the second. George W. already knew what a treasure he had found when he married Laura. Now the rest of the country knew as well.

Visiting the National First Ladies' Library

The president and Laura Bush do not accept visitors at their ranch in Crawford, Texas, nor is there a memorial to them in Midland, Texas. While they're in Washington, D.C., White House tours are available to the public, but one won't likely find the First Family in the accessible rooms there.

For a more educational visit, try the National First Ladies' Library in Canton, Ohio, which Laura dedicated in September 2003. Its expanding collection includes books about, or by, America's First Ladies, as well as the Abigail Fillmore White House Library Collection, and books related to other prominent women in American history. The collection also includes thousands of photographs and other images along with artifacts related to America's First Ladies. The center has a ninety-one-seat Victorian theater where films and documentaries on the accomplishments of the First Ladies are shown and frequent lectures and performances are held. Changing exhibitions concentrate on specific eras in American history and the impact of First Ladies on them. The library also has a rapidly growing electronic bibliography on America's First Ladies that can be accessed through its Web site: www.firstladies.org.

Below: The First Ladies National Historic Site in Canton, Ohio, is a great resource for information on every First Lady from Martha Washington to Laura Bush.

Guided tours of the special exhibitions are given mornings and afternoons, Tuesday through Saturday. Admission is $7.00 for adults, $6.00 for seniors, and $5.00 for children. The First Ladies' Library is located at 331 Market Avenue South in downtown Canton, Ohio, which is easily reached from north-south Interstate 77 or Route 30. For more information, call 330-452-0876.

Index

(photos indicated in **bold**)

I

J

K

N

Photo Credits

T = Top; B = Bottom; R =Right; L = Left

Abbie Rowe, National Park Service/ Courtesy of Harry S Truman Library: 510; Ash-lawn Highland: 86; Associated Press, AP: 565, 566; Belle Grove Plantation: 67 R, 67 L; Buffalo and Erie County Historical Society: 196 B, 198 L; Clinton Presidential Library: 674 T, 674 B, 675 T, 675 B, 676, 678 T, 678 B, 680, 681, 683, 684 T, 684 B, 685, 687, 688, 689 T, 689 B, 691; Dwight D. Eisenhower Library: 522 T, 522 B, 523, 524, 525, 526, 529, 533, 535, 537; FEMA/Photo by Dave Gatley: 690; Franklin D. Roosevelt Library Digital Archives: 480, 481, 482 T, 483, 484, 485 T, 485 B, 486, 487, 488, 489, 490, 491 T, 491 B, 492, 494, 496, 497, 499, 500; Frick Art Reference Library: 100 B; Gerald R. Ford Library: 610 T, 610 B, 611 T, 611B, 612, 613, 614 T, 614 B, 615 T, 615 B, 619, 620 B, 623 T, 623 B; George Bush Presidential Library: 656 T, 656 B, 657 T, 657 B, 658 T, 658 B, 659, 662, 664, 666, 667, 668, 669, 670 T, 670 B, 671, 697, 698 T, 698 B, 699, 700 T, 700 B, 701, 702; George Eastman House: 181 B; Herbert Hoover Presidential Library and Museum: 468 T, 468 B, 469 T, 469 B, 470 T, 470 B, 475; James K. Polk Home: 174, 177, 179 B, 180, 182, 183; James Monroe Museum and Library: 87; Jimmy Carter Library: 620 T, 626, 627 T, 627 B, 629, 630, 631, 633, 635 T, 635 B, 636, 637 T, 637 B, 638 T, 638 B, 639 T, 639 B; John F. Kennedy Library and Museum: 540 T, 540 B, 543, 554, 553, 554, 555, 556, 557, 558, 559, 560 T, 560 B, 562, 563, 567; LBJ Library: 570 T, 570 B, 571, 572, 573, 576, 583, 584 T; LBJ Library photo by Austin Statesman: 578; LBJ Library photo by Cecil Stoughton: 561 B; LBJ Library photo by Charles Bogel: 587 B; LBJ Library Photo by Frank Muto: 579; LBJ Library Photo by Frank Wolfe: 582, 587 T; LBJ Library photo by Robert Knudsen: 580, 584 B, 585; LBJ Library Photo by Yoichi R. Okamoto: 586 T, 586 B; Library of Congress, Manuscript Collection, The Papers of William M. Evarts: 303 BL; Library of Congress, Manuscript Division: 17, 42 T, 54, 305 T; Library of Congress, Prints & Photographs Division: vi, 2 T, 3 T, 3 B, 4, 5 T, 7 T, 8 T, 9 T, 9 B, 12 R, 12 L, 18, 20, 23 B, 27, 29, 33, 37, 38, 39, 58, 62, 63 T, 64, 71, 72, 73 B, 74, 78, 81, 82, 84, 88 B,

94, 95, 96, 97 T, 98, 101, 102, 105, 121 TL, 121 TR, 123, 124, 125 B, 127, 130, 132 T, 134, 136 T, 137 T, 138 T, 139, 141, 142, 144, 146, 147 T, 147 B, 148, 149, 152 T, 154, 158, 159 T, 159 B, 162, 163, 165 T, 165 B, 169, 171 T, 172, 173, 175, 176, 184, 186 T, 186 B, 187 B, 188 T, 188 B, 189 T, 192, 194, 196 T, 197 B, 199 T, 200, 202 T, 202 B, 203, 204 T, 205, 207 B, 208, 209 TL, 209 TR, 212, 213 T, 216, 218, 220 B, 221, 227, 228 B, 230 T, 230 B, 232, 233, 234 T, 234 B, 235 T, 235 B, 236, 237, 240 B, 241, 243 T, 243 B, 244, 245, 246, 248, 253 T, 254, 260, 261 T, 261 B, 263 TR, 263 BR, 264, 266, 268 T, 269 B, 271, 272 T, 272 B, 273 B, 274, 275 TR, 276, 278, 282, 283, 287 B, 288 T, 288 B, 296, 298 T, 298 B, 302 B, 303 T, 303 BR, 304 T, 304 B, 306, 308, 310, 311, 312, 313, 314, 315 L, 316, 317, 318, 320, 322 B, 324 T, 324 B, 325, 327 T, 328, 330, 333, 334, 335, 337, 338, 339, 340, 342 T, 343, 345 T, 346, 348, 349, 351 B, 353, 354, 355 T, 355 B, 357, 358, 359, 360 T, 360 B, 361, 364 T, 364 B, 365, 368, 370, 371, 372, 374 T, 374 B, 375 B, 376 T, 376 B, 378, 379 T, 380, 382 T, 382 B, 383 T, 383 B, 384 B, 385 T, 385 B, 387 T, 388 T, 388 B, 389 B, 390, 392, 396, 399, 400, 402, 405 T, 405 B, 408, 410, 412, 413, 414, 415, 417, 418, 420, 421, 425 T, 426, 430, 434, 436, 437, 438, 442, 443, 444, 446, 449, 450, 452 T, 453 T, 453 B, 455 T, 455 B, 456, 457 T, 457 B, 458 T, 458 B, 459 T, 459 B, 460 T, 461, 465 T, 465 B, 466, 471 T, 471 B, 472 T, 472 B, 473, 474 T, 476 B, 478, 502, 520, 527, 538, 561 T, 568, 588, 608, 624, 640, 642, 654, 672, 682; Library of Congress, Prints & Photographs Division, Frances Benjamin Johnston Collection: 286, 300 B, 327 B, 342 B, 352, 367, 369 T, 369 B, 373, 377 T, 377 B; Library of Congress, Prints & Photographs Division, Brady-Handy Photograph Collection: 138 B, 140, 210, 222, 224, 226, 238, 239, 250, 258, 270 T, 273 T, 275 TL, 281, 285 T, 287 T, 292, 300 T; Library of Congress, Prints & Photographs Division, Civil War Photographs: 240 T; Library of Congress, Prints & Photographs Division, Detroit Publishing Company Collection: 6 B, 28, 42 B, 65, 92; Library of Congress, Prints & Photographs Division, FSA-OWI Collection: 474 B, 493, 495, 694; Library of Congress, Prints & Photographs Division, George Grantham Bain Collection: 167 T,

322 T, 329 T, 344 B, 362, 384 T, 389 T, 393, 397, 401, 406, 419, 482 B; Library of Congress, Prints & Photographs Division, Gottscho-Schleisner Collection: 24, 460 B; Library of Congress, Prints & Photographs Division, Historic American Buildings Survey: 6 T, 9, 22, 32, 57, 63 B, 77, 80, 88 T, 121 B, 128 B, 133 T, 133 B, 137 B, 143 T, 153, 155, 164, 170, 171 B, 191, 213 B, 214, 256, 265, 268 B, 269 T, 275 B, 290 B, 301, 305 B, 315 R, 329 B, 332, 345 B, 379, 424, 425 B, 476 T, 477, 511; Library of Congress, Prints & Photographs Division, NYWT&S Collection: 551; Library of Congress, Prints & Photographs Division, Photochrom Collection: 104 T; Library of Congress, Prints & Photographs Division, Prokudin-Gorskii Collection: 97 B; Library of Congress, Prints & Photographs Division, Theodor Horydczak Collection: 15, 47, 93; Library of Congress, Prints & Photographs Division, Toni Frissell Collection: 549; Library of Congress, Prints & Photographs Division, U.S. News & World Report Magazine Collection: 528 B, 596, 603, 617, 618, 622; Library of Congress, Prints & Photographs Division, Works Projects Administration Poster Collection: 132 B; Library of Congress, Rare Book and Special Collections Division: 89 B; Library of Congress, Swann Collection, Prints & Photographs Division: 69; Massachusetts Historical Society: 36; Monticello/Thomas Jefferson Foundation, Inc.: 43, 45, 46, 48, 49, 51, 52, 53, 55, 57; National Archives and Records Administration: 536, 602, 604 T, 604 B, 605 T, 606 B; National Museum of American Art: 119 B; National Park Service: 156, 387 B, 514, 228 T, 247; National Park Service, Andrew Johnson Historic Site: 252, 253 B, 262 B; National Park Service/Adams National Historical Park: 25, 31, 34, 119 T, 120; National Portrait Gallery: 189 B; National Society Daughters of the American Revolution/NSDAR Archive: 344 T; New Hampshire Historical Society, Franklin Pierce Collection: 206; New York Public Library, Humanities and Social Sciences Library, Print Collection, Miriam and Ira D. Wallach Division of Art, Prints, and Photographs: 112 T, 197 T, 284 T, 284 B, 323 T, 323 B, 326; New York Public Library, Humanities

and Social Sciences Library: 7 B, 70, 75, 76, 104 B, 107, 118, 160, 161, 204 B, 207 T, 209 B, 217 T, 217 B, 219 B, 251 T, 291, 302 T, 341; New York Public Library, Humanities and Social Sciences Library, Rare Books Division: 386; New York Public Library, Mid-Manhattan Picture Collection: 2 B, 5 B, 8 B, 10, 11, 13, 23 T, 40, 56, 60, 61, 66, 89 T, 109, 116, 131, 136 B, 150, 152 B, 167 B, 178, 179 T, 181 T, 198 B, 199 B, 220 T, 251 B, 262 T, 263 TL, 270 B; Nixon Presidential Materials: 593 T, 605 B, 606 T; Ohio Historical Society: 431, 433, 435, 439, 440, 445; Michael Reed/www.thecemeteryproject.com: 143 B; Picture History: 111, 112 B, 114 B; Ronald Reagan Presidential Library: 643 T, 643 B, 644 T, 644 B, 645 T, 645 B, 646, 647, 648, 649 T, 649 B, 650, 651, 652, 653; Rutherford B. Hayes Presidential Center: 279, 280 T, 280 B, 285 B, 290 T, 294, 295; Smithsonian Institution: 114 T, 187 T, 190; Tennessee State Museum Collection: 126; The Calvin Coolidge Memorial Foundation: 452 B; The Hermitage: Home of President Andrew Jackson, Nashville, TN: 125 T, 128 T, 129 T; The Ladies Hermitage Association: 129 B; The Marion County Historical Society: 447; The Montpelier Foundation: 83; The Montpelier Foundation and the National Trust for Historic Preservation: 73 T, 79; The National First Ladies' Library: 709; The President Chester A. Arthur State Historic Site, Vermont Division for Historic Preservation: 319; The Richard Nixon Library and Birthplace Foundation: 590, 592, 593 B, 597, 599, 600, 607; The William McKinley Presidential Library and Museum, Canton, Ohio: 350 TL, 350 TR, 350 B, 351 T; Truman Presidential Library and Museum: 504 T, 504 B, 505 T, 505 B, 506 T, 506 B, 507 T, 507 B, 508, 511, 513, 515, 516, 518, 519 T, 519 B, 528 T, 530; U. S. Naval Historical Center: 219; White House Historical Association, photo by Bruce White: 90; White House Historical Association, photo by Bruce White: 91, White House Historical Association, photo by Will Brown: 375 T; White House photo by Eric Draper: 703; White House photo by Joyce Naitchayan: 707; White House photo by Susan Sterner: 704, 705, 708; White House photo by Tina Hager: 692.

Color Insert

Inaugural Gowns and Other Ceremonial Dresses:
Ida McKinley: The William McKinley Presidential Library and Museum, Canton, Ohio. Martha Washington: Library of Congress, Prints & Photographs Division, Theodor Horydczak Collection. Lady Bird Johnson: LBJ Library Photo by Robert Knudsen. Sarah Polk: James K. Polk Home. Barbara and George H. W. Bush: George Bush Presidential Library. Bess Truman: Truman Presidential Library and Museum. Caroline Harrison: National Museum of American History, Smithsonian Institution. Elizabeth Monroe: Ash Lawn-Highland. Edith Wilson: White House Historical Association. George and Laura Bush: White House photo by Eric Draper. Rosalynn and Amy Carter: Jimmy Carter Library. Angelica Van Buren: White House Historical Association. John and Jackie Kennedy: The John F. Kennedy Library and Museum. Eleanor Roosevelt: National Museum of American History, Smithsonian Institution. Lucy Hayes: Rutherford B. Hayes Presidential Center. Helen Taft: White House Historical Association. Louisa Adams: Library of Congress, Prints & Photographs Division. Betty Ford: Gerald R. Ford Library. Lucretia Garfield: National Museum of American History, Smithsonian Institution. Mamie Eisenhower: Dwight D. Eisenhower Library. Julia Tyler: New York Public Library, Humanities and Social Sciences Library. Edith Roosevelt: White House Historical Association. Pat Nixon: National Archives and Records Administration. Florence Harding: National Museum of American History, Smithsonian Institution. Ronald and Nancy Reagan: Ronald Reagan Presidential Library. Bill and Hillary Clinton: Library of Congress, Prints & Photographs Division. Mary Todd Lincoln: National Museum of American History, Smithsonian Institution. Grace Coolidge: White House Historical Association.

Suits and Business Attire:
Eleanor Roosevelt and Madame Chiang Kai-Shek: Associated Press, AP. Laura Bush: Associated Press, AP. Nancy Reagan: Ronald Reagan Presidential Library. Lucy Hayes: Rutherford B. Hayes Presidential Center.

Barbara Bush: George Bush Presidential Library. Rosalynn Carter, Betty Ford and Lady Bird Johnson: National Archives and Records Administration. Abigail Adams: White House Historical Association. Mamie Eisenhower: Dwight D. Eisenhower Library. Bill and Hillary Clinton: Clinton Presidential Library. The Ford Family: Gerald R. Ford Library. Jackie Kennedy: The John F. Kennedy Library and Museum.

Casual Attire:
Frances Cleveland: New York Public Library, Humanities and Social Sciences Library, Print Collection, Miriam and Ira D. Wallach Division of Art, Prints, and Photographs. Lady Bird Johnson: LBJ Library Photo by Frank Wolfe. Laura Bush: Getty Images. Jimmy and Rosalynn Carter: Jimmy Carter Library. Bess Truman: Truman Presidential Library and Museum. Hillary Clinton: Clinton Presidential Library. Gerald and Betty Ford: Gerald R. Ford Library. Barbara and George Bush: George Bush Presidential Library. Kennedy Family: The John F. Kennedy Library and Museum. Mamie Eisenhower: Dwight D. Eisenhower Library. Pat Nixon: National Archives and Records Administration. Nancy Reagan: Ronald Reagan Presidential Library. Dolley Madison: Courtesy of The Montpelier Foundation and The National Trust for Historic Preservation.

Extensive searches of copyright registration have been conducted for all images reproduced in this book and every effort has been made to obtain appropriate permissions and clearances. The author and publisher apologize for any inadvertent oversight and, if made aware, will include an appropriate acknowledgment in all future printings.